Culture and History of the Ancient Near East

VOLUME 32

Reconstruction of the funeral ceremony held before the burial of the king. Tumulus MM is shown under construction in the background.

THE GORDION WOODEN OBJECTS
VOLUME I

THE FURNITURE FROM TUMULUS MM

Elizabeth Simpson

TEXT

With contributions by

Harry Alden   Benjamin Held
Burhan Aytuğ   Walter Hopwood
Mary W. Ballard   Joseph Koles
Robert A. Blanchette Patrick E. McGovern
Roland Cunningham   Lynn E. Roller
Laure Dussubieux   Krysia Spirydowicz

BRILL

LEIDEN • BOSTON
2010

This book is printed on acid-free paper.

Library of Congress Cataloging-in-Publication Data

Simpson, Elizabeth, 1947-
     The furniture from Tumulus MM / Elizabeth Simpson ; with contributions by Krysia Spirydowicz ... [et al.].
     p. cm. – (University Museum monograph. Gordion special studies ; 4)
     (Culture and history of the ancient Near East ; 32, v. 1)
     A two-vol. set. First vol. is text; second vol. is illustrations.
     ISBN 978-90-04-16539-7 (v. 1 & 2 : alk. paper) 1. Gordion (Extinct city) 2. Furniture–Turkey–Gordion (Extinct city) 3. Excavations
(Archaeology)–Turkey–Gordion (Extinct city) 4. Turkey–Antiquities. I. Spirydowicz, Krysia. II. Title. III. Series.

     DS156.G6S56 2009
     684.100939'26–dc22

                                                                                          2008019707

ISSN: 1566-2055
ISBN: 978 90 04 16539 7

This book is dedicated with appreciation to
Machteld J. Mellink
who first suggested that I restudy the Gordion furniture.

"Symmetry, as wide or as narrow as you may define its meaning, is one idea by which man through the ages has tried to comprehend and create order, beauty, and perfection."

–Hermann Weyl, *Symmetry*

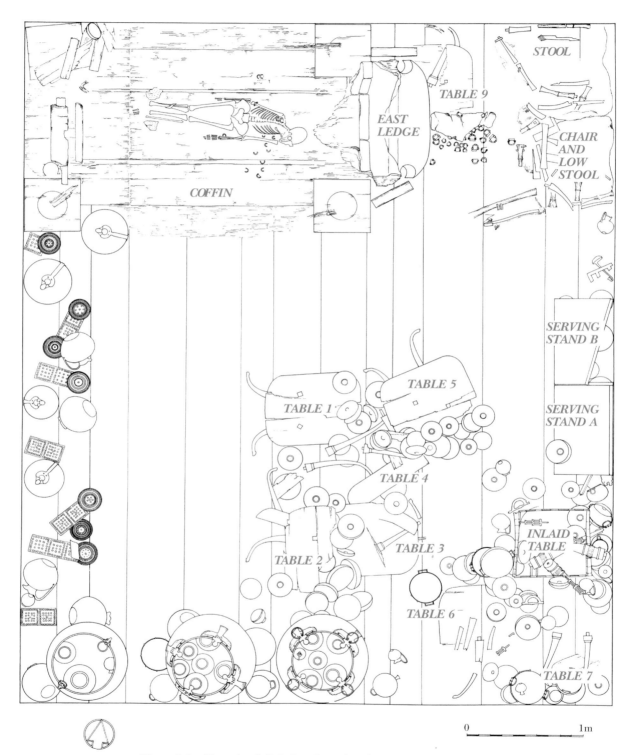

STOOL

TABLE 9

EAST
LEDGE

CHAIR
AND
LOW
STOOL

COFFIN

SERVING
STAND B

SERVING
STAND A

TABLE 5

TABLE 1

TABLE 4

INLAID
TABLE

TABLE 3

TABLE 2

TABLE 6

TABLE 7

0   1m

Plan of the Tumulus MM chamber, showing the furniture *in situ*.

CONTENTS

TEXT VOLUME

Plan of the Tumulus MM Chamber viii
List of Color Plates.. xiii
List of Figures.. xv
List of Plates xix
List of Text Figures... xxvii
List of CD-Figures xxix
Preface xxxv
Acknowledgments.. xxxvii
   Photographic Credits xxxix
   Art Credits... xxxix

Introduction 1

PART ONE. DISCOVERY AND EARLY INTERPRETATION

Chapter 1. The Excavation of Tumulus MM and the Contents of the Burial 7

Chapter 2. Early Interpretations of the Furniture from Tumulus MM 13
   The Tables... 13
      Plain Tables.. 13
      Inlaid Table (The "Pagoda Table")... 15
   The "Screens" 18
      "Screen A" 20
      "Screen B" 20
   The Furniture from the Northeast Corner 21
   The "Bed" 22

PART TWO. CATALOGUE AND COMPARANDA

Chapter 3. The Inlaid Table.. 31
   Form and Decoration 32
      Internal Bracing System 32
      Frame... 33
      Corner Pieces 34
      Top Struts and Handles 34
      Leg Struts.. 37
      Legs and Table Top 38
      The Reconstructed Table 39
   Comparanda: Form and Function 39

Comparanda: Other Ancient Tables 40
  Early Banquet Tables 41
  Near Eastern Tables in the First Millennium B.C. 44
  Evidence from East and West in the First Millennium B.C. 47
Comparanda: Designs 48
  Mazes and Swastikas on the Inlaid Table 50
  Fertility Symbols and Genealogical Patterns 52

Chapter 4. The Plain Tables 57
  Table 1 58
  Table 2 58
  Table 3 59
  Table 4 59
  Table 5 60
  Table 6 60
  Table 7 61
  Table 9 61
  Comparanda 62

Chapter 5. The Serving Stands 65
  Serving Stand A ("Screen A") 65
  Serving Stand B ("Screen B") 70
  Form and Function 73
    Comparanda: Other Ancient Vessel Stands 74
  Designs on the Serving Stands 77
    Comparanda: Designs 83
    Stars and Rosettes as Symbols of Near Eastern Goddesses 87
    Iconography of the Phrygian Goddess Matar 91
  Furniture as Cosmic Metaphor 99

Chapter 6. The Furniture from the Northeast Corner 111
  Form and Function 111
  Comparanda: Stools and Chairs 114

Chapter 7. The Coffin 119
  Form and Function 120
  Comparanda 123

Chapter 8. Conclusions—The Burial of the King 127

APPENDICES

Appendix 1. Conservation of the Wooden Furniture from Tumulus MM (Krysia Spirydowicz,
  Queen's University, Kingston, Ontario) 137
Appendix 2. Reconstruction of the Inlaid Table and Serving Stands for Display (Elizabeth
  Simpson) 159
Appendix 3. Wood Species Analysis (Burhan Aytuğ, Istanbul University; Robert A. Blanchette,
  University of Minnesota; and Benjamin Held, University of Minnesota) 165
Appendix 4. Assessment of Wood Deterioration in the Furniture and Coffin from Tumulus MM
  (Robert A. Blanchette, University of Minnesota) 171
Appendix 5. Chemical Identification of the Beverage and Food Remains in Tumulus MM
  (Patrick McGovern, University of Pennsylvania Museum of Archaeology and
  Anthropology) 177

Appendix 6. Graffiti on the Wooden Serving Stands from Tumulus MM (Lynn E. Roller,
    University of California, Davis) 189
Appendix 7. Woodworking Tools and Techniques (Elizabeth Simpson) 197
Appendix 8. Preliminary Analyses of Textiles Associated with the Wooden Furniture from
    Tumulus MM (Mary W. Ballard, Harry Alden, Roland H. Cunningham, Walter Hopwood,
    Joseph Koles, and Laure Dussubieux, Museum Conservation Institute, Smithsonian
    Institution) 203
Appendix 9. Concordance 225

Bibliography 227

Index 251

ILLUSTRATIONS VOLUME

Color Plates
Figures
Plates
CD-Figures (located on the CD inside the back cover)

LIST OF COLOR PLATES

Frontispiece   Reconstruction of the funeral ceremony held before the burial of the king.
Color Plate I   The excavation of Tumulus MM.
                   A. Tumulus MM during its excavation in 1957.
                   B. Remains of the king and his log coffin, as found in 1957.
Color Plate II   The excavation of Tumulus MM.
                   A. East ledge of the coffin, as it fell outward onto the tomb floor. Top of Table 9, at
                      right, with the bag of bronze fibulae that fell from the table when it collapsed.
                   B. Furniture fragments in the northeast corner, with the fibulae removed and some
                      pieces repositioned.
Color Plate III   The excavation of Tumulus MM.
                   A. The serving stands leaning against the east wall of the tomb, with the inlaid table
                      to the south. Tables 1, 4, and 5 are visible in the foreground.
                   B. The inlaid table as it was found in 1957.
Color Plate IV   The excavation of Tumulus MM.
                   A. Serving stand A, with a bronze omphalos bowl found leaning against the face.
                   B. Serving stand B with a small bronze cauldron, ladle, and other vessels that had
                      fallen behind it.
Color Plate V   The excavation of Tumulus MM.
                   A. Table 2 and bronze omphalos bowls. Table 3 is in the background.
                   B. Tables 2 and 3 (far left) and large cauldrons (MM 2 and MM 3) at the south of
                      the tomb.
Color Plate VI   Bronzes from Tumulus MM.
                   A. Large bronze cauldron (MM 2), with pottery jars containing the remains of food.
                   B. Small bronze cauldron (MM 10), found behind serving stand B.
                   C. Bronze ladle (MM 47), found behind serving stand A.
Color Plate VII   Bronzes from Tumulus MM.
                   A. Bronze lion-headed situla (MM 45), before cleaning; found partly behind serving
                      stand A.
                   B. Bronze ram-headed situla (MM 46), after cleaning; found behind serving stand
                      A.
Color Plate VIII   The inlaid table as assembled for display in the Museum of Anatolian Civilizations,
                   1989.
Color Plate IX   The inlaid table, mounted for display, seen from the left rear corner of the table.
Color Plate X   Color diagrams of serving stand A, showing the main designs, derivatives, and
                   design groups (see also CD-Figures 66–69).
Color Plate XI   Color diagrams of serving stand B, showing the main designs, derivatives, and
                   design groups (see also CD-Figures 70–73).
Color Plate XII   Serving stand A, assembled for display in the Museum of Anatolian Civilizations,
                   1999.
Color Plate XIII   Serving stand A, as mounted for display, back view.
Color Plate XIV   Serving stand B, assembled for display in the Museum of Anatolian Civilizations,
                   1999.

Color Plate XV   Serving stand B, as mounted for display, back view.
Color Plate XVI   Replicas and reconstructions.
                   A. Replica of the Tumulus MM chamber, Museum of Anatolian Civilizations, 1993,
                      containing a reproduction of the coffin and original bronzes from the tomb.
                   B. Artist Richard Neave from the University of Manchester putting the finishing
                      touches on a reconstruction of the head of "King Midas."

LIST OF FIGURES

Figure 1   Early reconstruction drawing of the inlaid table from Tumulus MM. Dorothy Cox.

Figure 2   Early drawing of "screen A," as seen from the back. Dorothy Cox.

Figure 3   Early drawings of the king's "bed," reconstructed from Young's field notes and subsequent publications.

Figure 4   Inlaid table. Schematic top plan, with the table top and decorative top struts removed.

Figure 5   Inlaid table. Front frame piece (frame piece A) with decorative top struts.

Figure 6   Inlaid table. Back frame piece (frame piece D) with decorative top struts.

Figure 7   Inlaid table. Right frame piece (frame piece B) with decorative top struts.

Figure 8   Inlaid table. Left frame piece (frame piece C) with decorative top struts.

Figure 9   Inlaid table. Mazes on the frame.

Figure 10   Inlaid table. Right leg strut (leg strut B).

Figure 11   Inlaid table. Left leg strut (leg strut C).

Figure 12   Inlaid table. Front leg strut (leg strut A).

Figure 13   Inlaid table. Handle at left on front frame piece (handle A1).

Figure 14   Inlaid table. Handle at right on front frame piece (handle A5).

Figure 15   Inlaid table. Handle at left on back frame piece (handle D1).

Figure 16   Inlaid table. Handle at right on back frame piece (handle D5).

Figure 17   Inlaid table. Mazes on the handles.

Figure 18   Inlaid table. Left rear leg (leg C).

Figure 19   Inlaid table. Front leg (leg A).

Figure 20   Inlaid table. Right rear leg (leg B).

Figure 21   Inlaid table. Reconstruction drawing.

Figure 22   Inlaid table. Inlaid bands on the table's leg tops.

Figure 23   Inlaid table. Inlay on the tops of the table's feet.

Figure 24   Inlaid table. Isometric reconstruction of the joinery at the corners of the frame.

Figure 25   Inlaid table. Reconstruction of one of the missing corner pieces, in its simplest possible form.

Figure 26   Inlaid table. Construction details showing the way in which the decorative struts that supported the table top were joined to the top and frame.

Figure 27   Inlaid table. Construction details showing the way in which the legs were attached to the table top.

Figure 28   Inlaid table. Grain configuration on the left rear leg (leg C).

Figure 29   Plain tables. Legs of the eight plain tables (tables 1–7 and 9).

Figure 30   Profiles of the tops of the eight plain tables and the inlaid table.

Figure 31   Table 1. Sections of the legs and diagram of the table as seen from the top.

Figure 32   Table 2. Sections of the legs and diagram of the table as seen from the top.

Figure 33   Table 2. Grain configuration on both sides of the front leg.

Figure 34   Table 2. Grain configuration on both sides of the right rear leg.

Figure 35   Table 3. Sections of the legs and diagram of the table as seen from the top.

Figure 36   Table 4. Sections of the legs and diagram of the table as seen from the top.

Figure 37   Table 5. Sections of the legs and diagram of the table as seen from the top.

Figure 38   Table 5. Sections of the legs and table top.

Figure 39   Table 5. Section and diagram of the left rear leg, showing details of the table's construction.

Figure 40   Table 5. Reconstruction drawing.
Figure 41   Table 6. Section of leg and diagram of the table as seen from the top.
Figure 42   Table 7. Section of legs and diagram of the table as seen from the top.
Figure 43   Table 9. Section of leg and diagram of the table as seen from the top.
Figure 44   Serving stand A. Sections and top view of the carved top piece of the stand.
Figure 45   Serving stand A. Inlaid right edge of the stand's face with adjoining inlaid right side piece.
Figure 46   Serving stand A. Inlaid left edge of the stand's face with adjoining inlaid left side piece.
Figure 47   Serving stand A. Side view of the stand, reconstructed, showing construction details.
Figure 48   Serving stand A. Back view of the stand, reconstructed, showing construction details.
Figure 49   Serving stand A. Diagram of the front face, showing construction details.
Figure 50   Serving stand A. Front face of the stand with inlaid decoration.
Figure 51   Serving stand A. Reconstruction drawing, back view.
Figure 52   Serving stand B. Sections and top view of the carved top piece of the stand.
Figure 53   Serving stand B. Inlaid right edge of the stand's face with adjoining inlaid right side piece.
Figure 54   Serving stand B. Inlaid left edge of the stand's face with adjoining inlaid left side piece.
Figure 55   Serving stand B. Side view of the stand, reconstructed, showing construction details.
Figure 56   Serving stand B. Back view of the stand, reconstructed, showing construction details.
Figure 57   Serving stand B. Diagram of the front face, showing construction details.
Figure 58   Serving stand B. Front face of the stand with inlaid decoration.
Figure 59   Serving stand B. Reconstruction drawing, back view.
Figure 60   Serving stand A. Left front foot block, showing construction details.
Figure 61   Serving stand B. Right front foot block, showing construction details.
Figure 62   Serving stand A. Front face of the stand, with numbered boards and graffiti locations.
Figure 63   Serving stand A. Graffiti on tenons (A1–A7).
Figure 64   Serving stand B. Front face of the stand, with numbered boards and graffiti locations.
Figure 65   Serving stand B. Graffiti on tenons (B1–B3).
Figure 66   Serving stands. Graffiti on broken tenons.
Figure 67   Serving stands. Inlaid rosettes at left below central medallions.
Figure 68   Serving stands. Method of cutting and joining segments of wood to make the inlaid
              designs.
Figure 69   Serving stands. Inlay method, showing a meander square from serving stand A (row 2,
              square 11) and the segments from which it was made.
Figure 70   Serving stand B. Inlay method, showing the background inlay and the guidelines used to
              lay out the patterns.
Figure 71   Serving stands. Evolution of the swastika design symmetrical with respect to rotations of
              180 degrees.
Figure 72   Serving stand A. Inlaid meander squares that occur on the face of the stand.
Figure 73   Serving stand A. Diagram of the face of the stand showing the positions of the numbered
              designs.
Figure 74   Serving stand B. Inlaid meander squares that occur on the face of the stand.
Figure 75   Serving stand B. Diagram of the face of the stand showing the positions of the numbered
              designs.
Figure 76   Reconstructed stool leg ("short leg") from the northeast corner of the tomb.
Figure 77   Fragmentary carved stretcher from the northeast corner of the tomb.
Figure 78   Carved stretcher from the northeast corner, reconstructed, with the slats that fitted into its
              lower edge.
Figure 79   Coffin. Diagram showing the way that the height and position of the east ledge were
              ascertained.
Figure 80   Coffin. Reconstructed side view, looking north, as placed in the tomb.
Figure 81   Coffin. Reconstructed side view, as placed in the tomb, with cross-section of the coffin
              body, corner-block cuttings, nail holes, and the slat on the slope below the east ledge
              indicated by dashed lines.
Figure 82   Coffin. Side view, as assembled for the ceremony before the burial.
Figure 83   Coffin. Reconstruction as placed in the tomb, seen from above.

Figure 84   Coffin. Reconstruction as placed in the tomb, with the edges of the corner blocks and
             pieces of the rails that were covered by the coffin body indicated by dashed lines.
Figure 85   Coffin. Schematic reconstruction as placed in the tomb, top view, with the rails
             reconstructed to their original form and length.
Figure 86   Coffin. Reconstruction, as assembled for the ceremony, seen from above.
Figure 87   Coffin. Reconstruction, as placed in the tomb, viewed from the east end.
Figure 88   Coffin. Reconstruction, as placed in the tomb, from the east, with cross-section of the
             body, corner-block cuttings, nail holes, and rails indicated by dashed lines.
Figure 89   Coffin. Reconstruction, as assembled for the ceremony, seen from the east end.
Figure 90   Coffin. View as assembled for the ceremony, before it was disassembled for placement in
             the tomb.
Figure 91   Comparanda. Inlaid serving stand from Tumulus P, Gordion. Reconstruction drawing of
             the front face.
Figure 92   Comparanda. Pebble mosaic from Megaron 2 in the destruction level of the city mound,
             Gordion.
Figure 93   Comparanda. Büyük Kapı Kaya. Drawing of the façade.
Figure 94   Comparanda. "Doodle stone" drawing from the city mound, Gordion (ST 263a).
Figure 95   Comparanda. "Doodle stone" drawing from the city mound, Gordion (uncatalogued,
             DSD 29).
Figure 96   Comparanda. "Doodle stone" drawing from the city mound, Gordion (ST 436).
Figure 97   Comparanda. "Doodle stone" drawing from the city mound, Gordion (ST 450).
Figure 98   Comparanda. "Doodle stone" drawing from the city mound, Gordion (ST 841).
Figure 99   Comparanda. "Doodle stone" drawing from the city mound, Gordion (ST 446, left).

LIST OF PLATES

Plate 1   Inlaid table *in situ* in the Tumulus MM chamber.
Plate 2   Inlaid table. Dowels from the inner support structure.
Plate 3   Inlaid table. Front frame piece (frame piece A).
              A. Frame piece A, with decorative top struts.
              B. Frame piece A, without top struts, back view.
Plate 4   Inlaid table. Decorative top struts from the front frame piece (frame piece A).
              A–D. Handle A1, four views.
              E–F. Strut A2, front and back views.
              G–H. Strut A3, front and back views.
Plate 5   Inlaid table. Decorative top struts from the front frame piece (frame piece A).
              A–B. Strut A4, front and back views.
              C–F. Handle A5, four views.
Plate 6   Inlaid table. Inlaid panels on the front frame piece (frame piece A).
Plate 7   Inlaid table. Curved front leg strut (leg strut A).
Plate 8   Inlaid table. Front leg strut, pieces at upper left and right.
Plate 9   Inlaid table. Inlaid details on front leg strut, bottom piece.
Plate 10   Inlaid table. Inlaid details on front leg strut, bottom piece.
Plate 11   Inlaid table. Right frame piece (frame piece B).
              A. Frame piece B, with decorative top struts.
              B. Frame piece B, without top struts, back view.
Plate 12   Inlaid table. Decorative top struts from the right frame piece (frame piece B).
              A–B. Strut B1, front and back views.
              C–D. Strut B2, front and back views.
              E–F. Strut B3, front and back views.
              G–H. Strut B4, front and back views.
Plate 13   Inlaid table. Inlaid panels on the right frame piece (frame piece B).
Plate 14   Inlaid table. Right leg strut (leg strut B).
Plate 15   Inlaid table. Left frame piece (frame piece C).
              A. Frame piece C, with decorative top struts.
              B. Frame piece C, without top struts, back view.
Plate 16   Inlaid table. Decorative top struts from the left frame piece (frame piece C).
              A–B. Strut C1, front and back views.
              C–D. Strut C2, front and back views.
              E–F. Strut C3, front and back views.
              G–H. Strut C4, front and back views.
Plate 17   Inlaid table. Inlaid panels on the left frame piece (frame piece C).
Plate 18   Inlaid table. Left leg strut (leg strut C).
Plate 19   Inlaid table. Back frame piece (frame piece D).
              A. Frame piece D, with decorative top struts.
              B. Frame piece D, without top struts, back view.
Plate 20   Inlaid table. Decorative top struts from the back frame piece (frame piece D).
              A–D. Handle D1, four views.
              E–F. Strut D2, front and back views.
              G–H. Strut D3, front and back views.

Plate 21   Inlaid table. Decorative top struts from the back frame piece (frame piece D).
              A–B.   Strut D4, front and back views.
              C–F.   Handle D5, four views.
Plate 22   Inlaid table. Inlaid panels on the back frame piece (frame piece D).
Plate 23   Inlaid table. Left front corner of the table, showing the joinery and residue that is the
              evidence for the missing corner piece.
Plate 24   Inlaid table. Front leg (leg A), left side and front views.
Plate 25   Inlaid table. Front leg (leg A), right side and back views.
Plate 26   Inlaid table. Right leg (leg B), left side and front views.
Plate 27   Inlaid table. Right leg (leg B), right side and back views.
Plate 28   Inlaid table. Left leg (leg C), left side and front views.
Plate 29   Inlaid table. Left leg (leg C), right side and back views.
Plate 30   Inlaid table. Carved, inlaid top sections of legs A, B, and C.
Plate 31   Inlaid table. Details of the feet of the table's three legs.
Plate 32   Inlaid table. Fragments of the table top.
Plate 33   The inlaid table as reconstructed.
Plate 34   The inlaid table as reconstructed, front view.
Plate 35   The inlaid table as reconstructed, back view.
Plate 36   Plain tables. Tables 1–5 and 6–7 *in situ* in the tomb.
Plate 37   Table 1, after removal from the tomb.
Plate 38   Table 1, face down, after early treatment with wax and attachment of the legs to the top.
Plate 39   Table 1. Legs.
Plate 40   Table 1. Table top, top view.
Plate 41   Table 1. Table top, underside.
Plate 42   Table 2, after removal from the tomb.
Plate 43   Table 2. Legs.
Plate 44   Table 2. Table top, top view.
Plate 45   Table 2. Table top, underside.
Plate 46   Table 3, after removal from the tomb.
Plate 47   Table 3. Legs.
Plate 48   Table 3. Table top, top view.
Plate 49   Table 3. Table top, underside.
Plate 50   Table 4, after removal from the tomb.
Plate 51   Table 4. Legs.
Plate 52   Table 4. Table top, top view.
Plate 53   Table 4. Table top, underside.
Plate 54   Table 5, *in situ* in the tomb.
Plate 55   Table 5, after removal from the tomb.
Plate 56   Table 5, in a wooden storage drawer in the Museum of Anatolian Civilizations, 1965.
Plate 57   Table 5. Legs.
Plate 58   Table 5. Table top, top view.
Plate 59   Table 5. Table top, underside.
Plate 60   Table 6, after removal from the tomb.
Plate 61   Table 6. Legs.
Plate 62   Table 6. Table top, fragmentary remains, top view.
Plate 63   Table 7, after removal from the tomb.
Plate 64   Table 7. Legs and detail showing the way the leg tenons fit into the collars of the table
              top.
Plate 65   Table 7. Table top, fragmentary remains, top view.
Plate 66   Table 9, after removal from the tomb.
Plate 67   Table 9. Remains of legs and fragments of collars from the table top.
Plate 68   Table 9. Large fragment of the table top, top view and underside.
Plate 69   Serving stands A and B leaning against the east wall of the tomb chamber.
Plate 70   Serving stand A *in situ* in the tomb chamber.

Plate 71   Serving stand A, as removed from the tomb.

Plate 72   Serving stand A. Face, front view, after cleaning and conservation.

Plate 73   Serving stand A. Face, back view, after cleaning and conservation.

Plate 74   Serving stand A. Carved top piece.

Plate 75   Serving stand A. Back piece and diagonal back struts; short back strut.

Plate 76   Serving stand A. Inlaid side pieces.

Plate 77   Serving stand A. Detail of central rosette.

Plate 78   Serving stand A, assembled for display in the Museum of Anatolian Civilizations, 1999.

Plate 79   Serving stand A, as mounted for display, back view.

Plate 80   Serving stand B, as found in the tomb.

Plate 81   Serving stand B, as removed from the tomb.

Plate 82   Serving stand B. Face, front view, after cleaning and conservation.

Plate 83   Serving stand B. Face, back view, after cleaning and conservation.

Plate 84   Serving stand B. Carved top piece.

Plate 85   Serving stand B. Back piece and diagonal back struts; short back strut.

Plate 86   Serving stand B. Inlaid side pieces.

Plate 87   Serving stand B. Detail of central rosette.

Plate 88   Serving stand B, assembled for display in the Museum of Anatolian Civilizations, 1999.

Plate 89   Serving stand B, as mounted for display, back view.

Plate 90   Serving stand A. Details of the right front foot.

Plate 91   Serving stand A. Details of the left front foot.

Plate 92   Serving stand B. Details of the left and right front feet.

Plate 93   Serving stand A. Graffiti on tenons (A1–A7).

Plate 94   Serving stand B. Graffiti on tenons (B1–B3); graffiti on loose tenons.

Plate 95   Serving stands. Details of inlay wedges.

Plate 96   Serving stands. Inlay at top of left and right side boards.

Plate 97   Serving stands. Details of inlay over pegs, joints, and patches.

Plate 98   Serving stands. Details of joinery.

Plate 99   Serving stands. Main designs on serving stands A and B.

Plate 100   Furniture from the northeast corner. Fragmentary furniture remains *in situ* in the tomb chamber.

Plate 101   Furniture from the northeast corner. "Short legs" and other fragments, as removed from the tomb.

Plate 102   Furniture from the northeast corner. "Medium legs" and other fragments, as removed from the tomb.

Plate 103   Furniture from the northeast corner. "Long legs" and other fragments, as removed from the tomb.

Plate 104   Furniture from the northeast corner. Carved stretcher, main fragment and details.

Plate 105   Furniture from the northeast corner.
              A. Carved stretcher, main fragment, with two adjoining slats.
              B. Largest fragment from the group of "short legs."

Plate 106   Miscellaneous.
              A. Leg fragments, with carved molding, possibly from the northeast corner.
              B. Textile fragment, with impression of cording from a seat.
              C. Clumps of plaster, possibly used as fill for imperfections in wooden furniture.

Plate 107   Coffin *in situ* in the Tumulus MM chamber.

Plate 108   Coffin. East ledge *in situ*.

Plate 109   Coffin. Remains near the west wall of the tomb.

Plate 110   Coffin. Rails *in situ* on the tomb floor.
              A. South rail uncovered, looking north.
              B. Both rails uncovered, looking north.

Plate 111   Coffin. East ledge.

Plate 112   Coffin. East and west ledges, with the iron bars that served as reinforcements.

Plate 113   Coffin. Iron fragments associated with the coffin.

Plate 114   Coffin.
              A–B. Iron bosses associated with the coffin.
              C. Coffin rails. Fragments of the long rails.
              D. Coffin rails. Fragments of the short rails.
Plate 115   Coffin. Corner blocks.
Plate 116   Comparanda.
              A. Detail of the stone tablet of Nabû-apla-iddina from Sippar. Neo-Babylonian. British
                 Museum.
              B. Cult statue of the goddess Narundi, dedicated by Puzur-Inshushinak at Susa. Louvre.
              C. Initiates in Arnhem Land, Australia, wearing painted "genealogical patterns."
              D. Two dancing maidens, shown on a sherd (P 3763) from the city mound, Gordion.
Plate 117   Comparanda.
              A. Clay figurine from Cucuteni, Moldavia. National Antiquities Museum, Bucharest.
              B. North Syrian ivory horse frontlet (BI 432), found in the Terrace Building (TB 2),
                 Gordion.
              C. Orientalizing period amphora, Boeotia. National Archaeological Museum, Athens.
Plate 118   Comparanda.
              A. Relief of Matar from Gordion (S 59). Museum of Anatolian Civilizations, Ankara.
              B. Relief of Matar from Ankara/Bahçelievler. Museum of Anatolian Civilizations,
                 Ankara.
              C. Head of Matar from Salmanköy. Museum of Anatolian Civilizations, Ankara.
              D. Relief of Kubaba from Carchemish. Museum of Anatolian Civilizations, Ankara.
Plate 119   Comparanda.
              A. Statue group from Boğazköy. Museum of Anatolian Civilizations, Ankara.
              B. Double idol from Faharet Çeşme, set into a wall at the site of a spring.
              C. Relief with enthroned figure (S 86), Gordion.
              D. Relief of King Warpalawas, Ivriz.
Plate 120   Comparanda. Arslan Kaya.
Plate 121   Comparanda.
              A. Arslan Kaya. Detail of the scene in the niche showing the goddess Matar with her
                 attendant lions.
              B. Büyük Kapı Kaya. Matar, in the niche, was once flanked by two figures that are now
                 missing.
Plate 122   Comparanda.
              A. Pair of stone lions, Göllüdağ.
              B. Stone lion, Gordion (S 35).
              C. Stone lion, Gordion (S 43).
Plate 123   Comparanda. Midas Monument, Midas City.
Plate 124   Appendix 1.
              A. Removal of wax and dirt from fragments of the inlaid table using toluene.
              B. First mount for the inlaid table, showing damage to the acrylic sheet.
              C. Board from serving stand B (board 5) during cleaning.
Plate 125   Appendix 1.
              A. Large steel tank first employed for consolidation of the serving stands in 1983.
              B. Excavation of fills of wax and sawdust prior to the removal of the legs of table 1.
Plate 126   Appendix 1.
              A. Table 1 during treatment: softening of wax by application of a solvent-gel poultice.
              B. Wax residue on the surface of table 1 after consolidation.
              C. Fragments of table 6 encased in silkscreen pouches and sewn to the metal tray in
                 preparation for consolidation.
Plate 127   Appendix 1.
              A. Ethafoam storage mount for the carved stretcher from the northeast corner of the
                 tomb.
              B. Placing fragments of table 5 in a storage mount of ethafoam and Plexiglas.

Plate 128   Appendix 1. Legs of table 2 and table 4 housed in the new steel storage cabinets in their
              mounts of ethafoam and Goretex.
Plate 129   Appendix 2.
              A. Pieces of the inlaid table laid out in preparation for its reconstruction in 1983.
              B. Installation of the newly mounted table in its display case in the Museum of Anatolian
                 Civilizations, Ankara, 1983.
Plate 130   Appendix 2.
              A. Constructing the Plexiglas frame for the inlaid table's second mount, 1989.
              B. Attaching the struts and frame pieces to the new mount.
              C. Fitting the curved metal supports for the table's legs.
              D. The new metal leg supports attached to the original iron tripod stand.
Plate 131   Appendix 2.
              A. Plexiglas backing for the right rear leg strut being attached to the new mount.
              B. Painting the angle deck with shellac, after the old glue had been stripped from the
                 surface.
              C. The angle deck covered with fabric, attached without the use of adhesives.
Plate 132   Appendix 2.
              A. The newly mounted table being returned to the exhibition hall of the museum, 1989.
              B. Adding the evil-eye charm to the display.
Plate 133   Appendix 2.
              A. Parts of the top pieces, side pieces, back pieces, and diagonal back struts of the serving
                 stands, as sorted out in 1983.
              B. Attaching the wood of serving stand A to the Plexiglas backing, 1984.
Plate 134   Appendix 2.
              A. Making the Plexiglas replacement leg for the face of serving stand A.
              B. Two iron stands that supported the Plexiglas mounts of the serving stands.
              C. The wood of serving stand A being attached to the mount.
Plate 135   Appendix 2.
              A. The serving stands on display on their first mounts, 1984.
              B. Transporting the serving stands back to the museum laboratory in preparation for
                 remounting, 1999.
Plate 136   Appendix 2.
              A. Reconditioning the old Plexiglas mount of one of the serving stands.
              B. Cleaning the top piece of serving stand B.
Plate 137   Appendix 2.
              A. Sculpting metal hooks for the new mounts.
              B. Painting the padded metal hooks.
              C. Reattaching the wood of serving stand A to its Plexiglas mount.
Plate 138   Appendix 2.
              A. Attaching the wooden side pieces and back struts to the mount of serving stand B.
              B. The two serving stands on display in their new case, 1999.
Plate 139   Appendix 4. Transverse and radial sections of sound *Juglans* and *Buxus*.
Plate 140   Appendix 4. Transverse and radial sections of sound *Cedrus*, *Juniperus*, and *Taxus*.
Plate 141   Appendix 4. Transverse sections of decay in wood from the tops of table 6, table 7, and
              table 4.
Plate 142   Appendix 4. Degraded areas in wood from the tops of table 9 and table 4, with wood
              borer damage and frass present in voids in the wood.
Plate 143   Appendix 4. Transverse sections from boxwood legs of table 2 and table 7.
Plate 144   Appendix 4. Radial sections of vessel elements from fragments of the top of table 6,
              showing thickenings in walls of the vessels characteristic of *Acer* or *Prunus*.
Plate 145   Appendix 4. Transverse sections of decayed wood from the tops of the inlaid table and
              serving stand A.
Plate 146   Appendix 4. Transverse sections of wood from the tops of table 6, table 7, table 5, serving
              stand B, and leg of table 9, showing ultrastructural characteristics of soft rot.

Plate 147   Appendix 4. Scanning electron micrographs showing decay in wood from the coffin body
             and northeast corner block.

Plate 148   Appendix 4. Soft-rot cavities in radial sections of decayed pine wood from the northeast
             corner block, *Cedrus* coffin body, and sound cells of *Taxus* showing helical thickenings.

Plate 149   Appendix 4. Iron pseudomorphs of wood cells found in the coffin near iron bars and
             nails.

Plate 150   Appendix 7.
             A. Tenon fragments from serving stand A or B, with fine, straight saw cuttings.
             B. Tenon fragment from serving stand A or B, with marks of a chisel that was held at an
                angle, producing side compression of the wood fibers.
             C. Tenon from serving stand B, with clearly visible tool marks caused by a nicked chisel.
             D. Detail of the foot of the left rear leg (leg C) of the inlaid table, showing a line of drilled
                holes in a channel that had held a strip of inlay.

Plate 151   Appendix 7.
             A. Detail of handle A5, showing two of the recesses that had once held inlay.
             B. Detail of the face of serving stand B, showing a line of drilled holes used to facilitate
                the carving of a channel for a strip of inlay.
             C. Top of the right rear leg of table 5, showing evidence of an ancient repair.
             D. Tenon of the front leg of table 5, with the hole drilled for the wood pin that secured the
                tenon in the collar of the table top.

Plate 152   Appendix 7.
             A. Bottom of the foot of one of the legs of table 7, showing the compass marks used to
                determine the shape of the foot.
             B. Underside of one of the collars of table 6, showing a section of the compass-inscribed
                circle used to define the position of the mortise.
             C. Boxwood trees at Carter's Grove, Virginia, showing bent branches of the sort used to
                make the legs of the plain tables from Tumulus MM.

Plate 153   Appendix 8. Woven textile from the coffin (sample 2003-Tx-1).
             A. Scanning electron micrograph (SEM) showing plain weave (tabby) with microbial
                debris and mechanical damage.
             B. Detail of individual fibers within a single yarn (SEM).
             C. Detail of a single yarn, after solvent cleaning to remove microbial debris (SEM).
             D. Evidence of sheath remaining: detail of individual fibers within a single yarn after
                solvent cleaning (SEM).

Plate 154   Appendix 8.
             A. Woven textile from the coffin (2003-Tx-1). Hollow core of extant fiber shape: detail of
                damaged condition of individual fibers (SEM).
             B. Woven textile from the coffin (2003-Tx-1). Nonfibrous surface of individual fibers
                (SEM).
             C. "Mattress" material from the coffin (2003-Tx-5). Mass on surface (SEM).
             D. "Mattress" material from the coffin (2003-Tx-5). Detail of Plate 154C, indicating
                microbial origins of fine strands (SEM).

Plate 155   Appendix 8.
             A. Cushion or upholstery on "stool #2," northeast corner (2003-Tx-6). Detail of two
                layers on the upper surface, with fragments and impressions of the fine threads.
             B. Cushion or upholstery on "stool #2," northeast corner (2003-Tx-6). Detail of extant
                woven structure on the underside. The cording that was once strung across the seat
                stretchers of the stool is also visible on this sample.
             C. "Bag" on "stool #2," northeast corner (2003-Tx-7). Fine dark yarn of the fabric (SEM).
             D. "Bag" on "stool #2" northeast corner (2003-Tx-7). Detail of Plate 155C, showing the
                fragmentary and degraded condition of the fibrous mass (SEM).

Plate 156   Appendix 8.
     A. "Bag" on "stool #2," northeast corner (2003-Tx-8, front). Detail, showing the tendency of the dark fibers to crack, a property of the degradation of fiber (SEM).
     B. "Bag" on "stool #2," northeast corner (2003-Tx-8, front). Detail of a single yarn, an amalgamated mass (SEM).
     C. "Bag" on "stool #2," northeast corner (2003-Tx-8, back). Yarn from a second fabric on the fragment (SEM). This fabric is tan in color and a balanced plain weave.
     D. "Bag" on "stool #2," northeast corner (2003-Tx-8, back). Detail of Plate 156C showing the tan yarn, which has a coagulated and coated surface (SEM).

Plate 157   Appendix 8. Cloth from the floor behind serving stand A (2003-Tx-11, Yarn #1).
     A. Example of the finely spun yarn found in the cache of this sample, after the removal of surface debris by solvent cleaning (SEM).
     B. Detail of the finely spun yarn shown in Plate 157A (SEM).
     C. The fibers of the smooth strands, with coated surface (SEM).
     D. The fibers of the smooth strands are seen to be hollow, with coated surface (SEM).

Plate 158   Appendix 8.
     A. Cloth from floor behind serving stand A (2003-Tx-11, Yarn #1). Detail of Plate 157B, showing the longitudinal surface of the yarn's fiber (SEM).
     B. Cloth from floor behind serving stand A (2003-Tx-11, Yarn #2). Example of dark (black) yarn found in the cache of this sample, after the removal of surface debris by solvent cleaning (SEM).
     C. Cloth from floor behind serving stand A (2003-Tx-11, Yarn #2). Detail of a strand of dark yarn shown in Plate 158B (SEM).
     D. Cloth from floor behind serving stand A (2003-Tx-11, Yarn #2). Detail of Plate 158C, showing evidence of microbial activity (SEM).

LIST OF TEXT FIGURES

Plan of the Tumulus MM chamber, showing the furniture *in situ*, p. viii.

Chart, p. 80. Number of occurrences of square designs and design groups on the serving stands.

Text Figure 1, p. 180. DRIFTS spectra showing the principal absorptions of Tumulus MM beverage samples from different vessel types.

Text Figure 2, p. 181. DRIFTS spectra of representative beverage sample from Tumulus MM, showing the principal absorptions as explained by synthetic calcium oxalate, calcium tartrate, and modern beeswax.

Text Figure 3, p. 182. DRIFTS spectra showing the principal absorptions of Tumulus MM food samples from two different vessel types and a clump of material in a large cauldron.

Text Figure 4, p. 185. DRIFTS spectra of representative beverage sample from Tumulus MM, showing the principal absorptions as explained by modern lamb's fat and beeswax.

Text Figure 5, p. 186. A high-performance liquid chromatogram of a chloroform-methanol extract of the food residue from Tumulus MM.

Text Figure 6, p. 198. Illustrations of Egyptian carpenters' tools (Kenyon, *Jericho I*, figure 227).

Text Figure 7, p. 206. Comparison spectra of goethite and the gold-colored yarn seen on the "back" of 2003-Tx-2.

Text Figure 8, p. 210. Two-strand weft twining, shifted clockwise 90 degrees, or two-strand warp twining; wrapped soumak substituting for a weft shed, shifted clockwise 90 degrees; simple gauze weave.

Text Figure 9, p. 210. Twined yarns, which retain their twist; wrapped soumak and adjacent yarns; gauze yarns, detached.

Text Figure 10, p. 216. Comparison of pure cellulose with yarn from 2003-Tx-10, by FTIR.

Text Figure 11, p. 219. Gold-colored Fabric #1 of 2003-Tx-11 and its blue stain, compared with the mineral goethite and the spectrum of indigo, by FTIR.

Text Figure 12, p. 220. The FTIR spectra of the dark tiger-stripe components of Fabric #2, 2003-Tx-11, compared with those of indigo and the gum resin, myrrh.

Table 1, p. 205. Weight percentage of inorganic elements present on the recto of textile fragment 2003-Tx-1, as analyzed by SEM-EDS.

Table 2, p. 207. Weight percentage of inorganic elements present in the mixed reddish powder in 2003-Tx-3, as analyzed by SEM-EDS.

Table 3, p. 207. Weight percentage of inorganic elements present in the brightest red powder in 2003-Tx-3, as analyzed by SEM-EDS.

Table 4, p. 208. Weight percentage of inorganic elements present in the white powder, 2003-Tx-3, front, as analyzed by SEM-EDS.

Table 5, p. 209. Weight percentage of inorganic elements present in the fibers on the surface of 2003-Tx-5, as analyzed by SEM-EDS.

Table 6, p. 209. Weight percentage of inorganic elements present in the fiber residue of 2003-Tx-5, as analyzed by SEM-EDS.

Table 7, p. 212. Weight percentage of inorganic elements present in the reddish/purple powder, 2003-Tx-6, as analyzed by SEM-EDS.

Table 8, p. 214. Weight percentage of inorganic elements present in the dark fiber, 2003-Tx-7, back, as analyzed by SEM-EDS.

Table 9, p. 214. Weight percentage of inorganic elements present in the dark warp, 2003-Tx-8, as
    analyzed by SEM-EDS.

Table 10, p. 214. Weight percentage of inorganic elements present in the dark yarn, 2003-Tx-9, as
    analyzed by SEM-EDS.

Table 11, p. 218. Weight percentage of inorganic elements present in the dark strands, 2003-Tx-11, Yarn
    #2, as analyzed by SEM-EDS.

Table 12, p. 221. Weight percentage of inorganic elements present in a single bicomponent yarn,
    2003-Tx-11, Fabric #2, as analyzed by SEM-EDS.

LIST OF CD-FIGURES

Appendix 8: Preliminary Analyses of Textiles Associated with the Wooden Furniture from Tumulus MM

CD-Figure 1   Woven textile from the coffin (sample 2003-Tx-1). Optical microscopy showing plain weave, after solvent cleaning. Detail shown is 1.5 mm wide × 1.35 mm high.

CD-Figure 2   Woven textile from the coffin (sample 2003-Tx-1). Optical microscopy showing plain weave with white microbial debris, prior to cleaning. Detail shown is 5.4 mm wide × 4.0 mm high.

CD-Figure 3   Fragment of fiber (sample 2003-Tx-1) showing the cell wall with numerous perforations.

CD-Figure 4   Cell wall fragments (sample 2003-Tx-1). Polarized light microscopy (crossed polars with a λ plate and ¼λ plate added). Note large fragments' red color.

CD-Figure 5   Same fragment as in CD-Figure 4, but rotated 90 degrees. Polarized light microscopy (crossed polars with a λ plate and ¼λ plate added). Note prominent blue color. The color change could indicate a right-handed bast fiber like flax or ramie.

CD-Figure 6   Woven textile from the coffin (sample 2003-Tx-2, back) in its entirety. The fragment shows layers that have been overlaid in different directions.

CD-Figure 7   As seen by optical microscopy, a detail of CD-Figure 6 shows a doubled weft running diagonally towards the lower right; sections running at different angles indicate various layers of fabric. Detail shown is 17 mm wide × 12.5 mm high.

CD-Figure 8   Mass of possibly proteinaceous fibers from the front (red matted) side of sample 2003-Tx-2.

CD-Figure 9   Mass of possibly proteinaceous fibers from the front (red matted) side of sample 2003-Tx-2.

CD-Figure 10   Back view of fragment 2003-Tx-3 with yarn-like shapes visible in lighter color. Note small burr at right of center.

CD-Figure 11   Side view of fragment 2003-Tx-3; the stratified layers are also differentiated by their color.

CD-Figure 12   Detail of back view of fragment 2003-Tx-3, showing the cross-section of a pair of yarns forming a spiral shape. The uppermost is a Z-plied yarn; the dark spaces between the lighter yarns indicate the possible locations for a perpendicular element, perhaps the weft. The yarn is 1.37 mm wide.

CD-Figure 13   A "fruit" of *Medicago spp.* (burr clover, *Fabaceae*) observed on the back of sample 2003-Tx-3. It is about 4.8 mm × 5.6 mm.

CD-Figure 14   Highly degraded fiber fragments (sample 2003-Tx-3).

CD-Figure 15   Highly degraded fiber fragments (sample 2003-Tx-3).

CD-Figure 16   Cracked fragmentary agglomerations (2003-Tx-4) contain remnants of textile structure, top center. See detail, CD-Figure 17.

CD-Figure 17   Detail of textile fragment 2003-Tx-4, as seen by optical microscopy at low magnification. The crossing of a pair of yarns makes a spiral shape at the upper central edge of the fragment. Each yarn is about 0.2 mm wide.

CD-Figure 18   Highly degraded fiber fragments (sample 2003-Tx-4).

CD-Figure 19   The twined fabric on the back of sample 2003-Tx-5, difficult to discern because of the mottled debris.

CD-Figure 20   At higher magnification with optical microscopy, the interaction of the twined vertical elements of sample 2003-Tx-5 are visible. The width of one of these yarns appears to be 0.2 mm wide.

CD-Figure 21   A well-preserved fiber (sample 2003-Tx-5) embedded in a granular matrix. Polarized light microscopy (crossed polars with a λ plate and ¼λ plate added).

CD-Figure 22   Close-up of CD-Figure 21 showing thick cell wall with dislocations, indicating a bast fiber. Polarized light microscopy (crossed polars with a λ plate and ¼λ plate added).

CD-Figure 23   Another well-preserved fiber (sample 2003-Tx-5) embedded in a granular matrix. Polarized light microscopy (crossed polars with a λ plate and a ¼λ plate added).

CD-Figure 24   Same fiber as CD-Figure 23, but rotated 90 degrees. Polarized light microscopy (crossed polars with a λ plate and ¼λ plate added). The color change indicates a right-handed bast fiber like flax or ramie.

CD-Figure 25   Upper surface of the cushion or upholstery fragment from "stool #2" from the northeast corner of the tomb (2003-Tx-6).

CD-Figure 26   Underside of cushion or upholstery fragment from "stool #2" from the northeast corner of the tomb (2005-Tx 6). Two cording yarns are visible in the right lower central section of this fragment; additional yarns running parallel to them are partly visible.

CD-Figure 27   Detail of CD-Figure 26, as seen by optical microscopy, showing the upper left edge of the underside of the cushion or upholstery fragment from "stool #2" (2003-Tx-6), with the stratigraphic layers visible. The depth from the upper edge to the uppermost red layer is 2–3 mm.

CD-Figure 28   Detail of CD-Figure 26, showing a microscopic view of the lower edge of the underside of the cushion or upholstery fragment from "stool #2" (2003-Tx-6), with the stratigraphic layers visible. An ovoid space (1.37 mm wide × 0.75 mm high) marks the spot where a textile element once lay; its longitudinal counterpart, a reddish yarn with an apparent Z twist, lies beneath it.

CD-Figure 29   Upper surface of the cushion or upholstery fragment from "stool #2" from the northeast corner of the tomb (2003-Tx-6). The detail shows the twining, with clear horizontal spacings of 1.5 mm.

CD-Figure 30   Upper surface of the cushion or upholstery fragment from "stool #2" from the northeast corner of the tomb (2003-Tx-6). Detail of the twining, at a slightly higher magnification, showing another type of patterning, possibly a *verso*. The vertical yarns appear to be about 0.44 mm wide.

CD-Figure 31   Mass of fibers from sample 2003-Tx-6 resembling those in sample 2003-Tx-2 (see CD-Figures 8–9).

CD-Figure 32   Mass of fibers from sample 2003-Tx-6 resembling those in sample 2003-Tx-2 (see CD-Figures 8–9).

CD-Figure 33   Mass of fibers from sample 2003-Tx-6 resembling those in sample 2003-Tx-2 (see CD-Figures 8–9).

CD-Figure 34   Fragment of the "bag" on "stool #2" from the northeast corner (2003-Tx-7). The fragment has textile twining, but it is obscured by a tan powdery mass.

CD-Figure 35   Mass of unknown fibers from sample 2003-Tx-7.

CD-Figure 36   Mass of unknown fibers from sample 2003-Tx-7.

CD-Figure 37   Mass of unknown fibers from sample 2003-Tx-7.

CD-Figure 38   Fragments of the "bag" on "stool #2" from the northeast corner (2003-Tx-8). These fragments also have textile twining, again obscured by a tan powdery mass.

CD-Figure 39   Fragments of the "bag" on "stool #2" from the northeast corner (2003-Tx-8). On the opposite side, the fragments have a balanced plain weave (tabby) in a light golden tan atop a dark yarn textile; the pattern of the latter cannot be read optically, but appears to be related to the twining.

CD-Figure 40 Fragment of the "bag" on "stool #2" from the northeast corner (2003-Tx-8). In this detail of CD-Figure 39, the fabric lies in layers, sometimes pressed into the surface and sometimes running at different angles.

CD-Figure 41 Fragment of the "bag" on "stool #2" from the northeast corner (2003-Tx-8). This photomicrographic detail of CD-Figure 39 shows the tabby fabric, with the S-plied yarns unevenly twisted.

CD-Figure 42 Fragment of the "bag" on "stool #2" from the northeast corner (2003-Tx-8). This photomicrographic detail of CD-Figure 39 shows the dark fabric, perhaps twining, that lies below the light golden tan tabby fabric. The dark yarns appear to be slightly S-twisted singles, 0.18–0.24 mm in diameter.

CD-Figure 43 Mass of unknown fibers from sample 2003-Tx-8.

CD-Figure 44 Mass of unknown fibers from sample 2003-Tx-8.

CD-Figure 45 Mass of unknown fibers from sample 2003-Tx-8.

CD-Figure 46 Fragment of the "bag" on "stool #2" from the northeast corner (2003-Tx-9). The fragment has textile twining, but it is obscured by a tan powdery mass.

CD-Figure 47 Fragment of the "bag" on "stool #2" from the northeast corner (2003-Tx-9). This photomicrographic detail of CD-Figure 46 shows a cross-section of a pair of yarns twining about one another. The spacing between the (missing) perpendicular elements is 0.76 mm.

CD-Figure 48 Fragment of the "bag" on "stool #2" from the northeast corner (2003-Tx-9). With optical microscopy, the illustrated detail shows an area 20.25 mm wide × 15 mm high.

CD-Figure 49 Fragment of the "bag" on "stool #2" from the northeast corner (2003-Tx-9). This detail of CD-Figure 48 shows the twined pairs placed 1.38 mm apart, with the elements running perpendicular to them spaced 0.5 mm apart. The yarns are fine, 0.12–0.15 mm in width.

CD-Figure 50 Mass of unknown fibers from sample 2003-Tx-9.

CD-Figure 51 Mass of unknown fibers from sample 2003-Tx-9.

CD-Figure 52 "Pieces of fine material lifted from fibulae" on "stool #2" from the northeast corner. This detail of the plain weave fragment (2003-Tx-10) shows an irregular coating on some of the yarns. Detail shown is 0.5 mm wide × 0.4 mm high.

CD-Figure 53 Detail from sample 2003-Tx-10, bast fiber, showing cell wall dislocations. Polarized light microscopy (crossed polars with a λ plate and $\frac{1}{4}\lambda$ plate added).

CD-Figure 54 Detail from sample 2003-Tx-10, bast fiber. Polarized light microscopy (crossed polars with a λ plate). Note predominant yellow color.

CD-Figure 55 The same bast fibers seen in CD-Figure 54, but rotated 90 degrees. Polarized light microscopy (crossed polars with a λ plate). Note blue color. The color change indicates a right-handed fiber like flax or ramie.

CD-Figure 56 "Cloth" found "on the floor behind Throne Back A [serving stand A]." Overview of the fragment group examined (sample 2003-Tx-11).

CD-Figure 57 "Cloth" found "on the floor behind Throne Back A [serving stand A]." Detail of Fabric #1 of textile sample 2003-Tx-11, seen at the lower right of CD-Figure 56.

CD-Figure 58 "Cloth" found "on the floor behind Throne Back A [serving stand A]." Detail of Fabric #4 of textile sample 2003-Tx-11, seen at the top center of CD-Figure 56.

CD-Figure 59 "Cloth" found "on the floor behind Throne Back A [serving stand A]." Detail of Fabric #3 of textile sample 2003-Tx-11, seen at the "6 o'clock" and "7 o'clock" positions of CD-Figure 56.

CD-Figure 60 "Cloth" found "on the floor behind Throne Back A [serving stand A]." Detail of Fabric #2 of textile sample 2003-Tx-11, seen at the "3 o'clock" position, extreme right center in CD-Figure 56.

CD-Figure 61 "Cloth" found "on the floor behind Throne Back A [serving stand A]." Detail of the bicomponent yarns of Fabric #2 of textile sample 2003-Tx-11, seen in CD-Figure 60.

CD-Figure 62 Degraded fiber from Fabric #2 of textile sample 2003-Tx-11 with a highly perforated cell wall similar to that seen in textile sample 2003-Tx-1.

CD-Figure 63 Another detail of the highly perforated cell wall seen in sample 2003-Tx-11.

CD-Figure 64   Fiber fragments from sample 2003-Tx-11. Polarized light microscopy (crossed polars with a λ plate).

CD-Figure 65   The same fiber fragments shown in CD-Figure 64, but rotated 90 degrees. Polarized light microscopy (crossed polars with a λ plate). The color change indicates a right-handed bast fiber like flax or ramie.

Serving Stands A and B, Color Diagrams (Color Plates X–XI)

CD-Figure 66   Color diagram of serving stand A, with each main design shown in a different color (Color Plate XA).

CD-Figure 67   Color diagram of serving stand A, with each main design shown in a different color; derivatives of the main designs are shown in the same colors as the designs that they are meant to replace (Color Plate XB).

CD-Figure 68   Color diagram of serving stand A, with each main design *group* shown in a different color (Color Plate XC).

CD-Figure 69   Color diagram of serving stand A, with each main design *group* shown in a different color; derivatives of the main design groups are shown in the same colors as the groups they are meant to replace (Color Plate XD).

CD-Figure 70   Color diagram of serving stand B, with each main design shown in a different color (Color Plate XIA).

CD-Figure 71   Color diagram of serving stand B, with each main design shown in a different color; derivatives of the main designs are shown in the same colors as the designs that they are meant to replace (Color Plate XIB).

CD-Figure 72   Color diagram of serving stand B, with each main design *group* shown in a different color (Color Plate XIC).

CD-Figure 73   Color diagram of serving stand B, with each main design *group* shown in a different color; derivatives of the main design groups are shown in the same colors as the groups they are meant to replace (Color Plate XID).

Additional Comparanda: Monuments of the Phrygian Highlands

CD-Figure 74   Diagram of the geometric pattern on the carved façade of Arslan Kaya in the Phrygian highlands to the west of Gordion. The complex decoration can best be understood by extending the pattern beyond the extent of the façade. Two sets of interconnected swastikas are embedded in the pattern, one group oriented counterclockwise (red and yellow) and the other clockwise (blue and green).

CD-Figure 75   Inscription mentioning Midas on the face of the Midas Monument, Midas City, carved above the façade, to left.

CD-Figure 76   Inscriptions on the Midas Monument, Midas City. Left (no. 5): graffiti on inner right side post of façade niche, mentioning Midas and Matar. Right (no. 2): inscription carved on the façade frame.

CD-Figure 77   Arslan Taş, Phrygian Highlands.

Additional Comparanda: Iconography and Ethnographic Parallels

CD-Figure 78   Two bronze plaques depicting sphinxes, Syria, ninth-eighth century B.C. Metropolitan Museum of Art, New York.

CD-Figure 79   "Rebus" pectoral, tomb of Tutankhamun, 14th century B.C. Egyptian Museum, Cairo.

CD-Figure 80   Bronze standard, Alacahöyük, third millennium B.C. Museum of Anatolian Civilizations, Ankara.

CD-Figure 81   Lead "idol," Troy, third millennium B.C.

CD-Figure 82   "Bell idol," Boeotia. Late Geometric, eighth-seventh century B.C. Louvre.

CD-Figure 83   "Bell idol," Boeotia. Late Geometric, eighth-seventh century B.C. Museum of Fine Arts, Boston.

CD-Figure 84   Drawing of the painted scene on a ceramic polos, Boeotia, seventh century B.C. Stockholm National Museum.

CD-Figure 85   Relief pithos, Boeotia, seventh century B.C. National Archaeological Museum, Athens.

CD-Figure 86   Terra-cotta stamps or seals, Çatalhöyük, sixth millennium B.C.

CD-Figure 87   Wall painting, Çatalhöyük. Shrine E.VII/21, seventh-sixth millennium B.C.

CD-Figure 88   Wife of a Teke Khan, photograph before 1890.

CD-Figure 89   Turkmen baby's dress, 19th–20th century. Silk ikat and printed cotton with later addition of silver, carnelian, shell, and bead decoration. Collection of the author.

CD-Figure 90   Turkish traditional dress (right), Hubyar tribe, Almuş region.

CD-Figure 91   Turkish traditional dress, Sivas mountain region.

CD-Figure 92   Turkish traditional headdress, 19th century. Felt, string, and ribbon with silver, brass, coral, and bead decoration. Collection of the author.

CD-Figure 93   Turkish doll in traditional dress, made by Hanife Güneş, 2004. Sorgun, Keles mountain region. Collection of the author.

CD-Figure 94   Diagram of a "calendar" embroidery showing the year as a circle, divided into months, with each of the 365 days represented. Major feasts and the best planting days for various crops are indicated, along with the solstices and equinoxes. Historical Museum, Moscow.

CD-Figure 95   Two wooden door posts, said to represent the "ancestors," carved with lozenge patterns representing the multiple bodies of many generations. New Caledonia, South Pacific.

CD-Figure 96   Toba woman with facial tattoos, including a quartered lozenge, with dots in the quadrants, on her forehead, Argentina.

CD-Figure 97   Stele of King Warpalawas from Bor, eighth century B.C. Museum of the Ancient Near East, Istanbul.

CD-Figure 98   Representations of Assyrian dress from the reign of Tiglath-pileser III (r. 744–727 B.C.).

CD-Figure 99   Orthostat depicting the goddess Kubaba, Carchemish, tenth or ninth century B.C. Museum of Anatolian Civilizations, Ankara.

CD-Figure 100   Roman grave relief from Amiternum, first century B.C.(?). Aquila, Museo Aquilano.

PREFACE

Rodney S. Young, director of the University of Pennsylvania team that excavated the ancient Phrygian site of Gordion, Turkey, died in 1974, with the study of the wooden objects still in its preliminary stages. It was my job to prepare the final illustrations for Young's posthumous volume, *Three Great Early Tumuli: The Gordion Excavations Final Reports, Volume I* (hereafter *Gordion I*).[1] Comparison of the field drawings with the excavation photographs showed that many of the original drawings of the wooden artifacts from these three tombs—Tumulus MM, Tumulus P, and Tumulus W—were inaccurate. The editorial committee decided that the publication of Young's book should go forward, but Machteld Mellink, the chair of the committee, suggested that I undertake a new study of the Gordion furniture and other wooden finds. I agreed to the proposal and went to Turkey in 1981 to investigate the inlaid table from Tumulus MM. This initial work soon became a full-scale project conducted at the Museum of Anatolian Civilizations in Ankara, under the auspices of The University of Pennsylvania Museum of Archaeology and Anthropology.

The purpose of the Gordion Furniture Project, still ongoing, is the study, drawing, photography, conservation, reconstruction, and storage of the furniture and small wooden objects from the site. Results have been published in numerous articles and books, which are listed in the notes and bibliography. The most comprehensive treatment can be found in *Gordion Wooden Furniture* (hereafter *GWF*), published in 1999 in English and Turkish by the Museum of Anatolian Civilizations, Ankara.[2] The Tumulus MM furniture was the subject of my 1985 doctoral dissertation;[3] after 20 more years of work on the objects, all the information, drawings, and photographs in that preliminary study have been superseded. The Gordion wooden artifacts, once misinterpreted and even maligned,[4] are now recognized as the largest and most important group of well-preserved ancient wooden objects to be excavated from the Near East.

In 1981 I met Robert Payton, then conservator for the British Institute of Archaeology in Ankara, who was working in the laboratory of the Museum of Anatolian Civilizations at the time. He and I both realized that the objects could not be studied safely and effectively until the wood had been consolidated. Payton became the first conservator to work on the Gordion wood, followed by 11 conservators and 20 graduate interns. Since 1990, the conservation project has been headed by Krysia Spirydowicz of Queen's University, Kingston, Ontario, who has written the conservation summary that appears in this book (Appendix 1). The methods initiated by the conservation team now serve as a model for the conservation of dry archaeological wood.

Numerous scientists, wood specialists, photographers, preparators, artists, and archaeologists have also contributed to the results published here, including many valued Turkish colleagues at the Museum of Anatolian Civilizations. Burhan Aytuğ, Robert Blanchette, and Benjamin Held conducted the wood species analysis (Appendix 3); Robert Blanchette and his graduate students carried out the wood pathology analysis (Appendix 4); Patrick McGovern and his

[1] Rodney S. Young, *Three Great Early Tumuli, The Gordion Excavations Final Reports* I (Philadelphia, PA: University of Pennsylvania Museum of Archaeology and Anthropology, 1981). With contributions to the text by K. DeVries, E.L. Kohler, J.F. McClellan, M.J. Mellink, and G.K. Sams.

[2] E. Simpson and K. Spirydowicz, *Gordion Wooden Furniture (Gordion Ahşap Eserler): The Study, Conservation, and Reconstruction of the Furniture and Wooden Objects from Gordion, 1981–1998* (Ankara: Museum of Anatolian Civilizations, 1999).

This publication superseded the first edition of this book: E. Simpson, K. Spirydowicz, and V. Dorge, *Gordion Wooden Furniture (Gordion Ahşap Eserler): The Study, Conservation, and Reconstruction of the Wooden Furniture from Gordion, 1981–1990* (Ankara: Museum of Anatolian Civilizations, 1992). See also Simpson, "Phrygian Furniture from Gordion."

[3] Simpson, "Wooden Furniture from Tumulus MM at Gordion, Turkey."

[4] Young, "Phrygian Furniture from Gordion," 9; *Gordion I*, 183. For a complete discussion, see Chapter 2.

colleagues analyzed the food and drink remains found in Tumulus MM (Appendix 5); Lynn E. Roller studied the graffiti on the serving stands from this tomb (Appendix 6); Daniel Olson, John Scofield, Antoine Wilmering, and Geoffrey Killen contributed to the study of Phrygian woodwork-ing techniques (Appendix 7); and Mary Ballard and her associates have analyzed the textile re-mains related to the furniture (Appendix 8). The project's participants and our many interested friends and colleagues have all played a role in the dramatic discoveries presented in this book.

ACKNOWLEDGMENTS

Work on the wooden furniture and household objects from Gordion has been carried out under the auspices of the University of Pennsylvania Museum of Archaeology and Anthropology in conjunction with the Museum of Anatolian Civilizations, Ankara, and the General Directorate of Monuments and Museums, Ministry of Culture of the Turkish Republic.

Cooperating institutions and organizations include Queen's University, Kingston, Ontario; the British Institute of Archaeology, Ankara; the University of Minnesota; the University of California, Forest Products Laboratory; the Eastern Regional Research Center, U.S. Department of Agriculture; the Amber Research Laboratory, Vassar College; Scientific Instrument Services; Smith-Kline Beecham Pharmaceuticals; the Museum Conservation Institute, Smithsonian Institution; the Canadian Conservation Institute; the Conservation Technology Group; the Henry Francis DuPont Winterthur Museum; the Conservation Center of the Institute of Fine Arts, New York University; the Metropolitan Museum of Art; the Bard Graduate Center for Studies in the Decorative Arts, Design, and Culture; and, for the re-creation of the "Midas Feast," the Museum Catering Company and Dogfish Head Brewery.

Funding for the project has been contributed by The University of Pennsylvania Museum, the Gordion Foundation, Queen's University, the National Endowment for the Humanities, the National Science Foundation, the Samuel H. Kress Foundation, the 1984 Foundation, the Getty Grant Program, the National Geographic Society, the American Council of Learned Societies, the Center for Advanced Study in the Visual Arts of the National Gallery of Art, the Archaeological Institute of America, the American Research Institute in Turkey, the Anatolian Archaeological Research Foundation, the American-Turkish Council, T.C. Ziraat Bankası, the Institute for Aegean Prehistory, the Bard Graduate Center, the Metropolitan Museum of Art, the Dover Foundation, the Joukowsky Family Foundation, the Joseph Rosen Foundation, the Overbrook Foundation, the Kaplan Fund of New York, the Moore Collaborative, Mr. and Mrs. William S. Street, Michael R. DeLuca, Mr. and Mrs. Thomas F. Troxell, Jr., Benjamin Zucker, Daniel Olson, B. Gerald Wyckoff, Marquis C. Landrum, and several donors who wish to remain anonymous. The work of the project would not have been possible without the generous support of these institutions and individuals.

The following staff members have taken part in the study, conservation, and reconstruction of the Gordion furniture: Elizabeth Simpson, Director (1981–2009); Krysia Spirydowicz, Senior Conservator (1990–2009); Robert Payton, Conservator (1982–1985); Lisa Goldberg, Conservator (1988–1989); Andrew Todd, Conservator (1989); Valerie Dorge, Conservator (1990–1992); Marian Kaminitz, Conservator (1991); James Wermuth, Conservator (1994–1995); Elisabeth Joy, Conservator (1999); Alice Boccia Paterakis, Conservator (2007); Won Ng, Graduate Student Conservator (1991) and Conservator (1992–1993); Anne McKay, Graduate Student Conservator (1992) and Conservator (1993–1996); Nancy Love, Graduate Student Conservator (1994) and Conservator (1997–1998); Ellen Pratt, Graduate Student Conservator (1988); Emily Dunn, Graduate Student Conservator (1989); John Childs, Graduate Student Conservator (1990); Emily Kaplan, Graduate Student Conservator (1993); Marianne Weldon, Graduate Student Conservator (1994); Lisa Bengston, Graduate Student Conservator (1997); Joanne Boyer, Graduate Student Conservator (1998); Alexander Gabov, Graduate Student Conservator (1999); Stacy McLennan, Graduate Student Conservator (2000); Alison Whyte, Graduate Student Conservator (2000); Laura Lipcsei, Graduate Student Conservator (2000); Kimberly Cobb, Graduate Student Conservator (2004); Ariel O'Connor, Graduate Student Conservator (2007); Melanie Clifton-Harvey, Graduate Student Conservator (2008); Christine Moog, Graduate Research Assistant

(1993); Janis Mandrus, Graduate Research Assistant (1997–1999); Michelle Hargrave, Graduate Research Assistant (1999).

Special studies were carried out by Burhan Aytuğ, wood species analysis (1983–1989); Robert Blanchette, wood species and wood pathology analyses (1989–2009); Benjamin Held, wood species analysis (1999–2009); Arno Schniewind, wood studies and wood strength tests (1993–1995); Susan Buck and John Childs, wood finish analysis (1989–1990); Robert Gillespie, glue analysis (1983); George Reilly, glue analysis (1989–1990); Patrick McGovern, with Donald Glusker, Lawrence Exner, Robert Moreau, Alberto Nuñez, Curt Beck, Edith Stout, Eric Butrym, Chad Quinn, and Gretchen Hall, chemical analysis of food and drink remains (1998–2009); Daniel Olson, tools and techniques (1990–1999); Antoine Wilmering, tools and techniques (1990–1991); Gareth Darbyshire, Gordion tools (1998–1999); Lynn Roller, graffiti (1990–1995); and Mary Ballard, with Harry Alden, Roland Cunningham, Walter Hopwood, Joseph Koles, and Laure Dussubieux, textile analysis (2003–2009).

Exhibition mounts for the wooden objects were constructed with the help of Celal Alpüren, Cemal Alpüren, Abdurrahim Çulha, Alexander Gabov, Michelle Hargrave, Logan Hurst, Hamit Kaplan, Mehmetçik Kutkam, Janis Mandrus, Won Ng, Daniel Olson, Latif Özen, Robert Payton, Nancy Reynolds, Christine Smith, Krysia Spirydowicz, and Nazif Uygur. Denise Hoffman and Claire Zimmerman prepared several pencil renderings, and Janis Mandrus and William Schenck produced many of the ink drawings of the furniture illustrated in this book. Jocelyn Miller photographed numerous objects and printed many of the photographs that appear in the plates; the photographic archives were organized by Robin Miller. Martina Grünewald, Michelle Hargrave, Freyja Hartzell, Heather Jane McCormick, Kelly Moody, Kellie Sanborn, Beth Tedesco, and Yumi Yamamori helped with research, translation, and final preparation of the plates and manuscript for publication. The entire team must be credited with the results.

Special thanks are extended to our friends at the Museum of Anatolian Civilizations for their help and many kindnesses. The project is indebted to Director Hikmet Denizli and past Directors İlhan Temizsoy, Gürkan Toklu, İnci Bayburtluoğlu, Osman Aksoy, and Raci Temizer; Assistant Directors Emel Yurttagül and Nihal Tırpan; past Assistant Directors Memetçik Kutkam, Tahsin Saatçi and Doğu Mermerci; Behiç Günel, Hüseyin Şen, and the staff of the museum photography studio; and curatorial staff Işık Bingöl, Okan Cinemre, Nuray Demirtaş, Belma Kulaçoğlu, Özcan Şimşek, Ayşe Toker, and Remzi Yağci. This project is especially grateful to Nazif Uygur, Latif Özen, and the accomplished staff of the museum laboratory, past and present, including Rıfat Çelik, Abdurrahim Çulha, Cemal Uzundağ, and Fethi Ünlü, as well as Emine Yeşim Alagöz, Gülay Asılkazancı, Sinan Asılkazancı, Aynur Aslan, İmge Batur, Havva Boydaş, İlknur Elyıldırım, Sinem Güzeltepe, Leyla Kılıçtaş, Cengiz Özduygulu, and Songül Yılmazer. Our work has benefited from the support of the Department of Antiquities, in particular that of past Acting General Director of Monuments and Museums Kenan Yurttagül and past General Directors Altan Akat and Engin Özgen. We thank M. İstemihan Talay, Turkish Minister of Culture, for the award given to the project by the Turkish government in 1998.

We are grateful to our colleagues at the University of Pennsylvania Museum, in particular past Directors Jeremy A. Sabloff and Robert H. Dyson, Jr.; and Alan Waldt, Mary Dobson, and the Business Office staff. We wish to acknowledge the help of Janice Bellace, Deputy Provost of the University of Pennsylvania, and to thank the readers of the manuscript for their useful comments. We appreciate the support of Michiel K. Swormink and Patricia Radder at Brill, and we are especially indebted to Jennifer Pavelko, Acquisitions Editor at Brill USA, Inc., and Rebecca Blake, graphic designer, for the time and expertise they contributed toward the publication process. We thank David Schulman and Shapco Printing, Inc., for producing a handsomely illustrated book.

For their special help, the project thanks Andre Abad, Ann Bruck, Sam Calagione, Kory Cease, Suzanne Clappier, Toni Cross, Keith DeVries, Robert Forcier, John Haight, Pamela Hatchfield, Bruce Hoadley, Pamela Horowitz, Joel Jurgens, Mary B. Kelly, Jane Kergan, Geoffrey Killen, Robert Koestler, Peter Kuniholm, Greg Landrey, David Lidle, Richard Liebhart, Naomi Miller, Daniel Olson, Martha Phillips, Lynn Roller, Irene Bald Romano, G. Kenneth Sams, Fred Schock, John Scofield, Carlos Simpson, Steven Soter, Russell Stockman, Maya Vassileva, Karen Vellucci, Alexandra Walcott, Susan Weber, Richard Wolbers, B. Gerald Wyckoff, and our Turkish colleagues Özgen Acar, Celal Alpüren, Cemal Alpüren, Ekrem Aydemir, Ekrem Berik, Ragıp Buluç, Sevim Buluç, Birtan Collier, Cemil Eren, Zeynep Eren, Meral Gözübüyük, Cennet Köse, Alkan Oral, Osman Öztartan, Selahattin Öztartan, Nimet Özgüç, Erkal Saran, Selahattin Savaş, and Ekber Topal.

Finally, I am personally indebted to Rodney S. Young for encouraging me to study at the University of Pennsylvania and to the following colleagues for their expert guidance and unfailing support: Lisa Ackerman, Stuart Fleming, Georgina Herrmann, Ellen L. Kohler, Patricia Lawrence, Machteld J. Mellink, David Gordon Mitten, Oscar White Muscarella, James B. Pritchard, David Stronach, Charles K. Williams II, and Irene J. Winter.

Photographic Credits

All photographs are by the author except the following:

Gordion archives—Color Plates I–VII; Plates 1, 36–38, 42, 46, 50, 54–56, 60, 63, 66, 69–71, 80–81, 100–103, 107–110, 116D.
Gordion Furniture Project—Plates 130A–B, D; 131A; 134A; 135A; 136A.

Courtesy Robert Blanchette—Plates 139–149.
Courtesy Jocelyn Miller—Plates 40–41, 44–45, 48–49, 52–53, 58–59, 62, 65, 68.
Courtesy Museum of Anatolian Civilisations—CD-Figure 99.
Courtesy Daniel Olson—Plate 152C.
Courtesy Latif Özen—Plate 22A–B, E.
Courtesy Smithsonian Institution—Plates 153–158 and CD-Figures 1–65.
Courtesy University of Manchester—Color Plate XVIB.
Courtesy Antoine Wilmering—Plate 150A–C.

Akurgal, *Art of the Hittites*, plates 7, 115, 136—Plates 118D, 122A; CD-Figure 80. Photographs courtesy Ekrem Akurgal.
Akurgal, *Kunst Anatoliens*, plates 38, 52, 54, 60, 67—Plates 118B, 119D, 120–121A, 123. Photographs courtesy Ekrem Akurgal.
Arias and Hirmer, *History of Greek Vase Painting*, plate 11—Plate 117C.
Boardman, *Early Greek Vase Painting*, figure 101—CD-Figure 83. Photograph ©1998, Museum of Fine Arts, Boston.

Erden, *Anatolian Garment Culture*, 227, 237—CD-Figures 90–91.
Gimbutas, *Goddesses and Gods of Old Europe*, plate 204—Plate 117A. Reprinted by permission of the Estate of Marija Gimbutas.
Haspels, *Highlands of Phrygia*, figures 132; 183; 598:1–2, 5—Plate 121B, CD-Figures 75–77. Reprinted by permission of Princeton University Press.
Herrmann, *Furniture of Western Asia*, plates 64B, 76B—Plate 116B, CD-Figure 100. Plate 116B courtesy Musée du Louvre.
Kalter, *Arts and Crafts of Turkestan*, plate 61—CD-Figure 88.
Mellaart, *Çatal Hüyük*, plate 121—CD-Figure 86.
Mellaart, Hirsch, and Balpınar, *Goddess from Anatolia* 1, plate 5:3—CD-Figure 87. Photograph courtesy John Eskenazi, Ltd.
Muscarella, *Bronze and Iron*, no. 493a–b—CD-Figure 78.
Muscarella, "Fibulae Represented on Sculpture," figure 6—CD-Figure 97.
Orthmann, *Der alte Orient*, plate 248—Plate 116A.
Prayon, *Phrygische Plastik*, plate 15C (photograph Kurt Bittel)—Plate 119B. Photograph courtesy Ernst Wasmuth Verlag, Tübingen.
Schliemann, *Ilios*, 337, no. 226—CD-Figure 81.
Treasures of Tutankhamun, color plate 16 (cat. 26)—CD-Figure 79.
Vermaseren, *Cybele and Attis*, plate 1—CD-Figure 85. Courtesy National Archaeological Museum, Athens. Inv. no. 355.

Art Credits

All drawings are by the author except the following:

Dorothy H. Cox—Tomb plan, Figures 1–2.
Greg Harlin—Frontispiece.
Greg Harlin, William Schenck, and Elizabeth Simpson—Figure 40.
James S. Last—Figure 92.
Janis Mandrus after* Elizabeth Simpson—Figures 12–16, 19–20, 22–23, 26–39, 41–49, 52–57, 60–66, 68–70, 73, 75–76.

* The designation "after" indicates that the first artist listed produced the ink drawing based on an original pencil drawing by the artist listed second.

Janis Mandrus after Claire Zimmerman–Figures 24–25.

Lynn E. Roller–Figures 94–99.

William Schenck after Elizabeth Simpson–Figures 6–7, 58, 78.

William Schenck and Elizabeth Simpson–Figure 50.

Boardman, *Early Greek Vase Painting*, figure 235—CD-Figure 84. © The National Museum of Fine Arts, Stockholm.

Boehmer, "Phrygische Prunkgewänder," figures 17–19—CD-Figure 98.

Gimbutas, *Language of the Goddess*, figure 142—CD-Figure 82. Reproduced by permission of HarperCollins Publishers.

Haspels, *Highlands of Phrygia*, figure 522—Figure 93. Reprinted by permission of Princeton University Press.

Kelly, *Goddess Embroideries of Eastern Europe*, figure 9—CD-Figure 94. Courtesy Mary B. Kelly

Kenyon, *Jericho II*, figure 227—Text Figure 6. Courtesy Council for British Research in the Levant.

Schuster and Carpenter, *Patterns That Connect*, figures 260–261, 483—Plate 116C, CD-Figure 95. Courtesy Edmund Carpenter.

Schuster and Carpenter, *Social Symbolism in Ancient & Tribal Art* 1:2, figure 764—CD-Figure 96. Courtesy Edmund Carpenter.

Most of the drawings of the Tumulus MM furniture were photographed by Independent Printing Company, New York, under the supervision of Robert Carpenito and Anthony Novello; additional photographs and digital reproductions have been provided by National Reprographics, Inc., Queens Progress, Artcraft Digital, and Color Group of New York.

INTRODUCTION

In the 1950s, Rodney Young and his team of archaeologists excavated a remarkable collection of Phrygian wooden objects at the site of Gordion in Turkey. Recovered from three royal tumulus burials and the destruction level of the city mound, the fine furniture and small wooden artifacts constituted one of the most significant archaeological finds of organic objects ever discovered. The largest of the burial mounds, Tumulus MM, contained an impressive array of offerings, including the remains of 15 or more pieces of wooden furniture. Three of these pieces were elaborately carved and inlaid in contrasting woods with a variety of geometric patterns. The objects were quite well preserved when found, although virtually all of the wood had suffered some kind of deterioration. As a result, the collection presents some unusual problems, which bear on the present study.

Accurate measurements are difficult to obtain, since the pieces are warped, broken, or fragmentary in varying degrees. Photographs alone do not suffice for their depiction, as the wood now looks much different than it did originally. The once vivid contrast between the light base wood and dark inlay of the inlaid pieces has been lost, and many details are unclear in the photographs. And photographic images, while they can relay much of the beauty and fine craftsmanship inherent in the pieces, cannot convey an adequate impression of their original appearance. It was always obvious that drawings were needed, but during the course of the present study it became clear that these drawings would not be mere supplementary illustrations. Drawings could indicate almost all the new discoveries and would be the most concise and effective way of presenting this information. Finally, drawings allow the furniture to be reconstructed on paper, in versions that closely approximate the pieces in their original state. My colleagues and I have tried to make these drawings as accurate as possible, as they are an essential part of the scholarship.

As dimensions are problematic, only the basic measurements are given in the catalogue (Part Two). Measurements of the objects as they are now preserved are designated as *preserved* measurements.[1] In some cases, reconstructed measurements, designated as *estimated* measurements, are given for pieces as envisioned in their original form. Metric scales are included in some of the drawings; drawings and photographs without them have their scales noted in the captions where appropriate. Because of the condition of the wood, some of the dimensions given here cannot be considered definitive. In all instances, measurements were averaged to achieve a satisfactory compromise. But this averaging itself had a leveling effect, and the reader may consider most reconstructions to be approximately accurate. Abbreviations for measurements are as follows: G.P.L.—greatest preserved length, G.P.H.—greatest preserved height, G.P.W.—greatest preserved width, G.P.Th.—greatest preserved thickness, G.P.D.—greatest preserved diameter, Est.L.—estimated length, etc.

G.P.L. indicates the greatest possible *straight* measurement taken from a given object. In cases such as the curved table legs, this is the greatest diagonal measurement from the top of the tenon to the tip of the foot; a measurement taken along the curve of a leg would be neither consistent nor representative of the leg's true dimensions. Preserved measurements have been noted to help the reader envision the sizes and shapes of the extant pieces, and for the purpose of recording and identifying the objects and their constituent parts.

---

[1] The original field measurements taken in 1957 are on file in the Gordion archives at the University of Pennsylvania Museum.

Several pieces of furniture from Tumulus MM were left uncatalogued in 1957: tables 2, 3, 4, 6, 7, and 9; the furniture from the northeast corner of the tomb; and the king's coffin (Young's "bed") and associated finds. These have now been catalogued, with the new numbers appearing here in the catalogue entries. The wood catalogue numbers consist of an initial number (the number of the find in the Gordion running inventory series), followed by a "W" (indicating wood), and then a second number (the number of the object in the wood inventory series). Catalogue numbers should be distinguished from "MM" numbers, which were given to the objects for publication in Young's posthumous monograph (*Gordion I*). Some pieces remain uncatalogued, notably the "medium" and "long" legs from the northeast corner, as these have now deteriorated beyond recognition. The interpretation of the furniture from the northeast corner is still tentative, although one "short" leg and a carved stretcher have been identified and catalogued.

Standard American woodworking terms are used here in the catalogue descriptions. A *tenon* is a projecting element extending at the end of a piece of wood for insertion into a corresponding slot or *mortise* cut in an adjoining member. A *dowel* is a *pin* or *peg* fitted into corresponding holes in two pieces of wood to fasten them together.[2] The term *dowel* is used here for the internal bracing members that reinforced the frame of the inlaid table. *Pin* and *peg* are used interchangeably. *Free tenons* (also called *floating tenons, loose tenons, double tenons,* or *flat dowels*) are the small, flat pieces that secured the boards of the faces of the serving stands ("screens"). These *free tenons* were set into corresponding mortises cut in the edges of two adjoining boards and were normally secured by pins.[3]

The corners of the frame of the inlaid table were joined with an *open mortise* or *corner bridle joint*

with a locking pin: the projecting tenons of the front and back frame pieces fit into open slots at the ends of the side frame pieces.[4] A *halved joint* utilizes corresponding channels in adjacent faces of two members.[5] The curved front leg strut of the inlaid table was set into the top of the front foot in this manner. A *T bridle joint* allows a strip notched on both sides to be fit into a slot at the end of a piece running perpendicular to it. This is the joint used in the construction of the "rails" of the coffin.[6]

The word *grain* can function in many different ways, but the term is often used to describe the dominant longitudinal cells in a tree. The term *grain direction* is clearer and can be substituted regarding this meaning.[7] The structure of wood is normally considered in three-dimensional terms: the *transverse plane* or *cross-sectional plane* is perpendicular to the stem axis and can be observed typically at the end of a log or stump. A plane passing through the pith of the wood (as a radius of a circle) is called a *radial plane* or surface. A *tangential plane* or surface is a plane parallel to the pith but not passing through it, forming a tangent to the circular growth-ring structure.[8] *End grain surface* (or *end grain*) refers to the transverse or cross-sectional surface. *Side grain* or *longitudinal surface* indicates a plane running parallel to the pith: any radial or tangential surface is a longitudinal surface. Boards that are *flat cut* (or *flatsawn* or *plainsawn*) exhibit interesting side grain, which can be used for decorative effect.[9] The reader is referred to the books cited in the notes for additional clarification.

The woodworking tools and techniques used to make the furniture from Tumulus MM are discussed in detail in Appendix 7. Regarding the craftsmen, no distinction is made here between *artists* and *artisans*, and these terms are used interchangeably.[10] Regarding the transliteration of ancient names into English, it is difficult to avoid inconsistency, and I have not attempted to do so;

[2] Definitions are based on those in *Merriam-Webster's Collegiate Dictionary*, 11th edition (2003). For the mortise-and-tenon joint, see Hoadley, *Understanding Wood*, 183–186; Frid, *Tage Frid Teaches Woodworking*, 160. For a complete discussion of woodworking joinery and modern construction techniques, see Rogowski, *Complete Illustrated Guide to Joinery*.

[3] Rogowski, *Complete Illustrated Guide to Joinery*, 334–335. Steffy, *Wooden Ship Building*, 276, 297.

[4] Hayward, *Woodwork Joints*, 56, figure 22. Rogowski, *Complete Illustrated Guide to Joinery*, 232, 244.

[5] Hayward, *Woodwork Joints*, 22, figure 12c. This joint may also be called a "cross half lap" joint. Rogowski,

Complete Illustrated Guide to Joinery, 231.

[6] Blackburn, *Illustrated Furniture Making*, 124–126. Rogowski, *Complete Illustrated Guide to Joinery*, 232.

[7] For a full discussion of the word *grain* and its implications, see Hoadley, *Understanding Wood*, 7–23.

[8] These very precise descriptions are Bruce Hoadley's. Hoadley, *Understanding Wood*, 12–13.

[9] Ibid., 13–14.

[10] On the perceived difference, see Gunter, "Artists and Ancient Near Eastern Art," 11–12; Metzler, "Historical Perspectives on Artistic Environments," 143; and other articles in the same volume.

the reader will recognize these names, which conform to common usage.

In all cases, the drawings, photographs, and information presented here supersede those previously published elsewhere. References to Figures and Plates (capitalized) refer to the illustrations in this volume; illustrations from other publications are cited as figures and plates (lower case) from those sources. A CD has been included, containing color images of the Tumulus MM textiles (see Appendix 8), the color diagrams of the serving stands, as well as additional comparanda. A useful concordance has been included at the end of this book (Appendix 9).

PART ONE

DISCOVERY AND EARLY INTERPRETATION

CHAPTER ONE

THE EXCAVATION OF TUMULUS MM AND THE CONTENTS OF THE BURIAL

Tumulus MM at Gordion in Turkey was excavated in 1957 by the University of Pennsylvania Museum under the direction of Rodney S. Young. The capital of the ancient kingdom of Phrygia, Gordion was ruled at its height by the great King Midas, an historical figure who lived in the eighth century B.C. Tumulus MM, a gigantic burial mound some distance from the ancient citadel, stood 53 meters high with a diameter of nearly 300 meters at the time of Young's excavation. In 1955 and 1956, a series of 96 holes was bored into the earth of the tumulus in order to determine the location of the burial chamber beneath the mound.[1] The chamber's position and extent were outlined in the summer of 1956; in April 1957 a trench was opened in the mound's perimeter, and excavation of the tumulus was begun (Color Plate IA).[2]

The trench was dug from the southwest straight in toward the center of the mound in the direction of the tomb chamber. The trench ran for about 70 meters, at which point a tunnel was started.[3] The tunneling proceeded for another 67.7 meters,[4] when a stone wall was exposed, blocking the tunnel's path. The wall was about 3 meters high, made of roughly cut stone blocks.[5] The excavators breached the wall and found that the space beyond it was filled with rubble. On June 16, after much of the rubble had poured out, the team was able to pass through the breach. On the other side of the wall were two large logs resting on rubble at about the level of the top of the wall. Beyond these, a third log was exposed, which turned out to be part of a log wall at the west side of the tomb. Another such log wall was uncovered at the north. These two walls were part of a massive casing of juniper logs that surrounded the inner tomb chamber.[6] The excavators removed a section from the western log wall, and more rubble poured out, revealing the finished wooden wall of the inner chamber.

The chamber, made of pine planks,[7] was almost square, measuring 5.15 meters (east-west) by 6.2 meters (north-south) on the interior. The walls rose to a height of about 3.25 meters above the tomb floor.[8] The gabled roof was supported at the center by a composite crossbeam that spanned the width of the interior,[9] and at the north and south ends by pairs of double beams at the tops of the north and south walls. These ran out beyond the chamber's east and west walls and rested in cuttings in the upper logs of the tomb's outer log casing.[10] The inner chamber must have been built up in conjunction with the construction of the outer log casing. Since the outer logs did not form a free-standing, self-supporting structure, they must have been laid down, one by one, braced on both sides by rubble. This would have required that the surrounding stone enclosure wall be built up gradually along with the log casing. Young thought that successive ramps of clay might have been laid down outside the stone enclosure to facilitate construction of the

---

[1] For the dimensions, see Young, *Gordion I*, 79; for an account of the drilling program, 81 ff. For background on the Phrygian capital and an account of the earliest excavations at the site in 1900, see Körte and Körte, *Gordion*.

[2] Young, *Gordion I*, 83, plate 35B.

[3] The trench is reported to have been 70 m long at the top and 67.5 m at the bottom. Young, *Gordion I*, 84 ff. and plate 36.

[4] Ibid., 85 and n. 10.

[5] Ibid., 85 and plate 37A.

[6] Ibid., 86 ff. and figures 55–63. For analyses of these logs, see 291, sample 17; 292, samples 32–40, 42.

[7] Ibid., 291, sample 16; 292, samples 24–31. The samples taken from the floor of the tomb were identified as yew

(samples 21–22) and cedar (sample 23). Subsequent research has indicated that the floor planks formerly thought to be yew were actually cedar (see Appendix 3, p. 170). For a discussion of soft-rot decay that mimics certain characteristics of yew, see Blanchette and Simpson, "Soft Rot and Wood Pseudomorphs in an Ancient Coffin."

[8] Young, *Gordion I*, 96–98.

[9] Ibid., 99 and figure 65.

[10] Ibid., 89 and figure 63. Above the gabled roof were more logs, which were separate from the main tomb structure. In their original positions, these would have served to distribute weight away from the roof of the tomb. For details of their placement, see *Gordion I*, 94.

whole complex.[11] The inner chamber was eventually roofed, after the log casing had been raised to roof level.[12] The grave goods and body of the deceased were placed in the tomb after the floor and walls had been built but before the roof had been completed.[13] As there were no doors or openings in the walls,[14] the contents of the tomb must have been lowered into the chamber after the log casing, stone enclosure wall, and posited clay ramp had been constructed. The objects could have been carried up such a ramp, lowered into the tomb, and then placed in their respective positions.

This final disposition was revealed to the excavators when they cut through the west wall of the chamber and looked in on the marvelous scene. Directly before them was the tomb's occupant, clothed in the remains of a leather outfit, and lying on what Young thought was a four-poster bed (Plan, p. viii; Color Plate IB).[15] A board was put down, and the team entered the tomb (Plate 107A).[16] The skeleton of a man in his sixties was resting on a mass of textiles, which had cracked and separated into large chunks.[17] The upper part of this mass was a dense, purplish fabric that was thought to be felt;[18] beneath were many layers of fine, yellow-brown woven cloth, initially assumed to be linen.[19]

Under the textiles was deteriorated wood, which Young identified as the remains of the bed planks. At the corners of the "bed" were four massive square blocks. A flat, finished piece of wood carved with circular cutouts had fallen out

over the northeast and southeast "corner blocks" (Plate 108 and Color Plate IIA). A second, similar carved piece had been found at the west end, near the west wall of the tomb, but it had been removed before the board was put down by the excavators for entry. Young thought these carved pieces at the east and west were the headboard and footboard of the bed. Between the corner blocks, lying on the floor of the tomb under the "bed planks" were the remains of two long composite strips of light and dark wood, which Young identified as bed rails. Found along with these were shorter strips of the same design, which had apparently served as supports for the long "rails" (Plate 110). At the foot of the bed beside the northwest corner block was a damaged bronze bowl;[20] near the southwest corner block was a bronze pitcher.

According to Young, the "grave [was] very wet," especially at the edges, with a layer of slippery mud in the middle of the floor, "evidently from our own drilling" prior to the tomb's excavation.[21] Young believed that the water had been harmful to the wooden objects, which were especially degraded in the northeast corner of the tomb, east of the "headboard." Here were found many damaged furniture fragments and more chunks of textiles (Color Plate IIB and Plate 100), "well sodden in water."[22] Some of the fragments were obviously furniture legs, thought to represent stools of three different heights.

Under the carved headboard at the east of the bed were fragments of a three-legged table;

---

[11] Ibid., 89 and n. 12.

[12] This must have been the case, since, as noted above, the pairs of double beams at the tops of the chamber's north and south walls extended beyond the tomb's side walls and rested in cuttings in the top logs of the outer log casing. Young, *Gordion I*, 94. A new study of the tomb's architecture is being carried out by Richard Liebhart, along with a project to conserve, support, and monitor the structure. See Liebhart and Johnson, "Support and Conserve."

[13] Young, *Gordion I*, 94.

[14] Ibid., figures 60–62.

[15] MM 389. Ibid., 187–190. Young reported that the skeleton "evidently had been dressed in pants or a skirt of leather with fancy overlaid textiles and bronze studs on the outside," although some of these materials might have been the remains of a bronze-and-leather belt placed over the legs of the king. In addition, the body may have been covered by a shroud. Young, *Gordion I*, 101, and *Gordion Field Book* (hereafter *GFB*) 63, 183–184. Young's "bed" was not catalogued in the field.

[16] See also Color Plate IB and Plate 109. For Young's description of the contents of the tomb, see *Gordion I*, 100–102.

[17] Ibid., 101. The skeleton was examined by Muzaffer Şenyürek, Division of Palaeoanthropology, University of

Ankara, who reported that the tomb's occupant was male, age 61 to 65, height 1.59 m. The skull, now in the Museum of Anatolian Civilizations, Ankara, was the subject of a recent study. See Prag and Neave, *Making Faces*, 85–104, and below, p. 132.

[18] These textiles were subject to preliminary study and published in *Gordion I*. In Richard Ellis's appendix, the purplish material is called Fabric K. Ellis, "Textile Remains," 309.

[19] Ellis's Fabric A. Ellis, "Textile Remains," 301–302, and Young, *GFB* 63, 80. The yellow-brown color was once thought to have resulted from contact with the iron nails and other iron fragments associated with the "bed." Ellis also associated Fabric H with the "bed." Ellis, "Textile Remains," 308. For a new analysis of these textiles, see Appendix 8.

[20] Young, *GFB* 63, 194. See Young, *Gordion I*, 147, n. 74.

[21] Young, *GFB* 63, 65–66. The drill bit had been cooled with water, which was supposed to circulate but did not return properly to the surface, escaping instead into the earth of the mound. See Young, *Gordion I*, 81, n. 8. See Appendix 4 for a discussion of the deterioration of the wood from the tomb.

[22] Uncatalogued. Young, *GFB* 63, 165.

the table top had an upturned rim, giving it the appearance of a tray.[23] A bag of bronze fibulae that had been sitting on the table had fallen to the floor and broken open when the table collapsed (Color Plate IIA, Plate 100). Seven similar "plain tables" were found in the tomb—five at the center and two in the southeast corner (Color Plates IIIA, V; Plates 36, 54).[24] Many of the legs were well preserved, but the table tops were generally in fragile condition, having been affected by the moisture on the floor.[25] Stacks of bronze vessels that had been placed on the tables had tumbled to the ground when the joinery gave way. Some of the vessels contained desiccated residues,[26] and water remained in at least one of the bronze bowls.[27]

Near the east wall of the tomb, north of the two tables in the southeast corner, a carved, inlaid table had collapsed on the floor.[28] The square frame had fallen intact, and the curved legs tilted inward (Color Plate IIIB, Plate 1). Most of the wood was in good condition, but the table top had largely deteriorated. The frame and legs of the table were made from a light-colored wood, inlaid with darker wood in geometric patterns. The openwork frame was carved as a series of inlaid squares connected by double bars; carved, inlaid struts once rose from these squares, serving as supports for the table top. Dowels still in place in the legs indicated that there had been an internal bracing system that secured the legs to the frame. This table, too, had once been piled with bronze vessels.

North of the inlaid table, leaning against the east wall, were two inlaid panels that Young termed screens (Color Plates IIIA, IV; Plates 69–70, 80).[29] The "screens" had once had side and top pieces, supported by back legs and diagonal struts, but most of these elements had de-

teriorated and fallen to the floor.[30] Both screens were affected by the water that had entered the tomb, and the southernmost screen ("screen A") was wet and "rotted" along the upper edge.[31] The faces of the screens were made of light-colored wood, with rows of square designs inlaid in wood of a darker color. At the center of each "screen face" was a large medallion, which Young called a "rose window," inlaid with a rosette-like design. The rosette was surrounded by an inlaid beveled border, above which was an inlaid, pendant semicircle (or lunette).

The central rosette was supported from below by two curved leg elements, which were slightly rounded at the front, standing out from the plane of the screen faces. These curved legs ended in stylized, scroll-like animal-paw feet. Bronze vessels were found behind and near the screens, including numerous bowls, ten small cauldrons,[32] and two ladles[33] (Color Plates IV, VIB–C). Behind one of the screens (screen A) were two situlae, or buckets, which had been wrapped in cloth. One situla terminated in a lion's head and the other in the head of a ram (Color Plate VII).[34] Resting against the face of screen A was a bronze omphalos bowl (the Greek *phiale mesomphalos*), resembling a rosette with petals worked in relief (Color Plates IIIA, IVA; Plates 69, 70).[35]

Near the south wall of the tomb, west of the two plain tables, were three large bronze cauldrons on iron ring stands (Color Plate VB).[36] One cauldron had bull's head ornaments attached at the rim,[37] the second had four "sirens,"[38] and the third had two sirens and two "demons," as characterized by the excavator.[39] These attachments had held large ring handles, which were still in place on two of the cauldrons but were missing on the third.[40] Inside the cauldrons were bronze and pottery vessels; the pottery jars

---

[23] MM 387. Young, *Gordion I*, 181–182.

[24] MM 380–386. Ibid., 181–182.

[25] Young, *GFB* 63, 115–116.

[26] Samples of the food and drink residues from the tomb were initially analyzed but not identified. Young, *Gordion I*, 102, n. 28, and appendix IIA. New analyses were undertaken by the Museum Applied Science Center for Archaeology of the University of Pennsylvania Museum (hereafter MASCA); the outcome was published by McGovern, et al., in *Nature* 402 (1999): 863–864. For the details of these new analyses, see Appendix 5.

[27] Young, *GFB* 63, 72.

[28] MM 388. Young, *Gordion I*, 183–187.

[29] MM 378–379. Young, *Gordion I*, 176–181.

[30] Young, *GFB* 63, 155–156.

[31] Ibid., 156–157.

[32] MM 4–13. Young, *Gordion I*, 110–112.

[33] MM 47–48. Ibid., 123.

[34] MM 45–46. Ibid., 121–123. For the cloth wrapping, see *Gordion I*, 304, Fabric F, which was also associated with a small cauldron (MM 7) and a fibula (MM 187).

[35] MM 92. Ibid., 136.

[36] Two of the iron stands had three legs (MM 357–358), and one had four (MM 359). Young, *Gordion I*, 172.

[37] MM 1. Ibid., 102–104.

[38] MM 2. Ibid., 104–107.

[39] MM 3. Ibid., 107–110. The "sirens" are beardless, and the "demons" have beards.

[40] The rings were missing on MM 2, the cauldron with the four siren attachments.

contained the desiccated remains of food (Color Plate VIA).[41]

Nine large bronze jugs were lying on the floor near the west wall of the tomb (Plate 109B), and a tenth was found near the south wall, partially under the second large cauldron (Color Plate VB).[42] Near the jugs were nine bronze-and-leather objects identified as belts, with wide, decorated bands and large round discs.[43] A tenth belt, without a disc, was found near the legs of the skeleton.[44] Twenty-one smaller jugs were scattered throughout the tomb,[45] along with a total of 122 bronze bowls.[46]

Many of the bronze objects had once hung from iron nails driven into the west, south, and east walls of the tomb.[47] The west wall showed evidence of 20 nails, arranged in two rows of ten. The belts found on the floor had evidently been suspended from some of these nails: under the disc of one of the belts, the tip of an iron nail was preserved.[48] The south wall had two rows of 12 nails each, and the east wall had three rows with a total of 25 nails. The nails themselves had largely deteriorated, but their placement was deduced from dark stains on the wooden walls, discolored by iron corrosion (Color Plate IIIA).[49] Bronzes that had once hung on the walls fell to the floor when the nails broke. The contents of the chamber were recorded according to their placement on the tomb floor, and the objects were rendered on a plan of the tomb, drawn by Dorothy Cox at the time of excavation (Plan, p. viii).

The Tumulus MM burial produced a wealth of valuable finds, including 170 bronze vessels,[50] more than 180 fibulae, ten belts, 18 pottery vessels, and at least 15 pieces of fine wooden furniture. The splendid assemblage, along with the size of the tumulus, the largest burial mound at Gordion,[51] clearly indicated that the tomb's occupant was a powerful Phrygian king. Inevitably, the huge mound was associated with King Midas, a figure well known from ancient sources, and it acquired the initials "MM" (for "Midas Mound") which eventually became its official designation.[52] The furniture in the tomb recalled a passage in Herodotus, who commented on the famous throne of Midas at Delphi:

> Gyges was the first foreigner we know of, after King Midas of Phrygia, son of Gordias, to dedicate offerings at Delphi. Midas presented the royal throne from which he used to give judgment; it stands with Gyges' bowls, and is well worth seeing [ἀξιοθέητον].[53]

The historical Midas ruled at Gordion during the second half of the eighth century B.C., and reportedly committed suicide when the city was overrun by Kimmerian invaders. With this in mind, Young came to believe that the occupant of the tomb was more likely the father of Midas, whom he called King Gordios.[54] In Young's opinion, the Phrygians were surely in no position to build such a grandiose monument in the wake of the Kimmerian invasion. The tomb chamber itself cannot be dated definitively, but there is evidence to suggest that the outer logs may have been cut around 740 B.C. If so, then this provides a terminus post quem for the burial. The ques-

---

[41] Young, *Gordion I*, 173–176. Eighteen pottery vessels containing food residues were found in the cauldrons: twelve dinoi (MM 360–371) and six small amphorae (MM 372–377). Supra n. 26. The bronzes found in the large cauldrons had apparently hung on the wall, falling into the cauldrons when the nails gave way. *Gordian I*, 102.

[42] MM 16–25. Ibid., 114–116; plates 46B, 47B–C, 48A.

[43] MM 170–178. Ibid., 147–153; plates 46B, 47B–C, 48A. The way these "belts" were fastened is not clearly understood.

[44] MM 180. Ibid., 101, 148, 154.

[45] MM 14–15, 26–44. Ibid., 113–114, 116–121.

[46] MM 49–169. Ibid., 123–147; 21 of the bowls had handles. Supra n. 20, for the bowl found near the feet of the king.

[47] Young, *Gordion I*, 100, n. 26; "Gordion Campaign of 1957," 150–151.

[48] Young, *Gordion I*, 148, n. 79.

[49] The nail count given here derives from a reexamination of the tomb walls by Richard Liebhart. The south wall had 24, not 25 nails. Young, *Gordion I*, 100, n. 26.

[50] Ibid., 147, n. 74.

[51] And the second largest in Anatolia. Ibid., 79.

[52] The excavators' early nickname for Tumulus MM was "MMT" for "Midas Mound Tumulus," which became shortened to "MM." The mound was also called the "Great Tumulus," by which it is still known in Turkey today (Büyük Tümülüs). Young, *Gordion I*, 79–80.

[53] Herodotus 1.14. The throne was kept in the Corinthian Treasury. An ivory statuette found at Delphi was associated with Midas's throne by Keith DeVries in a 2002 lecture, and although the attribution was purely speculative, the theory was publicized as "news" in the *New York Times*. DeVries, "Throne of Midas?" Wilford, "Statuette is Traced to Midas." See also Schiering, "Löwenbändiger und Midas-Thron in Delphi." This idea, although completely hypothetical, has since been picked up and given credence by other scholars. Munn, *Mother of the Gods*, 88, n. 118.

[54] *Gordion Guide*, 50, and elsewhere, where Young uses the spelling Gordios. Herodotus refers to "Midas, son of Gordias," in his account of Midas's dedication at Delphi. For the Kimmerian invasion and suicide of Midas, see Strabo 1.3.21, and below, p. 133.

tion of the tomb's date and the identity of the king—whether Midas or his predecessor—is discussed in detail in the concluding chapter of this volume.[55]

Although no gold was found in the tomb, the hundreds of bronzes were of the highest quality, and the furniture, with its fine woods and detailed workmanship, must have been of incomparable worth. As initially published by Young, however, the spectacular nature of the furniture was not fully appreciated.[56] The brief preliminary study, rudimentary conservation treatment, and quickly executed drawings led to serious misconceptions about the pieces. Fortunately, the excavators' extensive documentation of the burial has allowed these errors to be rectified. Research conducted over the past 27 years has yielded surprising new results regarding the form, construction, and decoration of the furniture. These new discoveries rest ultimately on Young's early interpretations.

[55] The occupant of the Tumulus MM burial has never been identified with certainty. See Mellink in Young, *Gordion I*, 271–272, for the suggestion that the king was indeed Midas, but see Muscarella, "King Midas's Tumulus at Gordion," 9–10, who does not agree. The question is now further complicated by new dates proposed for the seeds from the destruction level of the city mound. See below, pp. 132–134.

[56] Young, "Phrygian Furniture from Gordion," and *Gordion I*, 176–190, 259–261.

CHAPTER TWO

EARLY INTERPRETATIONS OF THE FURNITURE FROM TUMULUS MM

The Tumulus MM furniture was recorded in the Gordion field books while the pieces were still in the tomb chamber.[1] Rodney Young described the "bed" and its removal in some detail and discussed the rest of the furniture briefly. Some of the tables were numbered, approximate measurements were made, and initial efforts were undertaken to conserve the wood. Parts of the bed, fragments from the northeast corner, and the tops of the "plain tables" were treated with a solution of Alvar, a polyvinyl acetal resin, while the pieces were still *in situ*. The inlaid table and two "screens" were removed from the chamber, dehydrated in a solution of alcohol and water, and then immersed in a bath of wax. Unfortunately, these well-intentioned efforts at conservation did not strengthen the wood appreciably and in fact caused some damage (see Appendix 1 for a full discussion of the early treatment).

In conjunction with the conservation and study of the finds, working drawings were made of the inlaid table, one plain table, and the inlaid screens.[2] Two drawings were published in Young's 1958 article in the *American Journal of Archaeology* on the Gordion campaign of 1957,[3] and additional drawings were featured in his 1974 article, "Phrygian Furniture from Gordion," for *Expedition*.[4] Young's final analysis of the furniture from Tumulus P, Tumulus MM, and Tumulus W appears in *Gordion I*, published posthumously in 1981, with commentary based on his own writings and augmented by the editors of the volume.[5] Subsequent study has shown that Young's original ideas were in need of revision. However, many of his observations are useful, and his excavation notes provide much important data. The early interpreta-

tions of the Tumulus MM furniture are presented here to provide the background against which all further research must be viewed.

The Tables

Young numbered the Tumulus MM tables from one through nine. A sketch in the field book shows how the tables were situated in the tomb and clearly indicates the numbers that Young had given them.[6] These numbers are shown here on the plan of the Tumulus MM chamber (Plan, p. viii). Only two plain tables were catalogued in 1957: tables 1 and 5 were assigned inventory numbers 5203 W 79 and 5202 W 78, respectively. The inlaid table, listed as table 8, was catalogued as 5212 W 80. The remaining five tables were not given inventory numbers at the time of excavation. In *Gordion I*, the plain tables are designated MM 380–387.

Plain Tables (MM 380–387)

In his field notes, Young described the plain tables as they were found on the tomb floor (Color Plates IIIA, V; Plates 36, 54, 108). He noted that the legs of the tables were made of hard, light-colored wood and that the tops were of dark wood, which was softer and not as well preserved as the wood of the legs. This indicated that tables' legs and tops had been made from different types of wood. Approximate measurements of the tops were taken, and the tables were removed from the tomb in the following manner. First, the upper surfaces of the table tops were painted with

[1] Young, *GFB* 63, 73–81, 115–117, 127, 131–133, 141–142, 155–158, 160–182, 187–194; *GFB* 70, 34–38.
[2] Most of these drawings were made by Dorothy Cox; Andy Seuffert drew the central medallion from "screen B." Later, for the *Gordion I* publication, I drew the face of "screen A" from photographs taken in 1957, re-drew one of the screen's side pieces, and reconstructed the "bed" from Young's excavation notes and subsequent publications.

Young, *Gordion I*, figures 104–113.
[3] Young, "Gordion Campaign of 1957," figures 23, 25, plate 27.
[4] Young, "Phrygian Furniture from Gordion," 2–13.
[5] Young, *Gordion I*, 62–77, 176–190, 217–218, 259–261, 264–265, and *passim*.
[6] Young, *GFB* 70, 36.

a thin Alvar solution. Sticks were then slid under the tops and raised slightly, the legs were pulled out from underneath, and plywood was placed under the tops, which were then removed on the plywood sheet (Plates 37, 42, 46, 50, 55–56, 60, 63, 66). Young stated "it is questionable if it is worthwhile to try to treat more than the two best preserved tables (#1 and 5), which if they can be preserved, will serve as examples typical of all."[7] This is no doubt the reason that the remaining five plain tables were not catalogued. In his published report on the Gordion campaign of 1957 he noted, "The eight plain tables were all alike, with slight variations in their dimensions."[8]

A reconstruction drawing of one of the plain tables appeared in Young's *Expedition* article and again in *Gordion I*.[9] The tables were described as having three legs and oblong tops with rounded corners. The tops were "dished" with a low, raised rim running around the edge, although this was not shown in the reconstruction drawing. The table tops measured approximately 75 by 60 cm; Young thought that each top was made from a single piece of wood. He believed that the legs were lathe-turned and then artificially bent, either by steaming or soaking. The ends of the legs, which had rested on the floor, were cut flat on their undersurface to form feet. Young noticed three rectangular cuttings in each table top, which had received the tenons at the tops of the three legs.

Young also noted peg holes in the legs' top tenons and in the round "collars" of soft wood that had been found surrounding many of the leg tenons. From this he concluded that the legs had been joined to the tops by means of separate collars, which had fit down over the leg tenons, providing a broader resting surface for the table tops. "The collar served to hold the tenon securely and to spread the bearing surface for the table top; no doubt it made a firm joint and prevented wobbling which might have damaged the table top where the end of the tenon passed through it."[10] In order to hold the

tops onto the collars, Young theorized, "quite a lot of strong glue must have been used."[11] The tops of tables 1–7 and 9 were assumed to be maple, based on the analysis of one fragment.[12] The tables were about 50 cm high, not high enough to sit up to, so Young thought that people may have sat near them on cushions or hassocks on the floor.

In *Gordion I*, the plain tables are listed with their MM numbers and illustrated in photographs taken *in situ* in the tomb chamber. Included are three photographs that show individual tables after their removal from the tomb.[13] In the *Gordion I* list, only two of the tables have catalogue numbers, and there is no detailed information in the separate entries. Although the tables are identified correctly in the *in situ* photographs, some confusion occurred when they were illustrated individually (*Gordion I*, plate 81C–E). A table called MM 384 (table 3) is supposedly shown in both plate 81D (reproduced here as Plate 56) and 81E (here Plate 38). Plate 81D shows a table in a wooden drawer, and 81E shows a restored table, which the caption calls a "composite restoration." It is clear from the photographs, however, that the legs of the restored table cannot possibly be those of the table shown in the drawer.

In fact, neither of these photographs shows table 3 (here illustrated correctly in Plates 46–49). The table in the drawer is MM 383 (table 5), and the "composite reconstruction" is actually MM 380 (table 1). This can be ascertained from the *in situ* photographs, which can be related to Young's field book diagram of the plain tables as found on the tomb floor. *Gordion I*, plate 81C shows MM 380 (table 1), accurately identified, after its removal from the tomb. This confusion resulted from the general similarity of the tables, which were not considered separately but classed as a group. By the time of their publication in *Gordion I*, the elegant tables, each a unique and important survival, were misidentified in the photographs taken after their excavation, and information about individual tables was almost completely lacking.

[7] Young, *GFB* 70, 38. For references to the various plain tables, see *GFB* 63, 115–117, 127, 131–133; *GFB* 70, 34–38.
[8] Young, "Gordion Campaign of 1957," 153.
[9] Young, "Phrygian Furniture from Gordion," 5, figure 2; *Gordion I*, 182, figure 108.
[10] Young, *Gordion I*, 182.

[11] Young, "Phrygian Furniture from Gordion," 7.
[12] Young, *Gordion I*, 181 and 291, sample 18. Just what this sample was taken from is unclear, as the wording is ambiguous: "similar to MM 380–387. Dark, powdery wood fragment from table top."
[13] Ibid., 182; plates 43, 45A, 48B, 49, 81C–E.

Inlaid Table (The "Pagoda Table") (MM 388)

A ninth table (called table 8) also had three legs and a tray-shaped top, but it was elaborately carved and intricately inlaid with geometric patterns (Color Plate III, Plate 1). The legs had fallen inward, and most of the decorative struts had broken off, but the frame had landed intact, and the basic form of the table could be determined.[14] Its frame was made of four carved pieces of wood, joined at the corners, featuring inlaid squares alternating with pairs of carved, dowel-like rungs. From each inlaid square rose a carved, inlaid strut, two of which were still in place at the time of excavation. These decorative struts had supported the table top; they came to be called the "pagoda" supports or struts because of their curving extremities and fanciful appearance.[15] The table's three legs had carved, inlaid top sections and inlaid feet. From the feet rose carved struts that supported the frame at its corners. The table top was in poor condition when found—its withered fragments lay draped over the other pieces of the table and the bronze bowls that had fallen in the area (Plate 1).

In his field book, Young stated that, in taking up the decorative struts that supported the table top, the excavators could "identify and record the original place of each." He noted several cylindrical dowels found with the table and supposed that they had once fastened the table's legs to the backs of the frame pieces. Two of these dowels were found still in place in two of the legs, visible in the *in situ* photographs. Young also recorded a number of "small cuttings" 2 cm long in fragments of the table top and suggested, correctly, that these cuttings had received the tenons at the tops of the "pagoda" struts.[16]

After the table was photographed, the pieces were removed from the tomb, dried in a bath of alcohol, and then immersed in a solution of wax and gasoline in an attempt to strengthen the wood. This treatment did not produce the desired effect, however, contributing instead to the wood's deterioration (see Appendix 1). Nonetheless, the table survived in fairly good condition, and the pieces were drawn and studied. A reconstruction drawing was produced by Dorothy Cox, for inclusion in Young's *AJA* report on the Gordion campaign of 1957.[17]

New information and three of Cox's drawings appeared in Young's subsequent article for *Expedition*.[18] He found that the table had been made from more than forty separate pieces. The four frame pieces had been joined together by "tongues" fitted into "slots" and held in place by pegs (see Plate 23). Eighteen decorative struts rose vertically from the inlaid squares of the frame, all of which, according to Young, could be fitted into their proper positions. Curiously, Young stated in *Expedition* that "no cutting was preserved" in the underside of the table top, even though he had noted several such cuttings while the table was still in the tomb (see Plate 32C).[19]

Young noted that dowels had been socketed into the legs and ran to the "back face" of the frame (Plate 1). He commented on the ingenious method by which the table's three legs had supported the four corners of the square frame. From the rear feet rose elaborate struts that propped up the frame at the back corners. A complex curved strut, composed of a lower "rocker" and two "R-shaped" pieces, had been joined to the front leg behind the foot.[20] This curved strut extended out and up to support the front corners of the frame. Young believed that the legs were "lathe-turned and tapered,"[21] with their carved, inlaid top sections made separately and later joined to the legs. He thought that glue must have been used for the joints, but he could not find any evidence for it. Young concluded, in his inimitable style, with his personal appraisal of the table's artistic merit:

> It was the dowels and tenons and mortises which afforded the clues which enabled us to reconstruct the whole and reveal it in its full horror. However much it may revolt us it must be admitted nevertheless that it is from

---

[14] Ibid., plates 45A and B depict the collapsed table in two other views; plate 45B was taken after some of the pieces had been removed and others rearranged.

[15] This terminology first appeared on the catalogue cards and was soon adopted for the name of the table. "Pagoda Table" was used in Simpson, "Reconstructing an Ancient Table," but later abandoned after Edith Porada called the picturesque but misleading term "pagoda" into question.

[16] Young, *GFB* 63, 141–142.

[17] Young, "Gordion Campaign of 1957," figure 23, plate 27.

[18] The following account is taken from Young, "Phrygian Furniture from Gordion," 7, 9. The reconstruction drawing of the table appears on page 6 as figure 3.

[19] Young, *GFB* 63, 142.

[20] For the term "R-shaped," see Young, *Gordion I*, 187.

[21] Young, "Phrygian Furniture from Gordion," 7.

a technical point of view a masterpiece of the cabinet-maker's craft and certainly worth looking at.[22]

The phrase "worth looking at" derives from Herodotus, writing about the famous throne that King Midas had dedicated in the sanctuary of Apollo at Delphi.[23] Although Young's assessment was meant to be witty, the table soon acquired a dubious reputation. This was reinforced by Cox's reconstruction drawing (Figure 1), which made the table look strange and ungainly.

Gordion I featured a more detailed description of the inlaid table and further comments on its construction and design.[24] The light wood from which the table was made was tentatively identified as boxwood, with a suggestion that the dark inlay might be yew.[25] The table was discussed part by part, beginning with the top, which Young thought had overhung the frame on all sides, being larger than the frame itself. He theorized that the top had covered the full extension of the legs and feet, giving it dimensions "at least 0.20 m greater than those of the frame."[26] The tenons at the tops of the legs were reportedly 6 cm long, with the lower, thicker part of the tenon recorded as 4.5 cm long and the smaller top section 1.5 cm. From this, Young estimated the thickness of the table top at 1.5 cm, with the smaller section of the leg tenon going all the way through the table top and showing on its upper surface.[27]

Noting again the short dowels that fastened the legs to the back of the frame, Young suggested that braces must also have run from leg to leg but said that these were not found or, if found, were not recognized as such. In fact, such

additional dowels are pictured in a number of photographs in the Gordion archives. Young estimated that "the whole rickety structure" was assembled from around 44 separate pieces.[28] To facilitate description of the table, some of the individual components were given letter or number designations: frame pieces A–D, legs A–C, struts type 1, 2, and 3.[29]

Type-1 struts (as in Plate 4E–F) resemble stylized trees. The type-1 strut features a single stem that supports a second tier of two inlaid vertical strips. These in turn support a third tier, composed of three vertical segments, the one at the center inlaid. Of the eight type-1 struts, one is slightly different from the rest (Plate 16E–F). Young called this unusual strut a variant. The six type-2 struts (Plate 16C–D) feature a symmetrical arrangement of two pairs of inlaid vertical strips, with a single cylindrical segment at the center.

Four type-3 struts "supported the handles placed at each corner of the table" (Plate 20A–D). Young thought that these were separate struts to which the table's handles were pinned, although the handles are actually incorporated. These struts have three tiers like the type-1 struts, but the bottom tier is wider, flat at the front, and inlaid, while the upper tiers are cylindrical, with projecting spool-like knobs where the members intersect. The curved part of the handle extends out from the lower segment and arches upward, returning to meet the supporting framework at the top. The faces of the curved elements are inlaid with geometric designs in panels, which alternate with recessed areas featuring tiny, irregular holes arranged in patterns. Only later were these

---

[22] Young, "Phrygian Furniture from Gordion," 9. For a more decorous version of these comments, see the editorial paraphrase in Young, *Gordion I*, 260. For Young's earliest statement on the merits of the table, see Young, "Gordion Campaign of 1957," 153: "This table demonstrates the great technical skill, if not the good taste, of the Phrygian cabinetmakers."

[23] Herodotus 1.14. See above, p. 10.

[24] Young, *Gordion I*, 183–187; figures 109–111; plates 45, 82–83.

[25] Ibid., 183. This was based on the analysis of six specimens from the Tumulus P "screen" (TumP 151), tripod table (TumP 153), and Mosaic Table (TumP 154). See Young, *Gordion I*, 290, samples 8–13. The light wood of the Tumulus P screen and tables was identified as boxwood and the dark wood as yew. Later analysis has shown that the wood of the frame and legs of the Tumulus MM inlaid table is indeed boxwood, but the dark wood of the inlay is juniper (see p. 31 and Appendix 3).

[26] Ibid., 183. Young's theory was correct, although he

does not clarify the meaning of "at least 0.20 m greater than those of the frame."

[27] These measurements are inaccurate and may have been taken from a drawing by Dorothy Cox of one of the table's legs. *Gordion I*, 185, figure 111H.

[28] Ibid., 183. Dowels are pictured as follows: neg. nos. 394:19/20, 102659, GO 5306, and GO 5307. All the dowels that made up the internal bracing system were found with the pieces of the inlaid table in storage in the Museum of Anatolian Civilizations, Ankara, in 1981.

[29] Young's designations, when facing the front of the table, were as follows: frame face A (front), B (back), C (left side), D (right side); leg A (left rear), B (right rear), C (front); leg strut A (left rear), B (right rear). These designations can be found on the original catalogue cards. For the sake of clarity, these designations have now been changed; each of the legs is here called by the same letter as the frame piece that it supported and the strut that rose from its foot. See Figure 4 for the new letter designations, which are used throughout this volume.

recessed areas recognized as sections of missing inlay.

Young arranged the struts on the frame as follows.[30] The four type-3 struts, which carried the handles, were positioned at the four corners of the frame, or, to be more exact, at the far left and right ends of the front and back frame pieces. This arrangement can be seen in an early photograph of the front frame piece (with top struts added) and in the Cox reconstruction drawing illustrated in *Gordion I*.[31] The six type-2 struts were placed over the central squares of the front and back frame pieces and over the far left and far right squares of the side frame pieces.[32] Young placed the eight type-1 struts "two at each side, alternated with the struts of type two."[33] His wording is somewhat confusing, but one may assign the type-1 struts to all the remaining positions. On the front and back frame pieces, from left to right, Young posited the following sequence: 3–1–2–1–3. On the left and right frame pieces was a different arrangement: 2–1–1–2.

Young's sequence for the front and back frame pieces is consistent with the photo illustrated in *Gordion I* and the Cox reconstruction drawing. But his arrangement for the sides is impossible. When the table was discovered, two top struts remained in place, extending up from the frame. On the left side of the table (clearly visible in Plate 1), the strut over the far left panel was of the first type and not the second.[34] The issue is further complicated by Cox's drawing, where the struts on both the left and right sides of the table are arranged, from left to right, in a 2–1–2–1 sequence. The *in situ* photographs show the drawing to be wrong in both cases. Thus, the placement of the "pagoda" struts was not well understood by either Cox or Young. If, as Young wrote in his field book, the excavators could "identify and record the original place of each" strut,[35] this information was not utilized for the reconstruction drawing.

Young thought that each of the table's three legs was made from two separate pieces: a lower, curved part and a decorated top piece, which

he called a "capital." He believed that "collars" had surrounded the top tenons of the legs, much like the system envisioned for the plain tables. The collars would have supported the table top from below, while the smaller top parts of the leg tenons would have been embedded in square cuttings in the table top. Earlier, Young had expressed his belief that the table's legs were "lathe-turned and tapered,"[36] and in *Gordion I* he added that they were "artificially bent outward at the bottom like those of the plain tables."[37] Actually, neither of these techniques was used for the legs of the inlaid table.

The legs were disposed in a triangular arrangement, with two "at one long side of the table at the corners," and the third "at the middle of the opposite long side."[38] As Young had earlier recognized, struts rose from the feet of the three legs and supported the frame's four corners. He did not discuss their exact placement, but this can be inferred from Cox's reconstruction drawing (Figure 1).[39] In the drawing, the table's two back legs point directly toward the back of the table, and the struts that rise from their feet support the back frame at its left and right ends. However, this cannot be the correct placement of the back legs and leg struts, as is clear from the photograph of the right frame piece illustrated in *Gordion I* (see Plate 11A).[40] At the far right, attached at the bottom of the frame piece, is a small segment of wood, which is certainly the missing top strip from the right rear leg strut (Plate 14).[41] Therefore, the rear leg struts must have supported the rear corners of the frame at the sides, and not at the back of the table. Just how the rear legs were disposed in order to accomplish this feat could not be determined from the written records or the excavation photographs.

Into the front leg was set the elaborate three-piece strut that supported the two front corners of the frame. Under each corner was an "R-shaped" strut, with the bottom of the "R" facing upward (Plates 7A, 8). These two struts were supported from below by the "rocker" (Plate 7), which was joined to the front leg behind the foot.

---

[30] Young, *Gordion I*, 186.
[31] Ibid., figure 109, plate 82B.
[32] "...the six struts of type two over the central square panels of the long sides of the frame, and over the outer panels at either end." Young, *Gordion I*, 186.
[33] Ibid., 186.
[34] The second strut found in place was a type-1 strut, which rose from the third square of the right frame piece.

The right side of the table lay along the tomb's east wall.
[35] Young, *GFB* 63, 142.
[36] Young, "Phrygian Furniture from Gordion," 7.
[37] Young, *Gordion I*, 187.
[38] Ibid.
[39] Ibid., figure 109.
[40] Ibid., plate 82A, top.
[41] Ibid., plate 83C.

The front leg strut is positioned accurately in Cox's reconstruction drawing, but the form and decoration of the strut are not correct.

Thus the inlaid table did not fare well in Young's publications. The inconsistencies in the written accounts, and the discrepancies between those accounts and the early illustrations, left many aspects of the table's construction unclear. In addition, close comparison of the early drawings with the field photographs revealed numerous problems with the rendering of the inlaid decoration.[42] Finally, Young considered the table an impressive accomplishment but, from an artistic standpoint, an exercise in poor taste. This judgment was supported and perhaps even prompted by the published drawings. However, careful observation of the photographs suggested that the inlaid table had been misrepresented; this would be confirmed by future study.

The "Screens"

In his field book, Young initially referred to the two inlaid panels found leaning against the east wall as "throne-backs" A and B. Later in his discussion, he suggested they might be "a sort of screen."[43] He described the objects briefly, indicating that they had been made from several boards, "doweled together," with the joinery secured by pegs. Some of the joints were still very "tight" at the time of excavation, being in some places almost invisible (Color Plates IIIA, IV; Plates 69–70, 80). Young observed that the separate boards of each "screen" had been pegged together before the whole was inlaid: the inlay seemed to him to be continuous over the entire surface, even covering some of the pegs that held the boards together (Plates 97–98).[44] Pieces had projected out from the backs of the screen faces at their tops, and one such piece was still in place on

the right side of the northernmost screen ("screen B") (Color Plate IVA, top left). The others had fallen to the floor, apparently broken off by the fall of several bronze vessels that had hung from nails in the tomb's east wall.

During the excavation of the tomb, the bronzes were removed from behind the screens, as Young believed they were putting too much strain on the joinery. Pieces of plywood were then slid behind the screen faces, and they were left in place in the tomb to dry slowly.[45] After a month, however, a green mold appeared on the wood, and Young decided to take the screens out of the chamber.[46] After their removal, they were conserved in the same manner as the inlaid table: immersed in a bath of alcohol for drying and then in a solution of wax dissolved in gasoline, in the hope that the wax would enter the pores of the wood (see Appendix 1). By Young's account, the operation was not successful, and after the pieces had undergone this treatment, they began to warp and crack.[47] The wood darkened, and the contrast between the light-colored wood of the background and the dark wood of the inlay was greatly reduced.

Nevertheless these screens were well enough preserved that an accurate reconstruction on paper could be made, and they served as models to solve the mysteries of restoration for the two similar screens found in Tumuli P (TumP 151) and W (TumW 80).[48]

Young discussed the back construction of the Tumulus MM screens in his excavation notes, in his *Expedition* article, and again in *Gordion I*.[49] Originally, two inlaid openwork side pieces had extended toward the rear at the top of each screen. These were connected at their ends by a long, narrow back piece, which was pierced with a row of square "cutouts." In the frame thus formed

---

[42] In one obvious example, figure 111F (Young, *Gordion I*, 185) shows the decoration on one of the handles in a roll-out drawing. This handle is also pictured in plate 82B, right, and plate 82E. The bottom of the handle was inlaid with rows of squares. In figure 111F, below these rows of squares, as though it too belonged to the decoration of the same handle, is a meander configuration. However, this is actually from the lower section of another of the handles (not illustrated in *Gordion I*, but see the handle here in Figure 5, at right). In another instance, the designs on the four frame faces as shown in photographs (*Gordion I*, plate 82A–B) are not reproduced accurately in the drawings (figure 110). In one case, the second square of the frame face pictured in figure 110C, the

artist has drawn six squares across and six squares down, for a total of 36. Actually, there were six squares across and seven squares down, making a total of 42. In fact, only three of the 22 panels depicted in figure 110 are correct.

[43] Young's discussion of the "screens" can be found in *GFB* 63, 155–164.

[44] Young, *GFB* 63, 157–158.

[45] Ibid., 155–158.

[46] Young, *Gordion I*, 176–177.

[47] Young, "AJA Draft," 23.

[48] Young, *Gordion I*, 177.

[49] Young, *GFB* 63, 160–164; "Phrygian Furniture from Gordion," 9–13; *Gordion I*, 180–181 and figure 105.

sat an openwork top piece, preserved in fragments found on the floor of the tomb behind the screen faces. Young concluded that the top piece was made up "of linked small rings within three rectangular panels, and near the center of each panel a much larger open ring."[50] Parts of the top had disintegrated, "but enough were recovered to assure the design," as well as provide the nickname "three-burner stove."[51] The top pieces of both screens were considered to be similar, and a reconstruction drawing was made by Dorothy Cox following the excavation (here reproduced as Figure 2). This was initially labeled "screen" in Young's *AJA* report on the Gordion campaign of 1957 and later in *Expedition*. However, by the time of *Gordion I*, the drawing was thought to represent screen A, and the caption was worded accordingly.[52]

The frame had been supported at the back by a single leg and two pairs of diagonal struts, which extended out from the sides of the leg. Young thought that no pegs had been run through the tenons of the diagonal struts, and supposed that the joinery was secured with glue.[53] The back leg shown in the Cox drawing is square in section, with an unusual configuration at the bottom involving a scroll-like foot. In *Expedition*, Young did not comment on the foot shown in the drawing, but in the field book he mentioned two "scrolled feet" which he said were found "still in place on the floor against the wall."[54] In *Gordion I* he noted these back feet again but suggested that the "scroll foot" in the drawing might be turned the wrong way.[55]

As Young had noted earlier in his field book, the front faces of the screens were made from several boards of wood, fastened together with "dowels" and pegs and then inlaid. In his *Expedition* article, Young identified the light-colored boards as boxwood and the dark wood of the inlay as yew.[56] However, the wood of the screens had not yet been analyzed,[57] as is clear from *Gordion I*: "On the analogy of the screen from Tumulus P (TumP 151), of which pieces were sub-

mitted for analysis, we assume that the light background wood is boxwood and the darker wood of the inlay, yew."[58] Set into the screen faces were the curved "legs" supporting the central rosette medallions; Young believed these legs were bent "by steaming or soaking to a curve."[59] These reminded him of the legs of the tables, which he thought were also artificially bent.[60]

The inlaid square designs on each screen numbered "nearly two hundred." They were set into a field of diamonds and triangles, and exhibited great variety in terms of their form and orientation.

> In some the swastika proper is of the dark inlaid wood, in others it is left in the light background wood; in some the swastika rolls from right to left, in others from left to right; and in many places the inlays do not form true swastikas at all but rather various patterns which give the same general effect. Between and around these inlays the entire face of the screen is sown with tiny inlaid lozenges and triangles arranged in rows, horizontal and vertical.[61]

Young realized that with such profuse and varied inlay, the screens would have taken a long time to make. He concluded that the screens had not been produced for the burial but were brought from the palace where they had been used during the king's lifetime. But just how these objects had functioned Young could not say with certainty. "Perhaps the best guess is that they were sumptuous backgrounds—throne backs, if you will—before which a magnate could sit in glory on a stool or on a hassock, serving the psychological, if not the physical, functions of a throne."[62] In the "Conclusions" to *Gordion I*, Machteld Mellink considered Young's interpretation, commenting that such decorative backrests might have been used in outdoor settings, tents, or chariots, as well as in rooms. The holes in the top pieces might have served to hold standards or parasols. The

[50] Young, "Phrygian Furniture from Gordion," 10.

[51] Ibid.

[52] Young, "Gordion Campaign of 1957," figure 25, plate 27; "Phrygian Furniture from Gordion," 10, figure 1; *Gordion I*, 180, figure 105.

[53] Young, "Phrygian Furniture from Gordion," 10.

[54] Young, *GFB* 63, 164. This statement is not substantiated by any drawings or excavation photographs.

[55] Young, *Gordion I*, 180.

[56] Young, "Phrygian Furniture from Gordion," 10.

[57] Supra n. 25, regarding the assumption that the inlaid table was made from boxwood and yew, based on the analysis of six samples from Tumulus P. See Young, *Gordion I*, 290, samples 8–13.

[58] Young, *Gordion I*, 177.

[59] Ibid., 179.

[60] Ibid., 182, 187, 258.

[61] Young, "Phrygian Furniture from Gordion," 10–11.

[62] Ibid., 13.

placement of the "screens" in the Tumulus MM chamber, with open space in front of them and tables with drinking vessels nearby, suggested to her that the area in front was reserved for guests of honor.[63]

"Screen A" (MM 378)

Young believed that the screen face or "screen proper" had been assembled from 11 pieces of wood.[64] These pieces were joined together by what he called "dowels" set into "slots" cut into the sides of the wood planks and secured by pegs. He thought that the pegs were "apparently inserted indifferently from the front or the back" of the screen. As evidence, he noted the presence of six pegs running down the top half of the long right side board (see Plates 69–70); these pegs indicated that "dowels" had joined the right side board to the three center boards or "crosspieces" immediately to the left. But there were no corresponding pegs in right ends of these crosspieces. As Young thought that such pegs were necessary to hold the "dowels" in place, he theorized that these pegs had been run in from the back, and were thus not visible on the screen's face. However, inspection reveals no such pegs on the back at the left and right ends of the crosspieces (Plate 73).

Young suggested that the channels for the inlay were made by boring a row of tiny holes with "a fine awl" and then cutting away the wood between them. By this process, a straight-sided "slot" was formed, in which the inlays were glued in place.[65] He thought the inlay was cut across the grain in straight segments, as well as in ⌐-shaped, ⌐-shaped, and even ⌐-shaped pieces. Young realized that the circular border of the central medallion—the "rose window"—was laid out with a compass, indicated by the prick at its center (see Plate 77). He thought that the curvilinear decoration within the circle might also have been laid out in this way. The arcs to the right and left above the rosette medallion were certainly constructed with a compass, as the central prick is visible at the left (although not at the right). A compass might also have been used for the pendant semicircle above the central medallion, but, if so, the center of the circle would have lain across the joint and on the neighboring board.[66] The face of screen A is illustrated in *Gordion I*, drawn by the present author, based on the 1957 photographs. The form and decoration are largely correct in this drawing, but the dimensions and some details are inaccurate.[67]

The side pieces that extended back at the top of the screen had tenons at one end, which fit into "cuttings" in the back of the screen's face (Plates 73, 76). Each side piece was inlaid and, when attached to the screen, revealed a design of eight square cutouts. The narrower back strip of the frame was not inlaid but was also pierced by open squares (Plate 75). In *Gordion I*, their number is given as 13, as shown in the reconstruction drawing (here Figure 2), although a photograph of the back piece (*Gordion I*, plate 80P) shows only 12 cutouts. The screen's top shelf, the "three-burner stove," is reconstructed in the Cox drawing with three large rings and smaller linked circles.[68] According to Young, the back leg of the screen was "incompletely preserved," although "the lower end remained, square in section," with a "scroll foot like those at the front of the screen."[69]

"Screen B" (MM 379)

Specific dimensions for screen B are not given in the *Gordion I* catalogue entry and are said to be "the same as those of MM 378" (screen A).[70] The brief description states that screen B was "put together in the same way" as screen A, and that the inlaid decoration of the face was "almost exactly the same," except for a variation in the decoration of the central rosette medallion and the pendant semicircle above it. A drawing of the central medallion concludes the entry.[71] Photographs of the pierced back strip (with 12 cutouts) and the

---

[63] Young, *Gordion I*, 264–265.

[64] This account, unless otherwise noted, is based on the catalogue entry for "screen A" in Young, *Gordion I*, 177–181.

[65] Ibid., 179 and note 110. Young states in the text that most of the inlay remained firmly in place and that it was not possible to ascertain the inlay method, except by analogy with the screen from Tumulus P. However, this is followed by a footnote detailing the inlay method and mentioning the use of "a fine drill." This anomaly no doubt reflects the difficulties inherent in the production of the posthumous publication.

[66] Ibid., 179, n. 112.

[67] Ibid., 178, figure 104. E. Simpson drawing, based on field photographs.

[68] Ibid., 180.

[69] Supra n. 55.

[70] Young, *Gordion I*, 181.

[71] Ibid., 181, figure 107.

diagonal struts are illustrated in *Gordion I*, as are fragments of the carved top piece, although the elements are incorrectly positioned.[72] As had occurred with the plain tables, the two screens were viewed as a set, and while screen A was addressed in some detail, little information about screen B was provided. As would eventually become clear, screen B was illustrated in the Cox drawing, not screen A, although the rendering of this second "screen" was inaccurate (Figure 2). And although the two objects were evidently made as a pair, their dimensions and decoration were different.

The Furniture from the Northeast Corner

The furniture fragments from the northeast corner of the tomb were not catalogued and do not have entries in *Gordion I*. However, they are shown on the tomb plan and illustrated in one *in situ* photograph (Plan, p. viii; Color Plate IIB).[73] In his *Expedition* article, Young referred to this furniture as "a scatter of pieces of smaller items of furniture, evidently stools and more tables, which had fallen apart and to a certain extent disintegrated."[74] In his field book, he called it simply "the Mess."[75]

Several objects "had evidently been stacked one on top of the other" and could not be easily sorted out and recorded.[76] The most specific information is given in the field books, which describe three pieces of furniture from the northeast corner, with legs measuring 20 cm, 30 cm, and 50 cm in height.[77] The wood was "blanketed" by the remains of textiles, very much like those from the "bed," which obscured the position of the pieces below. Young thought that the medium-sized legs had probably belonged to a four-legged stool ("stool #3"), 30 cm high, which stood by itself near the northeast corner. From the placement of the legs, he estimated the size of the seat as roughly 60 cm (north-south) by 45 cm (east-west along the north wall). The stool legs

had stretchers connecting them at the top and also further down near the middle. Textiles covered the stool legs, including "linen and colored wool," and on top of the textiles were several small wooden objects: "two wooden saucers, very small and deep, with lug handles…also the bowl of a spoon, and some handles, probably for spoon or similar implement."[78] These objects do not appear in Young's subsequent publications.

South of the medium-sized stool was a "jumble" of furniture fragments. This included the short legs that belonged to another piece of furniture ("stool #1"), which was apparently stacked on top of a larger piece with longer legs. Young referred to this larger piece as "stool #2," with some hesitation, as he could not tell whether it was actually a stool.[79] The size of the larger piece was estimated, according to the position of the legs on the floor, at about 80 cm (north-south) by 70 cm (east-west), extending out from the east wall of the tomb. The legs of "stool #2" were 50 cm high and showed evidence for stretchers at the top and middle of the legs.[80] At the east, the section of the "frame" that connected the legs "was evidently wrapped around and around with a band of cloth,"[81] and covering the legs was more fabric of two types, some of it pink and purple.[82] What may have been a cloth bag, containing at least one fibula, was found on top of the mass of fabric.

The cloth that covered "stool #2" was clearly beneath the short legs of "stool #1." This disposition suggested that several wood fragments found on top of the cloth should be associated with the short legs. These included a "crosspiece" (47 cm long) and two "cross-slats" (25 cm long) that had once run perpendicular to the crosspiece, "dowelled" into its edge. According to the position of the short legs on the tomb floor, Young suggested that "stool #1" measured approximately 25 by 48 cm and was around 20 cm high, with stretchers connecting the legs at the top. The textiles found in the northeast corner were associated not only

---

[72] Ibid., plate 81A–B.

[73] Ibid., plate 43B. The remains are briefly noted on page 101: "In the northeast corner was a mass of rotted wooden fragments from collapsed furniture."

[74] Young, "Phrygian Furniture from Gordion," 3.

[75] Young, GFB 63, 165.

[76] Young, Gordion I, 259.

[77] Young, GFB 63, 165–175; GFB 70, 35.

[78] Young, GFB 63, 173: "As found, these are somewhat shapeless and stuck together; they will have to be dried and sorted out." The small objects described in the field books

apparently did not survive, as they have not been identified among the extant fragments. Young thought that "stool #3" might have been a table or stand.

[79] Young, GFB 63, 170–171. Young thought that "stool #2" was possibly a table.

[80] Ibid., 170–171.

[81] Ibid., 170.

[82] Ibid., 166–167: "The cloth is much like the bed covering, made up of many layers of linen and ?wool, the latter colored pink and purple."

with the furniture but also with the walls of the tomb—Young noted "shreds of cloth still stuck to the wall face" on the north wall, 35 cm above the level of the floor.[83]

The "Bed"

The king's "bed"[84] presented a complex and confusing problem. The massive construction lay at the north of the chamber, running from the west wall eastward toward the northeast corner (Color Plates IB, IIA; Plates 107–109; and see Plan, p. viii). This very deteriorated object was difficult to decipher, but Young made an attempt, interpreting the fragments as he uncovered and removed them.[85] Thus, in the excavation records, the actual facts of the discovery and Young's interpretations are inextricably interwoven. The remains were indicated on Cox's tomb plan, but a reconstruction drawing of the bed was not made at the time of excavation.

The excavators had entered the chamber by means of a plank put down near the "foot" of the massive wooden bed, which had fallen to pieces on the tomb's floor. The extent of the debris suggested to Young that the bed was approximately 2.9 m long (east-west) and 1.9 m wide (north-south).

> Our door enters the tomb chamber at the foot of the bed, between the corner blocks on which it stood. By putting down a plank below the door and between the end blocks we can gain access to the chamber; but first we have to remove the end of the bed, between the blocks. This consists of a long wooden block—the foot-board, as it turns out, which is fairly firm on its right end, fallen and rotted at its left…The footboard would appear to have fallen *inward*, i.e., toward the east: probably it originally stood upright close against the west wall.[86]

Before the "footboard" was removed, Dorothy Cox sketched the fragments, later to be incorporated in her final plan of the Tumulus MM chamber. The discrepancies in the early accounts begin here, with the Cox drawings showing the footboard fallen outward toward the *west* and not the east. The "corner blocks" at the foot of the bed appear on the plan—one in the northwest corner of the tomb[87] and the other to the south along the west wall.[88]

A "heavy roll of material" made up of many layers of cloth was found partly covering the footboard. The cloth was "yellowish brown at the surface" and seemed to extend over the whole bed, apparently a "coverlet or mattress" on which the king had lain. Young's account continues:

> We take up the footboard; it rests on an iron bar turned down at one end, which probably served as a sort of clamp to hold down the long planks of the bed platform and keep them together; we note a succession of nail holes evenly spaced at about 16 cm apart in their upper faces. The space under them is hollow and we lift them, finding and clearing the floor of the tomb chamber. We put down a block and a plank, and so gain access to the room.[89]

The footboard was puzzling when first found and removed from the tomb. But on entering the chamber, the excavators found another piece just like it, lying farther to the east (Color Plate IIA, Plate 108). This piece—the "headboard"—was "enough to explain all."[90] Young's concept of the bed, as outlined in the following discussion, was reconstructed in a drawing, by the present author, for publication in *Gordion I* (reproduced here as Figure 3).[91]

Young proceeded to take up the bed, describing its constituent parts. These included the four corner blocks, which Young thought were solid, "cubical" blocks of wood.[92] The SE corner block (Plates 107–108), the best preserved of the

---

[83] Ibid., 175.

[84] Hereafter, the quotation marks on "bed" will be dropped; when the word bed is used, it will signify Young's interpretation of the piece of furniture on which the skeleton was found. The same will apply to the words "footboard," "headboard," "planks," "bed platform," "bedposts," and "rails," which, after their first appearance, will be used without quotes and will refer to the pieces that Young thought were the components of a four-poster bed.

[85] Young, *GFB* 63, 73–74, 78–81, 177–194.

[86] Ibid., 78–79.

[87] Hereafter the NW corner block.

[88] Hereafter the SW corner block.

[89] Young, *GFB* 63, 80–81.

[90] Ibid., 81.

[91] Young, *Gordion I*, 188, figure 112. E. Simpson drawing, based on Young's field notes and subsequent publications.

[92] Young at times referred to these corner blocks as "bedposts"; he later reserved the word bedpost for the "posts" that he thought rose from the tops of the corner blocks. *GFB* 63, 177 ff.

four, measured 50 cm (east-west) by 48 cm (north-south) by 33 cm in height. In the middle of its upper face, Young noted a shallow round "cutting" 25 cm in diameter. The four blocks were apparently originally the same size and shape, although they differed in their state of preservation when found in 1957.[93] Young thought the shallow cuttings had held "bedposts":

> The round cuttings on top must have held some sort of bed posts like those of a four-poster; in the NE cutting [i.e., the cutting in the top of the NE corner block] lies the end of a post of black wood at least 60 cm long, which has fallen toward the west and dribbles down the west face of the block and over the bed to some little distance. Fragments of a similar bedpost of black wood lie on the SE bedpost [i.e., the SE corner block] and fallen to the east of it. The fragment on the floor to the east, now not more than 10 cm in diameter, may have shrunk considerably, but was never big enough to be set in a cutting 25 cm in diameter. These posts must have been secured in place on the blocks below by separate doughnut-shaped pieces, such as crown the tops of the legs of all the tables found in the grave.[94]

The bedposts are indicated on Cox's tomb plan, visible especially at the east, where two rectangular posts with squared ends appear just to the east of the NE and SE corner blocks. However, these posts are not easy to recognize in the excavation photographs, although the SE bedpost should probably be identified with the rough piece of wood lying near the edge of the headboard (Plate 108A–B, foreground).

According to Young, the headboard, like the footboard, had fallen over toward the east, with its top resting on the floor:

> Its lower part seems to have been cut aslant as it now lies almost horizontally. The bottom of the visible part of the headboard is covered by a long iron bar, now entirely rust, extending from side to side and no doubt securing the headboard in position at either end.[95]

Young believed that the headboard, like the footboard, had rested on an iron bar that had somehow held together the planks of the bed platform. He found the same empty space beneath the planks at the east end that he had noted at the west. At the east, he calculated that this space was about 20 cm deep.[96] Young counted a possible seven planks for the bed platform, with the central plank being the widest.

> How these long planks were supported is not clear: at the foot evidently on a cross-piece between the corner blocks; but the fallen planks extend out to the south edge of the corner blocks and there was nothing underneath to support them unless their ends rested on top of the corner blocks—but there was no trace of these if they did.[97]

The textiles that had covered the bed and on which the skeleton lay were broken into chunks: "the individual planks of the bed have fallen and shrunk, so that there are long trenches between them now; and the mattress material lies also broken crosswise."[98] Cloth extended out over the headboard in an arc and ended further down in a roll, as it had on the footboard (Plate 108). Young thought the lower half of the thickness of the cloth might have been draped over the headboard, while the upper half could have been rolled or folded back above the body.[99] The disposition of the king's remains was somewhat unusual.

> The skeleton lies on its back with feet toward the west and head toward the east…The skull has rolled over toward the south (its left) and is somewhat disturbed: the mandible or lower jaw is upside down, there is a hole in the back of skull, and the position is very hunched and bent down. These minor damages were doubtless the result of the falling of the bed platform.[100]

In taking up the planks of the platform it was noticed that the "outermost" plank (represented by the southernmost fragments of wood on the floor) was thinner and not covered by cloth. Ac-

---

[93] The NW corner block was badly preserved "due to damp." Young, *GFB* 63, 177.
[94] Ibid., 177–178.
[95] Ibid., 179.
[96] Ibid., 179–180.
[97] Ibid., 180.
[98] Ibid., 180–181.
[99] Ibid., 181–182.
[100] Ibid., 182–183.

cording to Young, Cox thought this plank did not belong to the bed platform itself but had "stood vertically on edge under and supporting the edge of the first platform-plank." The second plank in (i.e., the plank to the north of the thin "outermost" plank) was taken up in order to allow access to the skeleton.[101] This second plank was reportedly in "horrible condition and could not be saved," but its width was measured as ca. 30 cm. The excavators removed the remaining cloth, exposing the rest of the bed planks, which had "gone to pieces in a big way" but seemed to confirm Young's earlier impression of a wide central plank, which he measured as approximately 58 cm wide and 4 cm thick.[102]

The removal of the second plank exposed two pairs of dark wood strips (Plate 110A). These were found under the wood of the bed planks, lying directly on the floor of the tomb. The longer pair of strips, preserved to a length of 1.23 m, had a squared east end, which lay 45 cm to the west of the west face of the SE corner block. The northern long strip was notched 28 cm west of the squared end. Beyond the long strips, near the notch, was a shorter pair of strips, 22 cm long and lying slightly askew. The southern ends of these short strips were notched, and the northern ends were squared. It thus seemed likely that the long and short strips had once fit together.

Each of these dark wood strips was said to be 1.5 cm wide and 2 cm thick. Fragments of light-colored wood lying between and to either side of the dark strips suggested to Young that the light and dark strips had been fastened together to form a sort of "five-layer sandwich."[103] This idea was confirmed by the discovery of small holes

in the dark strips, which must have held pins that fastened the "sandwich" together. Five strips, each 1.5 cm wide, would have made a composite piece 7.5 cm wide and 2 cm thick. Young thought that the long composite piece "would seem without doubt to have been a rail along the bed on its south side, running from corner block to corner block at the edge of the platform; the shorter pieces were the struts carrying the rail, probably with their lower ends doweled into the top face of the plank at its edge."[104] Although Young's concept of the bed was problematic, he had correctly understood the rail construction (Figure 3D).[105]

The removal of the bed planks at the north revealed another "rail" of the same light and dark wood (Plate 110B). The long strips of this second rail were preserved to a length of 1.35 m. Two short supporting struts lay perpendicular to the long rail, extending toward the south. The first short strut was 28 cm from the long rail's squared east end, and the second was 60 cm west of the first.[106] This placement suggested that there had originally been three short struts supporting each of the long rails. Assuming that the arrangement at the north was symmetrical, Young posited a third short strut 60 cm to the west of the second, with the rail extending another 28 cm to the west of this third strut. He thus arrived at a calculation for the rail's total original length, which roughly fit the space between the corner blocks, ca. 1.95 m.[107]

Young concluded his discussion with an unusual explanation of how the rails, which he thought had been socketed into the upper face of the bed platform, could have ended up underneath the platform itself. This disposition presented a serious problem, because the space be-

---

[101] Ibid., 187. On the afternoon of July 21, 1957, "M. Şenyürek took up the skeleton and carried it off to Ankara."

[102] Ibid., 187–188.

[103] Ibid., 188–191. In his field notes, Young says the wood was "1.5 cm in thickness" and "2 cm in width." In *Gordion I*, 189, the words width and thickness are used interchangeably, and both words can apply to the same dimension. Here, 1.5 cm will be taken to be the width of the strips, 7.5 cm as the width of the composite pieces, and 2 cm as the thickness.

[104] Young, *GFB* 63, 190–191.

[105] First published in Young, *Gordion I*, figure 113. This E. Simpson drawing was based on Young's description in *GFB* 63, 188–192.

[106] Young, *GFB* 63, 192. Young's wording, however, is somewhat ambiguous. The notch for the first short piece was presumably 28 cm west of the squared east end, just as it had been on the rail at the south (*GFB* 63, 189). But exactly where the second short piece lay with respect to the first is not totally clear. Was the second notch placed west

of the first with an intervening 60 cm between the inner edges of the notches? Or was 60 cm the distance between the inner edges of the 5-layer composite short pieces? There is a difference of 6 cm between these two interpretations of Young's observation.

[107] Ibid., 192. Young's wording here would seem to indicate that the outer short struts began 28 cm from the ends of the rails and that the 60 cm measurement was taken between the inner edges of the composite short struts. This runs counter to his earlier observation that the notch for the first short strut in the southern rail complex was cut 28 cm from the end of the long rail (*GFB* 63, 189). If Young's measurements were taken between the notches, the rails would have been 28 + 1.5 + 60 + 1.5 + 60 + 1.5 + 28 = 180.5 cm long. If his measurements were taken between the edges of the short struts, the rails would have been 28 + 7.5 + 60 + 7.5 + 60 + 7.5 + 28 = 198.5 cm long. Such details became important as I tried to reconstruct the bed in a drawing.

neath the platform had supposedly been inaccessible, closed off by the planks at the north and south sides, which had been set down vertically in order to support the outer edges of the platform. In Young's estimation, "On falling [each of the rails] evidently went under the edge of the bed after the supporting vertical planks had fallen out, and was finally covered on the collapse of the bed itself."[108] This would have entailed the north and south vertical planks falling outward and onto the tomb floor, the rails falling off the bed platform onto the floor, and these same rails moving in under the platform, before it finally collapsed on top of them. This is an imaginative scenario—but impossible for inanimate objects.

By 1974, Young felt considerably more confident about the bed's construction, as is evident from his comments in *Expedition*:

Iron bars running across the width at head and foot supported the ends of the lengthwise planks of the bed platform as well as the curlicued head- and footboards at either end. The footboard, which had fallen inward over the lower end of the bed, lay exactly inside the door cut through the wooden wall to gain entrance to the tomb; it blocked access and had to be removed. Beneath its base and running between the corner blocks lay the remains, now mostly rust, of a horizontal iron bar which must have supported it as well as the lower ends of the bed planks. At the head and underneath the thick wads of cloth which had been bedcoverings and had been dragged upward when the headpiece fell outward, lay a heavy line of iron rust, the remains of a similar bar. No doubt the ends of these bars were socketed in cuttings in the faces of the

corner blocks, though the socket holes were not preserved.[109]

Young described the bed planks with more assurance (see Figure 3). A central plank approximately 60 cm wide was flanked by two narrower planks that were about 20 cm wide and reached out to the inner edges of the corner blocks.[110] Outside these were two more planks, set between the corner blocks, carrying the width of the platform out to about 1.40 m.[111] Beyond these two planks were two "outermost planks," which "had probably been stood on edge underneath to support them and to close access to the space beneath the bed." These "outermost" planks were said to be 24 cm wide, thus suggesting the height of the bed platform.[112]

The rails had been supported in three places by "vertical posts," new terminology for the short composite struts of the field book. In *Expedition*, Young stated that there were tenons at the lower end of these posts, indicating that they had been socketed into the upper surface of the bed platform. However, there is no evidence for such tenons, either in the field books or the photographs. In fact, in his field notes Young noted that the short vertical struts had notches in their upper ends, while their lower ends were squared.[113] Young had originally thought that the squared ends of the short struts had been socketed into the bed platform.

That the bed had been a "four-poster" was attested by the shallow cuttings in the corner blocks and the "fallen fragments of round posts lying near them." Young reiterated his idea that these "posts" had been set into the corner blocks by means of collars of soft wood, "now entirely disappeared." Finally, he judged that the bed,

---

[108] Young, *GFB* 63, 192–193.

[109] Young, "Phrygian Furniture from Gordion," 3–4.

[110] Although Young does not give the width of these narrower planks, it can be calculated approximately from his field measurements. *GFB* 63, 73: "the bed measures approximately 1.90 m in width." *GFB* 63, 81: "The bed at its lower (W) end is 2.0 m wide from outside corner block to outside of corner block." *GFB* 63, 177: "width N–S 1.93 m." If one subtracts the widths of the corner blocks (48 cm, N–S) and central plank from 2.0 m, the result is ca. 44 cm. This gives a width of 22 cm for each plank. If one subtracts the widths of the corner blocks and central plank from 1.9 m, the result is 34 cm, giving a width of 17 cm for each plank.

[111] Young, "Phrygian Furniture from Gordion," 4. If the inner plank was 60 cm wide and each of the two narrow flanking planks was 20 cm wide, then Young's postulated width of 1.40 m would suggest that the planks that fit

between the corner blocks were each approximately 20 cm wide. Yet in *GFB* 63, 187, Young reports that the southern plank between the corner blocks was measured and found to be 30 cm wide. Two outer planks, each 30 cm wide, would bring the total width of the platform to 1.60 meters.

[112] Young, "Phrygian Furniture from Gordion," 4. It is unclear how Young arrived at a width of 24 cm for the "vertical" planks that stood on edge to support the platform.

[113] Young, *GFB* 63, 190. While the wording of this description is ambiguous, Young is apparently talking about the short vertical struts when he mentions "corresponding nail-holes through the two darker bits of wood near their squared ends. At their other ends both of the dark pieces are notched and the notches exactly fit the one in the long piece." *Gordion I*, plate 42B, shows that the short vertical struts had square ends with no evidence of tenons on their bottom edges.

while uncomfortable, was indeed fit for a king. "No doubt it was used by the king while he was alive, then placed in the tomb for further use in the other world."[114]

Finally, Young's description in *Gordion I* follows his report in *Expedition*, with added details about the bed's constituent parts and the way in which they were assembled.[115] According to the *Gordion I* account, both the headboard and the footboard were supported on iron crossbars:

A large quantity of iron rust was found along the length of the underside of the footboard when it was lifted, and subsequently a similar band of iron rust was found on the lower face of the headboard. These iron bars were set between the corner blocks of the bed at both ends—probably their ends had been fitted into cuttings in the side faces of the blocks, though the condition of the wood was so bad that no traces of cuttings were discernible. Iron crossbars at each end would have supported the ends of the planks of the bed platform, as well as the end boards.[116]

The reconstruction of the platform given in *Gordion I* closely follows the account in *Expedition*. The platform consisted of seven planks, each plank about 4 cm thick, for a total width of 1.40 m. The central plank was ca. 58 cm wide and was flanked by two narrower planks, which made up the rest of the distance between the north and south corner blocks. The width of the three planks together, which equaled the distance between the inner faces of the corner blocks, was approximately 95 cm. To each side of the central group of three planks was one more plank; these fourth and fifth planks had fit between the eastern and western corner blocks, "evidently supported beneath by lengthwise planks set on edge." The fourth and fifth planks would each have been approximately 22.5 cm wide, to make up the platform's total width of 1.40 m. The sixth and seventh planks would have stood on edge, supporting the fourth and fifth planks at the outside of the bed platform.[117] The height of the platform above the floor "cannot be exactly calcu-

lated; probably 0.25 to 0.30 m. The corner blocks are 0.33 m high above floor level; the level of the platform must have been somewhat lower."[118]

In the *Gordion I* account, there is no mention of tenons at the lower ends of the short vertical struts of the rails. "It is possible that there were holes through the outer plank, and that the supports were bedded in the edge of the supporting plank beneath."[119] The length of the rails is estimated at 1.985 m, which corresponded "almost exactly with the distance between the inner faces of the corner blocks" (i.e., the distance between the inner faces of the corner blocks at the east and those at the west). The width of the notches in the long strips is now given as 7.5 cm; this is clearly an error, which may have resulted from a misunderstanding of Young's original text.[120]

The four-poster theory is repeated in *Gordion I*, with the four bedposts gaining in substance:

On or near each of these sinkings was a piece of black wood, round in section and 0.10 m in diameter; the longest of these was preserved to a length of 0.60 m. It is likely that these are remnants of corner posts of the bed; the positions in which they lay suggest it, and they are not to be assigned to any other pieces of furniture.[121]

Although I managed to draw Young's bed from this evidence (Figure 3), nagging problems with the early interpretation persisted. These derived mainly from the ambiguous nature of many of the descriptions, as well as discrepancies between the information given in the field notes, the *Expedition* article, and the text for *Gordion I*. Adding to the confusion were conflicts between Young's commentary and Cox's drawing of the bed on the tomb plan. My reconstruction drawing was published in *Gordion I*, but several questions remained.

One of the most problematic aspects of the early interpretation was Young's discussion of the headboard and footboard. Young stated that the footboard fell inward, to the east, and from this he surmised that it had once stood upright

114 Young, "Phrygian Furniture from Gordion," 4.
115 Young, *Gordion I*, 187–190.
116 Ibid., 187.
117 Ibid.
118 Ibid., 189. Apparently Young had by this time given up trying to estimate the height of the bed based on the

width of the outermost planks (the sixth and seventh planks), due to their deteriorated condition.
119 Ibid., 189.
120 Ibid.
121 Ibid. The "sinkings" were 25 cm in diameter and 3 cm deep.

against the west wall of the tomb.[122] However, the footboard is shown fallen to the west on Cox's tomb plan (Plan, p. viii) and also in her preliminary drawings.[123] Before taking up the footboard, Young had to remove "a heavy roll of material that partly overlies it."[124] The roll of material appears on Cox's plan, lying over a long strip. One wonders if this strip is the iron bar to which Young had referred, although a second strip, pictured somewhat to the east, might be the iron bar instead. In his field notes, Young stated that the footboard "rests on an iron bar turned down at one end, which probably served as a sort of clamp to hold down the long planks of the bed platform and keep them together."[125] Yet he was not able to understand the means of attachment in detail.

The headboard was also supposedly supported by an iron bar, with its role likewise uncertain. According to Young's field book account of the headboard, "its lower part seems to have been cut aslant as it now lies almost horizontally. The bottom of the visible part of the headboard is covered by a long iron bar, now entirely rust, extending from side to side and no doubt securing the headboard in position at either end."[126] The iron bar can be identified in the *in situ* photographs as the corroded strip lying partly under and to the east of the cloth on the headboard (Color Plate IIA, Plate 108). However, this rusty strip is not at the bottom edge of the headboard but lying on its face. Also curious are the hollow spaces that Young noticed under the bed planks near the headboard and footboard.[127] At the east, this empty space was said to have been about 20 cm deep. At the west, Young noted nail holes 16 cm apart in what he thought were the ends of the bed planks. One wonders how these hollow spaces and nail holes figured into Young's ultimate solution.[128]

Also problematic was the evidence for the bedposts. In the field book, this was limited to fragments of wood lying on the SE corner block, to its east on the tomb floor (Plate 108B, left foreground), and "the end of a post of black wood"

on the NE corner block, "which has fallen toward the west and dribbles down the west face of the block and over the bed to some little distance."[129] Although these chunks were rough and fragmentary, which is obvious from the photographs, in *Gordion I* they were characterized as four posts, 10 cm in diameter, the longest of which was preserved to a length of 60 cm. Cox's tomb plan shows not the fragmentary remains of the bedposts, but what seem to be the bedposts themselves. The wood chunk to the east of the SE corner block has been transformed into a post-like piece with squared ends. Near the NE corner block a similar post is indicated, extending not to the west of the corner block but to the east instead. Remnants of a third fragmentary post lie on the SW corner block, and a fourth post is shown on the NW corner block, with another comparable piece nearby. Curiously, these finished posts do not appear on Cox's preliminary sketches.[130] At some point, the bedposts became entities—and were added to the final plan of the tomb.

Finally, the situation of the bed rails was one of the most troubling aspects of the early reconstruction. In order for the rails to have been socketed into the top of the bed platform but found beneath it, they would have had to fall off the sides and travel under the platform, which is not a viable option.

These, then, are the early interpretations of the furniture from the Tumulus MM burial. The pieces and their disposition were clearly of interest to Rodney Young and Dorothy Cox, both of whom tried seriously to understand the wooden fragments and the way they might have been assembled. However, the fragile condition of the wood and the problems associated with its conservation made the furniture considerably more difficult to study than the metal and pottery objects from the tomb. This situation was compounded by the unusual nature of the wooden artifacts, many of which were totally unprecedented in their form and decoration. Add to this the complexity of the inlaid designs, and it will

---

[122] Young, *GFB* 63, 78–79. He reiterates this in "Phrygian Furniture from Gordion," 3, and *Gordion I*, 187.

[123] On Cox's original sketch of the west end of the bed (Gordion plan 1957–6B), the footboard appears as it does on her final plan. She seems to have drawn the sketch from the door cut in the tomb wall, apparently before the footboard was removed. The original sketch is extremely helpful, although Cox's annotations on her sketch are difficult to decipher.

[124] Young, *GFB* 63, 79.
[125] Ibid., 80.
[126] Ibid., 179.
[127] Ibid., 80–81, 179–180.
[128] Young, *Gordion I*, 187.
[129] Young, *GFB* 63, 178.
[130] Gordion plan 1957–6B (west end) and 1957–1959 (east end).

be clear that the remarkable furniture from Tumulus MM could neither be understood nor ad-
equately drawn at the time of the tomb's excavation. Although much progress was made in subsequent investigations, at Young's death in 1974
many problems were still unresolved. Unfortunately, Young did not have the chance to revisit

these issues, as he surely would have for his final
publication of the Tumulus MM, P, and W burials. The present study was undertaken, then, with
all these concerns in mind, picking up the story
from Young, Cox, and then the editors and artists
of *Gordion I.* The catalogue that follows details the
results of the new research.

PART TWO

CATALOGUE AND COMPARANDA

CHAPTER THREE

THE INLAID TABLE

As research has now shown, the Tumulus MM furniture was refined and elegant—vastly different from the odd creations depicted in the early drawings. The imaginative forms, intricate inlaid ornament, and play with symmetry and pattern are unprecedented outside of Phrygia. The cabinetmakers who made these special pieces were clearly among the most talented artists of their time.

The collection included nine three-legged tables, two inlaid serving stands (Young's "screens"), two stools, a chair, and the massive log coffin (Young's "bed") in which the king was buried. The furniture was evidently used in conjunction with the many bronzes found in the tomb. The circumstances of the burial have produced evidence for the lavish funeral of the king, and chemical analyses of the food and drink residues from the vessels have provided the menu for the funerary banquet (see Chapter 8 and Appendix 5). The furniture found in the tomb was apparently used for the ceremony and subsequently interred with the king.

Of the nine tables found in the Tumulus MM chamber, eight were plain (see Chapter 4). The ninth, however, was extremely ornate, with an unusual frame construction and exquisite inlaid decoration. This was Young's "Pagoda Table," here called the inlaid table.[1] The table was made of boxwood, with a walnut table top, and the wood of the inlay was juniper—not yew, as originally suggested.

Inlaid Table (Table 8)

5212 W 80
(MM 388)
Frame, inlaid struts, legs, leg tenons, dowels, pegs: boxwood (*Buxus sempervirens* L.); inlay: juniper (*Juniperus* sp.); table top: walnut (*Juglans* sp.).[2]
Glue analysis inconclusive.[3]
Found along the east wall of the tomb, south of the two serving stands.
Color Plates III, VIII–IX; Figures 1, 4–28, 30I; Plates 1–35, 124A–B, 129–132, 150D, 151A.

---

[1] See above, pp. 15–18, for the early interpretation.

[2] The wood species analysis for the wooden objects from Tumulus MM was conducted by Burhan Aytuğ of the Forestry Faculty of Istanbul University and Robert Blanchette and Benjamin Held of the Department of Plant Pathology, University of Minnesota. Results of the analyses appear here in Appendix 3. Young correctly assumed that the wood of the table was boxwood, but he thought that the inlay was yew (*Gordion I*, 183).

[3] A dark residue was present on the corner joints of the frame of the table, and some of this material was removed in 1982 from the ends of the back frame piece (frame piece D) for analysis. The glue residue, which was available in only a very small sample, was subjected to testing in 1983 by Robert Gillespie of the U.S. Forest Products Laboratory and again in 1991 under the direction of George Reilly of the Science and Research Division, Winterthur Museum. Helpful comments were also contributed by Rudy Michel of MASCA, University of Pennsylvania Museum, and Robert Snider of Franklin International (Gordion Furniture Project archives). The sample was difficult to identify due to its small size and because it was determined to be contaminated. This is not surprising considering that the table was submerged in a solution of wax and gasoline in 1957, with the waxy surface subsequently attracting dust and dirt over the intervening 25 years (see Appendix 1). Interestingly, tests showed the likely presence of polyvinyl acetal resin, or Alvar, among the contaminants. The sample was taken before the wood of the table was consolidated by Robert Payton in the fall of 1982. Traces of similar residues were also noted by Payton on the top surfaces and the bottom tenons of the struts that supported the table top, in the mortises in the top of the frame that received the tenons of the top struts, on the ends of the dowels that secured the frame and legs, and in the recesses cut to hold the inlay (R. Payton, letter of 12/6/82, Gordion Furniture Project archives). The identification of ancient glue by chemical analysis is notoriously difficult, because of the typically small size of samples and contamination of glue residues, as well as the problem of differentiating between ancient and modern glue, the latter often used to repair the artifacts in question after their excavation. It has been said that ancient Egyptian glue was made from protein collagen, present in animal hides, bones, and connective tissue; sources of this protein could have included both animals and fish. See Newman and Serpico, "Adhesives and Binders," 475, 481–484, 492. Casein glue has also been suggested as a possibility for the glue used on the inlaid table.

Est.H. of table ca. 63 cm.

Table top. Est.L. ca. 78–80 cm (front to back).
Est.W. ca. 78 cm (side to side). Est.Th.
ca. 1.8 cm. G.P.Th. 1.7 cm.

Legs. Est.H. to top of tenon 63 cm. Est.D. reeded
section of top pieces 10.5 cm. Est.H. tenon
projection 4.5 cm.

Feet. Est.L. base 6 cm. Est.W. base 6 cm. Est.H.
foot 7.3 cm.

Frame. Frame piece A (front of table): G.P.L.
67.1 cm; G.P.H. 6.3 cm. Frame piece B
(right side): G.P.L. 58.9 cm; G.P.H. 6.3 cm.
Frame piece C (left side): G.P.L. 58.1 cm;
G.P.H. 5.9 cm. Frame piece D (back of table):
G.P.L. 66 cm; G.P.H. 6.1 cm.

Top struts (excluding top and bottom tenons).
Est.H. ca. 19.5 cm. G.P.H. 18.1–19.3 cm.

Dowels. G.P.L. 9.6–32 cm. G.P.D. 2.2 cm.

The table was made from 46 individual
components.[4]

Form and Decoration

The inlaid table was found near the east wall
of the Tumulus MM chamber, just south of
Young's "screens" A and B. Bronze vessels had
been placed on the table at the time of the
burial, and it had eventually collapsed on the
floor (Color Plate IIIB, Plate 1). The table's frame
had fallen almost intact, with at least one of its
corners still joined. The frame pieces were carved
as a series of panels connected by double bars,
the panels inlaid with geometric decoration. The
excavation photographs show two of the struts
that supported the table top still in place above
the frame, and two handles were lying where
they had fallen from the corners of the table.
These top struts and handles were also inlaid.
The three legs were found leaning inward; clearly
visible were their carved top sections, with inlaid
bands above and below. Extending up at the very
top of the legs were stepped tenons, surrounded
by fragments of wood—the remains of Young's

"collars." Dowels were still in place in two of the
legs, evidence of an internal bracing system. The
table top had largely disintegrated, although a
few degraded fragments were found draped over
the legs and frame. The excavation photographs
do indeed reveal the table's form, but this was
somewhat different from the way that Young and
Cox had envisioned it.

Internal Bracing System

Although no dowels appear in Cox's original
drawing of the inlaid table (Figure 1), all nine
dowels from the internal support system survived
(Plate 2). These dowels can be situated within
the table's frame, and it is this arrangement that
provides the key to the correct reconstruction of
the table (Figure 4).[5] The boxwood dowels were
round in section with squared tenons at the ends.
These tenons fitted into the table's legs and the
backs of the square panels of the frame. The front
leg of the table (leg A)[6] was attached by a short
dowel to the back side of the front of the frame
(Plate 2, dowel shown at bottom). The tenon at
one end of the dowel fit into a mortise cut in the
front of the leg below its carved top section (see
Figures 4, 21; Plates 1, 24B). The tenon at the
other end fit into a mortise cut in the back of
the central square of the front frame piece (frame
piece A; Plate 3B, center).

The two legs at the rear corners of the table were likewise attached to the frame by dowels (Figure 4). Two short dowels extended out
from the back legs and fitted into mortises cut in
the back frame piece (frame piece D; Plate 19B).
Two slightly longer dowels joined the legs to the
two side frame pieces, near the rear of the table
(Plate 11B, mortise in square at left; Plate 15B,
mortise in square at right). The two rear legs
were connected to each other by a long dowel
running between them. Another long dowel extended from the back of the front leg (Plate 25B)
and was mortised into the dowel that connected
the two back legs (Figure 4 and Plate 2, center).

---

[4] Excluding ancient repairs and the missing attachments (see below, pp. 34–35): nine dowels, four frame pieces,
18 top struts and handles, two rear leg struts, the front leg
strut (made of three pieces), three legs (each made of three
pieces), and the table top. The top was evidently made of
more than one piece of walnut, featuring fine edge joinery, but its fragmentary condition precludes reconstruction
of the original details. See below, p. 39.

[5] Dowels are recorded in Young, GFB 63, 141–142, and

photographs of five dowels and part of a sixth appear on the
catalogue cards. They do not appear in Cox's reconstruction
drawing, however, and in Gordion I, Young notes only two
dowels (Gordion I, 183). See above, pp. 15–16.

[6] Leg A is the leg most clearly visible in Plate 1A–B,
with its attached dowel pointing out to the right. As already
noted (Chapter 2, n. 29), Young's letter designations for the
pieces of the table have been superseded. For new letter
designations, see Figure 4.

Two more long dowels ran across the table from side to side, joined to the central dowel that extended back from the front leg. These two long dowels ran to mortises cut in the lower of the double bars at the center of the side pieces of the frame (Plate 11B, center; Plate 15B, center).

This reconstruction of the central bracing system is certain, and the position of all the dowels is now known. But there are more cuttings in the legs than were needed for the dowels of the support system. On the front leg is a square patch just above the mortise that held the front dowel (Plate 24B). This suggests that an upper mortise was cut and abandoned, later to be patched with a small block of wood. A second mortise was cut some distance below the first, and it was this second mortise that had held the dowel that joined the leg to the front frame piece. A close look at the table's three legs shows that the mortises for the dowels have all been cut twice. In several cases, the two mortises are so close together that they now appear contiguous (Plates 25B, 26A, 27A–B, 28B, 29A–B). These form long cuttings, which may have facilitated the insertion of the dowels into the mortises of the legs within the rigid frame. But at least two of the extra mortises were clearly not for this purpose, since they do not connect (Plates 24B and 28A). In the case of these mortises at least, the original placement was apparently abandoned when it proved problematic. They were then cut a second time in the correct locations, and the original mortises were patched. An unrelated cutting further down on the left rear leg (leg C) was not a mortise but held a patch, probably to mask an imperfection in the wood (Plate 29A). Two such patches are still in place in leg C. An unusual feature of the internal bracing system can be seen in Figure 4, which shows three of the rear dowels joining the frame at oblique angles. This is not the result of the wood's present condition but occurred in the original assembly.

Frame

Each side of the frame was cut from a single board of boxwood. The front and back frame pieces (frame pieces A and D, respectively) were carved as five square panels connected by pairs of bars, with squared tenons extending out from both ends (Figures 5–6; Plates 3, 19). The right

and left frame pieces (B and C, respectively) were slightly shorter than those at the front and back. These were carved in a similar manner, but with four square panels on each side and inlaid strips near the ends (Figures 7–8; Plates 11, 15). Two squared elements projected beyond each of these inlaid strips, forming slots to receive the tenons at the ends of the front and back frame pieces. These open mortise joints (or corner bridle joints) were secured with a locking pin (Figure 24, Plate 23).

The panels of the frame were elaborately inlaid with geometric decoration (Plates 6, 13, 17, and 22). The intricate designs were constructed from small pieces of juniper, set into carved recesses, and longer juniper strips that were inserted into channels. Some of these strips have fallen out, revealing the method by which the channels were created: a series of holes was drilled, and the channels were hollowed out along the line of the drillings. Young had seen this evidence on "screen A," but had suggested that the holes were "borings by a fine awl."[7] Instead, their regular, cylindrical shape indicates that they were made by a bow drill, used throughout the Near East in antiquity (see Appendix 7 and Plate 150D). Most of the panels are inlaid with rectilinear designs, while three feature curvilinear motifs (Figures 5–8). The various patterns include fields of squares or diamonds, lattices, rosettes with guilloche-like elements, "meander squares" (variations on the swastika), and complex configurations with hooks. Hooks and longer curved pieces of inlay were normally made from short, contiguous segments of wood.[8]

The inlaid patterns on the panels of the frame appear to be arranged somewhat unsystematically. Although the carved forms of the frame pieces are themselves bilaterally symmetrical, there is no such symmetry in the series of designs on any frame piece, and no obvious sequential coincidence (repetition in sequence) to the designs as they run around the table. But there are hints of bilateral symmetry and intentional interplay among the individual panels. Certain designs resemble each other, although no two are exactly alike. Elements of a design may be enlarged, reduced, or modified for use in another, and there is one clear instance of dark/light reversal (Figure 5, squares 2 and 4). These correspondences suggest the possibility of an underlying scheme for the decoration on the frame pieces, but careful scrutiny reveals no such organization. If the arrangement of designs was meaningful, this is not evident to the modern eye.

Several patterns seem wildly eccentric, with hooks and segments arranged in no apparent order (see Figure 6, squares 3 and 4; Figure 7, squares 3 and 4). These configurations were seen as idiosyncratic—until the designs were finally understood. The patterns are actually mazes (Figure 9), underscoring the puzzle-like nature of the table's decoration.[9] The viewer could negotiate these mazes, which feature apparent starting points, false leads, and one blind section (Figure 9D, lower left). The false leads indicate that these are "multicursal" mazes—that is, mazes that require a choice between paths (while "unicursal" mazes, with their single path, offer no such opportunity). Not mere games, however, the table's mazes were of special significance and may have been religious symbols (see below, pp. 50–52). Irrespective of their meaning, these clever designs highlight the exceptional nature of the inlaid table. While utilizing the rational principles of symmetry and repetition, the artisans dispensed with these principles at times, introducing anomalies and creating an element of surprise that occurs throughout the decoration of the table.

Corner Pieces

Further embellishing the inlaid frame were four decorative corner pieces, which do not survive but once certainly existed. These covered the four open mortise joints at the corners of the table. Eight small wood pegs were driven into the sides of each joint, unrelated to the actual joinery (Figure 24; Plate 23).[10] These pegs, along with the residue of the glue that had been liberally applied at the corners, provide clear evidence that the joints had been sheathed.[11] Impressions near the bottom of the table's four handles (Figures 13–16; Plates 4A, 5E, 20A, 21E, 23B) show that the

sheathing had covered the corner joints, risen up next to the handles, and curved out above the frame. The corner pieces can be envisioned in their simplest form (Figure 25), but given the complexity of the table's design, it is likely that they were more elaborate. Curiously, no trace of these corner pieces was recovered from the burial. This suggests that they were intentionally removed, a possibility that will be considered again in connection with the table's handles (see pp. 35, 39 below).

Top Struts and Handles

From each inlaid square of the frame rose a decorative strut. Eighteen of these struts connected the table top to the frame, supporting the top from below. As Young recognized, three different types of these supports were found on the inlaid table (see above, pp. 16–17). The form and placement of these top struts is now well understood. The first type, Young's type-1 strut, has three tiers and resembles a stylized plant or tree. At the bottom is a small, half-round base from which rises a slender cylindrical stem (e.g., Plate 4E–F).[12] The stem branches into two outturned leaves, which are inlaid with stripes and support the two vertical segments of the second tier. These two segments have inlaid, flat faces and rounded backs, ending in single, outturned leaves which are inlaid with stripes. This second pair of leaves supports the upper tier of the strut, which is composed of three more vertical segments. The outer two are cylindrical and rise from the tops of the leaves below them.[13] The central segment rises from between these two leaves; it is inlaid on its flat face and is rounded at the back. The three upper verticals are connected across the top by a half-round crosspiece. The flat top of this crosspiece was fit into a shallow cutting in the underside of the table top. A tenon at the top of the strut fit into a deeper mortise at the center of the shallow cutting, and the entire joint might be secured by tiny pins.[14] A tenon at the bottom of

---

[9] Simpson, "Phrygian Artistic Intellect," 28–29. Carlos Simpson first brought these mazes to my attention. This was the key that unlocked the mystery of the table's seemingly erratic decoration.

[10] Young thought that these pegs had secured the corner joints. See above, p. 15, and Young, *Gordion I*, 183.

[11] In some cases, the corner sheathing had covered the inlay at the ends of the side frame pieces: glue was found on the inlaid sections, and the pegs were sometimes driven through inlays (Figures 7–8; Plate 17A, F).

---

[12] This stem is not "square in section," as in *Gordion I*, 186.

[13] These cylindrical verticals are not "most often round in section"; they are always round in section. *Gordion I*, 186.

[14] These pins were run through the top crosspieces of many of the struts and into the corresponding mortises in the underside of the table top. In the case of strut A2 (Plate 4E–F) and two other type-1 struts (B1 and D4), no pins were utilized.

the type-1 strut fit into a mortise cut in the upper edge of an inlaid square panel of the frame (Figure 26).

There are eight struts of this first type, seven having the same form, but one that is different. This unusual strut rose from the third square of frame piece C, at the left side of the table (Strut C3: Plates 16E–F and see Figure 8). The single stem of strut C3 does not split but ends in a rounded top. To either side of this rounded top are short upturned leaves, from which rise the two inlaid vertical segments of the second tier. The upturned leaves and the top of the single stem combine to form a kind of wave with three curves, inlaid with triangles in an undulating pattern. The third tier of the strut rises from a similar wave with five curves inlaid with triangles. The outer verticals of the third tier are round in section; the central one is flat at the front and inlaid.[15] As a rule, the flat areas of the table's top struts coincide with the inlaid surfaces.

There are six struts of a second type, Young's type 2, which also incorporate floral-like elements (e.g., Plate 16C–D). As with the type-1 struts, type-2 struts have three tiers; although they utilize the elements in type 1's second tier, the type-2 struts are different in form. From the half-round base rise two vertical segments, inlaid on their flat front faces. At their tops are single outturned leaves, inlaid with stripes, which support a second tier consisting of a single vertical segment. This segment, round in section and tapering toward the middle,[16] supports the third tier, which is like the first but inverted, with the leaves of the upper

segments joining the top of the central element. At the top of the strut is a half-round cross-strip and a central tenon; these elements were fit into cuttings in the table top, as with the type-1 struts.[17] Likewise, tenons at the bottom of the struts fit into mortises cut in the upper edge of the frame's square panels.

At the corners of the table were four elaborate handles, Young's type 3,[18] which rose from the outer squares of the front and back frame pieces (Figures 13–16; Plates 4A–D, 5C–F, 20A–D, 21C–F). The curved extension of each handle had a flat outer surface, decorated with a series of inlaid panels. The inlaid panels now alternate with square, shallow depressions showing patterns of small holes (Plate 151A). These depressions had once held separate sections of inlay, now missing, with the small holes suggesting the designs' configuration. It is clear that the missing panels were forcibly pried out, as many of the edges that bordered the panels are broken, and the depressions show evidence of chipping. Thus the table had been robbed of 12 sections of its inlaid handles, and probably its four corner pieces as well. The missing parts must therefore have been worth stealing and may have been made of precious metal.[19]

The vertical elements of the handles are arranged in three tiers, as with the type-1 and type-2 struts. The bottom tier is a wide support with an inlaid, flat front surface. Above this are two cylindrical segments, rising from horizontal spool-like bases. At the tops of these segments are two more spools, connected by a crossbar run-

---

[15] Strut C3 was photographed at the time of excavation but was not found with the other parts of the table in the museum storeroom in 1981. It was therefore not conserved with the other pieces, which were subsequently mounted for display. Missing for many years, it was recovered by chance in 1995 from a storeroom in the citadel (Ankara kalesi). It was then conserved and photographed (Plate 16E–F) but does not appear in the display.

[16] This vertical is not "usually round in section," but always round in section. *Gordion I*, 186.

[17] Type-2 struts A3, C2, and D3 did not utilize small pins in the top joinery.

[18] Young suggested, mistakenly, that these were composite pieces made by attaching handles to struts that differed only slightly from those of type 1. The lower end of the handle extension is not always "pinned by a dowel" to the lowermost vertical, and the central member of the top tier likewise does not spread "to receive a dowel fastening the upper end of the handle." *Gordion I*, 186.

[19] Since the inlays were clearly pried out of the handles, a robbery seems the most plausible scenario. Regarding the case for precious metal attachments, it is clear that small holes were drilled in the panels of the wooden handles, and

square pegs were then driven into the drilled holes. The well-defined square openings that resulted suggest that the pegs were metal (Plate 151A). See Appendix 7. Numerous remnants of wooden furniture adorned with gold and silver sheathing or attachments have been preserved from antiquity. Some of the most complete examples come from Egypt. The remains of several such pieces were found in the tomb of Queen Hetepheres at Giza, dating to the middle of the third millennium B.C. See Reisner, *Tomb of Hetep-heres*, for the account of their excavation. For a well-preserved piece of wooden furniture with precious metal attachments, see the "cedar" chair from the tomb of Tutankhamun. This magnificent chair has four gold-sheathed brackets that secure the seat to the chair back, as well as decorations on the stretchers below the seat that are covered with gold foil (parts of these are now missing). The lion's feet have ivory claws and sit on gilded drums with bronze shoes. A gilded winged disc decorates the chair back at its top, and the whole is dotted with gold-capped studs that secured the joinery. The rest of the chair is left as natural wood. H. Baker, *Furniture in the Ancient World*, figures 95–96. *Treasures of Tutankhamun*, color plate 2 (cat. 12). Eaton-Krauss, *Thrones, Chairs*, 57–67.

ning between them. From these upper spools and from the middle of the crossbar rise three more cylindrical segments, which terminate in the half-round top strip that supported the table top at its corners. The curved part of each handle is inlaid on both sides—on three handles with rows of triangles and on the fourth with a scalloped pattern.

While the four handles are similar in form, each is constructed slightly differently. The handle at the table's left front corner (handle A1), which rises from the first square at the left of the front frame piece, was apparently assembled from at least two pieces (Figure 13; Plate 4A–D). The first-tier support is separate and was pinned to the rest of the handle. Three more joins are evident at the top of the handle, one of which seems to have involved an ancient repair. The joint between the first-tier base and the rest of the handle may indicate an ancient repair as well. The right front handle (handle A5), over the last square of the front frame piece, is assembled in an even more unusual manner (Figure 14; Plate 5C–F). It was made from two pieces, joined at the lower part of the curved section and also along its first-tier base with an interlocking joint. Most of the base was a single separate piece, but a thin section at the back was part of the rest of the handle. This may be the way the handle was originally made, or it too could indicate a repair. The right rear handle (handle D1, at the left when facing the back of the table) also shows a possible break line (Figure 15; Plate 20A–D). Only the left rear handle (handle D5) is made from a single piece of wood (Figure 16; Plate 21C–F).[20] The possibility that the handles were repaired in antiquity brings to mind the missing panels of inlay. Perhaps when the panels were pried out the handles were damaged in the process.

Three of the handles had small blocks of wood pinned to their tops to provide an additional bearing surface. The fourth (A5) may also have had a block, but this is uncertain, as the top of this handle is broken. A mortise for the top of one of the handles is preserved in a corner fragment of the table top (Plate 32C); between this cutting and the edge of the top is a shallow, square impression made by the small block at the top of the handle (Plate 32C, to the right of the recess).

Young's arrangement of the 18 top struts on the frame can now be revised. The illustration in *Gordion I* of the front frame piece and top struts shows the proper order of strut types, although none of the individual struts was placed correctly in the photograph.[21] For the sequence on the side pieces, however, neither *Gordion I* nor the Cox drawing was accurate. The key to the proper disposition can be found in the excavation photographs (Color Plate IIIB, Plate 1). These show the left side of the table, facing out toward the middle of the tomb chamber, with a type-1 strut still in place at the far left end of the frame piece. The photographs also show a type-1 strut extending up from the third square of the right frame piece (the side that had fallen next to the tomb wall). Finally, another type-1 strut can be seen near its original position at the front of the table. Using this information, and by matching the shapes of the mortises in the frame with the tenons at the bottom of the struts, the remaining pieces could be positioned and the four sides of the table reconstructed (Figures 5–8).

The struts at the front and back of the table were placed in a bilaterally symmetrical arrangement, while the struts at the sides alternated in sequence. The inlaid squares of the front and back frame pieces supported five top struts in the following positions: at the middle was a type 2 strut, flanked by two type-1 struts, and on both ends were the handles (Figures 5–6). The arrangement on the sides of the table was as follows: type 1 at the left of each frame piece, followed by type 2, then type 1, and ending with type 2 at the right (Figures 7–8). Thus when the table was assembled, the bilateral symmetry of the front and back faces was not carried through to the table as a whole (Color Plates VIII–IX, Figure 21, Plates 33–35).[22] Like the decoration on the frame, the placement of the top struts was eccentric, provoking the curiosity of the viewer.

---

[20] Two other struts show obvious signs of repair. C4 has two pegs running in from the sides, attaching the leaves at the base of the upper tier to the top of the central vertical segment between them. D2 is made in four pieces. The half-round base at the bottom of the strut is a composite piece, with the two sides pegged to the bottom of the first-tier vertical. In addition, there is an apparent break line between the left and right halves of the strut, which are pegged together at the base of the upper tier.

[21] Young, *Gordion I*, plate 82B. For a complete discussion of the early strut placement, see above, pp. 16–17.

[22] For instance, the first strut to the left of the left front handle, as the viewer looks around at the left side of the table, will be a type-2 strut. But the corresponding strut at the right beyond the right front handle is a type-1 strut, and so on.

The decoration on the struts and handles is equally inventive. The flat faces of the type-1 and type-2 struts are intricately inlaid with patterns composed of triangles or squares arranged in rows, crosses, or net-like fields, as well as stacked U-shaped or fork-like elements. The outturned leaves are inlaid with curving stripes, and the type-1 struts feature rosettes (and one lunette) at the top of the second tier. The four handles are inlaid on the outer face and sides of the curved handle proper, as well as on the front of the lower vertical support. The ornament on the handles exhibits great variety, featuring squares, diamonds, swastikas, hooks, and two obvious mazes: a complex, multicursal maze on handle D1 and a unicursal, squared spiral on handle D5 (Figure 17A, C). A swastika on D1 is maze-like as well (Figure 17B), with a short strip extending in from the border, in the manner of the "starting points" of the mazes on the frame (Figure 9A, C). The decoration of the struts and handles, like that of the frame, shows a sophisticated play of symmetry and pattern. The eye moves from strut to strut, from the struts to the frame and back again, in search of some scheme or correspondence. The viewer is drawn into an investigation of the complex artistry, which was apparently the intention of those who conceived it.

Leg Struts

Also ingenious is the lower support system of the table. The corners of the frame were propped up by carved, inlaid struts that rose from the table's three feet. The front leg strut (Figure 12; Plates 7–10) was composed of three pieces. The lower, curved section[23] features disc-shaped terminals at each end, inlaid with two types of rosette-like motifs on the front and back faces (Plate 9A–D). Panels of inlaid hooks decorate the front of this piece below the discs (Plate 10C–D), and the upper edge is inlaid at left and right with two rows of small idol-like shapes, "head" to "head" and divided by a scalloped pattern of inlay (Figure 12B; Plate 10A–B). Rising from the inlaid discs were vertical struts, which branched out to support the front frame piece at its corners (Plate 8).[24] These two branching struts are inlaid, in somewhat different arrangements, with patterns featuring hooks, squares, diamonds, and triangles. Tenons extended up from the tops of these two struts and fitted into mortises cut in the underside of the frame piece. At the bottom of the front leg strut, a large notch was carved in the underside at the center. This notch originally fit down over the top of the front foot in a kind of halved joint (Color Plate VIII; Plates 7A,C, 24A, 25A, 33; see Plate 9E for inlay).

Single inlaid struts rose from the foot of each rear leg to support the two back corners of the frame (Figures 10–11; Plates 14, 18). Young and Cox had situated these rear struts under the ends of the back frame piece (Figure 1), with the two rear legs extending out toward the back of the table. The *in situ* photographs, however, show that this was not their proper orientation.[25] Based on the correct reconstruction of the dowels of the internal support structure, the rear legs and struts could finally be positioned accurately (Figure 4). The legs had actually curved out toward the rear corners of the table, while the rear leg struts rose from their feet, twisted in an agile feat of carving, and joined the side pieces at their ends, supporting the frame from below (Figure 21; Plates 33–35). The rear leg struts, long presumed to be warped, were instead carved to look twisted, in a playful jest with a vertical supporting member.

The two rear leg struts are similar in form, varying slightly in their decoration (Figures 10–11). Each strut features a cylindrical base strip from which rise two vertical segments with flat, inlaid faces.[26] These end in single, outturned leaves that are inlaid with stripes, much as on the type-2 struts above the frame of the table. Rising from these leaves is a single cylindrical stem that tapers toward the top. The stem supports two stacked U-shaped pieces that are connected by a short vertical section; all these components are inlaid on their flat front surfaces. The arms of the uppermost U are connected by a half-round

---

[23] Young's "rocker" (as listed on the catalogue cards); see above, p. 15. This term is not used here.

[24] Young's "R-shaped supports" (as listed on the Gordion catalogue cards). The struts joined the frame below the inlaid squares at the ends of the front frame piece; the lower bars that extended in from these inlaid squares have been flattened at the bottom for some distance in order to facili-

tate the joinery (details pertaining to this joinery can be seen in Figures 5, 21; Plates 3, 6A, E).

[25] Young, *Gordion I*, 187. See above, p. 17, and Simpson, "Reconstructing an Ancient Table," 14–15.

[26] These two verticals are not, as Young says (*Gordion I*, 187), square in section.

crosspiece. From the top of this crosspiece rose a tenon, which fit into a mortise cut in the lower edge of the table's frame. The U-shaped sections resemble the lower part of the front leg strut, terminating in discs inlaid with triangles. Close comparison of the inlaid patterns on the two rear leg struts shows a whimsical play with design and symmetry.[27]

Legs and Table Top

The table's three legs look the same at first glance, but they, too, exhibit variations (Figures 18–20; Plates 24–29). The front leg has a tighter curve[28] while the two rear legs extend out a greater distance,[29] as necessitated by the table's design and construction (see Figure 4). The legs have carved, inlaid top pieces[30] and inlaid feet; these feet are based on the traditional Near Eastern lion-paw type, but appear here in a highly abstracted version. The three feet differ only in minor respects (Figure 23; Plate 31), but the leg tops vary significantly (Figure 22; Plate 30). The biconical mid-section of the front leg top has 32 carved reeds or ridges, while each of the back leg tops has 44. The inlaid decoration on the flat bands above and below the carved mid-sections provides an interesting study in contrast (Figure 22). Leg A's top band has meander-like running hooks, while its bottom band has a row of diamonds, bordered by inward-facing triangles. Leg B's top band has diamonds and triangles, with hooks in the band at the bottom. Leg C has hooks in the top band and diamonds and triangles below. This raises the possibility that leg B's carved top section might have been attached upside down. But if its orientation is reversed, the three top pieces are still not exactly alike, with the running hooks proceeding around the leg tops in different directions.

The table's three feet are inlaid with diamonds, triangles, and stripes, but only the front leg is inlaid: two rows of alternating triangles run down the face of the leg, changing to a pattern of squares near the bottom; these continue across the top of the front leg strut and over onto the front foot (Plate 24B, and see Figure 21). Beyond this, a cross of diamonds, framed by triangles, is inlaid separately on the front of the foot. The feet of the two rear legs show similar patterns (Figure 23). This diamond or lozenge cross occurs elsewhere on the table—on the front leg strut, one of the handles, and the frame. On the back and right frame pieces, the design appears singly and quadrupled, surrounded by a maze border (Figure 9). The pattern's association with the maze suggests that it may have had a special significance (see below, pp. 52–56).

The boxwood legs were apparently cut to their curved shape and not bent, as Young had surmised; this is indicated by the direction and configuration of the grain of the wood (Figure 28).[31] It is difficult to understand exactly which part of the tree was utilized for the legs, but it seems likely that each leg was cut from a curving branch, possibly incorporating part of the tree trunk. Each of the legs was constructed from three separate pieces (Figure 27): the curved lower section, the carved top piece, and a long square dowel, which fit down through the top piece and into a mortise cut in the top of the curved section.[32] The stepped top of this dowel formed a tenon, which fit into a corresponding mortise in the table top and apparently was exposed on the table's top surface.[33] The soft "collars" of wood attached to the top tenons when the table was found (Color

---

[27] The right rear leg strut (Figure 10) has triangles on its upper U and diamonds on the lower U, while the left rear leg strut (Figure 11) has diamonds above and triangles below. The two short vertical strips connecting the U's are inlaid with different hook configurations. Finally, the lower vertical segments are decorated with groups of squares disposed in varied patterns.

[28] The original extension of the front leg was about 23 cm from front to back.

[29] The rear legs extend out about 30 cm toward the table's back corners.

[30] Philadelphia woodworker Albert LeCoff, who specializes in wood turning, suggested that the leg tops might first have been turned on a lathe, with the reeding carved subsequently. There is no visible evidence to support this theory, although the lathe was in use by this time at Gordion. See

Simpson, "Use of the Lathe in Antiquity." For the animal-paw feet, see below, pp. 95–96.

[31] Young, *Gordion I*, 187. Burhan Aytuğ drew this conclusion after examining the table's legs in 1983, as did Valerie Dorge, Robert Blanchette, and Arno Schniewind, who examined the legs subsequently. It has been judged unlikely that boxwood pieces this thick would have been bent utilizing ancient steam-bending methods. See Appendix 7.

[32] Young thought each leg had been made from four pieces: the leg proper, which had a "tenon" at the top; the "capital," which had fit over the tenon; a stepped "vertical dowel" set into the capital; and finally a "collar" of wood that surrounded the dowel, "giving support to the table top from underneath." Young, *Gordion I*, 186.

[33] The fragmentary condition of the table top makes it impossible to confirm this with certainty.

Plate IIIB; Plate 1) were not separate elements, as Young had supposed. They were thicker parts of the table top itself, which extended down from its lower surface.[34] Fragments of the top survive, indicating that it was otherwise approximately 1.8 cm thick (excepting the collars) with a thinner edge that turned up in a graceful curve (Figure 30I; Plate 32). The preserved fragments show that the walnut top was made from at least two boards, joined edge to edge. These boards were cut to exhibit side grain, which was used for decorative effect (see Appendix 7).

The Reconstructed Table

The inlaid table has now been reconstructed in a drawing as it appeared at the time of the burial (Figure 21).[35] Its handles and tray-shaped top indicate that it was a portable banquet table. Small and delicate, the table was finely carved and meticulously inlaid with a profusion of inventive patterns. Although the wood is now darkened and damaged, the boxwood frame, struts, and legs were originally a light, creamy color. Inlaid into the boxwood were thousands of pieces of reddish-brown juniper, making up the complex geometric designs that covered much of the table. A walnut table top with figured grain completed the colorful assembly. Precious metal fittings had apparently adorned the corners of the frame and the outer faces of the handles. This dazzling production must have been one of the most valuable possessions of the Phrygian royal family. The actual pieces of the table have been mounted for display in the Museum of Anatolian Civilizations in Ankara (Color Plates VIII–IX, Plates 33–35, and see Appendix 2 for the table's reconstruction).[36]

Several questions remain regarding the condition of the inlaid table. Still unexplained are the extra cuttings in the legs, the apparent ancient repairs, the missing corner pieces and inlay from the handles, and the unusual strut (C3)

at the left side of the table. It is clear that the missing sections from the handles and the corner pieces were removed from the table before the tomb was sealed, indicating that the table had been damaged at some earlier point—either before the king's funeral or after the ceremony, during the final deposition. Evidence from the struts and handles suggests that the table was repaired in antiquity, and strut C3 was likely an ancient replacement. One wonders about the extent of the ancient repairs and what this might indicate about the use and age of the table. In any event, either the tomb was robbed before the roof was completed, or the table was damaged and repaired—but without its precious metal attachments—before it was placed in the chamber.[37]

Comparanda: Form and Function

Three-legged tables were common in ancient times: a table with three legs is the most stable type for the uneven floors that prevailed in antiquity. The inlaid table from Tumulus MM is one of these steady tables, despite its delicate appearance, and its inner dowel system would have added considerably to its strength. This sturdy construction was important, because the table was portable, as shown by its tray-shaped top and four handles. As ancient sources indicate, portable banquet tables were used to transport food. These tables could be heavily laden and might end up on any part of an irregular or sloping floor.

Ancient authors refer to three-legged tables being carried, always for meals. Homer speaks of food and tables being taken away together after the guests at a feast have retired.[38] Xenophon, describing Thracian dinners in the *Anabasis*, mentions 20 three-legged tables being carried in to the guests; the tables were covered with piles of meat attached by skewers to loaves of leavened

[34] Young, *Gordion I*, 183, and see p. 16, n. 27. Young's measurement for the top tenon projection (6 cm) should instead be ca. 4.5 cm; the smaller top step is about 0.7 cm, not 1.5 cm. This is important for the calculation of the thickness of the top and original height of the collars.

[35] For an account of how the reconstruction drawing was made and an analysis of the table in three dimensions, see Simpson, "Reconstructing an Ancient Table." The drawing published here as Figure 21 supersedes figure 24 in that publication.

[36] The first Plexiglas mount was designed and constructed in 1983, but by 1984, crazing of the Plexiglas began to occur within the sealed case. The table was finally removed and remounted in 1989. See Appendix 2 and also Simpson and Payton, "Royal Wooden Furniture"; Simpson and Spirydowicz, *Gordion Wooden Furniture* (hereafter *GWF*), 37–39.

[37] On the possibility that certain objects were damaged intentionally before they were placed in the tomb, see T. Özgüç, *Altın Tepe II*, 68 and n. 17.

[38] Homer, *Odyssey* 19.61; Athenaeus 1.12.

bread.[39] Xenophon and Athenaeus (who refers to this passage in his *Deipnosophistae*) use the Greek word τρίπους for this type of table. Petronius, in the *Satyricon*, describes Trimalchio's slaves taking away the tables used for one course, and bringing in more tables for the course to follow.[40] The Latin word *mensa* can in fact mean both course and table; Petronius's "*cum secundas mensas*" can refer to either a second course or second tables, and here seems to refer to both at once. Pindar speaks of the last course of a meal as the last tables, using the word τράπεζα.[41] The pavilion of Ptolemy Philadelphus at Alexandria is said to have contained one hundred gold couches, and beside each couch were two gold three-legged tables.[42] Ancient tables could be highly valuable and were certainly often numerous.[43]

The set of eight plain tables with tray-shaped tops from Tumulus MM suggests that the Phrygians, too, carried food on tables, with multiple tables on hand for separate courses or individual guests. The inlaid table is clearly such a banquet table, in a very fancy version. Food and drink residues were found in many of the vessels from the tomb, suggesting that they were used for a meal, which likely involved the tables. The inlaid table, with its ancient repairs, was apparently in use prior to the death of the king. This being the case, the literary evidence for sets of banquet tables suggests a possible explanation for the unusual strut C3. There may

have been two or more similar tables, with pieces that were virtually interchangeable; the strut C3 could have been taken from another such table to repair the one to be placed in the tomb. There is additional evidence from Tumulus P at Gordion that the Tumulus MM inlaid table may not have been unique.[44] In this regard, it can be noted that the Tumulus MM serving stands were evidently made as a pair (see pp. 77, 99–110).

Comparanda: Other Ancient Tables[45]

Although the inlaid table may originally have been part of a set, no other table found at Gordion resembles it. In its general form, it is similar to the eight plain tables from the tomb. All nine tables had three legs, tray-shaped tops, and collars extending down from the underside of the table tops to fit over the top tenons of the legs. But here the similarity ends, for the plain tables were much simpler, lacking inlaid ornament and without a frame, struts, handles, or internal bracing system.

Tumulus P at Gordion also contained several tables, three of which are catalogued in *Gordion I*. The tripod plain table (TumP 153) was similar to the plain tables from Tumulus MM, and there are fragments of at least one more plain table from the tomb.[46] The "Mosaic Table" (TumP 154) was inlaid on its flat, square top with large strips

[39] Xenophon, *Anabasis* 7.3.21, and Athenaeus 4.151. The reference to 20 tables, ὅσον εἴκοσι, occurs in one medieval manuscript of the *Anabasis* and appears in the text of Athenaeus; it is not accepted by the editor of the Oxford edition of the *Anabasis*. *Anabasis*, first half of the fourth century B.C.; Athenaeus, *Deipnosophistae*, ca. A.D. 200.

[40] Petronius, *Satyricon* 68. *Satyricon*, first century A.D.

[41] Pindar, *Olympian* 1.50–51. Pindar, first half of the fifth century B.C. For a discourse on τρίπους and τράπεζα, see Athenaeus 2.49. See Richter, *Furniture of the Greeks, Etruscans, and Romans*, for a statuette of a man carrying a three-legged table (figure 348) and a servant carrying food on a four-legged table depicted on a krater from Naples (figure 365).

[42] Callixeinus of Rhodes, as recorded in Athenaeus 5.196–197. Ptolemy II Philadelphus, 308–246 B.C.

[43] The use of multiple tables with tray-shaped tops was not limited to Greece and Egypt, as the Pazyryk tombs in Siberia attest. In these tombs (fourth-third centuries B.C.) tray-topped banquet tables were found in a developed form. Four of the five largest tombs contained more than one table. Rudenko, *Frozen Tombs of Siberia*, 35, 65–68, and see below, pp. 47 and 63–64. For a much earlier reference to the use of multiple tables (of indeterminate form), see Symington, "Hittite and Neo-Hittite Furniture," 122: at a banquet held in connection with a Hittite cult festival,

18 tables were set up for the king, queen, princes, and dignitaries, and 43 tables were used for the representatives of the outlying provinces.

[44] Although the inlaid table from Tumulus MM is the only surviving table of its type, it was probably not the only such Phrygian table made. An inlaid stool from Tumulus P at Gordion has carved front and back faces that are two-dimensional renderings of the front view of just such a fancy table. See Simpson, "Phrygian Artistic Intellect," 26–27, 35–38, figures 4–5, 13. In this extraordinary play with design and dimension, the artists who made the Tumulus P stool acknowledge a table type that was apparently made in more than one example. See also Simpson and Spirydowicz, *GWF*, 56–57, figures 67–70, and Simpson, "Phrygian Furniture," 204–206, plate 63A.

[45] For a general history of ancient Near Eastern furniture see Simpson, "Furniture in Ancient Western Asia." Detailed information on the furniture made in specific areas can be found in G. Herrmann, ed., *Furniture of Western Asia*.

[46] Young, *Gordion I*, figure 38; in this illustration, the table is shown, incorrectly, with four legs. For the second, fragmentary plain table (13022 W 132), see Simpson and Spirydowicz, *GWF*, 59–60. For a general discussion of the plain tables from Tumulus P, see Simpson, "Banquet Tables at Gordion."

in a simple, regular pattern.[47] The third table, the "Tripod Tray Table" (TumP 152), was imaginatively designed but not inlaid. The circular tray-shaped top had a wide, carved border running around much of the perimeter.[48] The legs of the Tripod Tray Table were unique among the Gordion table legs: although they were not understood initially, they can now be envisioned from the surviving fragments. At the top of each leg was a large open ring,[49] which was grasped above and below by stylized "fingers." From the bottom set of fingers extended the curved lower part of the leg, which ended in an abstract paw foot, carved to resemble the finger motif.[50]

Tumulus K-III at Gordion, excavated in 1900, had also contained several pieces of furniture, now preserved in badly degraded fragments. The excavators, Gustav and Alfred Körte, thought that the fragments represented a sarcophagus, a bed (kline), a chair carved in openwork and decorated with bronze studs, and a second inlaid chair. In light of further study, these identifications must be reconsidered. The remains from the second inlaid "chair" resemble those from the top of the Mosaic Table from Tumulus P. The "chair" may therefore be a table, but it was not like the inlaid table from Tumulus MM.[51] Fragments of another such "mosaic table" were found in Megaron 3, from the destruction level of the city mound at Gordion.[52]

Early Banquet Tables

Although no comparable table was found at Gordion, the inlaid table from Tumulus MM was at home in the ancient Near East. Depictions of fancy tables occur, and actual tables and fittings survive. Although evidence is more plentiful from

the first millennium B.C., the origins of such tables are to be found in the Early Bronze Age.[53] One famous table is shown on a lyre from the Royal Cemetery of Ur (ca. 2550 B.C.).[54] While this tall table is not ornate, it features a system of strutwork that supports the table top, which is piled with a leg and two heads of animals. The table is carried by a feline, which wears a knife in its belt, suggesting the means by which the heads and leg were severed.

Two actual tables, which were sheathed in bronze, were recovered from a tomb at Horoztepe in central Anatolia.[55] These small tables, dating to the late third millennium B.C., are the earliest surviving pieces of assembled furniture from the Near East—and the ancestors of the Gordion tables. Each of the Horoztepe tables had four hollow legs that ended in boot-like feet. The legs were attached to the table tops by means of cylindrical sections that were fastened to the undersides of the tops. These cylinders were fitted into the upper parts of the legs and secured by nails. The hollow legs had evidently contained cores of wood, and the thin metal table tops may have overlain wooden tops.

In 1974, excavations at the site of Ebla (Tell Mardikh) in Syria yielded numerous carbonized wooden furniture fragments dating to the third quarter of the third millennium B.C. These fragments, taken to represent a table and a chair, were found in a room in the palace (area G).[56] The table had a rectangular top (ca. 40×90 cm) made from three boards joined edge to edge and secured with "double-pronged bone studs." The top had a raised border that was inlaid at intervals with bone segments pegged to the wood. This upturned lip suggests that the top was a tray: if so, the Ebla table is the earliest wooden tray table for which there is evidence. Fitted into

[47] Young, *Gordion I*, figure 39; plate 30C–D. Simpson and Spirydowicz, *GWF*, 58–59, figures 74–75.

[48] Young, *Gordion I*, figure 37; plate 30A. Simpson, "Phrygian Furniture," figure 8, plate 62C–D. Simpson and Spirydowicz, *GWF*, 57–58, figures 71–73.

[49] The most completely preserved ring was originally thought to have belonged to the leg of the Tumulus P serving stand, and was placed incorrectly below the bottom of the foot. Young, *Gordion I*, figures 35–36.

[50] One of the feet survives and was catalogued as "foot with finger motif" (4244 W 47) but was not included in the Tumulus P catalogue in Young, *Gordion I*. This fragment has been incorporated in a new drawing of the leg; supra n. 48.

[51] Körte and Körte, *Gordion*, 43–53. The inlaid fragment that may be from a table is pictured on p. 50, figure 10.

[52] Young, *Gordion I*, plate 96J.

[53] Simpson, "Furniture in Ancient Western Asia," 1649–1651.

[54] For an illustration of the table depicted on the lyre from Ur see H. Baker, *Furniture in the Ancient World*, figure 247. Although the text of Hollis Baker's early study is outdated, the book contains many valuable insights and is an important source of illustrations. Unfortunately, the inlaid table from Tumulus MM is illustrated by Baker in the Cox drawing and an *in situ* excavation photograph that is printed upside down (figures 373–374).

[55] T. Özgüç and Akok, *Horoztepe*, 8–9, 42–43, figures 1–2, plates 2–3. See de Jesus, *Prehistoric Mining and Metallurgy*, 317, nos. 364–365 for analyses of the bronze sheathing. Simpson, "Banquet Tables at Gordion," figure 16.

[56] North Room L.2601. Matthiae, *Ebla: An Empire Rediscovered*, 88–92.

a "rail" on the underside of the table top was an openwork frieze of figures that ran around the sides of the table. The figures were 15 cm in height and were fixed to a "horizontal lower rail" that joined the legs of the table in some manner. The frieze included a scene of a lion attacking a bull; the lion was inlaid on its haunch with a rosette pattern. According to the excavator, the frieze featured scenes from myths and battles as well.

Also found at Ebla, in the Tomb of the Lord of the Goats (ca. 1700 B.C.), was a fragmentary bone frieze carved with figures.[57] One section shows a banquet scene, depicting a table that relates to the Tumulus MM inlaid table. The table shown in the frieze has curved legs that support the table top at its center, with a large "collar" extending down from the underside of the top. The feet of the table are ornately carved, and the table top is rounded on its underside, suggesting that the upper surface was concave. A large bundle or vessel rests on top, and a man is seated nearby on a folding stool.

This type of table, with legs that extend down from the center of the table top, curve out, and end in carved feet, must have been common in western Asia in the early part of the second millennium B.C. This is confirmed by the numerous depictions of such tables on the cylinder seal impressions recovered from Kültepe in central Anatolia. The Kültepe depictions are particularly relevant, because vertical struts rise from the feet of the legs to meet the table tops at the edge.[58] The feet are carved in the form of bull's hooves. The Kültepe tables occur in several versions, with legs of various shapes that sometimes splay out at the top to support the table top near its edges.

Remains of approximately 25 wooden tables were found in the Middle Bronze Age tombs at Jericho (ca. 17th–16th century B.C.).[59] Food was found on some of the tables, including roasted mutton.[60] Most of the tables were rectangular with three legs, two at one end and one at the other. Tenons at the tops of the legs fit into collars carved from the underside of the table tops. The tops variously had upturned rims or bordering strips set around the edge; some of the tops were concave or incorporated bowl-like depressions in their upper surface. The legs of the tables frequently curved out at the bottom, ending in feet that resembled boots or, as the excavator suggested, duck's feet or ram's heads.[61] Evidence of joinery was recovered, revealing a variety of construction techniques.[62] The Jericho tables show that already by the middle of the second millennium B.C. the collar-and-tenon system found later at Gordion was a standard method used to join the legs of a table to its top. At Jericho, this joint could be secured by a pin that ran through the collar and tenon. Such pins were not used for the leg/top joinery of the inlaid table, but all the plain tables from Tumulus MM had their leg tenons pinned in place in the top collars.[63]

Tombs at the site of Baghouz in Syria also contained wooden furniture, including seven tables that date to the early second millennium B.C.[64] Each of these tables had a round top made of three boards joined edge to edge and secured with "tongues" (free tenons or flat dowels). A rim ran around the edge of the table top, and the legs, which were detachable, might fit into the top at "thickenings" carved in the underside. These thickenings were rendered in steps near the edge

[57] Matthiae, *Ebla: Un impero ritrovato*, 182–183, figures 148–149.

[58] N. Özgüç, *Anatolian Group*, 55–56, plate I:1, II:6, III:8, IV:11a, and others. Plate XXVI:77 shows projections at the top of the vertical leg struts, which may represent handles. See also Symington, "Hittite and Neo-Hittite Furniture," plate 28D.

[59] Kenyon, *Jericho I* and *Jericho II*. The following tombs had contained furniture: B 3, B 35, B 48, B 50, B 51, G 37, G 46, G 73, H 6, H 11 (?), H 18, H 22, J 1, J 3, J 14, J 37, J 54, M 11, P 1, P 19, P 21, and P 23. See also Parr, "Jericho and Baghouz," 43–44.

[60] For instance, Kenyon, *Jericho I*, 317 (Tomb G 37), 455 (Tomb H 6), and 486 (Tomb H 18).

[61] For instance, table 2 from Tomb P 19, Kenyon, *Jericho II*, 399–400, figures 200–201.

[62] For woodworking techniques used for the Jericho furniture, see Ricketts, "Furniture from the Middle Bronze Age Tombs," figure 227 (tools); figure 228 (means of shaping the lower side of a table); and figure 229 (details of joinery), in particular 229:2, which shows a leg with a top tenon, the corresponding "collar" of the table top, the pin that secured the tenon in the collar, and wedges that strengthened the joint. Ricketts's figure 229 is published in H. Baker, *Furniture in the Ancient World*, figure 356, and elsewhere. See also Cartwright, "Bronze Age Wooden Tomb Furniture from Jericho," and Appendix 7 below.

[63] See below, pp. 62–63.

[64] Mesnil du Buisson, *Baghouz*, 36–39. The following tombs contained tables: Z 66, Z 67, Z 95, Z 121, Z 122, Z 123, and Z 144. Simpson, "Banquet Tables at Gordion," figures 17–18. See also Parr, "Jericho and Baghouz," 45–47.

of the table top and were pierced with oblique holes that ran through the table top from the upper to the lower surface.[65] This was a variation on the collar-and-tenon joinery used for the Jericho tables. Preserved on the tops of the tables from Baghouz were the remains of the funerary meal. This consisted generally of a piece of meat (the leg of a sheep), a small wood bowl, and sometimes other provisions.[66]

The Egyptians used tables as well, but the three-legged tray table with collar-and-tenon joinery was apparently a Near Eastern type. This foreign table type may have been adapted for a painted stool from the 18th Dynasty tomb of Tutankhamun (r. ca. 1332–1322 B.C.).[67] This unusual piece has a semicircular seat, with one straight side. The seat is dished and carved on its upper surface with two lions, bound head to tail. Running around the edge is a separate border carved with running spirals. The three legs are joined to the seat by means of collars; the legs curve out and end in flat paw feet. A stretcher runs between two of the legs, supporting an elaborate carved strut that rises up to the level of the seat.[68] The entire piece of furniture was gessoed and painted white. Carved strutwork was popular in Egypt for all types of furniture. Two chests, also from the tomb of Tutankhamun, are decorated with struts of alternating hieroglyphs that stand on stretchers and support the upper casework.[69]

Elegant carved ivory struts survive from Late Bronze Age sites in the eastern Mediterranean region, notably the site of Megiddo.[70] These were found in the Canaanite palace (level VIIA) in a three-room section that has been called the Treasury. A total of 382 ivories have been catalogued and published, all dating from the 14th through 12th centuries B.C. Several of the struts are stylized plants or trees; this type of strut is the ultimate ancestor of the struts on the Gordion table.[71] Fragments of an ornate ivory table were recovered from the royal palace at Ugarit (14th–13th centuries B.C.). The table had a round ivory top, carved with a rosette at the center, surrounded by scenes of animals and mythological beasts.[72] Several other Late Bronze Age examples could be cited; this was an age of prosperity for the Near Eastern kingdoms, and the trappings of luxury were highly coveted.[73]

Important written evidence for such costly furniture exists in Hittite texts and also the Amarna letters.[74] The latter, found at Amarna in Egypt, detail the correspondence between the Egyptian pharaohs Amenhotep III, Akhenaten, and Tutankhamun and their Near Eastern contemporaries. Of all the valuable objects listed in these letters, however, tables are not in evidence. This may be due to the fragmentary nature of the tablets, which often preserve an indication of the materials from which objects were made (even specifying which were inlaid) but are missing the names of the items. The Late Bronze Age Aegean was not without fine furniture, evidence of which occurs in the Linear B tablets.[75] One tablet (Ta713), lists a table (*to-pe-za*) of ebony (*ku-te-se-ja*) with ivory "strutting," and another (Ta715) lists two tables apparently made of yew (*mi-ra₂*) and boxwood (*pu-ko-so*), inlaid with a precious material, possibly silver (*pa-ra-ku-we*). The inlaid

---

[65] For example, Mesnil du Buisson, *Baghouz*, plate 49. The tables could have three or four legs, encircled by a wood ring at the center, allowing them to splay out above the ring (to join the table top) and below (to rest on the ground).

[66] Ibid., 38.

[67] H. Baker, *Furniture in the Ancient World*, 90–91, figure 105. Killen, *Ancient Egyptian Furniture I*, plate 71. Eaton-Krauss, *Thrones, Chairs*, 122–124. For simpler Egyptian three-legged stools with collar-and-leg joinery, see Killen, plate 70; H. Baker, figures 159, 212. For a related Egyptian three-legged table, see H. Baker, figure 237; Killen, plate 111.

[68] The strut is carved in the form of the lily and papyrus, tied around the hieroglyphic sign "to unite," symbolizing the unified lands of Upper and Lower Egypt. The strutwork is situated below the straight side of the seat.

[69] H. Baker, *Furniture in the Ancient World*, figures 106–107.

[70] Loud, *Megiddo Ivories*, including nos. 21–26 and 165–172, which have tenons at top and bottom for attachment to upper and lower elements.

[71] Ibid., plates 34–35, nos. 165–167 in particular.

[72] Schaeffer, "Ras Shamra-Ugarit," 59–61, plate 7:3–4,

figure 8; Caubet and Poplin, "Objets de matière dure animale," figure 20; Caubet and Yon, "Le mobilier d'Ougarit." The ivory table top was apparently inlaid with lapis lazuli and colored glass paste and may have been gilded. A vertical rim, carved in openwork scallops, ran around the edge of the top.

[73] Noteworthy is the carved sarcophagus of Ahiram of Byblos, which shows the king seated on an elaborate throne with sphinxes at the sides, facing a fancy table with curving legs and lion-paw feet. H. Baker, *Furniture in the Ancient World*, figure 337.

[74] See Symington, "Hittite and Neo-Hittite Furniture," 114–116, 122–125; and Moran, *Amarna Letters*.

[75] Ventris and Chadwick, *Documents in Mycenaean Greek*, 332–348, for the *Ta*- series tablets from Pylos. *To-pe-za* is the Linear B equivalent of the Greek τράπεζα on Ta642, 713, and 715. See also Krzyszkowska, "Furniture in the Aegean Bronze Age," 94–96, for two tables from Thera and other Aegean examples; Muhly, "Furniture from the Shaft Graves," for two wood tables from Shaft Grave V at Mycenae.

table from Tumulus MM had clear antecedents in the second millennium B.C.

Near Eastern Tables in the First Millennium B.C.

By the early first millennium, more furniture is evident, both in depictions and from actual surviving pieces. Among the most highly prized were the productions made in the region of the Levant, descendants of the luxurious Late Bronze Age furniture made in the area. Phoenician and Syrian furniture was collected by the Assyrians for their great palaces in northern Mesopotamia—through trade, tribute, or plunder. Most notable are the many ivory attachments from Nimrud, found in the Northwest Palace, Burnt Palace, and Fort Shalmaneser.[76] Numerous struts survive among the Nimrud ivories, including stylized floral plaques that are comparable to the struts from the Tumulus MM inlaid table. The Nimrud plaques are not as abstract, however, and feature recognizable vegetal forms.[77] Floral struts were made in wood as well, although few remnants survive; fragments of such struts made of boxwood have been recovered from excavations in Jerusalem.[78] A carved ivory pyxis from the Northwest Palace, Nimrud, depicts a table with curved legs connected by stretchers and ending in lion-paw feet. As the pyxis is carved in a North Syrian style, the table depicted is presumably a Syrian type. It recalls the form of the Gordion table in general, although the legs are less stylized, and there are no decorative struts. Fragments of actual tables, including curved legs ending in lion-paw feet, survive among the Nimrud ivories.[79]

The furniture pictured in Assyrian reliefs can be quite ornate, with elaborate turned legs, realistically rendered animal-paw feet, carved strutwork, and figural attachments. Such depictions can often elucidate the form but not the materials of the examples represented. Two somewhat similar tables from Nineveh may serve to illustrate what seems to be a common Assyrian type. The first is the table shown in front of the couch of Ashurbanipal (r. 668–627 B.C.) in the famous garden scene on a relief from Nineveh in the British Museum.[80] This fancy table has a dished top and three (or four) straight legs ending in lion-paw feet on tapered bases. The legs show decorative banding or turnings along their length, with the uppermost bands possibly indicating collar-and-tenon joinery. The table has two sets of horizontal stretchers, above and below the lion-paw feet, connected by a central support that runs up to support the table top. This support is carved with leaf-like capitals at intervals, suggesting four slender stacked columns. Ashurbanipal reclines, and his wife sits up to the table, and both drink from lobed bowls resembling those from Gordion.

A second, similar table is depicted on another relief from Nineveh, in a scene showing Ashurbanipal pouring a libation over four dead lions.[81]

[76] These include the Layard series from the Northwest Palace, furniture attachments carved in Egyptianizing styles; the Loftus group from the Burnt Palace, attachments carved in Syrian style; and also the 19 pieces of ivory furniture, evidently chairs, recovered from Room SW.7 at Fort Shalmaneser, the Nimrud arsenal. The earliest of these pieces apparently date to the ninth century B.C. For a summary see Simpson, "Furniture in Ancient Western Asia," 1658–1661. Primary publications include Barnett, *Nimrud Ivories*; Mallowan and Herrmann, *Furniture from SW.7*; Herrmann, *Small Collections* and *Ivories from Room SW 37*. See also Herrmann, "Ivory Furniture Pieces from Nimrud," and Winter, "Carved Ivory Furniture Panels from Nimrud," "Phoenician and North Syrian Ivory Carving," and "Is There a South Syrian Style?"

[77] For floral attachments that may have belonged to tables, see, for instance, Herrmann, *Small Collections*; nos. 41–46, 156–157, 296, 344, 424, 427, 429–431, 433, 478, 481–482; and *Ivories from Room SW 37*; nos. 764–846, 1075–1079, 1159, 1163–1164. Of the ivories from SW 37, nos. 764–766 are fragments of struts that took the form of a palm tree, with three fronds extending up from the top of the tree. Such a piece might have been the prototype for the type-1 struts on the Tumulus MM inlaid table. A strut such as no. 1163 (SW 37) might have served as inspiration for the table's type-2 struts.

[78] City of David excavations, "Burnt Room," stratum 10, destruction dated to the sixth century B.C. Shiloh, *Excavations at the City of David*, 19, plate 34:1. Shiloh, "Material Culture of Judah and Jerusalem," 139–140, figure 21. As boxwood is not native to the area, Shiloh believed that the furniture that had once incorporated the boxwood struts was imported from North Syria. The boxwood fragments are said to have once been painted, although no evidence or further explanation is given.

[79] For the ivory pyxis depicting the table with curved legs, see Herrmann, "Ivory Furniture Pieces from Nimrud," plate 40A; for another such example, see plate 43D. A prototype can be seen on the famous Late Bronze Age sarcophagus of King Ahiram of Byblos. Supra n. 73. For fragments of ivory legs and feet, see Herrmann, "Ivory Furniture Pieces from Nimrud," plates 40B–C, 43C; *Ivories from Room SW 37*, nos. 1396–1443.

[80] BM 124920. H. Baker, *Furniture in the Ancient World*, figures 304–305; Curtis, "Assyrian Furniture," 177 and plate 46B. The king's bed appears to have Syrian or Phoenician decorations, which suggests that the bed, and perhaps the other furniture shown in this relief, may have been imported.

[81] BM 124886. H. Baker, *Furniture in the Ancient World*, figure 308; Curtis, "Assyrian Furniture," plate 51A.

The dished top of this table is likewise supported by a slender central column, which terminates in a lotus flower. A relief from Khorsabad from the palace of Sargon II (r. 721–705 B.C.) shows a table of this type carried by two attendants.[82] In this case, two sculpted figures stand on the upper stretcher to either side of the central supporting column, their hands raised to brace the underside of the table top.

Another piece of furniture carried by attendants on a relief from Khorsabad is somewhat different and more closely recalls the Tumulus MM inlaid table. This object has been assumed to be a table, although it has also been interpreted as a seat. The piece has legs that terminate in lion-paw feet on tapering bases, with a square frame featuring ram's head finials and carved strutwork.[83] Three floral struts are shown supporting the table top, much in the same manner as the top struts on the inlaid table. Such floral imagery has been linked to the concept of agricultural abundance in Assyria.[84] At the corners of the frame, flanking the floral struts, are two standing figures, and similar figures appear below these, forming the table's legs. The ram's head finials extend out horizontally at the top and bottom of the frame. These finials recall the decorative attachments on numerous Assyrian stools depicted on reliefs, including the backless throne of Assurnasirpal II (r. 883–859 B.C.), shown on a relief from Nimrud in the British Museum.[85] Several actual animal-head attachments survive from Assyrian sites, along with various other types of metal fittings.[86] This evidence suggests that the missing corner pieces of the Gordion inlaid table might have been animal-head attachments.

Assyrian-style tables were also used in Iran to the east, and one such table appears on a relief from Susa.[87] A woman is shown spinning, seated on an upholstered stool in front of a table with a dished top; on the table are a fish and other food. Like its Assyrian counterparts, the table has straight legs, connected by a stretcher, and realistically rendered animal-paw feet. The leg tops are carved with decorative moldings, recalling those of the Tumulus MM inlaid table.

Assyrian furniture seems also to have influenced the productions of Urartu, which the Assyrians in turn admired and coveted. This is evident from Sargon II's account of his sack of the Urartian city of Musasir (714 B.C.), in which he acquired the silver bed of the god Haldi, covered with gold and jewels; an ivory couch; ivory tables; ten tables of boxwood; and what may have been chairs of maple and boxwood inlaid with gold and silver.[88] It is clear from Sargon's list of booty that fine furniture made from costly woods was a highly prized commodity and could incorporate inlay of gold and silver. This gives credence to the theory that the missing attachments from the Tumulus MM inlaid table were made from precious metal.

Urartian furniture from excavations is characterized by its metal and ivory fittings, although this is due in part to their survival in cases where the wood has decayed. The metal fittings resemble Assyrian furniture attachments: bronze lion-

---

[82] H. Baker, *Furniture in the Ancient World*, figure 295. For another example, see Curtis, "Assyrian Furniture," plate 51C.

[83] H. Baker, *Furniture in the Ancient World*, color plate XIII and figure 294; Curtis, "Assyrian Furniture," 176, plate 50C. Baker calls this piece of furniture a table on p. 185, but in the caption of the color plate he calls it a chair. For a less elaborate example on a relief from Khorsabad, see Curtis, plate 50B; this resembles the seats with calf's head finials shown on another Khorsabad relief (Curtis, plate 47B). See also comparable Urartian tables and seats in Seidl, "Urartian Furniture," 182–185, plate 54. From the available evidence, it seems that Assyrian and Urartian tables and footstools regularly had animal-paw feet, but stools and chairs did not. Thus, the object with carved floral struts depicted on the Khorsabad relief is likely a table.

[84] See Winter, "Ornament and the Rhetoric of Abundance." The repetition of plant forms as a sign of agricultural abundance can be seen as early as the fourth millennium B.C. on the Uruk vase, where two different plants, apparently flax and barley, alternate in a continuous sequence in the bottom register. Winter, "Representing Abundance: A Visual Dimension of the Agrarian State," 125–129.

[85] BM 124565. Curtis, "Assyrian Furniture," plate 47a. A detail is illustrated in Kyrieleis, *Throne und Klinen*, plate 1, and a drawing of the corner construction of the stool is shown in his figure 1, p. 8. Supra n. 83, for other examples.

[86] Curtis, "Assyrian Furniture," plates 48, 51B, 52–53.

[87] "Neo-Elamite" relief from Susa, 10th–8th centuries B.C. H. Baker, *Furniture in the Ancient World*, figure 363; Gunter, "Furniture in Elam," 217, plate 68B.

[88] Sargon's eighth campaign is recorded in a letter to the god Assur, preserved on a tablet in the Louvre. Although the translation of the text is problematic, many valuable pieces of furniture are listed. While some of these may have derived from areas outside Urartu, presumably many were Urartian productions. See Luckenbill, *Ancient Records 2*, 73–99. For a more recent study of this text, see Mayer, "Sargons Feldzug gegen Urartu." Wood types cannot be identified with certainty (see Appendix 7).

paw feet,[89] bronze corner pieces,[90] and leg fittings with hanging-leaf capitals.[91] A large table from Tomb 3 at Altıntepe had four wooden legs featuring bronze fittings with leaf capitals, and it may have incorporated a silver rod with lion's head terminals.[92] Tomb 3 had also contained two wooden stools with silver-plated legs.[93] Silver corner attachments have been preserved from the same tomb,[94] and the bottoms of some of the furniture legs were sheathed in silver.[95] Precious metal attachments are thus well attested on Urartian furniture.[96] Ivory plaques were also found at Altıntepe, indicating their use on furniture in Urartu as well as in Assyria, North Syria, and the Levant.[97]

Ornate tables were in use in eastern Anatolia in this period, as an orthostat relief from Karatepe shows. The local ruler is seated before a banquet table piled with food, ministered to by his attendants in the Assyrian manner. The table has fancifully carved animal legs and a curious figure crouching on the floor between them. The small man supports a horizontal stretcher on his head; a vertical strut apparently extended up above this stretcher to support the table top from below.[98] Fancy tables are therefore well documented throughout the Near East in numerous variations. However, the wooden versions are largely missing, although there must have been many such splendid creations. The extent of this loss can be gauged from the remarkable finds from the site of Pazyryk, in the valley of the Altai Mountains in Siberia.

[89] T. Özgüç, *Altın Tepe II*, plate 23. Barnett, "Toprak Kale," plate 3. See also Barnett, "Toprak Kale–Addenda."

[90] T. Özgüç, *Altın Tepe II*, 69, n. 19 and plate 21:1. Barnett, "Toprak Kale," plates 2, 4:3; also illustrated in Kyrieleis, *Throne und Klinen*, plate 7:1.

[91] Barnett, "Toprak Kale," plate 19. See Seidl, "Urartian Furniture," plate 55B for a leg fitting from the Melgunov kurgan; 181–186 for the relationship between Assyrian and Urartian furniture. See also Merhav, *Urartu: A Metalworking Center in the First Millennium B.C.E.*, 260–261, figures 7–9, for a large collection of bronze fittings. Unfortunately, as these are unexcavated, they reveal little about the identity of the furniture they once belonged to.

[92] T. Özgüç, *Altın Tepe II*, 70, plate 20; Seidl, "Urartian Furniture," plate 57 (below). A detail of the silver rod is shown in *Altın Tepe II*, plate 25:3.

[93] T. Özgüç, *Altın Tepe II*, 68, plate 19; Seidl, "Urartian Furniture," plate 57 (above). Tomb 3 had also contained a "well-preserved table in wood" (p. 68), two tables of walnut (p. 69, plate 21:1), and the remains of "several wooden stools, thrones, and tables" (p. 70). Tomb 3 has been dated by the excavator to the late eighth or early seventh century B.C.

[94] T. Özgüç, *Altın Tepe II*, plate 24:1–2, 3–4. In the text (both in English, p. 70, and in Turkish, p. 24) these are referred to as corner pieces. But in the list of illustrations, the pieces shown in plate 24:1–2 are called corner pieces and those in plate 24:3–4 are called feet.

[95] Ibid., plate 24:5.

[96] This phenomenon was obviously not confined to Urartu. According to Herodotus (1.50), the Lydian King Croesus burnt couches covered with gold and silver as part of a huge sacrifice to the Delphian Apollo. Herodotus also reports on the fabulous furniture from Babylon (1.181–183), which included a gold table from the lower shrine (apparently Esagila) and another in the shrine on top of the ziggurat. No precious metal attachments survive from Gordion, but a chair from Tumulus P (TumP 166) had short, cylindrical legs sheathed in bronze. Young, *Gordion I*, plate 33E–G; Simpson and Spirydowicz, *GWF*, 62.

[97] T. Özgüç, *Altın Tepe II*, 78–93, and particularly plates 46–47. Two similar ivory plaques have been recovered from the city mound at Gordion: 6670 BI 391 and a second plaque recently excavated in Building A (YH 69299). A fragment of a related ivory plaque was found in Tumulus D at Bayındır (Özgen and Özgen, *Antalya Museum*, cat. 56). Ivory plaques could be overlaid with gold and inlaid with stones and glass. Two well-known examples are the ivory plaques from Nimrud depicting "Ethiopian" boys attacked by lions. These were covered with gold leaf and inlaid with carnelian and lapis lazuli set in frit, producing the effect of precious stones in gold settings. Mallowan, *Nimrud and Its Remains*, 139–142, plates 81–84 and color frontispiece. One of these plaques is now in the British Museum; the other was in the Iraq Museum, Baghdad, but was stolen when the museum was looted in April 2003. Glass plaques might also be used to decorate furniture, such as the small, square panels excavated at Arslan-Tash in Syria and the unexcavated companion pieces in the Metropolitan Museum, Lands of the Bible collection, and elsewhere. Thureau-Dangin, *Arslan-Tash*, plate 47:113–117; Muscarella, *Ladders to Heaven*, 285.

In light of this evidence, one might ask whether the missing attachments of the Tumulus MM inlaid table incorporated ivory, glass, or stones. The corner pieces must have been metal, as these served not only to sheath but to strengthen the corner joints. The metal pieces may have been inlaid, although there is no evidence for this technique in Phrygia. The missing sections of inlay in the handles might have included ivory, and if so, it may have been overlaid with gold. There are various options for the materials used for the inlaid panels that were pried out of the table's handles. All must surely include precious materials, as otherwise the missing sections would not have been prone to plunder.

[98] Akurgal, *Art of the Hittites*, plate 143; Symington, "Hittite and Neo-Hittite Furniture," plate 33 (below). The Karatepe relief dates to the late eighth century B.C. and is contemporary with the inlaid table from Tumulus MM. Symington, 135–136, finds that this type of table is not depicted in the art of any other Neo-Hittite center. For a depiction of an elaborate table from Zincirli, see Symington, 135, figure 20, as reconstructed from fragments.

Evidence from East and West in the First Millennium B.C.

The rich tombs excavated at Pazyryk contained leather, fur, textiles, and wooden objects in exceptional condition, as the contents of the tombs had been frozen in ice. At least 12 wooden tables were found in the five largest tombs, barrows 1–5, now dated to the late fourth and third centuries B.C.[99] The Pazyryk tables were small, with four legs and dished table tops, many of which had collars that extended down from their lower surface. These collars were carved in one piece with the table tops to fit down over the leg tenons in the manner of the Gordion tables. This collar-and-tenon joinery method was surprisingly widespread considering the expense it involved: each table top was cut from a thick piece of wood, which was then carved away on the upper surface to form a tray, and cut away substantially at the bottom, leaving only the projecting collars. This joinery technique, in evidence from the mid-second millennium B.C. at Jericho and in use at Gordion, continued through the third century B.C. as far east as Siberia, demonstrating the range and continuity of ancient woodworking traditions.

The legs of many of the Pazyryk tables were carved, and two tables from barrow 2 had legs in the form of tigers, standing on their hind feet and supporting the table tops with their front paws and muzzles.[100] Sections of some of the legs were apparently sheathed in metal.[101] The leg tenons were not secured in their collars by pins, and the excavator believed that the tops were meant to be detachable, even though leather wrappings and wedges were used to make the tenons fit tight in the collars.[102] If so, these tables were easily transportable, suggesting that the collar-and-tenon system may have originated in the furniture of ancient nomadic peoples. The tray-shaped tops of the Pazyryk tables imply that they were used to carry food. Remains of food associated with the table tops were tentatively identified as the meat of horse and goat.[103]

In contrast to this wealth of information, Greek woodworking in the early first millennium B.C. is poorly documented. However, it can be surmised that early Greek tables were somewhat different from their Near Eastern counterparts. Greek tables could have three legs and were used to carry food,[104] but they apparently did not utilize the collar-tenon joinery technique, at least in the Orientalizing and Archaic periods (ca. 700–480 B.C.) when illustrations of furniture become plentiful.[105] Greek beds and seats (although not tables) are shown on Geometric funerary vases of the eighth century B.C., but the schematic depictions reveal nothing about construction and little about form or decoration.[106] Thus there is no evidence for contemporary Greek furniture that was anything like the Tumulus MM inlaid table. Herodotus was duly impressed with the royal throne that Midas dedicated at Delphi, which might suggest that such ornate furniture was not common in Greece during Herodotus's time or was unknown to him from earlier periods.[107] However, if the profusely decorated Geometric vases are any indication, Greek woodworkers might very well have produced fine furniture that was lavishly ornamented with geometric

[99] Rudenko, *Frozen Tombs of Siberia*, 35, 65–68. Simpson, "Furniture in Ancient Western Asia," 1668–1669. Simpson, "Banquet Tables at Gordion," figures 21–22. Barrow 1 was excavated in 1929, followed by the excavation of barrows 2 through 5 in 1947–1949 by the Hermitage Museum and Soviet Academy of Sciences.

[100] Rudenko, *Frozen Tombs of Siberia*, plates 50–51. Simpson, "Furniture in Ancient Western Asia," figure 20. Simpson, "Banquet Tables at Gordion," figure 22.

[101] According to Rudenko, "covered by tinfoil." *Frozen Tombs of Siberia*, 66.

[102] Ibid., 65.

[103] Ibid., 35. See also Polosmak, "Mummy Unearthed," 96, for two similar wood tables found with meat on their tops, excavated from the Ukok plateau in Siberia.

[104] Richter, *Furniture of the Greeks, Etruscans, and Romans*, 63 ff. Supra n. 38, on portable Homeric banquet tables.

[105] See, for instance, Richter, *Furniture of the Greeks, Etruscans, and Romans*, figures 311–317, for illustrations of Greek

three-legged tables. See also Simpson, "The Andokides Painter and Greek Carpentry," regarding depictions of furniture on Greek vases.

[106] Arias and Hirmer, *History of Greek Vase Painting*, plate 5; *Metropolitan Museum of Art: Greece and Rome*, 23. Ahlberg, *Prothesis and Ekphora*, 46–54, 101–104. Fragments of early Greek wooden furniture have survived in votive deposits from the sanctuary of Hera on Samos, but these undated pieces provide no indication of anything resembling the Tumulus MM inlaid table. See Ohly, "Holz"; Kopcke, "Neue Holzfunde aus dem Heraion von Samos"; and Kyrieleis, "Archaische Holzfunde aus Samos." However, there are remains of wood tables from Samos, and the incised designs on fragments of various types of furniture from the site are noteworthy. In particular, see the reconstruction drawing of a stool (or footstool) with sides carved in the form of horses and with geometric patterns incised on the top surface. Coldstream, *Geometric Greece*, 256, figure 83b.

[107] Herodotus, 1.14. See above, p. 10.

patterns.[108] Homer records wooden furniture that incorporated precious metals, such as chairs that were studded and inlaid with silver.[109] It therefore seems likely that early Greek furniture was more elaborate than might otherwise be envisioned. The discovery of a large collection of Villanovan wooden artifacts at the site of Verucchio gives some indication of the nature of the loss of the art of ancient Mediterranean woodworking.

Two tombs excavated in 1972 at Verucchio in northern Italy contained a wide variety of fine wooden objects dating to the late eighth or early seventh century B.C.[110] The finds from tombs 85 and 89 included wood tables, footstools, thrones, boxes, and bowls, along with other organic materials including fur and textiles. Several pieces of furniture were embellished over their surfaces with carved figural and geometric decoration. Three tables were found in tomb 85, each with a round top and three curved legs that ended in elaborately carved, lyre-shaped feet. The legs were fixed to the table top with a version of collar-and-tenon joinery: the top tenons of the three legs were inserted into mortises cut into a ring-shaped band that extended down from the underside of the table top.[111] The remains of a meal had survived on the tables in tomb 85: found on one table were dishes of fish and meat; on a second were large covered wine bowls and cups; and on a third were plates of nuts and grape seeds. These were offerings or vestiges of a funerary meal.[112] The Verucchio find proves that imaginative wooden furniture was made in Italy, as it surely was in Greece, in the late eighth and early seventh centuries B.C.

Seen within this context, then, the inlaid table from Tumulus MM has much in common with contemporary furniture from the areas to the east and west of Gordion. Despite these similarities, however, its particular form and style of decoration are without parallel. No other known table had handles, and none featured such detailed wooden inlay or the same profusion of carved strutwork. Above all, no other ancient furniture utilized natural forms abstracted to such a high degree, and the Phrygians' clever play with design and symmetry is unique. A brief study of the decoration on the table confirms its special character.

Comparanda: Designs

Although some of the geometric motifs on the Tumulus MM inlaid table may be found in the art of neighboring areas, the table's decoration is distinctively Phrygian. The swastika-type squares on the frame pieces and handles also occur on the two inlaid serving stands from Tumulus MM, although the swastikas on the table are freer and more idiosyncratic. The inlaid diamonds bordered by triangles found on the table's frame, struts, and legs appear on the stands in the background inlay pattern, which runs between and around the meander squares inlaid into the stands' faces (Figures 50, 58; Plates 69–72, 80–82). At the front of the table, the central square of the front frame piece contains a rosette-like motif, which recalls the central medallion on the serving stands' faces in its prominent central position (Figure 5, Plate 6C). One of the type-1 top struts at the front of the table (A2) has a rosette inlaid between the upper pair of outturned leaves, and the other (A4) features a half-circle, or lunette, in the same position (Figure 5, Plates 4E, 5A). These evoke, in miniature, the central rosettes on the stands' faces and the lunettes that appear above them. Small rosettes occur on all of the other standard type-1 struts of the table.

The designs on the inlaid table also find counterparts on the furniture from Tumulus P at Gor-

[108] See below, p. 50, for a discussion of Greek Geometric motifs as related to the decoration on the inlaid table. For a vase painter in the Archaic period who may also have been a furniture maker, see Simpson, "The Andokides Painter and Greek Carpentry."

[109] *Iliad* 18.389–390; *Odyssey* 7.162, 10.314–315, 19.55–58.

[110] The wooden objects from Verucchio, which were waterlogged when they were found, were conserved and placed on display in the Bologna Museum. Some of these pieces are now on view in the Museo Civico in Verucchio. Gentili, "Verucchio," 232–257; Gentili, *Verucchio Villanoviana*, 282–290, 293–311, plates 131, 136, 143, 147, VI, VIII–IX, CCLX, CCLXVII, CCLXXIII, CCLXXVI; von Eles, *Museo Civico Archeologico, Verucchio*, 36–38, 80–81; and see von Eles, *Guer-*

riero e sacerdote, and Bonfante, "The Verucchio Throne," for a discussion of the wooden throne from tomb 89.

[111] This construction is clearly visible in Gentili, *Verucchio Villanoviana*, plate CCLX, which shows the underside of the top of one of the tables (no. 18) from tomb 85. The legs of this table are decorated with incised geometric patterns (diamonds, zigzags, and complex crosses) that run down the front of the legs. Gentili, *Verucchio Villanoviana*, plate 131. Simpson, "Banquet Tables at Gordion," figure 20.

[112] Gentili, "Verucchio," 233; *Verucchio Villanoviana*, 284–285. The animal bones were those of a small herbivore, suggested to be a rabbit.

dion. The serving stand from Tumulus P (Figure 91) is inlaid with several patterns that are found on the table, including bands of diamonds and triangles, checkerboards, and running hooks. A large carved and inlaid rosette is featured at the center of the serving stand, and a lunette is shown above it. A second piece of furniture from Tumulus P, an inlaid, studded stool,[113] has designs composed of stacked U-shaped motifs and interlocking hooks, which are also found on the table's top struts, the squares of the frame pieces, and the curved front leg strut. Two stretchers from this stool are inlaid with connected, stacked U's that form two rows of interlocking hooks.[114] The decoration of the Tumulus P stool also includes wheel-like rosettes, which are studded with bronze tacks at their centers and around the perimeter. Finally, the "feet" of the stool are highly abstracted and inlaid with stripes, in a simpler version of the feet of the table.

Three bronze belts from Tumulus P are covered with incised patterns that recall the inlaid designs on the Tumulus MM table.[115] The decoration on the belts is arranged in square, framed panels containing swastikas, checkerboards, and a variety of idiosyncratic or maze-like patterns such as those found on the table.[116] The square designs alternate with rectangular panels containing hooks, zigzags, circles, and other configurations. A bronze and leather belt from Tumulus W at Gordion is quite different but also features schemes reminiscent of the designs on the inlaid table.[117] The extant fragments show a lattice as well as crossed figure-eights, the latter recalling the design at the center of the front frame piece of the table (Figure 5, Plate 6C).[118] The belt's

large, leather-backed bronze disc is ornamented in repoussé with attached studs to form an elaborate rosette-like element.

Many of the patterns on the painted pottery from Gordion are also related to designs on the inlaid table. Pottery from Tumulus P features checkerboards and diamond lattices for dominant and subsidiary decoration (TumP 51–53, 55–57).[119] The pottery from Tumulus W and Tumulus K-III exhibits these same patterns, as well as geometric designs in panels.[120] The painted ceramics from the city mound share these same motifs.[121] Rows of diamonds bordered by facing triangles occur on two circular stands;[122] these are found on the inlaid table's leg tops and leg struts (and will be seen again on the Tumulus MM serving stands). Finally, the famous pebble mosaic from the city mound at Gordion contained in its scatter of ornament many of the inlaid designs on the table (Figure 92).[123]

In the Near East, inlay with diamonds and triangles appears as early as the third millennium B.C. The inlaid strips dividing the registers on the "Standard of Ur" show this design in a basic version, with a row of diamonds arranged between upper and lower borders, producing inward-facing triangles in reserve.[124] When the bordering triangles are made slightly smaller, the design becomes somewhat removed from its original form, and more complex. The lyre from Ur in the British Museum shows the diamond-triangle design in three stages of progression.[125]

The diamond-triangle patterns on the leg tops of the Tumulus MM table show the elements pulled apart (Figure 22), lightening the effect, and introducing a dark/light interplay between

---

[113] Young, *Gordion I*, figure 42, p. 73, in an inaccurate drawing. See Simpson, "Phrygian Artistic Intellect," figures 4–5; Simpson and Spirydowicz, *GWF*, figures 67–70.

[114] Simpson and Spirydowicz, *GWF*, figure 69.

[115] TumP 34–36. Young, *Gordion I*, figures 9–11.

[116] See Young, *Gordion I*, figure 9E, for several such designs. The diamond-and-lattice pattern on the fifth panel in this illustration is very close to the pattern on the fourth square of the front frame piece of the inlaid table (Figure 5).

[117] Ibid., figure 126.

[118] However, the two arms of the cross on the belt are disposed differently than those of the design on the front of the table. The design on the belt is bilaterally symmetrical, and that on the table is symmetrical with respect to rotations of 90 degrees.

[119] Young, *Gordion I*, plates 16, 17.

[120] Ibid., plate 92G–I. Körte and Körte, *Gordion*, figures 18, 21–26.

[121] See, for instance, Sams, *Early Phrygian Pottery*, fig-

ures 24–30, 36–37, 41–46, 48; plates 92–93, 97, 123–125, 128–132; and, for the variety of stamped and painted motifs, figures 60–65.

[122] Ibid., plate 108, nos. 870, 871. An amphora (plate 126, no. 932) features this same design.

[123] The mosaic was uncovered in 1956 in Megaron 2 and published in Young, "Early Mosaics at Gordion," 10ff. and cover drawing. A comparison of the drawing (p. 11) with the *in situ* photograph (p. 10) shows that some of the designs are incorrectly or incompletely rendered in the drawing. The photograph reveals even more designs like those on the inlaid table, especially in the area to the left of the central six-petalled rosette.

[124] Strommenger and Hirmer, *Art of Mesopotamia*, color plate X. On the Standard of Ur, there are two types of arrangements: red limestone diamonds bordered by lapis lazuli triangles and lapis diamonds bordered by white limestone triangles.

[125] Ibid., color plate XIII.

the dark inlaid designs and those created in the reserved areas of the light base wood. This interaction between design and background is found on all the inlaid furniture from Gordion.

Throughout the history of ancient Near Eastern art, geometric ornamentation was a highly developed skill.[126] By the first millennium B.C., the Assyrians were utilizing regular symmetrical designs in canonical arrangements.[127] In Iron Age Iran, designs were freer but no less artfully conceived: patterned squares float on the sides of pots, and lively, irregular panels are arranged in rows,[128] recalling the squares on the frame of the Tumulus MM inlaid table. The meticulously executed inlay on the Gordion table partakes of both these approaches: some designs are absolutely regular, while others are surprisingly carefree. Parallels for both the symmetry and asymmetry exhibited in the table's decoration are found in the art of other Near Eastern cultures, but nowhere are the two combined so ingeniously as at Gordion.

Many of the motifs on the inlaid table find close comparisons on the painted pottery of Geometric Greece.[129] One famous example, the "Dipylon amphora," is covered with rows of triangles, diamonds, and meanders arranged above and below the central funerary scene.[130] A painted pyxis from the Athenian agora[131] has swastikas, checkerboards, and diagonal crosshatching in panels running around the body of the vessel. A giant "pyxis" from Argos with three strap feet also features many motifs from the Phrygian repertoire, such as swastikas, interlocking hooks, and rows of diamonds.[132] The designs on the Argos pyxis initially appear more freely

disposed than those on contemporary Athenian vases. But closer inspection of the Argos vessel reveals the same commitment to bilateral symmetry and regular, repeating patterns. Herein lies the distinction between Phrygian and Greek geometric ornamentation: both utilized common motifs, but the organization of these motifs was completely different. Greek geometric design involved elaborate decorative schemes, regulated by rules governing symmetry and sequence; Phrygian geometric design often followed no comprehensive rationale, and when rules do apply, they are sure to be broken.

Mazes and Swastikas on the Inlaid Table

The maze, hook, and swastika designs on the inlaid table are surely related, although the nature of their relationship is unclear to the modern viewer—as is the meaning of the designs themselves. The complex mazes are constructed largely of hooks (Figures 9, 17), which are also the elements of the swastika. Two actual swastikas occur on the table's handles (handles D1 and D5), and one of these (D1) apparently doubles as a kind of maze (Figure 17B). This is suggested by the small segment that projects inward from the inner border at the lower left of the panel. This seems to indicate a "starting point" like those on three of the other mazes (Figures 9A, 9C, and 17A).[133] The swastika on handle D1 is defined by the dark, inlaid strips of the design, whereas the maze utilizes the space *around* the inlaid strips for the path to be negotiated.

The maze on handle D5 at the back of the table consists of a single hook that spirals in to-

---

[126] For a very early instance, see the designs on the Çatalhöyük wall paintings in Mellaart, *Çatal Hüyük*, plates 29–36, especially plate 31, from the wall of a shrine (A.III.8) in Building Level III. The painting on a beaker from Susa of the fourth millennium B.C. shows the consummate artistry of the maker. Strommenger and Hirmer, *Art of Mesopotamia*, color plate III.

[127] See the designs on the skirt borders of guardian figures from the North Palace of Ashurbanipal at Nineveh, where floral and geometric motifs alternate in square panels. Barnett, *Sculptures from the North Palace*, plate IV. See also plate XXVII for decorated floor slabs with lotus crosses arranged in panels.

[128] See Ghirshman, *Sialk 2*, plates IX–XI for pots with square panels on their bodies (Cemetery B, late ninth-eighth centuries B.C. and possibly later). Plate X:4 shows several panels including a diamond lattice panel. Square tiles from the "Painted Chamber" at Baba Jan (ca. eighth century

B.C.) are painted freehand but skillfully with lattices, crosses, X's, and wheels. See C. Goff, "Excavations at Baba Jan, 1967," 126–129, plate 4, and "Excavations at Baba Jan, 1968," 144–148, plate 3.

[129] The fragments of wooden furniture recovered from Samos suggest that Greek furniture was decorated with many of the same geometric motifs as the vases. Supra n. 106.

[130] Athens 804. J.N. Coldstream, *Greek Geometric Pottery*, plate 6.

[131] Agora P 4784. Coldstream, *Greek Geometric Pottery*, plate 10k. The animals on the lid recall sculpted animals on the lids of Gordion pieces; an animal group was certainly on the lid of a cauldron from Tumulus K-III. See Körte and Körte, *Gordion*, 68, figure 45.

[132] Argos C 209. Coldstream, *Greek Geometric Pottery*, plate 26.

[133] See above, pp. 34, 37.

ward the center of the panel. This maze is uni-cursal, or one-directional (Figure 17C); the path from the "entrance" at the lower border leads directly toward the center, without false leads requiring a choice on the part of the viewer. The terms maze and labyrinth are often used interchangeably, although some scholars of the subject reserve the word labyrinth for unicursal configurations.[134] It has been assumed that the unicursal labyrinth is the only type depicted in the art of antiquity, a position that must now be abandoned in light of the multicursal mazes on the inlaid table.[135]

The most famous ancient maze was the Cretan labyrinth of Greek legend.[136] This structure was attributed to Daedalus, the legendary Athenian craftsman, who built it to contain the minotaur born to Pasiphae, wife of King Minos of Knossos.[137] The hero Theseus negotiated the maze, killed the minotaur, and found his way back out again using a skein of thread given to him by Ariadne. The fact that Theseus needed

this thread shows that the Cretan labyrinth was *multicursal*. This labyrinth is represented much later by *unicursal* mazes on numerous coins of Knossos from the fifth century B.C.[138] Contemporary with these are other Knossian coins depicting a minotaur on the obverse, running with arms and legs arranged to evoke a swastika, and a maze-like configuration or actual swastika on the reverse.[139] This suggests that the swastika could be used to symbolize the labyrinth, at least in the art of Crete in the fifth century B.C. Homer refers to a dance floor that Daedalus constructed at Knossos; this and other evidence suggest to some scholars that the pattern of the labyrinth may have been connected to early dance.[140]

Depictions of maze-like patterns occur as early as the third millennium B.C.[141] The mysterious symbol of the swastika is even older, with examples appearing well before the beginnings of recorded history.[142] Early designs that take this form are often constructed with figures, such as

[134] Kern, *Through the Labyrinth*, 23 and 316, n. 1: "labyrinths and mazes offer the walker totally different experiences: in a labyrinth, there is a single, undeviating path to the center… By contrast, the path to the center of a maze is determined by the choices the walker makes at intersections … The center of a maze can be found only if the walker takes the initiative, by constantly working to orient and redirect him- or herself toward the goal. In a labyrinth success is a natural consequence of the path's design." This distinction is not made by all scholars. See, for instance, Matthews, *Mazes and Labyrinths*, 2; Doob, *Idea of the Labyrinth*, 1. I will use the words maze and labyrinth interchangeably here.

[135] Kern, *Through the Labyrinth*, 23: "the earliest depiction of a [multicursal] maze dates from about 1420 CE." As Kern acknowledges, ancient literary tradition indicates that multicursal architectural mazes were known in ancient times, the most dramatic being the Cretan labyrinth.

[136] The Cretan labyrinth was one of several famous ancient architectural labyrinths, noted by Pliny, Herodotus, and others. These include the great Egyptian labyrinth near Lake Moeris (supposedly the model for the Cretan labyrinth), the Etruscan labyrinth or tomb of Lars Porsena, and the Samian Heraion of Theodoros, Rhoikos, and Zmilis. Pliny's text refers to the latter as "Lemnian," which scholars have supposed is an error. Kern, *Through the Labyrinth*, 57–65; Matthews, *Mazes and Labyrinths*, 6–41; Doob, *Idea of the Labyrinth*, 20–38. On the "Lemnian" labyrinth, see also Pollitt, *Art of Ancient Greece*, 181 and n. 2; Simpson, "Use of the Lathe in Antiquity," 781.

[137] Diodorus 4.77.1–4, in Pollitt, *Art of Ancient Greece*, 14; Kern, *Through the Labyrinth*, 41–55; Doob, *Idea of the Labyrinth*, 11–13.

[138] Kern, *Through the Labyrinth*, 54, nos. 50–58. A square or circular labyrinth is shown on the reverse, with a male or female head on the obverse.

[139] Ibid., 53, nos. 39–43. The swastika may have a rosette motif at the center.

[140] *Iliad* 18.590–592. Pollitt, *Art of Ancient Greece*, 13. Kern, *Through the Labyrinth*, 25–30; 43–47.

[141] Kern, *Through the Labyrinth*, 35, figure 7.

[142] Recent research on the history of the swastika has been constrained by its use as a Nazi symbol, with few scholars venturing into this area of inquiry since the end of World War II. The most comprehensive early history was written by Thomas Wilson at the end of the 19th century; this major study has been the basis for much of the work that has followed. The word "swastika" is Sanskrit, meaning "well-being," although the symbol occurred in many early contexts that were culturally and geographically distant from India. Because of this distinction, some scholars of the subject have chosen not to use the term "swastika" when referring to the image outside of India, substituting instead the image in their written texts. Wilson produced evidence that the swastika could symbolize "a great number" (China), and by extension "long life, a multitude of blessings, great happiness," etc.; "benediction," "good augury," or the four stages of the soul (India); the winds and wind songs (Kansas American Indians); and "good luck" (Kickapoo, Sac, Pottawatomie, Iowa, and Winnebago Indians). He found swastikas on many kinds of small objects in common use and thus deduced that the sign acted mainly as a charm or amulet signifying good luck, long life, or benediction. Wilson, *Swastika*, 768–791, 799–806, 894–895, 948–952. Heller, *Swastika*, 7–10, and others.

animals disposed in a wheel-like arrangement with 90-degree rotational symmetry.[143] The classic swastika occurs in Anatolian art by the third millennium B.C., notably on objects from Troy and Alacahöyük (CD-Figures 80–81).[144] The meaning (or meanings) of these early manifestations is unknown, although the symbol has been shown to connote "good fortune" in various later contexts.[145] This association apparently pertains as early as the fourth century B.C., when the swastika occurs in a pebble mosaic labelled "ΕΥΤΥΧΙΑΚΑΛΗ" ("good luck is beautiful") from a house at the site of Olynthos.[146] The connotation of "good fortune" suggests that the sign was apotropaic, meant to ward off evil, a known function of the swastika in numerous cultures.[147] What the swastika meant to the Phrygians is hard to discern, although its prominent use on the Gordion royal furniture suggests that here too it was apotropaic. This is not to suggest that the swastika symbolized only good fortune. As with many apotropaic devices, the swastika must once have had a more specific meaning. Whether or not it did at Gordion—and, if so, what this meaning might have been—cannot be known with certainty. However, the context of the many swastika-like designs on the inlaid serving stands from Tumulus MM indicates that they functioned in a design system that included religious symbols.[148]

Fertility Symbols and Genealogical Patterns

Several other motifs on the inlaid table may be associated with magic and protection, and perhaps more specifically with concepts of fertility and divinity. This idea is supported by a great variety of ancient and ethnographic parallels. Motifs on the inlaid table that may reflect such concerns include stacked U's or fork shapes, rows of "idols," crosses, patterns of small squares, and particularly the ubiquitous diamonds or lozenges, which occur in small groups or net-like fields, with and without borders or lattice-like divisions.

The lozenge and lozenge cross occur from very early times over a wide area, appearing on pottery, in wall painting, and incised into the bodies of female figurines from sites in the Near East and Europe. Although these lozenges may reflect different meanings at various times and places, some are clearly associated with reproductive and agricultural fertility. Such designs may take the form of a lozenge or square (a lozenge rotated 45 degrees), divided by an interior cross into four sections, normally with a dot or small depression at the center of each section. The arms of the cross may extend out to the four corners of the larger figure[149] or to the middle of each of the four sides. Numerous examples of the latter type are found on the abdomens of chalcolithic female figurines from Cucuteni sites in the area of Mol-

---

[143] For instance, the grouping of four horned animals arranged around the interior of a shallow bowl from Hassuna, Samarra culture, ca. 5000 B.C. or earlier. Strommenger and Hirmer, *Art of Mesopotamia*, color plate I, plate 2. Four female figures may also be disposed in this way, as may birds or branches, and an actual swastika is sometimes seen at the center of the composition. B. Goff, *Symbols of Prehistoric Mesopotamia*, 3–5, figures 32–41. This type of design appears on the painted pottery from Susa in Iran, ca. 4000 B.C. See, for example, Strommenger and Hirmer, *Art of Mesopotamia*, plate 8, lower left. The swastika sign is also found on Susa pottery, such as Louvre Sb 3153, which depicts two-headed animals alternating with swastikas, arranged around a central cross. See also the Early Dynastic seal impressions from Ur in Legrain, *Archaic Seal-Impressions*, nos. 393 and 518.

[144] For instance, the swastikas on a bronze "standard" from Alacahöyük (CD-Figure 80), and on spindle whorls and other objects from Troy, levels 2 and later. One of these is a small lead "idol" depicting a female (no. 226) with a prominent swastika on the pubic triangle (CD-Figure 81). Akurgal, *Art of the Hittites*, plate 7, top. Schliemann, *Ilios*, 337, no. 226; 345–354; 561–563, nos. 1215, 1218, 1220. Easton, *Schliemann's Excavations at Troia*, figures 134, 136–137, 140–141, 144, 146, 150, 153, 157–158, 160, 164, 166–167, 169, 180–181, 184, 193. Wilson, *Swastika*, 810–833. For a discussion of the swastika and other designs with rotational symmetry, see below, pp. 83–87.

[145] Supra n. 142. Various swastika-type motifs found on Anatolian carpets and kilims have been catalogued and designated "motifs related to protection of life." Erbek, *Anadolu Motifleri*, 136–137.

[146] Robinson, "Villa of Good Fortune," figure 1. The meaning of "ΕΥΤΥΧΙΑΚΑΛΗ" is debated, and although "good luck is beautiful" has been suggested by the excavator, it is also possible that the reference is to a divinity or a person. The room with the swastika is in the northeast corner of the villa, to the east of an anteroom with the inscription "ΑΓΑΘΗΤΥΧΗ" or "good fortune," for which the villa is named. The two inscriptions, combined with the mosaics' iconography, suggest that "good fortune" is indeed the message meant to be conveyed by both mosaics. Swastikas appear prominently in a mosaic from the courtyard of House A xi 9 at Olynthos. Robinson, "Villa of Good Fortune," plate 31. See also, Dunbabin, *Mosaics of the Greek and Roman World*, 6–8. For a swastika in a pebble mosaic from the city mound at Gordion, see Figure 92; supra p. 49.

[147] Dunbabin, *Mosaics of the Greek and Roman World*, 8. Wherever the swastika has symbolized "good luck," it can be taken to be apotropaic. See, for instance, Wilson, *Swastika*, 803 (India).

[148] See below, pp. 77–110.

[149] See for instance Mellaart, *Çatal Hüyük*, plates 30, 36. Mellaart, Hirsch, and Balpınar, *Goddess from Anatolia* 1, plate 5:3 (here, CD-Figure 87).

davia. This sign can also be rendered as a single lozenge with a small depression at the center, found decorating the female abdomen and in other contexts.[150] In one famous instance, a quadripartite lozenge, with dots, is shown on the stomach of a clay female figurine from the site of Cucuteni (Tripolye), dated to the fifth millennium B.C. (Plate 117A).[151]

Prehistoric figurines are notoriously difficult to interpret, with some scholars identifying a large number of types with deities, while others are skeptical about assigning specific meanings and functions to most of these early objects.[152] This problem is particularly acute with respect to "goddess" types, of which the Cucuteni figures are examples. The quadripartite (or single) lozenge has been associated with a "sown field" and the dots with the "seed," giving rise to the theory that such figurines were used to invoke agricultural fertility in general, or such specific advantages as increased crop yield or rain at the right time and in the right quantity.[153] While such an explicit interpretation might seem untenable,

there is additional evidence for the use of such figures to secure agricultural fertility. Certain figurines, from Cucuteni and elsewhere, show depressions on their bodies resulting from impressions of actual grain made in the clay; alternately, grain might be embedded in the clay fabric, mixed in before the figurine was molded.[154]

In Anatolia, the neolithic sites of Hacılar and Çatalhöyük have yielded additional evidence that female figurines may have been used to effect agricultural fertility. While wild grains are attested at these sites, domesticated cereals were also cultivated, including emmer, einkorn, and bread wheat, as well as naked six-row barley.[155] At both Hacılar and Çatalhöyük, numerous female figurines were found in contexts associated with grain. Some were found in grain bins, such as the enthroned goddess flanked by felines from Çatalhöyük,[156] while others were recovered in or near grain deposits. An exceptional find was made at Çatalhöyük in 2002: a clay figurine with an opening in the middle of the back, into which had been inserted a seed, which was determined to

---

[150] For photographs and drawings of several of these figurines, see Gimbutas, *Goddesses and Gods*, 205–207.

[151] Gimbutas, *Goddesses and Gods*, 206, figures 204–205, front and back views. Versions of this symbol are still found on traditional costumes of eastern Europe and south Russia, often woven or embroidered over the stomach or pubic area. Kelly, "Living Textile Traditions of the Carpathians," 167, and see below. The motif also survives in Turkmen textiles and jewelry, notably on large silver plaques decorated with carnelians (or small silver appliqués) placed at the corners or in the divisions of the field. Schletzer and Schletzer, *Old Silver Jewellery of the Turkoman*, 118–130; and see CD-Figure 89. These charms are worn at the front or back of the body; a late 19th-century photograph of the wife of a Teke Khan shows a lozenge-shaped plaque worn over the stomach (CD-Figure 88). Kalter, *Arts and Crafts of Turkestan*, 80, plate 61.

[152] The former stance can be epitomized by the works of Marija Gimbutas, including *Goddesses and Gods*, *Civilization of the Goddess*, *Language of the Goddess*, and her final book on the subject, published posthumously, *Living Goddesses*. Contra Gimbutas, see Meskell, "Goddesses, Gimbutas, and 'New Age' Archaeology." For the advantages of a broader perspective, see Ucko, "The Interpretation of Prehistoric Anthropomorphic Figurines" and *Anthropomorphic Figurines of Predynastic Egypt*; Talalay, "Rethinking the Function of Clay Figurine Legs" and *Deities, Dolls, and Devices*; and Voigt, *Hajji Firuz Tepe*, 186–195.

[153] The "sown field" theory is advanced by Gimbutas, *Goddesses and Gods*, 205, and elsewhere, after B.A. Rybakov and S.N. Bibikov. See Rybakov, "Cosmogony and Mythology of the Agriculturalists," part 1, 21: "For 6,000 years this complex symbol has retained not only its form but its meaning with respect to marriage ritual. An interesting supplement is provided by 19th-century Belorussian ethnography: when a new house was built, a square of this type was first

drawn on the ground. Then the head of the family visited each of the four fields around the farmyard, and brought from each a rock carried on his head, which he then placed in the center of each quarter of the square. As a result there appeared on the site...our Tripolyan square with four cells, and a rock as dot in each of them. Thus the hypothesis offered relating this symbol to a field and seeds finds confirmation."

[154] Gimbutas, *Goddesses and Gods*, 204, figure 156; Rybakov, "Cosmogony and Mythology of the Agriculturalists," part 1, 19.

[155] Cereals were cultivated at Hacılar and Çatalhöyük in the 7th–6th millennia B.C. Mellaart, *Çatal Hüyük*, 224; Helbaek, "First Impressions of the Çatal Hüyük Plant Husbandry"; Helbaek, "Plant Husbandry of Hacılar." Whereas wild varieties can be cultivated, "domesticated" crops are mutants that have been selected for cultivation by man; domesticated varieties normally survive only under the conditions of cultivation. See Helbaek, "Plant Husbandry of Hacılar," 194–195: "a cultivated plant need not necessarily be domesticated—indeed, cannot by any means so be from the outset—whereas on the other hand, a domesticated plant can exist only as a cultivated plant."

[156] For the enthroned goddess with felines (Level II: shrine A.II.1), see Mellaart, *Çatal Hüyük*, 183–184, figure 52, plates 67–68, IX; "Excavations at Çatal Hüyük, 1962 Season," 46, 93, 95, plate 24. For other figurines found in granaries see Mellaart, "Excavations at Çatal Hüyük, 1962 Season," 95, and "Excavations at Çatal Hüyük, 1961 Season," plate 9a–b; *Excavations at Hacılar*, 167. For figurines associated with grain or peas: "Excavations at Çatal Hüyük, 1961 Season," plate 8b; "Excavations at Çatal Hüyük, 1962 Season," 95; "Excavations at Çatal Hüyük, 1963 Season," 75; *Excavations at Hacılar*, 17, 167. Despite this evidence, Ian Hodder sees only a "possible and weak association with plants." Hodder, *Leopard's Tale*, 213.

be wild. The presence of a seed pressed into the mid-section of a female figure would seem to confirm the connection between this figurine and the wish for high agricultural yield at the site.[157] All this evidence suggests that numerous female figurines, including those displaying the lozenge or lozenge-and-dot motif (whether single or quadruple), were associated with agricultural fertility at sites in Eastern Europe and Anatolia in the neolithic and chalcolithic periods.

The lozenge-and-dot motif occurs on female figurines from Çatalhöyük and particularly Hacılar, in effect, in its anthropomorphized version: the prominent, lozenge-shaped belly with a large navel, framed by the groin and breasts. The schematic lozenge-and-dot occurs on other types of objects, including painted pottery vessels from Hacılar[158] and "stamp seals" of clay and stone from Çatalhöyük (CD-Figure 86).[159] The patterns on most of the stamps feature multiple lozenges framed within maze-like hook configurations. The stamps may have been used to decorate cloth or to apply paint to the body.[160] Comparable lozenge and hook configurations appear on the clothing shown on "goddess" figures from Europe and the Balkans.[161] Grids of lozenges, or "net" patterns, also decorate the clothing of figurines from this area, attested from the sixth millennium B.C. down to the time of the Tumulus MM burial (CD-Figure 82).[162] This use of the lozenge pattern on textiles is of particular interest in terms of its persistence, as textile designs can have great longevity. Indeed, the quartered lozenge and lozenge-and-dot have continued in use on women's dowry textiles, headgear, and ritual cloths from rural communities in Europe and Anatolia down to the present (CD-Figures 90–93). The motif has not always retained its specific meaning, but it is considered to afford protection from the evil eye, give strength and beauty, and promote reproduction, especially when worn on an apron.[163] This devolved interpretation of the lozenge as a symbol of good luck, fertility, and protection can be seen in the many lozenge-based symbols on Anatolian carpets and kilims—and the generalized meanings given to them by present-day artisans and ethnographers.[164] Although one cannot be certain that

[157] The figurine was found in a foundation trench at the top of the mound, probably to be associated with Level III or IV. Because the seed was wild, Ian Hodder, the director of excavations at the site, used the figurine to support a very different line of reasoning: "It is as if people at Çatalhöyük were not really interested in agriculture." His suggestion that wild seeds were necessarily unrelated to "agriculture" is curious; undomesticated varieties could of course be cultivated and no doubt were (supra n. 155). Hodder, "The Lady and the Seed," 159; Balter, *Goddess and the Bull*, 309–311. The wild seed was not further identified in either publication.

[158] Many lozenges or squares occur on Hacılar painted vessels, with and without dots. See, for instance, Mellaart, *Excavations at Hacılar*, figures 67:12, 74:2–3, 79:15, 97:10, 115:16, 115:18, 116:12, 116:14–15, 120:14, and others. A remarkable female "effigy vase" has five lozenges incorporated in the painted decoration, figure 249:1.

[159] Mellaart, *Çatal Hüyük*, plate 121 (CD-Figure 86); "Excavations at Çatal Hüyük, 1963 Season," 96. See Hodder, *Leopard's Tale*, plate 23, for a stamp that shows a schematic lozenge-and-dot motif on the belly of an animal. One of the stamps from Hacılar also carries the lozenge-and-dot motif. Mellaart, *Excavations at Hacılar*, figure 187:1.

[160] One of the reliefs from a Çatalhöyük "shrine" shows a large frontal "goddess" with arms and legs spread, covered with a garment or veil (shrine VII.23). This textile, if that is what is represented, is decorated with a red, net-like pattern, which features a row of lozenges running down the chest of the figure. Mellaart, *Çatal Hüyük*, 113–114, color plate VII.

[161] For a variety, see, for instance, Gimbutas, *Language of the Goddess*, figures 128, 224, 257; *Goddesses and Gods*, figures 102–103, 210–211. Vessels and furniture are also decorated with the lozenge-and-dot pattern: see *Goddesses and Gods*, figures 93–94.

[162] Dating to the late eighth or early seventh century B.C. is a Boeotian terra-cotta "doll" or "bell idol," now in the Louvre, which wears an ornate dress, boots, and jewelry (CD-Figure 82). On the front of her dress is a net-like pattern, set within a nest of rectangular borders; to either side of the rectangular panel is a bird, and above each bird is a tree or branch. Also on the figure's dress are star-like designs, perhaps versions of the rosette, and she has two swastikas on each of her arms. Gimbutas, *Language of the Goddess*, figure 142. For a comparable figure in Boston, see Boardman, *Early Greek Vase Painting*, figure 101 (CD-Figure 83). On the dress of the Boston figure are two birds flanking a star-like design, swastikas, and other patterns; on each arm are two swastikas. For geometric decoration on an actual ancient garment fragment from a Hallstatt period tomb in Southwest Germany, see Barber, *Prehistoric Textiles*, 189, figure 7.3. The reconstructed pattern includes a swastika within a lozenge and rows of hooks.

[163] There is extensive literature on this subject, both scholarly and popular. See, for instance, Kelly, "Living Textile Traditions of the Carpathians," 161–163; Mladenovic, "Threads of Life," 99, 103; Williams, "Protection from Harm," 146–152; Erbek, *Anadolu Motifleri*, 67, 122; and Erden, *Anatolian Garment Culture*, 35, 66, 183, 184, 227 (CD-Figure 90), 237 (CD-Figure 91), 243, 246–247, 249, 348. See Allen, *Birth Symbol*, plates 5, 9, 13, 35, et al., for the use of the motif over a wide geographical area. For a connection between weaving techniques and metrical poetry, see Tuck, "Singing the Rug," implying that ancient textile patterns may have persisted through the use of mnemonic weaving devices.

[164] Erbek, *Anadolu Motifleri*. For the survival of Phrygian motifs in textiles and other media, see Türck, "Die phrygischen Muster und ihr Weiterleben."

the Phrygians at Gordion attached the idea of fertility and protection to the lozenge motif, the surprising continuity of this connection makes the notion plausible. Comparative evidence from Assyria suggests that the alternating floral struts of the Tumulus MM table may have connoted agricultural abundance (see above, p. 45).

More can be learned about the designs on the inlaid table through a different avenue of inquiry. A vast body of ethnographic data on ancient and tribal symbols was compiled and published by Carl Schuster and Edmund Carpenter, who studied the body painting, clothing, and artifacts of traditional societies.[165] This research showed that certain forms and motifs carried the same or related meanings through time and in different areas of the world. Working from surviving cultures and first-hand historical accounts, Schuster and Carpenter were able to ascribe specific meanings to many of these symbols and, in some cases, project those meanings back into the past. The overriding theme of the "decorative" designs in the art of traditional societies was the representation of one's ancestors and, in some cases, ultimate ancestor (or ancestors) of the tribe—the original progenitor(s) as creator deity.[166] Body decoration, including clothing, served—and can still serve—to clothe the individual in his or her tribal ancestry, invoking the legitimacy, means of identification, and protection that this can provide (Plate 116C).

These "genealogical patterns" are composed of repeated and interconnected elements that represent one's guardian ancestors, usually in highly schematized form. The patterns may also be abridged, utilizing a part in place of the whole, with the same implied meaning. Such schemata might take the form of opposing hooks (arms/legs); hourglass figures (bodies); rows of lozenges (bodies); lattices (arms/legs); or "grids" of multiple lozenges or squares, which might form crosses (crossed bodies), set within a larger lozenge or square border.[167] These motifs clearly recall the designs on the Tumulus MM inlaid table.[168] In some cultures these schemata are named appropriately, such as the hourglass-shaped back shields worn by Yami women on Botel Tobago, off Taiwan, which are known by the name "Mother."[169]

Obviously this subject is complex, involving many cultures and a wide variety of motifs, combined in a seemingly endless array of configurations, and found on all kinds of objects, from door-posts to pebbles, weapons, and skin clothing. Some of these designs have now lost their original meaning and relate generally to fertility or protection, while others are merely "decorative," lacking any obvious significance.[170] However, as the writings of Schuster and Carpenter show, much of the geometric art we now consider "ornament" stems ultimately from these "genealogical patterns." The widespread occurrence of these motifs, they believe, "lies in the dispersal of peoples in pre-ceramic times."[171] Thus,

[165] A selection from Carl Schuster's extensive archive of notes, correspondence, and photographs, now in Basel, was published after his death by Edmund Carpenter in a 12-volume compilation; this was followed by a single summary volume in which Schuster's main ideas are outlined and substantiated. Schuster and Carpenter, *Social Symbolism in Ancient & Tribal Art* (1986–1988), and *Patterns That Connect* (1996). This magisterial resource has gone largely unnoted by the archaeological community.

[166] Schuster and Carpenter, *Social Symbolism in Ancient & Tribal Art* 1:1, 47–123, 127 ff. For a warning against the uncritical use by scholars of "the omnipresent ancestor," without reference to supporting ethnographic studies, see Whitley, "Too Many Ancestors."

[167] Schuster and Carpenter, *Social Symbolism in Ancient & Tribal Art*, 1:1, "Excerpted Figures," 185 ff.

[168] See, for instance, the fields of lozenges found on two door-posts from New Caledonia in the South Pacific: each door-post represents the "ancestors" (plural) of one side of a family (CD-Figure 95). Schuster and Carpenter, *Patterns That Connect*, 95, figures 260–261. The lozenges on the door-posts were identified by a New Caledonian as "stomachs." *Social Symbolism in Ancient & Tribal Art* 2:3, 660. Stacked U's or fork-like elements originally derive from stacked torsos with arms or legs (depending on the orientation), sometimes

connected by a single spine, resembling branching trees. *Social Symbolism in Ancient & Tribal Art* 1:2, 463; *Patterns That Connect*, 112. Rectilinear designs composed of hooks are found as body decoration among the Kashinawa Indians, Peru. *Patterns That Connect*, 168–169, figures 470–471; see also *Social Symbolism in Ancient & Tribal Art* 1:2, figure 524. The lozenge-and-dot occurs as a tattoo on the forehead of a Toba woman in Argentina; the quartered lozenge here appears to be the body of a figure (CD-Figure 96). *Social Symbolism in Ancient & Tribal Art* 1:2, figure 764. True genealogical patterns, consisting of net-like lattice designs of lozenges, are still painted on the bodies of young initiates in Arnhem Land, Australia (Plate 116C). *Patterns That Connect*, 176–177, figures 483–484. The rows of tiny facing "idol" motifs on the front leg strut of the inlaid table are among the most obvious of the "genealogical patterns" in the table's décor.

[169] Schuster and Carpenter, *Social Symbolism in Ancient & Tribal Art* 1:1, 206–207. These shields are also produced in miniature and worn as pendants.

[170] "I think there was a tendency, especially in later times when meaning faded, for genealogical designs to break up, at which point their various parts were equated with whatever else they happened to resemble." Ibid., 323.

[171] Ibid., 314.

by the time of the Gordion table, the specific meaning of the motifs could well have been lost. Nonetheless, the genealogical origin of these motifs is worth noting. The designs on the table may have retained religious significance, particularly in terms of a creator deity, and they may have been related to reproductive or agricultural fertility. Finally, they may infer a group or clan—perhaps the dynasty of Midas. These ideas will be explored further regarding the decoration on the Tumulus MM serving stands (see Chapter 5).

CHAPTER FOUR

THE PLAIN TABLES

Eight plain three-legged tables were found in the Tumulus MM chamber. These tables were numbered (1–7 and 9) by Young and drawn by Dorothy Cox on the tomb plan.[1] Only two of the tables were catalogued at the time of excavation; all were later given MM numbers for the *Gordion I* publication (MM 380–387). Although the tables are drawn properly on the plan published in *Gordion I*, two of the tables are confused in the text, and the published photographs of individual tables are labeled incorrectly.[2] The table listed as MM 383, "not catalogued," had actually been catalogued as 5202 W 78, and the table listed as MM 384, "W 78," had not been catalogued at the time of the *Gordion I* publication. This resulted in the incorrect identification of these two tables on the tomb plan. The original numbers of the tables (1–7 and 9) have been adopted here in order to avoid further confusion (Plan, p. viii).

One table (table 9) was found at the north end of the chamber in fragments beneath the east ledge of the coffin (Young's headboard) (Color Plate IIA; Plates 100, 108A). Five tables (1–5) were arranged in a group near the center of the tomb,[3] west of the two serving stands and the inlaid table (Color Plates IIIA, V; Plates 36, 54). Two more tables (6 and 7) lay to the southeast of the central group, with Table 7 in the southeast corner of the tomb (Plate 36B, left rear). Bronze bowls and other vessels had been stacked on the tables, falling to the floor when the tables collapsed. Many of the legs were intact, while others were much more fragmentary. The table tops had broken, and several were in fairly good

condition, but some were extremely degraded. All the tables' legs were boxwood, and the tops of Tables 1–5, 7, and 9 were walnut. The top of Table 6 could not be identified with certainty but was possibly maple or cherry (Appendix 3).[4]

The plain tables had tray-shaped tops, like the top of the inlaid table, with varying but similar profiles (Figure 30). Each top was apparently made from a single piece of wood, with a beautiful, pronounced grain pattern that enhanced the upper surface.[5] As with the inlaid table, collars had originally extended down on the underside of the table tops, fitting over the tenons at the tops of the legs (Figure 39). The collars were not separate "intervening" members[6] but were cut from the wood of the table tops, which had been carved away substantially on the bottom to create the projecting collars. The tenons at the tops of the legs were secured in the collars with wood pins, which ran from side to side on the front legs and normally from front to back on the rear legs.[7] At least one tenon-collar joint was secured by a wedge or shim, driven in from the top of the table.[8] The elegant legs curved out, ending in small, plain feet with rounded or flat faces. The legs of four of the tables had flat, raised bands at the top, while the legs of the remaining four tables were unarticulated.[9] Otherwise, the plain tables' legs were similar, differing only slightly in size, shape, and decorative detail (Figure 29). At least four tables had rear legs that curved out toward the rear corners (tables 1, 2, 4, and 7); the legs of table 3 extended out to the back, and those of table 5 toward the sides. The legs of the plain

---

[1] The inlaid table was called table 8.

[2] The original numbers (1–7 and 9) were not used in Young, *Gordion I*, which may have contributed to the confusion (see above, p. 14). See *Gordion I*, 182, for the catalogue entries. For a summary of the problem, see Simpson, "Banquet Tables at Gordion."

[3] Not in two rows, as in *Gordion I*, 181.

[4] Young's statement that the tops were maple (*Gordion I*, 181) is based on one sample taken, although it is unclear whether this sample was actually from one of the Tumulus MM plain tables: "similar to MM 380–387. Dark, powdery wood fragment from table top." *Gordion I*,

291, sample 18.

[5] This cannot be proven in every case, because of the fragmentary condition of the table tops.

[6] As in Young, *Gordion I*, 182.

[7] An exception to this rule is table 3, which had pins running from side to side in all three legs. The direction of the pins in the rear legs of tables 6 and 9 could not be determined because of their fragmentary condition.

[8] The left rear collar of table 7 (see below).

[9] Contra *Gordion I*, 182, where all the legs are said to have banded tops.

tables were evidently made from naturally curving or trained branches (see Appendix 7).[10] According to the measurements of the extant pieces, the tables were ca. 48–55 cm high, and the table tops ca. 64–77 cm long and 49–65 cm wide. As the wood is now degraded, the original dimensions may have been greater.

Table 1

5203 W 79
(MM 380)
Legs: boxwood (*Buxus sempervirens* L.); table top: walnut (*Juglans* sp.).
Found in center of tomb.
Color Plate IIIA; Figures 29A, 30A, 31; Plates 36A, 37–41, 125B, 126A–B.
Est.H. of table ca. 49.5 cm. (Est.H. of table is equal to Est.H. of legs for all the plain tables.)
Table top. Est.L. ca. 73.5 cm. Est.W. ca. 56 cm. G.P.L. ca. 73 cm. G.P.W. ca. 54 cm. G.P.Th. 2.1 cm.[11]
Legs. Est.H. ca. 49.5 cm. G.P.L. ca. 52 cm (right rear leg).[12]
Grain direction follows curve of legs. Rear legs curve out toward rear corners of table.

Table 1 is correctly shown, after its removal from the tomb, in *Gordion I*, plate 81C (here Plate 37). The restored table shown in *Gordion I*, plate 81E (here Plate 38), labeled as MM 384 (table 3), is actually table 1.[13] Although few fragments of the original front leg survive, the two rear legs are in excellent condition.[14] The legs have raised bands at the top, and their feet are flat on the bottom.

The curve of the legs continues down through the feet, with a smooth transition from curved to flat surface, and the feet are squared off on their front faces (Figure 31).[15] As with all the plain tables, the tenons of the legs projected up through the collars, and the tops of the tenons were visible on the table top's surface.[16] The curve of the grain follows the curve of the legs, suggesting that the legs were made from branches that reproduced the desired curve. The figured grain on the table top has been obscured by an earlier conservation treatment.[17]

Table 2

12516 W 124 (previously uncatalogued)
(MM 382)
Legs: boxwood (*Buxus sempervirens* L.); table top: walnut (*Juglans* sp.).
Found in center of tomb, south of table 1.
Color Plate V; Figures 29B, 30B, 32–34; Plates 36B, 42–45, 128.
Est.H. of table ca. 52.5 cm.[18]
Table top. Est.L. ca. 77 cm. Est.W. ca. 57 cm. G.P.L. ca. 70 cm. G.P.W. ca. 57 cm. G.P.Th. 2.8 cm.[19]
Legs. Est.H. ca. 52.5 cm. G.P.L. ca. 52 cm (right rear leg).
Grain direction follows curve of legs (see Figures 33–34). Rear legs curve out toward rear corners of table.

The legs of table 2 have plain tops and rounded feet with flat, circular bases. All three legs are now warped, but their original curve has been

---

[10] Not, as in *Gordion I*, 182, "artificially bent by pressing, by soaking, or by steaming." See above, p. 14.

[11] As many of the fragments are shrunken or swollen and delaminated, the G.P.Th. of the table top will not accurately indicate the top's original thickness.

[12] For the G.P.L. measurement for the curved legs, see above, p. 1.

[13] See above, p. 14. Young, *Gordion I*, plate 81E, shows the restored table as though it were standing, with a grey background dropped in.

[14] The front leg shown in Plate 38 is a modern reconstruction.

[15] The cross-section (and, in this case, the front view) of the foot is shown in Figure 31B. Cross-sections of the feet of tables 1–7 and 9 are included in the drawings of the legs, with section lines indicated for clarification where necessary.

[16] The placement of the pins running through the rear collars is approximate. The position of the pin in the front collar is impossible to determine accurately and is therefore

indicated in dashed lines. This convention has been utilized for the drawings when the reconstruction of any aspect of a table is tentative.

[17] The table as shown in Plate 38 was coated with wax in an attempt to conserve and restore it. This apparently occurred in 1964; the process had been completed before this photograph was taken by R.C. Bronson in 1965. This early treatment caused considerable damage to the wood and was particularly detrimental to the table top. Table 1 has since been re-treated, for which see Appendix 1.

[18] This measurement has been estimated based on the reconstructed curve of the legs (see below).

[19] Due to the deteriorated condition of the wood of the table top, the surviving fragments have been identified and arranged with some difficulty. Photographs of the table top after its removal from the tomb (Plate 42) show many of the fragments out of order. The length and width of the top cannot be determined with certainty, and it is likely that the original width was greater than is suggested by the width of the combined fragments.

reproduced for the reconstruction drawings (Figures 32–34).[20] Fragments of the collars of the table top still adhere to two of the leg tenons (Plate 43). The wood grain pattern is spectacular on these legs, with decorative swirls evident over much of the surface (Figures 33–34). The grain pattern suggests that the legs were cut from a curved stem or branch that was relatively close in diameter to that of the finished legs (see Appendix 7). The curve of the two back legs is tighter than that of the front leg, which has a slightly shorter extension.

Table 3

12517 W 125 (previously uncatalogued)
(MM 384)
Legs, pin from collar: boxwood (*Buxus sempervirens* L.); table top: walnut (*Juglans* sp.).
Found in center of tomb, west of inlaid table (table 8).
Color Plate V; Figures 29C, 30C, 35; Plates 36B, 46–49.[21]
Est.H. of table ca. 52 cm.
Table top. Est.L. ca. 72 cm. Est.W. ca. 65 cm. G.P.L. ca. 71 cm. G.P.W. ca. 62 cm. G.P.Th. 3.2 cm.
Collars. G.P.D. ca. 8.3 cm.
Legs. Est.H. ca. 52 cm. G.P.L. ca. 54 cm (combined fragments left rear leg).
Grain direction follows curve of legs. Rear legs curve out toward back of table.

The legs of table 3 are badly damaged but can be reconstructed in drawings (Figure 35A–C).[22] Their tops are plain, and their feet are rounded at the front with flat, circular bases. All the tenons have broken off the legs, but the three leg collars survive with fragments of the tenons still inside them (Plate 47, above). The three legs appear to have a similar curve, although this is difficult to confirm because of the legs' condition. The grain direction on the collars and the orientation of the leg tenons in the mortises indicate that the rear

legs of table 3 curved out toward the back of the table (Figure 35D).[23] The table top is almost square with gently rounded corners (Plate 48).

Table 3 (MM 384) was not catalogued after its removal from the tomb and was listed incorrectly in *Gordion I* as W 78.[24] In *Gordion I*, plate 81D–E is said to illustrate this table. However, plate 81D is actually a photograph of table 5 (MM 383), and plate 81E, as noted earlier, shows table 1 (MM 380). The *Gordion I* catalogue entry states that table 3 was restored in the laboratories of the Museum of Anatolian Civilizations, Ankara. However, as noted above, it was table 1 that was restored and not table 3. The reconstruction drawing in *Gordion I* (figure 108), "based on MM 384," gives a general idea of the table's appearance but is incorrect in several particulars. The tops of the legs of table 3 are plain, although raised bands occur in the drawing. The form and curve of the legs is wrong, and the feet are rendered incorrectly. Finally, the table top was actually much wider than it appears in the early drawing, and the edge of the top formed a lip.

Table 4

12518 W 126 (previously uncatalogued)
(MM 381)
Legs: boxwood (*Buxus sempervirens* L.); table top: walnut (*Juglans* sp.).
Found in center of tomb, south of tables 1 and 5.
Color Plate IIIA; Figures 29D, 30D, 36; Plates 36, 50–53, 128.
Est.H. of table ca. 54.5 cm.
Table top. Est.L. ca. 72 cm. Est.W. ca. 60 cm. G.P.L. ca. 67 cm. G.P.W. ca. 56 cm. G.P.Th. 2.2 cm.
Legs. Est.H. ca. 54.5 cm. G.P.L. ca. 56 cm.
Grain direction follows curve of legs. Rear legs curve out toward rear corners of table.

The legs of table 4 are the most distinctive of the group (Figure 29D). The tops have raised bands, and the slender legs extend straight down

[20] Dimensions of the front foot have been reconstructed based on the foot of the left rear leg.
[21] The arrangement of the leg fragments shown here in Plate 47 supersedes that in Simpson, "Wooden Furniture from Tumulus MM at Gordion, Turkey," plate 31, where the fragments of the front and right rear legs were placed incorrectly.
[22] The curious way in which the three legs are broken makes it appear as though each of the legs was made from

two pieces of wood. However, the grain patterns show that each leg was made from a single piece of wood, as with the legs of the other plain tables.
[23] This can be deduced from the evidence, although the arrangement would seem to be less stable than one in which the legs curved out to the sides or corners.
[24] 5202 W 78 is actually table 5 (MM 383). Young, *Gordion I*, 182.

and curve out decisively toward the bottom.[25] The feet are cut flat at the front and on the resting surface. At the base of the curve of the legs, a short reverse curve forms the back of the feet. The tenons are still intact, and pieces of the three collars of the table top survive, one still attached to the tenon (Plate 51). The table top is fragmentary, but its size and shape can be reconstructed. The placement of the legs can be determined; the rear legs curved out toward the corners of the table.

Table 5

5202 W 78
(MM 383)
Leg, pin from collar: boxwood (*Buxus sempervirens* L.); table top: walnut (*Juglans* sp.).
Found in center of tomb, west of serving stands A and B.
Color Plate IIIA; Figures 29E, 30E, 37–40; Plates 36A, 54–59, 127B, 151C–D.
Est.H. of table ca. 50.5 cm.
Table top. Est.L. ca. 73.5 cm. Est.W. ca. 50.5 cm. G.P.L. ca. 73 cm. G.P.W. ca. 55 cm. G.P.Th. 2.3 cm.
Legs. Est.H. ca. 50.5 cm. G.P.L. ca. 49.5 cm (left rear leg).
Grain direction follows curve of legs. Rear legs curve out toward sides of table.

Table 5 is one of the best preserved of all the plain tables. Since its form and dimensions can be reconstructed with some confidence, a series of drawings of this table has been included here (Figures 37–40). This may serve to help illustrate the construction of all the plain tables. The legs of table 5 have banded tops, and its feet are rounded at the front, with flat, circular bases. The top of the right rear leg shows an ancient repair secured with two small pins (see Plate 151C and Appendix 7). The front leg has a tighter curve than the back legs (Plate 57, Figure 37A–C); the back legs curved straight out toward the sides of the table.[26] The tray-shaped table top (Plates 58–

59) was made from a single piece of wood, as can be determined from the grain pattern on the underside.

The collars, although originally carved in one piece with the table top, were torn off the top when the table collapsed, breaking off neatly along the line of the grain. This can be seen on the underside of the table top, in the slight, uneven circular depressions surrounding the square mortises (Plate 59). The tenons of the legs extended up through these mortises, showing through as squares on the top surface (Figure 40). As the legs were of boxwood, these squares would have been lighter in color than the expanse of the walnut table top. The pins that secured the leg tenons to the top ran through all the collars in the same side-to-side direction (Figure 37D).[27] Figure 39 illustrates the way in which the legs were joined to the table top. This was the method by which all the plain tables were constructed.

Table 5 (MM 383) is listed in *Gordion I* as "not catalogued." In fact, table 5 was catalogued at the time of excavation as 5202 W 78. Plate 81D in *Gordion I*, which supposedly illustrates table 3 (MM 384), actually shows table 5 instead.

Table 6

12519 W 127 (previously uncatalogued)
(MM 385)
Legs, pin from collar: boxwood (*Buxus sempervirens* L.); table top: severely degraded, possibly maple (*Acer*) or cherry (*Prunus*).
Found in southeast corner of tomb, southeast of table 3.
Figures 29F, 30F, 41; Plates 36B, 60–62, 126C, 152B.
Est.H. of table ca. 51 cm.
Table top. Est.L. ca. 63.5 cm. Est.W. ca. 49 cm. G.P.L. ca. 62 cm. G.P.Th. 1.7 cm.
Legs. Est.H. ca. 51 cm. G.P.L. ca. 51 cm.[28]
Grain direction follows curve of legs. Rear legs curve out toward back or sides of table.

---

[25] All three feet are restored in the drawings based on the dimensions of the foot of the left rear leg.
[26] The legs are now warped, and their original curve has been reconstructed in the drawings. The front foot has been lengthened somewhat in Figure 37C; the foot is now shrunken, and its original length is difficult to estimate.
[27] In the front leg, the pin ran through the tenon from

side to side, and in the rear legs, the pins ran through the tenons from front to back. This is the normal placement of the pins in the tables' leg tenons. The exception to this rule is table 3, where the pins ran side to side in all three leg tenons.
[28] The length of the legs cannot be ascertained with certainty.

The wood of table 6 is degraded, and the legs and table top are in very poor condition. Their basic shape and approximate dimensions can nonetheless be determined. The legs had plain tops, and their feet were flat on the front and bottom.[29] The curve of the legs continued through to the bottom of the feet, although the feet themselves are badly shrunken. The general form of the legs is clear (Figure 41A), but their exact height, and therefore the height of the table, is uncertain. The position of the rear legs cannot be reconstructed, but the grain direction on the collars shows that the legs curved out toward either the back or sides of the table (Figure 41B, Plate 152B). The width of the table top cannot be accurately measured, but table 6 was one of the smaller tables; its top was comparable in size to those of tables 7 and 9.

Table 7

12520 W 128 (previously uncatalogued)
(MM 386)
Legs: boxwood (*Buxus sempervirens* L.); table top: walnut (*Juglans* sp.).
Found in southeast corner of tomb, south of the inlaid table (table 8).
Figures 29G, 30G, 42; Plates 36B, 63–65, 152A.
Est.H. of table ca. 48 cm.
Table top. Est.L. ca. 65 cm. Est.W. ca. 49 cm. G.P.L. ca. 62 cm. G.P.Th. 1.5 cm. G.P.Th. top fragment with collar ca. 5.2 cm.
Legs. Est.H. ca. 48 cm. G.P.L. ca. 48 cm.
Grain direction follows curve of legs. Rear legs curve out toward rear corners of table.

As with table 6, the top of table 7 is so degraded that its width cannot be accurately measured.[30] One of the legs is preserved in a fragment, and the other two legs are broken and split. The wood of the legs is otherwise in excellent condition, however, with the wood grain prominent and figured.[31] The legs have banded tops, and the feet are rounded at the front with flat, circular bases. The two well-preserved legs are now somewhat different in size, due to varying degrees of shrinkage. The leg with its tenon intact (Plate 64A, right) has a longer extension and larger foot, which was laid out with the aid of a compass (Plate 152A).[32] This was apparently the table's front leg, as its tenon has a pin run in from the side. While the top of Table 7 is badly damaged, one very important fragment is well preserved (Plates 63, above center; 65, left center). This is one of only two collars still attached to a piece of a table top,[33] and it can be fitted down over the tenon of the best-preserved leg in what was apparently its original position (Plate 64B). The other surviving collar from table 7 (Plate 63, center) resembles the loose collars from the other plain tables. This collar broke off the table top neatly along the line of the grain and retains the top tenon from the left rear leg of the table. Preserved in the collar is a wooden wedge or shim, which once served to tighten the joint. The direction of the grain on this collar proves that the rear legs curved out toward the corners.

Table 9

12521 W 129 (previously uncatalogued)
(MM 387)
Legs, pin from collar: boxwood (*Buxus sempervirens* L.); table top: walnut (*Juglans* sp.).
Found along north wall of tomb, partly under the east ledge of the coffin.
Color Plate IIA; Figures 29H, 30H, 43; Plates 66–68, 100, 108A.
Est.H. of table ca. 50.5 cm.
Table top. Est.L. ca. 64.5 cm. Est.W. ca. 49 cm. G.P.L. ca. 30 cm (fragment group). G.P.W. ca. 50 cm. G.P.Th. ca. 2.1 cm.
Legs. Est.H. ca. 50.5 cm. G.P.L. ca. 48 cm (longest leg fragment).
Grain direction follows curve of legs. Rear legs curve out toward back or sides of table.

The legs of table 9 are the most poorly preserved of all the plain table legs. The soft-rot fungi that had affected much of the wood at the north

---

[29] The feet have been reconstructed in the drawings based on markings at the bottom of a foot fragment, as well as on the feet of the legs of table 1, which are similar.
[30] The fragments of the top have been placed in a tentative arrangement in Plate 65, and the size has been reconstructed provisionally in Figure 42C. The legs' positions have also been reconstructed in the drawing, although the orientation of the rear legs is certain.

[31] Burhan Aytuğ remarked that the wood of this table's legs was so well preserved that the pieces looked like they had been recently cut and worked.
[32] See Appendix 7, p. 200.
[33] The other attached collar is from table 9, but the tenons are broken from the tops of its legs, and the collar and legs cannot be fit together.

end of the tomb clearly contributed to the legs' deterioration (see Appendix 4). Nonetheless, the basic form of the legs is evident: the tops were not banded, and the feet had flat bottoms and front faces (Figure 43A).[34] The preserved end of the table top shows the front leg collar still attached (Plate 68B). The collar was stronger than the leg tenon in this instance,[35] and the top of the tenon broke off, remaining inside the collar. The rear section of the table top had degraded to such an extent that the position and orientation of the two rear legs could not be determined with certainty (Plate 66). However, it is clear from the grain on the collars that the legs curved out toward either the back or sides of the table. The table top was apparently made from a single piece of walnut, with the wood grain prominent on the upper surface.

Comparanda

Like the inlaid table, the plain tables from Tumulus MM were portable banquet tables.[36] They were small and light enough to be carried and had tray-shaped tops to facilitate this function. At least two similar tables were found in Tumulus P at Gordion, one of which is well preserved and illustrated in *Gordion I*.[37] This table had three banded legs,[38] which curved like the legs of the Tumulus MM tables.[39] The legs' top tenons fit

into collars carved in one piece with the table top, and the feet had flat faces much like the feet of tables 1, 6, and 9 from Tumulus MM. A second plain table from Tumulus P is represented by a previously uncatalogued group of fragments.[40] Pieces of the table top are preserved along with the upper parts of three legs.[41]

As already noted, three-legged wooden tables have been found at other ancient sites. The earliest comparable group was excavated at Jericho.[42] Approximately twenty-five wooden tables were found in the Middle Bronze Age tombs, which have been dated to the 17th or 16th centuries B.C., around 900 years earlier than the Tumulus MM tables.[43] The Jericho tables were "plain," without decorative strutwork, although the legs were sometimes carved in a kind of haunch at the top, with the feet shaped to resemble duck's feet or ram's heads.[44] These tables were rectangular with two legs at one end and a third at the other. Some of the table tops featured separate borders joined to the central board by means of mortise-and-tenon joinery.[45] On some tables, the two rear legs evidently pointed straight out toward the back of the table, while on others they angled out to the corners.[46]

Perhaps the most significant similarity between the Jericho and Gordion tables lay in the collar-and-tenon joinery used to attach the legs to the table tops. The leg tenons of the Jericho tables were secured in their collars with pins run in

---

[34] The dimensions and curve of the front leg have been reconstructed in Figure 43.

[35] Usually the opposite is true.

[36] See above, p. 39.

[37] TumP 153. Young, *Gordion I*, 67–68, Plate 30B. Simpson, "Banquet Tables at Gordion," 137, figure 11.

[38] Not four, as in the early reconstruction drawing. Young, *Gordion I*, 68, figure 38.

[39] The legs were not straight, as shown in the early drawing. As evident in *Gordion I*, plate 30B, the legs of the Tumulus P plain table are severely deformed, which was no doubt the cause of the misunderstanding.

[40] 13022 W 132. See Simpson and Spirydowicz, *GWF*, 59–60. Simpson, "Banquet Tables at Gordion," figure 12.

[41] Two other related pieces are represented among the fragments from Tumulus P. These include what is apparently a miniature plain table (13023 W 133) and a table (or seat) with a square top and rounded, raised rim (13024 W 134). Simpson, "Banquet Tables at Gordion," figure 13. This second piece featured square collars that extended down from the underside of the top at the corners. These unusual collars, one of which is preserved, received the square tenons of the legs in the manner of the plain tables. Evidence of a round circle on the bottom of the extant square collar indicates that cylindrical leg tops

were joined to the square collars. Also of interest are several wooden tray-shaped objects, excavated from the Terrace Building complex on the city mound at Gordion. These objects, identified as "kneading troughs" by the excavators, were carbonized and reportedly could not be saved. Young, "Gordion Campaign of 1959," 242 and plate 62, figure 28.

[42] See above, p. 42.

[43] See Kenyon, *Archaeology in the Holy Land*, 169–170, 190, 192, for comments on dates for the Middle Bronze Age and duration of the tombs' use. See Parr, "Middle Bronze Age Furniture from Jericho and Baghouz," 41–42, for the difficulties of dating the Jericho tombs.

[44] See above, p. 42, n. 61.

[45] For instance, tables 20 and 54 from Tomb P 19 (Kenyon, *Jericho II*, 398, figure 199; 401, figure 202). For a diagram showing the type of joinery used, see Kenyon, *Jericho I*, 530, figure 229:1. Separate free tenons were fit into mortises cut in the edges of the central board and the bordering strips, such as would later be used for the edge-to-edge joinery of the Tumulus MM serving stands.

[46] The rear legs seem to point straight back on table 2 from Tomb P 19 (Kenyon, *Jericho II*, figure 200; reconstruction drawing, 400, figure 201) and toward the rear corners on table A from Tomb P 23 (*Jericho II*, figure 141, top).

through the collars.[47] The technique was conveyed in an illustration in *Jericho I*, which showed the addition of shims driven down into the top of the mortise to anchor the tenon tightly in the collar.[48] As noted above, shimming was also employed for the Tumulus MM plain tables.[49] While some of the collars of the Jericho tables were carved and added separately, most appear to have been made in one piece with the table tops.[50] In this case, much of the lower surface of the table tops was carved away, excepting the three collars, which were left to extend down to accommodate the legs' top tenons.[51] It is remarkable that this expensive and labor-intensive method of manufacture was utilized at both Gordion and Jericho, considering the difference in date of the furniture from these two sites and the geographical distance between them. Clearly, by the time of the Gordion tables, the collar-and-tenon system had become a standard joinery technique in western Asia.

By the early first millennium B.C, this system was also employed in eastern Anatolia in the kingdom of Urartu. In addition to the elaborate, metal-plated furniture found in the tombs at Altıntepe, evidence for wooden tables has been recovered from this and other Urartian sites.[52] The remains of three tables were excavated at Adılcevaz in chamber tomb I, including one complete example and table legs from two others.[53] The complete table had a round top and three legs, which were attached to the top by means of collar-and-tenon joinery. The leg tenons extended up through the collars and table top and were visible on the top's surface, in the manner of the Tumulus MM plain tables.[54] One set of table legs was decorated with incised patterns of diamonds and triangles.[55]

These woodworking techniques occur again in contexts dating to the fourth or third century B.C., where the banquet tables from Pazyryk in Siberia continue the tradition.[56] The Pazyryk tables had four legs and dished tops with rounded corners, and in most cases the tops were attached to the legs with collar-and-tenon joinery.[57] While the leg tenons fit into top collars, the tenons seem not to have gone all the way through the table tops.[58] Pins were not used to secure the tenons in the collars, suggesting that the tops were meant to be removable.[59] The Pazyryk tables would thus have been portable in two senses: as assembled tables used to carry food, like the Gordion tables, and also disassembled when broken down for the transport of household belongings. Some of the table legs were plain, while others were decorated with carved moldings,[60] and several of the tables

---

[47] Kenyon, *Jericho I*, plate 32:5.

[48] See Kenyon, *Jericho I*, Appendix B, 529–531, and figure 229:2 for the collar-and-tenon system of joinery. See also H. Baker, *Furniture in the Ancient World*, figure 356b. The illustration conveys most of the pertinent information clearly but is misleading in one respect: the pin is shown running through the collar as though to pierce the leg tenon at its edge rather than through one of the flat faces.

[49] See above, pp. 57, 61. Shimming may have been more common at Gordion than suggested by the extant remains (see Appendix 7).

[50] For collars added separately, see table 27, Tomb G 73 (Kenyon, *Jericho II*, 458–460 and figure 241). For collars cut in one piece with the table top, see for instance table 2, Tomb P 19 (*Jericho II*, 399–400, figures 200–201).

[51] Ricketts illustrates this technique in *Jericho I*, 529–531, figure 228.

[52] Although much of the wood from the Altıntepe tombs had disintegrated, the remains of several wooden tables are noted by the excavators. See T. Özgüç, *Altın Tepe II*, 68–70, for wood tables from Tomb 3, dated to the late eighth or early seventh century B.C. (see above, p. 46). No evidence for collar-and-tenon joinery is reported from Altıntepe.

[53] Felsen H, Kammergrab I. Öğün, "Die urartäischen Bestattungsbräuche," 660–661, plate 163:47. Öğün, "Die urartäischen Paläste," plates 21, 26a–c. C. Işık, "Tische und Tischdarstellungen," 426–427; figures 4, 6–8; plates 6–13. The reconstructed table and other table legs from Adılcevaz are on display in the Museum of Anatolian Civilizations,

Ankara. For reconstruction drawings of two of these tables, see Simpson, "Banquet Tables at Gordion," figure 19.

[54] C. Işık, "Tische und Tischdarstellungen," plate 7, shows the Adılcevaz table top from below, with the three collars clearly visible. The leg tenons were not pierced, indicating that the tenons were not secured in the collars by pins.

[55] C. Işık, "Tische und Tischdarstellungen," figure 4. These legs are reconstructed in a drawing with feet in the form of hooves supported by molded bases with hanging-leaf capitals. Although the table top was not preserved, the tenons at the tops of the legs were pierced, suggesting that they had fit into collars and were secured by pins. The second set of legs from the tomb also had hoof feet and pierced top tenons.

[56] See above, p. 47.

[57] Rudenko, *Frozen Tombs of Siberia*, 65–68. Most of the Pazyryk tables had leg collars carved in one piece with their tops; at least one had no collars but mortises cut through the table top. Rudenko, 67, figures 18–19.

[58] See also Polosmak, "Mummy Unearthed," 96. Some of the Pazyryk table tops had been lifted off their legs by grave robbers and used as trays to carry objects out of the tombs. Several tops were lost, and exact details of top/leg construction are unavailable for these examples.

[59] See above, p. 47.

[60] Rudenko asserts, but does not demonstrate, that some of the legs were turned on a lathe. *Frozen Tombs of Siberia*, 66 and 199.

were colored bright red with cinnabar.[61] The excavator thought that the food found on the tables had been meant to sustain the dead during their journey to the netherworld.[62]

As these examples indicate, the construction methods used for the Tumulus MM plain tables must have been common in the first and second millennia B.C., although good evidence survives at only a few sites. Numerous variations are also known, such as those found at Baghouz and Verucchio.[63] The wooden banquet table with collar-and-tenon joinery can thus be recognized as a table type of great antiquity, which was in use over a long period of time and throughout a wide area. These tables had three or four legs and dished tops that were round or rectangular.

Their legs might be pinned to the table tops or easily detachable. This type of construction, although widespread, was not universal, as is evident from the furniture of Egypt. The Egyptians were aware of the collar-and-tenon system, however, which was used for a carved stool from the tomb of Tutankhamun.[64]

Descendants of these wooden tray tables are still in use throughout Europe and the Middle East, with examples noted from Macedonia to Turkmenistan. Some of these later tables have legs that are fit into collars or thickened sections on the underside of the table tops. Others are low to the ground, with stubby legs, carved in one piece with the table tops, which may derive from the collars of their ancient predecessors.[65]

---

[61] Ibid., 65–67.

[62] Ibid., 118.

[63] See above, pp. 42–43, 48. Not quite similar but still related is a plain, rectangular wooden table top found on Samos, with no collars on the underside of the top but mortises cut to receive the top tenons of three legs. Pins ran in through the sides of the table top and passed through the leg tenons. Kopcke, "Neue Holzfunde aus dem Heraion von Samos," 135–136; figures 15–16; plate 75.

[64] See above, p. 43. See Killen, *Ancient Egyptian Furniture I*, plates 105–106, for a First Dynasty low table with four stubby feet, which resemble the collars of later stools and tables.

[65] Examples can be found in the Museum of Ethnography in St. Petersburg, in a one-room house in Macedonia (*Amnesty International Calendar*, 2002), and in the desert of northern Sinai (Slackman, "Out of Desert Poverty").

CHAPTER FIVE

THE SERVING STANDS

Young's enigmatic "screens" have now been identified as serving stands, each with an inlaid front face, openwork top piece, inlaid side pieces, and elaborate supporting structure. The back legs of both stands had decomposed, and the top pieces and supporting members had fallen to the tomb floor, leaving the faces leaning against the east wall (Color Plates IIIA, IV; Plates 69–70). The southernmost serving stand ("screen A") had stood to the north of the inlaid table (Color Plate IVA; Plate 70). The second serving stand ("screen B") was found directly to the north of the first (Color Plate IVB; Plate 80).[1] These two pieces of furniture may now be designated more accurately as servings stands A and B respectively. Of all the structural elements from the rear of the stands, only the right side piece of stand B remained in place, holding the top right corner of the front face out away from the wall of the chamber (Color Plate IVA, upper left, and IVB). Ten small cauldrons (MM 4–13), two ladles (MM 47–48), and the ram and lion situlae (MM 45–46) were found on the tomb floor behind or near the stands. Young and his colleagues theorized that these bronzes had hung on nails on the east wall and, in falling, had broken the stands' top and back sections.[2]

Young reported that both stands were wet when found, especially the top of stand A, which appeared "rotted," as is visible in the *in situ* photographs (Color Plates IIIA, IVA; Plates 69–70). A darkened area can be seen on the tomb wall above the damaged top of stand A, which may indicate that water ran down the wall and onto the stands' faces. Young thought that the water damage might have been caused by the

drilling program carried out in 1955 and 1956, prior to the tomb's excavation in 1957.[3]

As noted, the stands were left in the tomb to dry slowly, but when mold began to appear on the wood, they were removed on sheets of plywood.[4] They were then placed in an alcohol bath for drying, followed by immersion in a solution of wax dissolved in gasoline. By Young's own account, the treatment was not a success (Plates 71, 81).[5] The serving stands were subsequently moved to the Museum of Anatolian Civilizations, Ankara, where the face of stand A was put on display in the museum, and the remaining parts of both stands were placed in storage (Plate 133A). Beginning in 1983, the Tumulus MM serving stands were retreated, restudied, drawn, photographed, and eventually reconstructed in the Museum of Anatolian Civilizations (see Appendices). Their form and function have now been ascertained, and their complex decoration is largely understood. The creation of the stands was clearly a time-consuming process, suggesting that these objects were made for ceremonial use at Gordion and not specifically as grave goods for the king's burial.

Serving Stand A ("Screen A")

5229 W 81
(MM 378)
Screen face, side pieces, back piece, back struts, pegs, foot blocks: boxwood (*Buxus sempervirens* L.); curved front legs, top piece, tenon in right front foot block: walnut (*Juglans* sp.); inlay: juniper (*Juniperus* sp.).

---

[1] Young, *Gordion I*, 176–177. For catalogue entries and discussion of the "screens," see pp. 176–181.

[2] For the iron nails, see above, p. 10. Many of the bronze objects found in the tomb must originally have hung from these nails and fallen when the iron corroded and broke. The end of an iron nail was found resting under the disc of one of the bronze "belts" that lay on the ground near the west wall. Young, *Gordion I*, 148, n. 79.

[3] See Young, *GFB* 63, 156–157; Young, *Gordion I*, 81–83, for an account of the drilling.

[4] "The screens were left in place for as long a time as possible in the hope of a slow and gradual drying." Young, *Gordion I*, 177.

[5] Ibid., 177. See Appendix 1 for a full account of the early conservation.

Found along east wall of tomb, directly north of the inlaid table.

Color Plates IIIA, IVA, X, XII–XIII; Figures 44–51, 60, 62–63, 67A, 68–69, 71–73; Plates 69–79, 90–91, 93, 95A, 96A–B, 97A–B, 98A–B, 99A–D, 133–135, 137C, 138B; CD-Figures 66–69.

Inlaid face. G.P.H. without front feet ca. 93 cm; with feet ca. 94 cm. G.P.W. without front feet ca. 77.5 cm; with feet ca. 80.5 cm. G.P.Th. ca. 3 cm. G.P. outer diameter central medallion ca. 17 cm.

Inlaid side pieces. G.P.L. including tenons ca. 25.5 cm. G.P.H. ca. 14 cm.

Pierced back piece. G.P.L. ca. 72 cm. G.P.H. ca. 10 cm.

Openwork top piece. G.P.L. ca. 70 cm. G.P.W. ca. 19.5 cm. G.P.Th. ca. 3.5 cm.

Back struts. G.P.L. 21.5–58 cm. G.P.W. 2.1–4.5 cm. G.P.Th. ca. 2.2 cm.

Back leg (not extant). Est.H. ca. 84 cm. Est.W. ca. 5.5 cm. Est.Th. ca. 3 cm.

Right front foot. G.P.H without foot block ca. 7 cm.

Inlaid meander squares outside front legs. G.P.H. ca. 3.3 cm. G.P.W. ca. 3.3 cm. G.P.W. inlay pieces ca. 0.2–0.3 cm. G.P. depth of inlay ca. 0.35 cm.

Compass pricks preserved in: 1) center of central rosette; 2) arc at left above rosette; 3) arc at right above rosette.

Grain direction follows curve of front legs.

The most imposing part of serving stand A is its inlaid front face, which featured fine woods of contrasting colors, areas worked in relief, and an amazing array of geometric patterns. The rectangular face was made from eleven boxwood boards inlaid with thousands of tiny diamonds, triangles, and strips of juniper (Figure 50; Plates 70, 72).[6] Two curved front "legs" were made separately and set into the stand's face. These legs were flat at the back (Plate 73) and rounded on their front surfaces, projecting slightly beyond the plane of the inlaid face. Each front leg was carved from a single piece of walnut,[7] terminating in a scroll-like, animal-paw foot. The front feet sat on boxwood foot blocks, joined by connecting pieces that were locked into the blocks and pinned to the feet (Figure 60; Plates 90–91).[8] The grain direction follows the curve of the legs (visible in Plate 73), suggesting that they were made from naturally bent or trained branches.[9] At the top of each front leg is an inlaid disc, ornamented with a star rosette, oriented with its axis slightly off the vertical (Figure 67A).[10] Directly above the star rosettes and dominating the decoration of the face of the stand is a large central medallion, supported from below by the two front legs.

The central medallion (Young's "rose window") has a raised border, which is inlaid on its beveled surface with three concentric bands of diamonds and triangles (Plate 77).[11] Within the circular border is a large, elaborate inlaid rosette. The rosette pattern is composed of curved double hooks,[12] circles, droplets, chevrons, diamonds, and triangles, laid out with the aid of a compass, as indicated by a small prick visible at the center. The large rosette is aligned along the vertical and horizontal axes, unlike the smaller star rosettes below it. Rising from the border of the central medallion are two striped arcs, each made from five concentric bands of inlay that curve up at the left and right. These arcs were also laid out with a compass.[13] Directly above the central medallion, supported by the two striped arcs, is a pendant half-circle containing a "meander square" composed of hooks, set between two quarter-round wedge-shaped patterns.[14] The outer curve of the

---

[6] Figure 50 supersedes Young, *Gordion I*, 178, figure 104, my original drawing of the face of stand A, which was reconstructed from excavation photographs. This early drawing incorporates numerous errors, concerning inlay details, peg placement, and the appearance and construction of the front legs and feet.

[7] The walnut legs were joined to the central board (Figure 62, board 7), which was made of boxwood; part of the legs at the top were carved from this boxwood board (Figures 49–50; Plate 72). If the colors of the different woods were not altered to mask the joint, this unusual feature would have been prominent.

[8] Such a locking joint is found on a wood fragment from Samos. Ohly, "Holz," 121.

[9] Young thought the front legs were artificially bent.

Gordion I, 179. On this question, see Appendix 7.

[10] In my drawing in *Gordion I*, figure 104, these rosettes are positioned incorrectly, with a uniform, vertical orientation.

[11] This motif was also used on the inlaid table: on the leg tops (Figure 22), on the top sections of the curved front leg strut (Figure 12A), and on the rear leg struts (Figures 10–11).

[12] Young's terminology in *Gordion I*, 179.

[13] According to Young, the compass prick was visible at the left but not at the right. Now, after cleaning and conservation, both pricks are visible. In addition, a third prick can be seen at the center of the left arc (Plate 77).

[14] The term "maeander-square" was used on the Gordion catalogue cards to denote these inlaid squares and has been adopted for the present publication.

half-circle is inlaid with four concentric rows of double, inward-facing triangles, the whole combination suggesting a crescent or "lunette."[15]

In the area above and to the sides of the rosette, lunette, and curved front legs are 190 additional meander squares (or portions thereof) composed of hooks in various configurations (Figure 50). These are set within a lattice ground of tiny inlaid diamonds and triangles, which serves as a sumptuous backdrop for the hook designs. Between the curved front legs are 18 more such squares, some of which are arranged in groups. These are also surrounded by a border of diamonds and triangles, its pattern somewhat different from that of the main lattice field.

Two inlaid, openwork side pieces originally projected out toward the back of the serving stand at the top of the front face (Figures 45B–C, 46A–B, 47; Plate 76). These had broken off and fallen to the tomb floor. When attached to the stand's face, the inlaid designs on the side pieces continued over onto the edges of the face, forming an uninterrupted pattern (Figures 45–46, 51; Plate 96A–B). The inlaid pattern featured rows of small squares and solid strips, which served to surround and accentuate the eight square openings in each side piece. The left side piece (when facing the front of the stand) has 20 inlaid squares running down its left end (Figure 46B), while the inlay on the edge of the stand's face has 25 squares running down at the right of the composite design (Figure 46C). On the side piece, six inlaid squares border each side of the square cutouts, but the corresponding pattern on the edge of the front face has seven. The inlay on the fragmentary right side piece shows similar discrepancies (Figure 45). This suggests that the side pieces were inlaid separately and later joined to the stand's face.

The square cutouts in the side pieces reflect a continuation of the first two rows of the meander squares on the stand's front face, although as a kind of negative manifestation of the pattern. The top row of the cutouts in each side piece is continued in the single row of openings cut in the long, pierced back piece (Plate 75A). The

back piece was joined to the side pieces at their ends, forming a frame for the openwork shelf that projected back from the top of the stand's face (Figures 44, 51; Plates 74, 79). This shelf was carved from a single piece of wood as a series of three open rings, surrounded by arcs and connecting strips. The top shelf was joined to the side pieces by means of tenons, two of which extended out at each end, and to the pierced back piece and screen face with six free tenons, secured by pins (Figures 44D, 47–48, 51).

Young had understood the general form of the stand's back section (the "three-burner stove"), although his description of the top and back pieces was at variance with the surviving fragments.[16] This no doubt occurred due to the early reconstruction drawing (Figure 2), published in *Expedition* and reproduced in *Gordion I*.[17] The drawing was said to depict stand A ("screen A") but was actually a rendering of stand B, although still incorrect in many details. Comparison of the early drawing with the new reconstruction (Figure 51) shows the extent of the inaccuracy. When the remains of the top, back, and side pieces of stands A and B were stored together after their removal from the tomb, the pieces had evidently been mixed up.[18] As a result, the carved top piece of serving stand A was never understood correctly.

The pierced back piece of stand A was supported from below at its center by a straight back leg. Although this leg did not survive, its basic form can be determined. The leg was rectangular in section, as shown by the projection that extends down from the lower edge of the back piece at the center. The dimensions of the back leg can be derived from this projection, which was cut with a mortise to receive a tenon at the top of the leg (Figures 48, 51). Four diagonal struts ran up from the leg to support the back piece from below. The outer two struts were longer and fit into projections extending down at the two ends of the back piece. All the diagonal struts are preserved and can be fit into position (Plate 75A); although the struts are now deformed, they can be reconstructed in drawings (Figures 48, 51). The flat, lower ends of the diagonal struts had fit flush against the sides of the back leg, showing that the

---

[15] Rows of facing triangles also appear on the inlaid table: on the rear leg struts (Figures 10–11), the sides of three of the handles (Figures 13–15), and the bands of inlay running up the front leg (Figure 19).

[16] Young, *Gordion I*, 180–181, and see above, pp. 18–19.

[17] Ibid., 180, figure 105.

[18] After the serving stands' excavation and early treatment, the face of stand A was laid out horizontally in a display case in the Museum of Anatolian Civilizations, Ankara. The face of stand B was stored in a large drawer, and in a second drawer were placed all the remaining pieces from both serving stands.

leg was straight and providing further confirmation that the leg was rectangular in section. A short strut joined the straight leg to the back of the stand's face (Figures 47, 51; Plates 75B, 79).[19] Based on this evidence, the back leg has been reconstructed in the new drawings and restored in Plexiglas for the stand's reconstruction in the museum (Color Plate XIII, Plate 79).

In the early drawing of "screen A," a curious foot was included at the bottom of the back leg (Figure 2), recalling the feet of the curved front legs of the stands. This detail corresponds to a reference in Young's field book, which states that two "scrolled feet" were found behind the stands on the tomb floor. Young thought these feet had belonged to the stands' back legs, as they were found "still in place on the floor against the wall."[20] In *Gordion I*, these feet are discussed again, although with the proviso that "quite possibly the foot has been turned the wrong way in the restored drawing."[21] Unfortunately, no evidence survives for these feet beyond Young's brief comment.[22] In fact, it is unlikely that the stand's back leg had ended in a "scrolled foot" as represented in the drawing, whether turned toward the stand or away from it. Based on other evidence from Gordion, such a scroll foot would never be found on a straight leg, especially one that was rectangular in section. It thus seems probable that Young's "scrolled feet" were not the feet of the stands' back legs—but were actually two feet that had broken off the curved front legs. In the case of stand A, the left front foot had become detached by the time the stand was removed from the tomb (Plate 71).[23] This foot survived and has been reintegrated with the stand (Plates 72–73, 78–79). Since there is no way of knowing whether there was a back foot (or what it may have looked like), a simple block has been rendered in the drawings, replicated in Plexiglas for the stand's reconstruction (Figure 51; Plate 79).

The face of stand A was made from fifteen separate pieces of wood (numbered in Figure 62).[24] The three top boards (boards 1–3) were joined edge to edge using free tenons, which were fit into mortises cut in the edges of the adjoining boards (Figure 49). This joinery was secured with pegs run through the boards and tenons, showing through on the front and back surfaces of the boards (Figures 48–49; Plates 72–73, 98A–B). In order to maximize the strength of the assembly, boards 1–3 (and all the other elements of the stand as well) were cut with the wood grain running lengthwise; in this case, the grain ran horizontally, in the context of the assembled stand. As wood is strongest along the direction of the grain, tenons could viably be cut extending from the ends of the boards, but any tenons that extended from the edges of the boards would have been prone to breakage along the line of the grain. This is clearly the reason that separate, free tenons were used for the edge joints of the stand.

Also joined with free tenons were boards 5 and 6 and boards 8 and 9; the curved front legs were joined to board 7 (the central board) in the same manner. This was apparently a common technique, as it is widely attested in ancient coffins and ships (see Appendix 7). As is evident from the construction diagram of the stand's face (Figure 49), long expanses were joined edge to edge without the use of tenons. This arrangement suggests that glue was used as the primary means of joining the boards. The free tenons would have secured the joints; the pins, if driven through holes drilled slightly offset, could have served to pull the boards tightly together, facilitating the gluing process (see Appendix 7). Whether or not the pins served this purpose, it is possible—and even probable—that the boards were clamped tight while the glue was setting.[25]

Boards joined edge to end, with the grain of one running perpendicular to that of another, uti-

---

[19] This short strut provides further confirmation that the leg was straight. The strut was only long enough to accommodate a leg that extended straight down from the back piece. The short strut was joined to the face of the stand at the back of board 3, at the center near the bottom of the board. The mortise cut in the back of the face (Plate 73, center) received a tenon at one end of the short strut; the tenon broke off and is still in place, pinned into the mortise by a peg that was run in from the lower edge of board 3.

[20] Young, *GFB* 63, 164, and see above, p. 19.

[21] Young, *Gordion I*, 180.

[22] In 1981, two scroll feet were located at Gordion in an unlabeled box, but these could not have belonged to the

serving stands, since they were the feet of two curved legs that were round in section, not rectangular.

[23] In the case of stand B, both front feet had become detached (Plate 81).

[24] This number does not include the separate, free tenons used in the joinery of the stand's face. Young thought the "screen proper" was made from eleven pieces of wood. Young, *Gordion I*, 177.

[25] Phrygian woodworkers were capable of stupendous feats of glued joinery, as is shown by the Tripod Tray Table from Tumulus P. The large tray top was made from ten thick boxwood boards, butted edge to edge and glued, with no supporting mechanical joinery. Each of the complex legs was made from at least eight separate pieces of boxwood,

lized standard mortise-and-tenon joinery: tenons cut from the ends of boards were fitted into mortises cut in the edges of adjoining pieces. By this means, the three-board unit at the top of the stand's face (boards 1–3) was attached to the two long side boards (boards 4 and 10). All three top boards had tenons at the left and right ends, extending out along the direction of the grain. These tenons fit into mortises cut in the inner edges of the long side boards, the grain of which ran lengthwise from top to bottom. Other such combinations were joined using the same method (boards 5–9 joined to boards 1–3 and to the curved front legs; board 7 joined to board 11). These joints were secured by pins that were run through the boards, passing through the tenons.[26]

Young did not fully understand the mortise-and-tenon joinery of the serving stands, mistaking some of the standard (single) tenons for free (double) tenons (which he called "dowels"). This led to some confusion about the placement and function of the pegs, which he thought were "apparently inserted indifferently from the front or the back" of the stand's face.[27]

Thus the three pairs [of pins] which attest three dowels [free tenons] fastening the upper part of the framing piece at the right [board 10] to the ends of the three crosspieces beside it [boards 1–3] are not balanced by corresponding pegs at the other ends of the same dowels, for those were run in from the back and did not come through to the front.[28]

However, as is obvious from the rear view of the face of serving stand A, there are no pins at the ends of boards 1–3 at the back (Plate 73, at left). This is because this joinery utilizes single and not double tenons, as noted above. With one exception, the pins securing the joinery run all the way through the stand's face.[29] These pins would most likely have been run through from front to back, to maintain control over the working of the front surface and restrict potential breakout to the area of the back.

Young thought that the boards of the serving stands were first joined together and then inlaid, noting that inlay runs across joints and over pegs. He thought that the two long side boards were the last pieces to be added before the inlay work was begun.[30] Young's observations were valid, although the situation is somewhat more complex. The side boards of each serving stand (boards 4 and 10) seem to have been inlaid *before* they were joined to the central boards of the stand. Clear gaps in the background pattern, where it should run smoothly across the joints, were filled by adding pieces of inlay that do not always serve to align the patterns on the two adjoining pieces perfectly.[31] Furthermore, some of the meander squares on the side boards do not line up exactly with their counterparts on adjacent boards.

Such irregularities occur elsewhere; these are indications of the craftsmen's efforts to coordinate patterns on surfaces that were inlaid separately.[32] From this evidence, it appears that boards 1–3 were first assembled and then inlaid as a unit. Boards 5 and 6 were assembled and then inlaid, as were boards 8 and 9 and also boards 7 and 11 (with 12 and 13). The long side boards 4 and 10 were inlaid individually. All these separately inlaid units were then joined together and secured with pins. Finally, the gaps between the

---

with only one pin used in the entire assembly. The only mortise-and-tenon joinery was at the point where the legs were affixed to the table top. This indicates that some kind of clamping mechanism was used for the glued joints of the Tripod Tray Table. Simpson and Spirydowicz, *GWF*, 57–58, plates 71–73; Simpson, "Phrygian Furniture," 201–203.

[26] Pins are lacking in only three cases, all involving free tenons: the tenon joining boards 3 and 8, and the two tenons joining boards 9 and 10. The free tenon joining boards 3 and 8 is pegged all the way through the screen face at the bottom of board 3, but it is pegged from the back only on board 8 (indicated by a dotted pin in Figure 49). This joint must originally have featured a single tenon that extended up from the top of board 8. This tenon apparently broke off, necessitating the cutting of a mortise in the upper edge of board 8 to accommodate a new, free tenon. The two free tenons that joined boards 9 and 10 were unpegged, from

either the front or the back. Half of the original tenon is still in place in the upper mortise.

[27] Young, *Gordion I*, 177.

[28] Ibid. Young refers to the tenons at the right side of the top unit (boards 1–3) and the three pairs of pins visible at the top of the long right side board (board 10). As he assumed that these boards had been joined using free tenons, he looked for additional pins at the left of the joint.

[29] Only one pin appears at the back and not at the front; this is the pin at the top of board 8. Supra n. 26.

[30] Young, *Gordion I*, 177–179.

[31] This can be seen in the reconstruction drawing of the face of stand A (Figure 50), especially near the bottom of the common edge of boards 9 and 10. These boards no longer join properly in their present condition (Plate 72).

[32] For instance, the border pattern at the lower edge of board 3 doesn't coordinate flawlessly with the border pattern at the top of boards 5–9.

inlaid units were masked with added pieces of inlay, and the inlay was reworked over the pins (Plate 97A). The distribution of the inlaid designs on the face of stand A provides further evidence for this scenario (see below, p. 81, and Color Plate X).

The stand was inlaid in the same manner as the inlaid table: small pieces of wood were inserted into cavities and longer strips set into channels, which were first drilled and then carved out with a chisel (Plate 151B). Complex designs, such as the meander squares, were composed of multiple strips set into recesses cut in the shape of the designs (Figures 68–69). Before any cutting or drilling was done, the inlaid patterns were first drawn out with a knife, as indicated by faint guidelines visible in places on the stand's face. The carvers took advantage of the adjacent tenons, using them as surfaces on which to practice; this is evident from the incised graffiti found on seven such tenons, which would not have been visible after the stand's assembly (Figures 62–63; Plate 93; and see Appendix 6). One of these graffiti (A2) shows a group of four diamonds such as those in the inlaid background pattern on the stand's face. Another (A3) is reminiscent of the design of the central medallion. At least two are apparently efforts to test or prime the edge of the knife (A4, A6). After the inlay was completed, the surface was finally smoothed off by rubbing or scraping (see Appendix 7).

Serving Stand B ("Screen B")

5230 W 82
(MM 379)
Screen face, side pieces, back piece, back struts, tenons, pegs: boxwood (*Buxus sempervirens* L.); curved front legs, top piece: walnut (*Juglans* sp.); inlay: juniper (*Juniperus* sp.); foot blocks: yew (*Taxus baccata* L.).
Found along east wall of tomb, directly north of serving stand A.
Color Plates IIIA, IVB, XI, XIV–XV; Figures 52–59, 61, 64–65, 67B, 68, 70–71, 74–75; Plates 69, 80–89, 92, 94A–C, 95B, 96C–D, 97C–D, 98C–D, 99E–F, 124C, 133A, 135, 136B, 138, 150C, 151B; CD-Figures 70–73.

Inlaid face. G.P.H. without front feet ca. 92.5 cm; with feet ca. 94 cm. G.P.W. without front feet ca. 80 cm; with feet ca. 82 cm. G.P.Th. ca. 3.2 cm. G.P. outer diameter central medallion ca. 18.3 cm.
Inlaid side pieces. G.P.L. including tenons ca. 23.5 cm. G.P.H. ca. 13 cm.
Pierced back piece. G.P.L. ca. 79 cm. G.P.H. ca. 7.6 cm.
Openwork top piece. G.P.L. ca. 68 cm. G.P.W. ca. 17 cm.
Back struts. G.P.L. 9.5–67 cm. G.P.W. 3.2–4.5 cm. G.P.Th. ca. 2.3 cm.
Back leg (not extant). Est.H. ca. 86.5 cm. Est.W. ca. 5.8 cm. Est.Th. ca. 2.7 cm.
Left front foot. G.P.H. without foot block ca. 5.7 cm.
Inlaid meander squares outside front legs. G.P.H. ca. 3.7 cm. G.P.W. ca. 3.7 cm. G.P.W. inlay pieces ca. 0.2–0.3 cm. G.P. depth inlay ca. 0.25 cm.
Compass pricks preserved in: 1–2) center of rosette; 3–7) along outer circumference of rosette, just inside the solid inlaid circular strip.
Grain direction follows curve of front legs.

The catalogue entry in *Gordion I* for serving stand B reads "dimensions the same as those of MM 378" (serving stand A).[33] It states that stand B was put together in the same way as stand A, and that the inlaid decoration of the face was "almost exactly the same," except for variations in the pattern of the central medallion and lunette. No other information is given, nor were any other details recorded: the catalogue cards say "Same basically as W 81" (serving stand A). The cards indicate that differences occur in two places in the inlaid design: in the lunette above the "rose-window"; and in the "four clusters of maeander-squares under rose window." Finally, they note, incorrectly, that the openwork top piece has "slightly larger simpler circles" in the spaces between the three large rings.[34] However, as subsequent research has shown, there is much more to be said about this second serving stand.

Stand B did indeed resemble stand A in its basic form and decoration, suggesting that the two

---

[33] Young, *Gordion I*, 181.
[34] Gordion catalogue cards, Gordion archives, University of Pennsylvania Museum. This comment surely contributed toward the confusion between the top pieces of serving stands A and B.

stands were made and used together as a pair (Figures 50 and 58; 51 and 59). This is underscored by their placement next to one another in the Tumulus MM chamber (Plate 69). Like stand A, stand B was made of boxwood, inlaid with juniper, with a walnut top piece and curved front legs (Plates 82–84). The legs were flat at the back and rounded at the front, projecting from the surface of the inlaid face; the direction of the grain followed the curve of the legs, evident from surviving fragments. The front legs were crowned by star rosettes and ended in scroll-like feet, pinned to separate base blocks (Figure 61; Plate 92). Both foot blocks survive, but only one front foot is extant.

Above the star rosettes and supported by the front legs was a magnificent rosette medallion with a beveled border (Plates 69, 80, 87). Although the walnut legs have almost completely disintegrated, the central boxwood board with its inlaid medallion is in fine condition. Two arcs extend up from the beveled border, connecting it to the pendant half-circle above. Outside this central complex, the face of stand B is covered with rows of inlaid meander squares, like those on stand A, set into a field of inlaid diamonds and triangles. On both stands, meander squares also appear between the curved front legs, singly and in clusters, set into a second type of background pattern.[35]

The form of the two stands was also similar. Stand B had two inlaid, openwork side pieces, connected at their ends by a long, pierced back piece (Figures 53–56; Plates 85A, 86). Into the frame thus formed fit a carved top piece, featuring three large rings connected by subsidiary openwork patterns (Figure 52; Plate 84). As with stand A, a straight back leg (now gone) had once supported the back piece of stand B (Figures 55–56, 59). Four diagonal struts ran from the back leg up to the lower edge of the back piece (Plate 85A), and a short strut connected the back leg to the back of the stand's face (Plate 85B, 89).

The face of serving stand B was made from fifteen separate pieces of wood (Figure 64, with boards numbered). The faces of the two stands were constructed in a similar manner, from the same number of pieces, utilizing the same kind of joinery (Figures 49, 57; Plate 98). Groups of boards were first joined to form units, the units were inlaid, and the inlaid groupings were then assembled to make the stands' faces (see above, pp. 69–70). Both stands were inlaid according to the same method: the patterns were first drawn out with a knife on the boxwood, the depressions and channels were cut, the juniper inlay was inserted, and the surface was smoothed off. Like stand A, stand B had graffiti incised on some of its tenons (Figure 65, Plate 94A–C). With these similarities in mind, one may consider the ways in which the two works differ.

Serving stand B was somewhat shorter and wider than serving stand A (Figures 50, 58). The dimensions vary only slightly, but the effect produced is markedly different. Stand A looks taller and thinner, its central medallion is placed higher up on the stand's face, and the lunette above the medallion is less than a full half-circle. The front legs of stand A appear longer and have an upward thrust, while those of stand B seem compressed by the weight of its larger rosette/lunette complex. Stand B's front feet are simpler, lacking the double moldings of the feet of A. At the top of the legs, the star rosettes are also different: those on stand B are more detailed, composed of many more pieces of inlay (Figure 67B). The star rosettes on both stands are oriented slightly off the vertical.

The beveled border of stand B's central medallion is different from that of stand A. On both stands, the central, raised band of the border is inlaid with a row of diamonds flanked by inward-facing triangles. This familiar pattern is featured on the legs and struts of the inlaid table (see, for instance, Figure 22). This same pattern also occurs on the outer bevels of the stand A border. On stand B, however, the outer bands display a different pattern: that of the lattice-like background that surrounds the meander squares on the stands' inlaid faces.

Within its beveled border, stand B's central rosette was laid out with a compass, as indicated by seven small pricks visible at the center and around the periphery. The design features inlaid droplets and triangles of various shapes and sizes, all united by a continuous, undulating curve. At

---

[35] The background pattern between the curved front legs is essentially the same on both stands. An anomaly on stand B occurs above the two swastikas at the center of the field. Here, sections of a different inlaid pattern have been inserted, apparently due to a spacing problem that was not anticipated. This filling ornament is also found elsewhere on stand B, below the meander squares in the bottom row of designs to the left and right of the curved front legs.

first glance, this appears very different from the rosette of stand A, but closer inspection reveals that the two designs are actually closely related. The continuous curve of the stand B rosette can be formed by connecting the four predominant curves of stand A's rosette; the orientation can be aligned by rotating either design 45 degrees. This type of clever manipulation is reminiscent of the ornament on the inlaid table. The two arcs and lunette above stand B's rosette are decorated with the familiar pattern of diamonds bordered by inward-facing triangles.[36]

On stand B, there are 181 inlaid meander squares (or portions thereof) above and to the sides of the two front legs and rosette/lunette complex.[37] Fourteen squares run across the width of both serving stands: stand B has fifteen rows of squares running from top to bottom, while stand A has sixteen, adding to the impression of its greater height. Serving stand B has the equivalent of ten square designs between the curved front legs, fewer than the 18 designs in the bottom panel of stand A.[38] In addition, the inlaid side pieces of the two stands differ in their decoration. The inlaid outer border on stand B's side pieces is formed by a solid strip running around the perimeter (Plate 86; Figures 53–54). Similar strips border the eight square cutouts of each side piece, and between these strips run single rows of squares. This is a kind of reversal of the inlaid design on the side pieces of stand A, which have rows of squares for the borders and solid strips running between them (Figures 45–46). This overt play with pattern again recalls the designs on the inlaid table.[39]

Serving stand B's pierced back piece seems to have had a straight lower edge (Plate 85A; Figures 56, 59). Although the piece is damaged at the center, it has no projections extending down at the left and right ends (as on stand A), suggesting that there was also no projection at the center. As with stand A, mortises in the lower edge of the back piece received tenons at the top of the back leg and diagonal struts, all of which supported the back piece from below.

Stand B's openwork top piece is quite unlike that of stand A. Its three large rings were cropped by the framing border and connected to one another by crosses, the longer arms of which reached out to the borders (Figure 52D). In the quadrants formed by the crosses are small rings, carved to look as though they are strapped together with thin, flat bands. These relief bands appear only on the tops of the small circles; on the underside, the circles are beveled and the bands are absent. A similar arrangement can be recognized in the early drawing by Dorothy Cox (Figure 2), which is supposed to represent "screen A," but features a rendition of stand B's top piece. In the Cox version, however, there are far too many small circles in the quadrants created by the crosses. This hybrid surely contributed to the confusion over the top pieces of the two serving stands.[40]

The border of stand B's top piece is largely missing, and the surviving fragments are degraded and shrunken. Although the top view can be reconstructed in a drawing (Figure 52D), it is difficult to produce a definitive section. The three large rings may have been thicker than the border, extending somewhat at the top and bottom of the frame (Figure 52A–B); it is also possible that the rings extended beyond the frame only at the bottom or not at all (Figure 52C).[41] In the reconstruction drawings included here (Figures 55–56, 59), the first option has been adopted.[42] Stand B's elaborate top piece was carved from a single piece of wood.

---

[36] Andy Seuffert's drawing of the central medallion of serving stand B is correct in its essentials but does not show the design as circular. Young, *Gordion I*, 181, figure 107.

[37] Or 182, if one counts the fifth design in the bottom row, to the left of the left front leg, which is triangular and lacks the hooks of the other designs.

[38] There are actually eight proper meander squares in the area between the two front legs on stand B's face. The elongated hook configuration at the top left appears to be made from two separate square designs joined together.

[39] The left side piece of stand B has 17 squares running down its left end, but the corresponding inlay on the left edge of the stand's face shows only 13 squares (Figure 54). This suggests that the side pieces were inlaid separately and then attached to the face, as was the case with stand A.

[40] The situation was further exacerbated by a photograph published in *Gordion I* showing fragments of the

"screen B" top piece with the pieces placed incorrectly. Young, *Gordion I*, plate 81A.

[41] The preserved corner section seems to indicate that the large rings were thicker than the border; the edge strip attached to the ring at the other end suggests that the rings and border may have been the same thickness. Because of the condition of the wood, the relationship between the rings and border cannot be understood with certainty.

[42] All damage aside, if the border were thick enough to accommodate the three big rings, as in either of the alternatives shown in Figure 52C, it would be thicker than the height of the top sections of the side pieces above the first row of cutouts (see Figure 55). The frame would have then hung down into the area of these cutouts, partially blocking the view through the openings. This seems inconsistent with the aesthetic preferences of the Phrygian cabinetmakers.

The serving stands' faces were constructed in a similar manner, although their joinery was not identical (Figures 49, 57). In three instances, where tenons were secured with a single pin on serving stand A, two were used for the comparable joint on stand B. The reverse is also true, noticeably in the case of the six double tenons that secured the edge joints of the top three boards (Plate 98). Stand B featured a few more tenons, including two free tenons that joined the curved front legs to the bottom board (board 11).[43] One of stand B's mortises was begun and abandoned: a mortise was cut in the right edge of board 9 (see hatched rectangle in Figure 57), and a corresponding mortise was outlined but never cut in the edge of board 10. On stand B (as on stand A), the pins were run through the boards of the face, passing through the tenons, and were normally visible on the boards' front and back surfaces.[44] On both stands, glue was surely used in combination with mortise-and-tenon joinery.

The walnut front legs of stand B had simple scroll feet that sat on blocks of yew (Plate 92). The blocks were joined with T-shaped elements that were fit into mortises cut in the feet and pinned (Figure 61). Both feet had broken off their legs and are missing in photographs of the stand after its removal from the tomb (Plate 81). One of the feet is extant, still pinned to its foot block; the other disintegrated, but its block has survived (Plates 82, 92). The well-preserved foot, found loose on the tomb floor, may have been wrongly associated with the stand's back leg by Young (see above, p. 19).

Finally, the face of stand B provides additional information about the inlay process. Faint, incised lines are visible in areas, indicating that preliminary grids were drawn to serve as guidelines for the elements of the inlay patterns (Fig-

ure 70). One triangle at the left of board 11 was sketched out but never inlaid (Figure 70C–D; visible in Figure 58, to the right of the left front foot); a second occurs below the central medallion, at the upper left corner of the field of inlay (Figure 58). These vestiges suggest that the entire inlaid pattern was first drawn out on the wood by incision. As three extant graffiti show, the artists who incised this pattern practiced their technique on the exposed tenons (Figure 65; Plate 94A–C).[45] Graffito B1 is the most complex, incorporating a six-petalled, compass-drawn rosette, straight cut-lines, and what look like four characters. Two unplaced tenon fragments also bore graffiti (Figure 66; Plate 94D). These fragments were certainly from the serving stands, but their exact location could not be determined (see Appendix 6).

Form and Function

The identification of the Tumulus MM "screens" as serving stands was prompted by research carried out on the "screen" from Tumulus P at Gordion, prior to its conservation in 1983.[46] The Tumulus P "screen" had a top piece featuring two large rings, set within a rectangular frame and connected by a group of four lunate segments. The large rings are octagonal in section, and deposits of bronze were found on the inner bevels of both rings.[47] This indicated that round-bottomed vessels had once sat in the rings: if bronzes had merely fallen on the wood as it lay on the floor of the tomb, the bronze residue would surely have appeared on areas other than the inner bevels. The large rings of the top pieces of the Tumulus MM serving stands were then examined, and depressions and dark patches were noted on their inner top surfaces (Plates 74A, 84A), suggesting

---

[43] On stand A, the front legs were not joined directly to the bottom board with mortise-and-tenon joinery except at the board's left and right ends, which ended in tenons that were fit into mortises cut in the scroll feet.

[44] There were three exceptions. In the first case, a single pin was run into the back of the right side board (board 10) at the bottom. The pin runs out the side of the board and into the adjacent board (board 9). This pin, not visible on the front face, is indicated by a small oval at the bottom of the board shown at the left (board 10) in Figure 56 and Plate 83. In addition, two other pins were run in from the back of the stand's face: these were to secure the short strut that ran from the back leg of the stand to the back of the face. The pins were run in at an angle, one on either side of the mortise cut in the back of board 7, to secure the

tenon at the end of the short strut (visible in Plate 83). They were effective—the tenon broke off and is still in place in the mortise. Serving stand A also featured a pinned tenon joining the short strut to the back of the stand's face. The pin was driven up through the bottom edge of board 3 along the joint and is visible as a small depression at the top of board 7 (Plate 73).

[45] As with serving stand A, there may be more graffiti on the tenons that remain inside the mortises.

[46] Simpson and Spirydowicz, *GWF*, 52–54.

[47] These deposits are visible in the upper left quadrant of the left ring and the lower right quadrant of the ring at the right, as shown in Simpson and Spirydowicz, *GWF*, figure 65. The top piece was carved from a single boxwood board.

that they had also held bronze vessels.[48] While these dark, damaged areas are not as dramatic as the bright green bronze deposits of the Tumulus P stand, the bronze vessels associated with the three stands confirm that all served the same purpose.

Found near the collapsed stand on the floor of the Tumulus P chamber were 20 bronze bowls, two bronze ladles (TumP 8–9), and a matched pair of small bronze cauldrons (TumP 3–4).[49] The size of the small cauldrons suggests that they had sat in the rings of the top piece. The two ladles were undoubtedly used with the cauldrons, to transfer whatever they had contained into the bronze bowls found nearby. East of the serving stand against the south wall was a large bronze cauldron (TumP 2). This may also have been used in conjunction with the serving stand and other bronze vessels.[50]

The same types of bronze vessels were found near the serving stands in Tumulus MM, but in much greater quantity (see above, pp. 9–10). Ten small cauldrons (MM 4–13), in matched pairs, and two bronze ladles (MM 47–48) were found behind and near the serving stands along the east wall of the tomb (Color Plate VIB–C). The small cauldrons had evidently been hung on the wall above the stands, suspended from iron nails, and had fallen to the floor when the nails broke.[51] Also in the vicinity were two fine bronze situlae, one ending in a ram's head (MM 46), found behind stand A, and the other ending in a lion's head (MM 45), found to the south of stand A against the wall (Color Plate VII). Three large cauldrons (MM 1–3) sat on iron stands near the south wall of the tomb (Color Plate VB; Plate 36B). Inside the large cauldrons were pottery jars containing desiccated chunks of food (Color Plate VIA). Strewn over the area were bronze jugs and bowls, some of which contained organic residues (Color Plate IIIB). Analyses of the residues from the bronzes have allowed us to identify the food

and drink remains (see Appendix 5); this has shown how the vessels were used with the serving stands, enabling us to reconstruct the funeral ceremony that took place before the king's burial (Frontispiece; see Chapter 8).

Comparanda: Other Ancient Vessel Stands

The Tumulus MM and P serving stands had the same general form and fulfilled the same function but differed in several respects. The Tumulus MM stands were larger and could accommodate up to three vessels each, while the Tumulus P stand could hold only two. The top pieces of the Tumulus MM stands are more elaborately carved and were supported by back pieces, inlaid side pieces, back legs, and diagonal struts. The Tumulus P stand's top piece projected out toward the back with nothing to support it except the back leg and two diagonal struts.[52] This leg curved out toward the rear and ended in a scroll foot.[53]

The front faces of all three stands are exquisitely inlaid, with some similar motifs, but many of the designs are different. The lower part of the Tumulus P stand's face is constructed in openwork, and the 15 large squares at the top include patterns not found in the Tumulus MM repertoire (Figure 91). This is also true of the design of the rosette, which is carved in openwork; the ornate inlaid configuration beneath the rosette; and the three small squares below it. By contrast, the Tumulus MM stands' faces are solid wood, completely covered with intricate inlay, and featuring a grid of square designs set into a lattice-like background, itself composed of thousands of tiny diamonds and triangles. All three stands feature a prominent rosette medallion, with two arcs rising at the top to support a lunette-shaped crowning element. On the Tumulus P face, this top section is surrounded on three sides by a checkerboard border.

---

[48] The best-preserved ring of serving stand B has a fairly uniform indentation along the inner part of the ring; the middle ring has depressions at the top and bottom with deposits; and a deposit can also be seen at right on the inner part of the right-hand ring. The top piece of stand A shows an apparent depression along the inside of the right-hand ring. The middle ring is shiny and dark toward the inside at the top, and the left-hand ring shows the same kind of damage over its entire top and inner surface.

[49] Young, *Gordion I*, reconstructed plan of Tumulus P, opposite p. 7. The serving stand, bronze vessels, and other furniture fragments were found in the southwest corner.

[50] Other objects were found in the southwest corner of the tomb, including juglets, jugs, one glass bowl, wood plates, and at least three stools. The bronzes may have been stacked on tables, perhaps the two three-legged plain tables, whose location in the tomb was not recorded. Simpson and Spirydowicz, *GWF*, 59–60.

[51] Young, *Gordion I*, 110–111. Their disposition on the floor suggests that they had hung on the wall arranged in pairs.

[52] Simpson and Spirydowicz, *GWF*, figure 64.

[53] As has been demonstrated, this was not the case with the Tumulus MM stands. See above, p. 68.

Curved front legs support the central medallions on all three stands. Those of the Tumulus MM stands are rounded at the front, while those of the P stand are flat and inlaid with a bold checkerboard pattern. The front feet of the Tumulus P stand are highly abstract, with flat faces inlaid with vertical stripes, although the back foot has toes or claws and resembles the scroll-like front feet of the Tumulus MM stands. This suggests that the front feet on all the stands represent animal paws, in varying degrees of abstraction. Despite certain differences between the three serving stands, several features remain constant, particularly regarding the main elements of the composition on the lower part of the stands' faces. These common features are the key to understanding the symbolism of the decoration and will be addressed below (pp. 87–110).

Assemblages from Tumulus W and Tumulus K-III at Gordion suggest that there had also been serving stands in these tombs. In Tumulus W, a very fragmentary "screen" was found, collapsed on the tomb floor.[54] The "screen" was carved from several boxwood boards in a series of openwork panels, featuring lattices of squares and lozenges as well as rosette-like patterns, all studded profusely with hemispherical bronze tacks.[55] Although no top piece or legs were preserved, the dimensions of the surviving fragments and the nature of the decoration suggest that this was a serving stand nonetheless. This impression is born out by the collection of bronze vessels and implements found near the "screen." These included two small cauldrons (TumW 3–4), two ladles (TumW 7–8), two large cauldrons (TumW 1–2), and 15 bronze bowls.[56] The ladles and bowls had all been placed in one of the large cauldrons (TumW 2).

Tumulus K-III contained fragments of wooden furniture that were carved in openwork, resembling the lower half of the face of the Tumulus P stand, and studded with bronze tacks, recalling the decoration on the Tumulus W "screen." The excavators thought this piece was a chair back,[57] but its form and decoration suggest that it was a serving stand instead. Evidence of a top piece survived, in the form of fragmentary wooden rings. Two rings were found connected, and two bronze bowls had sat in their tops.[58] The archaeological context provides support for this identification, as the K-III bronzes included four small cauldrons; one medium-sized cauldron; a large, lidded cauldron on an iron tripod stand; one ladle; and 27 bronze bowls.[59]

Finally, there may also have been a serving stand in Megaron 3, from the destruction level of the city mound:

Nearby were small strips cut in varying shapes—chevrons, zigzags and so forth—which had once been the inlay in a piece of furniture with inlaid decoration similar to that of the screens from the Royal Tomb [Tumulus MM] and Tumulus P. More substantial bits, probably from the outer framework of a screen or chair-back, had been liberally decorated with round-headed bronze studs, recalling the furniture fragment from Tumulus Pauline [Tumulus W]. Yet another fragment pierced by openwork squares recalled again the fragment from Pauline, and the throne-back from Tumulus P.[60]

These fragments are catalogued as the "first piece of furniture" from Megaron 3.[61] A "nest of corroded bronzes," including a ladle and an omphalos bowl, was found in the same room.[62] Whether the "first piece of furniture" was a serving stand or not, the bronzes suggest that there may have been one in the room.[63]

Elsewhere in the ancient Near East, three- or four-legged stands for individual vessels were

---

[54] Young, *Gordion I*, 217–218, plate 94G.

[55] The reconstruction drawing in Young, *Gordion I*, figure 129, has been superseded. See Simpson and Spirydowicz, *GWF*, 68–70 and figures 91–96.

[56] See Young, *Gordion I*, 199–207 and figure 116 (tomb plan). The remains of the small cauldrons are shown in figure 118 and plate 88B–C.

[57] Körte and Körte, *Gordion*, 49–51 and figure 9.

[58] Ibid., 52, no. 6.

[59] Ibid., 68–75.

[60] Young, "Gordion Campaign of 1959," 239–240. See also Mellink in *Gordion I*, 264–265, after Young. Tumulus W acquired the nickname "Pauline" from "the old-time movie

serial *The Perils of Pauline*" because of the dangers associated with its excavation. *Gordion I*, 193.

[61] 5817 W 83, 5916 W 90; 5813 B 1186, 5815 B 1188, 5816 B 1189. The "first piece of furniture" cannot be clearly identified in terms of the extant fragments.

[62] Young, "Gordion Campaign of 1959," 239.

[63] Other finds of bronze vessels, but without any furniture, suggest the possible presence of additional serving stands at Gordion. Two small cauldrons and fragments of a third were found in Tumulus K-IV; in one of the cauldrons was a ladle. With these were found bronze studs, which the excavators thought might have belonged to a "sarcophagus." Körte and Körte, *Gordion*, 100–101. The presence of the

widely used. Multiple-vessel stands were much less common, however, to judge from extant examples, representations, and descriptions in ancient texts. Single-vessel stands with splaying legs and oblique strutwork survive in wood from New Kingdom Egypt and appear in reliefs and in paintings.[64] Similar types occur in the Near East; in both areas, multi-vase stands are found infrequently.[65] Depictions suggest that the Near Eastern types might be made of wood or wicker, although metal may also have been used, as indicated by Urartian examples.

Metal tripod cauldron stands with oblique strutwork are known from Urartu, along with a few unusual metal stands for multiple vessels.[66] Two rare multi-vase stands made of bronze rods are attributed to Urartu, but nothing is known of their find spots, as they were not scientifically excavated. One has a square top piece with openings for four vessels, supported by two sets of crossed legs that end in hoof feet.[67] The second has three legs in a crossed arrangement, which support a top piece of three conjoined rings; another small tripod can be set up at the middle of the top piece to hold a fourth vessel at a higher level.[68] Although some wooden furniture has been excavated at Urartian sites, no wood serving stands have survived.[69]

Elaborate metal versions were known in western Anatolia, as attested by Athenaeus, who records Hegesander's comments on the iron vessel stand dedicated at Delphi by the Lydian king Alyattes. Herodotus called the stand a ὑποκρητη-ρίδιον.[70] According to Athenaeus:

But I too have seen it where it stands as an offering in Delphi, truly worth seeing on account of the figures of insects worked in relief upon it, as well as other tiny creatures and plants; it is capable of holding upon it mixing-bowls and other vessels besides.[71]

Regarding stands for single vases, Athenaeus states that in his day "The poor have one of wood; the rich, of bronze or silver."[72]

The Assyrians had stands for multiple vessels, which are known from several depictions. One is represented on an Assyrian-style ivory plaque from Nimrud, showing a banquet scene with a king or dignitary seated on a chair before a fancy table.[73] To his right, guests sit on stools and drink from bowls and cups. At the left is the stand, which holds three vessels with pointed bottoms and narrow, flaring necks. The vessels appear to be superimposed on the stand's top piece, the artist's convention to indicate that the vessels were sitting in rings or holes in the top. The stand has animal legs and lion-paw feet, which occur in other Assyrian examples.

A similar but taller stand is shown on a fragment from the Balawat gates in the Louvre.[74] Here again is a banqueting dignitary, seated before a table and attended by servants. To his right is the vessel stand, holding two large jars, which extend down below the level of the top piece. This stand apparently has four legs, connected by a stretcher, and lion-paw feet, as well as decorative corner fittings that extended out at the level of the top piece.

K-IV ladle in one of the small cauldrons shows that the ladles and cauldrons were used together. Fragments of three ladles were found at Gordion in the seventh century B.C. Tumulus S-1. Young, *Gordion I*, 227–229; Kohler, *Lesser Phrygian Tumuli*, 121, 124. Two ladles were found in Middle East Technical University excavations in Ankara: one from the Great Tumulus and a second from Tumulus I, found inside a small cauldron. Buluç, *Ankara Frig Nekropolünden Üç Tümülüs Buluntuları*, 101–104; plate 12:8–9.

[64] For two well-preserved wooden examples, see Killen, *Ancient Egyptian Furniture 1*, plates 116–118 (18th Dynasty, British Museum). For a painted depiction, see the tomb of Djeser-ka-re-seneb, Thebes. Lange and Hirmer, *Egypt*, color plate XXV. The same type is shown in relief in the tomb of Kheruef, Thebes. Lange and Hirmer, plates 166–167.

[65] Gubel, *Phoenician Furniture*, 262–270, and figures 62–63. Collon, *Cylinder Seals V*, plate IX. For early evidence of what appears to be a multiple-vessel stand from Mesopotamia, see an Early Dynastic seal impression in H. Baker, *Furniture in the Ancient World*, figure 254.

[66] For the large bronze tripod stand and cauldron from Altıntepe, dated to the late eighth or seventh century B.C., see Azarpay, *Urartian Art and Artifacts*, plate 30. For two

unexcavated (plundered) examples of the eighth or seventh century B.C., see Merhav, *Urartu*, 236, no. 30a (Karlsruhe); and 242, no. 39a (Munich).

[67] Merhav, *Urartu*, 258, no. 4 (Munich), dated to the eighth-seventh century B.C. See also Seidl, "Urartian Furniture," plate 56.

[68] Merhav, *Urartu*, 206–207, no. 2 (Les Arcs), supposedly dated to the reign of Ishpuini, ca. 830–810 B.C., based on the four inscribed bowls now associated with the stand. As the stand was unexcavated, the bowls cannot be attributed to the stand with certainty, and thus the stand cannot be dated by the inscribed bowls.

[69] See above, pp. 45–46 and 63.

[70] Alyattes, ca. 610–560 B.C. Athenaeus, *Deipnosophistae* 5.210, and Herodotus 1.25.

[71] Athenaeus 5.210. According to Athenaeus, after Herodotus, the stand of Alyattes was made by Glaucus of Chios.

[72] Ibid. Athenaeus, ca. A.D. 200.

[73] Metropolitan Museum, New York, No. 59.107.22. Mallowan and Davies, *Ivories in Assyrian Style*, plate V:7; Dentzer, *Le motif du banquet couché*, 33, plate 5, figures 31–32.

[74] Louvre AO 22.280/81. Dentzer, *Le motif du banquet couché*, 49, plate 13, figure 80.

A third stand is pictured on a relief showing an Assyrian camp, from the Northwest Palace at Nimrud.[75] At the right, prisoners are being led in, and in the center, horses are groomed and watered. At the left is a circular enclosure divided into four sections, in which a meal is being prepared. In the upper left quadrant is a vessel stand that holds four vessels. These are arranged in two tiers, although this may be the artist's convention to indicate four jars in a level top piece. Aside from the two-tiered effect, this stand is like those in the other depictions, with four legs, connected by a stretcher, and lion-paw feet.

A provincial variant is shown on a relief from Karatepe.[76] As with the Assyrian examples, this stand is part of the banqueting equipment of a dignitary, who sits enthroned in front of a table. The exact form of the vessel stand is not certain, although it seems to be a kind of bench with a tray-type top that holds two jars. The Karatepe rendering, along with the evidence from Assyria and Urartu, leaves little doubt that the Gordion stands are exceptional. A close examination of the designs on the stands' faces indicates the extent of their sophistication and complexity.

Designs on the Serving Stands

Comparison of the inlaid ornament on the two serving stands supports the impression that they were made as a pair. Already noted is the correspondence between the inlaid patterns on the side pieces, as well as the close relationship of the central medallions on the stands' faces. The most intriguing evidence can be found in the inlaid square designs, or "meander squares," on the faces of the two stands. The correlations among these square designs are not immediately apparent but can be discerned through an analysis of the designs and their groupings. The meander squares are arranged in rows, producing the appearance of order and symmetry. The order breaks down, however, when the individual squares are considered. Although the faces of the stands exhibit general bilateral symmetry, this does not carry through to the form of the square designs or their distribution. The mean-

der squares are composed of hooks in a great variety of configurations. An initial examination of the various distinct designs yields no indication of any rigorous system of organization.

This is evident in the first row of squares running across the top of stand A's face (Figure 50). Five different types of patterns appear in this row, in no obvious orderly sequence. The second row features eight different types, five of which occur also in the first row. Some of these types alternate, but not with any regularity. The first square in the second row is the same as the second square in the first row. This suggests that the designs might run diagonally. However, the second square in the second row differs slightly from the first square in the first row, calling this theory into question. Moving along, the third square in the second row is the same as the first in that row, and therefore the same as the second square in the first row. If one looks at the third row, the theory of diagonals is again suggested. However, the fourth square in the third row is different from some of those running diagonally above and below it.

The arrangement in the upper right-hand corner of the serving stand complicates the issue further. New designs run down the far right side, on the long side board of the stand's face (board 10). These new designs do not find counterparts in the adjacent section at the left (boards 1–3). This seemingly intractable situation can be resolved by a series of color diagrams (Color Plate XA–D, CD-Figures 66–69) through which the patterns on the stand can be decoded. If the individual designs on stand A are numbered (Figure 73), and then each design is assigned a color, one can immediately grasp their distribution on the stand's face (Color Plate XA, CD-Figure 66). A look at this first color diagram shows that the designs run diagonally only in certain areas, with no general organization apparent. However, a kind of underlying scheme does exist, but it cannot be recognized by considering the individual designs and their distribution. Instead, the key is a particular *type* of design that appears in various manifestations.

At first glance, the first and last designs in the top row on stand A's face seem to be mirror images of one another, in an arrangement that is

[75] Assurnasirpal II, r. 883–859 B.C. Smith, *Assyrian Sculptures, Shalmaneser III*, plate XVI:1. Mallowan, *Nimrud and Its Remains*, figure 44 (after Layard, *Monuments of Nineveh*). A drawing appears in H. Baker, *Furniture in the Ancient World*,

figure 333.
[76] Banquet relief, South Gate, eighth century B.C. Symington, "Hittite and Neo-Hittite Furniture," plate 33.

bilaterally symmetrical. In more common terms, it appears that the first design has been flipped over in order to form the second.[77] A closer look reveals that this is not true. The first design (at the far left) is a kind of swastika, but two of the arms do not meet at the center; the arms that do meet form a continuous strip running horizontally through the middle of the design. The last design (far right), although similar to the first, instead has a continuous strip running vertically through the middle. The last design can be formed from the first, by rotating the first design 90 degrees and then flipping it. This unusual swastika differs significantly from the standard form of the design.

The classic swastika is based on a cross, which has both bilateral and rotational symmetry.[78] Arms are added at the ends of the bars of the cross, running perpendicular and extending in uniform direction (Figure 71A–B). This produces a swastika, and destroys the bilateral symmetry of the cross, leaving only the rotational. The incipient rotation is overt, although the cross (with its bilateral symmetry) is still embedded in the pattern. This is what makes the swastika such a dynamic figure.

The standard swastika is symmetrical with respect to rotations of 90 degrees. That is, if the design is rotated a quarter turn (in either direction), the resulting design will replicate the original. The swastikas on the serving stands, while resembling the classic type, have one of the bars of the cross pulled apart at the juncture, which further limits the symmetry (Figures 71C–D). Such a design must be rotated 180 degrees in order to replicate the original. The swastika with

broken central bar epitomizes most of the designs on both serving stands. Although these designs take many forms, almost all are symmetrical with respect to rotations of 180 degrees.

Any of these special designs, when rotated 180 degrees, will reproduce the original. However, all other operations on these designs will yield something different. Although the number of possible operations is unlimited, only three other square designs can be produced in place of the original:[79] the original design rotated 90 degrees, the original design flipped,[80] and the original rotated 90 degrees and then flipped.[81] This is true no matter how many times the initial design is rotated or flipped (or in what sequence or combination). Including the original design, then, exactly four possibilities exist for each of these special configurations. The Phrygian artisans understood this phenomenon, manipulating a few basic designs to create the seemingly endless variety that covered the serving stands' faces.[82]

There are actually only three basic or "main" designs on serving stand A and two on serving stand B, all with 180-degree rotational symmetry. Numerous transformations were created by turning and flipping them, forming groups based on the main designs. Finally, there were several subsidiary designs on both stands that did not fall within the main groups. These utilized elements from the main designs but did not have their special symmetry. A total of 17 square designs occur on stand A (Figures 72–73), although most of the meander squares were based on the three main designs (Figure 72:1–3).[83]

The first main design, A1, is the swastika with broken central bar (Figure 72:1; Plate 99A).

---

[77] Weyl, *Symmetry*, 4–5 and figure 1. In the case of these essentially two-dimensional designs, the mapping that results in a mirror image (or reflection in a central line) is equivalent to a rotation of 180 degrees in space, or "flipping," around the central line (or axis). Here, the term flipping will be used for this kind of mapping, as it appears likely that a template was actually flipped to create certain of the variations described below.

[78] Ibid., 66. If a cross is flipped around either its vertical or horizontal axis (or reflected in a vertical or horizontal line), the same design will appear. The cross can also be replicated by a rotation of 90 degrees (or any multiple).

[79] That is, any of these operations, singly or in combination, will produce only three other square designs that are aligned along the vertical and horizontal axes and occupy the same plane. This is assuming that such operations are performed on the intact original design, without alteration to the design's basic form. Outside the main design groups such alterations do occur, but this changes the symmetry of the designs that are affected (see below, pp. 79–81).

[80] Flipping one of these special designs around either the horizontal or vertical axis will produce the same result.

[81] These two operations may also be performed in the reverse order with identical results.

[82] Simpson, "Phrygian Artistic Intellect," 29–34. Young was prompted to note in *Gordion I*, 179, that no two of the squares of serving stand A were alike, even though "the variations of actual pattern may be only six or eight in number."

[83] "Main" designs and their transformations have been ordered here according to the frequency of their appearance. Within design groups, the design taken to be the "main" design is that which occurs most frequently, the first transformation of that design is next, and the second transformation (if such exists) occurs with the least frequency within the group. One elongated design occurs on stand A (Figure 72:10); if added to the square designs, a total of 18 different inlaid "meander square" designs occur in the field of the face of stand A. For the purpose of this discussion, the hook design in the lunette above stand A's central medallion

Formed from this is a second design, which may be designated A1T1, with "A1" indicating the first main design on stand A, and "T1" its first transformation (Figure 72:1T1). A1T1 is the original design rotated 90 degrees and flipped, in its first (and in this case only) transformation. These two meander squares form the first design group on serving stand A.[84] They are familiar from the previous discussion: A1 is the first design in the first row of squares on the face of stand A, and A1T1 is the last in this row, at the upper right corner.

The second main design, A2, is a squared figure-eight, running diagonally, with hooks extending out at the top and bottom to fill the empty quadrants (Figure 72:2; Plate 99B). Although A2 differs from the swastika, it has the same kind of symmetry. This design was used in two transformations: A2T1, the original design rotated 90 degrees (Figure 72:2T1); and A2T2, the original rotated and flipped (Figure 72:2T2). These three designs comprise the second design group on stand A.

The third main design, A3, is a closed square with hooks extending in from the four sides (Figure 72:3; Plate 99C). This too is different from the swastika design, although a swastika can be recognized in the light background pattern created by the dark inlay. Two transformations of design A3 are utilized for the third design group: A3T1, the original design flipped (Figure 72:3T1); and A3T2, the original rotated 90 degrees (Figure 72: 3T2). The artists who devised stand A's ingenious decoration created three separate designs that were symmetrical with respect to rotations of 180 degrees. Each was unique, and each satisfied the exact conditions required for this limited type of symmetry.

Thirteen individual square designs occur on serving stand B, although most of the squares of the face are variations on the two main designs

(Figures 74–75). The first main design, B1, is a closed square with hooks projecting in from the four sides (Figure 74:1, Plate 99E). This resembles design A3 on stand A, but the hooks that project from the left and right sides of B1 are joined at the center. This creates a horizontal median line, which differentiates B1 from A3 and results in yet another special design with 180-degree rotational symmetry. The first design group on stand B consists of B1 and two transformations: B1T1, the original design rotated 90 degrees and flipped (Figure 74:1T1); and B1T2, the original rotated 90 degrees.

The second main design on stand B is the familiar swastika with broken central bar (Figure 74:2, Plate 99F; see also Figure 71D). Design B2 is a variation of A1 (A1 flipped), the first main design on stand A. Two transformations of B2 occur: B2T1, the original design rotated 90 degrees (Figure 74:2T1); and B2T2, the original rotated 90 degrees and flipped (Figure 74:2T2). The second design family on stand B is related to the first on stand A, and both stands include one particular design: B2T1 is essentially the same as A1T1, except that the arms of B2T1 each have one extra turn.[85]

In total, then, four distinct designs, all with the same type of symmetry, are used in five main groups on the Tumulus MM serving stands. On serving stand A, *group 1* designs occur 87 times, *group 2* designs 49 times, and *group 3* designs 31 times. On serving stand B, *group 1* designs appear 88 times, and *group 2* designs 89 times (82 times in the main field outside the curved front legs).[86]

Besides its main design groups, each serving stand has a number of subsidiary designs, some of them forming groups themselves (Figure 72:4–10; Figure 74:3–8). With only two exceptions (A6 and B4), these subsidiary designs stand outside the main scheme, for they do not have the same

is not considered here; it is ultimately a derivative of design A1 (see below, p. 100, n. 229). Two of the subsidiary designs on the stands do have 180-degree rotational symmetry (A6 and B4); these designs are discussed below.

[84] The numbers allotted here to design groups reflect the frequency of the main designs on which they are based. In general, *group 1* designs are most frequent, *group 2* designs are second most frequent, and so forth. On stand A, this order is clear; on stand B, the two main groups occur with almost the same frequency (see below, n. 86).

[85] The meander squares on stand B are slightly larger and somewhat more ornate than those on stand A. The arms of the hook configurations on stand B generally feature more turns than those of their stand A counterparts.

[86] The design groups on stand A are ordered in a clear hierarchy, with group 1 designs occurring by far the most often. On stand B, the designs of groups 1 and 2 occur 88 and 89 times respectively—that is, with almost the same frequency. Group 1 is based on design B1, which occurs 46 times, more often than any other design on the stand's face. Designs of group 2 occur with a total greater frequency, but those of group 1 are more numerous in the main field outside the curved front legs of the stand. Seven group-2 designs appear in the central panel between the curved front legs, below the central medallion; a doubled square ("2T2D") occurs at the upper left of this panel. The designs in this area are not part of the complex system that functions within the main field of the stand's face.

restricted symmetry as the five main groups.[87] Some have rotational and bilateral symmetry (A4 and A9), some have bilateral symmetry only (B3 and B6), and the remainder are asymmetrical configurations, composed of elements from the other designs (A5, A7, A8, A10, B5, B7, B8).[88]

Except for A4, which is the sole occupant of the area between the curved front legs of serving stand A, the subsidiary designs are confined to brief appearances. The frequency of the various designs and their groups can be tabulated (see chart below).

	Serving stand A			Serving stand B	
Design	*Occurrences of square designs*	*Occurrences of design groups*	*Design*	*Occurrences of square designs*	*Occurrences of design groups*
1	44	} 87	1	46	
1T1	43		1T1	26	} 88
			1T2	16	
2	27		2	44	
2T1	15	} 49	2T1	38	} 89*
2T2	7		2T2	7	
3	23				
3T1	6	} 31	3	4	} 6
3T2	2		3T1	2	
4	20	} 23	4	1	
4T1	3		5	1	
			6	1	
5	2		7	1	
5T1	1	} 4	8	1	
5T2	1				
6	4				
7	1				
8	1				
9	1				

*Group-2 designs occur 82 times in the main field outside the curved front legs.

Number of occurrences of square designs and design groups on the serving stands.

Some of the subsidiary designs are obvious derivatives of others (indicated by the notation "D" in Figures 72–75).[89] For instance, A6 is a derivative of A1, with the horizontal median bar of A1 broken at the center. Others are apparent derivatives, but the relationship is less overt. B3 can be derived from B1 through a more complex series of transmutations: B1 is first rotated 90 degrees, and the left (or right) half is then flipped to form the other half of B3. By extension, B3

---

[87] Subsidiary design B4 is unusual, as it is the same type as A2, one of the main designs on serving stand A. However, it appears only once on stand B and occurs in no transformations.

[88] Design A10 is a variant, formed of a square design (although compressed) with an added hook configuration extending from the right border. A few design fragments (and one doubled square) occur on the stands' faces. The fragments are found to either side of the curved front legs and were used to accommodate their curve within the rectilinear grid. Some of these fragments derive from the square

designs, although they have not been considered "meander squares" for the purpose of this discussion. The fragments are indicated on the diagrams shown in Figures 73 and 75 with a "D" for "derivative" following the numbers of the designs from which they may have been taken. On derivatives, see below.

[89] For example, (1D) following the number of a design indicates that the design in question has been derived visibly from the first main design. In the overall design scheme, derivatives may be used in place of the designs on which they are based, but they do not always fulfill this function.

is related to the entire first group of designs on stand B. This is true for all the design derivatives. The close relationship among the main designs is underscored by these derivatives, which can be tied to any number of designs through various permutations. A5 is particularly interesting, as it can be seen as a derivative of A1 (with the lower left quadrant flipped) or of A2 (with the upper right quadrant reconfigured). As will be apparent, this dual aspect of A5 is surely not a coincidence (see below). A few subsidiary designs, such as B8, are highly distinctive but can still be related to their various counterparts. This principle of derivation is borne out when one considers the general layout of the designs in their groups.

As already noted, the meander squares on stand A fall into no general pattern if the individual designs are identified and charted separately (Color Plate XA, CD-Figure 66). Some of the designs alternate to produce running diagonals, but this occurs only in certain areas and is not consistent over the face of the stand. Various designs from groups 1 and 2 predominate on the upper part of the face (boards 1–3), whereas an assortment from groups 1, 3, and 4 occurs on the lower sections (boards 5–6, 8–9). A1 and A2T1 alternate on the left side board (board 4), but A1T1 and A3 run down at the right (board 10). The scheme on the top three boards (boards 1–3) coordinates with the left side board (board 4) but not the right (board 10), which aligns more closely with the designs on the lower part of the face. The great variety of pattern can be appreciated from the first color diagram. Finally, the squares between the two front legs show no alternation, as they are all of one design (A4).

Stand B exhibits the same seemingly unsystematic distribution, but with the designs laid out in rows instead of diagonals (Color Plate XIA, Figure 75, CD-Figure 70). The top part of the face (boards 1–3) features designs B1 and B2 along with a few other designs. The left side board (board 4) shows B1T2 alternating with B2T2, except at the top (B3). The right side board (board 10) has the same design at the top (B3) but otherwise B1T1, B1T2, and B2T1 alternate. As with stand A, a different set of designs occupies the lower part of the face. Squares of design B2T1 occupy most of the area between the curved

front legs. The first color diagram shows several blank squares, which signify the subsidiary designs. Most of these are derivatives of the main designs, which, when considered as close variations, can be given the colors of the designs from which they are derived. This is reflected in the second color diagram for stand B (Color Plate XIB, CD-Figure 71). This produces a more uniform arrangement, with the various design units more clearly demarcated.

In terms of stand B's inlaid decoration, boards 1–3 are a unit, each side board is a separate unit, and so are the board groups to either side of the central medallion complex (boards 5–6 and boards 8–9). These board groupings are the same as those that were recognized earlier, when the stands' joinery and inlay methods were considered (see above, pp. 68–71). The distribution of the individual designs on stand B's face bears out the theory that each of these board groups was joined and inlaid separately, before the entire face of the stand was assembled. The distribution of designs on the face of serving stand A also supports this idea. When the design derivatives on stand A are given the same colors as the designs from which they derive, the units become clearer (Color Plate XB, CD-Figure 67), although the patterns are not as consistent as those on stand B. The derivative designs on stand A are most informative when the main design *groups* are charted.

If each main design group on stand A is assigned a separate color, a more coherent pattern emerges (Color Plate XC, CD-Figure 68). On the top three boards (boards 1–3), designs of groups 1 and 2 alternate in diagonals, except at the center left, where several subsidiary designs appear. This pattern coordinates with that on the left side board (board 4), on which designs from the same groups alternate from top to bottom. The right side board (board 10) shows alternating designs from groups 1 and 3, and this aligns with the patterns on the lower part of the stand's face. Here also, designs from groups 1 and 3 alternate in diagonals, although the pattern is disrupted by subsidiary designs to the right of the front legs. The meander squares between the curved legs are all of design A4 (Plate 99D), which was clear from the first two color diagrams.[90] The rest of the

[90] Design A4, which does not have the same symmetry as A1–A3, is nonetheless an important feature of stand A's inlaid decoration. It was used mostly in the bottom panel, but it also appears on the main part of the stand's face five times. In total, it occurs 23 times on stand A and is therefore treated in the design analysis.

configuration is new, however, and much simpler, proving that the designers did indeed start with an underlying scheme as the basis for the stand's complex inlaid decoration.

Designs from group 1 predominate over the face of stand A, alternating with those from the other two main groups. In terms of pattern, boards 1–3 were conceived as a unit, as were each of the two side boards (boards 4 and 10) and the areas to the left and right of the front legs (boards 5–6 and 8–9). The overall scheme was first established, based on design groups, and then individual designs were turned and flipped to add variety and even a sense of mystery, as is shown by the deliberate attempt to obscure the underlying rationale. The subsidiary designs on stand A yield additional information about the inlay process and provide an unexpected glimpse of the artists at work. As has been noted, subsidiary designs could act as substitutes for the main designs.[91] Thus A6, a derivative of A1, was used in place of A1 for the second design in the second row, fitting nicely into the diagonal program of the upper left-hand corner. A6 and the other derivatives can be assigned the colors of their respective design groups for the fourth color diagram (Color Plate XD, CD-Figure 69). However, four of the subsidiary designs are not so easily rendered. These form a fifth group and occur on the top section of the face, to the left of center.

The designs of the unorthodox group 5 are difficult to classify. A5 and its transformations A5T1 and A5T2 resemble both A1 *and* A2 and might be considered derivatives of either (see above, p. 81). A5 is in fact a combination of the two: the left half of A5 is essentially the left of A2; the right half of A5 is the right of A1. For the purpose of the color diagram, each of these bipartite designs can be assigned the two colors of A1 and A2. These two-colored squares are part of an irregular arrangement on the upper face that interrupts the diagonals of the underlying pattern. For the source of this anomaly, one must turn to the design and construction processes and, ultimately, to the woodworkers who planned, sketched out, and inlaid the patterns.

Fourteen meander squares run across the face of stand A at the top, forming the first of 16 rows of squares that cover the surface (Figure 73). The top part of the face, above the central medallion complex, features eight full rows and 14 columns. As already shown, the three-board unit at the top of the stand (boards 1–3) was joined and inlaid before being attached to the side boards (boards 4, 10). This three-board unit had 12 inlaid squares in the top row (numbered 2–13 on Figure 73). Thus, there is an even number of designs running across in rows, whether one considers the full face of the stand or the three-board unit. In the upper left corner of the face, designs from groups 1 and 2 alternate for some distance in the first row, beginning with group 1. They also alternate in the second row, beginning with group 2, and so forth. This kind of alternation in rows and columns will produce the diagonals that characterize the underlying pattern (see Color Plates XC–XD, CD-Figures 68–69).

If carried through across the width of the stand, this system would create a uniform field of alternating diagonals. It seems clear that this was the intent, at least regarding the central three-board unit. At both the left and right of this unit, designs from groups 1 and 2 alternate in rows and columns (with only one exception) until the scheme is interrupted.[92] This occurs in the area of the anomalous group-5 designs, beginning with column 4 and ending with column 7. The reason for this interruption relates to the assembly of the face from the board units. This technique was clearly employed in order to facilitate the inlay process: such relatively small units would provide greater access to the areas to be inlaid. Even with such manageable units, however, the artists would have needed to work in from all the edges. This was particularly true of the top section (boards 1–3), which was the largest of the board groups with the greatest amount of inlay. Working in this manner, the artists made an inadvertent error that was not discovered until they reached the area of columns 4–7.

A design from group 2 (A2T1) occurs at the upper left of the three-board unit. This appears as the second design in the first row on the stand's

---

[91] As indicated in Figure 72, subsidiary designs A6 and A7 are derivatives of A1. As already noted, A6 is similar to A1, but with the horizontal median bar broken at the center. A7 also resembles A1, but with its lower right quadrant flipped around the vertical axis. A8 may be considered a

derivative of A2: A8 is A2T2 with its lower right quadrant rotated 180 degrees.

[92] The exception is square 11 in row 1, which is a group-1 design (A1), although it should be group 2.

assembled face (Figure 73). Another design from group 2 (A2) occurs at the upper right of the unit (square 13 in the first row). This choice created an unanticipated problem. As the design groups must alternate in order to produce the pattern of diagonals, the groups at the far left and right *should have been different*, because there is an *even* number of squares in each row. The pattern on the fourth color diagram suggests the probable scenario. Two artists, working from the left and right sides of the top unit, each began with a group-2 design in the top row. They met to the left of the center, only to realize that they could not align their inlaid sections. The group-5 designs were enlisted, along with other variations, to coordinate the two sections and mask the error.[93]

The situation on serving stand B is more straightforward. In terms of individual designs, the top unit (boards 1–3) features the main designs B1 and B2, and their derivatives, running across the stand in alternating rows (Color Plate XIB). B1 designs fill the entire top row, with B2 designs in the second row, B1 designs again in the third, and so forth. The two long side boards (boards 4 and 10) have various designs from groups 1 and 2 alternating along their length, except at the top.[94] The board groups to the left and right of the central medallion (boards 5–6 and 8–9) show designs of groups 1 and 2 running across in alternating rows.[95] Finally, the area between the two front legs features mainly B2T1, with some additional ornament.

The distribution of the subsidiary designs on stand B can be recognized in the uncolored squares of the first color diagram (Color Plate XIA, CD-Figure 70). Many of these were derived from the two main designs and were substituted for them (Figure 74:3, 5–7). One of these designs, B4, is not an obvious derivative, and in fact replicates design A2 on serving stand A. However, its position in row 2, which is filled with group 2 designs and derivatives, suggests that it, too, was considered a group 2 subsidiary. Designs B3 and B3T1 occur in six places, in place of both B1 and B1T1. This kind of substitution makes sense when

the individual designs are set aside and the design *groups* are considered.

When each main design group is assigned a separate color, a surprisingly uniform scheme appears (Color Plate XIC, CD-Figure 72). Rows of group 1 designs alternate with rows of group 2 designs, from top to bottom, with a few subsidiaries intervening. When the derivatives are given the colors of their respective design groups, a completely regular grid appears (Color Plate XID, CD-Figure 73). This simple series of alternating rows provides the basis for the complex system of designs on stand B. As with stand A, the designs were rotated and flipped to add variety and obscure the basic plan. This orderly design grid, although hidden from the viewer, contributes to the *gravitas* projected by stand B. This can be contrasted with the high-keyed energy of stand A, which arises from its dynamic underlying pattern.

The system of ornament on the stands' faces can thus be apprehended. The dazzling effect of the inlaid decoration derives ultimately from the nature of the meander squares and their artful manipulation. When considered within their visual context, these designs achieve an even greater power. The field of diamonds and triangles into which the squares are set has the complete symmetry of a lattice, producing an impression of regularity and static balance over the surface of the stands' faces.[96] This highlights the restricted symmetry of the meander squares, which evoke a whirling motion within the lattice border. The squares also embody the potential to interact with their various counterparts in the complex design system. The powerful, subliminal effect produced by the serving stands' ornamentation results from this juxtaposition.

Comparanda: Designs

The swastika and other hook designs, as well as lozenge and lattice patterns, have been discussed above in terms of the inlaid table (pp. 50–56). As the evidence suggests, these motifs were very likely protective or apotropaic—and may have

---

[93] It is of course possible that the same artist did all the inlay on this three-board unit, first working from one side and then the other. The problem arose because the underlying scheme was not correctly anticipated.

[94] Designs B1T2 and B2T2 alternate down the left side board; designs B1T1, B1T2, and B2T1 run down at the right.

[95] Rows 9, 11, 13, and 15 feature designs B1T1 and B1T2;

these alternate with rows of design B2T1. On boards 8–9, the designs in five of the rows find exact counterparts on the adjoining side board at the right.

[96] The lattice has bilateral and translational symmetry (repetition in sequence) and is also symmetrical with respect to rotations of 90 degrees.

had more specific meanings relating to Phrygian religion and the ruling political dynasty. The inlaid decoration on the Tumulus MM serving stands provides further support for this theory. The individual designs, as well as the prominent rosette/lunette grouping with supporting curved legs, can be elucidated through comparison with the arts of neighboring areas.

Designs with rotational symmetry were used in the Near East from a very early period. In Mesopotamia and Iran, these designs were often composed of figures and can be found on neolithic and chalcolithic pottery. Examples include human figures as well as horned stags, goats, or birds alternating with fish in a circular arrangement.[97] This figural component is retained into the third millennium B.C., as featured in the archaic seal impressions from Ur, which depict remarkable motifs based on humans and animals. One seal impression shows a group of four crossed figures in a complex arrangement, with eight legs akimbo and four arms bent in the form of a swastika, reaching out to grasp four ankles of the adjacent figures. This design is symmetrical with respect to rotations of 90 degrees.[98] Another seal impression shows two men, back to back, legs and arms extended, with each figure holding the ankle of his neighbor's rear leg. This motif has the restricted symmetry of the meander squares on the Tumulus MM serving stands—it is symmetrical with respect to rotations of 180 degrees.[99] The Ur seal impressions show several other designs with this restricted

symmetry: two snakes set within a rectangular panel,[100] four heads (two men and two bulls) arranged around a central pivot,[101] and several abstract renditions.[102]

These radial patterns composed of four figures have counterparts in a wide variety of cultures.[103] The four components can represent four divisions of a tribe, and, ultimately, the mythical ancestors of cosmic "genealogical clans." Such quadripartite designs may have local interpretations or involve the four cardinal points, the four winds, the "four quarters" of the universe, or the four seasons of the year—all of which are, themselves, metaphors for a genealogical tetrad system.[104] A common origin for the form has been suggested, based on its wide distribution, although if there was an original common meaning, this has now devolved, accompanied by progressively schematic types of representation. It is possibly this devolution, in remote antiquity, that produced the swastika and its variations.[105]

Designs with rotational symmetry are found in Anatolia as early as the neolithic period, but these are schematic and not figural as in Iran and Mesopotamia. The lozenge-and-dot motif on the stamps from Çatalhöyük, with the "dot" framed by opposing hooks, exhibits 180-degree rotational symmetry.[106] Patterns with rotational symmetry are also found on stamps and pottery from Hacılar, particularly in the interiors of painted bowls.[107] By the third millennium B.C., fully developed schematic systems appear in the art of Alacahöyük, Mahmatlar, and elsewhere.

---

[97] Mellaart, *Earliest Civilizations of the Near East*, 65; Mallowan, *Early Mesopotamia and Iran*, 33; and see above, p. 52, n. 143.

[98] Legrain, *Archaic Seal-Impressions*, plate 21:393. Another example, with the same type of symmetry, shows four figures arranged in a square, arms and legs extended; the right hand of each figure holds a dagger, and the left hand of each grabs his neighbor's ankle. A more abstract motif is formed by four bull's legs, arranged as a wheel with a swastika at its center. Legrain, plates 25:454, 30:518.

[99] Ibid., plate 15:286. Next to the two men is an emblem formed by two intertwined snakes. While this design is imperfect, clearly it was intended to have the same restricted symmetry. The seal impression shown in plate 14:274 shows two men arranged in a similar configuration.

[100] Ibid., plate 15:284.

[101] Ibid., plate 21:394. Number 398 on the same plate shows a slightly different design made with the same components and having the same type of symmetry.

[102] Although not perfectly symmetrical with respect to rotations of 180 degrees, these designs were meant to evoke this type of symmetry. Legrain, *Archaic Seal-Impressions*, plates 21:398, 401; 23:417–418, 421–422.

[103] Schuster and Carpenter, *Social Symbolism in Ancient & Tribal Art*, 1:2, 523–609, on "split and quartered patterns."

[104] Ibid., 570–571, patterns from the Solomon Islands, Sumatra, Micronesia, West Africa, and North America (Navaho Indian); 601, from Siberia, the Sahara, Chile, Mongolia, and North America (Winnebago Indian). Within the quarters of these patterns can be found schematized human figures, animals, or more abstract motifs, including quartered circles with dots, whorls, and swastikas.

[105] See, for instance, B. Goff, *Symbols of Prehistoric Mesopotamia*, 8; figures 32–35, which show that four females in a radial arrangement may be symbolized by a swastika.

[106] Mellaart, *Çatal Hüyük*, plate 121 (CD-Figure 86); 220, figure 56, right. Levels VI–II, sixth millennium B.C. This motif is discussed above, in relation to the Tumulus MM inlaid table, p. 54.

[107] Sixth millennium B.C. Both 90-degree and 180-degree rotational symmetry are represented here. See, for instance, Mellaart, *Excavations at Hacılar*, figures 187:2,3 (stamps); figures 89:4, 125, 126:1–3, 130:2 (painted pottery). An interesting design painted on both sides of a bowl resembles a swastika, although one deviant arm breaks up the symmetry (plate LXIX:1).

Classic swastikas occur on the bodies of vessels,[108] on their bases,[109] and on a famous bronze "standard" from Tomb B at Alacahöyük (CD-Figure 80).

The openwork standard takes the form of a lozenge, containing 16 swastikas arranged in a grid.[110] The lines of the grid serve as borders for the swastikas, and run parallel to the four sides of the lozenge. In the main field, two versions of the swastika are used, one with the arms bent clockwise and the other counterclockwise. These two versions are interrelated, since the flipping of one version will produce the other. The two forms alternate within rows of the grid but repeat along the diagonals. Because of the orientation of the lozenge, the diagonals of the grid become the "rows" of the lozenge. Thus, the swastikas repeat in these "rows," which run in alternating directions from top to bottom. Larger designs are produced in the field, and the openwork adds an aspect of dark/light interplay to the patterns. At the apex and two side corners hang single, loose swastikas in lozenge panels; these are suspended so that they can actually flip, in a physical manifestation of the alternating patterns on the standard.

The scheme on the Alacahöyük standard is clearly a progenitor of the design system on the Tumulus MM serving stands. However, no comparable geometric ornament survives from the intervening period in Anatolia.[111] After more than a millennium, complex pattern-based decoration appears again, as if without precedent, in the art of Phrygia. Although the Phrygians may have brought this style with them when they migrated to Anatolia, presumably from the Balkans,[112] the standard from Alacahöyük shows that the im-

pulse existed in central Anatolia already. The style may have been transmitted through textiles, which have already been noted as carriers of artistic tradition.[113] Some of the serving stands' designs did occur on textiles, both at Gordion and in neighboring areas.

Geometric patterns are preserved on textile fragments from Tumulus P at Gordion. One of these has been reconstructed as a meander square with 180-degree rotational symmetry, closely related to the third main design on serving stand A. Also preserved are lozenges, which have been reconstructed with quadripartite divisions.[114] Carbonized textiles were recovered from the destruction level of the city mound, and these, too, have been reconstructed in drawings.[115] No meander squares are evident, but S-shaped hooks occur, forming figure-eight designs as well as intervening patterns—both symmetrical with respect to rotations of 180 degrees. Other motifs include lozenges, containing single crosses or groups of four; squares, bordered by rows of crosses; and stepped zigzags, in thin stripes or wide bands. While none of these reproduces the patterns on the serving stands exactly, the fragments show that the patterned textiles at Gordion were magnificent.

A stone relief from the city mound shows the lower part of a figure, seated on a throne cushioned with decorative textiles (Plate 119C).[116] These feature hook configurations that recall the patterns on the serving stands and inlaid table. Some additional evidence exists on a sherd from Gordion, depicting two women, with arms raised, holding each other's hands (Plate 116D).[117] They appear to be dancing, perhaps also singing, and they hold the hands of two other figures at

---

[108] K. Bittel, *Die Hethiter*, 31, figure 12.

[109] Akurgal, *Art of the Hittites*, plate 15, lower left.

[110] Ibid., plate 7, top. Supra, p. 52, n. 144. The swastika at the bottom is incomplete, squared off to accommodate the base of the standard.

[111] Several seal impressions from the site of Acemhöyük (19th–18th centuries B.C.) show designs with radial patterns. One such design has four griffin protomes, facing left, arranged around a central pivot (90-degree rotational symmetry). Another shows a guilloche-cross at the center, superimposed on a pattern of four interconnected spirals (180-degree rotational symmetry). N. Özgüç, "Seal Impressions from the Palaces at Acemhöyük," figures III-50, III-55. See also the contemporary seal impression from Kültepe in N. Özgüç, *Seals and Seal Impressions*, plate XIC, and whorl designs on seal impressions from Karahöyük, such as Alp, *Zylinder- und Stempelsiegel*, 252, figures 248–249. These carry on the tradition of the Ur sealings. Although these designs indicate a high level of artistry in Anatolia in the Assyrian Colony Pe-

riod, they provide no evidence for the type of sophisticated system of interrelated designs that characterizes the geometric ornament on the Alacahöyük standard. For a comparable design on a stamp from Central Asia, see Pittman, *Art of the Bronze Age*, 57, figure 26C.

[112] On the Phrygian migration, see Muscarella, "Iron Age Background to the Formation of the Phrygian State," and Drews, "Myths of Midas and the Phrygian Migration from Europe."

[113] See above, p. 54.

[114] Ellis, "Textile Remains," Fabric G, 305–308, figures 147–148, plate 101C–D. Figure 148 and plate 101D show a square design with hooks coming in from the sides. This is a permutation of design A3, with a swastika in reserve.

[115] Bellinger, "Textiles from Gordion," plates 10–16.

[116] 7689 S 86. City mound, TBT-CC/CC2. The patterned elements seem to indicate cushions and not part of the throne itself. See p. 115 below.

[117] 9399 P 3763. Surface find, 1967.

the left and right. Their robes, presumably Phrygian, are covered with a network of lozenges, each lozenge containing a dot.

The most important visual resource for central Anatolian textiles of the period is the relief sculpture of King Warpalawas, king of Tyana, known from Assyrian annals as a contemporary of Tiglath-pileser III (r. 744–727 B.C.). Warpalawas is depicted on a monumental rock relief at Ivriz (Plate 119D),[118] near Konya, and on a stele from Bor (CD-Figure 97).[119]

On both reliefs, Warpalawas very possibly wears Phrygian clothing, or clothing made of Phrygian textiles. This is suggested by the motifs, which are known from Phrygian pottery and furniture; many of these designs are found on the serving stands from Tumulus MM. On both reliefs, the king wears a long robe, covered with geometric patterns, and a cape with bands of decoration. At Ivriz, this is pinned with a Phrygian fibula.[120] Warpalawas also wears a fitted cap and shoes with upturned toes, as well as a bracelet, a necklace, and a Phrygian-style studded belt.

At Ivriz, the predominant pattern on the king's robe is a grid of squares, each with a dot at the center. At the bottom is a border of swastikas, with broken central bars and 180-degree rotational symmetry.[121] Of the two visible swastikas, one is the first main design on serving stand A, and the other is the first swastika flipped—and also the second main design on stand B. The sumptuous robe is edged at the hem with fringe, and fringe also decorates the king's cape. Three bands of lozenges occur on the cape, such as those seen on various parts of the Tumulus MM

inlaid table. The king stands before a colossal god of vegetation, who wears a kilt and horned cap, and holds sheaves of grain in his left hand and a vine with grapes in his right.

On the Bor stele, the king wears a fringed robe with a deep bottom border, consisting of four rows of elaborate patterns. These include rosettes, complex hook designs, classic swastikas, groups of four swastikas, volute and cross patterns, and, apparently, pairs of S's (design 6 on serving stand A).[122] The king's cape shows three bands of decoration, two with lozenges and one with square designs. Just why Warpalawas should have been wearing Phrygian-style clothing can only be surmised. He may have been a close ally, received the cloth as a diplomatic gift, or perhaps was dressed in the latest and most prestigious fashion. Support for this last idea comes from the realm of Assyria.

A new style of Assyrian clothing became popular during the second half of the eighth century B.C., characterized by square panels that covered the entire garment in a grid-like arrangement. This style appears on the reliefs of the Assyrian king Tiglath-pileser III, worn by both the king and members of his retinue (CD-Figure 98).[123] Toward the end of the century, small towers are introduced into the square panels, during the reign of Sargon II (r. 721–705 B.C.).[124] These paneled textiles were apparently a royal prerogative, and were also associated with deities.[125] The Assyrians have been seen as the originators of this style of garment, which may have been adopted by their neighbors, including the Urartians and the Phrygians, finally making its way to Greece. Thus the clothing of Warpalawas may show the

[118] Akurgal, *Art of the Hittites*, 139–140, color plate XXIV, plate 140. Boehmer, "Phrygische Prunkgewänder," figure 3.
[119] Northeast of the site of Ivriz. Boehmer, "Phrygische Prunkgewänder," figure 4. Bittel, *Die Hethiter*, figures 330–331. Muscarella, "Fibulae Represented on Sculpture," 84 and figure 6.
[120] Only the Ivriz relief shows the king wearing a fibula. The Bor stele is broken and part is missing (as shown in CD-Figure 97), although a fibula has been restored based on the relief from Ivriz. Muscarella, "Fibulae Represented on Sculpture," 83–84, figure 6, right.
[121] The swastikas on the king's robe are simpler versions of their counterparts on the Tumulus MM serving stands.
[122] Boehmer, "Phrygische Prunkgewänder," 152. Boehmer theorizes that some of these designs were embroidered. See Pliny, *Natural History* 8.196, for the claim that the Phrygians invented embroidery. For an earlier origin, see Dalley, "Ancient Assyrian Textiles and the Origins of Carpet Design," 119.

[123] Boehmer, "Phrygische Prunkgewänder," figures 16–19.
[124] Ibid., figure 21. This type of panel decoration is carried through to Persian garments, visible in color on the glazed brick portrayals at Susa (late sixth century B.C.). Harper, Aruz, and Tallon, *Royal City of Susa*, 226, cat. 155. The pattern makes its way farther east, found in barrow 5 at Pazyryk (fourth/third century B.C.), decorating an actual textile. Rudenko, *Frozen Tombs of Siberia*, plate 177B.
[125] For paneled garments worn by images of deities, see Pritchard, *ANEP*, figure 538; Oppenheim, "Golden Garments of the Gods," 183, figure 11. From Smith, *Assyrian Sculptures, Shalmaneser III*, plate 10. In this relief from Nimrud, four statues of deities are paraded by the army of Tiglath-pileser III as booty from a conquered town; one of these deities is most probably Ishtar, or one of her foreign counterparts. The decoration on such garments may have represented the celestial sphere. See Oppenheim, "Golden Garments of the Gods," 180–181, on AN.MA, "garment of the sky."

influence of Assyrian textiles.[126] It is also possible that the Phrygians developed these paneled textiles, given their tradition of geometric art. Whatever their local origin, the patterns go back to a much earlier source. The square designs arranged in a grid, as well as the lozenge-and-dot and lozenge network, are all related to the ubiquitous "genealogical patterns." These patterns seem to have retained their religious significance, whether in a specific or general sense, and were utilized by the Assyrian kings as protective royal devices.[127]

Additional evidence for Assyrian textile designs has been recognized in the sculpted stone slabs that decorated the thresholds of Assyrian palaces. Twenty-six examples have been catalogued, dating from the eighth and seventh centuries B.C.[128] The earliest is from the palace of Tiglath-pileser III at Nimrud; six slabs date to the reign of Sargon II (Khorsabad, Nimrud). The latter are characterized by fields of square panels arranged in an overall grid. The panels contain rosettes or quatrefoil motifs, such as found on the Pazyryk carpet.[129] These carved reliefs recall the Assyrian royal garments, and also the inlaid faces of the Tumulus MM serving stands. All this evidence suggests the possibility that the panel-and-grid decoration on the stands was meant to evoke textiles. However, the central rosette/lunette complex, along with its curved

legs, finds no counterpart in the textile comparanda. To understand this group of elements, one must first examine the symbol of the rosette in the Near East, which had a long association with major female deities. The rosette and curved legs on the serving stands' faces can ultimately be related to the great Phrygian mother goddess Matar.[130]

Stars and Rosettes as Symbols of Near Eastern Goddesses

Rosettes and stars as well as sun and moon symbols were widely used in the Near East to represent deities. In Mesopotamia, the sun-disc symbolized the sun-god Shamash, the crescent or lunar disc the moon-god Sin, and the rosette or star the Akkadian goddess Ishtar or her Sumerian counterpart Inanna, "Queen of Heaven and Earth."[131] The stone tablet of Nabû-apla-iddina, king of Babylon, provides clear evidence for the meaning of these signs in the ninth-century B.C. (Plate 116A).[132] The tablet shows Shamash enthroned in his shrine at Sippar; in front of the god is a large sun-disc on a stand. At the left, the king is being led into the presence of the god by a priest.[133] Three symbols can be seen above the sun-god: a lunar disc, a sun-disc, and a star rosette, which are labeled, "Sin, Shamash, and Ishtar."[134]

The rosette seems to have symbolized the great goddess Inanna, "guardian of essential cos-

[126] Boehmer, "Phrygische Prunkgewänder," 160–166. It should be noted that the local resident Assyrians were importing textiles into Anatolia as early as the Kültepe tablets, early second millennium B.C. Barber, *Women's Work*, 168–171.

[127] On the protective function of ornamental Mesopotamian textiles, see also Oppenheim, "Golden Garments of the Gods," 190–191; Stronach, "Patterns of Prestige in the Pazyryk Carpet," 24.

[128] Albenda, "Assyrian Carpets in Stone," 12–18. Strommenger and Hirmer, *Art of Mesopotamia*, plate 230 (Sennacherib).

[129] Albenda, "Assyrian Carpets in Stone," plates 2–7. Rudenko, *Frozen Tombs of Siberia*, plates 174–175.

[130] See Simpson, "Symbols on the Gordion Screens," for the initial statement of the arguments. For a discussion of the term "symbol," the migration of "live" religious symbols, and the "lingua franca" of symbolism, see Goodenough, *Jewish Symbols in the Greco-Roman Period*, 27–38.

[131] Van Buren, *Symbols of the Gods in Mesopotamian Art*, 82–85 (star); Van Buren, "Rosette in Mesopotamian Art" (rosette). The star is sometimes found in contexts not obviously associated with Ishtar/Inanna, making it difficult in these cases to determine whether it symbolized the goddess or had a more general astral significance; the star might also accompany other deities. Van Buren, *Symbols of*

the Gods in Mesopotamian Art*, 82. For the various aspects of Inanna/Ishtar, see Bahrani, *Women of Babylon*, 80–90, 141–160; Westenholz, "Goddesses of the Ancient Near East," 72–75.

[132] British Museum, BM 91000. Pinches, "Antiquities Found by Mr. H. Rassam at Abu-Habbah (Sippara)." King, *Babylonian Boundary-Stones*, 120–127. Woods, "Sun-God Tablet of Nabû-apla-iddina Revisited." Pritchard, *ANEP*, figure 529. The tablet records the restoration of the shrine of Shamash, which had previously been desecrated, by Nabû-apla-iddina (r. ca. 887–855 B.C.).

[133] Woods, "Sun-God Tablet of Nabû-apla-iddina Revisited," 45–50.

[134] The lunar disc contains a pendant crescent at the bottom. The sun sign resembles the large disc on the stand in front of the shrine. The sun-disc encloses a four-pointed star, with four wavy elements alternating with the arms of the star and emanating from a small circle at its center. The star or star rosette has eight points (or petals) radiating from a circle at the center. The inscription was read by King as "Sin, Shamash and Ishtar are set over against the heavenly ocean, within the divine judge." King, *Babylonian Boundary-Stones*, 121, n. 2. It was read by Woods as "Sin, Šamaš, and Ištar are depicted opposite the Apsû, between Nirah (and) the pillars." Woods, "Sun-God Tablet of Nabû-apla-iddina Revisited," 62.

mic sources," as early as the late fourth–early third millennium B.C.[135] It appears on vessels, in inlay, and on wall decorations from the Eanna precinct of Inanna at Uruk, as well as on re-lated seals.[136] These early rosettes commonly had eight petals, with pointed ends, a feature that may have led to the star-like rosette of Ishtar in later periods.[137] Perhaps this later manifestation was connected with the worship of the goddess as the morning and evening star.[138] An attribute of Inanna/Ishtar was the lion, which could ac-company her, support her, or adorn her throne.[139] The lion and rosette were also adopted for the goddess's foreign counterparts. This occurs in an example from Iran, a statue of the goddess Narundi from Susa of the late third millennium B.C. (Plate 116B).[140] Narundi sits on a throne decorated with four guardian lions, one at each side and two at the back. At the front of her footrest are two confronted lions, flanking a cen-tral rosette, in a symbolic version of the subject of the larger sculpture.

This transference of motifs continued into the second millennium B.C., as attested by numer-ous depictions of a West Semitic goddess type, standing on a lion.[141] These have been diffi-cult to identify, with candidates ranging from Asherah, the "Mother of the Gods" and con-sort of El at Ugarit, to Anat, Astarte (Akkadian Ishtar, Hurrian-Hittite Shaushga), or Qedeshet (*qdš*, Akkadian *qadištu*), all three of whom hold the title "Lady of Heaven, Mistress of All the Gods."[142] A likely candidate is Qedeshet, a Syro-Palestinian goddess worshipped in Egypt, shown with a lion in all representations in which she is identified by inscription.[143] These deities, shown with and without lions, are often nude, with outstretched arms, holding flowers, snakes, or pairs of animals. They may wear their hair as a Hathor-style wig, with various types of head-dresses, such as a disc with crescent, or horns sur-mounted by a sun-disc or rosette.[144] The adop-tion and adaptation of these common motifs make it difficult to identify individual deities from

---

[135] "The Exaltation of Inanna," third hymn of Enhedu-anna, priestess of Nanna at Ur and daughter of Sargon, king of Akkad (r. ca. 2334–2279 B.C.). Meador, *Inanna*, 171. Pritchard, *ANET*, 579–582.

[136] Late Uruk period, ca. 3500–3000 B.C., and the sub-sequent Jemdet Nasr. Van Buren, "Rosette in Mesopota-mian Art," 99–103. B. Goff, *Symbols of Prehistoric Mesopotamia*, figures 479–480; see also Strommenger and Hirmer, *Art of Mesopotamia*, plate VI, top. Walls and columns within the Eanna precinct were decorated in the cone-mosaic tech-nique, with patterns of zigzags, alternating triangles, and the ubiquitous lozenge-and-dot motif—a powerful protec-tive device that may have been associated with agriculture and fertility. Goff, *op. cit*, figure 481; see also Strommenger and Hirmer, *Art of Mesopotamia*, plate 13. Van Buren, *Symbols of the Gods in Mesopotamian Art*, 115–119.

[137] Van Buren, "Rosette in Mesopotamian Art," 105. See Steinkeller, "Stars and Stripes in Ancient Mesopotamia," 362–364, on the essential identity of the "flower" and "star" as symbols in Mesopotamian art. See Finkel, "On the Rules for the Royal Game of Ur," for Mesopotamian game boards with rosettes associated with abundance—of sexual love, well-being, food, and drink, all of which were well within the purview of Inanna/Ishtar.

[138] The planet Venus. Barber and Barber, *When They Severed Earth from Sky*, 188–190. Westenholz, "Goddesses of the Ancient Near East," 73. The Sumerian goddess Inanna was worshipped as the morning and evening star ("Morning Inanna" and "Evening Inanna"), attested in the archaic texts from Uruk. Szarzyńska, "Offerings for the Goddess Inana in Archaic Uruk," 8–10, 16–22. Steinkeller, "Archaic City Seals," 253–254. The equation of deities with celestial bodies, including Ishtar with Venus (Akkadian MUL.*Dilbat*), is explicit in a late scholastic list. Rochberg, *Heavenly Writing*, 188.

[139] Pritchard, *ANEP*, figures 522, 525–526.

[140] Cult statue dedicated by Puzur-Inshushinak, ca. 2100 B.C., inscribed with the name of the goddess, probably Narundi or Narunte. Harper, Aruz, and Tallon, *Royal City of Susa*, 90–91, no. 55.

[141] Budin, *Origin of Aphrodite*, figure 8 f. Cornelius, *Many Faces of the Goddess*, plates 5.1–5.12, 5.14–5.21, and others. See also Pritchard, *ANEP*, figures 470–474. The Hittites' main state deity, the Sun Goddess of Arinna (the Hurrian Hepat), is not to be classed with this type; although she is shown standing on a lion in Chamber A at Yazılıkaya (Boğazköy), the lion is not her regular attribute. Collins, "Politics of Hittite Religious Iconography," 85–87.

[142] Cornelius, *Many Faces of the Goddess*, 92–93 (Anat), 93–94 (Astarte), 94–99 (Qedeshet), and 99–100 (Asherah). The Mesopotamian goddess Ishtar (Hurrian Shaushga) was associated with a lion and worshipped by the Hittites. Bryce, *Life and Society in the Hittite World*, 146–147; Collins, "Politics of Hittite Religious Iconography," 85.

[143] Cornelius, *Many Faces of the Goddess*, plates 5.1, 5.3–5, 5.7, 5.16–17. In depictions of the other goddesses, as iden-tified by inscription, Anat is shown without an animal, As-tarte is shown without a lion but on horseback, and Asherah cannot be associated definitively with any iconography. Al-though in some cases *qdš* may be an epithet for Asherah, the "Mother of the Gods" cannot certainly be associated with the lion. Cornelius, 89–90, 99–100. The identity of *qdš*/Qedeshet is problematic; although she occurs in Egyp-tian texts as an independent goddess, she is not identified as such in Syro-Palestinian and Ugaritic sources.

[144] A beautiful ivory panel from Ugarit, which was once part of a bed, shows a winged goddess suckling two youths. She wears a Hathor-style wig, with two horns rising from her forehead, supporting a type of rosette. Cornelius, *Many Faces of the Goddess*, plate 3.11; Orthmann, *Der alte Orient*, plate 427.

their attributes, particularly in the absence of texts.[145]

These representations occur in various media, including metal pendants, or "Astarte" plaques, typically made of sheet gold and found throughout the Syro-Palestinian region.[146] A related type is a pendant medallion, decorated with a star or rosette, associated with the goddess Astarte/Ishtar and perhaps with other deities.[147] Both types of pendants—goddess and star—were found in the Uluburun shipwreck, dating to the 14th century B.C.[148] Three copper star/rosette medallions were found at Gordion in a Hittite-period burial, apparently evidence for the worship of the Hittite goddess Ishtar (Hurrian Shausga) there.[149]

This iconography carries into the early first millennium B.C. Close parallels are found in the nude "goddesses" shown on North Syrian horse trappings from the Near East and Greece. A bronze frontlet from Samos shows four nude female figures, three of which stand on lion's heads, arranged in two tiers below a winged disc.[150] Ivory horse frontlets from Nimrud also depict the nude goddess, who may stand on a lion or hold two lions, one in each hand, dangling by their hind legs.[151] As with her Bronze Age predecessors, this "Mistress of Wild Beasts" may hold other types of animals.[152]

Although the Assyrians imported such ivories, their own goddess Ishtar is shown fully clothed, retaining the attributes of the lion and rosette.[153] Ishtar may wear an elaborately patterned garment and a high polos headdress, topped with a star rosette.[154] Rosettes are also associated with the North Syrian goddess, as shown by imported ivory horse trappings found at Gordion, excavated in the Terrace Building (TB 2) of the destruction level on the city mound.[155] On one frontlet, the goddess holds two winged sphinxes and wears a high polos headdress, ornamented with panels of rosettes (Plate 117B).[156] Presiding over this scene is an elaborate winged sun-disc with curled tendrils above and below.

Rosette decoration on the polos of a goddess recurs in an orthostat relief from Carchemish in eastern Anatolia. The fragmentary basalt relief (Plate 118D) shows a goddess from the long wall of sculpture, dating to the tenth or ninth cen-

---

[145] See, for instance, a gold pendant from Minet el-Beida, depicting a nude goddess standing on a lion and holding two gazelles. This goddess has been identified variously as Astarte (Budin, *Origin of Aphrodite*, 238, figure 8f), Anat (van der Toorn, "Goddesses in Early Israelite Religion," 86, figure 31), and Qedeshet (Cornelius, *Many Faces of the Goddess*, 130). Deities with familiar attributes may remain completely unknown, such as a Cretan goddess, standing on a mountain flanked by two lions, depicted on a series of seal impressions from Knossos (mid-second millennium B.C.). Marinatos, *Goddess and the Warrior*, 118; 120, figure 6.8.

[146] Cornelius, *Many Faces of the Goddess*, 62–65; Maxwell-Hyslop, *Western Asiatic Jewellery*, 138–140.

[147] Maxwell-Hyslop, *Western Asiatic Jewellery*, 140–144. See, for instance, the Late Bronze Age star pendants from Alalakh (Maxwell-Hyslop, plate 100), Lachish (plate 101), Ugarit (plate 109), and Tell el-Ajjul (plates 108, 111). For star and figural pendants, see Negbi, *Goldwork from Tell el-Ajjul*, 30–32, plates 3–5, 7, 9, 11–35. Some of these stars or rosettes may have been solar symbols. See Maxwell-Hyslop, 141, and the ivory panel from Ugarit, supra n. 144. Mesopotamian versions of these medallions are found on the "Dilbat necklace," a collection of unexcavated jewelry in the Metropolitan Museum of Art, reported by the dealer to have been found in a jar at Dilbat, near Babylon. These have been dated to the 19th–17th centuries B.C., but without an archaeological context neither the date of the objects nor the find spot can be substantiated. *Metropolitan Museum of Art: Egypt and the Near East*, 104–105; Maxwell-Hyslop, 88–91. Aruz, Benzel, and Evans, *Beyond Babylon*, 24–25.

[148] Bass, "Oldest Known Shipwreck," 718–719; Pulak, "Uluburun Shipwreck: An Overview," 206–207. The gold finds include a pendant depicting a nude goddess holding a gazelle in each hand, and four medallions decorated with stars.

[149] B 463, burial H 41: (a) a seven-rayed star with a raised dot at the center and seven more between the arms of the star, (b) an eight-petalled star rosette with a raised dot at the center and four others in the field, and (c) a similar example. Mellink, *Hittite Cemetery at Gordion*, 41, plate 23:h-j. Maxwell-Hyslop, *Western Asiatic Jewellery*, 143–144.

[150] Ninth century B.C. Marinatos, *Goddess and the Warrior*, figures 1.33–34. For the goddess with lions on armor, see 18–24.

[151] Orchard, *Equestrian Bridle-Harness Ornaments*, plate 28: 135 (goddess standing on a lion); plate 29:136; plate 30:137–139; plate 31:147 (holding two lions by their rear legs). See also Budin, *Origin of Aphrodite*, figures 9c–d; Cornelius, *Many Faces of the Goddess*, figures 48a–b.

[152] Orchard, *Equestrian Bridle-Harness Ornaments*, plate 31: 143 (two goats).

[153] See, for instance, Collon, *Cylinder Seals V*, 127–129, plate 19:240–243.

[154] Collon, *Cylinder Seals V*, plate 33:240. Pritchard, *ANEP*, figure 522. And see *ANEP*, figure 538, for the statues of two deities dressed in this manner.

[155] Destruction level, late ninth or eighth century B.C. Young, "1961 Campaign at Gordion," 166–167. Sams, "Gordion and the Near East," 552. On the date of the destruction level, see below, pp. 133–134.

[156] 7652 BI 432. Young, "1961 Campaign at Gordion," plate 46. Sams, "Gordion and the Near East," plate 95. On the rosette in Mesopotamia and North Syria, see Winter, "Carved Ivory Furniture Panels from Nimrud," 46.

tury B.C.[157] She carries a pomegranate or poppy-head in her right hand and wears a robe with a scalloped border. She is depicted in profile, so her hair shows only one curl, and she wears a high polos, decorated with rosettes in panels, with a horn at the front and a veil that trails down the back. The profile rendering suggests that she had a Hathor-style hairdo and crown with two horns; in keeping with Mesopotamian tradition, her horned headdress is surely an attribute of divinity.[158] A fragmentary inscription indicates her divine status but not her name, although her iconography allows her to be identified as Kubaba, the "Queen of Carchemish."[159] Kubaba may be associated with the gods Tarhunzas and Karhuhas, and she is linked to the bird, which occurs as a logogram in her name.[160]

The goddess Kubaba appears again on a Carchemish orthostat, seated on a high-backed throne (CD-Figure 99).[161] She wears a polos that is covered by a veil, which extends over her body to conceal her figure. Her throne sits on a recumbent lion, and her feet rest on its head.[162] A procession of female figures approaches the goddess from the right, carrying various items, including mirrors, a bowl, a small animal, and sheaves of grain.[163] Following these figures is a parade of men bearing gazelles. Although the exact meaning of this procession cannot be known with certainty, the symbols of nature's bounty are here on display. Kubaba herself holds a poppy-head or pomegranate, as on the fragmentary relief, which apparently signifies fertility and abundance.[164] She also holds a mirror, which may represent some kind of magical or regenerative power.[165] The offering bearers bring a cup, perhaps containing saved seeds or life-giving water; sheaves of grain, reflecting the fertility of the fields; and animals, probably in preparation for sacrifice. These gifts are surely meant to induce

---

[157] Museum of Anatolian Civilizations, Ankara. Attributed to the long wall although found some distance from it. Woolley and Barnett, *Carchemish III*, 165, plate B.39A. Akurgal, *Art of the Hittites*, plate 115. Naumann, *Ikonographie der Kybele*, cat. 6, plate 2:3. Roller, *In Search of God the Mother*, 48, figure 4.

[158] The "naked goddess" at Carchemish, also from the long wall of sculpture, is depicted face front, revealing the form of her horned helmet—from which two horns extend, one to each side. She also has a standard Hathor-style hairdo, with curls at the left and right. Woolley and Barnett, *Carchemish III*, plate B.40.

[159] Bittel, "Kubaba: Ikonographie," 262, 2.3. Kubaba is attested in North Syria and Anatolia beginning in the second millennium B.C. Hawkins, "Kubaba: Philologisch," 257.

[160] Kubaba's name, as written in Luvian hieroglyphs, is transcribed as (DEUS)*ku*+AVIS, which may or may not be followed by -*pa* or -*pa-pa*. The designation AVIS signifies a picture of a bird, which is apparently a logogram using the symbol of the goddess. Hawkins, "Kubaba: Philologisch," 258. Kubaba may also have the epithet ATA, which has not been otherwise identified. Hawkins, "Kubaba at Karkamiš," 167–169:23a-24. For ATA and BABA in Phrygian inscriptions, see Brixhe and Lejeune, *Corpus*, 283–284, 288 (index). ATA occurs on one of the inscribed bronze bowls from Tumulus MM (MM 69), and in other contexts at Gordion. Young, *Gordion I*, 130, 273–275, figure 134c, plate 97c.

[161] Museum of Anatolian Civilizations, Ankara. Woolley, *Carchemish II*, plate B.19A. Naumann, *Ikonographie der Kybele*, cat. 2, plate 1:3. Symington, "Hittite and Neo-Hittite Furniture," plate 31B. Bittel, "Kubaba: Ikonographie," 262, 2:2. Kubaba has been identified as the subject of this relief in part due to an inscription that refers to "the procession" of Kubaba, on which, see below. Hawkins, "Kubaba at Karkamiš," 147.

[162] Kubaba may be associated with the lion, although male deities are as well. See, for example, a relief from Malatya, where Kubaba's throne sits on a bull while the god Karhuhas stands on a lion. Hawkins, "Kubaba at Karkamiš," 169: no. 25. Naumann, *Ikonographie der Kybele*, cat. 1, plate 1:2. Thus the lion as an attribute is not specific to Kubaba. Collins, "Animals in the Religions of Ancient Anatolia," 331.

[163] Woolley, *Carchemish II*, plates B.17a, B.19–24. Akurgal, *Art of the Hittites*, plate 114.

[164] A poppy-head may be depicted (as opposed to the pomegranate), as suggested by its small size and thick stem. Baumann, *Greek Plant World*, 50, 69–72. Both had much the same significance, in the Greek world and elsewhere, due to the many seeds they contained.

[165] Roller suggests that the mirror of Kubaba symbolized femininity and beauty. Roller, *In Search of God the Mother*, 48. While this may be true, Kubaba's mirror surely had spiritual significance as well, perhaps relating to divination or the cycle of rebirth. The mirror was symbolic as well as useful in many cultures, including that of ancient Egypt, where mirrors could symbolize the sun and moon, the eyes of the sky and bringers of illumination, connoting the triumph of life over death. Priestesses of the goddess Mut took part in a ritual in which they offered mirrors to the goddess, reanimating the deity and dispelling darkness. This ritual is attested in the Ptolemaic period but is thought to reflect an earlier tradition. Bianchi, "Reflections of the Sky's Eyes," 14–15. Mirrors were associated with prophecy by the Etruscans, and might even have been used for divination. Many were buried with their owners, for whom they may have provided protection and symbolized immortality. De Grummond, "Mirrors and Manteia"; "The Etruscan Mirror," 34. On mirrors in the tombs of Eurasian nomads, found in both female and male burials, see Rubinson, "Through the Looking Glass." The practice of using mirrors for divination has survived up to the present in central and eastern Europe. See Barber, "Curious Tale of the Ultra-Long Sleeve," 123–124. Mirrors have had magical significance among Siberian shamans, although their meaning varied from tribe to tribe. By looking into a mirror, Tungus shamans could see the dead person's soul. Eliade, *Shamanism*, 153–154.

a high crop yield, a wealth of natural resources, and an advantageous future for the city of Carchemish.[166] Several other images of Kubaba are extant, depicting similar iconography.[167]

Rosettes are not confined to the costumes of deities in eastern Anatolia and North Syria; they were also used by the king and his court. A king from Malatya wears a fillet decorated with rosettes, surely in emulation of Assyrian royalty, who used the rosette as a kind of official insignia, beginning in the ninth century B.C.[168] The prominence of the rosette in Assyrian iconography no doubt reflects the importance of the goddess Ishtar as patron deity of the royal house.[169] Assurnasirpal II (r. 883–859 B.C.) wears garments with rosettes in the border decoration, a headdress with a rosette at the front, and bracelets with large single rosettes—a type that could also be worn by his attendants.[170] Such bracelets were used by Assurnasirpal's successors, down to the time of Ashurbanipal (r. 668–627 B.C.).[171] Fine rosette fillets are shown on offering bearers in reliefs from the palace of Sargon II (r. 721–705 B.C.) at Khorsabad,[172] and an actual gold fillet, with agate-and-gold rosettes, was discovered in 1989 at Nimrud in tomb II, dating to the eighth century B.C. This was the burial of Atalia, queen of Sargon II, and two other royal wives, Yaba and

Baniti.[173] Finally, rosettes were featured on Assyrian threshold slabs, which suggests that they also appeared on carpets.[174] Such rosette motifs were surely considered to be protective, in Mesopotamia and elsewhere, invoking the deities they symbolized.[175]

Iconography of the Phrygian Goddess Matar

The Phrygians of the ninth and eighth centuries B.C. thus had an ample supply of religious iconography to contemplate, available on the monumental sculpture of eastern Anatolia, as well as in the textiles, jewelry, and ivories that must have made their way from the east to Gordion. Some such items were indeed imported into the city, as shown by the North Syrian ivory horse trappings found in the Terrace Building (TB 2). In keeping with the transfer of religious attributes so common in the Near East, the high polos of the eastern goddesses, along with the symbol of the rosette, were adopted for the Phrygian mother goddess Matar. The goddess Matar, whose name occurs in inscriptions, was the chief Phrygian deity—and the only deity attested in this early period. Although few representations of Matar survive, a head of the goddess from Salmanköy shows the Phrygian adoption of Near

[166] Inscriptions refer to offerings for Kubaba of "annual bread," "one ox and one sheep" (A11), as well as a pledge to fill the goddess's granary (A18). Hawkins, "Kubaba at Karkamiš," 150–151, 160. See also Collins, "Animals in the Religions of Ancient Anatolia," 320, for Hittite processions and sacrifice. For evidence that the cup might have held saved seeds, see below, p. 107, n. 277. For parallels in the art of Assyria, see Winter, "Ornament and the Rhetoric of Abundance."

[167] Naumann, *Ikonographie der Kybele*, cat. 1, 3–5, 7–10, plates 1:2, 2:1–2, 3. Bittel, "Kubaba: Ikonographie," 261–264. A few reliefs identified as grave stelai also show this iconography, with a figure supposed to be the dead woman wearing a veil and polos decorated with rosettes. She may hold a mirror or spindle, as on two stelai from Maraş. Akurgal, *Art of the Hittites*, plates 138–139.

[168] Colossal statue of a king from Malatya, ca. eighth century B.C. Museum of Anatolian Civilizations, Ankara. Akurgal, *Art of the Hittites*, 133, plates 106–107. See also the princess on a stele from Zincirli, who wears rosettes on her bracelet and diadem. Akurgal, *Art of the Hittites*, plate 130. Albenda, "Assyrian Carpets in Stone," 9.

[169] Dalley, "Ancient Assyrian Textiles," 125.

[170] Dalley, "Ancient Assyrian Textiles," figure 8. And see, for instance, Strommenger and Hirmer, *Art of Mesopotamia*, plates 191, 194–195: reliefs from the Northwest Palace, Nimrud. The king might also wear a necklace with pendants symbolizing various deities, including the star rosette of Ishtar; he does so on the Banquet Stele from Nimrud, which also features symbols of the gods above the king, as on the

tablet of Nabû-apla-iddina. Mallowan, *Nimrud and Its Remains*, 62–64.

[171] On a relief from the North Palace, Nineveh, Ashurbanipal hunts onagers wearing a rosette bracelet on one wrist (the other hand holds a bow, and his arm is covered by a guard), one on each upper arm, a fillet with rosettes in panels, a belt with a rosette and other divine symbols, and a sumptuous garment covered with rosettes of various types and sizes. The trappings of the king's horse feature rosettes as well. Strommenger and Hirmer, *Art of Mesopotamia*, plate 258.

[172] Ibid., plate 227.

[173] Oates and Oates, *Nimrud*, 82, plate 4B.

[174] See above, p. 87.

[175] Stronach, "Patterns of Prestige in the Pazyryk Carpet," 24. Oppenheim, "Golden Garments of the Gods," 191: regarding the decorative devices of the star, rosette, and lion, "The function of these designs is in all cases to ward off dangers and evil influences, to inspire awe, and to impress the adversary." The rosette and other protective motifs, such as the swastika and lozenge-and-dot pattern, are staples of the geometric repertoire of the Greeks in the early first millennium B.C. For an early rosette pendant, see the gold pendant worn on a necklace of gold and faience beads by the woman buried in the long building at Lefkandi, early tenth century B.C. Popham, Touloupa, and Sackett, "Hero of Lefkandi," plate 23B. See Popham, Calligas, and Sackett, *Lefkandi II*, plate 13, for a drawing showing the necklace *in situ*.

Eastern imagery (Plate 118C).[176] She wears a high polos decorated with a frieze of large rosettes, and a veil descends from the back and sides of her headdress. The hair of the goddess twists into two curls, recalling the Hathor-wig, but shorter. The high polos, veil, and characteristic hair style occur in other images of Matar. The rosettes of the goddess's headdress recur in a different context: the designs on the Gordion serving stands. A close relationship between Matar and the serving stands is revealed by a group of Phrygian stone monuments. There is much disagreement over the date of these works, which have been placed variously between the eighth and sixth centuries B.C.

Three well-preserved reliefs of Matar have been found in central Anatolia, at the sites of Gordion, Ankara, and Boğazköy. On all three the goddess wears a high polos, veil, and long, pleated garment, with the corner of her veil tucked into her belt. The reliefs from Gordion and Ankara show the goddess in a niche within an architectural frame, which is topped by a gabled pediment (Plate 118A–B).[177] She holds a bird in her left hand and a jug (Ankara) or bowl (Gordion) in her right.[178] The bird of prey and vessel are among Matar's attributes and appear elsewhere in related contexts.[179] These attributes recall the bird of Kubaba—the logogram that is part of her name—and the bowl that is carried in her procession. The Ankara relief is preserved almost completely, showing the entire gable; two horn-like projections rise from the apex to form an akroterion. The lintel extends out beyond the doorway, and to either side of the door is a vertical band of hooks. These hooks recall the designs on the inlaid table and serving stands from Tumulus MM. Also familiar is the frieze of lozenges that decorates the polos of the Ankara Matar.

The goddess from Boğazköy was placed in a niche as well, but the architectural frame was made separately (Plate 119A). She was found in her original context, set into the Phrygian wall in the area of the city gate.[180] Her torso was not recovered, so it is not clear what she was holding, although her left hand has been restored with a pomegranate. She wears a towering polos, a veil and pleated garment, and is flanked by two small figures of musicians, one playing a double flute and the other a harp. A fourth relief, found in Ankara (Etlik), shows Matar standing in a niche, although most of the right half of the relief is missing.[181] The goddess wears a high polos, veil, and pleated gown; in her right hand she holds a vessel, but her left arm is incomplete. The gable has a central akroterion, and a large, curling horn that rises from the roof. To the left of the door is a figure of a standing lion-demon, with arms raised, beneath two winged motifs.[182]

All these niche monuments are abbreviated versions of the house of the goddess, with an

---

[176] Circa seventh-sixth century B.C.(?) Museum of Anatolian Civilizations, Ankara. Naumann, *Ikonographie der Kybele*, cat. 24, plate 7:2. Roller, *In Search of God the Mother*, figure 11. Although the fragment is not otherwise identified, the familiar attributes indicate that this is a head of Matar.

[177] Museum of Anatolian Civilizations, Ankara. Naumann, *Ikonographie der Kybele*, cat. 18–19, plate 5:2–3. Roller, *In Search of God the Mother*, figures 7–8. The figure from Gordion was discovered in 1957–1958 in the old riverbed of the Sangarios. The relief was dated provisionally by Mellink to the seventh-sixth century B.C. but may be earlier. Mellink, "Comments on a Cult Relief of Kybele." The Ankara relief was found in 1959 in Bahçelievler, reused in a grave of the Hellenistic period. Temizer, "Ankara'da bulunan Kybele Kabartması." Berndt-Ersöz suggests a date in the second half of the eighth century B.C. Berndt-Ersöz, *Phrygian Rock-Cut Shrines*, 113, 117–118.

[178] For the bird of prey and vessel, see Mellink, "Comments on a Cult Relief of Kybele," 351–354. For an earlier representation of a goddess holding a cup and bird, dating to the Assyrian Colony period, see Collins, "Politics of Hittite Religious Iconography," 83, figure 1. The goddess is enthroned on a goat, with her feet resting on a lion.

[179] Several other representations of Matar exhibit these attributes. A fragmentary statuette from Gordion in the Istanbul Museum holds a bowl in her right hand and a bird in her left; a second fragmentary statuette from Gordion holds a bowl in her right hand, but her left hand is not preserved. An incomplete alabaster figure from Gordion holds a bowl in her left hand and a bird in her right. A fragmentary red stone figure from Gordion holds a bowl in her right hand, a bird in her left, and two more birds are shown on her skirt—one is holding a fish while the other eats it. Hawk figurines have also been found at Gordion. Mellink, "Comments on a Cult Relief of Kybele," plates 72–73. For a statue from Ayaş holding a bird and bowl, see Bittel, "Phrygisches Kultbild aus Boğazköy," plate 11C–D.

[180] Early sixth century B.C. or earlier. Museum of Anatolian Civilizations, Ankara. Naumann, *Ikonographie der Kybele*, cat. 23, plates 6:3, 7:1. Roller, *In Search of God the Mother*, figure 10. Bittel, "Phrygisches Kultbild aus Boğazköy." For shrines at city gates in Mesopotamia and the ritual activity conducted there, see M. Cohen, *Cultic Calendars of the Ancient Near East*, 347–351.

[181] According to the viewer's perspective. Museum of Anatolian Civilizations, Ankara. Naumann, *Ikonographie der Kybele*, cat. 20, plate 5:4. Roller, *In Search of God the Mother*, figure 9.

[182] Such "demon" figures are found at Carchemish and elsewhere and seem to relate to the Assyrian genii. Akurgal, *Art of the Hittites*, plate 112.

open doorway in which she stands. Comparable monuments occur in the Phrygian highlands to the west of Gordion, carved in the native rock.[183] Some of these are modest and others colossal, simulating the entire façade of Matar's shrine. Unfortunately, several of these works have now been damaged due to recent plundering activity.[184] Among the numerous examples that have been catalogued and studied, five may serve for the present discussion.[185] These five monuments all have—or had—a statue of Matar in the niche.

Küçük Kapı Kaya is a small niche monument carved in a rock outcrop, with gable, akroterion, and a standing goddess in the niche.[186] The construction resembles that of the Ankara monument (Plate 118B), although the akroterion is smaller, the sides are undecorated, and steps lead up to the door. A similar monument, Kumca Boğaz Kapı Kaya, was cut in a rock that had been trimmed down to accommodate the niche.[187] The simple frame had a gable, which is now missing; the goddess in the niche wore a polos, which reached up to the ceiling. In both these works, the surface of the figures is worn, and it is not clear whether they held any objects. In other respects, however, these niche shrines are similar to their counterparts from Ankara and Gordion.

A larger monument, Büyük Kapı Kaya, is a low wide rock, with a sculpted façade, facing west, and a niche at the center (Figure 93,

Plate 121B).[188] As with the Ankara relief, geometric patterns decorate the rock to either side of the niche. At Büyük Kapı Kaya, however, the patterns occupy two large, square panels, filled with concentric crosses forming a quadripartite design. No gable has been sculpted above the niche, as the architectural form implied here is much larger than that of the small niche monuments. In fact, the entire lower part of a building façade is suggested, cropped off at the top to conform to the shape of the rock. A lintel-like band runs across the width of the monument above the niche, and above this band is a checkerboard pattern, interrupted at the center by a pendant crescent. At the far left and right of the façade, as though supporting the "lintel," are two vertical "posts" and adjacent bands of lozenges. Inside the niche stood a goddess (now destroyed), wearing a pleated garment and a high polos that reached the ceiling.[189] On either side of the goddess was a low block, apparently the base for a sculpture. The two figures that stood on these bases were secured to the walls of the niche, as indicated by holes and traces of the bronze fittings. These were apparently lions, flanking the goddess, as suggested by another monument, the impressive Arslan Kaya.

Arslan Kaya was cut from a mass of rock that juts up above the surrounding plain (Plates 120, 121A).[190] Carved onto each side of the rock is a

---

[183] Rock-cut niches are also found to the east in Urartu, such as Meher Kapısı, near Van, and Taş Kapısı, in Yeşilalıç. These are related to the Phrygian niche monuments, although no figure is found in the Urartian doorways. An inscription on the back wall of the niche at Meher Kapısı states that the Urartian rulers Išpuini and Menua erected a "door" to the god Haldi. Salvini, "Historical Background," 205.

[184] Berndt and Ehringhaus, "Langsam stirbt Kybele." Hemelrijk and Berndt, "Phrygian Highlands, a Postscript." Although the monuments were carved from solid rock, thieves have mistakenly assumed that there was "treasure" inside. Because of the recent damage, older photographs show the monuments in better condition and are therefore published here.

[185] A full description of the highland monuments can be found in Haspels, *Highlands of Phrygia*, and Berndt-Ersöz, *Phrygian Rock-Cut Shrines*. Roller lists 23 monuments within the area defined by the cities of Eskişehir, Kütahya, and Afyon. Roller, *In Search of God the Mother*, 84.

[186] "Small door rock." Haspels, *Highlands of Phrygia*, 89; figures 185, 524:1. The monument faces north. Küçük Kapı Kaya was well preserved until 1986, but the rock was dynamited, and the upper right section is now missing, including much of the gable. Hemelrijk and Berndt, "Phrygian Highlands, a Postscript," 8–10, figures 12–13. The dates of this

and the other rock monuments discussed here have not been conclusively determined. Berndt-Ersöz suggests a date after 600 B.C. for the Midas Monument and Arslan Kaya (see below), but although her arguments are detailed, they are largely speculative. Berndt-Ersöz, *Phrygian Rock-Cut Shrines*, 89–118.

[187] "Door rock in the sandy mountain pass." Haspels, *Highlands of Phrygia*, 89–90; figures 159, 524:2. The monument faces southeast. The frame of the niche and the goddess have suffered some damage. Hemelrijk and Berndt, "Phrygian Highlands, a Postscript," 10–11, figures 14–15.

[188] "Large door rock." Haspels, *Highlands of Phrygia*, 87; figures 182–184, 522.

[189] Tragically, this monument has been irreparably damaged. The photograph reproduced here (Plate 121B), taken from Haspels, was shot before this damage occurred. By 1996, the central part of the figure in the niche had been cut away, and a hole was driven through it into the back wall. By 1997, the goddess had been destroyed completely. Hemelrijk and Berndt, "Phrygian Highlands, a Postscript," 6–7, figures 6–8.

[190] "Lion rock." Haspels, *Highlands of Phrygia*, 87–89; figures 186–191, 523. By 1993, Arslan Kaya had been dynamited, such that a large area of the façade at the upper right of the niche is now missing. Hemelrijk and Berndt, "Phrygian Highlands, a Postscript," 7–8, figures 9–10.

huge guardian animal figure.[191] The monument faces southeast and replicates a complete building façade, with a doorway, gable, and akroterion. The pediment contains a central king post that rises to the apex, flanked by two confronted sphinxes. A "tie beam" or "lintel" runs across the top of the façade at the bottom of the pediment, carved with an inscription, which is now barely legible but may have mentioned Matar.[192] At the far left and right, supporting the lintel, are two "posts," decorated with bands of lozenges. Surrounding the niche is an extraordinary pattern of interconnected squares that covers the façade, without any obvious symmetry. This puzzle-like pattern does have a rationale, although it is not immediately apparent. In order to understand the underlying scheme, the pattern must be extended over a continuous area, without the interruption of the niche (CD-Figure 74). When this is done, the basic elements can be recognized as a series of interrelated swastikas. These are oriented both clockwise and counterclockwise, and the underlying arrangement has been deliberately obscured. This recalls the decoration on the faces of the Tumulus MM serving stands, and suggests that the monument and the stands are very likely contemporary.[193]

On half of the squares in the main field of decoration on the Arslan Kaya façade, the sides extend out to form a kind of swastika with 90-degree rotational symmetry. The arms of the swastika hook around to terminate in the four adjacent squares (see, for instance, the swastika highlighted in red in CD-Figure 74, oriented counterclockwise). The square terminations also form the ends of neighboring swastikas oriented in the same direction (for instance, the red and yellow examples in CD-Figure 74). These contiguous swastikas run across the façade horizontally and vertically, leaving some extra squares outside the pattern. These extra squares form the centers of additional swastikas—of the same form but oriented in the opposite direction (for instance, the blue and green examples in the CD-figure, oriented clockwise). These resemble the original swastikas, but *flipped*, and they are interconnected with them. The additional swastikas run over the façade in the same manner, although jogged diagonally with respect to their counterparts. The interlocking swastika pattern produces squares and L-shaped sections in reserve, which attract the eye and detract from the solution to the puzzle. Finally, the whole configuration is cropped and surrounded by a border, and the niche breaks up the pattern completely. This kind of game playing is also found on the Tumulus MM serving stands. The Gordion woodworkers and the architects of Arslan

---

[191] Although the figures are worn, the one on the right is certainly a standing lion; the one at the left has been identified as a lion or griffin. Haspels, *Highlands of Phrygia*, 89; Roller, *In Search of God the Mother*, 86.

[192] According to Haspels, *Highlands of Phrygia*, 294, no. 20 (after Körte): [—]μ[-]τματεϱαν[—]. According to Brixhe and Lejeune, *Corpus*, 43–45, no. W-03:]m[ ]t[ ]m[ ]m[. The date of the inscription is contested.

[193] The method of extending the pattern beyond the limits of the façade was advanced by Berndt-Ersöz in her attempt to analyze the decoration. Although she made some interesting observations about the design structure, she did not recognize the swastikas of the underlying pattern. Consequently, she did not realize the close formal relationship between the Arslan Kaya façade pattern and the design scheme on the Tumulus MM serving stands. Believing them to be very different in character, she suggested a much later date for the monument. Berndt-Ersöz, *Phrygian Rock-Cut Shrines*, 36–37, 99; figures 101–102. Haspels was also unaware of the sophistication of the pattern on the face of Arslan Kaya, calling the decoration "slight and restless, even somewhat hesitant." Likewise, Roller saw the decoration as a simple variation on the meander pattern. These sources date the façade to the sixth century B.C., after Akurgal and others. Akurgal, *Die Kunst Anatoliens*, 86; Berndt-Ersöz, 125; Haspels, 105–106; Roller, *In Search of God the Mother*, 101.

Proponents of a late date for Arslan Kaya have also focused on the confronted sphinxes in the pediment, asserting that their form and disposition are Archaic Greek. See Berndt-Ersöz, 115: "Animals antithetically placed in a gable field indicate Greek influence…the sphinxes indicate a Greek influence, and stylistically they belong to the 6th century B.C." However, confronted sphinxes of this type occur in the Near East at an earlier date. See, for example, a pair of North Syrian bronze plaques depicting what were apparently confronted sphinxes (CD-Figure 78). The two plaques are unexcavated, but they are clearly North Syrian, dating to the ninth or eighth century B.C. *Metropolitan Museum of Art: Egypt and the Near East*, 127, figure 91. Muscarella, *Bronze and Iron*, 365–367, no. 493a–b. Like the Arslan Kaya sphinxes, the Syrian sphinx plaques are shown in profile with frontal faces, which has wrongly been considered a Greek trait. The motif of guardian figures, placed antithetically and flanking a post, plant, or tree, is common in the Near East and Egypt from an early period. Thus one need not look to Archaic Greece for the origin of the composition. Nor should one assume that orientalizing Greek sphinxes somehow influenced their Near Eastern counterparts. Finally, antithetical figures in the pediments of Greek temples do not necessarily have chronological implications for Arslan Kaya. Little is known about Near Eastern gable decoration, as superstructures seldom survive. This makes the Phrygian façade monuments all the more important for the history of ancient architecture.

Kaya shared an unusual intellectual approach to the art of geometric ornament.[194] The scene in the niche at Arslan Kaya reveals an even more striking correspondence.

Standing in the niche is a representation of the goddess Matar, flanked by two lions standing on their hind legs and touching her head with their paws (Plate 121A). The goddess wears a long robe and high polos that reaches up to the ceiling of the niche. Although the surface of the figure is abraded, it is clear that she holds an animal by its hind legs, perhaps a lion, so that it dangles down in front of her body. The sides of the niche are sculpted as the doors of Matar's shrine, opening inward, in effect, to reveal the goddess. As appropriate for a door, the niche occupies the lower section of the façade at the center. The rosette/lunette complex and supporting curved legs of the serving stands are located in much the same area on the stands' faces. This suggests that the rosette grouping on the stands may relate to the niche of the façade or the scene within it.

The most obvious correlation is between the rosette and the head of the goddess, which are found in comparable positions in their respective settings. This suggests the possibility that the large rosette at the center of the group symbolized the goddess Matar. As our comparative study of the rosette has shown, this is an entirely plausible proposition.[195] The lunette and horn-like projections above the rosette might then represent the goddess's polos headdress. And the two curved legs that support the rosette, with their paw-like feet, might stand for her attendant lions. This interpretation can also be advanced for the motifs on the Tumulus P serving stand.[196] To in-vestigate this possibility, the legs from the Tumulus MM stands must be examined in detail.

Each of the front legs on both serving stands ends in a "scroll foot," as Young called it,[197] which has moldings on the front and back faces and three "toes" at the outer edge. These features are visible on the best-preserved foot, from the leg at the right on serving stand A (Plate 90). The toes of the front feet are easily recognized in the reconstructed back views of the stands (Figures 51, 59). The feet on the stands can be identified as lion's paws, by comparison with a small wooden lion from Tumulus P,[198] and two stone lions from the city mound at Gordion. One of these lions (S 43) has a similar "scroll foot," with his four toes curled around a circular motif (Plate 122C). The second stone lion (S 35) has a comparable foot, although his toes curl into a spiral (Plate 122B). These two fierce beasts, found in the foundations of Middle Phrygian Building G, once decorated an early Phrygian structure.[199]

The stylized paws of the two Gordion stone lions find counterparts in other Anatolian examples. A more realistically rendered pair of lions from Göllüdağ shows the kind of curled paws that the Gordion sculptors emulated (Plate 122A).[200] Such lions could guard monumental entrances in the Assyrian manner and could also support the statues of deities.[201] It is this last effect that the designers of the serving stands were striving for, when they positioned the curved lion legs under the rosette medallions. At the tops of the curved legs were small, inlaid star rosettes, which may have served to mark the lion's haunch (Figure 67), also doubling as the short curls of Matar's hair style, placed strategically below the

---

[194] The idea of setting up a complex correspondence and then obscuring or negating it is also seen in the designs on the inlaid table from Tumulus MM. This concept occurs in the later arts of the Islamic world and is particularly noteworthy in architectural tile decoration. For the discovery of an amazingly sophisticated underlying mathematical system, see Lu and Steinhardt, "Decagonal and Quasi-Crystalline Tilings in Medieval Islamic Architecture."

[195] See above, pp. 87–91.

[196] See above, pp. 74–75. The "headdress" on the Tumulus P stand includes two "horns" at the bottom and a lunette motif at the top. The entire "polos" is surrounded by a band decorated with a checkerboard motif, recalling the "veil" associated with the Matar's polos in numerous representations. The "horns" of the headdress may indicate divinity, as found at Carchemish and elsewhere throughout the Near East.

[197] Young, Gordion I, 180: "scroll feet."

[198] 4030 W 2 (TumP 107). The "scroll feet" of the toy lion confirm the identification. In Young, Gordion I, plate 22C–F, the rear foot is shown attached (mistakenly) to the front leg. This foot was reattached correctly in 1994. Simpson and Spirydowicz, GWF, figure 81.

[199] 3522 S 35 and 3856 S 43. Young, "Campaign of 1955 at Gordion," 262, figures 42–43. Sams, "Aspects of Early Phrygian Architecture," 214, n. 10. Middle Phrygian Building G overlay the remains of Megaron 2 of the destruction level of the city mound.

[200] Kayseri Museum, ca. 700 B.C. Akurgal, Art of the Hittites, plate 136. Tezcan, "1968 Göllüdağ Kazısı," 218, plates 14–16.

[201] See, for instance, the guardian lions from Zincirli, Sakçagözü, and Malatya, and the statue base from Zincirli. Akurgal, Art of the Hittites, plates 103, 126, 132, 135.

large rosette.[202] Finally, this unusual configuration may have been inspired by the Syro-Palestinian winged discs, such as those on the ivory horse trappings from the Terrace Building at Gordion (Plate 117B). The discs at the center of these winged motifs feature various radial designs including sun symbols and rosettes, with curling tendrils extending down from the discs in the manner of the stands' curved legs. More tendrils curl out at the top, in the position of the "horned" headdress.[203]

The close formal relationship between the faces of the Tumulus MM serving stands and the façade of Arslan Kaya allows the symbols on the stands to be decoded. The placement of the rosette medallions on the stands corresponds to the position of the head of the goddess as she appears in the niche of the façade. The rosettes on the stands are supported by two curved lion's legs, much as the rearing lions of Matar reach up to touch her head with their paws.[204] One may conclude that the rosettes are symbols of the goddess Matar and the curved legs

represent her attendant lions. The complex designs that cover the rock façade find their counterparts in the inlaid decoration on the stands' faces. The Tumulus MM serving stands were apparently portable shrines of the goddess, shown in a symbolic epiphany. This impression is confirmed by the magnificent Midas Monument, cut into the cliffs at Midas City.

Yazılıkaya, the so-called Midas Monument, was named for an inscription that includes the name Midas (MIDAI) and runs along the rock face above the left half of the pediment (Plate 123, CD-Figure 75).[205] Another inscription runs down the right side of the façade, and graffiti mentioning Midas and Matar are carved on the inner side posts of the niche (CD-Figure 76).[206] The monument faces east, cut into a huge rock outcrop, carved to replicate a temple façade in the manner of Arslan Kaya. The pediment is bordered at the top by a raking "cornice," decorated with a row of lozenges and crowned with an akroterion. The interior of the pediment is framed by recessed bands of lozenges, stepped back from the level

---

[202] A cross, swirl, or rosette to mark the haunch (of both animals and humans) occurred throughout the Near East in the early first millennium B.C. and was transmitted to Greece as an orientalizing device. Akurgal, *Art of Greece: Its Origins*, figures 13, 15, 130–132; plates 16, 47. Akurgal, *Die Kunst Anatoliens*, plate 184, for an ivory goat. For a cross on the haunch of a lion orthostat from Ankara, see Akurgal, *Spaethethitische Bildkunst*, plate 36B. For concentric circles marking the haunches of a toy bull from Tumulus P, see Young, *Gordion I*, figure 24A.

[203] A solar-type symbol occupies the disc on the ivory frontlet from the Terrace Building at Gordion. Sams, "Gordion and the Near East," plate 95. For a rosette disc, see examples from Zincirli, Sakçagözü, and Nimrud. Akurgal, *Art of the Hittites*, plates 130, 134. Mallowan and Herrmann, *Furniture from SW.7*, plates 76–79.

Although the origin and meaning of the winged disc in the Near East are a matter of controversy, the motif seems to relate ultimately to the Egyptian winged scarab, such as that on the "rebus" pectoral of Tutankhamun (CD-Figure 79). Aldred, *Jewels of the Pharaohs*, 223, plate 106. *Treasures of Tutankhamun*, color plate 16 (cat. 26). The correspondence is particularly notable in the case of the North Syrian examples: the curved tendrils that extend down from the disc frame a "tail," and the tendrils themselves seem to be derived from the legs of the winged scarab. The claws of the scarab on the rebus pectoral grasp the hieroglyphic "shen" sign ("all that is encircled," "eternity," "totality"), which closely resembles the scroll feet of the Gordion serving stands. Gardiner, *Egyptian Grammar*, sign V.9. If this resemblance is meaningful, then the scroll feet on the stands may indicate a universal or solar aspect for the rosette that symbolizes the Phrygian goddess. This use of the shen sign is carried into the Egyptian Late Period. Müller and Thiem, *Gold of the Pharaohs*, figure 432 (tenth century B.C.), figure 452 (ninth century B.C.). Stierlin, *Gold der Pharaonen*, 208–209

(ninth century). See also Winter, "Carved Ivory Furniture Panels from Nimrud," 46–47, on the Syrian winged disc and the resemblance of the curled tendrils to the hairdo of Hathor.

For Old Babylonian plaques depicting what may be the ultimate prototype of the symbolic grouping on the Tumulus MM serving stands, see Woods, "Sun-God Tablet of Nabû-apla-iddina Revisited," 59–62 and figures 25–27. Here, two bull-men flank a sun-disc shown at the top of the trunk of a date-palm tree; one hand of each bull-man touches the sun-disc, supporting it from below.

[204] A similar arrangement can be seen on the front of Arslan Taş, a rock-cut monument (commonly identified as a tomb) with two lionesses flanking a pillar on the façade (CD-Figure 77). Haspels, *Highlands of Phrygia*, 118–119, figures 131–132.

[205] "Rock with writing." Haspels, *Highlands of Phrygia*, 73–76, 289–291 (inscriptions); figures 8–13, 510 and 598–599:1–5. According to Haspels, 289, no. 1: ατες | αρχιαεϝαις | ακενανολαϝος | μιδαι | λαϝαπταει | ϝανακτει | εδαες. According to Brixhe and Lejeune, *Corpus*, 6–9, no. M-01a: ates | arkiaevais | akenanogavos | midai | lavagtaei | vanaktei | edaes. The date of the inscription is uncertain; Brixhe and Lejeune have suggested that the name "midai" may refer to the late eighth-century B.C. king Midas of Gordion, and, based on an archaic usage (absence of yod), that the inscription could be contemporary with this ruler. *Corpus*, 6.

[206] Haspels, *Highlands of Phrygia*, 289–291, nos. 2, 4–5. Brixhe and Lejeune, *Corpus*, 9–15, nos., M-01b, c, d; see also M-01e. Haspels dates the Midas Monument to the eighth century B.C., contemporary with the Tumulus MM furniture; although the monument has been dated as late as the sixth century B.C. by other scholars, Haspels's early date is borne out by the present study. Haspels, 102–104.

of the face. A king post once stood at the center but is now almost completely worn away, due to a crack caused by weathering at the center of the façade. The "tie beam" or "lintel" at the base of the pediment is carved in panels, bordered at the left and right, featuring a design that evokes crossed diagonals, with four lozenges at the corners and a square at the center. This same pattern, doubled and without divisions, runs down the left and right side "posts" that function as "supports" for the lintel. Comparable lozenge-cross or square-cross groupings are found on the inlaid table from Tumulus MM.[207]

At the bottom of the façade is a niche with a double frame, in which a statue of Matar is presumed to have stood. This theory is based on a mortise cut in the ceiling of the niche, which must have secured the statue.[208] The niche is surrounded by an elaborate carved pattern that covers the face of the monument. This is composed of large, rectilinear quatrefoil designs, bordered by smaller crosses. These large quatrefoils are elaborate variations on the lozenge-cross groups of the posts and lintel. Six quatrefoils occur above the niche, and one to each side. This recalls the pattern on the façade of Büyük Kapı Kaya, which features a related quadripartite design at the left and right of the niche (Figure 93). On both Büyük Kapı Kaya and the Midas Monument a "beam" is indicated at the top of the niche, running across the face of the monument. The distinction is clear at Büyük Kapı Kaya, as the decoration changes markedly above the beam. On the Midas Monument, the division is subtle, but the pattern below the beam is indeed different from that of the top section. The quatrefoils below the beam are smaller, to accommodate the width of the niche. Curiously, this causes the small crosses that run through the beam to break up at the center. Since the overall design is disrupted at the level of the beam, the separation of top and bottom must represent a meaningful architectural feature.[209]

This distinction between top and bottom is emphasized in the decoration of the Tumulus P serving stand, which was surely a portable shrine of the goddess (Figure 91). Here, the top section of the stand is clearly demarcated, set off by a border of lozenges and inlaid with different designs from those of the bottom section. Fifteen large, square panels occupy the upper area, recalling the large quatrefoil motifs in the upper part of the façade of the Midas Monument; the lower part of the stand is carved in an openwork grid, which is inlaid with smaller panels. The Tumulus MM stands exhibit no such overt demarcation, but the distinction between top and bottom is nonetheless present. This can be seen in the color diagrams that were used to analyze the designs on the stands (Color Plates XB, XIB, and see above, pp. 77–83). The top three boards were inlaid as a unit, featuring a particular set of individual designs. The bottom sections were inlaid with a different set of designs, found at the left and right of the rosette/lunette grouping and outside the curved front legs. The long side boards were inlaid with yet another set, distinguished in this way from the interior panels. Thus, the design scheme on the Tumulus MM serving stands respected the architectural elements exhibited in the façade monuments. The architectural metaphor is more obvious on the stand from Tumulus P, with its lozenge-decorated "posts" and "lintel."

Given all these correspondences between the serving stands and rock monuments, one might wonder if the function of the monuments was related to that of the stands. Several highland monuments have a shaft cut into the rock, descending directly behind the niche. The rear wall of the niche is pierced by one or more holes, which communicated directly with the shaft at the back. Although there is no clear evidence for the purpose of these shafts, they may have been used for divination or sacrificial rites relating to the wor-

---

[207] See Figures 9–11, 23. Such groupings are particularly noticeable in the frame panels with maze borders. Here, they are composed of five lozenges or five squares, arranged to suggest crossed diagonals. The lozenge and lozenge-cross are featured on numerous architectural terracottas from Gordion and Pazarlı; the terra-cottas have been dated variously and cannot be used to date the rock monuments. Glendinning, "A Decorated Roof at Gordion." F. Işık, "Entstehung der tönernen Verkleidungsplatten."

[208] Haspels, *Highlands of Phrygia*, figure 510:2.
[209] The façade of Arslan Kaya does not observe this distinction. Haspels thought that the workers who sculpted the façade of the Midas Monument proceded from the top down and then altered the design when they reached the bottom section in order to accommodate the niche. She did not note the line of demarcation between the upper and lower sections. Haspels, *Highlands of Phrygia*, 102.

ship of Matar.[210] The ritual may have involved animal sacrifice or the pouring of libations.[211] These
activities recall the function of the serving stands
(see Chapter 8, below). The Midas Monument,
Arslan Kaya, and Büyük Kapı Kaya were not
among the monuments with shafts. However, this
does not preclude the possibility of sacrificial ritual associated with them. In fact, if such rites occurred at the shaft monuments, it is likely that
they took place at the other shrines as well. In the
absence of Phrygian religious texts, one may turn
to Urartu for an indication of the ritual associated with the rock monuments there. The Urartian niche monument at Meher Kapısı, near Van
(Tushpa), bears a long inscription enumerating
the types of animal sacrifice to be carried out in
the open-air sanctuary.[212]

Matar's "house," as represented by the rock
façades in the Phrygian highlands, surely evoked
a mountain habitat. This idea is supported by
several early inscriptions, which feature the name
of the goddess and provide her epithets. The
name Matar, or "Mother," appears ten times
in Paleo-Phrygian inscriptions, all found on cult
façades or niches.[213] Occurring twice is the epithet *kubileya* or *kubeleya*, an adjective used to mod-
ify the name Matar. This has been taken to designate a mountain associated with the goddess,
perhaps called Kybelon, based on the writings
of Strabo and others. This epithet of the Phrygian Matar apparently lies behind the name Kybele, used for the Greek goddess Meter, Matar's
Hellenic counterpart. The term may also re-

late to Kubaba of Carchemish or to the goddess
worshipped at Sardis, Kubaba or Kybebe, although firm evidence for these hypotheses is lacking.[214] Based on Byzantine sources, which provide various etymologies for the term Kybele, the
Phrygian "Matar Kubileya" might be translated
"Mother of the Mountain."[215]

Although this designation is hypothetical, the
mountain abode is considered to be the strongest
evidence for Matar's domain. Her predatory
"hunting bird" and lions have been related to
this wild mountain setting. Her monuments were
also found within settlements, such as the relief
from Boğazköy, which was built into the wall of
the city.[216] Thus, the goddess was versatile, with
the power to transcend the boundaries between
the natural and urban environments.[217] Beyond
these general assumptions, however, the Phrygian
Matar has remained elusive. There is little concrete data concerning her cult in Phrygia, and the
inscriptions on her monuments cannot be understood. Old ideas of a universal cult of the Mother
Goddess have been jettisoned by modern scholars, in favor of a more reasoned approach to the
evidence. The Anatolian Matar has been separated from her Greek and Roman counterparts,
and it is now considered inadvisable to look for
aspects of the original Phrygian goddess in these
later manifestations. Although this process has
been useful, it has left us with a relatively colorless
character in place of the once-awesome Matar.[218]
Circumstantial evidence, including ancient texts,
can yield additional insights into the domain of

---

[210] The monuments with shafts are Delikli Taş, Mal Taş,
the Bakşeyiş Monument, the Değirmen Monument, and a
monument at Fındık that consists of a shaft behind a plain
panel. In the Değirmen Monument, two small holes were
cut in the façade, communicating with the shaft behind
it. Haspels, *Highlands of Phrygia*, 100, n. 147, figures 163–
164, 520:4, 521:1. Roller, *In Search of God the Mother*, 96–
98, n. 127. See also Berndt-Ersöz, *Phrygian Rock-Cut Shrines*,
191–193, and "Phrygian Rock-Cut Cult Façades" for the
suggestion that the shafts were connected with some kind
of divination. The Değirmen Monument has now been
destroyed. Hemelrijk and Berndt, "Phrygian Highlands, a
Postscript," 6.

[211] It has been supposed that the Phrygian rock façades
were used in conjunction with springs and water, although
evidence is scant for significant sources of water near most
of the monuments in antiquity. Haspels, *Highlands of Phrygia*,
99, n. 140. Berndt-Ersöz, *Phrygian Rock-Cut Shrines*, 147–148,
183–188 on evidence for libations at the niche and step
monuments.

[212] Salvini, "Historical Background," 205–207. The inscription, dating to the ninth century B.C., stipulates the
sacrifice of large numbers of oxen and sheep to be made
to the various Urartian deities, presumably on the rock ter-

race below the monument. König, *Handbuch der chaldischen
Inschriften*, 54–56. Supra n. 183.

[213] See Roller, *In Search of God the Mother*, 65–71, for a
survey of the Matar inscriptions. For the main corpus of
Phrygian inscriptions, see Brixhe and Lejeune, *Corpus*.

[214] Based on available evidence, Matar Kubileya and
Kubaba cannot be related etymologically, although they can
be connected through their attributes. Supra n. 160 for the
bird logogram in the name of Kubaba. Roller, *In Search
of God the Mother*, 44–53, makes a case for the distinction
between the two deities, although her discussion of their
attributes does not employ their full iconography.

[215] Ibid., 68.

[216] See above, p. 92.

[217] Roller, *In Search of God the Mother*, 113.

[218] In her comprehensive review of the evidence for the
Phrygian mother goddess, Roller concluded that she was
a deity in "a position of power over the natural environment," which in turn afforded protection to the Phrygian state and its people. She found no convincing evidence that Matar was associated with childbirth, agricultural or animal fertility, or any universal concept of the
creative force. Roller, *In Search of God the Mother*, 6, 15,
114.

the Phrygian goddess. The symbols on the inlaid furniture from Tumulus MM can contribute to this picture.

Furniture as Cosmic Metaphor

Missing from the modern concept of Matar is an understanding of her relationship to the daily life of the ancient Phrygians—their reliance on animal husbandry and farming, and their obvious stake in the fertility of the land. Associated with this was their need for water, as well as their acute awareness of the weather, the passing of time, and the progression of the seasons of the year. This was all dependent on the movement of the celestial bodies and the workings of the upper cosmos, which governed the natural world, the politics of the state, and, ultimately, the lives of the people. The iconography of the Phrygian Matar, as conveyed through the designs on the Tumulus MM furniture, suggests a connection with these phenomena.

The Tumulus MM serving stands, made for the royal family, evidently depicted the state's official religious insignia. This consisted of a symbolic rendering of the goddess Matar, with a high "headdress," supported by her attendant "lions." This heraldic-like imagery was situated within an "architectural" context, which represented the façade of Matar's shrine. That this iconography was state sanctioned can be deduced from its occurrence, as rendered more realistically, on the rock monuments from the Phrygian highlands.[219] To this combination of motifs may be added the bird and vessel, which appear on the niche monuments from the heartland. Both on the serving stands and the monuments, these official attributes of the goddess were set against a background of traditional motifs, which had been passed down over thousands of years as symbols of protection and fertility. The swastikas and other meander squares on the stands' faces fall into this category, as does the lattice of diamonds and triangles that forms the bordering pattern. These, too, played their role in the official iconography, evoking the sumptuous paneled textiles worn by Assyrian and Phrygian monarchs.[220]

Religious symbols are found on the inlaid table as well, featured prominently among its many magical motifs.[221] Small rosettes decorate the type-1 top struts, which resemble stylized trees (Figures 5–8; Plates 4E, 12A, 12E, 16A, 20E, 21A). On all but two of the type-1 struts, rosettes occur between the upper pair of outturned leaves.[222] On one of these struts, A4 at the front of the table, a lunette appears in place of the rosette (Figure 5, Plate 5A). Thus the two type-1 struts above the table's front frame piece feature a rosette and lunette, the symbols from the central groupings on the serving stands, signifying the goddess Matar with her "headdress." Three rosette designs also occur on the frame of the table, which may refer to the goddess as well.

Other designs on the table include meander squares and various hook motifs, grids of squares, fields of lozenges, including the lozenge-and-dot, and additional "genealogical patterns." Mazes are prominent and may surround a single or quadruple lozenge cross (Figures 9, 17). Some of these designs appear on the Phrygian rock monuments, particularly the hook design and lozenge or lozenge cross. Many occur at Gordion, incised on the walls of a building from the destruction level, where the maze, cross, and lozenge field are associated with the rosette, lion, bird, and building façade (Figures 94–99). Young called these rudimentary drawings "doodles" and thought that they were drawn by the "common citizens" of the town.[223] Although he believed that they reflected everyday life at Gordion, the "doodles" were replete with religious symbols.[224]

The graffiti were incised on the exterior face of numerous stone blocks from the walls of Megaron 2. This building contained the imaginative pebble mosaic (Figure 92) and may also have incorporated the two stone lions (Plate 122B–C).[225] The drawings overlap one another and appear to

---

[219] Ibid., 111, on the official nature of the cult.

[220] Although there is no direct evidence for the kinds of textiles used for Phrygian royal garments, the costume of Warpalawas of Tyana suggests that the Phrygian kings and their retinue also wore paneled textiles. See above, p. 86.

[221] For a discussion of the designs on the inlaid table, see Chapter 3.

[222] One of these struts is the unusual strut C3, which was

apparently an ancient replacement. See above, p. 35.

[223] Young, "Doodling at Gordion," 270. These graffiti are the subject of a forthcoming publication by Lynn Roller.

[224] Simpson, "Symbols on the Gordion Screens," 638–639.

[225] The lions were found in the foundations of Middle Phrygian Building G, which overlay Megaron 2. Supra n. 199.

have been incised at random. The subject matter includes humans, such as warriors and hunters, as well as many birds and lions. Young recognized the bird of prey and associated it with the goddess Matar.[226] Several building façades are also depicted, with gables crowned by akroteria. In one group, two buildings are shown, with a rosette on one façade and a bird superimposed on the other (Figure 94). These buildings recall the stone niche monuments and rock façades, and may represent shrines of the goddess.[227] Birds are associated with lions (Figures 94–95) and rosettes (Figures 96), and the bird, lion, and rosette can appear together (Figure 97). The bird also occurs with the lozenge net and cross (Figure 99) as well as with two large mazes (Figure 98); accompanying these mazes was a lion and rosette.[228] The "doodles" tie together various symbols found on the rock monuments and the furniture, which were surely related to Matar.

The geometric designs on the serving stands provide additional elements of her iconography. The decoration on the goddess's "headdress" above the rosettes includes a meander square on stand A (Plate 77) and a series of vertical bands on stand B (Plate 87).[229] The bands in the lunette of stand B consist of rows of inlaid diamonds, flanked by triangles, with the reserved area forming vertical zigzags. Comparison with the decoration on a Phrygian "double idol" shows that the

motifs in both lunette crowns were attributes of the goddess, and that the pairing of the two designs was meaningful.

The stone double idol is now built into an Ottoman fountain, Faharet Çeşme, on the outskirts of Ankara (Plate 119B).[230] The figure consists of a square "body" with two disc-like "heads" above it. Etched into the stone below each head is a geometric pattern. At the left is a meander square with hooks extending in from the sides.[231] At the right is a panel filled with vertical lines, obscured at the bottom by a modern repair. Part of the right side has been plastered over, to cover a gaping hole where the water was once allowed to run through the relief.[232] Single and multiple "idols" occur at numerous Phrygian sites, carved into rock faces, forming the backs of stepped thrones or "rock altars," and carved as small, free-standing sculptures.[233] These aniconic images are apparently related to the cult of Matar and are thought to be early, schematic representations of the goddess.[234]

This relationship is suggested by the idols at Midas City, and particularly a double idol at the top of a stepped throne on the citadel.[235] The form of the idol is similar to that at Faharet Çeşme, although there is no decoration on the body. The two disc heads share a common Hathor-style hairdo, which curves over the tops of the contiguous discs and terminates in

[226] Young, "Doodling at Gordion," 275. In 1977, Mellink suggested that the hawk and lion "doodles" may have referred to attributes of the Phrygian goddess. Mellink, "Temples and High Places in Phrygia," 101. See Roller, "Early Phrygian Drawings from Gordion," for a general discussion of the "doodles."

[227] Mellink, "Comments on a Cult Relief of Kybele," 357–358.

[228] The large maze stone broke apart when it was removed from the back wall of the building. The remains were subsequently found in the Gordion depot and catalogued by Roller as ST 841 (DSD 14, 42). A photograph survives showing the maze stone in situ, sitting on top of another incised stone (GB 57-251, neg. 64596). Although the drawings are difficult to decipher, they seem to include two or three mazes, at least one bird, a lion at the left, a rosette below the lion, and another large rosette incised on the lower stone. Mazes, lozenges, and fields of lozenges also occur on other "doodle stones."

[229] The meander square in the lunette above the rosette of stand A is design A7 rotated 180 degrees and flipped (see Figure 72).

[230] Prayon, Phrygische Plastik, 207, cat. 47; Naumann, Ikonographie der Kybele, 94, plate 9F. Roller seems to suggest that the idol was carved into the rock near the spring that now supplies the fountain. Roller, In Search of God the Mother, 43, n. 11; 111. Although the idol may once have been carved into rock,

the block is now built into the later fountain; it is therefore unclear whether it was associated with the spring originally.

[231] The Faharet Çeşme design resembles 3T1 on serving stand A (Figure 72), but it is symmetrical with respect to rotations of 90 degrees instead of 180. The lines of the design create a swastika in relief.

[232] This is clearly visible in von der Osten, Explorations in Central Anatolia, plate 5B.

[233] Naumann, Ikonographie der Kybele, plates 9–11. Roller, In Search of God the Mother, 77–78. Roller notes five "idols" from Boğazköy and fifteen from Gordion, most of which are unpublished.

[234] Roller, In Search of God the Mother, 78. For a discussion of idols and theories regarding their identification, see Berndt-Ersöz, Phrygian Rock-Cut Shrines, 159–169. For evidence of the Hittite practice of replacing a non-anthropomorphic totem with a representational image as part of the refurbishing of cult, see McMahon, "Theology, Priests, and Worship in Hittite Anatolia," 1990.

[235] Haspels, Highlands of Phrygia, 291:7, figure 599:7. Naumann, Ikonographie der Kybele, plate 11A. Berndt-Ersöz, Phrygian Rock-Cut Shrines, figure 80. The dressed rock extending out to the left of the idols, at the top of the stepped structure, features a large inscription, in two rows, boustrophedon. According to Haspels: ακενανολαϝαν|τιξες|μοδροϝανακ|αϝαρς. According to Brixhe and Lejeune, Corpus, 21–23, no. M-04: akinanogavan|tiyes|modrovanak|[?]avara[?].

two short curls at the left and right.[236] This is the familiar hair style found on representations of Matar. The various double idols have been interpreted either as double images of the goddess, indicating two different aspects of the deity, or as symbols of a male and female deity, although evidence for the latter theory is lacking.[237] In fact, the Faharet Çeşme relief, in relation to the two serving stands from Tumulus MM, strongly supports the former hypothesis. The two squares of decoration on the relief approximate the inlaid designs in the two lunette crowns on the serving stands.[238] This suggests that Matar had two aspects, each of which was important iconographically, and that the two aspects were interrelated and meant to appear together.[239]

The meaning that the Phrygians ascribed to these two motifs is not so easily discovered. Bands or panels of straight or wavy lines are rarely noted in scholarly discussions, normally overlooked as simple, decorative filler. However, groups of such lines appear with great frequency on ancient artifacts, suggesting that they were

meaningful, particularly in the art of early peoples. Chalcolithic pottery from Cucuteni sites in Moldavia features many types of these line groupings, which have been interpreted as the upper sky with its supply of water, or rain, when the lines are slanted or vertical. Solar symbols and the path of the sun have also been seen on this pottery; sun and rain were the two indispensable elements necessary for the cultivation of crops.[240] While the interpretation of the Cucuteni designs is open to question, there is no doubt that the sun, the seasons, and access to water governed the lives of ancient farmers.

Comparable decoration occurs in early Anatolia, notably on the neolithic pottery from Hacılar, where bands of zigzags run down the outside of bowls and appear in radial designs in the interior.[241] Wavy or zigzag lines in bands and panels appear on many examples of Middle Bronze Age pottery from Kültepe, running horizontally around vessels, enclosed within panels, or disposed vertically in bands, in the manner of the

[236] For three comparable double idols see Berndt-Ersöz, *Phrygian Rock-Cut Shrines*, figures 81–82 (Midas City) and 115 (Sincan, Ankara). The Sincan relief, carved on a stele with rounded top, shows a double idol with a common Hathor-style hairdo, wearing what appears to be a fibula at the center, in the area where the "shoulders" meet. The figure(s) appear beneath a gable with akroterion in the manner of the rock façades. Metin and Akalın, "Frigya'da bulunan İkiz İdol," plates 4–5.

[237] See Berndt-Ersöz, *Phrygian Rock-Cut Shrines*, 161–166. Also Berndt-Ersöz, "In Search of a Phrygian Male Superior God," for the theory that the double idols, including the relief at Faharet Çeşme, represent Matar and a male deity. See Mellink, "Midas-Stadt," 155, for her statement that the double idol at Faharet Çeşme "suggests in its decoration that one of the figures wears a woman's costume, the other has a swastika and may be male." This statement was purely speculative, but the idea has since been promoted, without warrant, by other scholars.

[238] As each of the serving stands represents a portable shrine of the goddess, complete with her symbolic manifestation and specific headdress, then each half of the double idol at Faharet Çeşme, with its specific geometric motif, should represent the goddess in some particular regard.

[239] This theory may be supported by several later representations of Kybele, which show double images of the goddess, seated in a shrine and holding different attributes. Naumann, *Ikonographie der Kybele*, 99–100, 188–190, 334–336, plate 30:1. On the other hand, see Hanfmann and Waldbaum, "Kybebe and Artemis," on a relief from Sardis with two comparable (but not identical) images of female deities. See also Hadzisteliou-Price, "Double and Multiple Representations," for numerous Greek images and theories about

their identity. The author concluded (pp. 54–56) that Meter or Kybele might be duplicated for the purpose of "strengthening the quality of the deity." This "twinning" occurs in the art of Çatalhöyük and is not well understood but may refer to "dualism and complementarity, rather than the traditional Western response of polarity and difference." Meskell, "Twin Peaks," 50. For multiple "idols" as architectural decoration at Kerkenes Dağ, see G. Summers and F. Summers, "Kerkenes Project in 2006," 32–33. On duplication and repetition in Assyrian royal and religious imagery, see Winter, "Ornament and the Rhetoric of Abundance." On dual aspects of Assyrian kingship and the duality of the Mesopotamian cosmos, see Ataç, "Visual Formula and Meaning in Neo-Assyrian Relief Sculpture," 84–92.

[240] These resources were essential for the raising of animals, as well. Rybakov, in "Cosmogony and Mythology of the Agriculturalists," parts 1 and 2, has associated the designs on Cucuteni pottery and figurines with the concerns of the early agriculturalists. See above, pp. 52–53. These early farmers were dependent on the sun and water, in the form of rain, rivers, and springs, for the fertility of the land and protection of their plantings. Rybakov and others have seen solar, lunar, and celestial symbols in the decoration on Cucuteni pottery, as well as water symbolism, which he interpreted as a plea to the heavens for rain. See also Gimbutas, *Language of the Goddess*, figure 75, for a Vinča vase with decoration interpreted as "rain torrents," sixth millennium B.C.; figure 74, for two neolithic Greek vessels, one with streams descending in bands on the interior of a bowl (Peloponnese) and the other with groups of parallel lines curving over the outside of a jar (Thessaly), sixth millennium B.C.

[241] Mellaart, *Excavations at Hacılar*, plates 88–89, 91, 94–106, and others.

Hacılar versions.[242] Pottery from the destruction level at Gordion shows wavy lines running horizontally around the bodies of vessels, and, rarely, running vertically in panels.[243] The wooden "sarcophagus" from Tumulus K-III at Gordion was decorated with carved panels of parallel lines, recalling the motif on the idol at Faharet Çeşme, arranged in an overall pattern suggestive of a woven mat. The K-III panels were rotated 90 degrees, in effect, as they progressed horizontally and vertically over the carved surface.[244] While it is not certain that the Phrygians associated this motif with water, it is worth noting that other cultures did make this connection. The Egyptian sign for "water" was a zigzag line, which was multiplied to represent ponds or waterways in artistic representations.[245] Wavy lines were used to represent water in early Mesopotamian art, conforming with the ideographic sign for water in the Uruk tablets; the "flowing vase," associated with abundant waters, was depicted with streams of wavy lines flowing out and over the sides of the vessel.[246]

Whatever the design in the lunette of serving stand B signified, the meander square in the lunette of stand A must have been related to it. The meander square motif, derived from the inscrutable swastika, is surely a key to understanding the designs in the field of the stands' faces. As has been determined above, the swastika was apotropaic and a symbol of good luck and protection, although it must once have had a more specific meaning (or meanings). Its rotational aspect suggests that it was related to movement, and its various associations with spinning, fertility, religion, and natural phenomena mark it as a complex, multivalent symbol.[247] On a human level, it could relate to the life force[248] or, on a cosmic scale, the movement of the elements of the universe.[249] As a radial design, the swastika is connected in its form to the star, rosette, and sun-disc—cosmic emblems that symbolized the deities in Mesopotamia.[250] This suggests that the meander squares on the serving stands, and also the large central rosettes, might have had celestial significance in Phrygia.[251] While none of this evidence provides a specific meaning for the meander squares, when taken together it strongly suggests that these designs served as potent numinous devices. Although the two motifs in the lunette "crowns" of the serving stands cannot be understood with certainty, they must have represented two aspects of the goddess Matar or two forces within her power. If they were indeed symbols of water and "life," they may have been related to agriculture.

---

[242] For a variety of examples, see T. Özgüç, *Kültepe Kazısı Raporu*, plates 57, 59–60; *Kültepe*, plates 122–125, 144, 185–186. Numerous vessels featuring this decoration are exhibited in the Museum of Anatolian Civilizations, Ankara, and include a small juglet, a miniature jar, small cups, and chalices, which may have been ritual vessels.

[243] See Sams, *Early Phrygian Pottery*, figures 24, 28–29, 41–43; plates 50–51, 58–59, 72, 85, 90, 125.

[244] Körte and Körte, *Gordion*, 44, figure 6. This "rotation" created a scheme of diagonals, as on the face of serving stand A from Tumulus MM. In the case of the K-III "sarcophagus," the repeated design may have been meant to suggest basketry or a woven pattern.

[245] Gardiner, *Egyptian Grammar*, "water," sign N 35. Note also sign N 4, "moisture falling from the sky," which took the form of a sky symbol with four vertical lines descending from it; rain however, was not a common phenomenon in Egypt. For water indicated by rows of zigzag lines, see, for example, Wilkinson and Hill, *Egyptian Wall Paintings*, 60–61, 70, 94, 148–149.

[246] Winter, "Representing Abundance: A Visual Dimension of the Agrarian State," 125. Black and Green, *Gods, Demons, and Symbols of Mesopotamia*, 184–185. See also Van Buren, *Symbols of the Gods in Mesopotamian Art*, 124–131, on the flowing vase, which symbolized "the perpetually recurring streams of living water productive of the fruitfulness and abundance bestowed by divine munificence" (pp. 124–125). On a stone basin from the Ur III period, the "life-giving waters" were shown as deriving from the heavens, "for it portrayed little female divinities who lean from the clouds to let the streams from the vases they hold mingle with those bubbling up from the vases supported between them" (p. 126). On the "waters of abundance" in Assyrian texts and the theme of abundance in Assyrian royal iconography, see Winter, "Ornament and the Rhetoric of Abundance," 252–258. For the Mesopotamian god Enki/Ea and his realm of the Apsû, the body of sweet waters located below the surface of the earth, see Ataç, "Visual Formula and Meaning in Neo-Assyrian Relief Sculpture," 86–89. See also Woods, "Sun-God Tablet of Nabû-apla-iddina Revisited," 79–80, on the importance of water in Mesopotamian cosmogonic thought. On the persistence of the zigzag line as a symbol of water into the Romanesque, see Goodenough, *Jewish Symbols in the Greco-Roman Period*, 36.

[247] See above, pp. 50–52. On the "paradox" of symbols, see Goodenough: "As regards explanations, we must also bear in mind that in the case of a symbol of any deep importance, no single explanation of its power or scope ever suffices." *Jewish Symbols in the Greco-Roman Period*, 41.

[248] This was surely the implication of the swastika on the pubic triangle of a lead "idol" from Troy III. Schliemann, *Ilios*, 337, no. 226 (CD-Figure 81).

[249] See above, p. 84 and notes 103–105.

[250] See above, pp. 87–88.

[251] The large rosettes, symbols of the goddess Matar, may have been adopted from Mesopotamia via North Syria along with their celestial implications. For the connection between the central grouping of symbols on the stands and the winged sun-disc, see p. 96 and n. 203.

A count of the meander squares on the faces of the two stands provides a possible explanation for their pairing. If the designs outside the curved legs are considered, 180 complete meander squares are found on stand B and 184 on stand A; if the design in the lunette crown of stand A is counted, 185 complete squares are found on stand A. This makes a total of 364 or 365 complete square designs in the main field of the stands' faces, the area that participates in the complex turning and flipping of motifs to manipulate the overall pattern. Additional squares are found between the curved legs on both stands; these are disposed in a different arrangement and do not take part in the complex system. There are also fragmentary square designs, found at the bottom of both faces, which serve to accommodate the shape of the curved legs as they encroach on the design grid. Leaving these subsidiary designs aside, the total of 364 or 365 complete meander squares suggests the number of days in a year. To explore whether this tabulation is meaningful, one must consider the ancient calendar—or *calendars*, rather, because there was no uniform calendrical system in antiquity.

Pre-Roman calendars did not seek to represent an accurate progression of the complete solar year, but served primarily to provide a structure for the civic and religious year, designating the official holidays within the scheme of the agricultural cycle. These holidays involved important festivals and elaborate rituals, which might take place over an extended period. Throughout the ancient world, religious holidays were considered essential to the well-being of the state and were rigorously observed according to schedule.[252] The calendar was controlled by the political and priestly hierarchy, as a manifestation of the cosmic order.

Ancient calendars could be based on the solar year, the lunar months, or a combination of the two, which resulted in a "luni-solar" calendar.[253] This last type involved months of 29 and 30 days, with an extra month intercalated from time to time to bring the calendar into alignment with the solar year. The luni-solar calendar, with various systems of intercalation, was used in most areas throughout early antiquity. In the Babylonian calendar, a 13th intercalary month was added when necessary, in order to insure the proper placement of activities designated to occur in particular months, such as the barley harvest.[254] In Mesopotamia, intercalations were made by decree, as indicated by texts from the Old Babylonian through the Persian periods. The Babylonian year began in the month of Nisannu (March/April) around the time of the vernal equinox.[255] The Assyrians used a lunar calendar in the second millennium B.C. but adopted the Babylonian luni-solar calendar in the first millennium.[256]

The observation of the heavens was of great antiquity, and a star calendar based on celestial phenomena was also in use in Mesopotamia, well attested by the beginning of the first millennium B.C.[257] In this system, the year was determined by the return of a particular star or constellation to a specified area of the sky. This star-based

[252] The Hittites, for instance, believed that the gods required constant offerings and worship, in the form of daily ritual as well as major festivals, which were regulated through a complex religious calendar. These festivals might involve cultic journeys and processionals enacted by the king, his entourage, and images of the deities, and could last for several hours or extend over a period of more than 30 days. McMahon, "Theology, Priests, and Worship in Hittite Anatolia," 1993. For a comprehensive discussion of the festival year, see M. Cohen, *Cultic Calendars of the Ancient Near East*. On ancient astronomy, calendars, and the reckoning of time, see Evans, *Ancient Astronomy* 5–8, 163–190.

[253] But see Neugebauer, "Origin of the Egyptian Calendar," 400–403, on the complexity of ancient calendric concepts, the problematic nature of the designation "luni-solar," and the use of schematic calendars for practical purposes alongside those based on celestial phenomena.

[254] The duration of a month is approximately 29.5 days. This normally resulted in 12 months or "lunations" of either 29 or 30 days, for a total of 354 days in a lunar year, as opposed to the 365.25 days of the solar year. In most cultures, the length of a month was reckoned from the first appearance of the lunar crescent on the western horizon in the evening. Rochberg, "Astronomy and Calendars in Ancient Mesopotamia," 1931–1932.

[255] During the Neo-Babylonian period (626–536 B.C.), due to the variation in the length of the luni-solar year, the first of Nisannu might fall between March 11 and April 26. Rochberg, "Astronomy and Calendars in Ancient Mesopotamia," 1931.

[256] An early Assyrian lunar calendar has been reconstructed, which shows evidence of correlation with the solar year in terms of the naming of the year eponym. A lunar calendar without intercalation was in use in the Middle Assyrian period (14th–13th centuries B.C.), with the resulting slippage through the solar year. Rochberg, "Astronomy and Calendars in Ancient Mesopotamia," 1932. A lunar calendar is still in use for the Muslim religious year.

[257] Evidence for this system is found in the two-tablet astronomical compendium MUL.APIN ("Plough Star"), copies of which were found in Ashurbanipal's library (seventh century B.C.); the compendium is now thought to have been formulated as early as 1370 B.C. MUL.APIN includes the names and positions in the sky of fixed stars, the dates of their heliacal rising, astronomical seasons, dates for the solstices and equinoxes, gnomon shadow lengths, and the

year closely approximated the solar year and was correlated with the luni-solar calendar. The star-based system was used for the agricultural year, as most fully expressed in the *Works and Days* of the Greek poet Hesiod, who connected celestial and natural phenomena with the proper times to plow, plant, and harvest.

The Egyptians did not use a luni-solar system but had a religious lunar calendar and a separate civil solar calendar, the dominant calendar of ancient Egypt. The solar calendar had 365 days, consisting of 12 months of 30 days with five days added at the end.[258] The Egyptian solar calendar was in use from the time of the Old Kingdom and was considered to be advantageous because of its regularity. However, every four years the Egyptian solar calendar slipped back a day, getting progressively out of synch with the solar year on which it was based. The Egyptians knew that the actual year was somewhat longer than 365 days but did nothing to correct their calendar, which went through a complete cycle with respect to the actual solar year every 1,461 Egyptian years.[259]

The Greeks of the mid-first millennium B.C. used the luni-solar calendar, but each city had its own calendar and followed its own system of intercalation of a 13th month. Furthermore, extra days could be "inserted" by the authorities at will, which allowed religious activities to be moved within the calendar.[260] In 45 B.C., Julius Caesar instituted the Julian calendar, a solar calendar that adopted a mean length of 365.25 days for the year. This calendar, which took its final form by A.D. 8, was used until the Gregorian reform in A.D. 1582.[261]

This brief survey shows that of all the examples noted, the Egyptian solar calendar, with its 365 days, is the only one that might relate to the Tumulus MM serving stands, with their total number of 364 or 365 complete meander squares in the main field of the inlaid faces.[262] If this tabulation is meaningful, the correspondence is of interest, although it does not necessarily suggest that the Phrygians used the Egyptian solar calendar. What it may indicate, however, is a knowledge of the Egyptian calendric system, or, at least, an understanding of the 365-day solar year, as one would expect from such an advanced culture.[263] The length of the solar year could be approximated by reference to recurring phenomena, such as the equinoxes and solstices or the

position of the sun and moon relative to certain stars at the equinoxes and solstices. Also recorded in MUL.APIN is a stellar calendar mentioning winds, as well as a calendar of planets. Evans, *Ancient Astronomy*, 5–8, 27–31 (on the gnomon); Rochberg, *Heavenly Writing*, 6–7; Rochberg, "Astronomy and Calendars in Ancient Mesopotamia," 1930; and see Hunger and Pingree, *MUL.APIN*. The heliacal rising of a star is its first appearance on the eastern horizon just before dawn. The gnomon was a vertical stick that cast a shadow and was used to tell time, indicate the path of the sun, and determine the cardinal directions.

[258] The Egyptian calendric system has been the subject of much debate, with more than one lunar calendar posited, as well as a star calendar based on the heliacal rising of the star Sothis (Sirius) in July. This corresponded approximately to the time of the Nile inundation and was seen as its harbinger. However important the rising of Sothis was for the Egyptians, there is no conclusive evidence that it was the basis for an actual calendar. Depuydt, *Civil Calendar and Lunar Calendar in Ancient Egypt*, 2, 9–20. Clagett, *Calendars, Clocks, and Astronomy*, 47. The Babylonian, Macedonian, Julian, and Alexandrian calendars were used later in Egypt under the periods of Persian, Greek, and Roman domination.

[259] In 238 B.C., Ptolemy III tried to correct the problem by adding a leap year every four years, but the proposed reform was rejected by the priesthood and populace. Evans, *Ancient Astronomy*, 176, 207. Because of its regularity, and despite the slippage of a day every four years, the ancient Egyptian calendar was adopted by Ptolemy (second century A.D.) for his astronomical work, used by Copernicus, and continued to be utilized by astronomers up to the beginning of the modern era. Evans, 175.

[260] Each Greek city had its own month names, and the year might begin at different times in different cities. The only way that people from different cities could communicate a date to one another unambiguously was by means of star phases. The use of star calendars by Greek astronomers followed in the tradition of Hesiod (see below). Evans, *Ancient Astronomy*, 7, 20, 182–183.

[261] Three years of every four had 365 days, and the fourth was a leap year of 366. Evans, *Ancient Astronomy*, 163–168.

[262] While the resemblance may be fortuitous, it seems compelling nonetheless. The 365 days of the Egyptian calendar were grouped into 12 months of 30 days, with five days added at the end ($12 \times 30 + 5$). On the stands' faces, the square designs are organized into what seem to be groups of 30, if one follows a vertical path down and up through the columns of the complete square designs. Stand B has 180 complete squares outside the curved legs (6×30), and stand A has 184/185 ($6 \times 30 + 4/5$), for a total of 364/365 ($12 \times 30 + 4/5$).

[263] In the fifth century B.C., Herodotus wrote in praise of the Egyptian calendar (2.4). One of Herodotus's contemporaries, Xanthus of Lydia, noted the importance of the 365-day year at Sardis. Munn, *Mother of the Gods*, 203, n. 89. However, the actual use of the Egyptian solar calendar beyond Egypt is confirmed only much later, by Ptolemy in the second century A.D. and in the Alexandrian *astronomical canon*, a list of Babylonian (and then Persian) kings with their reigns recorded in 365-day Egyptian years. The date system in the *astronomical canon* has been taken to indicate that the Alexandrian astronomers translated the Babylonian data for use in their own system—and *not* that the Babylonians used the Egyptian calendric conventions to record the reigns of their rulers. Evans, *Ancient Astronomy*, 176.

appearance of particular stars or constellations.[264] The solar year, and the use of such phenomena to track the year's progression, was tied directly to the practice of agriculture.

This is elaborated in Hesiod's *Works and Days*, written in the seventh century B.C. The detailed agricultural treatise proceeds in the manner of a calendar, describing the preparations to be carried out in the summer months, the fall plowing and planting of grain, the activities that took place during the winter after the planting was done, the spring harvest, and the subsequent threshing and winnowing. Fruits and vegetables appeared in season, the grapes were picked in September and wine was made, and the cycle began again with the late fall plowing and planting. According to Hesiod, "When the Atlas-born Pleiades rise, start the harvest—the plowing, when they set."[265] The autumn rains arrive when "the star Sirius goes during the day only briefly above the heads of death-nurtured human beings and takes a greater share of the night"; this is the best time to cut wood for plows and wagons.[266] The voice of the crane signals the season of winter rain and the time to plow,[267] which should be completed before the winter solstice.[268] Winter tasks should be carried out "until the year is ended and you have nights and days of equal

length," interpreted as the spring equinox, when "Earth (Ge), the mother of all, bears again her various fruit."[269]

This cycle occupied a large part of the population in ancient agrarian societies, in which grain was the main subsistence food. Ancient political systems were based on the control of farming; the grain harvest was taxed, and state ideology and religious ritual reflected the farmer's world.[270] Major festivals and other events of the calendar promoted the stability of the annual agricultural cycle, on which the survival of the state depended. The Tumulus MM serving stands, with their official religious iconography, might have played a role in this system. The pair of stands, taken together, may have served as a calendrical metaphor—or possibly even an actual calendar—which was related to the solar year.

According to this theory, the meander squares should then represent the days of the year, or the passage of the sun (or celestial sphere) as it defined these days, or even the cycle of life itself. Each stand would represent half the year, perhaps the periods between the vital fall and spring equinoxes. Just such a division of the year into two six-month "equinox years" was observed in Mesopotamia.[271] Visually speaking, stand B is the likely candidate for the winter season, when the

---

[264] The Babylonian astronomical compendium MUL.APIN indicates that the solar year could be defined by the equinoxes and solstices. These could be determined in relation to celestial events or through the measurement of the lengths of the days and nights with a water clock. It is unclear how accurate such measurements might have been in the early first millennium B.C. Hunger and Pingree, *Astral Sciences in Mesopotamia*, 75. On MUL.APIN, supra n. 257. On Greek attempts to measure the length of the year accurately and determine the times of the equinoxes and solstices, see Evans, *Ancient Astronomy*, 205–211.

[265] *Works and Days* 383–384. Unless otherwise noted, the following passages from *Works and Days* are given in the Glenn Most translation. Hesiod's comment refers to the morning (heliacal) rising and morning (cosmical) setting of the Pleiades, which occurred in his day in the first half of May and late October/early November, respectively, according to Most's calculations. The morning rising of the Pleiades refers to their first appearance on the eastern horizon just before sunrise; their morning setting refers to their appearance on the western horizon just before sunrise. Evans, *Ancient Astronomy*, 4–5. Hannah, *Greek and Roman Calendars*, 11–12, 20–24.

[266] *Works and Days*, 414–422. In late September or early October.

[267] *Works and Days*, 448–451. In late October or early November.

[268] *Works and Days*, 479–482. Around December 21.

[269] *Works and Days*, 561–563. Around March 20. The translation given here is that of Evelyn-White, who sees a

reference to the spring equinox. Glenn Most interprets the text differently: "balance the nights and days until the end of the year."

[270] Eyre, "Agricultural Cycle, Farming, and Water Management in the Ancient Near East," 177–178, 184. Renfrew, "Vegetables in the Ancient Near Eastern Diet," 202. For pictorial evidence, see the complete relief of Warpalawas at Ivriz, where the king supplicates a colossal vegetation god who holds sheaves of grain and a vine with grapes. Akurgal, *Art of the Hittites*, color plate XXIV, plate 140.

[271] The vernal and autumnal equinoxes could be determined approximately at this period by the observation of celestial phenomena, the use of shadow measurements, or timing by water clock. Supra n. 264. Evans, *Ancient Astronomy*, 53–56. Clagett, *Calendars, Clocks, and Astronomy*, 65–111. For the division of the year according to the equinoxes in Mesopotamia, see Cohen, *Cultic Calendars of the Ancient Near East*, 6–7, 400–453. The six-month "equinox year" appears to have been an important factor in the organization of the Mesopotamian cultic calendar, with a new year's or *akītu* festival held in the first and seventh months, at the beginning of each "equinox year." On the respective merits of the summer and winter seasons in Mesopotamia, and the literary "Debate between Summer and Winter" in terms of the types of abundance the two protagonists provide, see Winter, "Representing Abundance: A Visual Dimension of the Agrarian State," 129, n. 16.

Virgil underscores the importance of the equinoxes in *Georgics* 1.208 ff., and symbols of the equinoxes played a key role in the cult of Mithras, which spread throughout the fields have been plowed and planted. Its regular alternating rows of two main designs may evoke the seeds in their furrows, lying in wait for the coming spring. Stand A, with its three main designs and energetic system of diagonals, suggests movement and growth and might represent the return of spring and subsequent growing season.[272] If the stands are calendrical, then the year must relate to the domain of the goddess Matar, since her symbolic presence dominates the field of the inlaid designs. She would thus oversee the agricultural year, its festivals and events, insuring the fertility of the land and promoting the welfare of the state. The serving stands would represent the passing of the seasons, the progression of the celestial bodies, and, by extension, the cosmic enterprise itself. While this thesis is speculative, there is some corroborating evidence for the domain of Matar.

Large-scale agricultural production is attested at Gordion in the 9th–8th century B.C. Evidence from seeds and plant parts recovered at the site shows that six-row barley, einkorn and bread wheat, lentils, and bitter vetch were cultivated.[273] Wheat and barley were abundant in most of the megaron units of the Terrace Building from the destruction level. The grinding of grain took place in the main rooms, as indicated by the numerous stone querns that were found *in situ*,

in one case with wheat still in place on the surface. Ovens were used to roast the grain as well as bake bread, and large, dished trays of wood or clay may have functioned as kneading troughs for the making of dough from flour.[274] Grain was also processed to make beer, which the Phrygians were known to appreciate.[275] Finally, flax was cultivated, spun, and woven into textiles, fragments of which have survived from the city mound and tumuli (see Appendix 8).[276] Thus, Gordion depended on sufficient crop yield and the stability of the agricultural cycle as did other ancient cities of the Near East and Europe. The survival of the state and well-being of its citizens were tied directly to the vagaries of farming. It would be surprising, then, if Phrygia's primary and only attested deity were not connected to agricultural fertility.

The designs on the inlaid table and serving stands from Tumulus MM are best appreciated in this connection. The motifs on these pieces include ancient fertility symbols and "genealogical patterns," found alongside symbols of the goddess Matar. It is therefore possible that these early motifs were not only protective but retained some of their original associations—with human and agricultural fertility, as well as with an ultimate ancestor or creator deity.[277] Matar, whose name means "mother," seems to reflect these qualities.

Roman Empire beginning in the first century A.D. Symbols of the equinoxes have been seen in the iconography of the mithraeum; and the tauroctony, or bull slaying, has been interpreted as a kind of code that foretold the precession of the equinoxes and the coming of a new astrological era. Ulansey, *Origins of the Mithraic Mysteries*, 62–64, 112–116. For a different view of the role of the equinoxes in the cosmic simulacrum of the mithraeum, see Beck, *Religion of the Mithras Cult*, 107–115.

[272] The fact that stand A has four or five more meander squares than stand B might be considered to support this division. The period between the spring and fall equinoxes, the "growing season," has up to seven more days than the fall/winter period, depending on which days are taken to designate the equinoxes. In contrast, the two periods between the solstices are approximately equal in length. However, in the eighth century B.C., the time of the equinoxes could only be approximated. According to modern calculations, in 750 B.C., the spring/summer period had 186 days, and the fall/winter period had 179.2 days. See Evans, *Ancient Astronomy*, 56, 205; *http://individual.utoronto.ca/kalendis/seasons.htm*.

[273] Miller, "Plant Use at Gordion," 304. Miller, "Archaeobotany: Macroremains," 92–93.

[274] Young, "Gordion Campaign of 1959," 241–242; plate 61, figure 26; plate 62, figures 27–28. DeVries, "Greeks and Phrygians," 39 and n. 29; figure 10. The querns occur regularly along the rear wall, numbering between five and eighteen, as well as elsewhere in the rooms. Wheat was found *in*

situ on a quern in TB 5. Large numbers of loom weights and spindle whorls were also found in these buildings, attesting to weaving on the premises. See Burke, "Textile Production at Gordion and the Phrygian Economy."

[275] Sams, "Beer in the City of Midas." See Chapter 8.

[276] A small jar of flax seeds was recovered from the Terrace Building (TB 2) at Gordion. Miller, "Archaeobotany: Macroremains," 93. DeVries, et al., "New Dates for Iron Age Gordion." For evidence of flax among the textiles from Tumulus MM, see Appendix 8. Louisa Bellinger published a preliminary examination of the Gordion textiles in 1962, identifying some of the fibers as flax or hemp, although until these particular fragments are re-examined, this identification must remain provisional. Bellinger, "Textiles from Gordion," 8, 13–16. The combined work of grinding grain and weaving textiles also took place in the palace of the Phaiakian king Alkinoös, as recorded in the *Odyssey*: "And in his house are fifty serving women, and of these some grind the apple-colored grain at the turn of the hand mill, and there are those who weave the webs and who turn the distaffs." *Odyssey* 7.103–105.

[277] See above, pp. 52–56. These patterns are still found on traditional costumes and textiles in eastern Europe, Russia, Turkey, and elsewhere, where they are associated with pre-Christian "goddess" symbols and other motifs that relate to human and agricultural fertility. Many such textiles survive in ethnographic collections, with abstract depictions of the "goddess" holding birds, "sun-discs," or tree-like branches. In spring festivals, ritual embroidered towels were

This ideology is expressed in early Greek texts relating to the Mother of the Gods, Earth (Ge or Gaia), and also to Rhea and Demeter, who could be identified or conflated with the Greek Mother (Meter). Meter was the manifestation of the Phrygian goddess Matar, worshipped widely in Greece beginning in the Archaic period.[278]

The Mother of the Gods, "mother of all gods and men," is addressed in the 14th Homeric hymn as "well-pleased with the sound of rattles and of timbrels, with the voice of flutes and the outcry of wolves and bright-eyed lions, with echoing hills and wooded coombes."[279] These associations recall the Phrygian Matar, with her mountain habitat and attendant lions. The 30th Homeric hymn is addressed to Earth (Gaia), "mother of all, eldest of all beings." This hymn is worth considering here, as it may reflect the domain of the Phrygian goddess:

> I will sing of well-founded Earth (Gaia), mother of all, eldest of all beings. She feeds all creatures that are in the world, all that go upon the goodly land, and all that are in the paths of the seas, and all that fly: all these are fed of her store. Through you, O queen, men are blessed in their children and blessed in their harvests, and to you it belongs to give means of life to mortal men and to take it away. Happy is the man whom you delight to honour! He has all things abundantly: his fruitful land is laden with corn [grain], his pastures are covered with cattle, and his house is filled with good things. Such men rule orderly in their cities of fair women: great riches and wealth follow them: their sons exult with ever-fresh delight, and their daughters in flower–laden bands play and skip merrily over the soft flowers of the field. Thus is it with those whom you honor O holy goddess, bountiful spirit.
>
> Hail, Mother (Meter) of the gods, wife of starry Heaven (Ouranos); freely bestow upon me for this my song substance that cheers the heart![280]

In *Works and Days*, Hesiod calls Earth (Ge) "the mother of all" who "bears again her various fruit" beginning at the time of the vernal equinox. Earth (Gaia) also appears in Hesiod's *Theogony*, as the initial force to issue from the primordial Chaos, the first state of the universe, which has been seen as a chasm or gap:

> In truth, first of all Chasm (Chaos) came to be, and then broad-breasted Earth (Gaia), the ever immovable seat of all the immortals …Earth first of all bore starry Sky (Ouranos), equal to herself, to cover her on every side, so that she would be the ever immovable seat for the blessed gods.[281]

---

tied to the branches of trees and also to the grave markers of one's ancestors. Ritual cloths were made to celebrate the harvest, depicting women holding cups containing the saved seeds that would be used for the next sowing. A calendar embroidery in the Moscow Historical Museum shows the 365 days of the calendar year arranged in a circle, surrounding a large rosette with a swastika at the center (CD-Figure 94). The circle is divided into months, with the major pagan festivals noted; the best days for planting various crops are marked, as well as the solstices and equinoxes. The meaning of these fertility symbols has faded, and although there has been a revival in some regions, "the urgent necessity to invigorate the fields by evoking the goddess, in the twentieth century became the work of the tractor and the fertilizer truck." Kelly, *Goddess Embroideries of Eastern Europe*, 61. Goddess images are now called "dolls" by the women who still embroider them, and although they avoid discussing their meaning, they admit to feeling compelled to reproduce them. For a Turkish doll dressed in traditional costume, see CD-Figure 93. This doll was made by Hanife Güneş, from Sorgun, who still wears such traditional clothing. On the lozenge-and-dot motif as a fertility symbol, see above, pp. 52–55. Textile motifs also appear in traditional woodworking, which has been deemed an important area for future research. Kelly, *Goddess Embroideries of Eastern Europe*, 9–29, 75–76, 111, 134–139; figure 9 ("calendar" embroidery) and see CD-Figure 94. Kelly, "Living Textile Traditions of the Carpathians," 166–

177. Breu, "Traditional Turkish Women's Dress," 38–49. Williams, "Protection from Harm," 152.

[278] Roller, *In Search of God the Mother*, 169–171. Roller seems to suggest that the Phrygian Mother entered Greece as a kind of blank slate ("there was little hint as to what she was the mother of") and was there assimilated as Earth, Rhea, and even Demeter and Hera. Instead, one might acknowledge the strong possibility that Matar came from Phrygia *as* a powerful fertility deity, the Mother of All, and that this is the reason she was so readily identified with her Greek counterparts.

[279] *Hymn to the Mother of the Gods* (XIV). In *Hesiod, the Homeric Hymns and Homerica*, 438–439.

[280] *Hymn to Earth Mother of All* (XXX) 1–18. *Hesiod, the Homeric Hymns and Homerica*, 456–457. Demeter, "bringer of seasons and giver of good gifts," takes on some of the powers of the Earth in the *Hymn to Demeter*; her mourning for the absence of her daughter Persephone caused the earth to be infertile: "The ground would not make the seed sprout, for rich-crowned Demeter kept it hid. In the fields the oxen drew many a curved plough in vain, and much white barley was cast upon the land without avail." *Hymn to Demeter* (II) 306–309. In *Hesiod, the Homeric Hymns, and Homerica*, 310–311. For the syncretistic character of the Greek Mother, see Roller, *In Search of God the Mother*, 169–177; however, Roller does not utilize the Greek sources as evidence for the domain of the Phrygian goddess Matar. Supra n. 278.

[281] *Theogony* 116–128, trans. Glenn Most. Subsequently

The realm of Earth, Mother of All, was likely the domain of the Phrygian Matar; like Earth, Matar must have been a creator deity, as she appears alone without a consort.

The cult of the Phrygian goddess had reached Greece by the sixth century B.C., recognized in numerous niche sculptures (*naiskoi*) from East Greece and then on the mainland.[282] She may have arrived earlier, if she is to be equated with Ge/Gaia, as suggested by the passages noted above. It has been supposed that this early manifestation represents *not* the Phrygian Matar but an indigenous Greek goddess.[283] However, a goddess with many of Matar's attributes is depicted on Greek pottery of the seventh century B.C. The most striking example is found on a Boeotian amphora (Plate 117C).[284] On the front of the vase, in the panel between the handles, stands a goddess with outstretched arms, flanked by two lions (below) and two birds (above). She wears an ornately patterned dress with a fish at the front, and wavy lines extend out from her waist and stream down to the ground. Two large leaf-like forms spring up from the ground

line, beneath the bodies of the lions. A bull's head and leg appear at the left and right, and six swastikas float in the field as "filling ornament."[285]

The goddess has long sleeves that cover her hands, so that her arms look almost like wings. This correspondence is accentuated by her sleeve decoration, a series of hatched lines, which also occur on the wings of the birds above.[286] On the back of the amphora, a large bird occupies most of the central panel. A hare is shown below, suggesting that the bird is a raptor. Two triangular forms rise from the ground line, perhaps indicating a mountainous setting, and the hare leaps over one of them as if to escape the bird's clutches. In the field is a large quatrefoil design, as well as small birds, swastikas, and crosses. The bull's head and leg on the front of the vase seem to represent a sacrifice that is being offered to the goddess.[287] With the exception of the sacrificial animal parts, almost everything in these panels is found in the iconography of the Phrygian Matar.[288] Other early Greek objects display equally intriguing imagery.[289]

---

from Chaos came Erebos and Nux (Night). After bringing forth the mountains and sea "without delightful love," Earth lay with Sky and bore Okeanos, Rhea, Kronos, and a host of other gods. *Theogony* 123 ff. The idea of a Mother creator deity arising from a chasm or void is seen in the religions of many peoples. Aditi, original ancestor and mother of the gods in the *Rig Veda*, has figured in the interpretation of the early Cucuteni artifacts. *Rig Veda* 10.72, et al. Rybakov, "Cosmogony and Mythology of the Agriculturalists," part 1, 23.

[282] Roller, *In Search of God the Mother*, 119 ff. Naumann, *Ikonographie der Kybele*, cat. 37–43, plates 12:4, 13, 14:1–2, et al. See also several statuettes from Ephesus, which may represent the Phrygian deity or participants in her cult, although these statuettes are neither identified nor dated conclusively. Akurgal, *Kunst Anatoliens*, plates 155–159, 167–173. For comparison, see the statuettes from Tumulus D at Bayındır, Antalya Museum. Özgen and Öztürk, *Heritage Recovered*, 26–27.

[283] Roller, *In Search of God the Mother*, 169–170. There is evidence for a powerful female deity in the Aegean in the Bronze Age if not earlier. See Ventris and Chadwick, *Documents in Mycenaean Greek*, 481, no. 306, for a Pylos tablet with the title "Divine Mother" (ma-te-re te-i-ja). For the famous Cretan seal impression showing a goddess flanked by lions standing on top of a mountain, see Marinatos, *Goddess and the Warrior*, figure 6.8. See also Goodison and Morris, "Beyond the 'Great Mother,'" 128–130.

[284] Arias and Hirmer, *History of Greek Vase Painting*, plate 11. Boardman, *Early Greek Vase Painting*, figures 102.1–2. For drawings of the front and back views, see Gimbutas, *Language of the Goddess*, figure 405.

[285] Motifs found on the inlaid furniture from Gordion also occur as "filling ornament" on many Orientalizing-period Greek vases. This interesting subject is beyond the

scope of the present discussion and will be treated in a separate study.

[286] Such long sleeves have occurred in the Balkans, southern Russia, and throughout the Middle East; in eastern Europe, they have been associated with ritual dance, in which maidens impersonated bird-spirits in order to channel their fertility. The bird-dance also occurs in ancient Greece, shown on later Greek pottery. Barber, "Curious Tale of the Ultra-Long Sleeve," 116–127. Coldstream, *Deities in Aegean Art*, 12–13.

[287] Piggott, "Heads and Hoofs," 112. The bull's head and leg may also have had cosmological significance.

[288] Painted fragments provide evidence of related, although simpler, scenes on Phrygian pottery. Prayon, *Phrygische Plastik*, figure 14a–c (14a is from Boğazköy and not Gordion). T. Özgüç, *Maşat II*, 132–133; plate 78:2, 3a–b; figures 152, 162. Bittel, *Hattusha*, figure 38.

[289] See, for instance, a Boeotian (or imported) relief pithos from Thebes, showing a goddess with raised arms in the center of a panel (CD-Figure 85). She is flanked by lions who rear up to the level of her hands. She wears a high polos headdress, from which issue two leafy sprigs, and a long robe decorated with a net-like lozenge-and-dot pattern. Two small figures stand to her sides, embracing her skirt, somewhat reminiscent of the two small musicians of the Boğazköy Matar (Plate 119A). Vermaseren, *Cybele and Attis*, plate 1. Marinatos, *Goddess and the Warrior*, figure 6.15.

Another Boeotian object, a painted ceramic version of a polos headdress in Stockholm, shows a goddess with outstretched arms, clad in a peplos with a large swastika on her breast and more swastikas running down the front of her skirt (CD-Figure 84). Also on her skirt, to either side of the panel of swastikas, are two wavy lines that stream down to the ground. She herself wears a polos, with circular decorations at the top and front, the one at the

The later Greek Mother (Meter), or Kybele, is outside the scope of this discussion, although it is worth noting that her cult was tied to the fertility of the land and involved the celebration of mysteries.[290] The Roman Magna Mater was imported directly from Phrygia, although by the time she was brought to Rome, the Phrygian cult had become Hellenized.[291] The Magna Mater retained her connection to agriculture; her festival, the Megalesia, was held in early April.[292] According to Lucretius, the Great Mother of the Gods was the mother of wild beasts, creator of humankind, and was identified with Earth (Tellus), the source of springs and of fire. She had the power to make the grain grow, produce fruitful trees, and provide rivers and pastures for animals.[293] Thus the later manifestations of the Phrygian Matar were creator and fertility deities, providing additional circumstantial evidence for the character of the original goddess.[294]

Finally, a depiction on a Roman relief from Amiternum may be considered in the context of this discussion.[295] The relief shows a funerary procession, with mourners and musicians disposed around the central scene (CD-Figure 100). Pallbearers carry the bier, which supports an image of the deceased lying on a bed; behind the bed is a large screen-like backdrop decorated with a star-and-crescent set within a field of stars. The backdrop has legs and suggests a stand of some sort. Although this piece of furniture is difficult to interpret, its celestial decoration implies a cosmological metaphor.[296] This symbolism again occurs in the crescent and seven stars (or planets) depicted on a coin of the deceased empress Faustina the Elder.[297] The theme of *aeternitas* dominates the posthumously issued coins of the deified Faustina, representing the ethereal sphere from which she could oversee the well-being of the Roman populace. This cosmic space appears on the fabulous shield of Achilles made by Hephaestus, as described in the *Iliad*:

> He made the earth upon it, and the sky, and the sea's water, and the tireless sun, and the moon waxing into her fullness, and on it all the constellations that festoon the heavens, the Pleiades and the Hyades and the strength of Orion and the Bear, whom men give also the name of the Wagon, who turns about in a fixed place and looks at Orion and she alone is never plunged in the wash of the Ocean.[298]

As has been demonstrated, many ancient cultures utilized cosmological and religious symbolism as a meaningful part of their decorative repertoire.

---

front resembling a star or rosette. Two birds fly to either side of her head, and she is flanked by two pairs of offering bearers, who wear poloi and have streams running down their skirts. Plants grow up from the ground, to meet a row of large swastikas (which can be flipped or have dots in the quadrants). More swastikas float in the field, along with two large rosettes. This goddess is associated with birds and rosettes and provides water for the plants, which grow under the influence of the swastikas. Simon, "Hera und die Nymphen," figures 1–3, 6; Boardman, *Early Greek Vase Painting*, figure 235.

For more of this symbolism, see the Boeotian "dolls" or "bell idols" mentioned above, p. 54, n. 162, and CD-Figures 82–83. Although Boardman notes the Boeotians' "backwardness of response" and calls their pottery "outdated" or "wholly imitative of others," they appear to be in the vanguard with respect to their Anatolian contacts and their worship of the Earth Mother Goddess. Boardman, 109–110. This goddess may also be evoked by a wooden statuette ("Hera") from Samos, who wears an ornate robe, belt, cape, and a high headdress that is decorated with designs in panels. Kopcke, "Neue Holzfunde aus dem Heraion von Samos," 102–107, plates 45–47. See also Prayon, *Phrygische Plastik*, 74–75, figure 13.

[290] Roller, *In Search of God the Mother*, 149 ff., 169 ff. By the fifth century B.C., Meter was equated with the goddess Demeter, although the two deities were worshipped with separate rites in their own sanctuaries. Euripides, *Helen* 1301–1337. This suggests that the worship of the goddess Matar in Phrygia may also have involved mystery rites, although there is no concrete evidence to support (or refute)

such a theory. See below, p. 135.

[291] Roller, *In Search of God the Mother*, 264–271. The Romans imported a small, dark stone from Pessinous (or Pergamon) in 204 B.C. According to Ovid, the stone was sought as the Mother of the Romans, who traced their origins to Phrygian ancestors. *Fasti* 4.259–274.

[292] Ovid, *Fasti* 4.179–190. The cultivation of grain was said to have originated in Phrygia, whence it spread throughout the world. Lucretius, *De Rerum Natura* 2.610–613.

[293] Lucretius, *De Rerum Natura* 2.589–599. For the Roman aspects of the cult of the Magna Mater in Lucretius, first century B.C., see K. Summers, "Lucretius' Roman Cybele."

[294] *Pace* Roller, *In Search of God the Mother*, 318.

[295] Aquila, Museo Aquilano. First century B.C.(?) Strong, *Roman Art*, 65, plate 60. Toynbee, *Death and Burial in the Roman World*, 46–47, plate 11. Calmeyer, "Achaimenidische Möbel," plate 76B.

[296] Toynbee, *Death and Burial in the Roman World*, 46, sees the decoration as "symbolic of celestial apotheosis." The designs on the Amiternum stand may relate to textiles, as with those on the Tumulus MM serving stands. On the possibility that Assyrian paneled textiles (or spangled textiles with gold stars or rosettes) represented the celestial sphere, see Oppenheim, "Golden Garments of the Gods," 180–181. Supra n. 125.

[297] As: head of Faustina (obverse); moon and seven stars (reverse), A.D. 141. Mt. Holyoke College Art Museum. Bergmann and Watson, *The Moon and the Stars*, 7; 26, cat. 23; frontispiece.

[298] Homer, *Iliad* 18.483–489.

The Phrygians were among those peoples who did so, as shown by their architectural monuments and wooden furniture. Symbols of the Phrygian goddess Matar and her attributes adorn the Tumulus MM serving stands, set within a schematic version of the cosmic universe, if one may argue from the evidence. It is within this metaphorical context that the iconography of the stands can best be understood.

CHAPTER SIX

THE FURNITURE FROM THE NORTHEAST CORNER

Carved stretcher
12522 W 130 (previously uncatalogued)
Short leg
12538 W 131 (previously uncatalogued)
Other fragments not catalogued.
Carved stretcher, short leg, tenon in short leg:
    boxwood (*Buxus sempervirens* L.); short wide
    slats: juniper (*Juniperus* sp.).
Found in northeast corner of tomb.
Color Plate IIB; Figures 76–78; Plates 100–106,
    127A.
Carved stretcher. G.P.L. ca. 32.5 cm. G.P.H.
    ca. 4.5 cm. G.P.Th. 1.9 cm. G.P.L. small
    fragment ca. 6.5 cm.
Short slats. G.P.L. better-preserved wide slat
    ca. 22 cm. G.P.W. ca. 6.6 cm. G.P.Th. .9 cm.
Short leg. G.P.H. ca. 15.8 cm. Est.H. ca. 18.8 cm.
    Est.D. at ring ca. 5 cm.

The furniture from the northeast corner of the tomb was in poor condition when it was found in 1957, preserved as a scatter of degraded wooden fragments interspersed with the remains of textiles (Color Plate IIB, Plate 100). The fragments were sketched by Dorothy Cox while they were still on the tomb floor.[1] The objects were recorded, painted with Alvar, and removed from the chamber on sheets of plywood, although some of the fragile pieces deteriorated in the process (Plates 101–103).[2] Cox's ink version of the Tumulus MM plan (p. viii) shows the fragments *in situ*, although they have not been reproduced exactly from her original sketch. Except for a few substantial pieces (Plates 104–105), the objects have now disintegrated into a group of amorphous chunks. The 1957 photographs, Cox's tomb plans, and Young's brief description constitute the main evidence for three or more pieces of furniture.[3]

The most recognizable elements were fragmentary furniture legs in three sizes, recorded by Young as belonging to short, medium, and high stools. These became known as "stool #1" (short legs), "stool #2" (long legs), and "stool #3" (medium legs), although Young thought that the last two objects were possibly tables or stands. Two of the short legs can be seen in the excavation photographs, lying near the west edge of the pile and adjacent to the bag of fibulae (Plate 100, center). To the north and south of the short legs, two of the long legs extend out obliquely. The medium legs, found near the north wall, are not clearly visible in the photographs. The dimensions of the three "stools" were approximated by Young and Cox, based on the position of the legs as found on the tomb floor.

Form and Function

The medium-sized stool (stool #3) had four legs that were 30 cm long. The legs were round in section and tapered downward from the top toward the middle, which was articulated with a ring-like molding. Below the ring, the legs flared out slightly and terminated in a banded molding at the base (Plate 102). At the top of each leg was a pair of through-mortises, running perpendicular, one above the other. These received the tenons at the ends of the seat stretchers, which apparently ran between the legs at two different heights. Halfway down each leg, in the area of the ring molding, two more shallow mortises were cut for a second pair of stretchers to reinforce the stool. Young measured the distance between the legs where they had fallen and estimated the dimensions of the seat at 60 cm (north-south) by 45 cm (east-west). However, the stool was proba-

---

[1] Gordion plan 1957–6A. Gordion Project archives, University of Pennsylvania Museum of Archaeology and Anthropology. The fragments are numbered on her sketch, but only a few of these numbers were recorded and identi-

fied in Young's field book. *GFB* 63, 169.
[2] Young, *GFB* 63, 159.
[3] Ibid., 165–176. See above, pp. 21–22.

bly square with a somewhat smaller seat, to judge from comparable examples found in Egypt.[4] Although this stool has not survived intact, it is the easiest to interpret of the three pieces of furniture from the northeast corner.

The short and long legs were found together to the south of "stool #3." The four short legs ("stool #1") were of the same type as the medium legs, although there was only one pair of mortises at the top of each leg. These mortises received the tenons of the seat stretchers of the stool (Plate 101). As the legs were less than 20 cm long, they did not require additional bracing at the middle. A large fragment of one of these legs has survived, allowing the short legs to be reconstructed in a drawing (Figure 76; Plate 105B). Young estimated the size of "stool #1" at 48 cm by 25 cm, although this stool too was probably square. Young's measurement of 48 cm was apparently derived from the length of a nearby "crosspiece," which he thought had belonged to the stool. This "crosspiece" had two "cross-slats" that had fitted into its edge. These and other fragments were initially associated with "stool #1" (Plate 101, right).

Young misunderstood the "crosspiece," thinking that it might have been one of the stool's seat stretchers. In fact, although it was a kind of stretcher, it did not form part of the stool's seat. In 1982, when the fragments were removed from storage for study, the broken "crosspiece" was turned over, revealing a delicately carved frieze that had never been noticed.[5] The carved stretcher was cleaned in 1989 but not consolidated, due to its fragility and the presence of red pigment on the surface.[6] Young had measured the preserved length at 47 cm, but only around 33 cm could be recovered from the surviving fragments. This included one large piece and a smaller fragment, depicting scenes of animals in panels (Plate 104). The wood of the stretcher, and that of the extant short leg, has now been identified as boxwood.

Although the stretcher is badly damaged, the charming scenes can still be appreciated (Figure 77). At the right is a lively horse, facing left, with a large eye and two pointed ears at the top of its head (Plate 104E). The eye of the horse, like those of the other animals, consists of a circular cavity, which was probably once inlaid. This panel was broken at the edge but seems to have been the end panel at the right of the stretcher. A tenon fragment is still in place behind the horse's front legs, indicating that a vertical strut supported the stretcher in this area. To the left of the horse are two confronted deer, flanking a central tree (Plate 104D). The small fragment showing their mouths suggests that the deer were nibbling at the leaves. To the left of the deer are two goats, also flanking a tree (Plate 104C). Beyond the goats is an animal combat scene, showing a bull and what seems to be a lion (Plate 104B). The bull gores the lion's breast, while the lion paws at the bull and bites its neck.[7] To the left of this scene is a fragmentary panel, with part of one animal's leg visible. The small, loose fragment (Plate 104F) shows the feet of two confronted animals; this piece can be assigned to the next panel at the left, based on evidence from the 1957 photographs. The animal at the right of the fragment has only three feet on the ground, suggesting another animal combat.

The carved stretcher once joined the two "cross-slats" and must have formed a crowning element (Plate 105A). Assuming that the arrangement was symmetrical, one can reconstruct the length and general appearance of the entire stretcher (Figure 78).[8] This was most probably the top rail of a chair back, which belonged not to "stool #1" but to "stool #2." This is the "stool" with long legs, measured by Young at 50 cm. Unfortunately, almost nothing survived of these legs after their removal from the tomb chamber (Plate 103). The in situ photographs are only partly helpful, because of the mass of textiles that obscured many of the wooden fragments. Fur-

[4] Egyptian stools of this type have been preserved, complete with their original woven seats. See below, p. 115.

[5] Simpson, "A Carved Stretcher from the Big Tumulus at Gordion." The carving was first recognized by Işık Bingöl.

[6] Simpson and Spirydowicz, GWF, figures 51–54. For the recent cleaning and consolidation of the fragments from the northeast corner, see Appendix 1.

[7] Two triangular depressions on the bull's body may once have held inlay. Curiously, the feet of the "lion" are rendered as hooves, which may indicate that it is some other

type of real or mythical beast.

[8] Because of the damage to the right end of the stretcher, the width of the two outer supports could not be determined with certainty. The tenon fragment still in place behind the legs of the horse at right does not indicate the width of the vertical strut that supported the stretcher at its end. An additional hole visible at the back of this panel may indicate that another piece had been joined to the panel. The position of the tenon fragment and extra hole in the last panel are indicated in Figure 77 by hatching.

thermore, the photographs themselves are problematic, because one group shows the pieces repositioned after the bag of fibulae had been removed by the archaeologists (Color Plate IIB).[9] Nonetheless, some information can be gleaned from the available evidence. The Cox sketch is useful in determining one characteristic of the long legs that suggests they belonged with the carved stretcher.

The four legs of "stool #2" were not simply longer versions of the short and medium legs. As is clear from the Cox sketch and also the photographs, the two visible long legs were actually somewhat different. The lower half of each of these pieces resembled the short and medium legs, while the upper half took the form of a strip that extended up from the top of the lower element. This is suggested on the final plan, in the schematic rendering of the long leg shown at the north of the chamber (Plan, p. viii, top right).[10] This leg type, with its upper extension, is also found among the stool legs from Tumulus P, in particular those of the bed.[11] The extension shows that "stool #2" had a superstructure, which must have included a chair back incorporating the carved stretcher as the top rail.

Additional information about this chair can be found in the 1957 photographs, which show that the stretcher fell toward the west, landing face down on the floor. The chair must therefore have been placed with its back near the east wall, facing the center of the chamber.[12] It was piled

with textiles, and on top of these was the stool with short legs. Eventually the joinery weakened and the chair collapsed, with the legs breaking away from the seat, and the chair back falling in toward the west. The two visible long legs, lying at the edge of the pile of fragments, must have been the front legs of the chair. One of the back legs can be discerned in the textile debris, with its top lying near the north end of the carved stretcher. Although the chair cannot be reconstructed completely, its basic form can be understood.

The dimensions may have been somewhat smaller than Young's original estimate of 70 by 80 cm.[13] The seat possibly measured around 60 by 60 cm, to judge from the original preserved length of the carved stretcher. The chair's low seat was apparently around 25 cm off the ground, bounded by four seat stretchers that connected the long legs at their midpoints.[14] Rising from the level of the seat on all four legs were the vertical extensions noted above. Based on the measurements proposed here, the extensions that rose from the two rear legs would have formed the sides of the chair back, projecting up at the left and right of the carved stretcher and joining it at its ends.[15] The chair may have had arm rests, running between the front and back legs and positioned at the tops of the four extensions.[16]

The maroon-colored textiles associated with the two stools and chair may have included cushions, although the remains were so extensive that

---

[9] Young, *Gordion I*, plate 43B. Gordion neg. 64367 and color slide G2336 (here Color Plate IIB).

[10] The long leg shown to the south is drawn somewhat inaccurately on the final plan. See Color Plate IIB, center at bottom. The long leg at the north of the chamber, including both the lower element and the upper extension, is rendered as a continuous piece on Cox's preliminary sketch. However, on the final plan, the upper extension appears to be separate.

[11] For the early reconstruction drawing of the Tumulus P bed, see Young, *Gordion I*, 71, figure 40; Simpson and Spirydowicz, *GWF*, figure 80. This drawing is correct in many of its essentials but includes some errors. Other similar legs with uprights were found in Tumulus P, representing as-yet-unidentified pieces of furniture.

[12] According to the tomb plan, the stretcher fell approximately 55–60 cm to the west of the east wall.

[13] This estimate was based on the positions of the long legs as found on the floor of the tomb. According to Young's measurements, the seat of the chair would have been 80 cm wide and 70 cm deep. However, one or more of these legs may have bounced or skidded as the chair fell to the floor, with its seat loaded with textiles, the small stool, and other items. The short legs definitely bounced, as shown by the *in situ* photographs; one of these legs fell far to the southeast of

the two legs visible at the west edge of the pile of fragments.

[14] One of the seat stretchers is visible in Plate 103, identified by the impressions of the woven seat preserved along its length. The seat stretcher, shown lying to the right of the tag on the plywood, appears to be preserved to a length of ca. 45 cm.

[15] If this theory is correct, the chair back had four vertical slats supporting the chair rail from below (two wide and two narrower slats; Figure 78), and two more joining the ends of the stretcher at the left and right. These two outer supports would have risen from the two rear legs. This type of construction is in keeping with that of the footboard of the Tumulus P bed. A second scenario is possible but not as likely: the seat may have been even smaller, ca. 50 × 50 cm, with the extensions of the rear legs rising up to support the chair rail from below. In this case, the chair back would have had a total of four vertical back slats, with the extensions of the rear legs forming the two narrow outer strips that flanked the two wider slats.

[16] Arm rests may be represented by the long, narrow strips that were found lying beside the two front legs. The identification of these strips is problematic, however, as they are rendered only partially on the tomb plans, and some of the photographs show the fragments repositioned after the cleaning of the area. Supra n. 9.

surely they represented more than just upholstery for the seating. One may conclude that additional pieces were placed on the stools as offerings. Young referred to the textiles as "blanketing," and suggested that they were wrapped
around or draped over the wooden furniture.[17]
He recognized a few bits of cloth stuck to the
north wall of the tomb, at a height of ca. 35 cm
in the vicinity of "stool #3." As the legs of this
stool were 30 cm long, these bits must have come
from textiles that had been placed on top of the
stool. Several clumps of the extant textile material
from the northeast corner show impressions of
the cording that was strung between the seat rails
of the stools to form the woven seats (Plates 106B,
155B).[18]

Samples of these textiles were analyzed for
the present study, although their degraded condition precluded definitive results in some cases
(see Appendix 8). The analyses suggest that the
maroon-colored material may represent felt, in
combination with interior batting or other compacted, non-woven material. No evidence of Tyrian purple was found, and the colorant that produced the reddish-purple hue has not been determined. Also recognized among the samples analyzed were fragments of fine twined textiles, as
well as plain woven textiles of bast fiber identified
as flax.[19] Young thought these fragments were the
remains of a "bag on stool #2." This "bag" had
apparently contained one or more bronze fibulae,
of which only fragments were recovered.[20]

To this "bag" with its contents may be added
the several small wooden artifacts found in the
area of "stool #3" at the north of the tomb.
These objects are attested only in Young's field
book records, as none of them has survived. The
small finds associated with the stool included
two wooden saucers and the bowl of a spoon.[21]
Also of interest are several degraded fragments
of wood, found later in storage, which may represent additional pieces of furniture from the northeast corner (Plate 106A).[22] Finally, several plaster-
like clumps were found with these fragments—
perhaps used as filler or patching material for the
wooden stools or chair (Plate 106C).[23]

Comparanda: Stools and Chairs

Many furniture legs were found in Tumulus P at
Gordion, including the legs of at least four stools
of the type found in Tumulus MM. These stools
were represented by Young's "baby legs," "small
legs," "elephant legs," and "long legs," published
in *Gordion I* under the designation TumP 156.[24]
The Tumulus P legs have now been restudied, conserved, and reconstructed, with additional leg fragments identified and catalogued.[25]
Other leg parts were found in the tomb and associated with the Tumulus P bed, although some
of these probably did not belong to it.[26] One
of the legs definitely does, as its upper section
joins the central part of the footboard. The bot-

---

[17] Traces of red pigment preserved on the carved stretcher may have been residue from textiles that were draped
over the back of the chair. The red pigment was found along
the top edge and most of the upper border above the carved
panels. There were slight traces of red on the bottom border,
on the bodies of some of the animals, and on parts of the
back of the stretcher near the top edge.

[18] This material could not be identified with certainty
from the impressions, but it may have been rush from marsh
grass or some combination of rush and straw. This was suggested by seating experts Mark and Margaret Rogers, based
on their examination of photographs showing the impressions of cording. These impressions have been examined
again recently and are discussed in Appendix 8, pp. 211–
213.

[19] See Appendix 8, pp. 215–216, for identification of flax
(or ramie) from the bast fiber group, for "pieces of fine
material lifted from fibulae" on "stool #2."

[20] Young, *GFB* 63, 170–171.

[21] Ibid., 173, and see above, p. 21.

[22] Now catalogued as 12208 W 122.

[23] Some of these clumps were stored with the textiles
from "stool #2," but others were found in unlabeled boxes.

These boxes apparently contained remains from the Tumulus MM coffin or the northeast corner of the tomb.

[24] Young, *Gordion I*, 70, 72; plate 31C–G. The furniture
legs from Tumulus P were published as the following groups:
(A) pair of legs, W 49; (B) pair of legs, W 50; (C) set of
small legs, W 48; (D) set of long legs, W 51; (E) square legs,
W 58. One of the legs from group B was reconstructed in a
drawing (*Gordion I*, figure 41), which is not entirely accurate.

[25] Simpson and Spirydowicz, *GWF*, 60–61, figures 77–
79. In 2004, the following furniture legs were recorded:
4245 W 48 ("baby legs," four legs preserved), 4246 W 49
("small legs," fragments of three or four legs preserved),
4247 W 50 ("elephant legs," parts of two legs preserved),
4248 W 51 ("long legs," parts of three legs preserved), 4255
W 58 ("square legs," fragments of two legs preserved), 13026
W 136 ("square legs," seven fragments preserved), and 13028
W 138 (miscellaneous stool leg fragments).

[26] 4251 W 54 (bed fragments, including legs) and 4249
W 52 (additional leg and leg fragments). These additional
fragments may belong to a stool. Simpson and Spirydowicz,
GWF, 63–64, figure 80. Young, *Gordion I*, 70, figure 40, and
plate 31A–B. The fragments in Young's plate 31A–B are
arranged incorrectly.

tom section resembles a stool leg; rising from the top of this element is a flat, board-like extension.[27] This is the leg type noted above, which is comparable to the "long legs" from the chair in the northeast corner of Tumulus MM.[28]

A few stool legs have been excavated from other contexts at Gordion. Found in Tumulus K-III was one complete leg, which probably belonged to a stool. However, the excavators associated it with two other fragments, one of which seems to have come from the face of a serving stand, mistaking the three pieces for the parts of a chair.[29] A fragment of a burned ivory leg was found in Megaron 3 from the destruction level of the city mound. The upper part of the leg survives, with a six-petalled rosette incised on its top surface.[30] Pieces of carbonized wooden legs were recovered from the destruction level, indicating that wooden stools were in use in the early Phrygian period.[31] Also found at Gordion is a fragmentary stone relief, which was apparently an orthostat from the early Phrygian city (Plate 119C).[32] This shows a figure seated on a stool or chair, padded with textiles exhibiting two types of hook patterns. The visible leg shows through-tenons at the top for the seat rails, and a set of stretchers below to brace the legs. The leg itself is more ornate than those from Tumulus MM, featuring a molding at the top and a high base with a scalloped band. This type of leg is reminiscent of examples from Urartu and Syria.[33]

The stool was ubiquitous in antiquity, being the most useful and portable type of seating furniture.[34] Stools are widely attested throughout the Mediterranean and Near East, with numerous examples surviving intact from Egypt, often with their original woven or leather seats. These well-preserved Egyptian stools can serve to indicate the general form and construction of the Gordion pieces. Various kinds of stools were made in Egypt, including fancy folding types, rudimentary three-legged stools, and "lattice stools" with elaborate strutwork supporting the seat.[35] One simple type is comparable to the Tumulus MM stools, having four short legs, banded near the bottom, and pairs of through-mortises at the top. The mortises received the four seat stretchers, which ran between the legs at two different heights.[36] These low stools did not require additional stretchers to brace the legs, as with "stool #1" from Tumulus MM. Higher stools with longer legs did utilize a second set of stretchers; the legs of these stools might be plain, banded, or carved in the form of lion's legs.[37] These serviceable Egyptian stools may have been the ultimate predecessors of the Gordion examples.

The remains of twenty-two or more stools were excavated from the Middle Bronze Age tombs at Jericho (ca. 17th–16th century B.C.).[38] Several of these were variations of the simple Egyptian four-legged type.[39] In terms of their construction, these were comparable to the stools from Tumulus MM. The legs were round in section and tapered toward the bottom, with a recessed band or waist at the point where the leg

[27] Young, *Gordion I*, 70. Young states that the lower element was a separate stool leg, with a groove in its top to receive the vertical board. Actually, the leg and board were made from a single piece of wood. The two side-board fragments shown at the left and right in plate 31A join, making a single board. This was the vertical extension that rose from the top of one of the legs.

[28] See above, p. 113. For fragments of a very different type of chair from Tumulus P, see Simpson and Spirydowicz, *GWF*, 62.

[29] Körte and Körte, *Gordion*, 50, figure 9.

[30] 5882 BI 355.

[31] 6537 W 110. Carbonized leg tops with through-mortises and other fragments from a stool or chair, Terrace Building (TB 3). 9927 W 116 are cylindrical fragments.

[32] 7689 S 86 (TBT-CC/CC2). Sams, "Sculpted Orthostates at Gordion," 448, plate 130:3.

[33] See, for instance, Seidl, "Urartian Furniture," figure 1, plate 55A–B; Herrmann, *Ivories from Room SW 37*, plate 390: 1455.

[34] Simpson, "Furniture in Ancient Western Asia," 1648.

[35] Killen, *Ancient Egyptian Furniture I*, plate 55 (folding stool, Middle Kingdom, Metropolitan Museum, NY); plate 69 (three-legged stool with dished seat, 18th Dynasty, British

Museum); plate 74 (lattice stool, 18th Dynasty, Brooklyn Museum); see also plate 71, which combines the last two types (tomb of Tutankhamun, Cairo). This last example resembles the Near Eastern type of three-legged table. See above, p. 43.

[36] Ibid., plates 51–53 (Ninth–12th Dynasty, Ashmolean Museum), plate 54 (early 18th Dynasty, Royal Scottish Museum, Edinburgh).

[37] Ibid., plates 49, 72–73, 79–84; and see plate 38, for a New Kingdom bed with plain legs with through-mortises, constructed in the manner of the stools. For a collection of New Kingdom stools from Deir el-Medina, see H. Baker, *Furniture in the Ancient World*, figure 214.

[38] Kenyon, *Jericho I and II*. Stool legs (or fragments that may have come from stools) were found in Tombs B 3, B 50, B 51, G 37, G 46, G 73, H 6, J 1, J 14, J 54, M 11, P 19, P 21, and P 23.

[39] H. Baker, *Furniture in the Ancient World*, figure 354. Kenyon, *Jericho I*, figure 154 (Tomb B 35); figure 200, plate 27:5 (Tomb H 6). Kenyon, *Jericho II*, figure 108 (Tomb M 11); figure 128 (Tomb J 54); figure 141:2 (Tomb P 23); figure 145; figures 206–207 (Tomb P 19); figure 227 (Tomb P 21).

began to taper. Pairs of through-mortises were cut at the top of the legs to receive the seat stretchers, which ran between the legs at different levels. Three stools were well enough preserved to determine their height (ca. 35–45 cm), which required a second set of stretchers to reinforce the legs. Comparable wooden stool fragments, dating to the early second millennium B.C., were recovered from the tombs at Baghouz in Syria.[40]

Similar stools must have been in use throughout the Near East in the second and first millennia B.C., although most were surely made of wood, which rarely survives.[41] Occasionally they are depicted, usually associated with artists or workers;[42] these simple stools were not for display but were practical pieces.[43] One might wonder, then, why such stools were included among the burial goods in Tumulus MM. They probably were not tomb gifts themselves but served primarily as stands for the precious textiles piled on top of them. In this connection, the chair ("stool #2") is of interest, as it was a more elaborate piece of furniture, although not in the category of the ornate inlaid table and serving stands.

Wooden chairs with backs and armrests survive from Egypt, although none is quite comparable to the chair from Tumulus MM. Low chairs have been associated with women in Egypt, although women are also shown seated on higher chairs.[44] Egyptian chairs have various types of legs, corresponding to those of the backless stools.

Chair backs feature top rails supported by slats, which are sometimes widely spaced but more often closer together. Two side boards normally support the ends of the top rail, but the back is frequently slanted and attached to the seat with angled braces.[45] Few low chairs have armrests, and only the most highly decorated Egyptian chairs have carved top rails. However, in terms of their basic construction, Egyptian chairs are related to the Tumulus MM example. Low chairs must also have been used outside of Egypt and in later periods, although they are not easily identified in ancient depictions.[46]

The most famous Near Eastern chairs are represented by fragments of 19 ivory chair backs found in situ in Room SW.7, Fort Shalmaneser, at Nimrud. The lavishly carved ivory fittings were made in Syria in the early first millennium B.C. and stockpiled by the Assyrians some time between the ninth and seventh centuries.[47] The backs were large, measuring ca. 65–80 cm in width, which led some scholars to suppose that they had belonged to beds.[48] The ivory facing was constructed of carved plaques, bounded above and below by rails, and in some instances enclosed at the sides by long vertical strips.[49] Some of the rails were carved, in one instance with a procession of bulls.[50] Also recovered from SW.7 were two halves of a long ivory stretcher, with a rosette at the center and four lion/bull combat scenes to each side.[51] This long stretcher was

---

[40] Mesnil du Buisson, *Baghouz*, plate 42 (Tombs Z 66–Z 67), plates 45–46 (Tomb Z 95), plate 48 (Tomb Z 121), plates 50–51 (Tombs Z 122–Z 123), plate 55 (Tomb Z 144). See also Parr, "Jericho and Baghouz," 45–47.

[41] Stool fragments of ivory and metal are occasionally found, but these represent fancier types than those from Tumulus MM. See, for instance, the remains of an ivory stool or footstool from Zincirli, approximately contemporary with the Tumulus MM stools. Von Luschan, *Kleinfunde von Sendschirli*, 125–128, plates 61–62. Similar fragments occur among the ivories from Nimrud.

[42] For the stools of an Old Babylonian carpenter, a harpist, and an Assyrian kitchen worker, see H. Baker, *Furniture in the Ancient World*, figures 280–281, figure 333.

[43] In Greece, however, the simple stool would become the seat of aristocrats and even gods, as shown on the reliefs of the Siphnian Treasury and the Parthenon. Richter, *Furniture of the Greeks, Etruscans, and Romans*, figures 203–204, 213 ff.

[44] See, for instance, the chairs of Hetepheres (Fourth Dynasty, 26th century B.C.) and Hatnofer (18th Dynasty, 15th century B.C.). H. Baker, *Furniture in the Ancient World*, 39–43; figures 28, 182; color plate 4A. Reisner, *Tomb of Hetepheres*, 28–32, figures 31–32, plates 15–16. Roehrig, *Life along the Nile*, 27, figure 42.

[45] Killen, *Ancient Egyptian Furniture I*, plates 85–102.

[46] Carved ivory legs and other attachments from a low chair with a back were looted from the site of Acemhöyük in Turkey and are now in the Metropolitan Museum of Art (19th–18th century B.C.). See Simpson, "Furniture in Ancient Western Asia," 1655.

[47] The ivory panels had originally been attached to wood backings, which had decayed along with the other wooden parts of the chairs. Herrmann, "Ivory Furniture Pieces from Nimrud." Mallowan and Herrmann, *Furniture from SW.7*. See also Winter, "Carved Ivory Furniture Panels from Nimrud."

[48] Herrmann, "Ivory Furniture Pieces from Nimrud," 154.

[49] Mallowan and Herrmann, *Furniture from SW.7*, plates 1 (ca. 76 × 60 cm), 6 (ca. 76 × 67 cm), 34 (ca. 82 × 56 cm); for a chair back that did not have the side strips, see plate 52 (ca. 72 × 42 cm). For the remains of an ivory chair dating to the eighth century B.C. from Salamis in Cyprus, see below, p. 129.

[50] Ibid., 112–113; plate 105, no. 104.

[51] Ibid., 113; plates 105–107, nos. 105a–b. The ivory facing was made in two pieces, which joined at the center; its dimensions are given as ca. 107 × 4.4 cm. For comparable ivory stretchers from Nimrud, see Herrmann, *Small Collections*, plate 29:137; plates 62–65:308–309; plate 72:351. These works recall the long stretcher carved with panels of

clearly not a chair rail, but it relates to the Tumulus MM stretcher in terms of its carved motifs. The Syrian chairs from SW.7 were larger and much more ornate than the Gordion chair, which was modest by comparison. Nearer to Gordion, the site of Kerkenes Dağ in central Turkey yielded a finely carved ivory stretcher, depicting a deer, two goats, and two sheep.[52] Dated to the sixth century B.C. by the excavators, this piece follows in the tradition of the Nimrud and Gordion stretchers.

The carved panels of the Tumulus MM chair rail contain whimsical little animals, almost cursorily rendered, shown in heraldic settings and scenes of mortal combat. This animal style, so different from the geometric art of the inlaid table and serving stands, seems to suggest a vernacular element in the Phrygian royal production. Similar animals are found on pottery from Gordion, both on painted and stamped pieces. Small stamped goats parade around the body of a storage jar, and schematically rendered deer and goats nibble at a tree.[53] Fancier animals, with decorated bodies, are shown in panels on pottery from Tumulus P, Tumulus K-III, and the city mound at Gordion.[54] These images recall the wooden animal sculptures from Tumulus P, which must have been the playthings of the royal child buried there. The collection includes two lions, two bulls, a lion and bull in combat, a yoked ox, a deer, a ram or goat, two hawks, and a griffin eating a fish.[55] Many of these animals appear elsewhere in Phrygian art in religious and official state contexts.[56] Thus the decoration on the chair from Tumulus MM, along with the wooden toys and other objects depicting animals, utilized the imagery of power.

charging animals from the couch of Ashurbanipal (r. 668–627 B.C.) on a relief from Nineveh in the British Museum. H. Baker, *Furniture in the Ancient World*, 190–191, figures 304–305. Curtis, "Assyrian Furniture," plate 46B.

[52] Dusinberre, "An Excavated Ivory from Kerkenes Dağ." The stretcher had a top border composed of amber beads and gilded spacers; the lower border was inlaid, perhaps with red glass paste, and the deer's spots may have been inlaid with silver.

[53] Sams, *Early Phrygian Pottery*, plates 126 (no. 932), 168B (city mound, destruction level). Animals painted in the style of no. 932 occur on Alışar IV pottery, and Sams, 162–163, suggests the possibility that this vessel was made somewhere in the region between Alışarhöyük and Gordion.

[54] Sams, *Early Phrygian Pottery*, plate 97 (city mound, destruction level). Young, *Gordion I*, plates 16E–F, 17A–F (Tumulus P). Körte and Körte, *Gordion*, figure 18, plates 2–3 (K-III). Akurgal, *Phrygische Kunst*, plates 12, 14A, 16, 19–20. The panels are bordered by bands of "genealogical patterns." See above, pp. 52–56. For related animals on painted terra-cotta plaques from Pazarlı, see *Phrygische Kunst*, plates 51–56.

[55] Young, *Gordion I*, plates 22–24, 28A–C. The Tumulus P animals have now been conserved and reconstructed. Simpson and Spirydowicz, *GWF*, figures 81–85. See also the Tumulus P miniature bronze quadriga with horses. Young, *Gordion I*, 21–26, figures 13–15, plate 13.

[56] In addition to those examples already cited, several large stone orthostats depicting animals have been found in the vicinity of Ankara. These belonged to one or more works of monumental architecture that may have incorporated reliefs of Matar. The animals include lions, griffins, a sphinx, a bull, and a horse. Buluç, "Architectural Use of the Animal and Kybele Reliefs," 16–18. Buluç, "Ankara Kabartmaları." For the fragmentary stone orthostats carved with similar subjects and associated with the early Phrygian period at Gordion, see Sams, "Sculpted Orthostates at Gordion." See Prayon, *Phrygische Plastik*, for other Phrygian animals.

CHAPTER SEVEN

THE COFFIN

Coffin assembly (wood)
12210 W 123 (previously uncatalogued)
Iron fragments associated with the coffin
12209 ILS 766
(MM 389)
Coffin body: cedar (*Cedrus libani* Loud.);[1] corner
blocks: pine (*Pinus sylvestris* L.); dark wood
of rails: yew (*Taxus baccata* L.); light wood of
rails (tentative): boxwood (*Buxus sempervirens*
L.); wood slat found on east slope of coffin
body (from frame or litter): boxwood (*Buxus
sempervirens* L.).
Found at the northwest of the tomb along the
north wall.
Color Plates IB, IIA, XVIA; Figures 79–90;
Plates 107–115.
Coffin as placed in tomb. G.P.L. from W edge of
W corner blocks to E edge of E corner blocks
ca. 2.9 m. G.P.W. from N edge of N corner
blocks to S edge of S corner blocks ca. 1.9 m.[2]
Coffin body. Est.L. as reconstructed ca. 3.27 m.
Est.W. as reconstructed ca. 1.07 m. Est.H. as
reconstructed ca. 46 cm. East ledge: G.P.L.
(edge of ledge to end of fragment, E–W)
ca. 96.5 cm; G.P.W. (across ledge, N–S)
ca. 107 cm; G.P.Th. (at outer edge) ca. 9 cm.
West ledge: G.P.L. (edge of ledge to end of
fragment, E–W) ca. 48 cm; G.P.W. (across

ledge, N–S) ca. 51 cm; G.P.Th. (outer edge)
ca. 8 cm.
Coffin as assembled prior to the burial. Est.L.
ca. 3.27 m. Est.W. between outer faces of
corner blocks ca. 1.79 m. Est.H. ca. 46 cm.
Corner blocks. NE corner block:[3] G.P.W. (E–
W) ca. 50 cm; G.P.W. (N–S) ca. 45 cm; G.P.H.
ca. 31 cm. SE corner block:[4] G.P.W. (E–W)
ca. 49.5 cm; G.P.W. (N–S) ca. 45 cm; G.P.H.
ca. 30.5 cm. Corner block and fragments:[5]
G.P.W. (E–W?) ca. 50 cm; G.P.W. (N–S?)
ca. 38 cm; G.P.H. ca. 23 cm. Corner block(?):[6]
G.P.W. (E–W?) ca. 50 cm; G.P.W. (N–S?)
ca. 42 cm; G.P.H. ca. 24.5 cm. Est.W. corner
blocks (E–W) ca. 50 cm; Est.W. corner blocks
(N–S) ca. 45–48 cm; Est.H. corner blocks
ca. 33 cm.
Rails. G.P.L. extant fragments of the long rails
ca. 95 cm. G.P.L. extant fragments of the short
rails ca. 23 cm. G.P.L. north rail (as found
on tomb floor) ca. 1.35 m. G.P.L. south rail
(as found on tomb floor) ca. 1.23 m. Est.L.
restored rails ca. 1.91 m. Est.H. restored rails
ca. 30 cm.
Iron bosses.[7] G.P.D. ca. 12.5–15 cm.

The remains of the interred king were found
lying on a mass of degraded textiles and wood,

---

[1] For a report on the problems of the identification of
the wood species of the coffin, see Blanchette and Simpson, "Soft Rot and Wood Pseudomorphs in an Ancient
Coffin."

[2] Young gives three different measurements in his field
book (*GFB* 63): L. 2.9 m and W. 1.9 m (p. 73); W. 2 m (p. 81);
and L. 2.93 m and W. 1.9 m (p. 177). I have used a width of
1.9 m for the purpose of my reconstruction drawings.

[3] A sample (GOR-43) was taken from the NE corner
block in the 1970s by Peter Kuniholm for his dendrochronological study of the tomb. Kuniholm believed that this block
was part of the section of the inner tomb wall that had been
cut by the excavators when they entered the tomb. The sample was subsequently reunited with the corner block and can
be seen in Kuniholm's original wrapping at the left rear
of the block, shown in Plate 115B. See Kuniholm, "Dendrochronology at Gordion," 10.

[4] The entire base of the SE corner block is preserved.

[5] This corner block was recognized from the end face
(Plate 115D), and although it must have been one of the
blocks at the west, its exact position could not be determined. A loose fragment with a shallow cutting in its top
surface was found on top of this corner block as stored at
Gordion (Plate 115A).

[6] This piece was found with several detached fragments
on top; it is preserved as two large individual pieces now
butted together.

[7] The remains of at least four iron bosses are preserved,
now deformed and larger than their original size. Radiogra-
phy was enlisted to try to determine their original size and
shape, but nothing of the original iron was observed within
the corrosion. These iron bosses have not been included in
the new drawings of the coffin, as their position and function
are uncertain.

which Young interpreted as a four-poster bed
(Color Plates IB, IIA; Figure 3; Plates 107–109).
Young thought the "bed" had a headboard, footboard, four cubical corner blocks with bedposts,
rails, and a platform made up of five planks,
with two more supporting the outer edges of the
platform at the sides (see above, pp. 22–28). According to Young's theory, the headboard and
footboard were supported from below by iron
bars, which had once been socketed into the
sides of the corner blocks. However, it was not
clear how the planks were supported, as a strange
empty space was noted beneath the area of the
iron bars on both the headboard and footboard.[8]
Young thought that the bars must have acted as
clamps of some sort to hold the planks of the
platform together. Even more curious were the
bed rails, which were found lying on the floor
after the textiles and bed planks were taken up
(Plate 110). Although these had lain beneath the
debris, Young thought that they had originally
extended up at the sides of the platform. This
would have necessitated the side planks falling
out, the rails falling off the platform and trav-
eling underneath it, and, finally, the whole bed
collapsing on top of the rails.[9] This interpretation
was not viable, as shown by the surviving fragments. However, Young's careful excavation and
commentary, the extensive photographic record,
and Dorothy Cox's tomb plans provided the information needed to determine the correct solution. The "bed" was not a bed, but a massive, uncovered log coffin, which had been used
for a funeral ceremony and then disassembled,
placed in the chamber part by part. The position of the pieces on the tomb floor yielded a
wealth of information, not only about the form
of the coffin but also the circumstances of the
burial.[10]

Form and Function

The king's coffin had been made from a huge
cedar log, hollowed out, with horizontal ledges
extending at both ends.[11] The "headboard" was
actually the ledge at the east end, which had
broken off the coffin body and fallen out onto the
floor (Color Plate IIA, Plate 108). This became
clear when the piece was located at Gordion
in 1981, stored with three of the corner blocks
and several boxes of unlabeled textiles apparently
from the coffin (Plates 111, 112A).[12] The east ledge
was found with a long iron bar sitting on its
upper surface, which had once been anchored to
the wood by five nails with tubular shafts. This
was the bar that Young thought had run along
the bottom edge of the headboard, supporting
it from below and securing the bed planks. The
actual purpose of the iron bar was to reinforce
the east end of the coffin, in order to keep the log
from splitting.[13] A very degraded fragment of the
west ledge was also found at Gordion, associated
with pieces of an iron bar that must once have
been attached to its upper surface (Plate 112B–C).
This was Young's "footboard," which was found
near the west wall and was taken up when the
excavators entered the tomb (Plate 109).[14] The
coffin must have had additional reinforcements,
as holes also occurred in the lower face of the
east ledge, and several loose iron fragments were
found among the remains of wood and textiles
(Plates 113, 114A–B).[15]

The east section of the coffin sloped down
from the ledge, tapering to a thin edge near the
break at the bottom (Plate 111A). The slope had
retained some textile fragments, which remained
in place below the iron bar. These were removed
and recorded in 1981, revealing the rings of the
tree from which the log had been cut (Plate 111B).

---

[8] Young, *GFB* 63, 80–81, 179–180. See above, pp. 22–23.

[9] Ibid., 188–193. See above, pp. 24–25.

[10] Simpson, "'Midas' Bed' and a Royal Phrygian Funeral."

[11] The coffin body was cedar and not yew, superseding Simpson, "'Midas' Bed' and a Royal Phrygian Funeral," 84. See Blanchette and Simpson, "Soft Rot and Wood Pseudomorphs in an Ancient Coffin," on the way in which soft-rot degradation in ancient wood can mimic the characteristics of yew.

[12] Simpson, *GFB* 175, 1–16. Interpretive comments in *GFB* 175 are here superseded. The boxed textiles appear to

be from the coffin, but as they were not labeled, they cannot be attributed with certainty.

[13] In fact, when the iron bar corroded, it contributed to the degradation of the wood. See Kohler, *Lesser Phrygian Tumuli*, 183, n. 3, on the problems of using large conifers.

[14] Young, *GFB* 63, 80–81.

[15] The holes in the lower part of the east ledge are indicated by dashed lines in the reconstruction drawings (Figure 79 and, by extension, Figures 81–82). A fragment of iron bar, which may perhaps be associated with the west ledge, retained a tubular double-clenched nail (Plate 113A); on this type of fastening, see Steffy, *Wooden Ship Building*, 46–48. On the iron bosses, supra n. 7.

A drawing was made of the east section of the coffin as found in the tomb, the thickness of the degraded bottom was estimated, and the east end was then righted in a reconstruction drawing, indicating its relationship to the SE corner block and suggesting the coffin's original height (Figure 79). This drawing indicates the reason for the empty space "about 20 cm deep" that Young had noticed in the area of the "headboard." He had observed the degraded lower edge at the bottom of the slope, which had tipped up when the end broke off and the ledge fell out onto the floor.[16]

Young's deteriorated "bed planks" were actually fragments of the log coffin, which had split apart along the grain and fallen in lengths on the floor. The textile remains had broken along with the wood, suggesting the appearance of planks (Color Plate IB, Plate 107A). The four pine "corner blocks" were not exactly cubical and did not serve as bases for "bedposts."[17] These "posts" were parts of the sides of the coffin, which had fallen out to the north and south. The "post" noted at the east of the SE block was apparently a chunk that had broken off the south wall of the coffin body (Plate 108B, bottom).[18] Crucial to an understanding of the coffin were the shape and dimensions of the "corner blocks" (Plate 115B–D). The inner edges of the blocks were cut off at an angle, as can be seen from the *in situ* photographs (Plates 108, 109B). These blocks were wedge-like supports, intended to be pushed up against the sides of the coffin to stabilize the rounded body. Finally, the "bed rails" were apparently rails, although they were found on the floor of the chamber.[19] More was learned about the pieces and

their placement as they were reconstructed in a series of drawings (Figures 80–90).

The position of the rails and corner blocks on the tomb floor is curious, since it appears to be at odds with their functions. As can be seen from the reconstructed side view of the coffin as placed in the tomb, the blocks are not in their proper arrangement (Figure 80). Those at the east appear to support the body of the coffin, while those at the west were found at the tomb's west wall. The blocks at the west were adjacent to the west ledge and not fulfilling their intended purpose. Only the NE corner block had been placed against the coffin body; the SE block was approximately 10 cm too far to the south (Figure 87). Thus three of the corner blocks were deposited in the tomb without regard for their original use. A study of the rails and their disposition reveals the reason for the blocks' positions.

The remains of the rails were measured by Young as they lay on the tomb floor, and several fragments have been preserved (Plate 114C–D). It was thus possible to reconstruct the rails in drawings and ascertain their original placement. The southernmost rail was found with its east end 45 cm to the west of the SE corner block (Plate 110A).[20] A short support lay to the north of the long rail, some distance from it and slightly askew. A notch in the long rail, 28 cm from the east end, indicates the position at which the long rail was joined to the short support.[21] Young noted that the rails and supports were made from strips of dark and light wood, which have been identified as yew and boxwood

---

[16] Young, *GFB* 63, 80–81, 179–180. Young noted the same kind of empty space in the area of the footboard, with holes spaced 16 cm apart in the "planks" above the space. These indicate an iron band for reinforcement, either the iron bar that was attached to the west ledge or an additional band around the exterior of the coffin body.

[17] Ibid., 177–178. See above, pp. 22–23, 25–26. The corner blocks did have shallow cuttings in their upper surfaces, as indicated by a fragment found with a corner block that shows this cutting (Plate 115A). It is not clear what these cuttings were used for; they may have held patterned inlay, although no evidence survives of such decoration. One might speculate, again without evidence, that they served as receptacles for incense or other funerary paraphernalia. Incense and spices were widely used as offerings throughout the ancient world, as attested in texts and depictions. See, for instance, 2 Chronicles 16.14 (royal burial), Exodus 30.1–9 (burning of incense in the Tabernacle), and Pliny, *Natural History* 12.52–71 (Arabian incense). The possibility remains that the circular cuttings were beddings for some sort of posts, which were used for the funeral ceremony but not placed in the tomb. The corner blocks were pine and

not yew, superseding Simpson, "'Midas' Bed' and a Royal Phrygian Funeral," 84. Supra n. 11.

[18] Although it did not have a finished surface, this fragment is the most regular of all the candidates for a "bedpost." The roll of fabric found near it had apparently been wrapped around its western end. Although this piece had most likely broken off the side of the coffin body, alternatively, it might have been a separate element, inserted into the adjacent circular cut-out in the east ledge in order to secure the textiles at the southeast end of the coffin.

[19] Although the function and position of the "rails" is not certain since the sides of the coffin were not preserved, the way that they have been reconstructed here seems to be the best of the possible options. See below and Figures 82, 89–90.

[20] Young, *GFB* 63, 189, and see above, p. 24. The squared east end of the long rail was found 45 cm to the west of the west face of the SE corner block.

[21] As shown in the photograph, the notch was cut in the dark strip at the north of the pair of long strips representing the southernmost rail.

(tentative).[22] These were pinned together in a kind of "five-layer sandwich," composed of three light and two dark strips, for a combined width of ca. 7.5 cm (Figure 3D). The southernmost rail was preserved to a length of 1.23 m, as reconstructed in Figure 84.[23]

The northern rail was found with its east end set against the NE corner block (Plate 110B).[24] Two short supports were lying perpendicular to the long rail, still in place on the floor. According to Young's measurements, the first support lay 28 cm from the east end of the rail, and the second was 60 cm to the west of the first (Figure 84).[25] Assuming that the arrangement was symmetrical, Young restored a third short support 60 cm to the west of the second, which produced an estimated length of 1.95 m for both of the long rails.[26] Based on these approximate measurements, the rails could be reconstructed to their full length as they had been placed on the tomb floor (Figure 85). Evidently both rails had been set down between the corner blocks, but the southern rail had been pulled to the west. The NW corner block was also found slightly askew. These anomalies suggest the likely sequence in which the parts of the coffin were deposited in the chamber at the time of the burial.

As the tomb had no doors, the coffin and king must have been lowered into the chamber, along with the other grave goods.[27] First, the two western corner blocks were set down against the west wall, with the NW block in the corner of the chamber. The rails were placed on the floor, with their west ends against the east faces of the corner blocks. The eastern blocks were then set down at the ends of the rails. The huge coffin body

was lowered into the tomb with ropes, which may have passed through the circular cutouts in the horizontal ledges. The massive log coffin was positioned on the floor between the corner blocks and pushed against the west wall. During this process, the south rail was kicked in by one of the workmen, and the coffin landed on the short supports, dragging the rail with it as it was moved to the west. After the pieces were in place, the body of the king was let down onto the coffin. There is evidence among the remains of the east ledge as to how this might have been done.

Found in 1981 beneath the textile debris on the slope of the east section was a boxwood slat, which is indicated in the reconstruction drawings (Figures 79, 81, 83–86). This was apparently part of a frame for a litter on which the king had lain. Small wood fragments discovered on top of the SE corner block may have belonged to this frame (Plate 108B, left). The roll of cloth to the west of the iron bar, mentioned by Young and visible in the photographs, seems to have been draped over the end of the litter.[28] The boxwood slat was found below a layer of reddish purple textiles, which had covered most of the remains of the coffin (Color Plate IB). Between the slat and the wood of the slope were a few layers of gold-colored fabric.[29] More of this golden cloth was found lying on the slope between the slat and the iron bar; one chunk exhibited 22 layers of fabric. The coffin textiles have now been analyzed in connection with the present study (Appendix 8).

The reddish or maroon textiles on which the king's body had lain have been identified tentatively as felt, although because of the degraded condition of the material, the identification can-

---

[22] The dark wood of the rails was easily recognizable when the fragments were found at Gordion. However, the light wood was essentially gone, except for a few small light-colored pieces found together with the dark wood. Samples of the dark and light wood were analyzed and identified as yew and boxwood. However, since the light wood had degraded into unrecognizable fragments, it is not certain that the samples analyzed were actually from the rails.

[23] Young, *GFB* 63, 188–189. Although given as 1.33 m in one typed transcript of *GFB* 63, the actual field book measurement is 1.23 m. The western end of the long rail at the south was badly deteriorated.

[24] Ibid., 191–192.

[25] "These lay the one 28 cm from the E end, the second 60 cm to the west of the first." Young, *GFB* 63, 192. It is possible that the first 28 cm measurement refers to the distance between the end of the rail and the first notch, as this same distance is recorded for the southern rail.

However, the 28 cm measurement might have been taken from the end of the rail to the first preserved piece of the first short support as it lay on the floor. It is not clear whether Young's second measurement of 60 cm was taken between the first and second notches or between the preserved pieces of the supports as they lay on the floor. See above, p. 24. As the latter seems more likely, I have based my reconstruction drawings of the rails on this premise.

[26] Ibid. I have calculated a restored length of ca. 1.91 m and used this measurement for my drawings. The total length was given as 1.985 in Young, *Gordion I*, 189, which was calculated according to a different understanding of the way in which Young took his measurements.

[27] See above, p. 8.

[28] A similar roll of cloth was noted in the area of the footboard. Young, *GFB* 63, 79. See above, pp. 22–23.

[29] For the early assessment of the dense, maroon-colored material and the yellow-brown woven cloth found beneath it, see above, p. 8.

not be considered conclusive (Plate 154C–D).[30] The red colorant has yet to be determined, although, as with the textiles from the NE corner of the tomb, there is no evidence of Tyrian purple. This maroon "felt" is comparable to the reddish material associated with the stools and chair from the NE corner. Twining has been recognized also among the coffin textiles, suggesting the possibility of lofted batting.[31] The gold-colored fabric found below the felt is a balanced plain weave of bast plant fiber (Plates 153, 154A–B). Thus Young was probably correct in his observation that the gold woven fabric was linen. Although this fabric was found in proximity to the iron bar, its color was apparently not the result of migrating iron corrosion. Instead, the cloth was found to be coated with a colorant containing the mineral goethite, which produced a uniform, bright gold color.[32]

Most of these beautiful textiles had overlain the frame of the litter, supporting the king's body as it was lowered into the chamber. The frame and textiles had also served a second purpose, as did the other parts of the coffin. The disposition of the pieces in the tomb, arranged without regard to their intended purpose, indicates that the coffin must have been assembled elsewhere prior to the burial. If the elements are reassembled, in effect, according to their original functions, the entire coffin can be reconstructed in drawings (Figures 82, 86, 89–90). In the drawings, the corner blocks have been moved in to support the coffin body, and the rails have been set into the sides.[33] The result is a sort of bier, which was used for the funeral. The body of the king lay at the top of the bier, supported on a frame that was covered with textiles. The rails protected the body as did the blocks, keeping the onlookers at a distance. Only after the viewing and funeral was the coffin dismantled for the burial. The other pieces of furniture found in the tomb were also likely related to the ceremony. The serving stands and banquet tables, along with the bronze ves-

sels and food remains, suggest that a funerary meal was served and the remains interred with the king. The food and drink residues have been analyzed, and the menu of the banquet can be determined (see Chapter 8 and Appendix 5).

Comparanda

As the Tumulus MM coffin was not a bed, it was not at all comparable to the bed from Tumulus P, although the two pieces were discussed together in the commentary section of *Gordion I*.[34] Also unrelated was the "sarcophagus" found in Tumulus K-III.[35] This piece is now too fragmentary for its form to be understood, and although it may have been some kind of "bed," it was surely not a log coffin. However, at least one other coffin was excavated at Gordion. A covered log coffin was found in Tumulus B, dating to ca. 630 B.C.[36] The Tumulus B coffin was apparently made from one great cedar log, cut in half and hollowed out, with half the log used for the body and the other half for the lid. Both the coffin and lid had short ledges on both ends, with iron nails noted in the ledges of the lower section, possibly for the attachment of iron bars.[37] Fragmentary iron banding was found in the vicinity of the Tumulus B coffin, and lead was used to fill cracks in the log where it had already split. Several other Gordion tumuli may have contained log coffins, on the evidence of iron bands or lead, including Tumulus S-1 (early seventh century B.C.) and Tumulus C (sixth century B.C.).[38]

Two other Phrygian sites have yielded the remains of what seem to be log coffins. In an Ankara tumulus in the area of the Atatürk Mausoleum (Tumulus 1), a section of half a log was found in the NE corner of the burial chamber. The excavators interpreted this piece as a bench or banquette (*Bank*), but it may have been part of the sloping end of a log coffin. The *Bank* had a kind of ledge that had fit over the top of the

[30] Appendix 8, samples 2003-Tx-2, front; 2003-Tx-3; 2003-Tx-4; 2003-Tx-5.
[31] See above, p. 114.
[32] Appendix 8, samples 2003-Tx-1; 2003-Tx-2, back.
[33] The original position of the blocks was determined for the purpose of the drawings through the construction of a scale model of the blocks and coffin body.
[34] Young, *Gordion I*, 259–260.
[35] Körte and Körte, *Gordion*, 43 ff., figure 6.
[36] Young, "Gordion—1950," 13–15, plate 6. Kohler, *Les-*

ser Phrygian Tumuli, 11–12, 17–18, figure 7, plates 5–6.
[37] Kohler, *Lesser Phrygian Tumuli*, 12. Young had believed that the iron was used to secure the bottom of the coffin to the top, although by analogy with the Tumulus MM coffin, the iron may have been used to reinforce the logs to keep them from splitting.
[38] See Kohler, *Lesser Phrygian Tumuli*, 183–185, for a list of tombs that may have contained log coffins, based on finds of iron and lead.

low wall of the wooden chamber.[39] Found in another Ankara tumulus burial (METU II) were iron bands and T-shaped lead bars, which may be evidence of a log coffin.[40] At Bayındır in the region of Elmalı, the occupant of Tumulus D was apparently buried in or on a log coffin, to judge from the wood fragments and two iron bars found at the north of the tomb.[41] The burial contained many fine artifacts, including two silver belts and other ornaments; silver and bronze bowls, small cauldrons, ladles, and fibulae; and one silver and three ivory statuettes.[42] According to the excavator, the finds at the south of the tomb may be the remains of offerings and a feast.

Log coffins were used in many areas of the ancient world and are well attested in northern Europe. Numerous European examples have been recovered from Bronze Age burial mounds in Denmark.[43] These coffins were made from oak tree trunks that had been split lengthwise and hollowed out, with half the log used for the body of the coffin and the other half for the lid.[44] The Danish coffins and their contents were particularly well preserved due to the composition of the bog water that had permeated the earth.[45]

Log coffins were also found in the tombs of Pazyryk in Siberia, which yielded a wide variety of organic objects that had survived encased in ice. Barrows 1–5 contained log coffins made from larch trunks up to one meter in diameter.[46] The lower part of each coffin was cut from a log and hollowed out. The lid was much shallower than the lower section and fit over its edges like a cap. The coffins had no ledges, although the wood at the ends was much thicker than that of the side walls. The excavator thought that the coffins had been lowered into the tombs by means of thick cords that had been passed through lugs carved at the ends.[47]

The two coffins of barrows 1 and 2 were covered with strips of birch bark, arranged diagonally and intersecting to form a pattern of lozenges. These coffins were also decorated with leather appliques in the form of animals.[48] For the coffin from barrow 1, the patterns had been attached to the coffin body without regard for its lid: when the lid was in place, the decoration was partly covered.[49] This suggests that the coffin may have had two functions, with the open coffin first used in a funeral ceremony in which the deceased had lain in state. After the ceremony, the coffin could have been closed and lowered into the tomb. Log coffin burials occur elsewhere in the Altai mountain region and in Tuva in southern Siberia, notably at Bashadar,[50] Tuekta,[51] and the Great Kurgan at Aržan.[52]

The Tumulus MM coffin finds counterparts over a wide area, from Scandinavia to the Far East. It seems likely that log coffin burials were more common than one might imagine from the surviving remains. In most situations, the wood coffins would have deteriorated in the earth, leaving little or no trace. Exceptions occur only when conditions at the burial sites allow for the preservation of organic materials. This is the case with the "coffins" from Qäwrighul and other sites in Central Asia, which consisted of wood planks to protect the body, without bottoms and often without lids. Pieces of these coffins survived due to the arid conditions and were eventually exposed by wind erosion.[53]

Traditional log coffins are still made today in Luidao, China, although the craft has been diminished by a government ban on their sale. The Luidao coffins are hewn from cedar logs, which are known to resist moisture and decay, although the harvesting of cedar is strictly controlled in an effort to curtail deforestation. Despite the current

---

[39] Özgüç and Akok, "Ausgrabungen an zwei Tumuli," 60; figures 5, 10, 12–13. Broken pottery vessels found on the floor to the west of the *Bank* may argue against this interpretation.

[40] Kohler, *Lesser Phrygian Tumuli*, 184, n. 8. Buluç, *Ankara Frig Nekropolünden Üç Tümülüs Buluntuları*, 24.

[41] Dörtlük, "Elmalı Bayındır Tümülüsleri," 173.

[42] Özgen and Özgen, *Antalya Museum*, 32–49, nos. 32–39, 41–42, 45–46, 48–59. Özgen and Öztürk, *Heritage Recovered*, 27. The occupant of Tumulus D has been identified as a woman.

[43] Glob, *Denmark*, 128 ff. Glob, *Mound People*, plates 2, 5–6, 14–16, 20, et al. For new information on the oak coffin burials from Denmark, see Randsborg and Christensen, *Bronze Age Oak-Coffin Graves*.

[44] Glob, *Denmark*, plates 51 and 52.

[45] Glob, *Mound People*, 17.

[46] Fourth-third centuries B.C. Rudenko, *Frozen Tombs of Siberia*, 14, 28 ff. See plates 5 (barrow 1), 18 (barrow 3), 19 (barrow 4), and 29–30 (barrow 5). The bodies had lain with their heads toward the east.

[47] Ibid., 29, plate 37c (barrow 1).

[48] Ibid., 29–31. The coffin from barrow 1 was decorated with appliques of cocks, and that of barrow 2 with deer.

[49] The edges of the coffin from barrow 2 had been damaged by robbers, so the leather decoration survived only at the ends. It is not clear whether the lid covered the appliques on this coffin.

[50] Rudenko, *Culture of the Population of the Central Altai*, plates 26–27.

[51] Ibid., plate 54.

[52] Grjaznov, *Der Grosskurgan von Aržan*, figures 3, 6–8.

[53] Barber, *Mummies of Ürümchi*, 80–81, 95, 102–105.

restrictions, there is still a demand for traditional log coffins in the city, which reportedly rose to fame when the body of a great ninth-century poet was preserved in a Luidao cedar coffin, "as fresh as the day he died."[54] There were surely important reasons for ancient log coffin burials beyond the preservative properties of the wood used to make them—perhaps relating to their boat-like shape or the symbolic significance of trees. Although this cannot now be determined for the Tumulus MM coffin, details of the interment allow the funeral ceremony to be reconstructed (see Chapter 8).

---

[54] Bradsher, "More Than a Billion Chinese but So Few Coffins."

CHAPTER EIGHT

CONCLUSIONS—THE BURIAL OF THE KING

The parts of the coffin as found on the tomb floor indicate that the coffin assembly had been dismantled for its final deposition in the tomb. Thus it must have been set up outside the chamber prior to the burial, with all the pieces fulfilling their intended functions. As is clear from the form of the assembled coffin (Figure 90), it had been part of the furnishings for the royal funeral, in which the king had lain in state on top of the bier.[1] Also found in the tomb were nine banquet tables, two serving stands, ten small bronze cauldrons and two ladles associated with the stands, along with a multitude of other bronze vessels, some of which contained organic remains. This suggests that the funeral had included a ceremonial banquet, with the trappings later interred with the king.

The menu of this banquet can be reconstructed, based on a recent analysis of the organic residues from the bronze bowls, situlae, and small cauldrons, as well as the desiccated food from the pottery jars stored inside the three large cauldrons at the south of the tomb (Color Plates VI–VII, and see Appendix 5).[2] The participants ate a spicy stew of sheep or goat, which probably included lentils and other vegetables.[3] The meat was apparently roasted on spits over an open fire before it was cut off the bone.[4] The drink was identified as a mixed fermented beverage of grape wine, barley beer, and honey mead.[5] This "barley wine," as it was called by the Greeks (κρίθινος οἶνος), was apparently known as bryton (βρῦτον) to the Thracians and Phrygians, who were said to enjoy this heady drink.[6]

---

[1] See above, pp. 120 ff. This practice is also attested in ancient Greece. The prothesis or display of the body provided an opportunity for the lament and allowed those concerned to pay their last respects. However in Greece this took place at home on a high couch, rather than in a massive coffin that was subsequently used for the burial. See Boardman, "Painted Funerary Plaques," 55, for the suggestion that the prothesis may have taken place outside the house. Prothesis scenes of this sort occur on late Geometric vases that are contemporary with the Tumulus MM burial. Kurtz and Boardman, *Greek Burial Customs*, 144; plate 4.

[2] McGovern, et al., "A Funerary Feast Fit for King Midas." The scientific team that performed the complex analysis was headed by Patrick McGovern and included Donald Glusker, Robert Moreau, Alberto Nuñez, Curt Beck, Eric Butrym, Lawrence Exner, Edith Stout, and Chad Quinn, with contributions from Stuart Fleming, then director of MASCA, University of Pennsylvania Museum of Archaeology and Anthropology.

[3] Fourteen food samples from the large cauldrons (MM 1–3) were tested, ten from pottery vessels and four loose clumps. The analysis revealed the presence of lamb or goat fat, honey (beeswax), pulses, olive oil, and anise or fennel (anisic acid). See Appendix 5. For lentils found in the Terrace Building (TBA2) at Gordion, see DeVries, et al., "New Dates for Iron Age Gordion." On the preference for

sheep and goats for Hittite ritual meals and offerings, see Collins, "Ritual Meals in the Hittite Cult," 89; on meat stew, 83.

[4] McGovern, et al., "A Funerary Feast Fit for King Midas," 863. This was implied by the presence of phenanthrene and cresol, a phenol derivative. See Appendix 5.

[5] Sixteen samples were analyzed, from the lion- and ram-headed situlae (MM 45–46), one small cauldron (MM 10), and 13 bronze bowls. Analysis of a sample from a second small cauldron (MM 13) was attempted, but the results were inconclusive because of the small size of the sample. Grapes were indicated by the presence of tartaric acid/tartrate salts, barley beer by calcium oxalate (beerstone), and honey by evidence of beeswax. See Appendix 5. The "Midas Feast" was reconstructed in 2000 at the University of Pennsylvania Museum. The spicy stew was prepared by the Museum Catering Company under the direction of Chef Pamela Horowitz. The beverage was brewed by Dogfish Head Brewery of Milton, Delaware, on the initiative of Sam Calagione; it was later made for sale as the award-winning "Midas Touch" (*www.dogfish.com*). See McGovern, *Ancient Wine*, 293–295.

[6] According to the seventh-century Greek poet Archilochus, as quoted in Athenaeus 10.447a–b. Xenophon noted this "barley wine" in Armenia, which was served in a large mixing bowl and drunk through straws (οἶνος κρίθινος ἐν κρατῆρσιν). *Anabasis* 4.5.26–27.

A similar potion appears in the *Odyssey*, mixed up (κυκάω) by Circe, from Pramneian wine, barley, honey, and cheese.[7]

The presence of the beverage in the small cauldrons, situlae, and bowls indicates the way in which the bronzes were used with the serving stands. As shown by the study of the stands, the small cauldrons had sat in the rings of the top pieces.[8] It can thus be inferred that the drink was ladled from the cauldrons into the many bowls found in the tomb (Color Plate VIB–C).[9] These included the omphalos bowls, which were found to contain beverage residues, suggesting that the mixture may have been poured as a libation as well as drunk by the guests at the funeral.[10] The two situlae were apparently used to transfer the drink into the small cauldrons from the three large vats found at the south of the tomb.[11] With this new information, the lavish funeral ceremony could be envisioned and is reconstructed here in a painting by artist Greg Harlin (Frontispiece).[12]

Magnificent funerals are known from ancient texts, and some are reminiscent of the Tumulus MM ceremony and burial. Taken together, they suggest the kinds of ritual activities that might have occurred at Gordion following the death of the king. As recorded in the *Iliad*, the funerals of the Greek hero Patroklos and the Trojan prince Hektor both included feasting and sacrificial ceremonies. The feast at the funeral of Patroklos entailed a massive sacrifice of oxen, sheep, goats, and swine, which were then roasted over a fire.[13] Elsewhere in the *Iliad*, the method of roasting meat is described: animals are killed, cut into pieces, spitted, and roasted, although the meat is eaten only after the appropriate portions have been dedicated to the deities.[14] A huge pyre was built for Patroklos, piled with sacrificed sheep and cattle, offerings of oil and honey, and horses and dogs, along with 12 noble sons of the Trojans.[15] Wine libations were poured at the pyre,[16] the body was burnt, the bones were interred, and the tomb was covered with an earth mound.[17] Writ-

---

[7] Circe's potion also contained drugs, which made it an even more lethal drink. *Odyssey* 10.233–236. A comparable Homeric potion, called *kykeon* (κυκεών), was mixed for Nestor in his golden cup, consisting of wine and grated goat's-milk cheese with white barley. *Iliad* 11.632–641. Sherratt, "Feasting in Homeric Epic," 207–208. See Powell, "Wine and the Vine in Ancient Mesopotamia," 104, for "sweet" beer made from barley malt and emmer wheat, probably sweetened with grape syrup. See also Gorny, "Viticulture and Ancient Anatolia," 153–154, for a Hittite beer/wine/honey concoction that was poured as a libation.

[8] See above, pp. 73–74.

[9] For a petalled bowl in association with a ladle, see the painting on the rear wall of the "Graeco-Persian" Karaburun tomb, fifth century B.C. This shows the tomb's occupant reclining, holding such a bowl (whether with or without omphalos is unclear). He is approached by a servant who holds an amphora with griffin handles in his right hand and a petalled bowl in his left. Hooked around the little finger of the servant's left hand is the end of a ladle, which appears meant to be used to transfer the liquid from the jar to the bowl. Mellink, "Excavations at Karataş-Semayük," 252, plate 54, figure 20." Özgen and Öztürk, *Heritage Recovered*, 47.

[10] The Near Eastern omphalos bowl, adopted by the Greeks as the *phiale mesomphalos*, was a libation vessel in the Mediterranean from the seventh century B.C., and its eastern antecedents may have served the same purpose. The omphalos bowl is difficult to drink from but functions efficiently for pouring. Strong, *Gold and Silver Plate*, 55–58. Luschey, *Die Phiale*. This type of bowl can perhaps be seen in use on Assyrian reliefs, notably those from the North Palace of Ashurbanipal at Nineveh, now in the British Museum. In one scene, the king pours a libation over four dead lions from a vessel that may well have been an omphalos bowl, to judge from the position of his fingers. At his

reclining banquet, he and his queen hold similar bowls, as if to drink from them, although it is not clear whether these bowls had omphaloi. Strommenger and Hirmer, *Art of Mesopotamia*, plates 241, 260. On the theory that phialai were used for both drinking and the pouring of libations, see Gunter and Root, "Artaxerxes' Silver Phiale," 23–26. See below.

[11] Lion-headed situlae were used this way in Assyria, as shown on a relief from Khorsabad (late eighth century B.C.). McGovern, "Funerary Banquet of 'King Midas,'" figure 3; after Stronach, "Imagery of the Wine Bowl," figure 12.3. The mixed fermented beverage from Tumulus MM may have been brewed in the large cauldrons, set over a fire on their iron stands. This idea was advanced a century ago by the Körte brothers for the cauldron from Tumulus K-III. Körte and Körte, *Gordion*, 83. Sam Calagione of Dogfish Head Brewery agreed that the beverage could have been brewed in the large cauldrons found in Tumulus MM. The process developed by Calagione for the reconstructed beverage entails the boiling of barley and water, its combination with honey and saffron at the end of the boil, and the addition of grapes during the primary fermentation after the beer mixture has been cooled.

[12] Simpson, "Celebrating Midas," 26. This painting was commissioned with support from the National Geographic Society and *Archaeology* magazine.

[13] Homer, *Iliad* 23.29–34. For the Homeric feast, see Sherratt, "Feasting in Homeric Epic," 181–191.

[14] *Iliad* 9.205–220.

[15] *Iliad* 23.163–177.

[16] *Iliad* 23.218–221. These libations invoked the winds, without which the pyre would not catch fire.

[17] *Iliad* 23.215–257. Achilles wished to be buried with Patroklos, and he expected that the small mound made for his friend would be greatly enlarged at the time of his own death.

ing in the fifth century B.C., Herodotus records a similar sequence for the funeral rites of prominent Thracians, for both cremations and inhumations.[18]

Homeric funerary ritual has been seen in the aristocratic tumulus burials in the necropolis of Salamis on Cyprus.[19] Tombs dating to the eighth-seventh centuries B.C. show traces of pyres in the dromoi, amphorae for offerings, human burials among the remains, and fully outfitted horses and chariots. Tomb 79, dated to the late eighth century B.C., is particularly noteworthy in relation to the Tumulus MM deposition.[20] The chamber had been looted, but the dromos was nearly intact and contained the furnishings of two consecutive burials. The finds included dishes with food residues, amphorae, iron firedogs and 12 iron spits, remnants of weapons and armor, and hearses and chariots pulled by horses, recalling the feast and funeral for Patroklos in the *Iliad*.[21]

Also recovered were several pieces of fine furniture. The wooden frames had disintegrated, although the outlines were preserved in the earth, along with fragments of ivory and metal sheathing and decorations. A bed, three chairs, and two stools were identified, as well as an ivory lion leg, which may have belonged to a table.[22] One of the chairs, "throne Gamma," was sheathed in ivory and had armrests and a back with rails, slats, and side pieces, resembling in its general form the chair from the northeast corner of Tumulus MM.[23] Two bronze cauldrons were found near the façade of the chamber, one with bull's

head attachments at the handles and the other with four sirens and eight griffin protomes at the rim.[24] The latter had sat in an iron tripod stand and was packed with pottery vessels. This recalls the three large cauldrons containing pottery jars at the south wall of Tumulus MM.[25] The finds from Tomb 79 at Salamis may represent a funerary meal or meals, made from ingredients that included eggs, chicken, ducks, birds, and fish.[26]

A 14-day Hittite funerary ritual is preserved in some detail from texts discovered at Boğazköy.[27] Although these are Late Bronze Age cremation rites and cannot be connected directly with the Phrygians, they are of interest because there was an earlier settlement and "Hittite" cemetery at Gordion, and vestiges of Hittite funerary customs may have persisted into the first millennium B.C. in the region.[28] Feasting, sacrifice, and purification rites appear frequently in the Hittite texts, with food and drink given to the dead as well as to the participants in the ritual. On the death of a king, those who took part included the newly installed king and his court along with various cult functionaries and wailing women.

To summarize, the first day's activities included the sacrifice of an ox at the foot of the corpse and the pouring of a wine libation. On the second day, the body was taken to the cremation site, and offerings of food were made to the sun-goddess of the earth,[29] the sun-god of heaven, the ancestral spirits, and the dead king. The body was apparently cremated on day three, and on the following day the bones were wrapped in linen cloth

---

[18] Herodotus 5.8. "When a rich Thracian is buried, the custom is to lay out the body for three days, during which, after a preliminary period of mourning, a feast is held of all sorts of animals slaughtered for the purpose; then the body is buried, with or without cremation, a mound is raised over it, and elaborate games set on foot." Both the Thracians and the Greeks of the *Iliad* held funerary games in honor of the deceased.

[19] The legendary founder of Salamis was Teucer, son of Telamon (king of the Greek island of Salamis) and brother of the Homeric hero Ajax. Karageorghis, *Salamis in Cyprus*, 7.

[20] The Assyrian king Sargon II (r. 721–705 B.C.), a contemporary of Midas, records the submission of the king of Salamis in the late eighth century. Karageorghis, *Salamis in Cyprus*, 23.

[21] Karageorghis, *Salamis in Cyprus*, 76–98; plates I–VIII, 33–56. Karageorghis, *Excavations in the Necropolis of Salamis III*, 4–122; plates A–H, I–CXXX.

[22] Simpson, "Furniture in Ancient Western Asia," 1661–1662.

[23] Karageorghis, *Salamis in Cyprus*, plates VI, 42. Kara-

georghis, *Excavations in the Necropolis of Salamis III*, 87–88; plates A, XXXII–XXXIV, LXI–LXIII, CCXL. The reconstruction of two ivory plaques below the armrests must be considered tentative. Traces of a cushion for the seat were reportedly found in the earth near the chair.

[24] Karageorghis, *Salamis in Cyprus*, plates I, 40–41. Karageorghis, *Excavations in the Necropolis of Salamis III*, 97–114, 214–221; plates H, X–XIV, CCXLIII–CCXLVI.

[25] Karageorghis, *Salamis in Cyprus*, plate 41.

[26] Karageorghis, *Excavations in the Necropolis of Salamis III*, 13, 259–269.

[27] Haas, "Death and the Afterlife in Hittite Thought," 2024–2027. Otten, *Hethitische Totenrituale*. See also Pitard, "Ugaritic Funerary Text RS 34.126," for a funerary ritual recorded in a tablet from Ugarit and the related *kispu* ritual in Mesopotamia.

[28] For the use of the term "Hittite" regarding the presence at Gordion, see Mellink, *Hittite Cemetery at Gordion*, 51–57. See also Gunter, *Bronze Age*, 102–105.

[29] The sun as it traveled underground at night. McMahon, "Theology, Priests, and Worship in Hittite Anatolia," 1985.

and put on a chair that was placed before a table set with food, with the participants sharing a
meal in the presence of the remains of the king.
On days six and seven, more animals were sacrificed, burnt offerings took place, and another
funerary meal was held in front of an image of
the deceased. On the eighth day, oxen, sheep,
horses, and asses were slaughtered near a spring
and presented to the dead king, whose image sat
on a cart. On day 12, the image was removed to a
gold throne in a ritual tent; a funerary meal was
held for the deities, the ancestral spirits, and the
soul of the deceased. Day 13 involved the sacrifice of live and artificial birds, the burning of the
image of the king, more animal sacrifice, and a
funerary meal. This brief excerpt from the elaborate sequence may serve as a reminder that Phrygian funerary rites were no doubt much more involved than is apparent from the Tumulus MM
assemblage. There was likely more than one feast
held in the context of the ritual, along with extensive animal sacrifice, libation, and rites of purification.

Following a ceremony held outside the Tumulus MM chamber,[30] the remnants of the banquet
and other grave goods must have been carried
up a ramp that was built around the tomb and
then lowered into the interior.[31] The objects were
arranged inside, and many of the bronzes were
hung from iron nails in the east, west, and south
walls (see Plan, p. viii).[32] At the west were 20 nails,
which held the large jugs and belts. There were
24 nails in the south wall, for small jugs and
bowls with handles. The east wall had 25 nails,

which held many of the bronzes found at the east
of the tomb (Color Plate IIIA). These included
small jugs, bowls with handles, the two situlae,
and the small cauldrons and ladles, although up
to six cauldrons could have sat in the tops of the
serving stands.[33] The situlae had been wrapped
in cloth, fragments of which still adhered to the
bronze; more cloth was found on the floor behind the stands.[34] One sample that was analyzed
showed bicomponent striped yarns that were colored with indigo (Appendix 8, sample 2003-Tx-
11). The omphalos bowls and other items had
been set on the nine tables (Color Plates IIA,
III, V), and textiles and small objects were placed
on the stools and chair in the northeast corner
(Color Plate IIB). Finally, the parts of the coffin
were lowered into the chamber, and the body of
the king was set down on the coffin (Color Plate
IB).[35]

With no Phrygian texts to explain this deposition, one is left wondering why the remains of the
funerary banquet were placed in the king's tomb.
While the deceased might require the amenities
of the present for his use in the afterlife, why
did he need such a quantity of ceremonial furniture, textiles, fibulae, belts, vessels, and perish-
able food? An answer can be found in the ancient concepts of ritual and sacrifice, and the role
they played in the maintenance of the cosmic
order—not only in terms of the natural world
but also regarding the state.[36] The impressive funeral, with its ritual activities and magnificent ac-
coutrements, served to promote the power of the
Phrygian royal house and facilitate the dynastic

---

[30] Whether this ceremony was held at the graveside or
elsewhere is uncertain.

[31] See above, pp. 7–8.

[32] See above, p. 10.

[33] The finds from Tumulus K-III suggest that some of
the bronze vessels found near the Tumulus MM stands may
have been placed in their top pieces at the time of the
deposition. Fragments of two wooden rings were found in
K-III with two bronze bowls sitting in them. This might
represent the collapsed top piece of a serving stand, with
two of the vessels that had sat in the rings. Körte and Körte,
Gordion, 52, no. 6.

[34] Young, *Gordion I*, 121.

[35] The burial is evoked by a model of the tomb chamber
in the Museum of Anatolian Civilizations (Color Plate
XVIA). The model chamber is half the size of the actual
structure, and a reconstructed coffin was built at a scale
of 2:3. Based on my drawings, the museum's coffin closely
approximates the appearance of the original, although the
parts had never been assembled inside the tomb. A "king"
has now been placed on the coffin, incorporating a model of
the head based on the king's skull (Color Plate XVIB). Prag
and Neave, *Making Faces*, plate I.

[36] A full discussion of ancient "sacrifice" is beyond the
scope of this study, although some comments may be of
interest here. Sacrifice was instrumental to the workings
of ancient theocracies, attested in detail, for instance, in
the Hittite texts. The king was the head of the state and
its bureaucracy as well as the chief priest, responsible for
the propitiation of the deities through sacrifice to insure
divine protection and promote the land's bounty. If the
gods received their due, they might look favorably on the
state and effect all manner of fertility and good fortune.
From a prayer to the god Telipinu on behalf of Murshili II
(late 14th century B.C.): "To the king, queen, princes,
and to the Land of Khatti give life, health, strength, long
years, and joy in the future! [And to them] give future
thriving of grain, vines, fruit, cattle, sheep, goats, pigs, mules,
asses—together with wild animals—and of human beings!"
Beckman, "Royal Ideology and State Administration," 529–
531. On the importance of sacrifice, followed by a meal,
for the Greek polities, see Detienne, "Culinary Practices
and the Spirit of Sacrifice," 3: "Political power cannot be
exercised without sacrificial practice." On the power of the
funerary ritual to insure continuity within the community,
see Burkert, *Homo Necans*, 55.

succession.[37] On analogy with the Hittite funerary rites, the feast was surely held in honor of the dead king and also the goddess Matar, both of whom would have participated by means of the food and drink offerings they received.[38] The mourners and officiants took part in the rituals and also shared in the meal. As a record of the splendid ceremony and sacrifice, the instruments were entombed with the king.

As such, the functional objects and food in the burial likely served as votive gifts, not only for the king but also for the Phrygian goddess.[39] The ritual assemblage, as placed in the tomb, would have represented the ceremony symbolically and honored the goddess with dedications on behalf of the dead king. The same kinds of objects were

dedicated in temples and sanctuaries elsewhere, often in large numbers, as indicated in texts and attested through excavation.[40] The most famous Phrygian votive was the throne of Midas, seen by Herodotus in the sanctuary of Apollo at Delphi.[41] Metal vessels were also prominent votive gifts, as shown by the vast array of gold and silver examples dedicated by the Lydian kings at Delphi.[42] Some of the same types have been recovered from graves, and are found in large quantities in the so-called "Lydian Treasure."[43] The group contained silver ladles and bowls, including numerous omphalos bowls, and silver and bronze jugs of various shapes and sizes.[44] A comparable assemblage of Phrygian objects was found in Tumulus D at Bayındır in southwestern Turkey. The

[37] The funeral in April 2005 of Pope John Paul II, the leader of a modern theocratic state, may offer some insights into the pomp and ceremony that must have accompanied the Tumulus MM funeral and burial. The funeral of the pope was orchestrated and administrated by the eventual successor Cardinal Joseph Ratzinger, which was taken as a sign that he would be chosen the next pope. The spectacle of the ceremony was calculated to overawe the members of the church (via world-wide television coverage), enable an orderly transfer of power, and promote the cohesiveness of the Vatican state ("As a spectacle, the funeral was an irresistible combination: a demonstration of mass spirituality veined by the political intrigue of the Medici court…"). Stanley, "When Mourning Becomes Television." A funeral mass was held for over two million people who had come to Rome to honor the pope. The coffin lay in state in the court of St. Peter's, carried in on a litter and placed at the center of a lozenge pattern on a huge oriental rug. Near the coffin were assembled 600 church officials and 1,000 current and former world leaders and royalty; at the bottom of the steps were 2,500 lesser dignitaries, and farther away still were 6,000 more people in the plaza. St. Peter's Square was said to accommodate 80,000 mourners. After the mass, communion (the sacrament of bread and wine) was shared, and the coffin was carried into the crypt and lowered into the tomb. Rosenthal, "Pilgrims Pay Last Respects."

[38] That the king was somehow a participant is suggested by the bronze bowl that was found near his feet (see above, p. 8). See Vernant, "At Man's Table," 24–25, on sacrifice to the gods at Greek ritual feasts; the offerings were made in order to honor the gods by inviting their participation in the meal.

[39] See Buluç, "Architectural Use of the Animal and Kybele Reliefs," 20, for the suggestion that objects from the Great Tumulus of Ankara might have been votive gifts for the goddess Matar (Kybele). See Vassileva, "Belt of the Goddess," 96, on the idea that the Phrygian belts found in burials were related to the cult of the goddess. And see Kramer, "Death and Nether World According to the Sumerian Literary Texts," 59–60, on earlier evidence in the Near East for the presentation of gifts to the deities of the underworld by the deceased. On this concept, as well as the idea that the deceased might hold a great feast to propitiate the netherworld gods, see A. Cohen, *Death Rituals*, 101, 103–104.

[40] See Muscarella, "King Midas of Phrygia and the Greeks," 337–341, for a list of Phrygian votive cauldrons, omphalos bowls, belts/belt clasps, and fibulae that were found in Greek sanctuaries, including Samos, Olympia, Perachora, and the Argive Heraion. See also Muscarella, "Fibulae Represented on Sculpture," 85, on fibulae as votive gifts. See Vassileva, "Belt of the Goddess," 93–96, on Phrygian belts dedicated in sanctuaries.

[41] Herodotus, 1.14. See above, p. 10.

[42] Herodotus 1.14, 1.25, 1.50–52. Gyges (r. ca. 685–657) dedicated six gold kraters (κρητῆρες) weighing 30 talents, which stood in the Corinthian Treasury with the throne of Midas. These were presumably large mixing bowls for some type of beverage. Alyattes (r. ca. 610–560 B.C.) made an offering of a great silver krater and iron krater-stand (ὑποκρητηρίδιον). Croesus (r. 560–546 B.C.) sought the favor of the Delphian Apollo through a number of outstanding sacrifices. This included the slaughter of 3,000 animals and the burning on a pyre of gold and silver couches, gold phialai (φιάλας), and purple robes (εἵματα πορφύρεα καὶ κιθῶνας). In addition, he sent to Delphi two huge kraters, one of gold and one of silver, which stood at the entrance to the temple of Apollo, as well as numerous other metal vessels. Such objects were also dedicated in Near Eastern sanctuaries, with extensive evidence coming from Urartu. Two large metal cauldrons were displayed on stands at the entrance to the temple of Haldi at Musasir, as shown in an Assyrian relief (now lost) from Khorsabad. Lloyd, *Ancient Turkey*, figure 44. An impressive selection of metal vessels and furniture is listed in the inventory of the temple, recorded as plunder by Sargon II. Luckenbill, *Ancient Records 2*, 92–98.

[43] This spectacular "treasure" consists of metal vessels, jewelry, and other precious objects that were looted from tombs in western Anatolia in the 1960s, acquired by the Metropolitan Museum of Art in New York (1966–1980), and finally returned to Turkey in 1993. Özgen and Öztürk, *Heritage Recovered*, 240–241 (concordance).

[44] Other types include silver alabastra and jars, as well as bronze and silver incense burners. Özgen and Öztürk, *Heritage Recovered*, 28–30, 55–56, 74–128 (nos. 11–83), 150–153 (nos. 106–107), 170–173 (nos. 122–124), 232–239 (nos. 222–228). Four fibulae are included in the group: 200–201 (nos. 165–167). For the objects as formerly held by the Metropolitan Museum of Art, see von Bothmer, *Greek and Roman Treasury*, 24–36, 38–45.

metal finds from this tomb included bronze and silver cauldrons, ladles, omphalos bowls, belts, and fibulae, all of which resemble the Gordion bronzes.[45]

Finally, several early tombs at Gordion contained banquet furnishings that relate to those from Tumulus MM.[46] In Tumulus P were found four tables, an inlaid serving stand, wooden spoons and plates, plain and painted pottery vessels, and numerous fine bronzes, including two large cauldrons, three small cauldrons, two ladles, two jugs, and 20 bowls.[47] Tumulus W contained a serving stand, wooden plates, and pottery vessels, as well as two large cauldrons, two small cauldrons, two ladles, two jugs, and 15 bowls of bronze.[48] K-III yielded fragments of several pieces of furniture, one of which was apparently a serving stand, pottery vessels, and bronzes, including five small cauldrons, one ladle, jugs, 27 bowls, and a large cauldron containing 43 vessels and possibly the remains of food.[49] K-IV contained pottery vessels and two small bronze cauldrons, one with a ladle found inside.[50] These grave goods point to the rites of sacrifice and feasting, with the equipment interred as votive gifts.[51] The popular notion that the bronze vessels found in the Tumulus MM burial were a "drinking set" for a festive "drinking party" or "symposium" overlooks the religious nature of the funerary banquet and the ritual significance of the objects.[52]

The inlaid table and serving stands were part of the ceremonial assemblage. Their iconography featured symbols of the goddess Matar, and the two stands evoked portable shrines. The inlaid motifs may also have had royal implications, perhaps adopted by the king and his dynasty as a kind of official insignia.[53] Elsewhere in the Near East, rosettes and other religious symbols were associated with royalty as well as deities,[54] and the grid of square patterns on the faces of the stands recalls Assyrian royal textiles of the mid-eighth century B.C. Such decoration was a prerogative of the king and his court in Assyria and North Syria, and may also have been a royal prerogative in Phrygia.[55]

As with other Near Eastern monarchs, the Phrygian kings were in charge of the state religion, overseeing the official cult and the festivals of the religious calendar.[56] The historian Diodorus Siculus, writing in the first century B.C., credits Midas with the establishment of the rites of Matar, and elsewhere he is called the son of the goddess.[57] Midas is also connected with Matar through the inscriptions on the Midas Monument at Midas City,[58] if indeed they refer to the historical king of the late eighth century B.C.[59] What this evidence does suggest is that Midas was the chief priest of the goddess Matar. Whether this king is to be identified with the occupant of Tumulus MM is a matter of question, but whoever was buried in the tomb was associated with the Phrygian goddess and interred with the instruments of her cult. An approximation of the likeness of the deceased king has been reconstructed (Color Plate XVIB).[60]

The recently proposed dendrochronological date of 740 B.C. +7/-3 for the felling of the

---

[45] Özgen and Öztürk, *Heritage Recovered*, 27, figure 31. Özgen and Özgen, *Antalya Museum*, nos. 32–39, 45–46, 48; see also no. 40 from Tumulus C. See above, p. 124.

[46] Tumuli P, W, K-III, and K-IV have been dated to the eighth century B.C. All four tombs had contained fibulae and belts, in addition to the banquet equipment described below.

[47] Young, *Gordion I*, 11–17, 32–46, 56–70. For the serving stand, tables, and small wooden objects, see Simpson and Spirydowicz, *GWF*, 52–54, 57–60, 66–67.

[48] Young, *Gordion I*, 199–207, 212–215, 216–218. For the wood plates and what was apparently a serving stand, see Simpson and Spirydowicz, *GWF*, 68–71.

[49] Körte and Körte, *Gordion*, 43–45, 49–75.

[50] Ibid., 100–101, 103–104. A third bronze cauldron was so fragmentary that its size and shape could not be determined. The roof of the tomb had collapsed, and the finds were badly damaged.

[51] See Winter, "Reading Ritual in the Archaeological Record," on the identification of ritual objects in burials, and the importance of understanding the activities they represented.

[52] See Simpson, "Celebrating Midas," 30–31. The assemblage of bronze vessels from Tumulus MM has been called "the most comprehensive Iron Age drinking set ever found." McGovern, "Funerary Banquet of 'King Midas,'" 22; after Moorey, "Metal Wine-Sets," 195: "the most comprehensive of all" metal "wine-sets" from the Iron Age. See also Özgen and Öztürk, *Heritage Recovered*, 32.

[53] See above, p. 99.

[54] See above, p. 91.

[55] See above, pp. 86–87.

[56] For the Hittite king as chief priest of the national deity, appointed by the deity and ruling under divine protection, see Beckman, "Royal Ideology and State Administration," 530.

[57] Diodorus 3.59.8. Roller, "Legend of Midas," 309.

[58] See above, p. 96, nn. 205–206, and CD-Figures 75–76, for inscriptions and graffiti on the Midas Monument.

[59] Roller, *In Search of God the Mother*, 69–70; "Legend of Midas," 301.

[60] Prag and Neave, *Making Faces*, plate I; and see Scurr, "Mask of Midas." Supra n. 35.

outer logs of the Tumulus MM chamber has suggested to some that the burial occurred around 740 B.C. However, this date has been subject to revision, and the Anatolian tree-ring chronology is still "floating" and not yet precisely secured.[61] Moreover, the date of the cutting of the outer logs gives only a terminus post quem for the construction of the chamber; the huge logs might have been dried or stored for years before they were put to use in this important tomb.[62] The Phrygian King Midas has been identified with Mita of Mushki, who appears in Assyrian records as a contemporary of Sargon II between ca. 718 and 709 B.C.[63] Later Greek sources put the death of Midas some time in the early seventh century B.C. According to Eusebius, Midas ruled between 738 and 696/95 B.C.; Julius Africanus puts his death at 676 B.C.[64] Strabo writes in his *Geography* that Midas committed suicide by drinking bull's blood when the Kimmerians overran Gordion.[65]

These sources suggest that the historical king known to the Greeks as Midas, and to the Assyrians as Mita of Mushki, ruled during the second half of the eighth century B.C. and died some time after 709 B.C., possibly as late as the early seventh century. If these dates are correct, it is still possible that Midas was buried in Tumulus MM, but only if the tomb was built in the late eighth century. If the tomb was completed before 709 B.C., the burial was that of Midas's predecessor, identified by Herodotus as King Gordias.[66] In this case, Midas would have officiated at the funeral as successor to the deceased king. In either case, Midas was the proprietor of the wooden furniture.

Young believed that the Kimmerian invasion had so taxed the resources of the city of Gordion that the huge Tumulus MM could not have been built following the invasion.

> Clearly an undertaking on this scale could not have been carried out immediately after the Kimmerian catastrophe; the burial must date from before it. The ancient sources say that King Midas was killed by the Kimmerians, or committed suicide immediately after their descent. For this reason the tomb is not likely to be that of King Midas; rather it should be that of his predecessor on the throne—presumably a Gordios [sic].[67]

Other scholars have followed this line of reasoning, particularly because of the extent of the devastation revealed in the destruction level on the city mound. This level had long been identified as the "Kimmerian destruction" and was originally dated to ca. 700 B.C.[68]

The situation is now complicated by new C-14 dates for seeds from the destruction level recov-

---

[61] For the date of 740 B.C. +7/-3, see DeVries, et al., "New Dates for Iron Age Gordion," published in 2003. Prior to this, in 2001, the date of 740 B.C. +4/-7 was proposed. Manning, et al., "Anatolian Tree Rings and a New Chronology," 2534. In 1996, 718 B.C. was proposed. Kuniholm, et al., "Anatolian Tree Rings and the Absolute Chronology of the Eastern Mediterranean," 782. In 1993, 757 B.C. ±37. Kuniholm, "Date-List," 373. It seems reasonable to imagine that the dating may undergo further revision. For the debate on the efficacy of dendrochronological dating of ancient wood from the eastern Mediterranean, see James, "The Dendrochronology Debate"; Keenan, "Anatolian Tree-Ring Studies Are Untrustworthy."

[62] No investigation has yet been undertaken, and no information published, on the question of whether the logs may have been dried (or stored) prior to their use in the tomb's casing. On the critical process of drying wood, see Hoadley, *Understanding Wood*, 147–157. Phrygian woodworkers were well aware of the pitfalls of using improperly dried wood, as can be seen from the cracks in the Tumulus B log coffin, which had to be filled with lead. See Kohler, *Lesser Phrygian Tumuli*, 11–12, 17–18, 183.

[63] Luckenbill, *Ancient Records* 2, 4 ff., in which Mita appears repeatedly in Sargon's annals (and other inscriptions) for years 5–13. Hawkins gives these dates as 718–709 B.C. in "Mita," 271. In 709, Mita finally submitted to Sargon. Körte and Körte, *Gordion*, 9–10, 18 (after Winckler); Mellink, "Mita,

Mushki and Phrygians," 318; Muscarella, "Iron Age Background to the Formation of the Phrygian State," 92. See these sources and also Sevin, "Early Iron Age," 97, for the idea that Mushki was a land to the east that had been incorporated into the Phrygian kingdom by the late eighth century B.C. King Mita had dealings not only with the Assyrians but also with his nearer neighbors, including the states of Carchemish, Tabal, and Urartu.

[64] Körte and Körte, *Gordion*, 20, 23.

[65] Strabo 1.3.21: "And those Cimmerians...often overran the countries on the right of the Pontus and those adjacent to them, at one time having invaded Paphlagonia, and at another time Phrygia even, at which time Midas drank bull's blood, they say, and thus went to his doom." See Roller, "Legend of Midas," 301, n. 15, on the bull's blood episode.

[66] Herodotus 1.14. The name Gordias has been considered by some to be apocryphal. Roller, "Midas and the Gordian Knot," 260–261. Young eventually came to believe that Tumulus MM was the tomb of Midas's predecessor. See above, p. 10. For an effort to sort out the kings of the dynasty that ruled at Gordion in the eighth century B.C., see Muscarella, "Iron Age Background to the Formation of the Phrygian State," 97.

[67] Young, *Gordion Guide*, 50. See above, p. 10, n. 54.

[68] Muscarella, "King Midas' Tumulus at Gordion," 9–10.

ered in recent excavations. The dates proposed
for these seeds would move the destruction level
back to the late ninth century B.C., although
some have argued against this early date.[69] If the
new chronology holds up, the widespread destruction of the citadel would then be unrelated
to the so-called Kimmerian destruction, which
was tied to the death of Midas by later ancient
authors. However, this does not rule out a Kimmerian attack on Gordion in the later eighth century. Several damaged objects were found in the
Tumulus MM chamber, most notably the inlaid
table, which showed evidence of plunder as well
as ancient repair.[70] As suggested above, attachments of precious metal were apparently pried
out of the table's handles and removed from the
corners of the frame.[71] One wonders whether this
theft was the work of invading Kimmerians—or a
robbery that took place at the time of the burial.

There is no doubt that the construction of
Tumulus MM was a monumental undertaking.
After the objects had been lowered down and
arranged in the chamber, the roof of the tomb
was completed, and a platform of transverse logs
was laid above the roof. Rubble was piled on to
a depth of around four meters, and the earth
of the tumulus was then built up, to a height
exceeding the 53 meters preserved today.[72] This
was a major engineering project that may have
taken years to complete.[73] Although there might
have been memorials at the tomb, there is no
surviving evidence of any such markers—only a
tantalizing Homeric epigram:

> I am a maiden of bronze and am set upon the
> tomb of Midas. While the waters flow and tall
> trees flourish, and the sun rises and shines and
> the bright moon also; while rivers run and the
> sea breaks on the shore, ever remaining on this
> mournful tomb, I tell the passer-by that Midas
> here lies buried.[74]

Some have seen the presence of Matar in this
maiden of the tomb, as the goddess was so
closely associated with the dynasty of Midas. In
any case, it is reasonable to assume that Matar
played a significant role in the funerary cult of
the Phrygian rulers.[75] Certainly, her worship must

---

[69] Barley, lentil, and flax samples from Terrace Building 2A have been dated to ca. 827–803 B.C. DeVries, et
al., "New Dates for Iron Age Gordion." But see also Muscarella, "Date of the Destruction of the Early Phrygian Period at Gordion," who takes exception to this early date,
based on a study of the artifacts from the destruction level.
Keenan, "Radiocarbon Dates from Iron Age Gordion Are
Confounded," argues that the new C-14 dates are problematic, due to anomalies present in the atmosphere at Gordion
in ca. 800 B.C. One looks forward with interest to the final
outcome of these interrelated studies.

[70] One of the large cauldrons (MM 2) was also damaged
and repaired (Color Plate VIA). The four ring handles were
apparently wrenched off, and the tails of two of the siren
attachments were broken in the process. The sirens were
subsequently reattached (minus the ring handles), with new
pins driven through higher up on the tail. Young, *Gordion I*,
104; plates 52A, 53A. Relatively minor damage is exhibited
by two jugs and six bowls, which were either missing studs
at the area of the handle or showed ancient repairs.

[71] See above, pp. 34–35, 39.

[72] Young, *Gordion I*, 94.

[73] Based on the current height and diameter of the
tumulus, the volume of earth contained in the mound is
approximately 1.25 million cubic meters. If the earth was
brought to the vicinity in wagons, and if 30 minutes is
allotted for each return trip of a worker from the place
the earth was dumped to the top of the tumulus, a worker
could make two return trips per hour. If the workers worked
12-hour shifts, completing 24 trips per day, and carried 50-
pound baskets of earth, it would have taken 1,000 workers
approximately seven years to build Tumulus MM. Different
scenarios might be imagined, such as return trips of 20
minutes and shifts of eight hours; this particular variation
would have produced the same result. For the calculation of
workload according to the volume of a mound, see Ford and

Webb, "Poverty Point, A Late Archaic Site in Louisiana,"
32, 128.

[74] *Homeric Epigram* 3, in *Hesiod, the Homeric Hymns, and
Homerica*, 466–467. I bring my study to a close with this
epigram in fond memory of Sevim Buluç, who loved this
poetic passage and mentioned it frequently.

[75] Some of the niche monuments of Matar and stone
orthostat reliefs depicting animals have been associated by
scholars with Phrygian funerary cult, although the arguments presented are highly speculative. Roller, *In Search of
God the Mother*, 52, 74, 251; after Buluç, "Architectural Use
of the Animal and Kybele Reliefs," 19–21. Some impressive
rock monuments in the Phrygian highlands have been identified as tombs, including the carved façade of Arslan Taş,
which is decorated with two gigantic lions carved in relief
(CD-Figure 77). The lions rear up, placing their paws on top
of a door frame that incorporates a niche, and flanking a
flat, vertical element that resembles a king post. Haspels, *The
Highlands of Phrygia*, 118–119, figures 130–134; Roller, *In Search
of God the Mother*, 102–103. See also Yılan Taş, Haspels, figures 141–156. However, one wonders if these so-called tombs
might originally have been monuments like Arslan Kaya or
the Midas Monument, only later to be adapted as burial
sites. As the chambers are now empty, the date of their construction cannot be determined, although the side chamber
at Arslan Taş is said to be Byzantine. See Haspels, 208, and
253–254 on the extensive reuse of Phrygian monuments in
the Byzantine period. See Berndt-Ersöz, *Phrygian Rock-Cut
Shrines*, 153, for a review of scholarship on the subject. There
is evidence for such secondary use of carved rock façade
monuments elsewhere, notably the Assyrian monument at
Bavian. This was built originally by Sennacherib (r. 704–
681 B.C.) but defaced by later chambers cut into the rock
face. Larsen, *Conquest of Assyria*, plate VII. Bachmann, *Felsreliefs in Assyrien*, plates 8–11.

have provided some kind of solace for ordinary Phrygians.

The abode of the goddess was a mountainous region, evoked by her rock-cut shrines in the Phrygian highlands.[76] The man-made mountains that covered the Gordion tombs may also have signified the realm of Matar. Although there is no clear evidence for the meaning of the mountain in the religion of ancient Phrygia, elsewhere in the ancient Near East mountains and mounds were associated with the netherworld and the primeval hill from which the earth was created.[77]

The house of the goddess, represented by the rock shrines, incorporated a door in which Matar appeared to her followers, and the façade was covered with complex designs. The decorative motifs on the furniture from Tumulus MM included symbols of the goddess and exhibited an even greater complexity. This imagery was intentionally obscure, as shown by the puzzle-like patterns on the serving stands and the mazes on the inlaid table. The unusual decoration is meditative, and it suggests a journey or a quest that can lead to a revelation. This may be the imagery of the mysteries, which involved a quest for spiritual rebirth through rites of initiation.[78] The cults of the Greek Meter and Roman Magna Mater were mystery cults, and this may have been a feature of the worship of the Phrygian goddess Matar as well. The rock shrines of the great goddess must have signified a mysterious and transcendent space, the abode of the mother of all things, from which one was born and to which one would return. Such metaphors were the language of Phrygian decorative art, which reached its finest expression in the Tumulus MM furniture.

---

[76] See above, pp. 93–98.

[77] For the early Mesopotamian association of the netherworld (*kur*) with the mountains, see Katz, *Image of the Netherworld in the Sumerian Sources*, 19–25, and elsewhere. On the Egyptian primeval hill, see Frankfort, *Kingship and the Gods*, 151–154, and elsewhere. For the concept of a Mesopotamian deity confined to, and liberated from, the mountain, see Frankfort, 321–325. For the primordial Sacred Mound at Nippur and its connection to fertility, see M. Cohen, *Cultic Calendars of the Ancient Near East*, 106–112; for the mountain or mound as entrance to the underworld, 111–112, 261, 357, 460.

[78] In this connection, see Schuster and Carpenter, *Patterns That Connect*, 278–281, on rebirth gaming boards, which take the form of a schematic rendering of the body of a god or goddess. See also Murray, *A History of Board-Games*, 15 (the Egyptian "hounds and jackals"); xiv, 22–23 (Near Eastern versions). Games of rebirth allow the players to transcend the hazards of earthly existence, ascend the world axis, and achieve spiritual rebirth by reaching the deity's head. Such games are still played today in India, Persia, and Tibet ("snakes and ladders"), although rebirth games are of great antiquity. Several examples were found among the cache of ivories from the Treasury of the Late Bronze Age palace at Megiddo, in a context dated to the 12th century B.C. Loud, *Megiddo Ivories*, plates 47:220, 48:221, 49:222, 50:223. These plaques have an "hourglass" shape, a motif used in tribal arts to signify a female ancestor. *Patterns That Connect*, 280. At the top is a rosette, in the position of the head of the figure. As this game had wide currency, the Phrygians may have known it, and the concept of spiritual rebirth might have been embedded in the configurations on the Tumulus MM serving stands and designs on the rock monuments. See also *Patterns That Connect*, 288–289, for divination charts that resemble rebirth gaming boards; 291–307 for the labyrinth as the path to the afterworld, as a means of achieving reunion with one's ancestors, and even as a symbol of an ultimate ancestor or creator deity. See Johnston, "Mysteries," 105–111, on the process of initiation and the role of secrecy. See Berndt-Ersöz, "Phrygian Rock-Cut Cult Façades," on the theory that some of the rock façade monuments in the Phrygian highlands served for the pronouncement of oracles, utilizing shafts cut within the monuments to make it appear as though the utterances were emanating from the niche—or from the cult statue within.

APPENDIX I

CONSERVATION OF THE WOODEN FURNITURE FROM TUMULUS MM

Krysia Spirydowicz

Art Conservation Program
Queen's University, Kingston, Ontario, Canada

Introduction

The stable environment that existed for centuries within the sealed earthen mound of Tumulus MM was largely responsible for the remarkable survival of the wooden furniture. Sampling of the tomb and furniture revealed that the wood had been attacked only by soft-rot fungi (see Appendix 4).[1] Robert Blanchette believed that the low moisture content, high pH, and lack of oxygen within the tomb favored the slow growth of soft-rot fungi to the exclusion of other more aggressive types such as basidiomycetes. Although there was little alteration in the external appearance of most pieces of furniture, the wood was generally very light in weight due to the loss of most of the wood components. What remained was essentially a framework of lignified material.

Post-excavation Treatment

The need for conservation of the wooden furniture found in Tumulus MM was recognized at the time of excavation. According to Young's field notes, the tomb was very wet when opened. Young attributed this to the results of the drilling process.[2] He remarked later that "it is probable that at one time water stood over the whole inside, though probably to no great depth—perhaps a couple of inches. This has been harmful to the wooden objects; of that there is no doubt."[3] Two different treatments were used on the wood soon after excavation. Portions of the king's coffin, the fragments recovered from the northeast corner, and the eight plain banquet tables were coated with a dilute solution of Alvar, a polyvinyl acetal resin, dissolved in acetone.[4]

The inlaid table and the two inlaid serving stands were subjected to a different preservative treatment that began with immersion of the pieces in a solution of alcohol and water. The alcohol content was slowly increased in order to drive out any remaining moisture. Individual pieces were then immersed in a bath of wax and gasoline in an attempt to stabilize the wood. It was anticipated that the wax would enter the cells of the wood, thereby preventing shrinkage, splitting, and warping.[5] It is difficult to ascertain from contemporary accounts exactly what materials were used in this treatment. Young referred to "a paraffin treatment" and then recounted that the wood was placed in "a bath of benzine …in which beeswax had been dissolved to saturation."[6]

In 1997, Elizabeth Simpson interviewed Ron Smith, a pilot who flew supplies to the Gordion excavations in the 1950s. Smith's interview elicited the following information regarding the materials employed in treatment. In 1957, he flew to Gordion, landing near Tumulus MM with supplies of gasoline, which were then used to treat the furniture. Smith recalled that he supplied aviation fuel (AVGAZ brand) and that it was light blue in color. He remembered that the use of avi-

---

[1] Blanchette, et al., "An Evaluation of Different Forms of Deterioration."
[2] Young, *GFB* 63, 66.
[3] Ibid., 72.
[4] See Simpson and Spirydowicz, *Gordion Wooden Furniture* (hereafter *GWF*). Information on the conservation of the wooden furniture was published in Simpson, Spirydowicz, and Dorge, *Gordion Wooden Furniture: The Study, Conservation, and Reconstruction of the Wooden Furniture from Gordion: 1981–1990* (1992), which has been superseded by Simpson and Spirydowicz, *GWF*. The inlaid table was also treated with Alvar initially but subsequently with alcohol/wax (see below).
[5] Young, "*AJA* Draft," 23.
[6] Ibid.

ation fuel left a blue stain on the treated pieces. When asked about the type of wax used in these treatments, Smith replied that it was probably beeswax, as paraffin wax was difficult to obtain in Turkey at that time, but beeswax was available everywhere. "All in a day's work for a bush pilot," said Smith, when he was thanked for his assistance to the Gordion excavations.[7]

In general, it can be concluded that neither treatment was effective in preserving the wooden furniture from Tumulus MM. The pieces that had been coated with a dilute solution of Alvar were in a very fragile state when examined in 1981.[8] Traces of a resinous coating were visible on seven of the eight plain banquet tables. It appeared that the Alvar solution had not penetrated much below the surface of the wood so that there was little strengthening effect.[9] Young's notes record that members of the field crew[10] as well as the excavation foreman[11] were assigned the task of "painting" the wood with an Alvar solution. Undoubtedly this resulted in many treatment variables. The inference is clear that this method was employed primarily as a first-aid measure to allow the most deteriorated pieces to be removed intact from the tomb.

The alcohol/wax method, a standard treatment for archaeological wood at the time, also proved problematic. While the initial immersion of the wood in alcohol solution was probably effective in reducing the moisture content of the wood, subsequent treatment in a bath of wax dissolved in gasoline was ultimately detrimental. Young was not entirely satisfied with the results at the time, admitting that a color change had occurred after the consolidation of the inlaid serving stands.[12] However he anticipated that the pieces would receive further treatment once they were transferred to the Museum of Anatolian Civilizations in Ankara. When the objects treated by this method were examined in 1981, it was found that the wax had remained at, or close to, the surface rather than penetrating the wood to any appreciable depth. The waxy surface attracted dirt over the years, while the wood beneath continued to deteriorate.

Assessment of the Furniture in 1981

During the preparation of Young's posthumous volume,[13] the field drawings of the wooden objects from Tumulus MM, Tumulus P, and Tumulus W were checked for accuracy, and many were found to contain errors. The need for further study of the individual pieces was recognized, and an assessment of the furniture began at the Museum of Anatolian Civilizations in 1981.

The inlaid table from Tumulus MM was the first piece to be studied. When the fragments of the table were removed from storage, it became apparent that the fragile wood was in urgent need of conservation. Examination of the rest of the Gordion wooden objects led to the same conclusion; all of the pieces had suffered significant deterioration since their recovery from the tomb. Shortly thereafter, under the auspices of the University of Pennsylvania Museum of Archaeology and Anthropology, the Gordion Furniture Project was established with the preservation, study, and publication of the wooden artifacts as its principal goals. All of the conservation treatments, with the exception of the earlier on-site interventions, were carried out during summer field seasons in the conservation laboratory of the Museum of Anatolian Civilizations.

Initial Testing

Robert Payton, the first conservator for the Gordion Furniture Project, carried out cleaning and consolidation tests in 1981, in preparation for the treatment of the inlaid table from Tumulus MM, the first piece of furniture to be conserved under the auspices of the new project.[14] Prior to cleaning, the surface of the inlaid table was very dark. Payton attributed this to the presence of the previously-applied consolidant, paraffin wax, which had imbibed dirt and soot during approximately 25 years of storage. It was important to remove the wax, Payton felt, since its presence prevented the penetration of any other consolidant. Toluene was found to be effective for the wax removal, and this solvent was used to clean the table the following year.

---

[7] Spirydowicz, notes on a telephone conversation between Elizabeth Simpson and Ron Smith, June 12, 1997.

[8] Simpson and Spirydowicz, *GWF*, 34–35.

[9] Spirydowicz, et al., "Alvar and Butvar."

[10] Young, *GFB* 63, 115.

[11] Ibid., 159.

[12] Young, "*AJA* Draft," 23.

[13] Young, *Gordion I*.

[14] Payton, "Conservation of an Eighth Century B.C. Table."

The type of consolidant to be used and its method of application were the most important considerations. The successful use of polyvinyl butyral as a consolidant for dry, fragile wood had been previously reported by Barclay.[15] Payton chose to experiment with a polyvinyl butyral resin of lower molecular weight and lower viscosity, i.e. Butvar B-98, rather than the slightly higher grade, Butvar B-90, used by Barclay. Payton recognized that polyvinyl butyral had a number of desirable characteristics for use as a wood consolidant on the Gordion furniture, including moderate to high strength, little discoloration, and solubility in a variety of solvents.

A 50/50 mixture of ethanol/toluene was selected by Payton to provide a polymer solution of low viscosity. The low surface tension of ethanol aided in wetting the wood fibers and increased the depth of penetration of the consolidant. Toluene was chosen because of its relatively slow evaporation rate, which inhibited the reverse migration of the consolidant towards the surface during drying.

Small, unprovenanced cubes of wood recovered from the Gordion tumuli were chosen for experimentation. These were consolidated with a 5% (wt/vol) solution of Butvar B-98 in equal parts of toluene and ethanol. The wood samples were immersed in the solution and left to absorb the consolidant. When the wood sank or floated just below the surface, indicating that most of the air in the wood had been replaced by the consolidant solution, the pieces were removed and air-dried.

Measurements taken before and after drying indicated that no shrinkage had taken place. This agreed with the results reported by Barclay, who recorded a minimal amount of expansion in test samples. In comparing treated and untreated portions of samples, Payton found that there was little color change. This result was particularly desirable for the treatment of the pieces of furniture containing inlay such as the inlaid table from Tumulus MM, where color contrast between woods was an important feature of the overall design. Payton judged that a 5% solution imparted sufficient strength to the otherwise fragile pieces, and the decision was made to proceed with treatment.

Conservation of the Inlaid Table

When found by Young in 1957 near the east wall of the tomb, the inlaid table had collapsed under the weight of the many bronze vessels that had been placed on it at the time of burial (Color Plate IIIB, Plate 1). The sections of the table had separated, but they had fallen in such a way that their original relationship could be determined. The table consisted of a square frame and three legs, with decorative struts supporting the tray-shaped table top. The frame, legs, and struts were inlaid with a dark wood in intricate geometric patterns. Later analysis indicated that the table was constructed of three different woods: boxwood (frame and legs), juniper (decorative inlay), and walnut (table top).[16]

When the table was found, the wood was judged to be in good condition, with the exception of the walnut top of which only shreds and small fragments were preserved.[17] Young reported that the wood was coated with a solution of Alvar while still *in situ*.[18] On removal from the tomb, the fragments of the table were immersed in a bath of alcohol in order to drive out moisture. The fragments were then consolidated in a bath of wax dissolved in gasoline.[19]

Payton's initial examination of the table in 1981 indicated that the wax had not penetrated the wood to any appreciable depth but instead had formed a sticky, dirt-attracting layer on the surface.[20] In 1982, Payton cleaned the surface of the wood using the following method. After removal of loose dirt with a soft brush, a cotton swab moistened with the solvent toluene was applied to the surface (Plate 124A). Usually three to four applications of toluene were required in order to remove all of the dirt and wax. During this process, the wood became noticeably lighter in color. A deep red-brown waxy material, consisting of a mixture of wax and powdered wood, was also removed. The latter appeared to be a deterioration product of the wood. Examination of cross-sections under the microscope indicated that most of the wax, which had penetrated no more than 0.2–0.3 mm in depth, was removed during cleaning.[21] After cleaning, the wood was considerably lighter in color, and the contrast was increased between the darker wood of the inlay

---

[15] Barclay, "Wood Consolidation."

[16] See Appendix 3 for all wood species identifications.

[17] Young, *Gordion I*, 183.

[18] Young, *GFB* 63, 115.

[19] Young, Letter to G. Roger Edwards, August 29, 1957.

[20] Payton, "Second Conservation Report 1982," 1.

[21] Ibid.

and the surrounding boxwood. Consolidation of the wood of the inlaid table was undertaken the same year.

Based on the results of previous experimentation, Payton chose to consolidate the table with a 5% (wt/vol) solution of Butvar B-98 dissolved in equal parts of toluene and ethanol. In order to ensure thorough penetration of the consolidant into the wood, Payton proposed the use of vacuum pressure. Because of the fragility of the wood, Payton judged that the use of a hand-operated vacuum pump offered the greatest control over the pumping rate and the resultant stresses imposed on the wood.

The smaller fragments of the table including the struts and dowels were treated in a glass vacuum desiccator. A specially designed tank of galvanized steel with a glass viewing window was used to consolidate the larger fragments such as the legs and frame pieces. A slow pumping rate was employed in both cases, and the vacuum pressure was increased in increments of 5 cm Hg. At each increment, most of the air was allowed to escape from the wood before the pressure was increased. The struts were subjected to a maximum pressure of 40 cm Hg while a maximum of 10 cm Hg was employed for the legs and frame.

Prior to consolidation, all of the pieces of the table with the exception of the legs and fragments of the top were weighed on a bilateral action balance. Measurements of each piece were taken in the longitudinal, radial, and tangential directions, using a metric ruler and Vernier calipers. Color photography provided a record of the color of the woods prior to treatment while photography with black and white film recorded the position of the pieces of inlay as well as the condition of the wood before consolidation.

All of the pieces containing inlay were wrapped in open-weave gauze in order to keep loose pieces in position. To counteract the tendency of the wood to float on the surface of the solution, the stronger pieces were anchored from below with lead weights. They were also weighted from above with stainless steel weights so that they floated just below the surface of the solution.

Fragile pieces were treated with greater caution. While floating on the surface of the solution, each piece was wetted with consolidant from a pipette. Once the lid of the tank was closed, a moderate vacuum pressure of 2–3 cm Hg was applied. After this was achieved, air was slowly allowed into the system, causing some absorption of consolidant. This vacuum-air cycle was repeated a number of times, with the vacuum pressure increasing at increments of 5 cm Hg each time, to a maximum of 40 cm Hg. Eventually, this process caused the fragments to sink below the surface of the solution. This procedure took a total of 3–4 hours. Afterward, air was slowly allowed back into the system. At this time, the wood was saturated with consolidant and sank to the bottom of the tank. Payton observed that there was a noticeable reduction in the level of the solution after treatment resulting from the absorption of the consolidant by the wood.[22]

The larger pieces of the table were treated in a similar manner. Individual pieces were placed in the solution, and the vacuum pressure was raised to a maximum of 10 cm Hg, using vacuum-air cycles as described above. Pressure was maintained over an 18 hour period in an effort to ensure penetration of the consolidant into the interior of even the thickest pieces of wood. When the wood was examined after treatment, it was noticeably lighter in color. In addition, the wax below the surface, previously evident in cross-sections, was no longer present. Payton therefore concluded that the choice of solvents combined with the flushing action of the vacuum-air cycles had removed the remaining wax from the wood.[23]

Drying was carried out very slowly in order to avoid problems such as splitting and cracking of the treated wood or reverse migration of the consolidant. After each piece was removed from the solution and any excess consolidant had drained from the wood, each fragment was placed in a polyethylene bag which was sealed shut, thus allowing the treated wood to dry slowly in an atmosphere of solvent vapors. Two methods were used to monitor the drying process. Periodic weighing of individual pieces in their polyethylene bags allowed the evaporation rate to be plotted on a graph. Payton judged that the end point had been reached when two or more consecutive readings of the same value were obtained. Color change was also used as an approximate indicator of the progress of drying. Immediately after consolidation, the saturated wood appeared black and shiny. As the solvents evaporated, the wood turned gradually from dark umber to reddish-brown and finally to a medium tan color.

---

[22] Payton, "Third Conservation Report 1983," 12.

[23] Ibid.

The greatest weight loss occurred within two to three days after removal from the solution. Most of the smaller pieces attained a constant weight after 12–14 days. Once this had been achieved, the polyethylene bags were opened slowly over a three-day period, to allow the wood to acclimatize to the laboratory atmosphere. On the third day, the wood was removed from the bags. Payton noted that a faint solvent odor emanated from the wood, but this disappeared within 24 hours.[24]

Although the wood was stronger after treatment, Payton felt that additional consolidant should be applied for two reasons: to strengthen the surfaces that exhibited deep hairline cracks and to provide a barrier against the fluctuating humidity (45%-68%) in the museum laboratory. Accordingly, a 10% (wt/vol) concentration of Butvar B-98 was applied with a brush to each piece. The number of applications varied, depending on the porosity of the individual fragments. Where the wood was particularly absorbent, consolidant was brushed on until an excess began to build up on the surface. The excess consolidant was then removed with an absorbent tissue moistened with a 50/50 mixture of ethanol and toluene. The use of ethanol alone caused a white bloom to occur on the surface due to the high ambient humidity. However this was preventable by the addition of 50% toluene. After this, each piece was placed in a polyethylene bag to dry slowly, as before. On drying, the wood was noticeably stronger although slightly darker than after the preliminary consolidation.

Weight gain measurements varied from about 22% to 168.5% after preliminary consolidation.[25] Absorption rates varied widely due to the variable condition of the pieces prior to treatment, the amount of exposed end grain vs. total surface area, and the general porosity of the wood. All of the pieces, with the exception of the decorative inlays, exhibited slightly expanded dimensions after treatment in the longitudinal, radial, and tangential directions. This was consistent with the results reported by Barclay. Payton also noted that consolidation appeared to diminish distortions evident in some pieces before treatment, for example some of the frame pieces, struts, and handles.[26]

Consolidation of the Table Top

The top of the inlaid table was in extremely poor condition when assessed by Payton in 1982. He reported later that "half the pieces were simply no more than powdered wood loosely held together. The rest was highly warped...extremely powdery and very light in color and weight."[27] Because some of the pieces retained information important to the analysis and eventual reconstruction of the table, it was decided to attempt consolidation of the wood (Plate 32). Solutions of polyvinyl acetate (AYAF), Acryloid B-72 and B-44, polyvinyl butyral, and ketone resin N were tested, although none of these thermoplastic resins imparted sufficient strength to the wood. The most promising results were obtained from tests of Rutapox R1210, an aliphatic long chain epoxy resin. The low viscosity of this thermosetting resin ensured deep penetration of the consolidant into the wood. In addition, the crosslinked structure of the cured bonds imparted considerable strength.

Payton was aware of the serious drawbacks of using this resin, namely that the treatment was irreversible and that it caused a significant alteration in appearance, rendering the wood dark and slightly shiny.[28] Because of the advanced state of deterioration of the table top, imparting strength to the fragile wood was of primary importance. Therefore Payton chose to use Rutapox R1210 in spite of its disadvantages.

Because the pieces of the table top could not be moved without causing further damage, the catalyzed resin was applied to the wood *in situ* in its storage drawer, using a pipette. Resin was applied to the point of saturation. Four hours later, it was possible to transfer the fragments to a non-stick polyethylene sheet. At the gel stage (i.e. between seven and ten hours), excess resin was removed from the surface of the wood using swabs soaked in acetone. After two days, the resin was fully cured. Payton reported that the wood was much darker after treatment as anticipated, although it was also much stronger. Individual fragments could be handled and studied safely. In subsequent years, the conservators who followed Payton concluded that the irreversible nature of the treatment, combined with the charred ap-

---

[24] Ibid., 14.
[25] Ibid., 20–27.
[26] Ibid., 16–17.

[27] Ibid., 18.
[28] Ibid., 19.

pearance imparted to the wood, made Rutapox an unacceptable choice for further treatments.

In the final phase of treatment, adhesives were used to join detached fragments and to readhere loose pieces of inlay. In most cases, a 20% (wt/vol) solution of Butvar B-98 in 50/50 ethanol/toluene was used. Where greater strength was required, HMG, a nitrocellulose adhesive, was employed. Some balsa wood fills were constructed to bridge gaps in the legs and one of the handles. These fills were adhered with HMG and painted with acrylic paints.

On completion of treatment, Simpson and Payton decided to reconstruct the inlaid table, although it was evident that the parts could not simply be rejoined by the use of adhesives. The design of the table was extremely complex, and some of the pieces had suffered permanent distortion resulting from the collapse of the table in the tomb. Thus they decided to mount the wood on a display support of clear acrylic sheet. Individual pieces of the table were fastened in place with small acrylic hooks. This system allowed the table to be reconstructed to a close approximation of its original appearance without placing undue stress on any individual elements. The acrylic hooks provided adequate support but did not restrict the wood from responding to environmental changes. In addition, the clear support allowed unobstructed viewing of the fragments of the table from a variety of angles (see Appendix 2 on the reconstruction of the inlaid table and serving stands for display).

In 1983, after the mount was complete, the reconstructed table was installed in a display case provided by the Ankara Museum. Gaps between the panes of glass forming the upper part of the case were sealed with silicone sealant in an attempt to exclude dust. It was expected that this measure would also assist in maintaining a fairly constant relative humidity inside the case. Unfortunately, problems became evident within a year. The acrylic support began to turn white due to the development of a network of fine cracks (crazing), and a strong smell was noticeable when the case was opened. It appeared that the damage to the acrylic sheet was due, at least in part, to the emission of fumes from the materials used in the display.

Recent conservation literature explores the problem of crazing. Clear acrylic sheet often con-

tains internal stresses as a result of the casting process. If these stresses are not relieved by annealing at the time of manufacture, crazing of the acrylic sheet may occur at a later date, particularly if it is kept in an unfavourable environment. Exposure to the vapors of aliphatic alcohols is now recognized as a common cause of crazing.[29] Subsequent weighing of consolidated fragments showed that the wood continued to lose weight for some years after treatment. Therefore it is likely that the slow release of ethanol vapors from the consolidant exacerbated the problem of crazing of the support.

In spite of repeated airing of the display case, off-gassing continued to be a problem, and the acrylic support showed signs of further deterioration (Plate 124B). During the 1989 season, the entire display was dismantled, and a second mount was made (Color Plates VIII–IX, Plates 33–35). A new support was constructed of craze-resistant Plexiglas (Rohm and Haas Plexiglas G). Painted brass hooks padded with ethafoam provided a strong yet unobtrusive means of supporting the fragments of the table. The original display materials were stripped from the case and new ones substituted, with minimal use of adhesives and sealants. The case was left unsealed in order to prevent vapor build-up. While the limited air circulation allowed some dust to enter the case, there were no further problems with the new Plexiglas support. The inlaid table was moved to a new, custom-designed display case in 1997 (see p. 162 below).

Conservation of the Inlaid Serving Stands

The two inlaid serving stands (A and B) were found leaning against the east wall of the tomb chamber, north of the inlaid table (Color Plates IIIA, IV; Plates 69–70, 80). Each stand consisted of a large, rectangular face decorated with dark wood inlay in elaborate geometric designs. The lower third of the face featured a central, inlaid rosette supported by two curved "legs." A horizontal shelf projecting from the rear incorporated three large wooden rings that had once accommodated small bronze cauldrons. Originally, the shelf had been supported by diagonal struts mortised into a vertical back leg. However at some point after burial, the rear sections of both stands

---

[29] Sale, "Eleven Adhesives," 327–328.

had collapsed. At the time of discovery, both of the shelves and their supporting structures were found in fragmentary condition, lying behind the faces of the stands, close to the wall of the tomb.

The excavation photographs reveal a distinct color contrast between the light brown of the boxwood face and the much darker juniper used for the inlaid designs (Color Plate IVA–B). Although the faces of the stands were in good condition when found, some of the joints had begun to separate, and the curved "legs" were deteriorating. The collapse of the rear shelf and supporting structure had caused the face of each stand to sag gradually over the centuries. Some of this tension had been released via cracks and breaks in the side panels of each stand.

Young's notes indicate that the two stands were left to dry slowly in the tomb, after completion of recording and photography. However, after a month green mold began to grow on the wood, prompting the removal of these objects from the burial environment.[30] Three of the fragile "legs" from the stands crumbled into small fragments on handling and thus did not survive the move. Once outside the tomb, the two stands were treated in a similar manner to the inlaid table. Each was first dewatered in alcohol baths and subsequently consolidated in a solution of wax dissolved in gasoline.[31] According to the excavators, the treatment was not successful, since the wood began to warp and shrink after removal from the consolidant (Plates 71, 81). Furthermore, the color contrast between the boxwood and the juniper inlays was much diminished.[32] After treatment, the stands were taken to the Museum of Anatolian Civilizations in Ankara.

When examined by Payton in 1983, stand B, which had been kept in storage, was covered in a thick layer of dust and soot. In contrast, stand A, which had been placed on display in a museum showcase, had been protected from such accumulations of dirt, although there was some dust on the surface. Payton noted that both stands were severely warped and distorted due to the previous conservation treatment,[33] and splits were evident between individual boards that had once been joined seamlessly. In addition, Payton noted fungal damage on both stands.[34] Those portions made of walnut, including the curved

front "legs" and the rings of the horizontal top shelf, exhibited considerable deterioration. This is consistent with the severe degradation evident in other pieces of tomb furniture fabricated from walnut, such as the tops of the banquet tables. The shrinkage of the boxwood faces caused by the initial conservation treatment resulted in the detachment or loss of many pieces of juniper inlay. In addition, a number of elements were missing, including the rear legs of both stands.

The procedure for the consolidation of the stands was similar to that used for the inlaid table. Cleaning and consolidation took place during August and September 1983. The two stands were cleaned using a 50/50 mixture of isopropyl alcohol and toluene applied on cotton swabs. This procedure was effective in removing both the wax and surface dirt (Plate 124C). A steel tank large enough to accommodate an entire stand was constructed in Ankara. Measuring 1 m by 1 m, the tank had a separate lid with a central viewing port of thick glass. Rubber tubing was used to form the seal for the tank. The tubing was laid into a bed of silicone sealant applied along the exterior flange of the steel base. A thin layer of silicone sealant was also applied to the inner edges of the lid, so that when the lid was in place, a seal was formed. When the tank was in use, "C" clamps were employed to clamp the lid to the base, ensuring a tight seal (Plate 125A).

The stands were photographed and then wrapped in perforated polyethylene sheeting. This was to ensure that any loose pieces of inlay would remain close to their original location, should they float out of position during treatment. Each stand was then immersed, in turn, in a 6% (wt/vol) solution of Butvar B-98 in a 50/50 isopropyl alcohol and toluene mixture. Using a hand-held vacuum pump, Payton applied vacuum pressure in increments of 5 cm Hg, up to a maximum of 20 cm Hg. Stand B was allowed to soak in the consolidant solution under a pressure of 18–20 cm Hg for a period of eight days, whereas the treatment time for Stand A was reduced to five days.

After consolidation, air was allowed into the tank very slowly until atmospheric pressure was reached. The lid of the tank was then removed, and the consolidated sections of each stand were

---

[30] Young, GFB 63, 158. Young, Gordion I, 177.

[31] Young, Gordion I, 177.

[32] Young, "AJA Draft," 23.

[33] Payton, "Conservation of Screens A and B 1984," 2.

[34] Ibid., 1.

carefully raised from the solution, supported on a thick polyethylene sheet. After excess consolidant had drained from the wood, each section of the stand was placed in a polyethylene bag, which was sealed in order to retard evaporation of the solvents. The pieces were then placed in a second polyethylene bag and returned to storage. The wood was allowed to dry over a period of nine months.

When the wood was removed from storage and the bags were opened, only a faint smell of residual solvents was noted.[35] The bags were opened one at a time, and as each piece of wood was exposed, the surface was further consolidated with one or two applications of 7%-8% (wt/vol) Butvar B-98 in 50/50 isopropyl alcohol/toluene. Payton judged that surface coating of the pieces was necessary, as it had been for the inlaid table, in order to provide a barrier against the fluctuating humidity levels in the museum laboratory. Further cleaning of some pieces was carried out prior to the application of the surface coating. This consisted in the use of a soft glass-bristle brush to remove dirt from previously inaccessible areas, as well as the use of a scalpel to shave mold residue from the backs of the stands and other areas.

Severely deteriorated portions of the stands, i.e. the walnut rings belonging to the top shelf and the remains of the front "legs," were further consolidated by repeated applications of a 10% (wt/vol) solution of Butvar B-98 in 50/50 isopropyl alcohol and toluene. These pieces were allowed to absorb the consolidant to saturation and then placed in polyethylene bags in order to control the drying process. This procedure had to be repeated in some cases. The right front foot of stand A required four separate applications of the stronger solution of consolidant in order to impart sufficient strength to the degraded wood so that it could be handled (Plate 90).

After consolidation, many of the pieces of inlay were loose but still in position. Because the stands were to be displayed in an upright position on Plexiglas mounts, there was considerable risk that some of the loose inlay pieces might fall out of their recesses. Payton therefore decided to secure each one in place with a dot of HMG adhesive applied to the back. Some pieces of inlay had become detached during consolidation. By consulting the photographs taken prior to treat-

ment, it was possible to return most of them to their original positions. These were also adhered in place with HMG adhesive.

Payton judged the treatment of the two stands to be successful, based on several factors. All of the pieces exhibited significant increases in weight: a comparison of the weights of three large fragments from stand B indicated a mean average weight gain, after treatment, of 16.47%.[36] Measurements of selected fragments in the longitudinal, tangential, and radial directions, both before and after treatment, indicated virtually no dimensional change. Payton observed that the thickness of the individual sections probably prevented any noticeable expansion of the wood, in contrast to some of the thinner pieces of the inlaid table, which had exhibited some swelling after treatment. Payton also concluded that the lengthy drying time had minimized dimensional changes within the wood. Slow drying was adopted as a standard procedure for all subsequent consolidations, with treated fragments left to dry for a period of one year on average.

After treatment, the appearance of the stands was greatly improved (Plates 72–77, 82–87). The color contrast between the boxwood background and the darker juniper inlay was enhanced, and details of the intricate geometric designs became clear, allowing accurate drawings of these pieces to be made. Subtle differences in color between the different types of wood used (boxwood, juniper, walnut, and yew) were also revealed. A considerable increase in strength was apparent, so that the pieces of the stands could be handled for drawing and photography without risk of damage. In 1984, the stands were mounted for display on Plexiglas supports, in a manner similar to the inlaid table. Modifications were made to the display mounts in 1999 (Plates 78–79, 88–89). The reconstructed "legs" that had been fashioned from Plexiglas were removed, and the acrylic hooks originally used to support the wood were replaced with brass hooks, padded with thin strips of Volara foam and painted with acrylic paint (see Appendix 2).

Conservation of the Eight Plain Banquet Tables

Eight banquet tables, called "plain tables" by the excavator, were found collapsed on the floor

---

[35] Ibid., 5.

[36] Ibid., 7.

of the tomb chamber (Color Plates IIIA, V; Plates 36, 54). All of these tables were of similar design, consisting of a tray-shaped top supported by three curved legs with tenons that fit into collars projecting from the underside of the table top (Figures 39–40). At the time of excavation, the tables were numbered 1–7 and 9. The inlaid table was designated as table 8. The banquet tables had collapsed under the weight of the bronze vessels that had been placed on top of them.

The condition of the tables varied, depending on their location in the tomb. Tables 1–5 (Plates 36–59), recovered from the center of the chamber, were in the best condition. The curved legs were found lying partially under, or close to, their respective table tops. Over the centuries, the wood of the table tops had gradually relaxed over the legs and the bronze vessels that lay beneath them. As a consequence, the table tops were broken, and much of the wood exhibited some deformation. In contrast, most of the legs of the tables were intact and appeared to be quite sound.[37] Later analysis identified the wood of most of the table tops as walnut and that of the legs as boxwood.[38]

Tables 6 and 7 (Plates 60–65), found in the southeast corner of the tomb, were in a badly deteriorated state. The tops were cracked and broken into cubical fragments typical of biologically degraded wood. The legs of table 7 were in fairly good condition, although most of one leg was missing. In contrast, although the legs of table 6 were extremely degraded, substantial portions of all three legs existed. Table 9 was discovered near the north wall of the tomb chamber, lying under the collapsed east ledge of the king's coffin. Only one end of the top was intact, and the legs were severely degraded (Plates 66–68).

While the tables were still *in situ*, the top of each one was painted with a thin solution of Alvar in an attempt to strengthen the wood.[39] The coating was applied to the upper surfaces of the table tops only, since the wood was too fragile to move without causing further damage. With reference to table 5, Young noted that "the bottom [i.e. the lower surface] is rather soft and spongy, but not too damp."[40] Tables 1 and 5

were removed from the tomb by "sliding sticks underneath and raising the tops enough so that we can draw out the fallen legs on which the tops rest, then sliding a piece of plywood underneath and lowering the table tops on to it."[41] Further damage to the wood may have occurred during the lifting stage. Young mentions that "Table #1 is now broken but we manage to get it out in fair condition" and "We get out #5 in fair condition—pieces but big ones; the whole top is fairly complete."[42] Although Young's notes give no further details, it seems likely that the rest of the tables were removed from the tomb in similar fashion. Ellen Kohler, the registrar at the Gordion excavations, recalled that mold growth was removed from the banquet tables by washing the surfaces with vinegar.[43]

Subsequently, two of the best-preserved tables (tables 1 and 5) were treated with the alcohol/wax method used for the inlaid table and serving stands. It seems probable that immersion in an alcohol bath would have dissolved much of the Alvar applied to the wood some weeks earlier. These treatments did little to strengthen the wood, which continued to deteriorate rapidly. By the early 1980s, most of the table tops were too fragile to be handled. Between 1988 and 1990, the eight banquet tables were consolidated with Butvar B-98, employing a similar procedure to that developed for the two inlaid serving stands. Treatment details for each table are outlined in the sections that follow.

Table 1

A photograph of table 1 taken at the time of excavation shows that the wood had a distinct whitish cast in places (Plate 37). A similar whitish or greyish layer was observed on the surfaces of other table tops, for example table 5. This appeared to be the Alvar that had been applied as a consolidant by Young. The dampness of the wood at the time may have caused blanching of the resin, resulting in a whitening of the surface of the wood. However, any traces of this and the subsequent alcohol/wax treatment

---

[37] Young, *GFB* 63, 77.

[38] The top of table 6 was so degraded that its wood species could not be determined with certainty. Later analysis by Blanchette has indicated that characteristics of woods such as maple or cherry are present. See Appendix 3, pp. 165–167.

[39] Young, *GFB* 63, 115.

[40] Ibid., 116.

[41] Ibid., 115.

[42] Ibid., 115–116.

[43] Ellen Kohler, personal communication to E. Simpson, Gordion Furniture Project archives.

were obscured by an attempt at reconstruction undertaken in 1964.

After the initial transfer of the tomb finds from Gordion to the Museum of Anatolian Civilizations in Ankara, table 1 was treated in the museum's conservation laboratory. No written information has been found regarding the procedures employed, although some details were obtained from the recollections of the Ankara Museum staff. The treatment consisted of applying melted beeswax to both sides of the table top. A hair dryer was reportedly used to drive the wax into the wood. Two of the legs were glued to the table top using a mixture of white glue and sawdust. A combination of beeswax and sawdust was used to fill voids. Small cracks were filled with a hard, lemon-yellow wax, probably paraffin, which was also used to coat the collars attached to the two original legs. A new leg was carved to replace the third fragmentary leg, and this was inserted into an original collar.

The purpose of this treatment was to allow the banquet table to be placed on exhibit in the museum. However, the application of excessive amounts of wax to the table top made the table so heavy that it could not be turned upright without risk of damage. Thus the table remained in storage, face down, for many years, until investigated by the Gordion Furniture Project conservators (Plate 38).

Examination

An initial examination of table 1 was undertaken during 1988.[44] The walnut table top was covered by a thick layer of dark brown wax which penetrated the wood to a depth of 2–3 mm. The interior of the wood appeared to be in poor condition, with a fair amount of wood dust evident. The two complete boxwood legs and attached collars appeared to be well preserved, although it was difficult to assess the condition of the wood accurately because of the dark, waxy coating that covered these pieces. In contrast, fragments of the original third leg were in very poor condition. One of the original legs had become detached from the top during storage.

In 1989, table 1 was reexamined and treated.[45] Emily Dunn noted that the table top had cracked into several pieces and surmised that this might have been the result of an attempt to turn the

table over for display. The table top was dusty and brownish-black in color when it was brought to the laboratory from storage. Some fragments of the table top and the incomplete collar had not been incorporated into the reconstruction of 1964. Among these, a large collar fragment and a fragment of a table edge were described as greyish in color and hard on the surface, indicating a previous resin consolidation. Others were coated with wax, although whether this was applied in 1957 or 1964 was not possible to determine.

Treatment

Removal of the wax and thorough consolidation of the fragile wood was considered essential for the long-term stability of table 1. Increased mechanical strength was another desirable objective of treatment, to allow for photography, drawing, study, and reconstruction of the fragments.

In order to detach the two legs (one original, one reproduction) still in place, excavation of thick fills of beeswax and sawdust was necessary (Plate 125B). Most of the work was accomplished using scalpels, although, on occasion, petroleum ether was injected by syringe to aid in dissolving the wax. The original legs were subsequently cleaned of wax by applying a mixture of toluene, ethanol, and acetone on cotton swabs. Because of the excellent state of preservation of the two complete boxwood legs, no further treatment was required. The two largest fragments of the incomplete leg were wrapped in silkscreen pouches and consolidated in a 10% (wt/vol) solution of Butvar B-98 in 60/40 ethanol/toluene. Collar fragments were consolidated locally by pipette using a 10% (wt/vol) solution of Butvar B-98 in 60/40 ethanol/toluene. These were covered with a piece of polyethylene to allow for slow drying over several days. Later, a complete collar was reattached to the table top using 30% Butvar B-98 in ethanol as the adhesive.

Removal of the heavy wax deposits from the table top began, using gel poultices of ca. 3% Klucel HF (hydroxypropyl cellulose) in a 50/50 solvent mixture of ethanol and toluene. Soon after application of a poultice to the surface, the gel became yellowish-brown in color, while the underlying wax turned white and soft (Plate 126A). The poultice was allowed to sit on the surface of the wood for ten minutes and was then re-

[44] Goldberg, "Conservation Report 1988," 41–47.

[45] Dunn, "Conservation Report 1989: Banquet Table 1."

moved with cotton swabs soaked in ethanol. Each area required several poultice applications until the wood appeared free of wax to the naked eye. At this point, Dunn was concerned that some of the wax had penetrated too far into the structure of the wood to be removed by this technique, and later, this proved to be true.

Once the entire lower surface of the top was cleaned of wax, the wood was padded with layers of absorbent cotton, tissue, cloth, and polyethylene sheeting. Two sheets of heavy cardboard were added on either side, and these were taped together. The top was then turned over to reveal the upper surface of the table, which was evenly coated with a thick layer of wax. In addition, there were several large pools of beeswax, which may have formed while the legs were being reattached. Dunn theorized that while the table lay face down, wax might have been poured through cracks and holes in order to seal them, in preparation for filling with a mixture of sawdust and wax. For the retreatment, this top surface was cleaned in the same manner as the under surface.

Dunn was careful to remove all visible traces of wax or sawdust to avoid redeposition of these materials during the consolidation process. After cleaning, the grain patterns in the wood of the table top were clearly revealed. One collar fragment was still attached to the under surface of the table top. Dunn was concerned about potential deformation of this piece during consolidation. The table top was therefore turned over once more onto a layer of silkscreen fabric, following the procedure described earlier, so that it would be resting on its upper surface during consolidation. The top was then transferred to a metal tank tray, which was subsequently used to support the fragile wood during immersion in the consolidant solution.

Another layer of silkscreen fabric was added, and the two layers were fastened together with straight pins, in order to create a large pouch that would serve to enclose the entire table top. Then the top was immersed in the consolidant, consisting of an 8% (wt/vol) solution of Butvar B-98 in 50/50 ethanol/toluene. The composition of this solution was slightly different from the standard solution used during the 1989 season— a 10% (wt/vol) solution of Butvar B-98 in 60/40 ethanol/toluene—for the following reasons. The slightly lower percentage of total solids, combined

with a slightly higher percentage of toluene, rendered the solution less viscous. This increased the ability of the solution to penetrate the wood, which was still impregnated with wax to some extent. Increasing the concentration of toluene, an excellent solvent for beeswax, thereby increased the efficiency of the solution to dissolve the remaining wax.

The table top was allowed to sit for about one hour on the surface of the solution, so that the solvent mixture would begin to penetrate and dissolve the wax lying just below the surface of the wood. However, the table top continued to float on the surface of the solution even after a vacuum of 20 cm Hg was pulled on the tank, using a hand vacuum pump. After 40 minutes, the vacuum pressure was released slowly. Dunn observed that the deposits of wax had turned white and softened considerably after this procedure. The table top was allowed to remain in the consolidant solution overnight.

Even after overnight immersion, the table top had not sunk to the bottom of the tank. Although the wood was totally immersed at this point, complete absorption of the consolidant had not been achieved. Deposits of wax were clearly visible on the surface. After the table top had been immersed for about 24 hours, it was removed from the solution and allowed to drain briefly. Then it was wrapped in polyethylene sheet and transferred to storage so that solvent evaporation could take place slowly over the following year.

Further Treatment

The table top was unwrapped in 1990.[46] Although the wood appeared to have been strengthened somewhat by the consolidation procedure of the previous season, the surface was covered with deposits of yellow wax (Plate 126B). These had been dissolved and redeposited as a result of immersion in the consolidant solution. Cupping, delamination, and shrinkage were observed in many areas. The interior of the wood was fragile and powdery. Some portions of the wood had a dry, parched appearance, whereas other areas were black in color where wax had collected at the surface.

Removal of excess wax from both sides of the table top was carried out between 1990 and 1994. Mechanical removal, using scalpels and

---

[46] Spirydowicz, "Treatment Record 1990: Table 1."

other small tools, was useful in reducing thick deposits of wax as well as the remains of previous fills. Poultices of 3 % Klucel HF in 50/50 ethanol/toluene were effective in absorbing the waxy film that had formed in patches on the wood surface after consolidation. These poultices were applied to the wood surface for a period of four to seven minutes. After the gel was scraped or wiped off, any remaining traces were removed by swabbing with 50/50 ethanol/toluene. In addition to extracting residual wax, the poulticing process softened and relaxed some of the thin, curled areas of the table top.

In 1993, fragments of the top were turned over to reveal the upper surface of the table.[47] Some fragments had suffered such severe delamination that further treatment was necessary before they could be moved. An adhesive was applied between the layers using a pin tool or a syringe. The adhesive consisted of Butvar B-98 dissolved in ethanol in concentrations of 15 % or 30 % (wt/vol), depending on the size of the fragments and the strength of join required.

The upper surface was in surprisingly good condition. There was little wax to obscure the surface, and the grain of the wood was clearly evident. Since the under surface of the table had lain uppermost throughout the consolidation and drying processes, it seems likely that residual wax was brought to the surface by solvent evaporation. Hence the lack of wax on the protected face of the table top.

As cleaning progressed, methods and materials were adjusted as required. For example, some areas responded to swabbing with solvent mixtures of petroleum ether and toluene (2/1) or ethanol/toluene (1/1) rather than to the application of a poultice. Adjustments in technique were made to avoid too much softening of the wood, which could have resulted in the inadvertent removal of some of the degraded surface.

In 1994, the treatment of table 1 was concluded.[48] A few areas were still obscured by wax, but the fragile wood beneath had a tendency to powder or crumble if solvents were used repeatedly. Therefore, in order to avoid further damage to the wood, treatment was discontinued. In spite of numerous interventions, it was not possible to return this object to its condition at the time of excavation. However, the substitution of Butvar

B-98 for the original wax consolidant has served to strengthen and stabilize the wood to a significant degree (Plates 40, 41).

In 1999, a permanent storage mount was constructed for table 1, based on a design developed during the previous season.[49] The table top was positioned on a rectangular sheet of clear Plexiglas, surrounded by a protective ethafoam border. For the legs, a single block of ethafoam was carved with recesses to accommodate the two intact legs, and a Goretex liner was added to provide a smooth resting surface for the wood. The mounts for the table top and legs were housed in a single storage drawer, along with the fragmentary third leg which was placed in a separate container. For a fuller account of the construction of the permanent storage mounts for all of the banquet tables, see p. 157 below.

Table 2

Examination

In 1988, table 2 was examined and treated.[50] The walnut top was found to be extremely friable, powdery, and light in weight. Many of the fragments had been disturbed to such an extent that the form of the table top was no longer apparent. Traces of a previous consolidant, probably Alvar, were evident as white or greyish patches across the surface. These surface discolorations indicated that the table had been partially consolidated after it was found (Plate 42). The three collars were no longer joined to the table top at the time of examination. Lisa Goldberg reported that the wood was friable and fragile and that the pieces were covered with a fine reddish-brown powder consisting of wood dust. During cleaning, additional fragments of the collars were found under portions of the table top.

The three boxwood legs were found to be in very good condition, apart from some superficial cracking and a slight warping from their original curvature (Plate 43). The tenons were in a somewhat more deteriorated state. A thick layer of grime covered all of the exposed surfaces, and there was evidence of a previous, partial consolidation in the form of patches and pools of a dark grey material.

[47] Spirydowicz, "Treatment Record 1993: Table 1."
[48] Spirydowicz, "Treatment Record 1994: Table 1."
[49] Spirydowicz, "Treatment Record 1999: Table 1."
[50] Goldberg, "Conservation Report 1988," 48–60.

Treatment

Accumulated dirt, debris, and wood dust were removed from the upper surface of the table top using a soft bristle brush and a vacuum cleaner adapted to deliver low suction. Fragments were then sorted and repositioned in their correct locations wherever possible. Intact areas of the surface were cleaned further with acetone applied on cotton swabs. This additional procedure was effective in removing dirt as well as previously applied consolidant so that the grain of the wood was exposed. In order to turn over the table top, the fragments were covered with a layer of silkscreen fabric followed by a sheet of Mylar, a layer of foam padding, and finally an extra-large board. Once the top had been turned and the underside revealed, it was cleaned in similar fashion to the upper surface.

In preparation for consolidation, a layer of silkscreen fabric was placed over the table top and attached to the underlying layer of fabric with straight pins. Severely distorted fragments were supported from below with cushions of silkscreen fabric stuffed with cotton wadding. The fragments were completely contained within this large silkscreen pouch, which was then transferred to the metal tank tray. The collars were placed in pierced tinfoil trays so that they could be consolidated along with the table top.

The metal tank tray was lowered slowly into the large steel tank. This had been partially filled with the consolidant, consisting of a 5%-10% (wt/vol) solution of Butvar B-98 in 50/50 ethanol/toluene. Prior to complete immersion, the wood was allowed to wick up the solution until completely wetted. Extra solution was gradually added to the bath until the wood was completely covered. The wood was allowed to soak in the solution for approximately 48 hours.

When the tank was opened, the table top and the collars were removed from the consolidant solution and allowed to drain briefly. The silkscreen pouch was then transferred to a board along with the collars and legs, and wrapped in multiple layers of polyethylene sheeting. The entire package was then transferred to storage to allow for slow drying over the following year.

The three legs of table 2 were not consolidated, because of their good condition. Some local consolidation of the more fragile tenons was carried out using a 5% (wt/vol) solution of Butvar B-98 in a 50/50 ethanol/toluene mixture.

Assessment

An assessment of the condition of the table top in 1990[51] indicated that the wood was still extremely fragile and that the fragments could not be handled without risk of further damage. It appeared that the concentration of Butvar B-98 had not been sufficient to strengthen the degraded wood. Accordingly, the decision was made to consolidate the table top for a second time in 1990, in a more concentrated solution of the same consolidant. Vacuum pressure was necessary in order to ensure that the consolidant entered the pores of the wood.

Retreatment

Because the fragments of the table top were too fragile to be moved from the silkscreen fabric on which they had been consolidated in 1988, this support was reused. A new silkscreen cover was cut to fit over the table top and sewn to the underlying layer. The entire envelope was then secured to the tank tray with heavy sewing thread, in order to prevent the wood from floating during treatment.

The large vacuum tank was filled with 75 liters of consolidant, consisting of a 10% (wt/vol) solution of Butvar B-98 in 60/40 ethanol/toluene. The tank tray was suspended on the surface of the solution for approximately ten minutes to allow the wood fragments to wick up consolidant gradually. Then the tray was lowered slowly into the tank until the fragments were completely submerged. The wood was left to soak overnight in the consolidant solution.

As with Payton's earlier treatment of the inlaid serving stands, a hand-operated vacuum pump was used to apply vacuum pressure gradually up to a maximum of 20 cm Hg. The application and gradual release of vacuum pressure took one-and-a-half hours in contrast to the total of five to eight days for the serving stands. The decision to reduce the amount of time under vacuum was based on two considerations: the

---

[51] Spirydowicz, "Treatment Record 1990: Table 2."

severely degraded condition of the table top in comparison to the excellent state of preservation of the stands, and the fact that different types of wood were being treated (i.e. boxwood for the stands vs. walnut for the table top).

After a total immersion time of 48 hours, the table top was removed from the solution and allowed to drain of excess consolidant. Then the silkscreen package was transferred to a storage tray which was wrapped in two layers of polyethylene sheet to inhibit rapid drying. The table top was returned to storage to allow for slow drying over the following year.

When the table top was unwrapped in 1991, the strength of the wood was considerably improved, allowing individual fragments to be handled safely. During the following season, the fragments were sorted, separated, and joined where appropriate, resulting in the reconstruction of an important piece of ancient furniture (Plates 44–45). In 1998, a permanent storage mount was constructed for the table top and legs. Further reconstruction of the table top took place, involving the joining of fragments with a 20 % (wt/vol) solution of Butvar B-98 in ethanol as the adhesive. A Butvar paste, consisting of a 15 % (wt/vol) solution of Butvar B-98 in ethanol, mixed with glass microspheres and tinted with dry pigments, was used to fill voids where necessary.[52]

Table 3

Examination

This table was examined and treated in 1988.[53] The table top appeared to be carved from a single plank of walnut with a centralized grain pattern or figure. Most of the top had been preserved, although the wood had delaminated into numerous small fragments. As with table 2, the wood was very light in weight, porous or spongy in character, and covered with a layer of fine reddish-brown wood dust. Goldberg noted areas of severe distortion and delamination as well as evidence (splashes and drips) of a previously applied consolidant. Many of the fragments appeared to have been disturbed and were no longer in their original positions (Plate 46).

All three of the collars had detached from the table top and the legs. These fragmentary collars contained pieces of tenons that had originally extended up from the tops of the legs. In contrast to the excellent state of preservation of the legs from table 2, the three legs from table 3 were extremely fragile, and all had broken where the curve of the leg begins (Plate 47). All showed evidence of severe delamination. The larger fragments were covered with reddish-brown wood dust, and there was a greyish cast to the wood that was interpreted as evidence of a previous consolidation.

Treatment

As with table 2, the table top from table 3 was cleaned of accumulated dirt and wood dust using a soft bristle brush and a vacuum cleaner adapted to deliver low suction. After cleaning, a number of fragments were repositioned in their original locations. Traces of the previous consolidant were removed successfully by using cotton swabs dampened with acetone or a mixture of toluene and ethanol. The rolling of swabs across the surface revealed the grain of the wood in some areas. The table top was turned over and then cleaned and consolidated using virtually the same methods and materials as previously described for table 2.

The legs were cleaned in a manner similar to that used for the table top. Once contained in silkscreen pouches, all of the leg fragments were consolidated along with the table top by soaking in a 5 %-10 % (wt/vol) solution of Butvar B-98 in 50/50 ethanol/toluene for approximately 48 hours. Upon removal from the tank, the fragments were allowed to drain briefly of excess consolidant. Then they were wrapped in several layers of polyethylene sheet and returned to storage for slow drying.

Assessment

An evaluation of the condition of table 3 in 1990[54] indicated that the table top was still fragile, although it was less distorted and had fewer losses than table 2. The leg fragments required very careful handling in order to avoid further damage. Thus the decision was made to reconsolidate

---

[52] Spirydowicz, "Treatment Record 1998: Table 2."
[53] Goldberg, "Conservation Report 1988," 61–73.

[54] Spirydowicz, "Treatment Record 1990: Table 3."

the table top and leg fragments from table 3 in 1990, using a 10% (wt/vol) solution of Butvar B-98 in 60/40 ethanol/toluene.

Retreatment

The consolidation procedure used for table 3 was much the same as for table 2. However the total immersion time was reduced from 48 to 24 hours in order to avoid the noticeable softening of the wood that had occurred during the treatment of table 2. After wrapping in polyethylene sheet, the table top and leg fragments were allowed to dry slowly over the following year.

When the table top was unwrapped in 1991, it was found to be in much improved condition. The wood was sufficiently strong to be handled without damage so that no further treatment was required (Plates 48–49). The legs required further local consolidation with a 10% (wt/vol) solution of Butvar B-98 in ethanol during the construction of a permanent storage mount in 1999.[55]

Table 4

Examination

This table was examined and treated in 1988.[56] The walnut table top had broken into numerous fragments with some sections missing. As with tables 2 and 3, accumulations of dirt and wood dust were evident on the surface as well as traces of a previous consolidant. Goldberg also noted a circular impression on the top that was surrounded by traces of a green corrosion product. This mark was presumably created by a bronze omphalos bowl that had landed upside down on the table (Plate 50).

The collars were no longer attached to the under surface of the table top at the time of excavation. One virtually complete collar was still attached to a leg when found, although the other two collars were in a fragmentary state. Goldberg described the condition of the wood of the table top as poor. The fragments appeared to have lost most of their original outer surface. In addition, the wood was spongy and porous and had a tendency to crumble if handled. However,

the legs were in good condition, although some cracking was evident. Goldberg observed some distortion in the curvature of the legs as well as evidence of a previously applied consolidant on the surface.

Treatment

As with table 2, the table top from table 4 was cleaned of accumulated dirt and wood dust using a soft bristle brush and a vacuum cleaner adapted to deliver low suction. The table top was turned over, then cleaned and consolidated using virtually the same methods and materials as previously described for table 2.

The attached collar was consolidated *in situ*. The consolidant solution, consisting of 5%-10% (wt/vol) Butvar B-98 in 50/50 ethanol/toluene, was applied to the wood with a pipette. Once the wood was saturated, it was wrapped in polyethylene sheet to allow for a slow evaporation of solvents. Fragments of the other two collars were consolidated in the same manner.

Subsequently, all three legs were cleaned. Residues of the previous consolidant were removed mainly by a poulticing technique. Klucel HF was prepared in ethanol and toluene to the consistency of a thick gel. When applied to the wood for approximately one minute, the gel poultice quickly softened the previous resin coating, which was then easily removed with a wad of cotton batting. This method proved to be generally more effective than swabbing the surface with solvents, as the removal of the resin coating was accomplished with greater speed and less manipulation of the wood surface. The legs from table 4 did not require consolidation due to their generally sound condition (Plate 51).

Assessment

In 1990, the condition of table 4 was assessed.[57] The table top as well as the collars were found to be very fragile even after consolidation, and none of the pieces could be handled without risk of damage. Reconsolidation of the table top and collars was undertaken in 1990 using a 10% (wt/vol) solution of Butvar B-98 in 60/40 ethanol/toluene.

---

[55] Spirydowicz and Joy, "Treatment Record 1999: Table 3."

[56] Goldberg, "Conservation Report 1988," 74–86.
[57] Spirydowicz, "Treatment Record 1990: Table 4."

152   APPENDIX I

Retreatment

The consolidation procedure used for table 4
was much the same as for table 3. The total
immersion time in solution was 24 hours. After
wrapping in polyethylene sheet, the table top was
allowed to dry slowly over the following year.

The fragmentary collars were treated separately. The consolidant solution consisted of 10%
(wt/vol) Butvar B-98 in 60/40 ethanol/toluene.
Once the fragments were immersed in solution,
they were transferred to a glass desiccating chamber so that they could be placed under vacuum
pressure briefly. They were then left to soak in the
solution for 24 hours. After removal from the solution, the fragments were wrapped in polyethylene sheet and returned to storage for slow drying.

When the table top was unwrapped in 1991,
the strength of the wood was much improved.
There was less delamination of the wood than
in tables 2 and 3, and the grain pattern was
clearly evident. The collars exhibited a less dramatic change but some improvement in strength
was apparent. During the following season, the
fragments were sorted, separated, and joined as
appropriate, using varying concentrations of Butvar B-98 in ethanol as the adhesive (Plates 52–53).
Butvar paste was used to fill voids where necessary.[58] A permanent storage mount was constructed in 1998.[59]

Table 5

Examination

Table 5 was examined in 1988.[60] The walnut table
top had been found relatively intact (Plates 54–
56); although broken into a number of fragments,
it was virtually complete. However the wood was
in fragile condition as indicated by the raised
grain and the quantity of reddish-brown wood
dust present. Prior to treatment, a further examination of table 5 was conducted in 1989. Andrew
Todd and Emily Dunn commented on the noticeable contrast between the upper surface of the
table top (greyish with white deposits) and the un-

der surface (pale brown and smooth) (Plates 58–
59).[61] The wood was covered overall with a thick
layer of dirt.

The three boxwood legs were well preserved
(Plate 57). Two were intact, and the third had
separated into two fragments. Although in poor
condition, portions of the walnut collars were still
attached to two of these legs. Todd and Dunn
noted traces of a previous consolidant that had
been applied to the surface of the legs. Goldberg
characterised the wood of the collars as porous,
fragile, and powdery.

Treatment

Treatment was carried out in 1989. The table top
was cleaned with a soft brush and low suction, using a pipette attached to a mini-vacuum cleaner.
Consolidation of the table top was carried out in
much the same manner as that of tables 3 and 4,
using a 10% (wt/vol) solution of Butvar B-98 in
60/40 ethanol/toluene.

Previously applied consolidant was removed
from the legs by swabbing with a solvent mixture
of 50/50 acetone and ethanol. Where the consolidant had been thickly applied, repeated swabbing with the solvent mixture was required for
complete removal. Occasionally mechanical removal (scraping with a scalpel) was used to reduce particularly heavy deposits. End-grain areas were cleaned using poultices of Klucel HF
in ethanol and toluene. Because of the excellent state of preservation of the wood of the legs,
consolidation was not required. The broken leg
was repaired using Acryloid B-72 (ca. 50% in
acetone) as the adhesive. Gaps in the repaired
leg were filled with a paste made from shred-
ded Japanese tissue and Ethulose 400 in 90%
ethanol/10% water. This fill material provided
repairs that were strong yet flexible and light in
weight.

Those pieces of the collars still attached to
the legs were consolidated locally using a 10%
(wt/vol) solution of Butvar B-98 in a 60/40
solvent mixture of ethanol and toluene applied
with a pipette. The collars were then wrapped
in polyethylene sheet to allow for slow drying.
Additional collar fragments were consolidated in

[58] Spirydowicz, "Conservation of Ancient Phrygian Furniture," 170.
[59] Spirydowicz, "Treatment Record 1998: Table 4."
[60] Goldberg, "Conservation Report 1988," 87–89.
[61] Todd and Dunn, "Treatment Record 1989: Table 5."

Plates 58–59 show the top of table 5 prior to its consolidation (photographed in 1982), in contrast with the after-
conservation photographs of the tops of the other plain tables. In this case, the earlier photos showed the grain of the
wood and evidence of the collars more clearly.

the same manner and left to dry slowly under polyethylene sheet.

The table top was unwrapped in 1990.[62] The strength of the wood had been improved significantly by the initial use of a 10% solution of the consolidant, and thus no further treatment was necessary. In preparation for the transfer of the table top to a permanent storage mount in 1998 (Plate 127B), some further local consolidation of the wood with a 10% (wt/vol) solution of Butvar B-98 in ethanol was carried out. Some fragments of the top were joined for ease of handling using a 20% (wt/vol) solution of Butvar B-98 in ethanol as the adhesive.[63]

Table 6

Examination

An initial examination of table 6 took place in 1988.[64] When found in the tomb, the table top and legs were in very poor condition (Plate 60). Approximately one third of the table top retained some structural integrity, although it was broken into a number of fragments. The remaining two thirds exhibited severe deterioration, having separated into many small cubical fragments as a result of fungal attack. The fragments themselves were severely deformed as most had curled along the grain.

A number of poorly preserved fragments remained from the three original legs. Goldberg noted that the fragments were delaminating along the grain and that significant amounts of reddish-brown wood dust were present. Some badly degraded sections of the collars were also identified (Plate 61).

Treatment

Table 6 was treated in 1989.[65] The table top and other fragments were cleaned using a soft sable brush and a vacuum cleaner fitted with a small nozzle. Because of the fragility of the wood, many pieces had to be consolidated *in situ* before they could be moved in preparation for consolidation in the large vacuum tank. Local consolidation

was carried out using a 10% (wt/vol) solution of Butvar B-98 in 60/40 ethanol/toluene. The solution was applied either by syringe or pipette. Many small pieces of the table top, as well as the fragmentary collars and legs, were consolidated using this method.

The table top and fragments of the legs and collars were then encased in silkscreen pouches and secured to the metal tank tray prior to consolidation (Plate 126C). Treatment was carried out in the large vacuum tank using a 10% (wt/vol) solution of Butvar B-98 in 60/40 ethanol/toluene. The procedures used were much the same as for tables 3, 4, and 5. After removal from the consolidant solution, the fragments were wrapped in polyethylene sheet and returned to storage for slow drying over the following year.

When the pieces of the table were unwrapped in 1990, they were found to be in much improved condition.[66] Even badly degraded fragments were strong enough to be handled without damage. In areas where excess consolidant had collected on the surface of the leg fragments, glossy patches were evident. These were removed by applying poultices of ca. 3% Klucel HF in 50/50 acetone/ethanol to soften the excess Butvar. After five to ten minutes, each poultice was removed with a microspatula, and the area was then given a final cleaning, using ethanol applied on cotton swabs. Several large fragments of the table top were repaired with the aid of Butvar paste (Plate 62).

In 1999, a permanent storage support was prepared. Some reconstruction of the fragmentary wooden legs took place using an adhesive consisting of 20% (wt/vol) Butvar B-98 in ethanol. Fragile areas were reinforced with Butvar paste.[67]

Table 7

Examination

Table 7 was examined in 1988.[68] The walnut table top was broken into many fragments (Plate 63). Portions of the top exhibited the same types of cubical checking and deformation evident in table 6. Goldberg described the fragments as being

---

[62] Spirydowicz, "Treatment Record 1990: Table 5."
[63] Spirydowicz, "Treatment Record 1998: Table 5."
[64] Goldberg, "Conservation Report 1988," 90–92.
[65] Todd and Dunn, "Treatment Record 1989: Table 6."

[66] Spirydowicz, "Treatment Record 1990: Table 6."
[67] Spirydowicz and Joy, "Treatment Record 1999: Table 6."
[68] Goldberg, "Conservation Report 1988," 93–96.

light in weight and light in color. They appeared to have retained some of their structural integrity and exhibited little tendency to powder. Traces of a previous consolidant were visible on the surface, and evidence of iron corrosion was noted on numerous fragments of the table top. Two of the boxwood legs were intact and in excellent condition in spite of significant cross-grain cracking. The lower part of the third leg was found in fragile condition, as were several collar fragments.

Treatment

Table 7 was treated in 1989.[69] The fragments of the table top were cleaned using a soft sable brush and a vacuum cleaner with a small nozzle. The fragments were then transferred to a sheet of silkscreen fabric lying on the tank tray. Some sorting and repositioning of fragments took place during this process. A pouch was created by placing a second piece of silkscreen fabric over the wood. The two pieces of fabric were pinned together around the perimeter and then secured to the tank tray with heavy sewing thread. Both intact legs and the fragmentary leg were sewn into separate silkscreen pouches and secured to the tray. Consolidation followed the procedures developed for tables 3, 4, 5, and 6.

The unwrapping of table 7 took place in 1990.[70] The condition of the wood was much improved after consolidation (Plates 64A, 65); the fragments were cleaned of excess consolidant as described for table 6. In 1999, repairs were made to one of the legs and some of the fragments of the table top, using an adhesive consisting of 20 % (wt/vol) Butvar B-98 in ethanol. Fragile areas were reinforced with Butvar paste. The same year, a permanent storage mount was constructed to house the table top and legs.[71]

Table 9

Examination

Table 9 was examined and treated in 1988.[72] Approximately one third of the walnut table top was relatively well preserved, including a virtu-

ally intact collar still attached to the underside. The remainder consisted of a jumble of small fragments (Plate 66). The well-preserved section had separated into a number of large fragments. In this area, the wood was very light in weight, with the exterior surfaces forming intact shells around the more degraded interior regions. A grey layer on the surface of the wood indicated that a consolidant had been previously applied. Details of the construction of the table as well as the grain pattern were clearly evident in these fragments.

Only fragments remained of the three legs and two detached collars, all of which were in very deteriorated condition. All three of the legs were suffering from severe delamination. Excessive powdering of the soft wood was noted by Goldberg.

Treatment

The table top was cleaned using a soft bristle brush and a vacuum cleaner adapted to deliver low suction. Residues of the previously applied consolidant were removed using cotton swabs dampened with toluene. The fragments from the well-preserved area of the table top were sewn into silkscreen pouches and consolidated along with the top of table 4. Some smaller fragments were consolidated in a glass vacuum desiccator, using a consolidant solution of ca. 5 % (wt/vol) Butvar B-98 in 50/50 ethanol/toluene. Other very fragile fragments were consolidated locally by applying the consolidant solution with a pipette. An assortment of small pieces was transferred to storage without consolidation.

Most of the fragments of the legs were consolidated locally to allow for reattachment of severely delaminated areas. Eventually the leg fragments were wrapped in silkscreen pouches in preparation for consolidation by immersion. However consolidation was not carried out until the following year, due to lack of time (see below).

Assessment

The consolidated portions of table 9 were unwrapped and their condition assessed in 1989.[73] Some fragments required reconstruction with an

---

[69] Todd and Dunn, "Treatment Record 1989: Table 7."

[70] Spirydowicz, "Treatment Record 1990: Table 7."

[71] Spirydowicz and Joy "Treatment Record 1999: Ta-ble 7."

[72] Goldberg, "Conservation Report 1988," 97–109.

[73] Todd and Dunn, "Treatment Record 1989: Table 9."

adhesive using either Acryloid B-72 (ca. 50% in acetone) or Butvar B-98 (10%-20% in ethanol). Some filling was required; glass microballoons mixed with Acryloid B-72 were used for this purpose.

Further Treatment

The three leg fragments which had been wrapped in silkscreen pouches the previous year were consolidated in 1989 using a 10% (wt/vol) solution of Butvar B-98 in 60/40 ethanol/toluene. They were removed from the solution after an immersion time of 24 hours and wrapped in polyethylene sheet for slow drying.

In 1990, the leg fragments were unwrapped and found to be in improved condition.[74] It was possible to reassemble parts of the legs and much of one end of the table top (Plates 67–68). In 1999, a permanent storage mount was constructed. At this time, further local consolidation of most fragments of the table top was carried out, using a 10% (wt/vol) solution of Butvar B-98 in ethanol. Joins were reinforced with Butvar paste.[75]

*Conservation of the Fragments
from the Northeast Corner*

The remains of several pieces of furniture interspersed with layers of textiles were found in the northeast corner of Tumulus MM (Color Plate IIB, Plate 100).[76] Three sets of legs were identified (Plates 101–103, 105B) as well as two slats and a stretcher; the stretcher was later found to be carved with a series of animals in panels (Plates 104, 105A). However most of the wood had deteriorated into a pile of scarcely recognizable fragments due to the presence of moisture in this area of the tomb. Young described the wood as "well sodden in water so that [it] is badly split, shrunk, and warped."[77] The wood was coated with Alvar while still *in situ*.[78]

Examination and Treatment

When the fragments were examined in 1989,[79] traces of a previous consolidant were observed on the legs as well as on the animal stretcher. In spite of this, many of the fragments were extremely fragile, except for the stretcher and one of the stool legs, which were noted to be in relatively good condition. These two pieces were cleaned but not consolidated, due to their satisfactory state of preservation. In addition, application of a consolidant could have caused undesirable changes to areas of red pigment that were found on the surface of the animal stretcher. An ethafoam mount was constructed which provided support as well as allowing examination without actual handling of this important piece (Plate 127A).

During the 1989 season, the remaining fragments from the northeast corner were wrapped in silkscreen pouches and consolidated under vacuum in a 10% (wt/vol) solution of Butvar B-98 in 60/40 ethanol/toluene. When these fragments were unwrapped in 1992, they were still in delicate condition.[80] However it was possible to reconstruct a few pieces, including a thin stretcher, using a 30% (wt/vol) solution of Butvar B-98 in ethanol as the adhesive. Additional reconstruction was carried out in 2001. Fragments were joined with an adhesive consisting of a 20% (wt/vol) solution of Butvar B-98 in ethanol, and excessively fragile pieces were reinforced with Butvar paste.[81]

Preservation of the King's Coffin

At the north end of the tomb chamber, the skeleton of the king was found lying on what Young took to be a bed (Color Plates IB, IIA; Plates 107–109). There were many layers of folded textiles beneath the skeleton, including what Young supposed to be linen and colored wool.[82] Young identified a headboard, a bed platform, and a foot-

[74] Spirydowicz, "Treatment Record 1990: Table 9."
[75] Spirydowicz and Joy, "Treatment Record 1999: Table 9."
[76] Young, *GFB* 63, 165–175.
[77] Ibid., 165.
[78] Ibid., 159.
[79] Todd and Dunn, "Examination Report 1989: NE Corner."
[80] Spirydowicz, "Treatment Record 1992: Furniture from the NE Corner."
[81] Spirydowicz, "Treatment Record 2001: Furniture from the NE Corner."
[82] Young, *GFB* 63, 74, 80.

board as well as four corner blocks.[83] The corner blocks and "headboard" were in relatively good condition (Plates 108, 109B, 111–112, 115); however the "central platform" was so degraded that Young misinterpreted the construction of the entire piece. According to Young, the "central platform" consisted of several long planks laid side by side,[84] whereas Simpson later proved that the "bed" was actually a massive, open log coffin with horizontal ledges at both ends.[85] The ledge at the western end of the coffin, interpreted by Young as the footboard, was only partially preserved and in very poor condition (Plate 112C).

A coating of Alvar was applied to the major fragments while the coffin was still *in situ* in the tomb chamber.[86] When Young attempted to remove the pieces, he found that the "planks" were in such poor condition that they could not be saved.[87] Removal of the degraded wood revealed lengths of dark and light-colored wood beneath, which Young identified as a pair of decorative bed rails (Plates 110, 114C–D).[88] By the end of the season, the four corner blocks, the "headboard," the "footboard," and the fragmentary rails had been removed from the tomb.

When the pieces of the coffin were located at the site of Gordion in 1981, they were in extremely degraded condition. To provide further protection, the pieces were brought to the Museum of Anatolian Civilizations in Ankara and placed in storage. A wooden storage case was made for the largest fragment, the so-called headboard, which was actually the coffin's east end.

In 1988, the east ledge of the coffin was examined.[89] This massive piece of wood had originally been reinforced by a heavy iron bar that had been attached to the surface with five iron nails (Plate 112A). The surface of the wood was obscured by a thick layer of dust and dirt. In general, the wood was brittle, and although it was quite solid, it had little mechanical strength. Some checking was apparent along the sides as well as around the iron nails.

The iron bar was covered with a thick layer of protective corrosion that ranged from dark brown to light orange in color. In 1988, no active corrosion was detected. The weight of the bar indicated that it still contained a considerable amount of metal. This observation also applied to the iron nails.

A study of wood samples taken from the ledges of the coffin, as well as from two of the corner blocks, revealed that this object had suffered extensive attack by soft rot, except in the areas immediately adjacent to the iron bars and iron nails.[90] In these areas, iron corrosion products and pseudomorphs were observed. In some cases, the pseudomorphs replicated the structure of the wood cells. Blanchette concluded that the high concentration of iron prevented the growth of soft rot in these areas. Blanchette speculated that the decomposition of the body and surrounding textiles might have provided nitrogen and other nutrients to enable the soft-rot fungi to flourish, since the coffin was most degraded below the remains of the king.[91]

The consolidation of the surviving fragments of the coffin has been deemed beyond the scope of the current project. While much larger pieces of wood have been treated successfully in other parts of the world, the specialized equipment and facilities required are not presently available in Ankara. Consolidation with Butvar B-98 may not be an appropriate or effective choice, given the poor condition of the wood and the large size of some of the fragments. Further research will be essential before the treatment of this important artifact can be undertaken.

Storage

The urgent need for the conservation of the wooden furniture provided the initial impetus for the Gordion Furniture Project. However, the importance of long-term preservation was also recognized. As the consolidation and reconstruction of the furniture neared completion, the attention of Project personnel focused on the safe storage of the fragments utilizing inert materials for enclosure and support.

Ethafoam planks were carved with recesses to accommodate individual pieces, and the surfaces of the recesses were covered with thin Goretex

[83] Ibid., 73.
[84] Ibid., 179.
[85] Simpson, "'Midas' Bed' and a Royal Phrygian Funeral."
[86] Young, *GFB* 63, 159.
[87] Ibid., 188.

[88] Ibid., 188–193.
[89] Goldberg, "Conservation Report 1988," 37–40.
[90] Blanchette and Simpson, "Soft Rot and Wood Pseudomorphs in an Ancient Coffin."
[91] Filley, Blanchette, Simpson, and Fogel, "Nitrogen Cycling."

fabric. The latter material was selected for its permeability to water vapor, thereby avoiding entrapment of moisture, and its slick surface, for protection of the wood. The storage mounts were designed so that related fragments could be grouped together in a single foam unit. Each foam unit can be removed independently from its storage drawer to allow for study and analysis with minimal handling of the fragments.

Because it was important to be able to view both sides of the tops of the plain tables, the storage of these pieces required a different strategy (Plate 127B). The fragments of each table top were positioned on a rectangular sheet of clear Plexiglas, cut slightly larger than the outer dimensions of the top. A protective ethafoam border ("bumper") was constructed to contain the wood fragments, fitting around the outer edge of each table top. The bumpers were constructed in four sections, which fit over Plexiglas pins attached at each corner of the Plexiglas sheet. The inner edge of each bumper section was lined with a thin strip of Volara foam, secured to the ethafoam with hot-melt adhesive. The Volara was covered with Goretex fabric, tucked into channels cut slightly beyond the upper and lower edges of the Volara. The bumper sections were secured to each other by means of Velcro strips attached with hot-melt adhesive to the exterior edges of the ethafoam.

Five steel storage cabinets for the Gordion wooden objects were installed in the museum's storage area with funding from the 1984 Foundation. The cabinets were fabricated in the United States and shipped to Ankara in 1997. Because the Museum of Anatolian Civilizations is a historic building, consisting of a restored fifteenth-century *han* or inn, the design of the units had to conform to the features of the building. Each cabinet had to be custom-built in three sections in order to fit through the narrow doorway of the Gordion wood storage depot. The five cabinets were designed to fit snugly within the storage room. When the cabinets arrived at the museum, each one was disassembled; the sections were moved individually into the wood storage room and then reassembled inside.

The storage cabinets were constructed of powder-coated steel so as to avoid the possibility of off-gassing of materials. Each unit has a 2½-inch base equipped with corner levellers. The cabinet sections have double lift-off steel doors that close on silicone gaskets. The units are fastened to each other by the insertion of screws on the inside. The reinforced drawers slide smoothly on ball-bearing extension brackets for vibration-free access. This feature allows the drawers to be removed individually for the safe transport of the objects to the museum laboratory. The ethafoam mounts made for the furniture and wooden objects from Gordion were designed specifically to fit into the drawers of the steel storage cabinets (Plate 128). In 2004, small furniture fragments were housed in archival Clear-View boxes with Mylar viewing windows and archival specimen trays. The floor of each box was padded with a layer of Volara foam. Heavy-duty archival tote boxes were used to store the textiles from the coffin.

Aside from central heating during the winter months, there is presently no climate control within the museum storage area. However the massive stone walls of this heritage structure help to buffer environmental extremes. Datalogger readings taken between 1992 and 1993 indicated that there were significant annual fluctuations in temperature (between 5° and 27° C) and relative humidity (between 28 % and 44 %) in the storage depot. In 1997, a single-pane window in the storeroom was blocked off with an insulating layer of Styrofoam, a vapor barrier of polyethylene sheet, and a final layer of drywall. This action proved effective in leveling out some of the drastic changes. In addition, the silicone gaskets of the doors of the new storage cabinets provide an effective seal that aids in buffering environmental fluctuations and in creating a more stable environment inside the cabinets. Datalogger readings taken in 1997–1998 and in 2004–2005 confirmed that annual fluctuations in relative humidity were reduced by ca. 5 % from previous levels. Conditions inside the display cases have tended to fluctuate to a greater extent; recent readings from the case containing the two serving stands show that relative humidity levels varied between a low of 22 % in August 2004 and a high of 49 % in March 2005. These variations should be mitigated by the climate control system that was installed in the museum galleries in June 2008.

Conclusion

The recovery of the furniture from Tumulus MM offered a unique opportunity to treat dry archaeological wood on a large scale. Butvar B-98, a polyvinyl butyral resin, was applied to a variety of ancient woods in differing states of preservation. Consolidation under vacuum with this low-viscosity resin provided a significant increase in strength as well as an improved appearance, in virtually all cases.[92] Additional practical applications of Butvar B-98 in this project included its use as an adhesive and as a component of a gap-filling paste for purposes of reconstruction.

Many conservators contributed to the success of the treatment phase of the Gordion Furniture Project (see above, pp. xxxvii–xxxviii). Their work ensures the survival of a unique collection of ancient wooden furniture and further guarantees that research can continue for the foreseeable future into the materials, tools, and techniques used by the ancient Phrygian cabinetmakers at Gordion.

List of Suppliers

Acryloid B-72: Rohm and Haas, Philadelphia, PA 19105, USA.

Butvar B-98: Monsanto Canada, PO Box 787, Streetsville PO, Mississauga, Ontario L5M 2G4, Canada.

Ethafoam (2-inch plank): Acme Foam, 900 Dean Street, Brooklyn, NY 11238, USA.

Glass microspheres: PQ Corp., Valley Forge, PA, USA.

Goretex: W.L. Gore & Associates, PO Box 1550, Elkton, MD 21921, USA.

HMG: Frank W. Joel Ltd., Oldmedow Road, King's Lynn, Norfolk PE30 4HH, UK.

Klucel HF: Hercules Inca., 300 Delaware Ave., Wilmington, DE 19899, USA.

Nalgene Hand Vacuum Pump: Thomas Scientific, 99 High Hill Rd., Swedesboro, NJ 08085, USA.

Plexiglas G (Rohm and Haas): Cadillac Plastics and Chemical Co., 1801 US Highway 1, Linden, NJ 07036, USA.

Silkscreen fabric (white mono polyester): Martin Supply Co., 2740 Loch Raven Rd., Baltimore, MD 21218, USA.

Storage boxes (Clear-View boxes, archival specimen trays, and heavy-duty artifact storage boxes): University Products, 517 Main St., PO Box 101, Holyoke, MA 01040, USA.

Storage cabinets (custom modular museum storage cabinets, steel with non-reactive, solvent-free, baked polyester powder coating): Delta Designs Ltd., PO Box 1733, Topeka, KS 66601, USA.

Styrofoam (extruded, pink): İzogül, Rüzgarlı, Ege Sokak 1/E, Ankara, Turkey.

Volara: University Products, 517 Main St., PO Box 101, Holyoke, MA 01040, USA.

---

[92] See Spirydowicz, et al., "Alvar and Butvar," for details on the effectiveness of the conservation treatment and information on the hardness tests conducted to assess the strength of the wood.

RECONSTRUCTION OF THE INLAID
TABLE AND SERVING STANDS FOR DISPLAY

ELIZABETH SIMPSON

Reconstruction of the Inlaid Table

The Inlaid Table (1983)

The inlaid table was first reconstructed for display in the Museum of Anatolian Civilizations, Ankara, in the summer of 1983, after the conservation of the wood of the table was completed (see Appendix 1).[1] This reconstruction allowed the inlaid table to be seen assembled for the first time in 2700 years. The pieces of the table were first laid out in order to determine whether they could be fit together on a mount (Plate 129A). Although some of the parts were misshapen, they had warped in conjunction with one another. The table must have sagged over a period of time, so that the legs and leg struts became progressively deformed while they were still joined. Eventually the table collapsed on the floor, but the structural damage was not significant (for the degradation of the wood itself, see Appendix 4, below). It was recognized that the original pieces could be fit together, with the exception of the internal dowel system.

The mount was designed by the author; the assembly of the mount and attachment of the wood was carried out by the author with Robert Payton, resident conservator of the British Institute of Archaeology in Ankara and first conservator of the Gordion Furniture Project, and Nazif Uygur, head of the laboratory of the Museum of Anatolian Civilizations. While a considerable amount of research went into the planning of the project, a mount of this complexity and for this purpose had never been made from acrylic sheet,[2] and the process turned out to be much more difficult than anyone had anticipated.

The mount was a kind of acrylic table, designed as a backing for the wood pieces, which were attached to the mount with 180 acrylic hooks. This large number of hooks was needed because, although the wood had been consolidated and was quite strong, hundreds of hairline cracks still ran through the pieces. The hooks were made from acrylic rods, which were cut, heated until they were flexible, and then bent to conform to the shape of the wood pieces. The finished hooks were inserted into holes drilled into the backing and glued or "welded" in place with dichloromethane (methylene chloride). This was applied with a syringe, which "melted" the surface of the acrylic at the area of the joint and effected a permanent bond. This system was devised so that the wood could be supported on the hooks but lifted off again if necessary. Although the hooks were glued securely in place, we did not want to constrain the wood by clamping it to the frame.

The backing was made from acrylic sheet, manufactured in Turkey, which was cut to the size and shape of the individual pieces of the table. This expert cutting was done by Cemal and Celal Alpüren of Alp Reklam, Ankara, who were hired with the help of Ekber Topal. Templates were made by the author, traced from the wood pieces, as a guide for the cutting of the backing. After each piece of the mount was cut at Alp Reklam, it was delivered back to us at the museum, and we

---

[1] Simpson, "Report on Conservation and Restoration 1983," 2–3, with sketches of the Plexiglas mount, adjustable wood stand, iron tripod stand, wood angle deck, and drawer that was attached to the underside of the original display case. Simpson and Payton, "Royal Wooden Furniture from Gordion," 45–46. Simpson and Spirydowicz, *GWF*, 37–39.

[2] Plexiglas, a trade name, will be used here to distinguish the Rohm and Haas product from Turkish acrylic sheet, although the name is used generically in Turkey.

filed, sanded, and polished the edges, with the aid of the museum's electric dental equipment (using *diş macunu*, or "tooth polish," which served as an effective mild abrasive). The mount's four side pieces were made first. Each comprised the backing for one of the sides of the table, including its frame piece, handles, and top struts. The acrylic top was made at the same time, so that the mount's frame could be constructed. The wood parts were positioned temporarily on the acrylic side pieces, to determine the placement of the holes for the hooks. These had to be drilled before the sides of the frame were joined.

The acrylic frame (four side pieces and top) was then assembled, by filing and sanding the surfaces to be joined until they fitted together perfectly, and then fusing the joints with dichloromethane. The four side pieces were joined together first, prior to their attachment to the top. A total of eighteen acrylic "struts" extended up on these side pieces, and the top edges of all of these extensions had to be filed and sanded to fit perfectly against the underside of the acrylic table top. When this had been accomplished, the extensions were joined to the top with dichloromethane. The wooden side pieces and top struts were mounted on the acrylic frame by means of the Plexiglas hooks.

The frame, with attached wood, was then set onto a wooden tripod stand, the height of which was adjustable. Only with the aid of this stand could the legs and leg supports be attached properly. The acrylic leg struts were fused to the undersides of the frame, and the acrylic "legs" joined to the top piece. These "legs" were flat acrylic strips that had been bent to conform to the curve of the table's three wooden legs, formed by heating the strips in plaster molds. Finally, the wooden leg struts and legs were mounted on their acrylic backing. Throughout the course of the project, the fitting and gluing of the parts of the mount progressed simultaneously with the wood montage. This was necessary because the effectiveness of the mount depended not only on the acrylic joinery but also on the relationship of the wooden parts to one another, as these had to fit together perfectly while on the acrylic backing. This provided us with first-hand knowledge (once removed) of the difficulties the Phrygian cabinetmakers must have faced as they assembled the parts of the table.[3]

This process was facilitated by the adjustable wood stand, which enabled us to determine the final height of the mounted table. This allowed us to design and commission an iron tripod stand from the ironworkers in Ulus, near the museum. The stand was then primed and painted by Alp Reklam. The iron stand had a triangular top, which was drilled with holes that were then threaded for attachment to the acrylic top with screws. The stand provided support for the acrylic frame, which hung from the acrylic table top; thus no pressure was put on the wood itself, which rested comfortably on the acrylic hooks. Once the mount was secured to the iron stand, the table was photographed in preparation for its installation in a display case in the museum.

This was a standard museum case, with an iron base and glass superstructure, opened by means of a sliding glass panel on one of the long sides. The case had already been in use and was emptied to receive the mounted table. For the new display, a wood angle deck was constructed, the top of which was drilled with a series of holes. This allowed for ventilation and the regulation of humidity inside the case, in conjunction with a metal drawer that was fitted under the floor of the case. A large area was cut out of the metal case flooring for attachment of the drawer, which could accommodate either a humidifying agent or a dessicant, as needed. The angle deck was covered with fine wool fabric, which was adhered to the wood of the deck with white glue. The glue was brushed onto the deck, and the fabric was then stretched over it and stapled to the lower perimeter of the base, without requiring seams. A small amount of white glue was also brushed onto the triangular top of the metal stand, for the attachment of felt strips to serve as a cushion for the acrylic top. This white glue was deemed safe at the time, but in fact it was problematic, as would become painfully apparent the following year. The acrylic sheet, rods, glue, and other mount materials used were all purchased in Turkey; the dichloromethane was brought from New York ("Weld-on" acrylic solvent cement).

At the end of the summer of 1983, the mounted table was carried into the museum and installed in its newly refurbished display case (Plate 129B). The metal tripod stand was secured to the angle deck, and the wooden dowels from

---

[3] See above, pp. 32–39.

the table's interior support system were set on the deck. We closed the glass door and sealed the sides of the case with silicone sealant, in order that no dust might enter through the gaps in the edges of the glass superstructure. This material, like the white glue, was to create problems for the acrylic mount (see Appendix 1, p. 142). These were apparent in 1984, when we returned to Turkey. After some days, we began to notice that the mount looked "dusty," and as it seemed to get increasingly dusty, we eventually cut through the silicone sealant and opened the case. A disturbing chemical smell wafted out, and we attempted to air out the case over the course of the summer season. Crazing had developed in the acrylic sheet, imparting a permanent cloudy appearance to the once-transparent surface.

By the following year (1985) the smell had diminished but was still noticeable, and the crazing had worsened (see Plate 124B for the condition of the acrylic top in 1989). We began to research the problem, eventually discovering the probable cause. The display materials, particularly the white glue and silicone sealant, had off-gassed inside the sealed case, and the ethanol used as a solvent for the wood consolidation had also released vapors in the closed environment. Because of the effectiveness of the sealant, the fumes could not escape from the case, resulting in damage to the acrylic mount. Although this had not affected the wood, the mount was becoming less and less attractive, and we began to make plans to remount the table. This was finally accomplished in 1989.

The Inlaid Table (1989)

Most of the materials for the new mount were purchased in the United States and brought to Turkey by project members. These included Rohm and Haas Plexiglas G, 1/4" acrylic sheet, craze resistant (table top); Rohm and Haas Plexiglas G, 3/16" acrylic sheet, craze resistant (frame and leg struts); Acrylic Solvent Cement, Craftics, Inc. (methylene chloride); Novus 1 and 2 plastic polish; acrylic paint; brown wool felt; silver solder; and contact cement (3M #4693). Brass rods for the hooks and brass strapping for the leg mounts were purchased in Turkey. We marshaled all available resources and enlisted a small army to remount the inlaid table, including Gordion Furniture Project team members and colleagues from the Museum of Anatolian Civilizations.

The new mount proceeded much in the same manner as had the first, with the cutting of

Plexiglas components (which this time was done in New York); the filing, sanding, and polishing of the edges; and the construction of the Plexiglas frame (Plate 130A). The Plexiglas top was joined to the frame construction as before, by means of fitting and bonding the 18 "struts" that rose from the frame to the underside of the Plexiglas top. The wood side pieces and top struts were then attached to the Plexiglas frame (Plate 130B). The wood was mounted using brass hooks, considered a better alternative to the acrylic hooks that had been used previously. The acrylic hooks had been fixed permanently to the backing, whereas the brass hooks were secured in the drilled holes with Acryloid B-72 (20% mixture in ethanol). This made it possible to remove and replace the brass hooks without damaging the mount, should this ever be necessary. The brass hooks were first dipped in the Acryloid B-72 solution to seal the metal, then thin ethafoam strips were attached with 3M contact cement, and the hooks and sides of the ethafoam padding were coated with acrylic paint. This provided a kind of camouflage, making the hooks less obtrusive.

New leg supports were made from brass strapping, utilizing silver solder (Plate 130C). This was a significant improvement over the acrylic strips that had been used to support the legs on the first mount. The brass leg mounts were stronger and very unobtrusive; these supports were attached to the original metal tripod stand, which was retouched and used again for the new mount (Plate 130D). The brass leg supports were coated with acrylic paint, and padding of brown wool felt was glued to the brass with 3M contact cement. The wood legs were secured to the brass strapping, and the Plexiglas frame and top were set on the metal stand, anchored to the stand with screws and without the use of any padding or adhesive. Finally, the wood leg struts were attached (Plate 131A), fragments of the wood table top were added, and the mount was complete (Color Plates VIII–IX, Plates 33–35).

The original wood angle deck was rehabilitated, by first removing the fabric covering and then planing off all remains of the white glue left on the surface. The stripped deck was then painted with shellac, an inert, natural material (Plate 131B). New fabric (35% wool, 65% polyester) was stretched over the wood deck and stapled to the lower perimeter, without the use of adhesive (Plate 131C). The refurbished angle deck was replaced in the display case, the newly mounted table was carried back into the museum (Plate 132A), and the table was reinstalled in its case. The metal tripod stand was secured to the angle deck, the dowels were set on the deck, and a datalogger was included to measure and record the temperature and relative humidity inside the case. Finally, we added a blue glass evil-eye charm in the shape of a horseshoe, given to us by a thoughtful museum curator (Plate 132B). The table and mount are now in good condition and were transferred to a new display case made in 1997.

Museum Display Cases (1997)

The new display cases were designed by the author and Erkal Saran of the Mob design firm in Ankara. Four cases were constructed at the Mob factory, under the direction of Erkal Saran, with funding from the National Geographic Society (see Plate 138B). The cases were made to accommodate (1) the inlaid table, Tumulus MM; (2) the two serving stands, Tumulus MM; (3) the carved stool, parasol, and fan, Tumulus P; and (4) the wooden animals, plates, spoons, and other small objects, Tumulus P. Each case was constructed on a steel base, covered with MDF (Medium Density Fiberboard)[4] veneered in dark wood, with a superstructure of laminated safety glass, made to coordinate with (but improve upon) the existing cases in the museum.

With the exception of the small case for the wooden animals, which had one opening, the cases opened on both ends, providing access to the artifacts from two directions. The glass ends of the superstructure were made separately and secured to the main frame on custom glide mechanisms, enabling the glass panels to slide outward to some distance. This made the area beneath the floor of the case accessible, should regulation of the humidity inside the case be required in the future. Goretex joint sealant with adhesive backing was applied to the edges of the glass doors, sealing the sides of the superstructure from dust but permitting ventilation. The cases were mounted on locking casters so that they could be moved within the museum.

Reconstruction of Serving Stands A and B

The Serving Stands (1984)

The parts of serving stands A and B were identified in 1983 (Plate 133A), and the wood was consolidated (see Appendix 1). In 1984 the two stands were mounted for display in the Museum of Anatolian Civilizations.[5] Plexiglas replacements were made for the missing back legs and three of the curved front legs, sculpted from large blocks of Plexiglas. Since thick acrylic sheet was not available in Turkey at the time, these blocks were brought from Philadelphia. As the display of the inlaid table became increasingly worrying, we decided to abandon our plans to use Turkish supplies for the mounts of the stands; craze-resistant Plexiglas sheet was ordered by phone and shipped by air from the United States. The imported Plexiglas was cut at Alp Reklam and finished by our team at the museum.

Plexiglas frames were constructed to accommodate the faces of the stands, along with the top, back, and side pieces. The frames were placed horizontally on tables for attachment of the wood face boards with Plexiglas hooks (Plate 133B). As the wood of the faces was heavy, several Plexiglas ledges were employed to carry some of the weight and keep pressure off the lower sections. Mortises and channels were cut in the Plexiglas replacement legs to accommodate the tenons and pegs.[6] The replacement legs were then set into the faces (Plate 134A), and the mounts were righted, one at a time, and placed temporarily on an adjustable wood stand. As with the procedure used for the inlaid table, the wood stand allowed the exact height of each mount to be determined. This permitted the design and production of iron stands to support the mounts in the display (Plate 134B). The Plexiglas frames, with the wood face boards attached, were transferred to the iron stands, secured to their tops with screws, and the side and back pieces of wood were attached to the mounts (Plate 134C). Replacements for the missing back legs were made in Plexiglas and joined to the frame. Finally, Plexiglas supports for the diagonal back struts were

---

[4] MDF with no formaldehyde emission.
[5] Simpson, "Report on Conservation and Restoration 1984," 1–2. Simpson and Payton, "Royal Wooden Furniture

from Gordion," 47. Simpson and Spirydowicz, *GWF*, 42.
[6] Where possible, pegs were removed (with their positions noted) for greater safety.

attached, and the wood back struts were added to the mounts. After six full months of highly concentrated work, the reconstruction of the serving stands was completed.

The stands were photographed, moved into the museum, and installed in a display case made on the model of the standard cases then in use (Plate 135A). This new case was required because none of the existing cases was large enough for the stands' display. The case was made with a drawer at the bottom to house either a dessicant or humidifying agent, should the humidity inside the case need to be regulated. No chemicals or glues were used in the 1984 display, and the sides of the case were not sealed. In 1997, the serving stands acquired a new Mob case, as did the inlaid table (see above).

The Serving Stands (1999)

Following our success in 1989 with the new mount for the inlaid table, we decided to remount the serving stands, utilizing the improved materials and techniques. The two stands, which had been reinstalled in a new display case in 1997, were removed from their case and transported back to the museum laboratory (Plate 135B). The wood was taken off the mounts, cleaned, and repaired in preparation for the new display (Plate 136B). The earlier Plexiglas mounts were reconditioned by drilling out the remains of the old Plexiglas hooks (Plate 136A). New hooks were made of brass, with each hook cut, shaped, and finished individually according to the size and form of the piece it was to support (Plate 137A). Serving stand A required 132 brass hooks, with 122 used for stand B. The hooks were padded with thin strips of Volara, adhered with Acryloid B-72 in acetone (50% wt/vol). The brass hooks were painted to match the wood (Plate 137B), and the finished hooks were glued in place with the Acryloid B-72 solution (Plate 137C). As with the inlaid table, these hooks could be removed if necessary without affecting the mount.

The original Plexiglas replacement legs that were set into the front faces of the stands were not employed in the new mounts. These replacement legs had rested on the bottom boards of the stands' faces; while their weight was not causing undue stress to the wood, their removal relieved all pressure. The Plexiglas back legs were left in place, along with the backing for the diagonal struts. As with the inlaid table, numerous small pieces of the stands had become detached during the conservation and prior mounting process, due to the dissolving of the original wax consolidant and the weakening of the early glued joins. In 1999 it was possible to incorporate many of these fragments, several of which had not been identified previously in terms of their original location.[7]

The mounts, with the face boards attached, were finally righted and replaced on their metal stands. The wooden side and back pieces were attached, as well as the back diagonal struts (Plate 138A). The carved top pieces were added, and the serving stands were re-photographed in their newly refurbished condition (Color Plates XII–XV; Plates 78–79, 88–89).[8] The stands were carried back into the museum and reinstalled in their display case accompanied by a datalogger, to measure the temperature and relative humidity, as well as an evil-eye charm (Plate 138B).

---

[7] Pegs removed for the first mounts were replaced, and additional peg fragments, formerly unplaced, were identified and adhered in their correct positions.

[8] Specifications and details of the mounting process are outlined in Mandrus, "Remounting of Serving Stand A," and Hargrave, "Remounting of Serving Stand B."

APPENDIX 3

WOOD SPECIES ANALYSIS

BURHAN AYTUĞ

Faculty of Forestry
Istanbul University

ROBERT A. BLANCHETTE AND BENJAMIN HELD

Department of Plant Pathology
University of Minnesota

Anatomical characteristics of wood are different among different genera of trees, but it is not usually possible to determine which species of tree the wood represents by examination of the wood micromorphology. Often, as in this study, the genus is determined by the wood anatomy, and the species designation is taken from the most common species that occurs in the area under investigation.

The identification of severely decayed wood can be difficult, since the microscopic features of the wood are disrupted by the deterioration, and anatomical details are not clearly evident. During the course of the investigation of the decay present in the Tumulus MM furniture, vessel elements from the top of table 6 were found to have wall thickenings when viewed with scanning electron microscopy. These wall thickenings are characteristic of woods such as *Acer* (maple family) or some fruitwoods such as *Prunus* (cherry) but not *Juglans* (walnut); see Appendix 4, Plate 144. The structure of this decay suggests that the wood is probably *Acer* (B. Aytuğ proposes the determination of *Acer trauvetteri*). Bruce Hoadley (University of Massachusetts, Amherst) and Harry Alden (US Forest Products Laboratory, Madison, WI) collaborated on the examination of samples from the top of table 6 and confirmed that it was *Acer* or a *Prunus* species.

The coffin body and corner blocks from Tumulus MM contained advanced stages of soft rot. This type of decay causes cavities to form within the cell walls (see Appendix 4). When samples from these parts of the coffin were first viewed microscopically by B. Aytuğ, spiral soft-rot cavities were noted within the cell walls. These appeared to resemble the helical thickenings that are characteristic of *Taxus* (yew). Because of this feature, the coffin body and corner blocks were originally identified as *Taxus*. In a later phase of this study, scanning electron microscopy of the decayed coffin wood clearly showed these structures to be cavities caused by a soft-rot fungus. Further investigation of the wood morphology revealed that the coffin body was *Cedrus libani* (Lebanese cedar) and the corner blocks a species of *Pinus* (pine), most likely *Pinus sylvestris* (Scots pine). As the wall and some timbers of the tomb chamber were of *Pinus*, it seems possible that the corner blocks of the coffin were cut from the same wood.

The woods from which the Tumulus MM furniture and coffin were made are characterized in brief below, followed by a detailed list of specific samples with their determinations. The floor boards of the tomb chamber were analyzed in the context of the study of the coffin.

Inlaid table
Frame, legs, struts, and interior dowels: boxwood
Inlay: juniper
Table top: walnut

Tables 1–5, 7, 9
Legs: boxwood
Table tops: walnut

Table 6
Legs: boxwood
Table top: severely decayed, possibly maple or cherry

Serving stands A and B
Faces, side pieces, back pieces, and back struts: boxwood
Inlay: juniper
Top pieces and front legs (set into the faces of the stands): walnut
Foot blocks: boxwood (stand A) and yew (stand B)

Furniture from the northeast corner
Carved stretcher and short leg: boxwood
Two slats: juniper

Coffin
Coffin body: cedar
Corner blocks: pine
Rails: severely degraded, but apparently boxwood and yew

Floor boards of the tomb chamber: cedar (8 boards) and pine (3 boards)

List of Wood Samples and Their Determinations

[1] Samples analyzed by Burhan Aytuğ, Istanbul University
[2] Samples analyzed by Robert Blanchette and Benjamin Held, University of Minnesota

Sample #	Description	Determination
Inlaid table (5212 W 80)		
1983-S-1[1]	Inlaid table: frame piece B	*Buxus sempervirens* L.
1983-S-2[1]	Inlaid table: inlay from frame piece B, square B-1	*Juniperus* sp., likely *J. foetidissima* Willd., since this is found in Turkey
1983-S-3[1]	Inlaid table: inlay from one of the feet (loose piece)	*Juniperus* sp.
1983-S-4[1]	Inlaid table: dowel connecting the two rear legs	*Buxus sempervirens*
1983-S-5[1]	Inlaid table: dowel connecting the central dowel to frame piece C	*Buxus sempervirens*
1983-S-6[1]	Inlaid table: wooden peg, front leg strut, top left	*Buxus sempervirens*

Sample #	Description	Determination
1983-S-7[1]	Inlaid table: table top, two samples (unconsolidated)	*Juglans* sp., likely *J. regia* L., since this species is found in Turkey
1983-S-22[1]	Inlaid table: leg C	*Buxus sempervirens*
1983-S-23[1]	Inlaid table: reeded top of leg C	*Buxus sempervirens*
1983-S-24[1]	Inlaid table: inlay from top of leg A	*Juniperus* sp.
1983-S-25[1]	Inlaid table: tenon at leg top	*Buxus sempervirens*
1983-S-26[1]	Inlaid table: strut A2, lower tenon	*Buxus sempervirens*
1983-S-27[1]	Inlaid table: strut C3 (upper right section)	*Buxus sempervirens*
1983-S-28[1]	Inlaid table: strut C4, lower tenon	*Buxus sempervirens*

Table 1 (5203 W 79)

1984-S-34[1]	Table 1: leg	*Buxus sempervirens*
1984-S-35[1]	Table 1: top	*Juglans* sp.

Table 2 (12516 W 124)

1984-S-43[1]	Table 2: leg	*Buxus sempervirens*
1984-S-44[1]	Table 2: top	*Juglans* sp.

Table 3 (12517 W 125)

1984-S-48[1]	Table 3: leg	*Buxus sempervirens*
1984-S-49[1]	Table 3: top	*Juglans* sp.
1984-S-50[1]	Table 3: peg from collar	*Buxus sempervirens*

Table 4 (12518 W 126)

1984-S-36[1]	Table 4: top	*Juglans* sp.
(inspection)[1]	Table 4: legs	*Buxus sempervirens*

Table 5 (5202 W 78)

1984-S-40[1]	Table 5: top	*Juglans* sp.
1984-S-41[1]	Table 5: leg	*Buxus sempervirens*
1984-S-42[1]	Table 5: peg	*Buxus sempervirens*

Table 6 (12519 W 127)

1993-WS-9[2]	Table 6: top	severely degraded, likely *Acer* or *Prunus*
1984-S-38[1]	Table 6: leg	*Buxus sempervirens*
1984-S-39[1]	Table 6: peg from tenon associated with collar fragment	*Buxus sempervirens*

Sample #	Description	Determination

Table 7 (12520 W 128)

| 1984-S-51[1] | Table 7: leg | *Buxus sempervirens* |
| 1984-S-52[1] | Table 7: top | *Juglans* sp. |

Table 9 (12521 W 129)

1984-S-45[1]	Table 9: leg	*Buxus sempervirens*
1984-S-46[1]	Table 9: top	*Juglans* sp.
1984-S-47[1]	Table 9: peg from collar	*Buxus sempervirens*

Serving stand A (5229 W 81)

1984-S-1[1]	Serving stand A: right curved "leg" set into face of stand	*Juglans* sp.
1984-S-2[1]	Serving stand A: left curved "leg" set into face of stand	*Juglans* sp.
1984-S-3[1]	Serving stand A: face, second board down from top [board 2], tenon at right	*Buxus sempervirens*
1984-S-4[1]	Serving stand A: peg from tenon in sample 1984-S-3 above	*Buxus sempervirens*
1984-S-5[1]	Serving stand A: peg from tenon at left of third board down from top [board 3]	*Buxus sempervirens*
1984-S-6[1]	Serving stand A: openwork back piece	*Buxus sempervirens*
1984-S-7[1]	Serving stand A: short back diagonal strut, at left when facing back of stand, tenon	*Buxus sempervirens*
1984-S-8[1]	Serving stand A: short strut connecting face at back to back leg	*Buxus sempervirens*
1984-S-9[1]	Serving stand A: right side piece, tenon	*Buxus sempervirens*
1984-S-10[1]	Serving stand A: top piece, large ring (loose fragment)	*Juglans* sp.
1984-S-11[1]	Serving stand A: inlay from front face	*Juniperus* sp.
1984-S-12[1]	Serving stand A: right front foot block	*Buxus sempervirens*
1984-S-13[1]	Serving stand A: tenon in right front foot block	*Juglans* sp.
1984-S-14[1]	Serving stand A: front face, right side board [board 10]	*Buxus sempervirens*
1984-S-15[1]	Serving stand A: inlay from front face	*Juniperus* sp.

Serving stand B (5230 W 82)

1983-S-8[1]	Serving stand B: front face	*Buxus sempervirens*
1983-S-9[1]	Serving stand B: foot of one of the curved legs that were set into the face	*Juglans* sp.
1983-S-10[1]	Serving stand B: right curved leg that was set into the face	*Juglans* sp.
1983-S-11[1]	Serving stand B: one of the front foot blocks	*Taxus baccata* L.
1983-S-12[1]	Serving stand B: inlay	*Juniperus* sp.
1983-S-13[1]	Serving stand B: peg from one of the tenons that secured the planks of the face	*Buxus sempervirens*
1983-S-14[1]	Serving stand B: one of the tenons that secured the planks of the face	*Buxus sempervirens*

Sample #	Description	Determination
1983-S-15[1]	Serving stand B: top piece, large ring	*Juglans* sp.
1983-S-16[1]	Serving stand B: top piece, small ring	*Juglans* sp.
1983-S-17[1]	Serving stand B: tenon that secured top piece to openwork back piece	*Buxus sempervirens*
1983-S-18[1]	Serving stand B: openwork back piece	*Buxus sempervirens*
1983-S-19[1]	Serving stand B: side piece	*Buxus sempervirens*
1983-S-20[1]	Serving stand B: long back diagonal strut, at right when facing back of stand	*Buxus sempervirens*
1983-S-21[1]	Serving stand B: short back diagonal strut, at left when facing back of stand	*Buxus sempervirens*

Furniture from the northeast corner

Sample #	Description	Determination
1984-S-21[1]	Short leg (12538 W 131)	*Buxus sempervirens*
1984-S-22[1]	Tenon lodged in short leg (see above)	*Buxus sempervirens*
1984-S-23[1]	Carved stretcher (12522 W 130)	*Buxus sempervirens*
1984-S-24[1]	Wide slat found with carved stretcher (see above)	*Juniperus* sp.

Coffin (12210 W 123)

Sample #	Description	Determination
1991-WS-24[2]	Coffin: east end of coffin body, ledge	*Cedrus libani* Loud.
1991-WS-17[2]	Coffin: west end of coffin body, ledge near iron bar	*Cedrus libani*
1991-WS-18[2]	Coffin: west end of coffin body, sloping section that had broken off from the ledge	*Cedrus libani*
1998-WP-39[2]	Coffin: NE corner block (C-TU-GOR-43), sound wood	*Pinus* sp., likely *P. sylvestris* L.
1998-WP-40[2]	Coffin: NE corner block (C-TU-GOR-43), decayed wood	*Pinus* sp.
1991-WS-23[2]	Coffin: SE corner block	*Pinus* sp.
1991-WS-22[2]	Coffin: fragment of corner block showing circular cutting	*Pinus* sp.
1998-WP-35[2]	Coffin: long strips of rails (dark wood)	*Taxus baccata*
1998-WP-36[2]	Coffin: short strips of rails (dark wood)	*Taxus baccata*
1998-WP-37[2]	Coffin: wood found with coffin rails–possibly the light wood of the rails	*Buxus sempervirens*
1998-WP-38[2]	Coffin: wood found with coffin rails–possibly the light wood of the rails	*Buxus sempervirens*
1984-S-30[1]	Coffin: wood slat that lay beneath the textiles at the east end of the coffin (interior frame?)	*Buxus sempervirens*

Miscellaneous

Sample #	Description	Determination
1998-WP-28[2]	Leg with white coating (12208 W 122), possibly from Tumulus MM	*Buxus sempervirens*

Sample #	*Description*	*Determination*

Floor boards from the Tumulus MM chamber

1999-TMM-1[2]	Floor board under west wall of tomb, first floor board	*Pinus* sp.
1999-TMM-2[2]	Second floor board	*Cedrus libani*
1999-TMM-4[2]	Third floor board	*Cedrus libani*
1999-TMM-7[2]	Fourth floor board	*Cedrus libani*
1999-TMM-9[2]	Fifth floor board	*Cedrus libani*
1999-TMM-12[2]	Sixth floor board	*Cedrus libani*
1999-TMM-15[2]	Seventh floor board	*Cedrus libani*
1999-TMM-16[2]	Eighth floor board	*Cedrus libani*
1999-TMM-18[2]	Ninth floor board	*Cedrus libani*
1999-TMM-19[2]	Tenth floor board	*Pinus* sp.
1999-TMM-21[2]	Eleventh floor board	*Pinus* sp.

APPENDIX 4

ASSESSMENT OF WOOD DETERIORATION IN THE FURNITURE AND COFFIN FROM TUMULUS MM

ROBERT A. BLANCHETTE

Department of Plant Pathology
University of Minnesota

In Tumulus MM, the wooden coffin and furniture were found in various stages of deterioration. The massive coffin and some of the tables had extensive decay, whereas other objects, such as the inlaid serving stands, were remarkably well preserved. The large number of wooden objects found in the tomb and the different stages of deterioration that were present provided a unique opportunity to investigate the degradation processes that affected these ancient works of art. In this study the types of deterioration were identified, and the current physical and chemical condition of the wood determined. The investigation also provided important new information on the biological and non-biological degradation processes that were found in the wood. These results provide data that were useful to help develop appropriate conservation and restoration techniques for the wood and for understanding deterioration processes that occur in other buried archaeological woods.

Extensive research has been done on the changes that occur in wood during decomposition. When microorganisms decay wood, they cause distinct morphological and chemical changes that are signatures of the causal organism. Examination of the degradation patterns can reveal what type of microorganism was responsible and also provide a great deal of information on the condition of the wood. Over the past several decades, numerous investigations have been carried out on the biodeterioration of wood.[1] This information can provide a guide for assessing the decay present in archaeological woods. Categories of microbial degradation include three major groups of fungal decay (brown-, soft-, and white-rot decay) and several groups of bacterial attack (pit membrane destruction, tunneling, erosion, and cavitation). For each group there may be several forms and subcategories depending on specific microbial physiology and cell wall decay patterns.

Abiotic causes of deterioration may also be present in archaeological wood. Deterioration from metal corrosion products, soluble chlorides, high concentrations of acids or alkaline substances, and other non-biological factors may be responsible for significant damage to wood. These decay patterns are usually distinctly different from those produced by microorganisms. Unfortunately, many of these abiotic deterioration processes are poorly understood because of the masking effect produced from decay by the ever-present microbial population, environmental influences that alter wood over time, and the difficulty of studying these slow processes. Non-biological deterioration was found within the Tumulus MM chamber in addition to microbial decay. The unusual condition of burial and preservation of the affected wood within the tomb provides an excellent opportunity to study the non-biotic factors responsible for the deterioration.

An assessment of deterioration can be made for archaeological wood by electron microscopy using extremely small samples. The samples obtained from the coffin and furniture from Tu-

---

[1] Blanchette, "A Guide to Wood Deterioration." Blanchette, "A Review of Microbial Deterioration." Blanchette, "Deterioration in Historic and Archaeological Woods."

Blanchette and Simpson, "Soft Rot and Wood Pseudomorphs in an Ancient Coffin." Nelson, Goñi, Hedges, and Blanchette, "Soft-Rot Fungal Degradation."

mulus MM were approximately 3×1×1mm or less and were taken from different locations to get a good representation of the decay present. Wood samples were sectioned and prepared for scanning and transmission electron microscopy. Segments of wood used for scanning electron microscopy were infiltrated with distilled water, frozen to -20° C and sectioned with a Cryo-cut freezing microtome. Sectioned wood segments were air-dried, or dehydrated through an ethanol series and critical point dried. Specimens were mounted on aluminum stubs, coated with gold, and examined. For transmission electron microscopy, small wood segments were fixed in 1% KmNO₄ for 15 minutes or 2.5% glutaraldehyde for two hours followed by 1% osmium tetroxide for an additional hour. Samples were then dehydrated through a graded ethanol series and embedded in Quetol embedding media. Transverse sections were cut on an ultra microtome and examined.

Micromorphology of Sound Wood

Micrographs of sound, modern wood are presented here to show the anatomical characteristics of the wood species present in the furniture that was found in the tomb (Plates 139–140).

Juglans: This semi-diffuse porous hardwood has scattered vessels that have simple perforation plates. Earlywood vessels are large, but vessel size gradually decreases through the annual growth ring into the latewood. Ray cells are up to five seriate (in width) and appear rounded in tangential view. Fibers range from thin to moderately thick-walled (Plate 139A–B).

Buxus: This wood has small, solitary vessels with few vessel-to-vessel contacts. Perforation plates in vessels are scalariform. Fiber tracheids are thick-walled with bordered pits. Both uniseriate and multiseriate rays may be present (Plate 139C–F).

Cedrus: The tracheids of *Cedrus* do not exhibit spiral thickenings on their walls. Rays are uniseriate, and pits between rays and tracheids are of the taxoid type. One distinguishing feature of *Cedrus* is the scalloped edge of the torus within border pits (best seen with high magnification light microscopy). No resin canals occur in normal wood, but traumatic resin canals may be found in trees that have been wounded (Plate 140A–B).

Juniperus: The tracheids of this wood are usually rounded and often have intercellular spaces in the area between cell corners. Rays are uniseriate and usually one to six cells in height. Tracheid walls are smooth (no longitudinal thickenings). No resin canals are present (Plate 140C–D).

Taxus: The most conspicuous microscopic features of this wood are the spiral thickenings on the walls of longitudinal tracheids. Bordered pits are usually in one row on radial walls. Pits between rays and tracheids are cupressoid. Rays are uniseriate and may range from one to 25 cells in height. No resin canals are present (Plate 140E–F).

Pinus: The distinguishing features of this wood include the presence of scattered resin canals among tracheids and large pinoid (window-like) pitting between rays and tracheids. Uniseriate rays are numerous, and fusiform rays are also frequently present with transverse resin canals. Micrographs of sound *Pinus* are not shown.

General Description of Deterioration in the Tumulus MM Furniture

Samples from the decayed regions of the furniture were exceedingly fragile and had lost a great deal of original wood strength. Transverse sections revealed wood that retained gross anatomical structure (vessel elements, fibers, and parenchyma cells were discernable), but cells had extremely thin cell walls. In many cells examined, the secondary wall layers of the cell wall were completely degraded, and only the middle lamellae between cells remained. This residual skeleton of the innermost zone of the cell wall was very fragile and often was distorted in shape and partially collapsed. In some cells only the disrupted remains of the residual middle lamella were found. Observations of wood with less severe evidence of decay showed cells in various stages of degradation. Cell walls where parts of the secondary wall remained had cavities and eroded zones in the secondary wall layer. This decay was typical of Type-1 and Type-2 forms of soft rot. Cell wall degradation by soft-rot fungi consists of conical-shaped cavities within the secondary wall (Type 1) or secondary walls that are eroded (Type 2). Although the secondary wall may contain large numbers of cavities or may be totally eroded, the middle lamella is not degraded. In the various wood samples examined from the furniture, cavities within the secondary wall appear to have preceded secondary wall removal. As decay progressed, cavities coalesced, and the fungus metabolized large portions of the secondary wall. In wood from some of the table tops, secondary walls within cells were completely degraded, and only a framework of weak cell wall middle lamellae was left.

Another feature observed in some of the wood from the tops and legs of the tables was the presence of voids in the wood. These relatively large voids had no intact cells present but were filled with minute oval pellets. The morphology of the pellets and meandering voids that were found suggest that they are insect frass from the larval stage of wood-boring beetles. Micrographs of the wood adjacent to the tunnels showed a border of cleanly cut cells similar to cells of modern day wood that have been attacked by *Anobium* beetles. Preference by the woodborers for certain woods was apparent, with greater occurrence in the walnut table tops, and a few instances were observed in boxwood table legs. *Anobium* beetles commonly attack the sapwood of many hardwoods and also attack the heartwood if decay is present. Some of the furniture apparently had been infested with eggs or wood-boring beetle larvae before being placed in the tomb, providing a population for reproduction that continued attack after the tomb was closed.

General Description of Deterioration in the Coffin

Soft-rot decay was the only form of biological degradation that occurred throughout the coffin. Advanced stages of soft rot were found in most samples examined from the cedar coffin and pine corner blocks. Numerous soft-rot cavities within the secondary wall layers were apparent. These cavities were aligned along the microfibrillar axis of cellulose fibrils and appeared as cylindrical chains of cavities with conical ends. In many parts of the wood, especially the pine corner blocks, the soft-rot cavities in the secondary wall extended out into the cell lumen. With light microscopy these spiral-oriented cell wall cavities resembled helical thickenings produced in the wood of *Taxus*, and were misidentified during

the first wood identifications made by Professor B. Aytuğ. Scanning electron microscopy clearly demonstrated that the wood was not *Taxus*, but *Cedrus* and *Pinus* with cavities caused by soft-rot fungi (see below).

In parts of the coffin where iron bars and nails were located, soft rot was not observed. Wood from the areas that were adjacent to the corroded iron displayed an unusual morphology. Iron corrosion products had infiltrated into the wood, forming a thin coating over the cell lumina, pit apertures, and pit chambers. The iron corrosion products apparently also induced cell wall dissolution and deterioration. The wood in these areas had been degraded leaving iron pseudomorphs of the cell structure (Plate 149). These cell replicas were well preserved and displayed the reverse image of tracheid and parenchyma cell morphology. Excellent detail of the wood structure was evident in the pseudomorphs, with even the fine structure of the pit membranes and warty layer of the cell wall evident. The pseudomorphs were most pronounced next to the iron bars and nails and were encountered less frequently in cells farther away from these areas.[2]

General Observations about Decay Found in the Tumulus MM Furniture

The unique environmental conditions within the tomb governed the type of deterioration that occurred. Soft-rot fungi are often associated with wood in environments that exclude other microorganisms. They often decay wood in very wet or dry conditions as well as wood that is buried in soil. All forms of microorganisms need some moisture for decay to occur. Although it is not known how moisture entered the tomb, or exactly when, a possible source could have been the layer of moist clay placed over the limestone rubble and tomb structure. At the time the tomb was closed and the tumulus built, moisture from the clay could have produced sufficiently high humidity for the soft-rot fungus to cause decay and for iron corrosion to occur. The moisture that entered the tomb had to pass through the limestone, resulting in an increased pH. The conditions of elevated pH do not favor Basidiomycetes, the major group of fungi that cause decay in

---

[2] Blanchette and Simpson, "Soft Rot and Wood Pseudomorphs in an Ancient Coffin."

wood, but apparently were ideal for the soft-rot fungi.

Nutrients are also a factor in governing the rate and extent of decay. The greatest amount of decay was found in the portion of the coffin that held the body. Even the floorboards of the tomb structure beneath and next to the coffin were decayed to a greater extent than other areas. The soft-rot fungi effectively utilized the increased amounts of nitrogen and other growth-promoting substances from the body, textiles, and funeral offerings, resulting in greater decay in areas of the tomb where they were located. The ability of fungi to translocate available nutrients and recycle nitrogen is well known and would allow the fungus to assimilate these resources to enhance decay over a large area.[3]

As moisture gradually diminished within the tomb, the soft-rot fungi, with their tolerance for reduced moisture, may have continued causing decay with just minimal amounts of water available. They also could utilize metabolic water generated by the degradation process to continue the decay processes for even longer periods of time. Undoubtedly, most of the decay took place in the years that immediately followed the closing of the tomb. But a slow progressive attack by the soft rot may have been active for decades or even centuries. The presence of soft rot in just about every cell of all the wooden items, and the time needed to decay the massive coffin made from rot-resistant *Cedrus*, suggest that the fungi were active for a very long period. Observation of decay in the large *Pinus* wood timbers used for the tomb's inner walls and in the *Juniperus* logs of the outer tomb structure also suggests that decay had occurred over an extended time period. Soft-rot fungi were also found in these woods, with decay extending into the center of the logs and timbers. The size of the logs and planks used for the construction of the tomb and the natural decay resistance of *Juniperus* wood indicate that an exceedingly long decay process was required for the extent of soft-rot degradation observed.

The species identity for the soft-rot fungi that caused the decay in the tomb is not known. After the tomb was opened, an influx of molds and decay fungi entered the tomb chamber and be-

came established. The presence of large amounts of moisture from the drillings used to locate the tomb within the tumulus (1955–1956), the opening of the tomb (1957) to the natural microflora, and the direct introduction of decay-infected timbers used during the excavation resulted in severe contamination of the woods by modern-day fungi. Attempts to isolate fungi from the tomb were successful, and some soft-rot fungi were found. However, it cannot be determined with certainty if these fungi were the original organisms that caused the damage or contaminants that arrived after the tomb was opened. A new threat to the tomb occurred with the appearance of brown-rot fungi after excavation. These aggressive Basidiomycetes are well-known wood destroyers and were brought into the tomb on infected wood used for supports during construction. Although this modern day brown-rot was found on the tomb structure (at many sites where wooded supports were used to prevent collapse of the roof), no evidence of this secondary invader was found in the furniture or coffin wood.

Micromorphology and
Ultrastructure of Furniture Samples

Wood decay in the samples from the tops of the various tables showed cell walls that were extremely thin and fragile. Cracks and fractured cells were common in severely decayed wood such as the decay found in table 6 (Plate 141A–B). Some cells had distorted shapes, and others appeared crushed. Cells that remained were eroded but not disconnected from one another. Fiber cells that typically display thick secondary walls in sound wood had little if any secondary wall layers left in the decayed wood examined (Plate 141C–D). Only a framework of middle lamellae from the original cell wall was left. Parenchyma cells were evident but were thin and eroded.

In many of the table-top samples, voids were found that were filled with oval pellets. In some samples, such as those from table 9 and table 4, large areas of the wood were affected. Remnants of vessels, fibers, and parenchyma cells were present in the wood remaining between the tunnels. These cells showed evidence of cell-wall

---

[3] Filley, Blanchette, Simpson, and Fogel, "Nitrogen Cycling."

erosion and thinning. Some areas were affected to a greater extent than others, with large zones of the wood removed (Plate 142A–B), whereas other samples had distinct meandering tunnels filled with oval pellets (Plate 142C–D). The morphology of the pellets and spatial relationship in the wood suggest that they are insect frass from wood-boring beetle larvae.

Patterns of decay similar to that observed in the table tops were found in the boxwood table legs (Plate 143). Cell walls were eroded, leaving the thin, middle lamella layer. The thick fiber cells of boxwood, however, were commonly seen with some secondary wall left and distinct cavities in the wall (Plate 143B). In samples with more extensive decay present (table 7, for example) the secondary wall was completely removed, and the altered wood resembled the decayed wood of the table tops (Plate 143C–D). Small tunnels with insect frass were found in only a few of the boxwood samples examined.

An interesting anatomical feature that helped to differentiate wood fragments from the tops of tables 6 and 7 was the presence of spiral thickenings within vessel elements (Plate 144A–B). The vessels of *Juglans* do not have this feature present in the wood. Samples from the tops of both tables showed that the top of table 7 was *Juglans* but the top of table 6 was a different wood. The fine, relatively even spaced spiral thickenings were characteristic of *Acer* and a few other hardwood species. It appears that the top of table 6 was likely made of *Acer* or possibly a *Prunus* species (such as cherry or some other fruit tree wood), and the use of this different species may account for the wood's severe deterioration. The sapwood of *Acer* or *Prunus* is considered much less resistant to microbial decay than the wood of *Juglans*.

Samples from the inlaid table and serving stands had similar patterns of cell wall degradation as observed in the plain tables. The *Juglans* top of the inlaid table had very advanced decay (Plate 145A). Cell walls were extensively eroded, leaving only the middle lamella behind as a skeleton of the wall structure. The delicate residual middle lamella was often broken, with groups of cells distorted and crushed. Ray parenchyma cells were still evident but were also eroded and disrupted. Oval pellets and tunnels resembling wood-borer damage were also observed in some samples (Plate 145B). In samples of boxwood from

the serving stands, less advanced stages of decay were apparent, but all cells had some soft-rot degradation. Cavities were seen in secondary walls of most thick-walled fiber cells (Plate 145C–D).

To further evaluate the degradation present in the furniture and to confirm that soft-rot fungi caused the decay, samples were fixed, sectioned, and examined by transmission electron microscopy. Samples from wood with the most advanced decay (table 6) showed distorted cells that were greatly altered from the normal cell structure of sound wood (Plate 146A). The only cell-wall layer remaining was the compound middle lamella. The convoluted and disfigured shapes of the remaining cells indicated that this residual framework of the cell wall had very little structural integrity. Eroded cell walls with only middle lamellae left were common features of all wood samples examined from the tables and serving stands. In some samples (table 7, Plate 146B; table 5, Plate 146C; serving stand B, Plate 146D), the middle lamella had differentiated zones still visible. The cell corner region was more electron dense and less affected than the middle lamella between cell walls. Particulate matter, which appeared to be remnants of the degraded secondary wall, was attached to the middle lamellae and seen to be dispersed within cell lumina (most likely displaced from the cell wall due to preparation techniques for microscopy). In sections of wood from the boxwood legs, some parts of the secondary wall were still evident, and distinct cavities in the wall were observed (Plate 146E–F). In some cells, numerous cavities coalesced together, and others had only a thin partition of secondary wall left between them. This intermediate stage of the decay clearly shows that soft-rot fungi destroyed the wall using a combination of cavity formation and cell-wall erosion (Type-1 and Type-2 soft-rot patterns of decay). In cells with advanced decay, the secondary wall was destroyed, and the middle lamella persisted relatively unaltered. The fractures and alterations in the residual walls of the decayed woods were likely due to mechanical damage from handling the fragile wood after excavation. Another possible reason for the alterations is the wetting and drying stresses that occurred when the water from the drilling used to locate the tomb chamber saturated much of the decayed furniture, followed by drying of the objects after the tomb was opened.

*Micromorphology and Ultrastructure of
Wood from the Coffin and Corner Blocks*

The most distinctive feature of decay in the coffin and corner blocks was the presence of soft-rot cavities within the cell wall (Plate 147A–F). In contrast to the decay in the furniture, no widespread erosion of secondary wall layers was observed. Cavities, however, were clearly evident in all transverse sections (Plate 147A–B). All cells of the wood examined from many different parts of the coffin were affected. Cavities were found in walls of both the latewood and earlywood cells but were more readily seen and abundant in the thick-walled latewood (Plate 147C–D). An extraordinary number of cavities were found in many cells, and the soft-rot decay represented one of the most advanced stages of this type of decay that has been reported anywhere. The corner blocks were identified as *Pinus* due to the presence of resin canals and large pinoid-type pitting that was present on tracheid-ray walls (Plate 147E–F).

Another distinct feature of soft-rot attack that was observed was the chains of cavities in the secondary wall that followed the microfibrillar orientation of cellulose. The cavities were produced in a spiral along the microfibrillar axis of the cellulose within the cell. In many cells examined from the coffin, soft-rot cavities were seen in radial and tangential sections as a series of cylindrical cavities with conical ends (Plate 148A–B). Fine hyphal penetration holes were seen entering the angular-shaped degraded zones of the cavities (Plate 148A–B). In some cells, the soft-rot cavities, as observed from the cell lumen, exhibited a series of spiraled cracks and checks (Plate 148C). These spiraled cracks gave the impression of spiraled cell-wall thickenings when the first wood identification studies were done in Turkey. With light microscopy, these spiraled alterations of the cells were misidentified as helical thickenings typical of the tracheids from *Taxus*. Scanning electron microscopy clearly shows the differentiation of these features in the two woods (Plate 148C–D). Investigators using light microscopy to identify decayed archaeological wood need to be aware of the microscopic characteristics of soft rot to avoid misidentification.

In wood from the coffin located near the iron bars or nails, a non-biological form of decay was present. Iron corrosion products had infiltrated the wood cells, deteriorated the wood, and left finely preserved wood pseudomorphs. The pseudomorphs made of iron corrosion products were exact replicas of wood cells and contained excellent fine detail of the cell structure (Plate 149A–D). The reverse image of the cell walls showed bordered pits with scalloped edges of the torus (a feature specific to *Cedrus*) and fine striations of the margo (Plate 149B–D). Even the warty layer found on the outer secondary wall was preserved as minute holes in the surface of the cell replica. No evidence of soft-rot degradation was evident in the replicas, indicating that the cells were sound when the iron corrosion process took place. Moisture originating from the clay heaped over the tomb when the tumulus was built was likely the inciting factor for the corrosion of the iron. This process, although relatively slow to achieve complete cell dissolution and pseudomorph formation, apparently occurred faster than the progressive attack by the soft-rot fungi. Little is known about the process of cell wall deterioration by metal corrosion products, but even under the most optimum conditions this is a very slow process. Only small amounts of remnant deteriorated cell wall matter were found between some of the pseudomorphs. As the distance from the iron increased, psuedomorphs were less frequent, and wood cells displayed greater evidence of soft-rot activity.

Acknowledgments

The analyses reported on in this appendix were carried out with the technical assistance of Andre Abad, Benjamin Held, Kory Cease, John Haight, and Joel Jurgens, research associates at the University of Minnesota.

APPENDIX 5

CHEMICAL IDENTIFICATION OF THE BEVERAGE AND FOOD REMAINS IN TUMULUS MM

PATRICK E. McGOVERN

Museum Applied Science Center for Archaeology
University of Pennsylvania Museum of Archaeology and Anthropology

Between 1997 and 1999, ancient organic remains contained in 29 of the bronze and pottery vessels from Tumulus MM were analyzed. Most of the chemical studies were carried out in the Molecular Archaeology Laboratory of the Museum Applied Science Center for Archaeology (MASCA) at the University of Pennsylvania Museum, with generous support from The Kaplan Fund of New York and in collaboration with Dr. Donald L. Glusker and Lawrence J. Exner. Selected samples, using a range of scientific techniques not available in MASCA, were also analyzed by the following investigators, with funding from the National Science Foundation and their home institutions and companies: Drs. Robert A. Moreau and Alberto Nuñez (Eastern Regional Research Center, U.S. Dept. of Agriculture, Wyndmoor, PA), Drs. Curt W. Beck and Edith C. Stout (Amber Research Laboratory, Vassar College, Poughkeepsie, NY), Eric D. Butrym (Scientific Instrument Services, Ringoes, NJ), and Dr. Chad Quinn (SmithKline Beecham Pharmaceuticals, King of Prussia, PA).

The main goals of the chemical analyses were to identify any ancient organic components that might shed light on whether they represented "leftovers" of a funerary feast held before the burial, as proposed by Dr. Elizabeth Simpson, and to refine MASCA analytical methods.

Three independent chemical techniques are typically used by the MASCA laboratory to detect organic compounds,[1] as outlined below. Samples were obtained by grinding up the solid ancient residue and extracting it twice with boiling methanol or chloroform for 20 minutes each.

1) Diffuse-Reflectance Infrared Fourier-Transform Spectrometry (DRIFTS) takes advantage of the nature of chemical bonds to stretch and bend when they absorb infrared (IR) light. Each chemical compound absorbs IR light at specific frequencies which can be precisely measured and shown on a spectrum. The technique is extremely versatile and precise, requiring as little as a milligram of material, which is ground up and mixed with potassium bromide, a transparent solid. The MASCA laboratory currently employs a Nicolet 5 DXB FT-IR spectrometer, with OMNIC 3.0 software and search capabilities. Spectra were deresolved at 8 cm⁻¹ wavenumber, a frequency unit used by spectroscopists for library storage, searches, and printing. Because the whole sample is analyzed simultaneously, the absorption peaks of individual compounds often overlap, sometimes frustrating accurate identifications.

2) High-Performance Liquid Chromatography (HPLC) is used for more precise identifications of mixed materials. Microgram amounts can be detected by MASCA's Hewlett-Packard 1090 Liquid Chromatograph, with an A06.01 ChemStation, which is run at 80 atm (ca. 1200 lbs/in²). A 10 or 20:1 sample, dissolved in methanol (or acetonitrile) is passed at 2 ml/min through a column (25 cm in length and 4.6 mm in diameter), which is lined with 3–10 micron diameter particles that preferentially absorb the compounds of interest. Depending on how strong the affinity or polarity is between the compound, moving solvent, and stationary substrate, the compound will take more or less time to pass through the

[1] McGovern, et. al., "Neolithic Resinated Wine," 480–481; McGovern, et al., "The Beginnings of Winemaking," 3–21; McGovern, et al., "A Funerary Feast Fit for King Midas," 863–864; McGovern, "Funerary Banquet of 'King Midas,'" 21–29; McGovern, *Ancient Wine*, 279–298.

column (referred to as the retention time). Once separated, the components are fed into an ultraviolet (UV)-visible spectrophotometer diode array, ideally yielding characteristic absorptions of chromophores by the compounds of interest. A database of several hundred relevant archaeological samples and modern reference compounds is then searched by the ChemStation software for the best matches at a specific retention time and UV wavelength (usually 210 nm).

3) Feigl chemical spot tests,[2] with microgram sensitivity, are used to test for specific compounds. For example, the presence of tartaric acid/tartrate, which occurs in large amounts naturally in the Middle East only in grapes (and therefore in wine), is confirmed by dissolving and heating an ancient sample in concentrated sulfuric acid. β, β'-dinaphthol is then added, to convert tartaric acid to a compound that exhibits green fluorescence under UV light. Calcium oxalate or "beerstone," which settles out at the bottom and along the sides of barley beer processing and storage vessels, is detected by reducing the sample with zinc granules in an acidic medium to glyoxalic acid, followed by reaction with phenylhydrazine and hydrogen peroxide, to give a distinctive pinkish red color.

In summary, the MASCA Molecular Archaeology Laboratory relies on three chemical techniques—DRIFTS, HPLC, and Feigl spot tests—to test an ancient organic sample for the presence of marker or fingerprint compounds, which are correlated to natural products of archaeological significance. A compound is said to be "present" only if it is attested by all three analyses. Follow-up liquid chromatographic-mass spectrometric (LC-MS) and gas chromatographic-mass spectrometric (GC-MS) analyses of some samples are useful in substantiating the findings, as well as in detecting additional compounds. Any assessment of the original organic material is also crucially dependent on and should be consistent with the archaeological context and the vessel types that contained the residues.

I. The "Mixed Beverage": Wine, Barley Beer, and Honey Mead

Sixteen residues were tested from a range of bronze vessel types from Tumulus MM,[3] which had contained more than 150 metal vessels, the most comprehensive Iron Age drinking set ever found, according to Moorey.[4] Based on banqueting protocol at a royal celebration—depicted on wall reliefs in the palace of the Assyrian king Sargon II at Khorsabad, which dates to about the same time as the burial in Tumulus MM—a preliminary judgment about how each vessel was used in a "funerary banquet" could be hypothesized. The ram-headed and lion-headed "buckets" or situlae, for example, would have been used to transfer the beverage from the three large vats (or cauldrons) to smaller cauldrons, mounted on two special wooden serving stands. From there, the beverage would have been ladled into 98 bronze omphalos bowls and 19 large two-handled bowls. This hypothesis was confirmed by the analyses undertaken.

As catalogued below, the residues from one small cauldron, two situlae, seven omphalos bowls, and six other bowls were analyzed in the MASCA laboratory. This represented 57% (of a total of 28) of the samples from "beverage vessels" which were brought back to the University of Pennsylvania Museum following the 1957 expedition. Any residue originally present in the three large cauldrons had been destroyed by immersion in hot sodium hydroxide when the vessels were conserved.

All the "beverage" residues have a very similar macroscopic and microscopic physical appearance. They are intensely yellowish in color, with dark-colored platelets dispersed through the matrix. These platelets are very shiny and rippled on one surface, and matte-textured on the other, suggesting a liquid that originally evaporated along the inside of a vessel and then flaked off. At 80× magnification, numerous bubbles and particles (on the order of a half to 2 microns in diameter) are visible in the platelets.

    [2] F. Feigl, *Spot Tests in Organic Analysis*.
    [3] See Young, *Gordion I*, for illustrations and discussion; the previous chemical analyses by A. Eric Parkinson are also included in this volume as an appendix. *Gordion I*, 277–284.
    [4] Moorey, "Metal Wine Sets," 195.

List of Analyzed "Beverage" Samples

MM10: bronze small cauldron; analyzed by DRIFTS, HPLC, and chemical spot test for oxalate.

MM45: bronze lion-headed situla; analyzed by DRIFTS, HPLC, thermal desorption (TD)-GC-MS (Eric Butrym), and chemical spot tests for tartrate and oxalate.

MM46: bronze ram-headed situla; analyzed by DRIFTS, HPLC, LC-MS (Chad Quinn), GC-MS (Curt Beck and Edith Stout), and chemical spot tests for tartrate and oxalate.

MM51: bronze bowl with lifting handles; analyzed by DRIFTS, HPLC, and chemical spot tests for tartrate and oxalate.

MM53: bronze bowl with lifting handles; analyzed by DRIFTS and HPLC.

MM56: bronze bowl with swiveling ring handles; analyzed by DRIFTS, HPLC, and chemical spot test for oxalate.

MM60: bronze bowl with swiveling ring handles; analyzed by DRIFTS, HPLC, LC-MS (Robert Moreau and Alberto Nuñez), GC-MS (Alberto Nuñez), and chemical spot test for tartrate.

MM86: bronze petaled omphalos bowl; analyzed by DRIFTS, HPLC, and chemical spot tests for tartrate and oxalate.

MM95: bronze petaled omphalos bowl; analyzed by DRIFTS, HPLC, and chemical spot test for tartrate.

MM104: bronze petaled omphalos bowl; analyzed by DRIFTS, HPLC, and chemical spot test for tartrate.

MM123: bronze petaled omphalos bowl; analyzed by DRIFTS, HPLC, and chemical spot test for tartrate.

MM128: bronze ribbed omphalos bowl; analyzed by DRIFTS, HPLC, LC-MS (Robert Moreau and Alberto Nuñez), and chemical spot tests for tartrate and oxalate.

MM137: bronze plain omphalos bowl; analyzed by DRIFTS, HPLC, and chemical spot tests for tartrate and oxalate.

MM144: bronze plain omphalos bowl; analyzed by DRIFTS, HPLC, and chemical spot test for tartrate.

MM168: bronze deep bowl; analyzed by DRIFTS and HPLC.

MM169: bronze deep bowl; analyzed by DRIFTS, HPLC, and chemical spot test for oxalate.

The chemical results for each group of samples—"beverage" and "food" (below)—were highly consistent within each group, but were very different from one another. When IR or HPLC searches were run on any given sample, its best matches were other samples in the same group. Thus, both the "beverage" and "food" represented in the tomb were of highly homogeneous chemical compositions.

The group of IR spectra shown in Text Figure 1 can be used to illustrate this conclusion. All the spectra have the same absorptions (variations in intensity are due to sample size or the amount of a given component), even though they come from a range of "beverage vessels," and contrast with those of the "food" (Text Figure 3). Starting with the higher frequencies on the left of Text Figure 1, the broad band centered around $3400\,cm^{-1}$ wavenumber is due to hydroxyl or water of hydration, and peaks at 2930 and $2860\,cm^{-1}$ are characteristic of the stretching between carbon and hydrogen atoms (i.e., hydrocarbons); then comes the carbonyl band of various organic acids and esters at 1730–$1710\,cm^{-1}$, followed by carboxylate or organic acid salt bands between 1670 and $1570\,cm^{-1}$. C–H bending frequencies show up at 1460, 1360, and $720\,cm^{-1}$, along with numerous other matches between the samples in the so-called "fingerprint region" between 1300 and $600\,cm^{-1}$.

By contrast, the "food" residues (Text Figure 3) are lacking the hydroxyl/water of hydration band around $3400\,cm^{-1}$. The hydrocarbon C–H stretch bands are there, as in the "beverage" samples, but a slight shoulder at $3000\,cm^{-1}$ sets them apart. A carbonyl band, which is often associated with organic acids and esters, is quite prominent, but it is much better defined in the "food," with a greater intensity and at a higher frequency (1750–$1730\,cm^{-1}$) than that of the "beverage." Moreover, the broad carboxylate salt band (1670–$1570\,cm^{-1}$), related to calcium tartrate and oxalate in the "beverage," is just barely present. At lower frequencies, C–H bending shows up at 1470, 1420, and $1390\,cm^{-1}$, and C–C stretching or C–H bending at 1170, 1120, and $720\,cm^{-1}$, as was also noted for the "beverage." But the fine structure of the "fingerprint region"—the shape, multiplicity, and intensity of the absorptions, representing any number of atomic vibrations—are very distinct for the "food" samples and quite unlike those of the "beverage" samples.

Petalled Omphalos Bowl (MM104)

Ram's Head Situla (MM46)

Bowl with Swivelling Handles (MM56)

Small Cauldron (MM10)

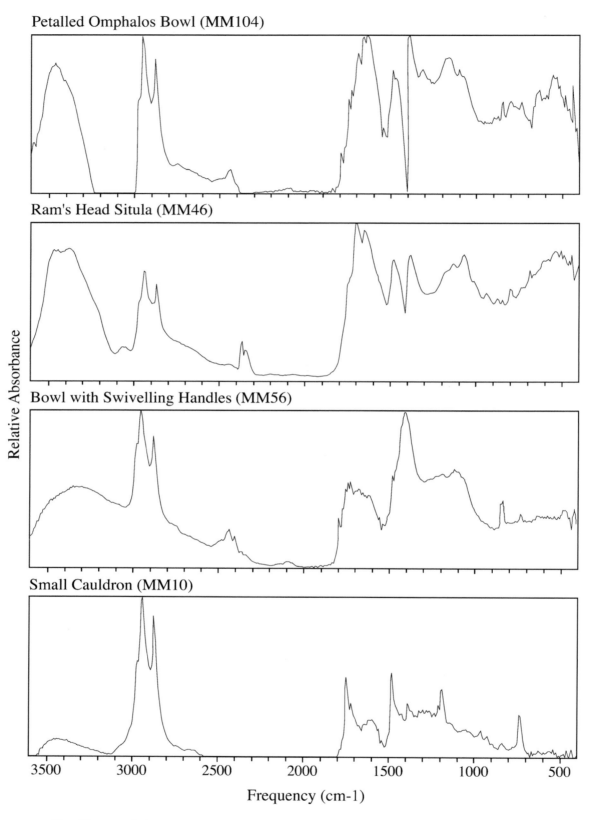

Relative Absorbance

3500   3000   2500   2000   1500   1000   500

Frequency (cm-1)

Text Figure 1. DRIFTS spectra showing the principal absorptions of Tumulus MM beverage samples from different vessel types. The *MM10* spectrum was less intense due to a smaller amount of material, accounting for its somewhat different appearance. See text for full explanation.

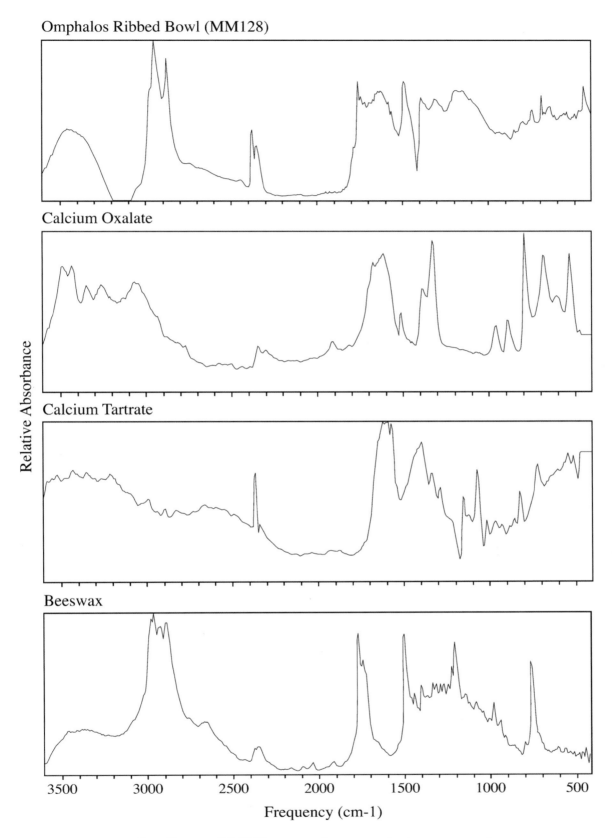

Text Figure 2. DRIFTS spectra of representative beverage sample from Tumulus MM, showing the principal absorptions as explained by synthetic calcium oxalate, calcium tartrate, and modern beeswax.

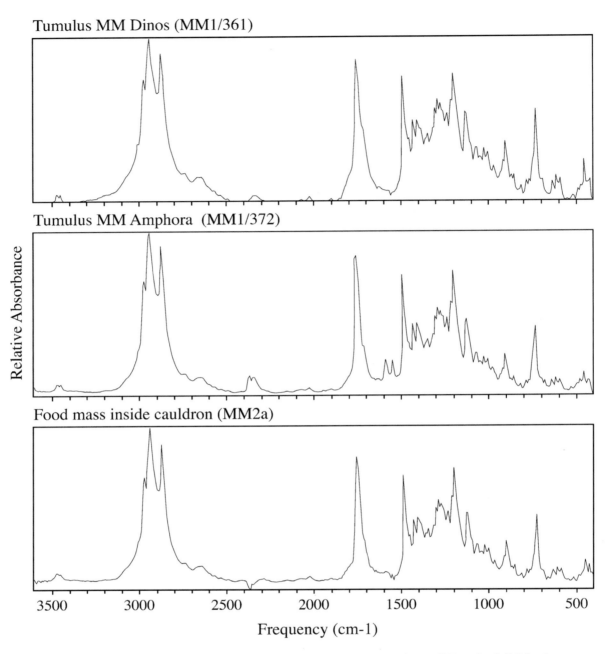

Text Figure 3. DRIFTS spectra showing the principal absorptions of Tumulus MM food
samples from two different vessel types and a clump of material in a large cauldron.

The IR results for the "beverage" samples can be explained as a mixture of grape, barley, and honey, most likely a combined fermented beverage of wine, beer, and mead, since naturally occurring yeast on grape skins and in honey become active in a liquid. Tartaric acid and tartrate salts are the fingerprint compounds of a grape product, because these compounds occur in large amounts naturally in the Mediterranean-Near Eastern region only in grape (*Vitis vinifera*). Outside of the Middle East and Europe, tartaric acid is also found in the African baobab tree and the fruit of the South Asian tamarind tree, but it is highly unlikely that products of these trees were traded during the early first millennium B.C. The insoluble potassium bitartrate and calcium tartrate salts are readily formed from the acid, and in unfiltered, unrefined wine, a crystalline accumulation of these salts, the so-called dregs or lees, will sometimes form on the bottom of a wine vessel. In Text Figure 1, tartaric acid is well attested by a sharp, intense carbonyl peak at 1720/1740 cm^{-1}, together with other absorptions at 1440 and 1250 cm^{-1}. Tartrate is especially pronounced in the samples, correlating with carboxylate absorptions at maxima of 1630 and 1560 cm[-1], with additional peaks at 1550, 1480, 1380, 1330, 1270, 600, 560, and 480 cm[-1] (cf. synthetic calcium tartrate in Text Figure 2). For all the samples tested, the presence of tartaric acid/tartrate was further borne out by positive Feigl spot tests and close HPLC matches with these compounds and other ancient and modern wine samples.

Calcium oxalate or beerstone, the marker compound for barley beer,[5] accounts for the organic acid absorption at the higher end of the salt bands, between 1670 and 1610 cm[-1]. This compound also accounts for the carbonyl stretch absorptions at 1505 and 1330 cm[-1] and some of the fine structure in the "fingerprint region" (cf. synthetic calcium oxalate, Text Figure 2). Positive Feigl spot tests for oxalate were obtained for all samples tested. HPLC gave close matches with the synthetic compound, as well as an ancient "ale" sample from New Kingdom Malkata[6] and a "mixed beverage" from Late Bronze Age Greece (see Conclusions).

While tartaric acid/tartrate and calcium oxalate contribute minimally to the hydrocarbon stretch bands at 2930/2860 cm[-1] (Text Figure 2), these peaks and a strong long-chain C–H bend absorption at around 725 cm[-1] substantiate the presence of beeswax. Greater complexity in the carbonyl region below 1710 cm[-1], coupled with doublet carbonyl peaks at 1730 and 1710 cm[-1] due to ester bonds in the wax compounds, provide further evidence for this identification. Beeswax—with characteristic long hydrocarbons (especially the C_{27} compound, heptacosane) and related acids (in particular, the C_{24} compound, lignoceric acid)—provides an excellent group of fingerprint compounds for honey. Although the sugars in honey rapidly degrade, beeswax is virtually impossible to filter out completely when processing honey, and its compounds can be very well preserved.[7] Curt Beck and Edith Stout identified the key compounds in beeswax by GC-MS in the samples that they analyzed. Close HPLC matches included beeswax, honey, mead (i.e., fermented honey beverage), potassium gluconate (the principal organic acid in honey), and "mixed beverages" with honey as one of the constituents from Mycenaean Greece and Mi-

noan Crete. A starting material of honey, when diluted down to a third by water, will be fermented to mead by osmophilic yeasts in the honey.

In summary, the "beverage" samples from Tumulus MM are all chemically consistent with one another, and are best interpreted as a "mixed fermented beverage" of wine, barley beer, and honey mead. Their uniform chemical composition in the various "beverage" vessels implies that the three components had been mixed or prepared according to a fixed formula.

II. *The "Food": A Lamb or Goat Stew*

The "food" residues were contained in 18 pottery vessels, six each inside the three large cauldrons, together with large clumps of similar-looking material randomly distributed in the cauldrons. If the large cauldrons were originally used to mix and serve the fermented beverage, then they must have been emptied before the "food" clumps and vessels were deposited in them.

Fourteen "food" residues, representing 54% (of a total of 26) of the samples brought back to Philadelphia, were tested. They included material from six dinoi and four small amphorae (types described and illustrated in Young, *Gordion I*), and four clumps, as catalogued below.

Examination of the "food" residues revealed that they consisted uniformly of a brownish material, with a more fused, dark-colored surface, that was extremely contorted and with large depressed areas and holes running through it—quite unlike the thin, shiny platelets and intense yellowish matrix of the "beverage" (above). Tiny bubbles (2 microns in diameter) were seen at 80× magnification, but no cellular structures, seeds, grains, or other plant or animal materials were observed. The physical characteristics were in accord with a thick liquid that had congealed into a solid.

List of Analyzed "Food" Samples

MM1/361: pottery dinos inside large cauldron MM 1; analyzed by DRIFTS, HPLC, LC-MS (Robert Moreau and Alberto Nuñez; Chad Quinn), GC-MS (Curt Beck and Edith Stout),

---

[5] Michel, et al., "Chemical Confirmation of Beer," 24; McGovern and Michel, "First Wine and Beer," 408A–413A.

[6] McGovern, "Wine of Egypt's Golden Age," 69–108.
[7] Evershed, et al., "Fuel for Thought," 979–985.

and chemical spot tests for tartrate and oxalate.

MM1/362: pottery dinos inside large cauldron
MM 1; analyzed by DRIFTS, HPLC, LC-MS
(Robert Moreau and Alberto Nuñez), GC-MS
(Curt Beck and Edith Stout), and chemical
spot test for tartrate.

MM1/372: pottery amphora inside large cauldron
MM 1; analyzed by DRIFTS, HPLC, LC-
MS (Robert Moreau and Alberto Nuñez), and
TD-GC-MS (Eric Butrym).

MM1a: large clump inside large cauldron MM 1;
analyzed by DRIFTS and HPLC.

MM1b: large clump inside large cauldron MM 1;
analyzed by DRIFTS, HPLC, GC-MS (Curt
Beck and Edith Stout), and chemical spot test
for oxalate.

MM2/366: pottery dinos inside large cauldron MM 2; analyzed by DRIFTS and
HPLC.

MM2/367: pottery dinos inside large cauldron
MM 2; analyzed by DRIFTS, HPLC, LC-
MS (Robert Moreau and Alberto Nuñez), TD-
GC-MS (Eric Butrym), and chemical spot tests
for tartrate and oxalate.

MM2/368: pottery dinos inside large cauldron
MM 2; analyzed by DRIFTS, HPLC, and
chemical spot test for oxalate.

MM2a: large clump inside large cauldron MM 2;
analyzed by DRIFTS, HPLC, GC-MS (Curt
Beck and Edith Stout).

MM3/370: pottery dinos inside large cauldron
MM 3; analyzed by DRIFTS, HPLC, and
GC-MS (Curt Beck and Edith Stout).

MM3/375: pottery amphora inside large cauldron
MM 3; analyzed by DRIFTS, HPLC, GC-MS
(Curt Beck and Edith Stout), and chemical
spot test for tartrate.

MM3/376: pottery amphora inside large cauldron MM 3; analyzed by DRIFTS and
HPLC.

MM3/377: pottery amphora inside large cauldron
MM 3; analyzed by DRIFTS and HPLC.

MM3a: large clump inside large cauldron MM 3;
analyzed by DRIFTS and HPLC.

As pointed out above, the "food" spectra shown
in Text Figure 3 all have the same absorptions (although magnitudes may vary with relative
amounts of each constituent and sample size), despite the fact that they come from different vessels.

The best reference matches in our IR database
for the MM "food" residues, in addition to their

matching one another, were modern lamb's fat
and beeswax (Text Figure 4). The slight shoulder
at $3000 \, cm^{-1}$ and a higher carbonyl absorption at
$1755 \, cm^{-1}$ set lamb's fat apart from beeswax. Although the latter is present, marking the presence
of honey, the overall congruity of lamb fat's IR
absorption with that of the MM "food" residues
implies that it makes up the bulk of the composition.

The HPLC results told a similar story: besides
being closely comparable to one another, the ancient "food" residues were most similar to modern lamb's fat, honey, mead, potassium gluconate
(the principal organic acid in honey), barley, calcium oxalate, and calcium tartrate. Relatively little absorption in the IR carboxylate region implied that tartrate, a marker for grapes or wine,
was not a major constituent. The Feigl spot tests
of the "food" samples confirmed the presence of
tartaric acid/tartrate and oxalate.

The significant IR and HPLC matches between the ancient "food" samples and lamb's fat
are best accounted for by triglycerides, as confirmed by the LC-MS analyses of Robert Moreau
and Alberto Nuñez. They showed that specific
triglycerides were very prominent in the MM
"food" remains, but not the "beverage" samples,
viz., palmitodistearin (m/z 864, protonated), with
lesser amounts of dipalmitostearin (836) and tripalmitin (808) (Text Figure 5). Small peaks at m/z
862, 892, and 890, respectively, are due to oleo-
palmito-stearin, tristearin and 2-oleodistearin, the
latter being prevalent in pulses (i.e., the seeds of
legumes). The diacylglycerides at m/z 608, 606,
580, and 552 are fragmentation products of the
analytical process.

Other components of the "food" samples were
identified by GC-MS and TD-GC-MS, carried
out by Curt Beck, Edith Stout, and Eric Butrym.
Their analyses showed that large quantities of the
straight-chained C_6, C_8, C_{10} saturated fatty acids—
commonly known as caproic, caprylic, and capric
acids, respectively—occur in the "food" but not
the "beverage" residues. When these acids are
found together, they are an excellent indicator of
lamb or goat fat, as the Latin root (*caper/capra*
meaning "goat") suggests. There is no way to
distinguish between the triglycerides or fatty acid
composition of lamb and goat's fat and meat, so
the exact composition of the ancient "food" must
be left open at present.

In addition to sheep or goat meat, a variety
of other ingredients were detected in the "food"
residues using GC-MS and TD-GC-MS. Phen-

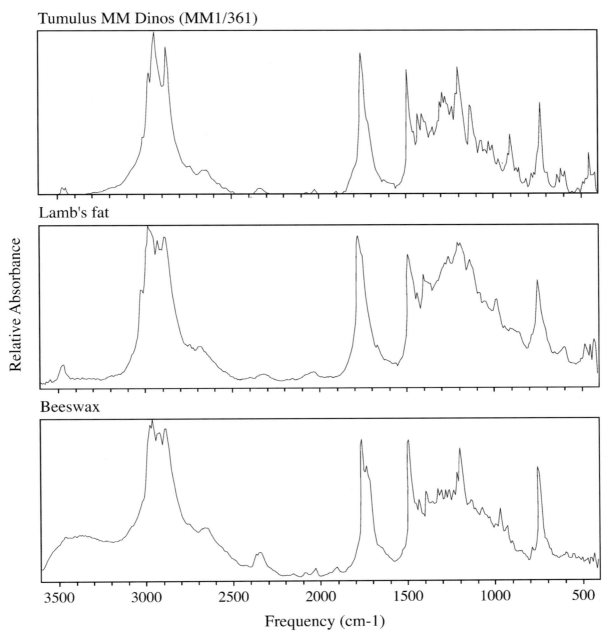

Text Figure 4. DRIFTS spectra of representative beverage sample from Tumulus MM,
showing the principal absorptions as explained by modern lamb's fat and beeswax.

anthrene, a stable aromatic hydrocarbon, and cresol, a phenol derivative, implied that the meat was first cooked over an open flame before it was cut off the bone. Honey, wine, and olive oil, which might have been used to marinate or barbecue the meat or to add their own distinctive flavors, were respectively represented by gluconic acid, tartaric acid, and oleic acid and its trans-isomer elaidic acid. Besides large amounts of cholesterol, which would be expected in a meat dish, a high-protein pulse—most likely, lentils—was present, as revealed by a related plant steroid,

chondrillasterol (and as already borne out by the triglyceride 2-oleodistearin, above).

Although some components of the ancient "food" might have been prepared separately or could have been added at different stages, the uniform chemical composition of the contents of ten pottery vessels and four clumps that were analyzed strongly suggests that the end-product was a homogeneous stew; otherwise, one must imagine the individual components being divided up and distributed equally to each vessel.

The finishing touches to this stew were pro-

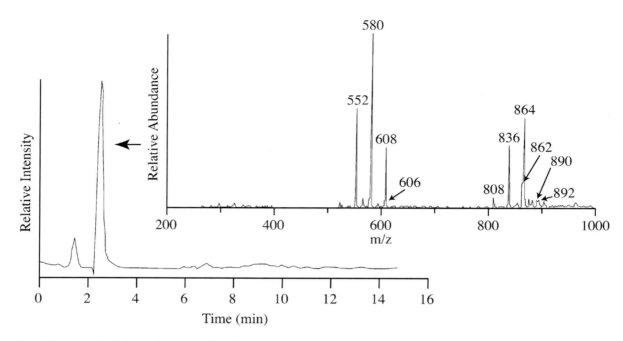

Text Figure 5. A high-performance liquid chromatogram of a chloroform-methanol extract of the food residue shows that triacylglycerols account for the major peak at a retention time of 2.55 min (total ions), representing 90% of the lipid fraction and approximately 10% of the ancient food residue. Its mass spectrum is dominated by protonated palmitodistearin (m/z 864), with lesser amounts of dipalmitostearin (836) and tripalmitin (808).

Small peaks at m/z 862, 892, and 890, are due to oleo-palmito-stearin, tristearin and 2-oleodistearin respectively, the latter being prevalent in pulses (i.e., the seeds of legumes). The diacylglycerides at m/z 608, 606, 580, and 552 are fragmentation products. The presence of tri- and diacylglyceride compounds is a good indication of excellent ancient organic preservation. (Graphic courtesy of Robert A. Moreau and Alberto Nuñez, Eastern Regional Research Center, U.S. Department of Agriculture, Wyndmoor, PA.)

vided by herbs and spices, according to the GC-MS and TD-GC-MS evidence: anisic acid (characteristic of anise or fennel) and α-terpineol and terpenoids found in various spices were identified. The sources of the latter compounds are unknown; bitter vetch (*Vicia*) and wild fenugreek (*Trigonella*), which grow around Gordion today, are possibilities, according to Dr. Naomi F. Miller of MASCA.

Conclusions

The chemical analyses of the "food" and "beverage" residues in Tumulus MM successfully identified the components of the hypothesized "funerary feast," whose "leftovers" were deposited with the deceased after the funeral. The main entrée was a spicy barbecued lamb or goat stew

with lentils and other vegetables (including barley). Noteworthy are the large stocks of lentils and cereals that were found in storage jars in the kitchens of buildings adjacent to what may have been Midas's palace on the Gordion citadel.[8]

The collection of bronze vessels used to serve the "mixed fermented beverage" of wine, beer, and mead has an importance that extends well beyond a Phrygian funerary feast. Later Greeks would have turned up their noses at such a concoction, but Homer describes a drink (Greek *kykeon*) that combines wine, barley meal, honey, and goat's cheese (*Iliad* 11:628–643; *Odyssey* 10.229–243). *Kykeon* is probably best translated as "mixture," and a range of ancient Greek texts,[9] extending down to Plato and the Eleusinian mysteries, suggests that any number of ingredients (herbs, spice, wine, milk, honey, oil, and water) might be tossed into the brew. Pliny the Elder

---

[8] DeVries, "Greeks and Phrygians," 39.

[9] Ridgway, "Nestor's Cup," 326–329.

(*Natural History* 14.113) claims that the best mead in the world was still being made in Phrygia in the first century A.D.

Recent chemical analyses by MASCA's Molecular Archaeology Laboratory of numerous late Mycenaean and Minoan drinking vessels, dated between 1400 and 1130 B.C., have shown that they were filled with a mixed fermented beverage nearly identical to that from Tumulus MM.[10] In other words, centuries before the Phrygians arrived in Anatolia, such a beverage was known and enjoyed in Greece and on Crete.

The main entrée of the funerary banquet also provided a strange, evocative parallel to Bronze Age Greek cuisine. As our evidence showed, a stew of sheep/goat, lentils, and other vegetables was eaten at the funerary feast associated with Tumulus MM. Similarly, lamb and lentil concoctions, sometimes flavored with olive oil, honey, wine, and various spices, figure prominently in Minoan and Mycenaean cuisines.

Acknowledgments

Dr. Elizabeth Simpson first proposed the project to the writer. In addition to my scientific colleagues on the project, other invaluable help was provided by Drs. Keith DeVries, Gretchen R. Hall, Ellen L. Kohler, Naomi F. Miller, Rudolph H. Michel, and G. Kenneth Sams. The chemical analyses of Mycenaean and Minoan pottery were done in collaboration with Drs. C. Holley Martlew and Yannis Tzedakis, with support from the European Union.

---

[10] See McGovern, "Retsina, Mixed Fermented Beverages." McGovern, Glusker, Exner and Hall, "Chemical Identification of Resinated Wine." Pain, "Grog of the Greeks."

APPENDIX 6

GRAFFITI ON THE WOODEN SERVING STANDS FROM TUMULUS MM

LYNN E. ROLLER

*Department of Art History
University of California, Davis*

Both of the two large wooden serving stands with inlaid decoration from Tumulus MM have several tenons that were incised with graffiti. In order to understand the relationship of the graffiti to the serving stands, it is useful to review briefly how these tenons functioned in the construction of the stands. The inlaid faces of the stands were made from boards or panels of wood, and the separate panels were then joined together with tenons fitted into mortises cut into the edges of the panels. Some of the tenons were separate pieces of wood that were inserted into mortises cut into two adjoining panels, while others were formed from the wood of the individual boards, appearing as tabs that extended from the ends of the panels (see Figures 49 and 57). Once inserted into the panels, the tenons were in most cases secured by wooden pins driven through both panel and tenon. Some groups of panels, e.g. boards 1, 2, and 3 (at the top center of each serving stand face); boards 5 and 6; 8 and 9; and 7 and 11 (at the lower left, right, and center respectively) were joined by tenons and pins and then inlaid. The two long side boards (boards 4 and 10) were inlaid separately (see Figures 62 and 64 for numbered boards and graffiti locations). Finally, the various sections of the serving stands were joined together with the same tenon-and-pin method (see pp. 68–71 and 81).

All of the visible graffiti occur on the tenons that extended from the ends of the wooden panels; none appears on a separate, or "free" tenon. The graffiti occur on tenons that were used to join the inlaid panel groups to adjacent boards, suggesting that the graffiti may have been incised while the groups were being inlaid.[1] In every case, the graffiti were incised onto the upper face of the tenon, i.e., the face nearest to the decorated face of the stands. Because the tenons were to be inserted into a mortise in an adjoining panel, none of the graffiti would have been visible after the serving stands had been fully assembled.

A total of 12 tenons now show graffiti.[2] Seven such tenons have been noted on serving stand A (see Figure 62) and three on serving stand B (Figure 64). The remaining two were loose pieces which had apparently broken off the stands; their original position remains uncertain.

Description of Graffiti

Serving Stand A

A1 (Figure 63A, Plate 93A)
Tenon extends down at the bottom of board 5, the left in the group of two vertical panels at the left of the large rosette in the center of the stand's face. Tenon originally fit into a mortise in the upper edge of the left curved leg, now missing. Pin hole in center.

To the left of the pin hole and overlapping its outer edge: a small incised compass-drawn circle, roughly the same diameter as the pin hole.

A2 (Figure 63B, Plate 93B)
Tenon extends down at an angle from the bottom of board 6, the vertical panel to the left of the

---

[1] As some of the groups of panels are still intact, with tenons and pins still in place, not all the tenons are visible; this suggestion must therefore remain hypothetical.

[2] For a preliminary discussion of the graffiti, see Simpson, "Wooden Furniture from Tumulus MM at Gordion, Turkey," 122–123 (serving stand A), and 130–131 (serving stand B).

central rosette. Tenon originally fit into a mortise in the upper edge of the left curved leg, now missing. Pin hole to the right of center.

Graffito near the left edge of the tenon: a series of four small diamonds, arranged as if on the four points of a larger diamond pattern. The two small diamonds at the two horizontal points of the larger diamond pattern each have a small incised point in their centers.

A3 (Figure 63C, Plate 93C)

Tenon extends out to the left from the left end of board 3, the lowest in the group of three horizontal panels forming the upper part of the serving stand face. Tenon fits into a mortise in the right edge of board 4, the long left side board. Two pin holes, near either side of the tenon.

Graffito incised between pin holes, touching the hole at right, as shown in Figure 63C: a complex pattern of four concentric circles with smaller arcs irregularly drawn within the confines of the outer circle. A point forms the center of the three small concentric circles whose diameters increase at roughly equal proportions. A fourth circle, the outer circle of the group, is notably larger than the three inner circles. Extending inward from the circumference of the outer circle at the four cardinal points are four arcs from circles of roughly equal diameter. The pin pricks of the centers of these arcs are visible on the circumference of the outer circle. Three additional arcs extend in towards the center, in two instances overlapping the central group of three concentric circles. Extending out from the periphery of the outermost of the central group of three circles is an arc from another, much smaller circle. All circles and arcs were drawn with a compass. Also visible are two short curves within two of the outer arcs and a line at the lower right that intersects at two points with the outer circle.

A4 (Figure 63D, Plate 93D)

Tenon extends from the right end of board 2, the middle in the group of three horizontal panels forming the upper part of the serving stand face. Tenon fits into a mortise in the left edge of board 10, the long right side board. Two pin holes. Edge of tenon is broken off beyond the left pin hole, as shown in Figure 63D; this edge is now missing, as is the corner at the lower right.

Graffito extends across the surface of the tenon: a series of nine lines, five parallel to one another, then four lines parallel to each other

but at a slightly different angle, all extending diagonally across the tenon.

A5 (Figure 63E, Plate 93E)

Tenon extends from the right end of board 1, the uppermost in the group of three horizontal panels forming the upper part of the serving stand. Tenon fits into a mortise in the left edge of board 10. Two pin holes. Tenon cracked with some wood missing.

Graffito near the outer edge of the tenon: two rows of small half-circles, each one formed with a compass, in a row on either side of an incised line, with a whole circle at either end. The central points of the half-circles lie approximately along the line. The ends of the arcs of the half-circles on one side of the line are used as the centers of the half-circles on the other side, so that the effect is roughly similar to an alternating scallop pattern running along a central line. At the inner part of the crack in the tenon, parts of two more incised circles are visible.

A6 (Figure 63F, Plate 93F)

Tenon extends from the left edge of board 2, the middle in the group of three horizontal panels forming the upper part of the serving stand. Tenon fits into a mortise in the right edge of board 4. Two pin holes.

Graffito between the pin holes: three concentric circles, two of them small and close to the center, the third larger. A small arc extending out from the innermost of the two small circles. All circles drawn with a compass. At the left of the circles, as shown in Figure 63F, two parallel lines incised into the wood, one nearly tangential to the outer circle, one beyond it. Several lines, lightly cut into the wood, randomly placed on the tenon face.

A7 (Figure 63G, Plate 93G)

Tenon extends from the upper end of board 6, the vertical panel at left of the central rosette. Tenon fits into a mortise in the lower edge of board 3, the lowest in the group of three horizontal panels forming the upper part of the serving stand. One pin hole.

Graffito adjacent to pin hole: two lines extending from pin hole to form a right angle; trace of an arc between them; an additional line below, almost forming a trapezoid. Two parallel lines, both parallel to the end of the tenon, and several other short lines.

Serving Stand B

B1 (Figure 65A, Plate 94A)
Tenon extends down at the bottom of board 5, the left in the group of two vertical panels at the left of the central rosette. Tenon originally fit into a mortise in the upper edge of the left curved leg, now missing. One pin hole. The wood of the tenon has split.

Complex pattern of graffiti extends across tenon: between the pin hole and the lower left corner, as shown in Figure 65A, a six-petal rosette inscribed within a compass-drawn circle. Next to this, four straight lines, with three or four alphabetic letters written over them. The pin hole cuts into one petal of the rosette. The arcs forming the rosette petals are segments of a circle with the same circumference as the surrounding circle; thus the rosette petals were drawn by a compass together with the circle and were intended as part of the same design pattern.[3] To the right of the pin hole are four straight lines, three of which fan out toward the lower right corner from a central point to the right of the pin hole; the fourth line, slightly to the left of the other three, extends down from the pin hole through the edge of the inscribed rosette. Across these lines were incised three letters, *o e s*; an additional mark, two lines forming a right angle as if intended to be the beginning of another *s*, can be seen to the right of the *s*. The *s* has three or four bars.[4] The *e* has three cross-bars and is written with the open side of the *e* pointing downward. The *o* resembles a diamond formed by four straight lines.

Because this tenon extends downward from the vertical panel of the serving stand, these letters have been read from left to right, as they would read if the tenon were in place. Since, however, the letters were clearly incised before the tenon was inserted into the curved leg, they could just as easily have been incised onto the tenon by someone holding the panel with the tenon in some other direction, in which case the letters could read *s e o*, with the additional angled strokes to the left of the *s*. Either reading, *s e o* or the reverse, *o e s*, would be possible from the form of the letters.

B2 (Figure 65B, Plate 94B)
Tenon extends up at the top of board 9, the second in the group of two vertical panels to the right of the central rosette. Tenon fits into a mortise in the lower edge of board 3, the lowest of the three horizontal panels forming the upper part of the serving stand. One pin hole.

Graffito between pin hole and lower left corner, as shown in Figure 65B: half of a compass-drawn circle. Compass prick visible at the center.

B3 (Figure 65C, Plate 94C)
Tenon extends up at the top of board 8, the vertical panel to the right of the central rosette. Tenon fits into a mortise in the lower edge of board 3, the lowest of the three horizontal panels forming the upper part of the serving stand. Two pin holes. The wood of the tenon has split.

Graffito between the pin holes: two arcs.

Tenons Whose Original Placement Is Unknown

Two broken tenons that bear graffiti remain unattributed. The first, U1, is broken but nearly complete and apparently once belonged to serving stand A or B; it has one pin hole. The second, U2, is very fragmentary, with only a small portion of the finished edge of the tenon and part of the pin hole preserved.

U1 (Figure 66, left; Plate 94D, left)
Tenon broken off from beyond the pin hole; preserved to the finished outer edge and now mended from two joining pieces. Graffito over much of the tenon: on one piece, two light parallel strokes, next to them two deeper strokes forming a V; on the other piece, one light stroke and two deeper strokes forming a right angle. Two small dots on each piece, to either side of the break line; this perhaps indicates that the tenon was broken and repaired in antiquity.

U2 (Figure 66, right; Plate 94D, right)
Fragment of a tenon, inscribed with two curved strokes forming a right angle.

---

[3] See p. 192.
[4] The drawing illustrated in Figure 65A shows three bars, the result of close examination of the tenon; the photograph (Plate 94A) gives the impression that a fourth bar was present, which remains a possibility.

Function and Meaning of the Graffiti

The graffiti appear to have served several different functions, including test cuts in the wood, practice designs for the decorative inlay of the serving stands' faces, and perhaps marks of personal identity by the artisans. Thus they permit some interesting observations on furniture making, craftsmen, and literacy at Gordion. One comment should be made at the outset: the graffiti were apparently not fitter's marks to indicate to the carpenters the way in which the stands were to be assembled. This is suggested by the random distribution of the tenons with graffiti and also their relatively small number. Serving stand B provides clearer evidence for this assumption than serving stand A.

Serving stand A had 39 tenons joining the panels and front legs of the stand's face, and these tenons provided 56 upper surfaces that would once have been available for graffiti— single tenons extending out from the ends of boards would have had one upper surface available, and double tenons (free tenons) would have had two. Of these 56 available surfaces, only seven show graffiti. However, only 20 of these 56 surfaces are still visible,[5] so there may well be more graffiti on tenons that are still in place in their mortises. Serving stand B had 43 tenons used to join the parts of the stand's face, with 63 tenon surfaces available for graffiti. Of these available surfaces, 25 are still visible. Yet only three of these tenon surfaces bear graffiti. Moreover, these serving stands were the only two pieces of furniture from the tomb that had graffiti inscribed on their tenons. All these details taken together suggest that the graffiti were not fitter's marks.

Some patterns among the graffiti on the serving stands can be observed. Several of them are basic forms, such as straight lines, compass-drawn circles, or partial circles, which comprise the foundational elements of the abstract designs that decorate the serving stand faces. Examples include the lines in graffiti A4, A6, and B1; the plain circle in graffito A1; and the simple arcs found in B2 and B3. These could be explained as the markings of an inlay artist who was making practice cuts in the wood, perhaps to test his tools before beginning the actual cuts on the serving stand face.[6]

Other graffiti depict more complex geometric designs, and it is possible that these were trial sketches for the complex geometric ornaments found on the serving stand faces. This seems a likely interpretation for A6, a series of concentric circles, and B1, a six-petaled rosette inscribed within a compass-drawn circle.[7] The most elaborate pattern drawn with a compass is that of A3, a series of overlapping concentric circles and arcs. This pattern of concentric circles and overlapping arcs is reminiscent of the central rosettes on both serving stand faces and may, in fact, indicate the technique used to lay out these designs.[8] Graffito A3 could have been a trial sketch for the central rosette of serving stand A. The pattern of graffito B1, the six-petaled flower, recurs in the inlay work on the faces of both serving stands, in the smaller rosettes at the upper ends of both curved legs where they touch the lower periphery of the large central rosette (see Figures 50, 58).[9] This suggests that several of the graffiti on the tenons may have been produced as reduced-scale sketches for the patterns to be inlaid on the front faces of the stands.[10] This explanation could also apply to A2, the set of four diamonds, the pattern found in the background inlay that covers the faces of the stands. Graffito A5, the scallop pattern, has no direct parallel in the inlay pattern of either serving stand face, but it does occur among the patterns inlaid on one of the handles of the ornate inlaid table from the tomb.[11]

---

[5] Some of the tenons are still in place in their mortises with their joints intact, some are broken off and still lodged in the mortises, and some are missing altogether. See above, pp. 68–69, for the mortise-and-tenon joinery.

[6] This theory was first proposed by Simpson, "Wooden Furniture from Tumulus MM at Gordion, Turkey," n. 171.

[7] This too was a type of decorative pattern found on other objects at Gordion, including a six-petaled flower in a circle on a polished knucklebone, unpublished, Gordion inventory no. BI 223, and a five-petaled flower on another bone, inventory no. BI 372. On these pieces its only function seems to have been ornamental.

[8] This theory was first proposed by Simpson, "Wooden Furniture from Tumulus MM at Gordion, Turkey," 122–123.

This possibility can be demonstrated by the presence of the pinprick used to fix the stationary arm of the compass, still visible in the center of the rosette as well as in the centers of the semicircles of the surrounding pattern. Young, *Gordion I*, 179, n. 112, and see above, pp. 66 and 70, for compass pricks visible on the faces of stands A and B.

[9] See above, pp. 66, 71.

[10] See above, p. 70.

[11] See Figure 16. As has been mentioned, such graffiti are not found on the table with elaborate inlay work from Tumulus MM. Therefore, the artists who inlaid the table were either practicing on separate pieces of wood or did not feel the need to execute such preliminary sketches.

There are several graffiti that do not fit this hypothesis, for they bear no resemblance to anything that could be called a sketch or trial design for the inlay work on the faces of the serving stands. These include the letter forms of B1 and the marks of A7, U1, and U2. The frequent occurrence of similar nonverbal graffiti at Gordion may contribute to an understanding of the markings on the stands' tenons. Such nonverbal graffiti were found throughout the site and on a variety of materials, including pottery, stone, and bone objects. One class of these nonverbal marks was incised on utilitarian objects, primarily pottery cups and bowls. This class, which includes non-alphabetic marks, individual letters, and pictures, is discussed and illustrated in *Gordion Special Studies I*.[12] Many of these nonverbal marks, particularly those found on pottery, appear to have been owners' marks, that is, marks that were applied by the owner of the vessel to signify personal possession.[13] Some of the graffiti on the furniture tenons bear a strong resemblance to such owners' marks. The plain circle, found in A1 (and in incomplete form in B2), was used as a non-alphabetic mark on a bowl from the destruction level at Gordion.[14] The markings of graffito U1 could be either non-alphabetic marks or letter forms; these marks are paralleled by several of the non-alphabetic symbols found on Gordion pottery[15] and may also be read as alphabetic letters, *l i i* and *i g* (both sinistroverse). The marks of A7 and U2 may be read as an alphabetic letter, in both cases as *g*. The presence of definite letter forms on B1 demonstrates that the tenons' graffiti could indeed include letters.

Whether alphabetic or non-alphabetic, the graffiti on the serving stands were surely not marks of personal ownership. The elaborate stands were clearly intended for use by members of the upper class and were not the property of the artisans who made them. Nor does it seem likely that any of those graffiti that include letter forms could be an artist's signature in the modern sense of an artist's public acknowledgement of his work: the tenons with graffiti would not have been visible once the serving stands were assembled.

Yet it is possible that both the letter forms and the geometric patterns could have been a form of personal expression by the artists. The regular use of complex patterns among the nonverbal graffiti found elsewhere at Gordion suggests that the designs of circles, lines, and diamonds could have served as another type of artistic signature. It seems evident that the artists who designed the inlays on the serving stand faces deliberately introduced a clever play with symmetry into the patterns.[16] The individuals who drew the graffiti may have been these same artists, who could have been making these markings for their own amusement. The use of such patterning as a form of personal signature was frequent on Phrygian pottery,[17] so it would not be surprising to find the phenomenon on the serving stands. Thus, the graffiti could be forms of playful artistic signatures, permissible because they would not have been visible. This suggestion follows the results of closer analysis of the geometric patterns in the inlay of the Gordion serving stands. Such analysis makes it increasingly certain that some of these patterns are not purely abstract, but were in fact laid out intentionally to communicate a message.[18] The individuals who drew the furniture graffiti could have been using these abstract symbols to communicate, perhaps simply their names, perhaps some aspect of the symbolism, most likely a religious symbolism, present in the same designs on the serving stands' faces, much as a Christian stone mason might carve a cross as a mason's mark on his work. The parallels between these graffiti and the other Gordion marks suggest that the artisans left the graffiti as a record of their individual personalities, even knowing that it would be ephemeral. In sum, the graffiti appear to have served several purposes. Some may have been practice cuts in the wood, some may have been sketches reflecting the inlay designs, and some may represent the artists' doodling, a form of playful design reflecting the artists' personalities.

---

[12] Roller, *Nonverbal Graffiti*.

[13] Ibid., 8–54.

[14] Ibid., nos. 2A-15. As noted above, these circles could also be the artisans' practice marks with a compass.

[15] These are illustrated in Roller, *Nonverbal Graffiti*, nos. 2A-140, 2A-169, 2A-208, 2B-43, 2B-69, 2B-83, 2B-140.

[16] See above, pp. 77–83, and Simpson, "Phrygian Artistic Intellect," 28–29; "Symbols on the Gordion Screens," 631.

[17] Roller, *Nonverbal Graffiti*, 10.

[18] See above, pp. 83–110, and Simpson, "Phrygian Artistic Intellect," 28–34; "Symbols on the Gordion Screens."

Finally, a few specific comments should be made on the letters in graffito B1. As noted above, these letters could be read in either direction, *s e o* or *o e s*, neither of which occurs as a name in the corpus of Phrygian inscriptions published by Claude Brixhe and Michel Lejeune. The former reading seems more likely, for then the letters would comprise the first three letters of an individual name. Inscribing groups of three or more letters on individual objects, usually pottery, was a frequent practice at Gordion, and these too have commonly been assumed to represent proper names.[19] The letter graffito on the furniture tenon offers one of the earliest examples of this practice, for clearly the graffito was incised onto the wooden tenon before the tomb was closed in the eighth century B.C.[20] Alphabetic writing was known in Gordion at this early date, and there are five examples of alphabetic texts on other objects from Tumulus MM. These occur on bowls placed in the tomb and were incised either directly onto the bowl (one bronze and one pottery example) or onto wax applied to bronze bowls.[21] Two of these graffiti also consist of three letters, and one contains four letters; the remaining two comprise longer words. Thus graffito B1 on the furniture tenon adds another valuable example to the corpus of Phrygian alphabetic inscriptions from the eighth century B.C. If the marks on the tenons A7, U1, and U2 are also letter forms, this would add further examples of early alphabetic marks to the early Phrygian epigraphical corpus.[22]

The position of the letters on the wooden tenon is also significant, as it indicates that this was clearly a casual graffito, not a formal public inscription, and was presumably inscribed by one of the artisans working on the furniture. This suggests strongly that already in the eighth century B.C. knowledge of alphabetic writing had spread beyond an elite class and was known to workers and craftsmen. The angular forms of the letters and their presence on wooden objects are also of interest. All Phrygian letter forms from eighth century inscriptions have this angular quality, suggesting that these letters were developed to be written on a hard medium, one in which every stroke was some form of a straight line. Such is clearly the case with graffiti on bronze and pottery, but the Gordion furniture graffito B1 indicates that this situation obtains for texts on wood as well.

This point is worth noting, since it may offer an explanation for the lack of complex texts in the Phrygian language, a circumstance that has long been remarked upon. A people with the artistic sensibility to create the fine wooden and metal objects such as those found in the Gordion tombs, and with the ready knowledge of alphabetic writing indicated by the frequency of alphabetic graffiti in various media, would very likely have had a tradition of literary and historical texts as well. Yet almost none is known from Phrygia.[23] Could the Phrygian alphabet have been developed to write on wooden tablets, or, more likely, tablets made of wood whose leaves

[19] Brixhe and Lejeune, *Corpus*, 95. Roller, *Nonverbal Graffiti*, 33–34. Brixhe, "Corpus, Supplément I," 24–99.

[20] The date of the tumulus, still a source of uncertainty, has recently been reexamined. A date in the late eighth century B.C., proposed in Young, *Gordion I*, 270, is considered by some to be about 30 years too low; this proposal is based on recent dendrochronological studies that indicate a date in the third quarter of the eighth century B.C. for the cutting of the outer logs of the chamber. Manning, et al., "Confirmation of Near-Absolute Dating of East Mediterranean Bronze-Iron Dendrochronology." For the purposes of this discussion, a shift of about one generation is not significant; what is important is that alphabetic writing was known and used in Gordion at the time of the Tumulus MM burial, as is clearly demonstrated by the presence of alphabetic inscriptions on five vessels found in the tomb. See Brixhe, "Graffites du grand tumulus."

[21] For publication of the graffiti on bowls from Tumulus MM, see Brixhe, "Graffites du grand tumulus," and Brixhe and Lejeune, *Corpus*, nos. G-105 through G-109.

[22] Apart from the graffiti on the tenons of the serving stands, there are six examples of Phrygian inscriptions from Gordion that can be securely dated to the eighth century B.C.: the five already noted from Tumulus MM (supra n. 21) and a series of graffiti on the lowest beam of the roofing system at the west side of the tomb chambers, first recorded in 2007.

[23] Roller, "Art of Writing at Gordion," 54–61, especially 60. Two exceptions to this pattern are two longer texts in the Phrygian language, one from Bithynia (Brixhe and Lejeune, *Corpus*, 62–63, no. B-01), probably a religious text, and one that may be an historical document (Brixhe and Lejeune, *Corpus*, 258, no. T-01).

were coated with hardened wax?[24] An abundance of wood, used for both structural and decorative purposes, was available at Gordion in the eighth century B.C.; it may have been through this medium that Phrygian intellectual activities were recorded—and because of the ephemeral nature of this medium that these creations are now lost.

[24] [Simpson author's note] A boxwood tablet with two leaves that were scored to receive a wax coating was found in the Late Bronze Age Uluburun shipwreck (although the wax was not preserved). See Bass, "Oldest Known Shipwreck Reveals Splendors of the Bronze Age," 730–731; also Payton, "Ulu Burun Writing-Board Set," and Warnock and Pendleton, "Wood of the Ulu Burun Diptych." This practice pertained in the early first millennium B.C. as well, as indicated by wood and ivory tablets found at Nimrud with writing surfaces scored to receive wax. These tablets have been dated to the later eighth century B.C. and are approximately contemporary with the Tumulus MM burial. See Mallowan, *Nimrud and Its Remains*, 152–162. Adhering to the surface of some of the wood boards from Nimrud were the remains of the original wax coating, with some of the cuneiform signs impressed in the wax still visible. One of the ivory writing boards had evidently once contained an important astrological text with omens derived from observations of the sun, moon, planets, and stars.

Although the Assyrian writing boards were utilized for the writing of cuneiform script, there is evidence that such boards were also used for alphabetic writing. The well-known stele of King Barrekub from Zincirli, dating to the eighth century B.C., shows the seated king and his scribe, who has a writing board tucked under his arm. Presumably the scribe would have been writing in the same Aramaic alphabetic script that is present on the stone stele itself. Akurgal, *Art of the Hittites*, plate 131. Such writing boards also appear in Greek literature, beginning with Homer. For an unusual occurrence of a Spartan writing directly on the wood of a tablet, see Mallowan, *Nimrud and Its Remains*, 159.

WOODWORKING TOOLS AND TECHNIQUES

Elizabeth Simpson

The Tumulus MM furniture provides substantial evidence for Phrygian woodworking techniques at Gordion. These have been discussed above, in relation to the various pieces of furniture from the tomb. It may be useful to summarize this information here and to situate the methods and materials used at Gordion within their wider context. The Phrygian tool kit was much like that from Egypt or elsewhere in the Near East (Text Figure 6),[1] and not very different from the assemblage employed by later cabinetmakers before the advent of mechanization and use of electricity.[2] The ancient tool kit, in essence, is still seen in many parts of the world today.

There is evidence from Gordion for the saw, axe, chisel, scraper, awl, knife, compass, and bow drill (Plates 150–152), as well as the lathe, although the clearest indication of the lathe is found not on the Tumulus MM furniture but on the wood plates from Tumulus W.[3] The adze must also have been used at Gordion, as it was known in the Near East by the second millennium B.C. The earliest depiction of a Near East-ern woodworker, on a terra-cotta plaque from the Old Babylonian period, shows a man seated on a stool wielding an adze to make a curved leg, much like those of the Gordion tables.[4] The versatile adze could be used to hew, trim, and true timber as well as shape more complex forms.[5] These tools can be seen in use in depictions from Egyptian tombs, such as the reliefs from the tomb of Ti at Saqqara (Dynasty V);[6] the model carpenter's shop from the tomb of Meket-re, now in Cairo (Dynasty XI);[7] and the painted scenes from the tomb of Rekhmire at Thebes (Dynasty XVIII).[8] Bronze and iron tools and tool fragments have been recovered from the city mound at Gordion, representing saws, axes, an adze(?), and several awls and chisels; two of the iron chisels were preserved with their bone handles intact.[9]

The woods used for the Tumulus MM furniture include cedar for the coffin body; pine for the corner blocks; yew and boxwood for the coffin rails;[10] and boxwood, juniper, walnut, yew, and possibly maple or cherry for the furniture

---

[1] Ricketts, "Furniture from the Middle Bronze Age Tombs," figure 227. For a recent analysis of the woods used for the Jericho furniture and a discussion of technology, see Cartwright, "Bronze Age Wooden Tomb Furniture from Jericho."

[2] Sloane, *Museum of Early American Tools.*

[3] Simpson, "Use of the Lathe in Antiquity." As Tumulus W is earlier than Tumulus MM, the lathe would have been available to the later woodworkers. The curved legs of the Tumulus MM tables were not formed on a lathe, contra Young, *Gordion I*, 260. The Tumulus MM pieces most likely to have been made on a lathe are the leg tops of the inlaid table (see below).

[4] Simpson, "Furniture in Ancient Western Asia," 1653, figure 8. Werr, "Domestic Furniture in Iraq," plate 10A.

[5] Killen, "Ancient Egyptian Carpentry," 15. The adze could serve much the same purpose as the modern plane. The plane (*runcina*) was in use by the Roman period. Pliny, *Natural History* 16.225. For a discussion of Roman tools, see Ulrich, *Roman Woodworking*, 13–58.

[6] Circa 2400 B.C. See H. Baker, *Furniture in the Ancient World*, figure 459, which shows the sawing of wood, work with the chisel and bow drill, and the smoothing of the surface of a bed by rubbing.

[7] Circa 2000 B.C. H. Baker, *Furniture in the Ancient World*, figure 462. Saleh and Sourouzian, *The Egyptian Museum Cairo*, figure 78. The carpenters saw planks, work with adzes, cut mortises with a chisel and mallet, and smooth the surface of a finished piece of wood.

[8] Circa 1420 B.C. H. Baker, *Furniture in the Ancient World*, figures 460–461. Killen, "Ancient Egyptian Carpentry," figure 7. The same kinds of activities are seen in the tomb of Rekhmire, including the assembly of a shrine and mounting of its decoration.

[9] One of the iron chisels with bone handles may have been a woodworker's chisel (9018 ILS 504). The candidates for woodworking tools from Gordion will be published in Simpson, *Gordion Wooden Objects II* (forthcoming).

[10] The identification of the light wood of the rails as boxwood is probable but not conclusive; see above, p. 122, n. 22, and Appendix 3.

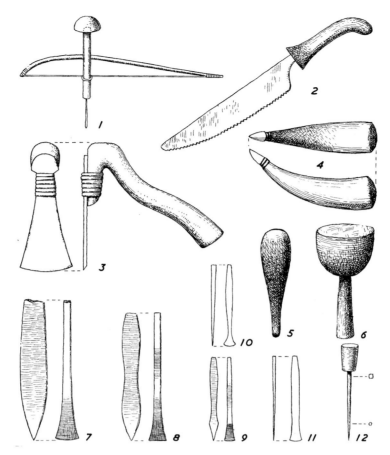

Text Figure 6. Illustrations of Egyptian carpenters' tools
(Kenyon, *Jericho I*, figure 227): (1) bow drill; (2) ripping saw
(Tomb of Rekhmire); (3) adze (ca. 1600 B.C.); (4) oil horn; (5)
mallet; (6) stone mason's mallet; (7) mortising chisel
(Tell el-Amarna); (8) mortising chisel (Thebes, New
Kingdom); (9) mortising chisel (Abydos, Old Kingdom);
(10) flat chisel (Tell el-Amarna); (11) flat chisel (Abydos,
Old Kingdom); (12) awl (Thebes, New Kingdom).

(Appendix 3).[11] These woods were available in the area of Gordion or could be procured from neighboring regions.[12] Boxwood was chosen for the frame, legs, and struts of the inlaid table; for the legs of the plain tables; for the face, side, and back pieces of the serving stands; and for parts of the furniture from the northeast corner. Walnut was preferred for all the table tops except one (table 6), and for the top piece and curved front legs of the serving stands.[13] Juniper was used for the decorative inlay of the stands and inlaid table, as well as for the back slats of the chair from the northeast corner. The small blocks below the front feet on the face of serving stand B were made of yew.

Boxwood is a hard, dense, fine-grained wood that is cream colored and well suited for carving. The boxwood elements of the Tumulus MM

---

[11] The results published here (Appendix 3) supersede Aytuğ, "Kral Midas'la Gömülen Mobilyalar" and "Le mobilier funéraire du roi Midas I."

[12] Miller, "Interpreting Ancient Environment," 18–19. Meiggs, *Trees and Timber*, 459. Hepper, "Timber Trees of Western Asia," 2–3, 6–8. For modern distribution, see Davis, *Flora of Turkey*, vol. 1: 72–74 (*Pinus sylvestris* L.), 71–72 (*Cedrus libani* Loud.), 76 (*Taxus baccata* L.), 82 (*Juniperus foetidissima* Willd.); vol. 7: 631 (*Buxus sempervirens* L.), 654 (*Juglans regia*

L.). On the difficulty of identifying cedar, pine, juniper, and walnut in ancient texts, see Meiggs, 410–422; Moorey, *Ancient Mesopotamian Materials and Industries*, 349–351. For boxwood, see below. Curiously, Vitruvius states that the Phrygians lived in the plain, without forests, and lacked timber, suggesting that by this time the main settlement areas may have been deforested. Vitruvius, *De architectura* 2.1.5.

[13] The top of table 6 was made from a different kind of wood, possibly maple or cherry.

furniture were originally light in color, although they have now aged to a dark, warm brown. The inlaid decoration, made from reddish-brown juniper inlay, would have stood out from the boxwood backing in striking contrast. The tops and accents of walnut provided yet a third color and grain configuration. Although lacking their original surface finish, clearly, the three pieces of inlaid furniture from Tumulus MM were once dramatic statements, featuring spectacular optical effects created through fine detailing in woods of contrasting colors. These effects are evoked by the pen-and-ink reconstruction drawings and color frontispiece in this volume (see, for instance, Figures 21, 50, 58, and Frontispiece). The inlaid table should also be envisioned with its precious metal attachments, which must have sheathed the corners of the frame and enlivened the inlaid panels of the four handles.[14]

Boxwood was widely appreciated in antiquity, as revealed in Near Eastern, Greek, and Roman texts. The Akkadian *taskarinnu* has been identified as boxwood, attested in the third millennium B.C. and used in the second millennium at Mari for stools, beds, and other types of furniture.[15] In the first millennium B.C., the Assyrians dedicated this costly wood to the gods and used it for their palaces, along with cedar, juniper, and pine.[16] The Urartians were also fond of boxwood; unfortunately, they lost much valuable boxwood furniture, some of it inlaid with gold and silver, when Sargon II sacked the city of Musasir in 714 B.C.[17] Boxwood is mentioned in the Bible, and actual

boxwood furniture fragments have been recovered from excavations in Jerusalem.[18]

Theophrastus discusses boxwood (πύξος) in his *Enquiry into Plants*, and here its identity is certain.[19] In his time, the largest boxwood trees grew in Corsica, but box was also found in Macedonian Olympos and in Kytoros (Κύτωρα), a mountain town in Paphlagonia on the south shore of the Black Sea. Pliny confirmed the habitat of boxwood (*buxus*), adding the Pyrenees and the mountainous Berecynthus district.[20] Berecynthus was located somewhere to the southwest of Gordion and was said to be sacred to Cybele, the Mother of the Gods.[21] Ovid calls Midas "Berecyntian hero," as he recounts the story of the king's fatal gift.[22] Thus boxwood was associated with the Magna Mater in Roman times and may have been sacred to the goddess Matar in the Phrygian period. Large boxwood trees are now rare, but a hundred years ago boxwood (*Buxus sempervirens* L.) was still plentiful on the south shore of the Black Sea.[23]

The Tumulus MM furniture was made from wood that was cut and seasoned, with the forms first roughed out and then finely finished. The boards used for the table tops and faces of the serving stands were flat cut, or cut through the log at its greatest diameter, as is evident from the grain pattern visible at the ends and on the surface.[24] Much of the forming must have been done with an adze (Text Figure 6:3), which was surely used to make the table legs and tray-like tops.[25] The curved legs of the inlaid table

[14] See above, p. 39.

[15] Reiner, *Assyrian Dictionary* 18, "T," 280–282. Salonen, *Die Möbel des alten Mesopotamien*, 225–226. Kupper, "Le bois à Mari," 167. But see Powell, "Timber Production in Presargonic Lagaš," 120, on the difficulty of identifying woods mentioned in Near Eastern texts; Van De Mieroop, "Wood in the Old Babylonian Texts," 160: *taskarinnum*, "boxwood(?)".

[16] Luckenbill, *Ancient Records 1*, 173, 186 (Assurnasirpal II); *Ancient Records 2*, 37 (Sargon II), 161 (Sennacherib). On the difficulty of identifying woods in texts, supra n. 15.

[17] Luckenbill, *Ancient Records 2*, 95–97.

[18] Isaiah 41.19; 60.13, in which boxwood is said to have grown in Lebanon along with cypress and pine. For boxwood finds from the City of David excavations, see above, p. 44, n. 78.

[19] Fourth – early third century B.C. Theophrastus, *Enquiry into Plants* 3.15.5. On the botanical writings of Theophrastus and Pliny, see Meiggs, *Trees and Timber*, 17–29. Boxwood was known to Homer (πύξινος). *Iliad* 24.269.

[20] Pliny, *Natural History* 16.70–71, in which he rates boxwood "in the first rank" for its smooth surface, pale color, and hardness. Theophrastus comments on the heaviness and hardness of boxwood. Theophrastus, *Enquiry into Plants* 5.3.1,

7. Pliny places the district of Berecynthus in Caria. Pliny, *Natural History* 5.108.

[21] Virgil, *Aeneid* 6.784, 9.82. Virgil also refers to "Berecyntian" boxwood flutes played in connection with the worship of the Magna Mater. *Aeneid* 9.617–620.

[22] Ovid, *Metamorphoses* 11.106.

[23] It has been estimated that, prior to 1864, a boxwood forest of 7,000 acres grew on the shore of the Black Sea. Lynn Batdorf, personal communication (March 2, 1987), Gordion Furniture Project archives. Record and Garratt, "Boxwoods," 18. For a map showing the current distribution of boxwood in Turkey, see Symmes, "Native Stands of Boxwood in Modern Turkey," 78.

[24] For the drying of wood, see Hoadley, *Understanding Wood*, 147–157; and see above, p. 133, n. 62. For flat-cut (or flatsawn) wood and figure in wood, see Hoadley, 14, 25–45. For the grain pattern characteristic of flat-cut boards, see also Ulrich, *Roman Woodworking*, figure 11.16 (top). The wide boxwood boards used for the faces of the serving stands were cut all the way through the log, incorporating the pith.

[25] See Simpson, "Furniture in Ancient Western Asia," 1653, figure 8, for such a leg in production. For the use of the adze for the fabrication of the tops of the Jericho tables, see Ricketts, "Furniture from the Middle Bronze Age

and plain tables were not steam bent but were made from naturally bent or trained branches (Plate 152C).[26] This is suggested by the grain pattern observable on the legs (Figures 28, 33–34). The legs of the plain tables were likely made from stems or branches that were relatively close in diameter to that of the final product. The front leg of the inlaid table was apparently made from a piece that was substantially larger in diameter than that of the leg; this was necessitated by the sharper curve at the bottom.[27]

The legs of the inlaid table were made from three separate pieces of wood: the curved lower part of the leg; the carved, inlaid top piece; and a square dowel that ran through the carved top piece and into a mortise cut in the curved leg (Figure 27). The square dowel extended up to form a tenon at the top of the leg; this tenon fit into a mortise cut into a "collar" that projected from the underside of the table top. This collar-and-tenon system was also used to join the legs to the tops of the plain tables from the tomb (Figure 39).[28] The three carved top pieces of the inlaid table's legs were possibly made on a lathe, carved into their finished form, and then inlaid.[29]

The compass was used extensively to lay out various carved elements. This included the feet of the plain tables (Plate 152A) and the collars of the table tops (Plate 152B). The inlaid rosettes were also laid out using a compass, which is indicated by the numerous compass pricks still visible in the wood. On stand A these can be seen at the center of the large rosette and in the two arcs at the left and right above the rosette (Plate 77); on stand B, two are visible at the center of the large rosette, and five occur along the rosette's outer circumference, just inside the solid circular strip of inlay at the bottom of the inner bevel (Plate 87). The compass was used not only to map out arcs and circles but also as a measuring device. Both these functions are evident in the graffito markings on the tenons of the serving stands (Figures 63, 65; and see Appendix 6).

The bow drill (Text Figure 6:1) was also used for a variety of purposes: to drill holes for the pegs that secured the mortise-and-tenon joinery (Plate 151D), to excavate areas for inlay (Plates 150D, 151A–B), and also for the occasional repair, which might be effected with the help of tiny pegs (Plate 151C).[30] The bow drill operated by means of reciprocal action, as did the ancient lathe.[31] The first step in the inlay process was the drawing of the pattern with a knife. The artists who marked out the complex patterns on the serving stands seem to have used the exposed tenons at the ends of the boards to cut practice designs and test their knives (Figures 63, 65). When the drawing was completed, the cavities to be inlaid were drilled out and then finished with a chisel. Small pegs and strips of juniper inlay were carefully cut, utilizing the grain direction for maximum strength, so that the inlay could be tapped in place without breaking. The inlay was secured in the recesses with glue, and, finally, the surface was finished by smoothing or scraping (Figures 68–70).[32] Evidence for

---

Tombs," figure 228. Like the Gordion tables, the Jericho tables had tops with "collars" that extended down from the lower surface. See above, pp. 42, 62–63.

[26] Contra Young, *Gordion I*, 179, 182, 187, 260; followed by Meiggs, *Trees and Timber*, 460. See above, pp. 38, 57–58. The first to suggest this idea was Burhan Aytuğ. Thick boxwood legs are not amenable to steam bending, but for the ease with which boxwood can be shaped by pruning, see Record and Garratt, "Boxwoods," 8. For steam bending of poles of wood by Egyptian carpenters, see Killen, *Egyptian Woodworking and Furniture*, 8. For the utilization of naturally bent wood, see Hesiod, *Works and Days* 427. For trained wood, see Virgil, *Georgics* 1.169–170.

[27] Robert Blanchette, personal communication (March 6, 2003), Gordion Furniture Project archives. Some of the legs of the plain tables failed (see Plates 47, 64), which may have resulted from the cutting of the lower part of the leg too far off center in order to achieve the desired curve. For a variation on the method described above, see Jagels, "Crook Timber," although crook timber (utilizing a branch and part of the trunk at the branch-trunk juncture) was apparently not used for the Tumulus MM plain table legs.

[28] There is evidence from table 7 that wedges or shims could be tapped into the mortise cut through the table top to tighten the collar-tenon joints. This is also attested at Jericho. Ricketts, "Furniture from the Middle Bronze Age Tombs," figure 229:2.

[29] Supra n. 3. The only other pieces of furniture from Tumulus MM that would have benefited from the use of the lathe are the stool and chair legs from the northeast corner (Figure 76), although not enough has been preserved of these legs to investigate this possibility. Contra Young, "Phrygian Furniture from Gordion," 7, in which he states that the legs of the inlaid table were "lathe-turned and tapered"; followed by Meiggs, *Trees and Timber*, 460, who states that the Tumulus MM table legs were turned on a lathe. See also Young, *Gordion I*, 260.

[30] For other ancient repairs see above, pp. 33, 36, 39, and Plate 97A–B (patching).

[31] Extensive study has been conducted on the use of the ancient bow drill in relation to the manufacture of cylinder seals. See, for instance, Gwinnett and Gorelick, "Copper Drills in Mesopotamia."

[32] See above, pp. 33, 70–71, 73. For the glue analysis, which was inconclusive, see p. 31, n. 3.

the drilling technique can be found in the holes at the bottom of channels where the inlay has fallen out. These drill holes are clearly visible on the front and left rear feet of the inlaid table (Plate 150D) and in some of the meander squares on the faces of the serving stands (Plate 151B). In general, the inlay has remained firmly in place, despite the passage of nearly three millennia.

The same technique was used for the metal inlay that once decorated the missing sections of the table's handles (Plate 151A). Holes for the inlay were first drilled with a cylindrical bit, and square pegs were then driven into the holes, anchoring some kind of plate or panel in each of the large rectangular cavities. This suggests an apparent sequence, which began with the making of the rectangular metal (or ivory) panels to fit within the cavities cut in the handles. Square holes for metal pegs were cut in the panels, the panels were set in the cavities, and the positions of the pegs were marked in the wood. The panels were then removed, the wood was drilled at the marked locations, the panels were replaced and glued into the cavities, and the metal pegs were tapped in. The missing metal inlay is difficult to reconstruct, although the designs must have resembled those of the adjacent wooden areas.

The inlaying of the designs on the serving stands' faces was carried out in conjunction with the joining of the boards (Figures 49 and 57).[33] The face of each stand was made from 15 separate pieces of wood (see Figures 62 and 64 for numbered boards). The top three boards (boards 1–3) were joined to form a unit. This top unit was then inlaid, according to the process described above. Boards 5 and 6 were also joined as a unit and inlaid, as were boards 8 and 9. The central board (board 7) was joined to the long strip at the bottom of the face (board 11), this group was joined to the two curved legs (12 and 13), and the four-piece unit was inlaid. The two long side boards (4 and 10) were inlaid separately, and the whole face was then assembled. Inlay was added over the joints to harmonize the overall pattern.[34]

This multi-panel construction was necessary in part because of the limited size of the boxwood boards, which would normally not have exceeded one foot in width, even when made from the largest boxwood trees.[35] The inlay was carried out on board units (rather than the assembled face) to provide better access for the inlay artists.[36] These considerations suggest a detailed construction sequence, particularly in light of the design error that occurred at the top of the face of serving stand A.[37] The boards were first cut and assembled temporarily so that the overall grid pattern could be drawn out with a knife (Figure 70). The large squares were delineated but without indication of the detailed designs in their interior. The face was disassembled, and the board units were glued up and pinned. These units and the long side boards were inlaid, with the artists working in from the edges of the large board groups. This process may have involved the use of metal templates to lay out the individual designs; such templates could easily have been rotated and flipped over to create the variety that served to obscure the underlying pattern on each stand. After the board units were inlaid, the complete face was assembled, and more inlay was added to coordinate the separately inlaid sections. Finally, the surface of the face was smoothed by scraping, rubbing with a stone or abrasive, or a combination of both. Evidence for this phase consists of remnants of scribe lines that remained visible in areas after the smoothing process.[38] No intention-

---

[33] See above, pp. 69–70, 81–83.

[34] See above, pp. 69–70.

[35] Boxwood trees require 200–300 years to achieve a trunk diameter of one foot; a few larger specimens have been recorded, with diameters up to two feet and heights of 50 feet. The boxwood trees used to make the boards of the Tumulus MM serving stands were large, old trees. Lynn Batdorf, personal communication (March 2, 1987), Gordion Furniture Project archives. A cargo of boxwood from a Roman shipwreck found at Comacchio contained logs that were, on average, 276 years old and only 17 cm in diameter. Ulrich, *Roman Woodworking*, 245. See also Record

and Garratt, "Boxwoods," 14, 19.

[36] See above, p. 82.

[37] See above, p. 82–83.

[38] See above, p. 73. The face of stand A was apparently scraped in an effort to remove the guidelines. Under magnification, a small area below the curve of the left front leg shows a smooth depression that was probably made by a metal scraper. Some of the guidelines remain in this area, indicating that they were too deep to be removed. For the smoothing of the surface of a board by rubbing, supra nn. 6–8. Pliny, *Natural History* 9.40 and 32.108, mentions the skin of a scaly fish that was used for finishing wood.

ally applied surface finish survives on any of the Tumulus MM pieces.[39]

In terms of construction, the serving stands were the most complex of all the pieces from Tumulus MM, particularly because the joinery of the stands' faces and side pieces had to be coordinated with the inlay process (Figures 45–46, 49–50, 53–54, 57–58). Boards that were joined edge to end utilized standard mortise-and-tenon joinery: tenons that extended from the ends of boards were fit into mortises cut in the edges of adjoining pieces. The boards that were butted edge to edge were joined by a different method. Corresponding mortises were cut in the edges of adjacent boards, and separate, free tenons were fit into the mortises and pinned.[40] This may have been a common technique for edge joinery in furniture, although most of the surviving evidence for this practice comes from ancient coffins and ships.[41] The method is attested in Egypt by the third millennium B.C., for panel construction on coffins and the hulls of ships, and continued into the Roman period and later.[42]

The joints of the stands' faces must have been glued and the boards clamped;[43] in addition, the holes drilled for the pins may have been slightly offset, serving to pull the boards tightly together when the pins were driven in. There is evidence from the plain tables that the pins may have been used for this purpose. The long pins that ran through the collars and leg tenons of table 6 showed compression on one side, suggesting that the holes had been offset and the pins utilized as a clamping mechanism. The effectiveness of this joinery method can be appreciated from the excavation photographs of the serving stands (Color Plate IV; Plates 69–70, 80), which show the faces in almost perfect condition. Nonetheless, the joinery did occasionally fail; apparently some of the boards had separated and were shimmed with inlay wedges (Plate 95).

The tools and techniques used by the Gordion woodworkers suggest that the artists worked well within established ancient craft traditions. Yet the fine carving, expert joinery, detailed inlay, and elaborate decoration set the Tumulus MM furniture apart. Fabulous wooden artifacts were surely made in other centers, though such evidence is rarely recovered.[44] Even so, the artistic inventiveness and intellectual ingenuity of the Gordion woodworkers place their furniture in a class by itself.

---

[39] In 1989–1990, 20 samples of surface residues from various pieces of furniture from Tumulus MM were analyzed for evidence of surface finish. This study was carried out by Susan Buck and John Childs of the Winterthur Art Conservation Program, in consultation with Greg Landrey and Richard Wolbers. The only sample that indicated a uniform finish layer was the residue from the inlaid table (sample 20). However, it could not be determined whether this layer was part of the original finish or had resulted from a later treatment. The bright fluorescence of the resin component in the sample seems to suggest the latter. Buck and Childs, "Sample Analysis," 4. It seems unlikely that the boxwood furniture was colored artificially, as boxwood does not lend itself to dyeing. Record and Garratt, "Boxwoods," 22. For the suggestion that boxwood furniture excavated in Jerusalem was painted, see above, p. 44, n. 78.

[40] See above, pp. 68–69. This effective joint will resist torsion, lateral tension, and compression. Weeks, "Roman Carpentry Joints," 163–164.

[41] This technique was used for some of the tables from Jericho and Baghouz. Ricketts, "Furniture from the Middle Bronze Age Tombs," figure 229:1. Mesnil du Buisson, *Baghouz*, plate 44. See Killen, *Ancient Egyptian Furniture 2*, 42–44, figure 55, for its use in an 18th Dynasty box.

[42] See Ward, *Sacred and Secular: Ancient Egyptian Ships and Boats*, 31–60, on Early Dynastic and Old Kingdom ship construction and related joinery in early coffins. The hull of the Uluburun ship (14th century B.C.) utilized this type of joinery. Pulak, "Uluburun Hull Remains." For additional evidence, see Steffy, *Wooden Ship Building*, 46 (Kyrenia), 61 (Athlit), 64 (Madrague de Giens), 69 (Kinneret), et al. The raft of Odysseus may have been made by this method: "he bored all the pieces and fitted them to one another, and with pegs and morticings did he hammer it together." *Odyssey* 5.234–257. But see McGrail, *Boats of the World*, 126, on the scholarly controversy surrounding the passage. For an example from the third century A.D., see McGrail and Denford, "Boatbuilding Techniques," 37–38, figure 3.13. For the use of free tenons in Roman wheel construction, see Ulrich, *Roman Woodworking*, 205–206.

[43] For evidence of gluing and clamping, see above, p. 68, n. 25. For glue residue on the inlaid table, see p. 31, n. 3. Lucretius remarks on the strength of bull's glue for joining wood. Lucretius, *De Rerum Natura* 6.1069–1071. According to Pliny, the finest glue was made from the ears and genitals of bulls. Pliny, *Natural History* 28.236. Animal glues are among the strongest of adhesives. T. Baker, "Glue," 206. For a discussion of clamping in the Roman period, see Ulrich, *Roman Woodworking*, 57–58.

[44] For the recently recovered examples from Verucchio, see above, p. 48.

APPENDIX 8

PRELIMINARY ANALYSES OF TEXTILES ASSOCIATED WITH THE WOODEN FURNITURE FROM TUMULUS MM

MARY W. BALLARD, HARRY ALDEN, ROLAND H. CUNNINGHAM, WALTER HOPWOOD, JOSEPH KOLES, AND LAURE DUSSUBIEUX

Museum Conservation Institute
Smithsonian Institution

Introduction

Many things happen to textiles when they are entombed. Instead of static "time capsules," reflecting their state at the time of burial, textiles are generally found to be degraded physically, chemically, and biologically. Decorative hangings can be pulled apart by their own weight, contact with metals can corrode fabrics, and enzymatic activity from microbes can dissolve textile fibers. It is fascinating to observe the results of these changes and attempt to deduce or reconstruct the original state of the fabrics, decorative furnishings, and textile regalia. As a group, the textiles themselves may be "animal, vegetable, or mineral"—protein, like silk or sheep's wool; cellulosic, like cotton or flax; or even mineral, like asbestos. Each group has its own susceptibilities for destruction.

Over the years, archaeologists and scientists have found intact textiles at frozen sites, but cellulosics especially are subject to many degradative soil bacteria.[1] Occasionally fibers will survive, especially when adjacent to antibacterial materials like copper.[2] However, metals can leach into fabric and transform the chemical structure into a metallic one. If the transformation occurs slowly, the surface or morphology of the fibers can remain intact, giving the appearance of the fabric, but now in a copper complex.[3] These are termed "pseudomorphs" since the identity of the fabric is retained, while its chemical structure has metamorphosed.[4] If the leaching occurs more quickly, the surface may be degraded, though the shape and volume of the space that the textile occupied survives.[5] Often wool textiles will disintegrate along with the flesh of the corpse (also protein); usually this enzymatic activity will also degrade a colorant. Interactions among decomposition systems can also produce unique synergies.[6]

Along with its own bacterial and chemical susceptibilities, each natural textile fiber has its own surface characteristics, chemical structure, working properties, methods of processing, and technology. Different fiber types lend themselves to different fabric structures, uses, and looms. Thus, identifying the fiber can provide circumstantial evidence for the science and technology, work habits, trade networks, and culture of a people. In her 1962 study of the Gordion textiles, Louisa Bellinger used this descriptive concatenation to assume that the matted compressed materials from Tumulus MM must be napped woolen fabrics or even felts.[7] Although this is technologically and culturally consistent with local tradition,[8] Bellinger's "felt" cannot be substantiated.

[1] The Pazyryk site is the best-known example. Siu, *Microbial Decomposition of Cellulose*, 129–147; Peacock, "Biodegradation and Characterization of Water-Degraded Archaeological Textiles," 52.

[2] See Wessel, "Textiles and Cordage," 424–445.

[3] See Jakes and Howard, "Formation of Textile Fabric Pseudomorphs."

[4] Ibid. See also Chen, Jakes, and Foreman, "Preservation of Archaeological Textiles through Fibre Mineralization," 1016.

[5] Gillard and Hardman, "Investigation of Fiber Mineralization Using Fourier Transform Infrared Microscopy," 180–181.

[6] See Filley, Blanchette, Simpson, and Fogel, "Nitrogen Cycling."

[7] Bellinger, "Textiles from Gordion," 12–13.

[8] See Gervers and Gervers, "Felt-making Craftsmen of the Anatolian and Iranian Plateaux"; Steinkeller, "Mattresses and Felt in Early Mesopotamia."

In another case, fabrics classified by Bellinger as "golden-brown goats-wool, probably mohair," were restudied in 1977–1978 by Richard Ellis, who used equally convincing structural similarities to conclude that these plain weave (tabby) fabrics from the tomb were "vegetable in appearance."[9]

Deductions based on simple observations can lead in contrary directions; analytical data can often clarify matters. Neither Bellinger nor Ellis was able to take advantage of modern optical microscopy or the advanced analytical equipment available today. In 2003, 11 diverse textile fragment groups from Tumulus MM were sent to the Smithsonian Museum Conservation Institute (MCI) for structural and chemical analysis, in conjunction with a review of the textiles recovered from the destruction level of the city mound at Gordion. The Tumulus MM textiles have characteristics quite distinct from those of the city mound and have provided some unexpected challenges.

First and foremost, many of the fragment groups from Tumulus MM have more than one type of textile incorporated in the fragment: the front and back of a fragment may actually reveal two different textiles amalgamated together. The textile on the back may have nothing in common structurally with the textile on the front; they are related only by proximity. For instance, textile fragment 2003-Tx-11 includes numerous unrelated specimens with different fibers and weaves. On the other hand, some of the fragments include only one type of textile, such as textile fragments 2003-Tx-1 and 2003-Tx-10, each of which has homologous, multiple layers or pieces of a single type. Second, the textiles have been biologically degraded in various ways: some remain visually intact but lack the physical and chemical properties associated with natural fiber textiles; others have disintegrated and been laminated together. The microbial activity appears to have been both fiber specific and location specific. In addition, an inorganic mineral coating has been found associated with one weave structure or fiber, and an organic bicomponent has also been identified. Yet two materials and two important fabric structures remain enigmatic. The following preliminary report provides some indication of the range of issues relating to the textiles associated with the furniture from Tumulus MM.

Textiles from the Tumulus MM Coffin

Textile 2003-Tx-1: a series of woven fragments.

Plates 153, 154A–B; CD-Figures 1–5 (and see CD-Figures 6–7 for a related sample).
Location: coffin, beneath the purple/red textile on which the body lay.
Fiber: bast plant fiber.
Yarns: 2 Z singles are S plied; this S-plied yarn is used in both warp and weft.
Weave: balanced plain weave (also known as tabby).
Weave count: 18 per centimeter ± 1 (46.6/inch ± 2.5) × 21 per centimeter ± 2 (54.2/inch ± 5.1).
Color: an even, level, deep golden color.[10]

The fibers are smooth, processed, and tightly packed longitudinally with diameters in the range of 10–20 microns (Plate 153B). They appear to be the processed stem bundles of bast plant fibers, a group that includes flax (*Linum*) and hemp (*Cannabis sativa*) plants. Chemically, bast vegetable fibers are composed primarily of cellulose. In most ancient societies they were used undyed. These fibers are staple (i.e. not continuous monofilament) and therefore require spinning in order to form yarns or threads (CD-Figure 1). There are no selvages on these fragments, but the warp is presumed to be the more deflected and highly packed direction with 21 yarns per centimeter. Although this set of yarns shows a higher variability, the proportion of thinner yarns is greater. The thinner, more highly twisted spun yarn is stronger and capable of greater tension, a requirement for warp yarns. Thicker, less tightly twisted weft yarns fill more space and would provide a faster weaving pace.

The individual fragments are small, and it is surprising to note the high number of spinning and weaving errors—uneven yarn diameters translate into an uneven weave count and give the fabric an uneven density or cover factor (CD-

---

[9] Bellinger, "Textiles from Gordion," 13–14. Ellis, "Textile Remains," 302. It is difficult to ascertain whether Ellis's "Fabric A" is Bellinger's "golden-brown goats-wool," although this seems to be the case.

[10] The specimen cannot be objectively measured with a tristimulus colorimeter because of its fragile, brittle surface and small size. This is true of all the specimens in this report. Fortunately, the color rendering in the digital images accompanying this appendix is quite accurate (CD-Figures 1–65).

Table 1. Weight percentage of inorganic elements present on the recto of textile fragment 2003-Tx-1, as analyzed by Scanning Electron Microscopy with Energy Dispersive Spectroscopy (SEM-EDS).

Element	Sample 1	Sample 2	Sample 3	Sample 4	Average[11]
Sodium	0.56%	0.63%	0.30%	0.43%	0.48%
Aluminum	0.73	0.60	0.46	0.30	0.52
Silicon	1.52	1.27	0.84	0.84	1.12
Phosphorus	0.78	0.62	0.56	0.44	0.60
Sulfur	–	0.28	0.24	0.21	0.18
Calcium	–	–	0.20	–	–
Iron	96.41	96.60	97.40	97.78	97.05

Figure 2). The loom system had an insufficient shed mechanism: alternate threads were not consistently lifted, so there are occasional mistakes in the weave, and a weaver's knot repairs broken threads. It is not clear at this time whether these errors are the result of a casual treatment. This might have been a utilitarian cloth, not meant to be considered as a fine and uniform fabric, perhaps the clumsier work of a beginning spinner and a beginning weaver. Alternatively, this fabric might have been woven at the limit of fineness for the technological system available. In this case, finer, more consistent yarns would not have been possible, and the weave count was beyond the scope of a more consistent fabric density—hence the repair of breaks with weaver's knots. However, considering the other evidence available regarding Phrygian textiles, the former scenario is more likely.

Condition: One side of the fabric appears to be napped, while the other side has no appreciable hairiness. A napped, brushed effect can be purposely induced to achieve a softened surface or be the result of deterioration. In the case of 2003-Tx-1, there is no pattern to the hairiness, and it occurs on the knot (bumpy) side of the fabric. Thus it is presumed to be the result of damage, the simple aggregation of surface yarns broken up during abrasion and caught on one layer, with the density of the fabric acting as a sieve or screen to hold the broken fibers.

On either side of the fabric, as seen in Plate 153B and CD-Figure 2, small white particles are distributed. These particles are fresh and intact, indicating that they are the result of fungal activity that occurred after the excavation of the tomb. At high magnification (700 diameters, Plate 153B), small white conidia and hyphae can be seen. Larger brown fungal spores are also present. The interior of the fiber is degraded; this would account for the low residual strength and non-plasticity of the fibers, and their tendency to fracture, as well as fractured fiber fragments themselves, observed as "nap." This evaluation is confirmed by the examination of cleaned yarns and fibers (Plate 153C–D).[12] At higher magnifications, it is evident that a hollow sheath of the fiber remains, but the actual fiber itself (Plate 154A–B) has disappeared. A coating or covering has taken on the appearance of the fibers, but the fibers are almost entirely missing.

The principal inorganic element of the fibers is iron (96–97% by weight using energy dispersive spectroscopy in a scanning electron microscope, SEM-EDS; see Table 1). An iron corrosion product (Fe_2O_3) can impart a dull orange hue to cellulosic fibers. As corrosion occurs, the fibers will be degraded in a pattern often radiating out from a primary source of iron (such as a thumbtack or nail). In this instance, the coloration is consistent, even, and level, as is the concentration of the iron. The textile fragment 2003-Tx-1 is related in weave structure and proximity to 2003-Tx-2 (CD-Figure 6), which was analyzed by Fourier Transform Infrared Spectroscopy (FTIR) for an infrared "chemical fingerprint." Its chief chemical component is goethite, α-FeOOH, an iron

---

[11] Elements with quantities less than 1% by weight are not always listed. Consequently weight percentage may not total 100%.

[12] Cleaned with sequential baths of xylene and acrylonitrile on a support of conductive polyester medical fab-ric. See Ballard, MCI Report #5277, Smithsonian Institution. Unpublished reports, Museum Conservation Institute archives, with contributors including Harry Alden, Roland H. Cunningham, Walter Hopwood, Joseph Koles, Laure Dussubieux, and Amandine Pequignot.

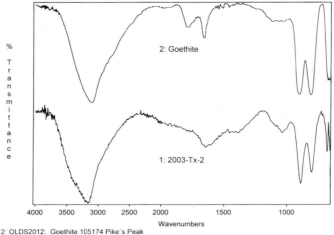

2: OLDS2012: Goethite 105174 Pike's Peak
1: YMBKING2: M. Ballard 2003-Tx-2 Back bright yellow thread

Text Figure 7. Comparison spectra of goethite
(source: Pike's Peak, CO) and the gold-colored yarn
seen on the "back" of 2003-Tx-2 (CD-Figures 6–7).

oxide hydroxide (Text Figure 7). This is a bacteriostatic, stable, conductive iron coating, of great light-fastness, and gold colored.

Related textiles: Textile 2003-Tx-2, back; some fragments of 2003-Tx-11 (see below).

References: Richard Ellis described other plain-weave fragments that he examined from the Tumulus MM coffin; he also noted weave errors. He designated this fabric "Fabric A," which he described as "vegetable in appearance."[13] This seems to contradict an earlier conclusion by Bellinger: Ellis identified his "Fabric A" with Bellinger's "golden-brown goats-wool."[14] The fine outside diameter of the fibers (14–18 microns) is comparable to that of cashmere or other fine goat hairs known to be present at other Anatolian sites; this, and the napped appearance of the surface, may have led Bellinger to attribute the fiber to goat. However, no features of goat hairs are present microscopically in textiles 2003-Tx-1 or 2003-Tx-2.

Textile 2003-Tx-3: a collapsed laminated mass.

CD-Figures 10–15 (and see Plate 154C–D and CD-Figures 8–9, 16–17 for related samples).

Location: coffin, beneath and adjacent to the body.
Fiber: indeterminate.
Yarns: indeterminate.
Weave: indeterminate.
Color: shades of red and purple.

At first glance this fragment appears to contain no textiles; it looks like a friable, flakey red clay lump of dirt, with white speckles, but the back view shows variegated swirls that might have once been fibrous (CD-Figure 10). On its side (CD-Figure 11) the lump is more clearly laminar, consisting of layers that are more or less porous, compacted, and monochrome. Upon closer examination, the back of the fragment has some extraordinary aspects. For example, there is a circular, spiral-shaped burr (from a burr clover, *Medicago* ssp.) visible at the center of CD-Figures 10 and 13.[15] This burr is dried and loose, but clearly nestled in the debris.

Nearby, fibrous yarn fragments seem to be present, perhaps some even in cross-section (CD-Figure 12). Weave structures that might be twill or some coarse, plain weave may be also present, but the fibers are indistinct and more collagenous than fibrous at higher magnification (CD-Figures 14–15). The degradation of the mass into

---

[13] Ellis, "Textile Remains," 301.
[14] Bellinger, "Textiles from Gordion," 13–14. Supra n. 9.
[15] W. J. Kress, Department of Botany, National Museum of Natural History, Smithsonian Institution. Personal communication, January 2005.

Table 2. Weight percentage of inorganic elements present in the mixed reddish powder in 2003-Tx-3, as analyzed by SEM-EDS.

Element	Sample 1	Sample 2	Sample 3	Sample 4	Average[16]
Magnesium	2.78 %	3.90 %	3.45 %	3.63 %	3.44 %
Aluminum	8.72	10.64	8.87	11.93	10.04
Silicon	11.29	13.59	10.49	15.93	12.83
Phosphorus	4.24	5.00	4.36	5.16	4.69
Sulfur	10.28	5.57	12.02	8.05	8.98
Potassium	1.99	2.06	1.23	2.59	1.97
Calcium	23.09	17.30	22.69	17.19	20.07
Iron	7.36	5.31	4.37	5.40	5.61
Nickel	1.24	7.52	5.63	3.57	4.49
Copper	29.00	34.42	26.89	26.54	29.21

Table 3. Weight percentage of inorganic elements present in the brightest red powder in 2003-Tx-3, as analyzed by SEM-EDS.

Element	Sample 1	Sample 2	Sample 3	Sample 4	Average[17]
Magnesium	2.87 %	5.49 %	3.33 %	–	2.92 %
Aluminum	11.38	12.15	10.57	5.97 %	10.02
Silicon	16.64	15.57	14.78	16.06	15.76
Phosphorus	5.50	5.08	4.43	4.92	4.98
Sulfur	7.19	6.63	6.03	8.45	7.08
Potassium	2.22	1.85	2.22	2.65	2.24
Calcium	17.02	17.31	17.03	21.26	18.16
Iron	6.12	5.91	8.53	8.44	7.25
Nickel	–	–	–	–	–
Copper	30.20	30.00	33.09	32.26	31.39

these indistinct shreds prevents standard microscopic identification of the fiber class. In addition, the ratios of the weight percentages of any inorganic elements present may be distorted by microbial deterioration or chemical degradation. Still, Tables 2 and 3 provide some indication of the nature of the red coloration.

As averaged, the inorganic content includes a high weight percentage of copper (29–31 %) and iron (5.6–7.3 %) as well as high levels of aluminum (10 %), silicon (12.8–15.8 %), and especially calcium (18–20 %). While these latter are often associated with soil and dirt, they may be indicative here of an inorganic complex associated with the coloration. The sulfur content (7 % to almost 9 %) is far too low for that of hair fibers or wool in an unmineralized, undegraded state, and too high for silk or leather, which inherently have no sulfur

content. The sulfur may be associated with the colorant. The material represented by this fragment has been described by Bellinger and Ellis as a "felt," the non-woven amalgam of wool or hair fibers as processed with heat, pressure, moisture, and alkali. Such processing might account for the high level of calcium shown in Tables 2 and 3, but not the low sulfur content. Even a shearling—fur left on leather—might not explain the data in these tables.

A white powder also exists on the surface of this textile fragment in discrete spots and in a laminar manner (CD-Figures 10–11). By weight percentage, this soft whitish powder contains significantly more sulfur (25.2 %), more calcium (36.9 %), and significantly less copper (8.4 %) than the reddish materials (see Table 4).

---

[16] Elements with quantities less than 1 % by weight are not always listed. Consequently weight percentage may not total 100 %.

[17] Elements with quantities less than 1 % by weight are not always listed. Consequently weight percentage may not total 100 %.

Table 4. Weight percentage of inorganic elements present in the white powder, 2003-Tx-3, front, as analyzed by SEM-EDS.

Element	Sample 1	Sample 2	Sample 3	Sample 4	Average[18]
Magnesium	1.08 %	1.75 %	0.46 %	1.17 %	1.12 %
Aluminum	6.44	8.25	2.68	6.31	5.92
Silicon	14.36	18.35	6.00	13.73	13.11
Phosphorus	2.08	2.49	0.83	1.59	1.75
Sulfur	22.35	17.77	36.28	24.45	25.21
Potassium	1.70	2.29	—	1.73	1.43
Calcium	35.94	27.66	47.62	36.35	36.89
Iron	6.66	8.36	2.89	6.55	6.12
Copper	9.39	13.07	3.24	7.75	8.36

An organic analysis for the white powder and for the red colorants remains to be completed. Nonetheless, the lack of the halogen bromine in the inorganic analysis by SEM-EDS indicates that the red coloration of the fragment is not caused by a residue of Tyrian purple (6,6'-dibromoindigo), a dyestuff associated with royalty from antiquity.

Related textiles: 2003-Tx-2, front; 2003-Tx-6, underside.

Reference: Ellis described "Fabric K," found on the remains of the Tumulus MM coffin, as felt; he also noted an interspersion of spun yarns in the "felt" fragments he examined.[19]

Textile 2003-Tx-5: A collapsed laminated mass with residual twining(?)

Plates 154C–D, CD-Figures 19–24.
Location: coffin.

Fabric #1
Fiber: indeterminate.
Yarn structure: none, matted.
Weave structure: none.
Color: shades of red, purple, and light brown with white specks.

Fabric #2
Fiber: indeterminate.
Yarns: Z twist(?)

Weave: twining.
Color: shades of red, purple, and light brown with white specks.

This textile fragment, along with 2003-Tx-4, yielded indistinct images. Textile 2003-Tx-5 includes two types of materials. One is the amorphous layer (Fabric #1) seen in the scanning electron microscope (SEM) images of Plate 154C–D; the other (Fabric #2) is a vague image of a twined textile with a horizontal thread running perpendicular to the twisting elements.

Both are covered and enveloped with an irregular, powdery white matter that interferes with visual analysis, optical imaging, and elemental analysis. Table 5 below shows a great inconsistency in the quantities of calcium, sulfur, silicon, aluminum, and iron found on various parts of the surface of the fibrous mass illustrated in Plates 154C–D. There may be uneven levels of contamination, alteration, or degradation, but the underlying fibrous "mattress" may also not have been homogeneous.

This fragment and others of similar appearance from the Tumulus MM coffin (2003-Tx-3 and 4) are associated with those identified as "mattress" or "felt" by Young,[20] Bellinger,[21] and Ellis.[22] Historically, it is quite evident that wool and goat (mohair) felts were produced in this time period and cultural milieu. At present, however, this sample cannot be identified unequivocally as "felt."

---

[18] Elements with quantities less than 1 % by weight are not always listed. Consequently weight percentage may not total 100 %.
[19] Ellis, "Textile Remains," 309. See also 2003-Tx-5,

below.
[20] Young, *Gordion I*, 189–190.
[21] Bellinger, "Textiles from Gordion," 12–13.
[22] Ellis, "Textile Remains," 309.

Table 5. Weight percentage of inorganic elements present in the fibers on the surface of 2003-Tx-5, as analyzed by SEM-EDS.

Element	Sample 1	Sample 2	Sample 3	Sample 4	"Average"[23]
Sodium	0.99 %	1.11 %	1.08 %	1.19 %	1.09 %
Magnesium	2.10	5.34	4.80	3.72	3.99
Aluminum	6.64	11.92	11.74	8.70	9.75
Silicon	20.52	40.07	36.19	25.89	30.67
Phosphorus	1.38	2.45	2.15	2.29	2.07
Sulfur	25.37	9.39	12.75	20.20	16.93
Potassium	1.89	4.13	3.80	2.51	3.08
Calcium	34.39	13.85	16.78	25.89	22.73
Iron	6.72	11.12	10.12	6.84	8.70
Titanium	–	0.63	0.58	0.54	0.44/0.58

Table 6. Weight percentage of inorganic elements present in the fiber residue of 2003-Tx-5, as analyzed by SEM-EDS.

Element	Sample 1	Sample 2	Sample 3	Sample 4	Average[24]
Sodium	0.87 %	1.08 %	0.62 %	1.41 %	1.00 %
Magnesium	2.10	1.81	2.02	2.85	2.20
Aluminum	8.18	8.90	8.72	11.94	9.44
Silicon	19.69	22.59	22.67	31.96	28.41
Phosphorus	1.37	1.76	1.63	2.13	1.72
Sulfur	25.45	21.97	22.44	16.45	21.58
Potassium	2.23	3.05	2.68	3.77	2.93
Calcium	33.29	30.24	29.78	20.84	28.53
Iron	5.96	8.07	6.81	8.39	7.31
Zinc	0.86	–	0.79	–	–
Titanium	–	0.53	–	–	–
Copper	–	–	1.82	–	–
Manganese	–	–	–	0.27	–

For Fabric #2, the fiber's inorganic residue has more consistency, as seen in Table 6. There is some birefringence associated with the fiber, as seen in CD-Figures 21–24. However, it is not clear whether this constitutes some residual, original optical property of the fiber or the effect of a subsequent absorption of a particular compound. The fibers of 2003-Tx-4 seen magnified under an optical microscope (CD-Figure 18) also show some ambiguity.

Fabric #2 of 2003-Tx-5 is a twined structure, visible in the left fragment of CD-Figure 19 and shown in detail in CD-Figure 20. A detail of its counterpart in 2003-Tx-4 can be seen at the upper left central edge of CD-Figure 17. The twining is not very clear, but a horizontal yarn may be distinguished running under angled and, per-haps, counter-angled, vertical yarns, as is visible in the detail of CD-Figure 20. This is not a plain weave fabric. It was not mentioned by either Bellinger or Ellis in their reviews of the fabrics present in Tumulus MM. There are several types of twined textiles that appear in antiquity: two-strand weft twining, tablet weaving, soumak wrapping, and gauze weave all produce a twined or twisted appearance, as seen in Text Figure 8 below.

By encircling the perpendicular yarns, the final woven structure tends to be more stable and less able to shift out of alignment.[25] Two-strand weft twining (or warp twining) can be used to produce bags and containers. Designs can be created by alternating the direction of the twining (Text Figure 8, left, is S twined), by

---

[23] Elements with quantities less than 1 % by weight are not always listed. Consequently weight percentage may not total 100 %.

[24] Elements with quantities less than 1 % by weight are not always listed. Consequently weight percentage may not total 100 %.

[25] Seiler-Baldinger, *Textiles: A Classification of Techniques*, 100.

WARP TWINING   SOUMAK   GAUZE

Text Figure 8. Left: two-strand weft twining, shifted
clockwise 90 degrees, or two-strand warp twining. Center:
wrapped soumak substituting for a weft shed (i.e. a weft
yarn), shifted clockwise 90 degrees. Right: simple gauze
weave (after Crowfoot and subsequently Forbes).[26]

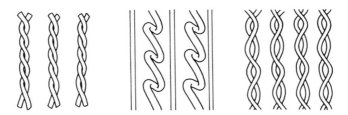

Text Figure 9. Left: twined yarns retain their twist.
Center: wrapped soumak and adjacent yarns
become loose threads. Right: gauze yarns are
also detached (after Crowfoot and Forbes).[27]

adding strands, or by switching the position of strand pairs.[28] When the organization is systematized by using pattern cards or tablets with a series of spaced holes, the technology is known as tablet weaving.[29] Soumak wrapping of yarns can be carried out on a loom, as a textile is woven (Text Figure 8, center). Soumak wrapping is much slower than passing a single weft across warps, but it permits the weaver to incorporate color or pattern, as well as producing stability in the finished fabric. Gauze is woven on a loom by manipulating the warps at an angle (Text Figure 8, right): the warps move out of plane; the wefts are not deflected. Of the three types, in their simplest forms, only soumak wrapping will appear different from front or back. Two-strand twining and gauze weave have identical faces.[30]

While these structures can look very similar when they are obscured by dust and dirt, they do not sustain a similar shape when their perpendicular, non-twined elements are damaged. In Text Figure 9, the soumak-wrapped fabric (center) and the gauze fabric (right) both become a series of individual loose strands, entirely disengaged from one another. On the other hand, in the two-strand weft twining shown at the left, the fundamental unit, in this case a pair of yarns, retains its twined relationship. If only a few perpendicular links were left in place, the whole pattern or texture of the textile would be maintained, as is the case in CD-Figure 20. Thus, the fine textile seen indistinctly can be described as a twined textile. This phenomenon is apparently the source of Bellinger's misunderstanding of the structure of her "felt" over a woven base (see below).

[26] Crowfoot, "Textiles, Basketry, and Mats," 430, fig. 271. R. Forbes, *Studies in Ancient Technology* 4, 190, fig. 26. However, in both instances, the simple gauze weave at right was sketched incorrectly, with the lowest (bottom) twining twisted. In Text Figure 8, that mistake has been corrected.

[27] Crowfoot, "Textiles, Basketry, and Mats," 430, figure 271. R. Forbes, *Studies in Ancient Technology* 4, 190, fig. 26. With the sketch of the undamaged gauze weave structure corrected, the degradation or absence of perpendicular el-

ements of the gauze weave produces a consistent uniform result.

[28] Seiler-Baldinger, *Textiles: A Classification of Techniques*, 61–62.

[29] Emery, *Primary Structure of Fabrics*, 199–200. Emery explains that warp twining can be carried out with or without tablet weaving technology. For a full discussion of tablet weaving see Collingwood, *Techniques of Tablet Weaving*.

[30] Emery, *Primary Structure of Fabrics*, 181, 197, 215.

Related textiles:

"Felt": 2003-Tx-2, front; 2003-Tx-4; 2003-Tx-6, underside.

Twining: 2003-Tx-4; 2003-Tx-6, back; 2003-Tx-7; 2003-Tx-8, front; 2003-Tx-9, front.

References:

"Felt": Ellis refers to this material as "Fabric K."[31] Bellinger also finds "felt" among the Tumulus MM textiles. She describes felt making as the layering of fibrous mats at right angles to each other, but she illustrates this point with a matted sample that bears some resemblance to 2003-Tx-5, illustrated here in Plate 154C.[32]

Twining: Ellis describes a weaving error, a crossing of occasional warps, and he also describes a starting border. Errors do not create a consistent pattern of oblique angles. Weaving errors are noticeable because they introduce irregularity into an otherwise regular pattern. With starting borders, the consistent pattern of warp crossing occurs only once, along one row, at the point of transition from starting border to main weaving.[33] Here the oblique angles of the warps occur repeatedly with several rows of weft. Bellinger illustrates a fragment of "tan wool" that she believes is the mat-like "base" of a felt "blanket" from the coffin; however, this sample seems to be related to the twined textile described above.[34]

Textiles from the Northeast Corner of the Tomb Chamber

Textile 2003-Tx-6: a collapsed laminated mass, cording, and residual twining.

Plate 155A–B, CD-Figures 25–33.

Location: amidst the furniture in the northeast corner of the tomb. The sample was originally labeled "blanketing under bag resting on stool #2."

Fabric #1
Fiber: indeterminate.
Yarn structure: floss (imperceptible twist).
Weave structure: twining.

Weave count: rows are 1.5–1.7 mm apart.
Color: dark brown weave on a powdery tan substrate.

Fabric #2
Fiber: indeterminate.
Yarns: S-twisted "cords" about 1 mm in diameter.
Yarns: spaced 4–5 mm apart.
Weave: none apparent.
Color: maroon to purple with white specks.

Other Fabrics
Fiber: indeterminate.
Yarn structure: none, matted.
Weave structure: none.
Colors: maroon to purple matte areas with white specks.

On the upper side of the fragment (Plate 155A) lies the remnant of a fine twined textile structure, Fabric #1, similar in quality to those twined textiles seen on fragments 2003-Tx-4 and 2003-Tx-5. The remnants are nestled against a white powdery substance (see CD-Figures 29–30). This substance bears the impression of the verso of the textile's structure, along with bits of the fiber, even though the textile has fallen away. Beneath this whitish layer may lie another twined structure, but this cannot be readily ascertained.

Details of a cross-sectional view of the fragment (see CD-Figures 27–28) show a compression of distinct colored layers, voids, and white powder. In the midst of the red layer visible in CD-Figure 28 is an ovoid pit measuring approximately 0.8 mm × 1.4 mm. This void appears to correspond to the S-twisted "cords" of Fabric #2 that are extant elsewhere on the underside of the fragment and shown in Plate 155B. These "cords" or plied materials are spaced 4–5 mm apart in an orderly manner. Where they are no longer extant, raking light shows a slight depression or trough at 4–5 mm intervals.

Between these "cords" are other fabrics, a matted complex, dark in color, as seen in CD-Figure 26. It is possible that this matted complex is evidence of a wool felt. Felts are compacted and condensed matted arrangements of wool or hair fibers; paper is the equivalent for

[31] Ellis, "Textile Remains," 309.
[32] Bellinger, "Textiles from Gordion," 18, plate 3D.
[33] Ellis, "Textile Remains," 298–299; figs. 141, 143. Bel-linger also discusses starting borders. Bellinger, "Textiles from Gordion," 11–12.
[34] Bellinger, "Textiles from Gordion," 12–13, plate 3D.

Table 7. Weight percentage of inorganic elements present in the reddish/purple powder, 2003-Tx-6, as analyzed by SEM-EDS.

Element	Sample 1	Sample 2	Sample 3	Average[35]
Magnesium	2.82 %	3.02 %	2.73 %	2.86 %
Aluminum	8.95	8.65	8.66	8.75
Silicon	13.42	14.02	13.84	13.76
Phosphorus	4.06	4.04	4.15	4.08
Sulfur	15.60	14.50	16.72	15.61
Potassium	1.86	2.25	1.79	1.95
Calcium	23.40	22.81	23.98	23.40
Iron	4.13	5.07	5.06	4.75
Copper	25.77	25.64	23.07	24.83

cotton fibers. It has been suggested that sample 2003-Tx-6 represents a cushion or some kind of upholstery padding found on one of the stools placed in the northeast corner of the tomb (stool #2). While such a layer would be practical directly above the tensioned string-course of upholstery, some intermediate layers of uncompacted lofted fibers could be expected. For comfort, a soft, resilient batting would be a reasonable selection. That is, an *uncompacted*, even teased beehive or pillow of fibers might be found, together with intermediary yarns or webs to hold these battings in place. Unlike heavily compacted felts, battings are light, mostly air, and can compact down to 2–3 % of their original thickness. The various striations at the top and bottom rims of the textile fragment seen in CD-Figures 27 and 28, are possible evidence of such lofted battings and their restraints seen in cross-sectional view, now degraded and compacted, as well as the traditional felt.

Condition: Thus, it is suggested that the generic "felt" associated with this and the purple and maroon coffin material from Tumulus MM may be divided into actual "felt," purposely made, in combination with batting or other uncompacted, non-woven, material now compacted due to degradation. Microbial degradation is likely. As regards the reddish coloration, this textile fragment seems to share the lumpish character of textile 2003-Tx-3—a laminated mass with a dark

red coloration, white powdery marks, and indistinguishable textile residues. The reddish purple coloration of sample 2003-Tx-6 (see Table 7) shares with its counterpart, sample 2003-Tx-3, high copper and calcium contents (respectively, 25 % and 23 % by weight), susbstantial levels of sulfur and silicon (16 % and 14 %), and significant amounts of aluminum and iron (9 % and 5 %).

Again, this reddish purple coloration lacks any bromine. Bromine at the 6 and 6' locations on the indigo molecule are both the cause for the purple hue and a distinguishing chemical feature of Tyrian purple. In the absence of bromine, no Tyrian purple can be associated with this fragment. Indeed, in this instance a sample was analyzed with Inductively Coupled Plasma-Mass Spectrometry (ICP-MS) to determine if any traces of bromine could be found. A 6,6'-dibromoindigo-dyed reference was procured and compared to confirm this finding. The precise cause of the reddish purple coloration has yet to be determined.

The dark, almost twistless fiber associated with the twining on the upper layer was examined by optical microscopy (see CD-Figures 31–33). The fibers are thin, fragmentary, degraded units locked in what appears to be a microbial film.

Related textiles:
Twining: 2003-Tx-4; 2003-Tx-5; 2003-Tx-7; 2003-Tx-8, front; 2003-Tx-9, front.
"Felt": 2003-Tx-2, front; 2003-Tx-4; 2003-Tx-5.

---

[35] Elements with quantities less than 1 % by weight are not always listed. Consequently weight percentage may not total 100 %.

References:

"Felt": Bellinger noted "different consistencies" among the various fragments of felts,[36] and she illustrated the striations and the juxtaposition of "felt" to woven fabric. Ellis observed "spun yarns lying between layers of randomly arranged felted fibers" for his "Fabric K" felt.[37] Associated with his "Fabric K," Ellis found yarns grouped but not spun, lying adjacent to each other, 5–10mm apart, occasionally crossed, but with no apparent weaving intended. Perhaps the textile fragments he examined had less extant twining than the samples analyzed here. In this context, the current study found a fine, reddish, random fibrous amalgam, reminiscent of a collagenous suede, on the front of textile 2003-Tx-2.

Cordage: Cordage is not discussed by either Bellinger or Ellis. No attempt was made during the current study to identify this material, which is now largely evident from impressions left in the textile remains. It should be noted that various reeds, "cat gut," or other membranes might be used as load-bearing, tensioned cords in stool construction. Impressions on one textile sample from the northeast corner were assumed to be "probably rush," according to a 1985 study (unpublished), although this conclusion was based on the observation of a photograph (see above, p. 114, n. 18, and Plate 106B).

Textiles 2003-Tx-7, 8, and 9: twined textiles.

Textile 2003-Tx-7: fragments of twined textile.

Plate 155C–D, CD-Figures 34–37.
Location: "bag on stool #2, east side, near northeast corner."
Fiber: indeterminate.
Yarns: floss (almost imperceptible S-twist single).
Weave: twining.
Weave count: paired yarns (spirals) are spaced 1.4mm apart; rows (perpendicular to the paired yarns) are 0.5mm apart.
Color: dark brown weave on a powdery tan substrate.

Textile 2003-Tx-8, front: fragments of twined textile.

Plate 156A–B, CD-Figures 38, 42.
Location: "bag on stool #2, east side, near northeast corner."
Fiber: indeterminate.
Yarns: floss (almost imperceptible S-twist single).
Weave: twining.
Weave count: paired yarns (spirals) are spaced 1.4mm apart; rows (perpendicular to the paired yarns) are 0.5mm apart.
Color: dark brown weave on a powdery tan substrate.

Textile 2003-Tx-9: fragments of twined textile.

CD-Figures 46–51.
Location: "bag mixed with blanketing under it, on stool #2, northeast corner."
Fiber: indeterminate.
Yarns: floss (almost imperceptible S-twist single).
Weave: twining.
Weave count: paired yarns (spirals) are spaced 1.4mm apart; rows (perpendicular to the paired yarns) are 0.5mm apart.
Color: dark brown weave on a powdery tan substrate.

These textiles share the same fiber and weave structure seen above with 2003-Tx-4 and 2003-Tx-5. Whether viewed by scanning electron microscope (Plate 155C–D) or with optical microscopy (see CD-Figures 35–37), textile 2003-Tx-7 also exhibits the same fragmentary damage and coating visible on the fibers. The textiles are made with the same fibers, yarns, and weave structure, although these cannot be precisely classified. Yet the fibers of textile 2003-Tx-7 have a significantly higher iron content than that found in either textile 2003-Tx-8 or textile 2003-Tx-9, as indicated in Tables 8–10 below. The latter two have a high level of copper, while 2003-Tx-7 has none. For all three textiles, the samples have inconsistent levels of iron, copper, potassium, sulfur, and silicon—proportionally changing from a major quantity to a less significant one, varying from sample to sample. This could indicate a capacity of the fiber for absorption, for contamination, or it could indicate a heterogeneous environment in terms of the tomb context. The samples are highly inconsistent.

---

[36] Bellinger, "Textiles from Gordion," 13; plates 3C–D, 4.

[37] Ellis, "Textile Remains," 309.

Table 8. Weight percentage of inorganic elements present in the dark fiber, 2003-Tx-7, back, as analyzed by SEM-EDS.

Element	Sample 1	Sample 2	Sample 3	Sample 4[38]
Magnesium	1.85 %	3.00 %	–	1.10 %
Aluminum	14.54	15.82	26.43 %	23.75
Silicon	43.30	42.12	9.92	15.13
Phosphorus	1.77	1.66	5.51	4.19
Sulfur	3.22	4.43	26.85	21.82
Potassium	8.18	6.88	18.00	14.39
Calcium	4.08	1.06	4.91	5.64
Titanium	1.65	1.06	0.68	0.33
Iron	21.41	18.06	7.40	12.47

Table 9. Weight percentage of inorganic elements present in the dark warp, 2003-Tx-8, as analyzed by SEM-EDS.

Element	Sample 1	Sample 2	Sample 3[39]
Magnesium	0.31 %	3.06 %	2.48 %
Aluminum	0.49	5.48	4.84
Silicon	1.12	13.92	9.84
Phosphorus	–	2.11	2.03
Sulfur	38.06	5.31	19.32
Potassium	–	1.39	1.12
Calcium	50.80	22.95	27.48
Iron	–	3.49	2.73
Copper	9.22	42.30	30.16

Table 10. Weight percentage of inorganic elements present in the dark yarn, 2003-Tx-9, as analyzed by SEM-EDS.

Element	Sample 1	Sample 2	Sample 3[40]
Magnesium	1.28 %	4.11 %	1.53 %
Aluminum	2.46	8.57	4.34
Silicon	6.45	25.58	11.61
Phosphorus	–	1.57	1.12
Sulfur	34.10	5.58	25.03
Potassium	0.92	3.56	1.47
Calcium	44.68	10.60	33.35
Titanium	–	0.85	0.31
Nickel	–	0.83	–
Iron	2.63	8.22	3.97
Copper	7.46	30.52	17.27

[38] Elements with quantities less than 1 % by weight are not always listed. Consequently weight percentage may not total 100 %.

[39] Elements with quantities less than 1 % by weight are not always listed. Consequently weight percentage may not total 100 %.

[40] Elements with quantities less than 1 % by weight are not always listed. Consequently weight percentage may not total 100 %.

Related textiles:
Twining: 2003-Tx-4, 2003-Tx-5, 2003-Tx-6.

References: Twined textiles are a well-defined group, but they can be manufactured by different technological methods. The twined structure of the present samples, like those examined previously, could have been made with or without tablet technology. Several authors provide knowledgeable definitions, examples, and comparative structures, among them: Emery, *Primary Structure of Fabrics*; Burnham, *Warp and Weft: A Dictionary of Textile Terms*; and Seiler-Baldinger, *Textiles: A Classification of Techniques*. A more complicated and decorative format can be carried out with tablets (sometimes referred to as "cards"), which can produce paired warps making confronting S and Z patterns—or other textures, depending upon the threading and holes, as well as the sequence of turning. Collingwood, in *The Techniques of Tablet Weaving*, describes the structural variation and technical intricacies possible. While tablet weaving is generally considered suitable for narrow bands, tapes, and belts, it may be used for wider textiles. Such complexity in a degraded fabric would render the weaving difficult to analyze and to reconstruct. With the current samples, the precise method of weaving is obscure, and tablet weaving offers a possible, but speculative, explanation.

Textile 2003-Tx-8, back: plain weave fragment.

Plates 156C–D; CD-Figures 39–41, 43–45.
Location: "bag on stool #2, east side, near northeast corner."
Fiber: bast plant fiber.
Yarns: 2 Z singles are S plied; this S-plied yarn is used in both warp and weft.
Weave: balanced plain weave (also known as tabby).
Weave count: 28 warps/cm × 23 wefts/cm (71/inch × 59/inch).
Color: golden, light tan.

Textile 2003-Tx-9, back: plain weave fragment.

Location: "bag mixed with blanketing under it, on stool #2, northeast corner."
Fiber: indeterminate.
Yarns: 2 Z singles are S plied; this S-plied yarn is used in both warp and weft.
Weave: balanced plain weave.

Weave count: perhaps 35 warps/cm × 35 warps/cm (89/inch × 89/inch).
Color: golden, light tan.

Textile 2003-Tx-10: plain weave fragment.

CD-Figures 52–55.
Location: "pieces of fine material lifted from fibulae, northeast corner on stool #2."
Fiber: flax (or ramie).
Yarns: 2 Z singles are S plied; this S-plied yarn is used in both warp and weft.
Weave: balanced plain weave.
Weave Count: 35 warps/cm × 35 wefts/cm (89/inch × 89/inch).
Color: brown.

The light tan or gold-colored fabric found on the back of 2003-Tx-8 is a finely woven, lustrous, balanced plain weave. Yet as seen in Plates 156C–D, the fibers are coated and obscured with debris. In part, this is due to a white powdery substance, seen in CD-Figure 41, which was also observed on 2003-Tx-1. Again, this undetermined white material may be a by-product of biological degradation. Microscopically, the fiber is fragmentary and breaks into brittle chunks, with a coated bubbly surface, as seen in CD-Figures 43–45. These images match the optical microscopy of the plain weave textile 2003-Tx-2. Small fragments of balanced plain weave also exist on the back of 2003-Tx-9. The largest is pulled, distorted, and partially covered by other layers of debris.

The case of 2003-Tx-10, the brown plain weave fabric (CD-Figure 52) is anomalous. It is a darker, slightly hairier, finely woven plain weave fabric. It has several layers folded upon each other, crumbled together; the fabric has a tarry (tar-like) coating over parts of it. With polarized light microscopy the fiber was identified as a right-handed bast fiber, flax or ramie (its Far Eastern equivalent), as can be seen in CD-Figures 53–55. Not only was the microscopic character of the fiber intact, the working properties of the yarns remained pliant and flexible. Its cellulosic character is confirmed by Fourier Transform Infrared Spectroscopy (FTIR), as seen in Text Figure 10. FTIR takes the chemical "finger-print" of the major constituent, so that minor components of the bast fiber—lignin or pectins, or even the tarry stain—do not necessarily figure against the dominant component, which, for modern flax, is cellulose. The tarry

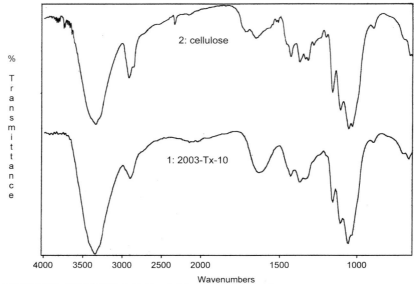

2: XGUMCELL: CELLULOSE, Schleicher & Schuell No. 289 filter pulp
1: YMBYLO10: M. Ballard swatch TX 10 yellow thread

Text Figure 10. Comparison of pure cellulose with yarn from
2003-Tx-10, by Fourier Transform Infrared Spectroscopy (FTIR).

substance partly coating textile 2003-Tx-10 has not yet been identified.

Related textiles: While the plain weave textiles of 2003-Tx-8 and 2003-Tx-9 share the same weave structure as 2003-Tx-1 and the back of 2003-Tx-2, the quality of their yarns is more lustrous, smoother, and less golden. They resemble more closely the "smooth yarns" found among the fragments of 2003-Tx-11. Textile 2003-Tx-10 is unrelated to the other plain weave fabrics in color and texture, but appears to share its fine weave count with 2003-Tx-9.

References: Reference to these fabrics cannot be discerned from Ellis's descriptions of fabric types that he catalogued from Tumulus MM.[41] Bellinger illustrates four plain weave fabrics of different fibers.[42] The sheen of the fabric illustrated in Bellinger's plate 17C is reminiscent of that of textile 2003-Tx-8, back. However, she lists it as linen. Of the group of textiles discussed in the current study, 2003-Tx-10 is the firmest candidate for attribution to flax; this textile is a dulled, matte, dark fabric with no sheen.

Textiles Found behind Serving Stand A

Textile 2003-Tx-11: various yarns, plain weave fragments.

Plates 157–158; CD-Figure 56 (overall view of fragments), CD-Figures 57–65.
Location: floor behind serving stand A.

Yarn #1
Plate 157A–D, Plate 158A.
Fiber: indeterminate, smooth appearance.
Yarn: 2 Z singles, S plied.
Color: gold colored.

Yarn #2
Plate 158B–D.
Fiber: indeterminate.
Yarn: 2 Z singles, S plied.
Color: dark (black).

Fabric #1
CD-Figure 57.
Fiber: indeterminate.
Yarn: 2 Z singles, S plied in both directions.

---

[41] Ellis, "Textile Remains."

[42] Bellinger, "Textiles from Gordion," plate 17.

Weave: balanced plain weave (tabby).

Weave count: 13 "warps"/cm × 18 "wefts"/cm (33 "warps"/inch × 46 "wefts"/inch).

Color: gold colored and, in part, green.

Fabric #2

CD-Figure 60.

Fiber: indeterminate.

Yarn: filled, 2 Z singles, S plied in both directions.

Weave: balanced plain weave.

Weave count: 18 yarns/cm × 17.5 yarns/cm (46 yarns/inch × 44 yarns/inch).

Color: gold colored with dark blue-black S-slanted markings in the yarns.

Fabric #3

CD-Figure 59.

Fibers: indeterminate.

Yarn: "warp" is Z single, gold colored; "weft" is filled, 2 Z single, S plied.

Weave: weft-faced plain weave/warp-faced plain weave.

Weave count: 14 "warps"/cm × 24 "wefts"/cm (36 "warps"/inch × 61 "wefts"/inch).

Color: tarry coated tan appearance (predominant yarn).

Fabric #4

CD-Figure 58.

Fibers: indeterminate.

Yarn: "warp" is filled, 2 Z single, S plied; "weft" is Z single, gold colored.

Weave: balanced plain weave.

Weave count: 20 "warps"/cm × 23 "wefts"/cm (51 "warps"/inch × 59 "wefts"/inch).

Color: gold colored with mottled darker areas.

A group of diverse textile fragments, including unraveled yarns and woven fabrics, was found near the east wall of the tomb, behind the inlaid serving stand A. Two types of yarns that were recovered did not appear to be associated with any of the woven fabrics. Yarn #1 could be recognized as a smooth, homogeneous spun yarn, once its surface debris was removed by mild solvent cleaning, as seen in Plate 157A.[43] Details of this yarn's fibers reveal an undifferentiated morphology, which at high magnification is seen to be composed of rows of convex bubbles (see Plates 157C, 158A). These bubbles are punctured at their top with small-diameter "blow-holes" as though for gas to escape. Running longitudinally through these bubbles are fine hairline cracks. In Plate 157D, the bubbled surface is seen to cement the left center fiber to its neighbor, and the fiber itself is hollow. That is, the coating has replaced the fiber, leaving a molten, melted-looking surface that gives a smooth appearance macroscopically.

Dark individual yarns, Yarn #2, were also found in this group. These yarns are especially friable or brittle. They are set with the permanent deflection or undulating wave that arises from ageing in place in a plain weave fabric. Yarn #2's counterpart, perhaps the weft, has disintegrated entirely, leaving these dark yarns disengaged. Once cleaned of debris, the surface of the dark yarn becomes clearer, as seen in Plates 158B–D. Again, this surface is not typical of a natural fiber: it is as though the outer cover of the fiber, whatever its origin, has been dissolved or eaten away. Indeed, the small spheres visible under high magnification are indicative of microbial activity (Plate 158C).

Samples of Yarn #2 were analyzed for their inorganic content. As seen in Table 11, they have a very high iron content (90%), though slightly lower than that found in the gold-colored textile fragments, 2003-Tx-1 (Table 1). Further examination of these yarn fragments may provide a definitive identification of the fabrics and fibers associated with these yarns, and explain the dark coloration.

In addition, four fabric fragments among the many from 2003-Tx-11 are of particular interest. Fabric #1, seen in CD-Figure 57, is a balanced plain weave. It has a tarry red stain near the center, but most peculiarly half of it is green and half of it is gold colored. Some of the yarns have a slight dark mark that follows the angle of the yarn's ply, emphasizing the S direction of the ply. This marking occurs in both warp and weft and is most apparent where the fabric is green. Green coloration on antique fabrics can be due to a combination of dyes, usually a yellow flavonoid mordanted onto a protein fiber and an indigoid vat. In archaeological contexts, copper mineral

---

[43] Cleaned with sequential baths of xylene and acrylonitrile on a support of conductive polyester medical fabric. See Ballard, MCI Report #5277, Smithsonian Institution.

Table 11. Weight percentage of inorganic elements present in the dark strands, 2003-Tx-11, Yarn #2, as analyzed by SEM-EDS.

Element	Sample 1	Sample 2	Sample 3	Sample 4	Sample 5	Sample 6	Average[44]
Magnesium	0.30 %	0.19 %	0.43 %	0.63 %	0.26 %	0.56 %	0.40 %
Aluminum	1.26	0.85	0.78	0.83	0.48	0.59	0.80
Silicon	2.43	1.97	2.77	2.00	1.34	3.16	2.28
Phosphorus	0.43	0.57	0.98	1.29	0.92	0.68	0.81
Sulfur	0.58	0.48	1.00	0.88	0.66	1.52	0.85
Potassium	1.05	0.75	0.23	0.28	0.26	0.50	0.51
Calcium	1.69	0.93	1.43	1.72	1.43	2.41	1.60
Iron	88.89	94.27	90.79	89.43	90.72	86.27	90.06
Nickel	0.71	—	—	—	—	—	—
Copper	2.67	—	1.58	2.94	3.90	4.31	2.56/3.08

salts are well known to produce green staining.[45] Indeed, some of the bronze vessels that had fallen behind the stand were apparently wrapped in or contained 2003-Tx-11 fabrics.[46] However, the FTIR spectrum for Fabric #1 produced an unusual indication of the mineral goethite for the yellow, top-dyed with indigo (see Text Figure 11 below).

It is unusual to find a dyestuff or dyeing better preserved than the fiber with which the dye is associated. The yarns of Fabric #2 (see CD-Figure 60) share the S-direction yarn markings and were also examined. In this instance the classic microchemical reduction test was carried out as well as FTIR on a microscopic scale to confirm the presence of indigo.[47] In this Fabric #2 the indigo has not been vatted; it lies inside the yarns, and it is what forms the dark tiger-stripe, perhaps painted on one of the two Z singles before they were plied. When viewed under the microscope, these stripe markings have a tarry appearance (see CD-Figure 61). A tentative identification of myrrh as the binder for the indigo powder has been made, as the FTIR in Text Figure 12 shows.

Indigo is vatted at about 50° Celsius in a reduced or oxygen-depleted, aqueous bath. In this reduced state, the pigment becomes soluble and can migrate into the fibers of a textile. Once it reoxidizes in the air, it is no longer soluble and is locked inside the fiber. Early illustrations of the process typically depict plain fabrics being submerged in vats of chemicals and dyes. Yet, there is no logical prohibition to dressing a yarn with the dye matrix, especially in the case of indigo, where the insoluble dyestuff diffuses into a fiber only in its leuco (reduced) state. Vatting a bicomponent fabric like Fabric #2 could easily produce a well-dyed, wash-fast product.

Vatting a plain, unprepared cloth runs the risk—characteristic of modern blue jean manufacture—of having the indigo vat not diffuse well through the fibers, so that the dye lies on the surface. Once poorly dyed indigo re-oxidizes and dries, the dye rubs off or "crocks" off as pigment particles. Whether it was more economical to paint yarns prior to spinning them than to dye plain cloth with more chemicals, a longer bath time, etc. is not known. Common reducing agents are odiferous; a smaller quantity might be necessary, or the duration of the bath might be shorter using painted yarns. Such fabrics could be stored as is, unreacted, for a very long time. Finally, it may have been the intention to use the indigo as a blue-black pigment, rather than as a dye. In that case, the texture of the subtle tiger-stripe was the goal, and the indigo was not simply a means to coloration.

---

[44] Elements with quantities less than 1 % by weight are not always listed. Consequently weight percentage may not total 100 %.

[45] See for example, Chen, Jakes and Foreman, "Preservation of Archaeological Textiles through Fibre Mineralization"; Gillard and Hardman, "Investigation of Fiber Mineralization Using Fourier Transform Infrared Microscopy"; Jakes and Howard, "Formation of Textile Fabric Pseudo-

morphs."

[46] Young, *Gordion I*, 111 (small cauldron, MM 7), 112 (small cauldron, MM 13), and 121 (lion- and ram-headed situlae, MM 45–46). These can be identified with Ellis's fabrics A and F.

[47] Hofenk de Graaff, "A Simple Method for the Identification of Indigo," 54–55.

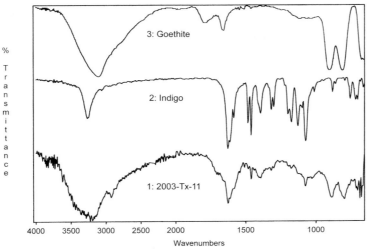

3: OLDS2012: Goethite 105174 Pike's Peak
2: XPIGBLUI: INDIGO from jo
1: YMBYLN11: M. Ballard swatch TX 11 yellow fiber segments plus blue agglomeration

Text Figure 11. Gold-colored Fabric #1 of 2003-Tx-11 and its
blue stain (bottom) are compared with the mineral goethite
(top) and the spectrum of indigo (center) by FTIR.

The inorganic elements of the bicomponent yarn were analyzed. In Table 12, the high iron content (63%) is considerably lower than in Yarn #2 or in 2003-Tx-1 (Tables 11 and 1 respectively). In the "bicomponent fabric" there is a higher copper content, a higher phosphorus content, and a higher calcium content. These inorganic elements are not directly related to the myrrh or the indigo, since they are organic in chemical structure, but they may be auxiliaries associated with the binding matrix or chemicals (additives) for subsequent dyeing. The inorganic elements may also represent contamination and migration with microbial decay.

With optical microscopy, the fibers of the bicomponent yarn appear curiously mottled, covered with particulate matter that is translucent but orange or black in color (see CD-Figures 62–63). Individual fragments of fiber do appear to have some birefringence (see CD-Figures 64–65). These characteristics appear related to those seen earlier in textile 2003-Tx-1 (compare with CD-Figures 3, 4, and 5).

Fabric #3, seen in CD-Figure 59, is a mixed fabric or "union cloth": the fine Z-spun warps do not share the same degree of twist, color, and other fiber characteristics with the larger weft yarns. The wefts are smooth 2 Z-spun singles S plied, with a tar-like filling, somewhat more irregularly coated than in Fabric #2. Upon close examination, the weft yarns of Fabric #3 appear quite similar to those of Yarn #1 and of textile 2003-Tx-1. The tar-like matrix on the weft yarns does not touch the warps, so the coating was applied prior to weaving. With the goal being to produce a weft-faced closely packed fabric, the weaver could simply have used an untarred, not-yet plied Z single. In weave constructions, a Z-spun yarn nestles on the perpendicular with an S-plied yarn. This weave structure compacts neatly. Yet, an entirely different fiber type was chosen for the Z-spun yarn, perhaps because it was stronger or cheaper. Is this a consciously crafted fabric or a finishing end? Fabric #4 is its plain weave counterpart (see CD-Figure 58, the warps set horizontally). Also a "union cloth," Fabric #4 is a balanced plain weave in somewhat more deteriorated condition. In this instance, the wefts appear more variegated than tar covered and are thus reminiscent of Fabric #2.

Related textiles: Yarn #1 may share its smooth character with textiles 2003-Tx-8 and 2003-Tx-9. Fabric #1 shares appearance and composition with textiles 2003-Tx-1 and 2003-Tx-2. Fabric #2 is linked to Fabric #1 by the presence of indigo and to Fabric #3 and Fabric #4 by the structure and technology of their weft yarns.

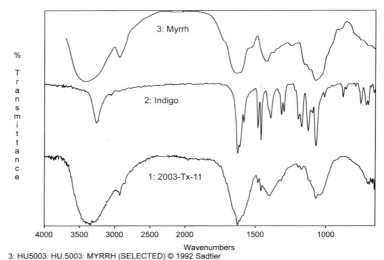

3: HU5003: HU.5003: MYRRH (SELECTED) © 1992 Sadtler
2: XPIGBLUI: INDIGO from J. Olin
1: YMBYLOGN: 2003-Tx-11 dark blue within brown threads

Text Figure 12. The FTIR spectra of the dark tiger-stripe
components of Fabric #2, 2003-Tx-11 (bottom), compared with
those of indigo (center) and of the gum resin, myrrh (top).

References: The "union" fabrics, Fabric #3 and
Fabric #4, seem to match Ellis's "Fabric F,"
which he describes as having a Z single yarn
weft and a 2 Z single S-plied warp yarn of unrelated origin. He suggests that the plied yarn
is "vegetable" and that the single is "animal."[48]
His plate 100D shows a starting border, which
can provide a tape-like edge or selvage to anchor
and space individual warps. This would place the
plied yarns as warps and the Z single as weft. If
the fibers were respectively bast and wool or mohair, such a choice would be sensible, since the
bast fiber would be stronger and capable of sus-
taining greater tension, as warps must necessarily do.[49] However, the identification of the fibers
for Fabric #3 and Fabric #4 remains problematic at this time, due to their degraded character.
Ellis noted areas on his samples where the Z single yarn was purple or dark red. This was not
seen on Fabrics #3 or #4. He also found areas
where the plied yarn was black and somewhat
melted in appearance. These dark yarns should
not be confused with those described above as
Yarn #2 (Plates 158B–D). They would seem to
be consistent with the staining seen in Fabric
#1.

Conclusions

The initial purpose of this project was to characterize and identify the fibers and fabrics physically associated with the wooden furniture in Tumulus MM. By achieving a better understanding
of the textiles related to the furniture, the role of
upholstery or cushioning might also be explored.
As the examination of the fragments got under-
way, the complexity of the extant material became apparent, as did the sophistication of the
textile workers of Gordion. The following concluding remarks summarize the samples according to category.

Textiles from the Tumulus MM Coffin

2003-Tx-1 and 2003-Tx-2, back: gold-colored balanced plain weave (tabby).

What appeared to be a straightforward tabby
or balanced plain weave from the coffin (2003-
Tx-1) is actually mineralized fabric. It is difficult
to find any organic material present, except for
some adventitious post-excavation surface fungal
and bacterial residue. Only with serious search-
ing into the least disturbed fibers could birefrin-

---

[48] Ellis, "Textile Remains," 304, plate 100E.

[49] Ibid., 298–299, 304.

Table 12. Weight percentage of inorganic elements present in a single bicomponent yarn, 2003-Tx-11, Fabric #2, as analyzed by SEM-EDS.

Element	Sample 1	Sample 2	Sample 3	Average[50]
Magnesium	1.28 %	1.51 %	1.91 %	1.57 %
Aluminum	1.61	1.33	1.33	1.42
Silicon	3.85	3.15	3.08	3.36
Phosphorus	4.97	5.82	5.83	5.54
Sulfur	1.28	1.37	1.39	1.35
Chlorine	0.60	0.54	0.43	0.52
Potassium	0.87	0.96	0.84	0.89
Calcium	6.98	7.65	7.28	7.30
Iron	64.32	61.82	63.72	63.29
Copper	14.23	15.84	14.20	14.76

gence be found to suggest the anisotropic behavior of flax. Yet, technically, this positive mineralized cast of a fiber does not conform to the image of a "pseudomorph" since the metal is iron, rather than copper. Iron is reputed to produce negative casts and destruction to the preservation of the textile shape.[51] Corroded textile residues might be expected due to the proximity to the iron bars and other reinforcements on the coffin. However, analyses of the extant textiles more closely conform to the results of an intentional coating, which appears to be goethite.[52] Iron oxide hydroxide is also present on the back of another fragment associated with the coffin (2003-Tx-2) and others found behind serving stand A (2003-Tx-11). Were these "gold" textiles a source for the legend of King Midas's "golden touch"?

2003-Tx-2, front; 2003-Tx-3; and *2003-Tx-5:* "mattress."

The issue of felt, matting, or "mattress" material remains perplexing. Whatever the fabric or fabrics once were, 2003-Tx-2, front; 2003-Tx-3; and 2003-Tx-5 have degraded into laminar, chunk-like entities that have only a tenuous connection to a felt or its lofted opposite, a bat-

ting. Bellinger and Ellis recognized the strong cultural and historic connection of felted materials, made of sheep's wool or of goat's wool (mohair), to the geographical area.[53] Yet in the extant fragments there appears to be no organic material remaining in a cohesive and identifiable condition. Optical microscopy cannot identify anything so completely degraded; FTIR is often ambiguous about proteins. Even amino acid analysis with High-Performance Liquid Chromatography (HPLC) cannot provide a definitive association with particular amino acids because of the absence of coherent organic residues.[54] The remnant strata suggest that, for the most part, the fibers were not mineralized, negatively or positively, since the space and volume the fibers originally occupied have shrunk to thin, flat layers.

These layers now appear to be composed of colorants, organic or inorganic. These compounds may be the actual residue original to the unknown textile-like materials as they lay in place in the tumulus. That is, these layers might indicate additional intentional colored coatings on fabrics. Throughout the tomb, other proteinaceous materials without a colored, mineral content have disappeared entirely: the flesh and hair of the king himself are gone, and only his

---

[50] Elements with quantities less than 1 % by weight are not always listed. Consequently weight percentage may not total 100 %.

[51] Gillard and Hardman, "Investigation of Fiber Mineralization Using Fourier Transform Infrared Microscopy," 180–181. See Blanchette and Simpson, "Soft Rot and Wood Pseudomorphs in an Ancient Coffin," for pseudomorphs of iron corrosion products that replicated wood cells from the Tumulus MM coffin.

[52] Kuhn, "Adsorption at the Liquid/Solid Interface: Metal Oxide Coated Textiles," 283.

[53] See also Gervers and Gervers, "Felt-making Crafts-

men of the Anatolian and Iranian Plateaux"; Steinkeller, "Mattresses and Felt in Early Mesopotamia." This reasoning is reinforced by economic pragmatism: the internal stuffing matter of cushioning tends to be low cost and ubiquitous—in western Europe and North America, horsehair was widely used as an upholstery stuffing.

[54] Personal communication, Dr. Amandine Péquignot, Musée National d'Histoire Naturelle, Paris. Dr. Péquignot prepared a sample of the red verso of 2003-Tx-2 and conducted amino acid analysis by High-Performance Liquid Chromatography (HPLC) at MCI. See Ballard, MCI Report #5277, Smithsonian Institution.

highly mineral (calcium) bones remained. Like the bones, the possibly inorganic colored compounds may be acting as circumstantial evidence that substantial protein fibers and fabrics once existed. The exact mechanisms of microbial decomposition lie outside the purview of the current discussion, but the extant material is consistent with microbial degradation.[55]

2003-Tx-3, 2003-Tx-4, and *2003-Tx-5*: twined textiles.

Twined textiles were not previously recognized among the residues from Tumulus MM. Two twined textiles, from samples 2003-Tx-4 and 2003-Tx-5, are difficult to characterize by yarn and twist, due to the presence of debris, mineralization, or other degradation. Yet, in a fiber taken from 2003-Tx-5, traces of the birefringence typical of flax fiber were discovered. Within 2003-Tx-3, also associated with the coffin, a small area has the darker yarns and oblique angles observed with the other group of twined fabrics, found in the northeast corner of the tomb chamber (see below).

Textiles from the Northeast Corner of the Tomb Chamber

2003-Tx-6: "blanketing."

This sample ("blanketing") closely resembles 2003-Tx-2, front; 2003-Tx-3; and 2003-Tx-5 from the coffin, discussed above. It was described by the excavators as "blanketing" on "stool #2." About this sample, it is possible to gather some information, which can then be applied to the comparable material from the coffin. Distinct layers confer the possibility of successive homogeneous materials, multiple upholstery materials with different (mineral) compositions, as seen along the rims of textile fragment 2003-Tx-6. The aperture where no yarn now exists, seen in CD-Figure 28 (textile fragment 2003-Tx-6), and the large yarn seen in CD-Figure 12 (textile fragment 2003-Tx-3) share a common diameter and provide plausible evidence for the use of the heavy (400–700 gram) loom weights excavated at the city mound.[56] In order for non-woven felt to support the weight of a human body without sagging or splitting apart, it would be prudent

to strengthen it with a network of strong interlaced yarns—a coarse woven underlayer and perhaps successive interlayers. These might correlate to the spun fabric that Bellinger described; she also saw the multiple colors as an indication of multiple layers and intentional patterning of the "felt."[57]

Distinct from these woven and non-woven interlayers are the S-twisted cords that lay beneath the "felts" of 2003-Tx-6, visible now largely as impressions imbedded in the textile sample (seen in Plate 155B). The small fragment shows only vertical cords, but they would likely have been locked with perpendicular cording, perhaps to form some kind of knotted netting, in order to support weight and distribute it. And clearly the cording did hold its place unsplayed, since the cords are still aligned. These cords were originally a material unrelated to the fiber of the "felts," for they have not undergone drastic flattening or dissolution. This cording is thought to have formed the seat of "stool #2" (see above, pp. 114, 211–213).

2003-Tx-6, 2003-Tx-7, 2003-Tx-8, and *2003-Tx-9*: twined textiles.

Most of the extant twined textiles (fragments 2003-Tx-6, 2003-Tx-7, 2003-Tx-8, and 2003-Tx-9) seem to share a similar fiber, yarn, coloration, and spacing. The fiber for both warp and weft seems to be dark, and the yarns have a low, almost imperceptible twist. Twist is necessary with short fibers ("staple") in order to connect them and to form a continuous yarn; more twists increase yarn cohesiveness and strength. Long continuous fibers, called "monofilaments," are actually weakened by twisting. Consequently, monofilaments like silk often have little twist, just enough to keep them bundled as yarn units. The yarns of the twined textiles from Tumulus MM appear to share this property. In addition to silk from the *Bombyx mori* moth, originally native to the Far East, true silk-like monofilaments are extruded by other moths and insects. Characteristics of silk are exhibited by other materials, from sinew to byssus.[58]

One alternative, "sea-silk" or byssus, is reported to have been favored as an Assyrian lux-

---

[55] For an interesting discussion of the complexity of microbial activity, see Filley, Blanchette, Simpson, and Fogel, "Nitrogen Cycling."

[56] Burke, "Textile Production at Gordion and the Phrygian Economy," 75–78. However, heavy loom weights can

also be used for fine yarns, according to Hoffman, *Warp-Weighted Loom*, 20–22.

[57] Bellinger, "Textiles from Gordion," 13.

[58] R. Forbes, *Studies in Ancient Technology* 4, 50–58.

ury good.[59] Byssus is the anchoring fiber produced by molluscs, notably the *Pinna nobilis* Linné and can be harvested.[60] Modern samples of byssus may reach 3 inches (8 cm) in length,[61] but this is not as long as flax fiber or many wools can be. All of these fibers require a substantial number of spinning twists for strength. Other alternatives are Coan silk from the *Pachypasa otus* Drury, a large moth native to the central and eastern Mediterranean,[62] or *Saturnia pyri*, the source of a strong and glossy dark brown silk.[63] One interesting aspect of *Bombyx mori* silk is its inherent resistance to microbial degradation;[64] perhaps these other more likely sources of the twined yarns share silk's measure of bacterial immunity.

All of the twined textiles appear to be very regular and fine. The yarns are thin, and the row spacings are narrow, as with a sheer, detailed netting. It should be noted that even monochromatic twined structures can be altered to produce designs and patterns. This kind of alteration may have been a feature of the Gordion textiles, and might account for the difficulty in deducing the weave structure and its technological origins. There are two contexts for these twined weavings. Fragments 2003-Tx-3, 2003-Tx-4, and 2003-Tx-5 are associated with the reddish-purplish material of the coffin. For the rest, textiles 2003-Tx-6, 2003-Tx-7, 2003-Tx-8, and 2003-Tx-9 were found in the northeast corner of the tomb and are most often layered with a white powder, not yet identified. For fragment 2003-Tx-3, there is, amidst the reddish-purplish fragments associated with the coffin, a small area in which the dark yarns are set vertically at oblique angles, with a white powder layer disposed in a laminar manner (see Table 4 above). The twined textiles appear to have a specific context, or designated use, that unites them, even in their pattern of degradation, and despite their different locations in the tomb. From our modern perspective, we might imagine twined textiles used for the decoration of pillows or for open-weave lined hangings; the twined weavings might also have been used as storage containers for light-weight valuables, food or feathers, which now survive as the degraded white powder. The excavators' theory that there was a "bag" on "stool #2" in the northeast corner may point to these twined textiles.

Plain Weaves from the Northeast Corner and Floor behind Serving Stand A

2003-Tx-8, back; *2003-Tx-9, back*; *2003-Tx-10*; and *2003-Tx-11*: balanced, faced, bicomponent, and union plain weaves.

The bicomponent tabby weave found behind serving stand A (2003-Tx-11, Fabric #2) shows an inventive method of incorporating indigo within a fabric. It may have been carried out using an active and passive yarn-plying technology, as suggested by another tan textile fragment (2003-Tx-8, back). Flax (or ramie) fiber from the bast fiber group was positively identified as the basis of the "pieces of fine material lifted from fibulae" on "stool #2" in the northeast corner (2003-Tx-10), but this fabric lacks congruency in yarn character and weave count with the other plain-weave fabrics. It may be that this fabric (2003-Tx-10) was imported or anomalous for some other reason. Coarser fabrics may have been considered more suitable for the application of a metallic coating—or for bedding.

As the study of the Gordion textiles is an ongoing project, the findings presented here may be augmented in the future. Some of the problems relating to the fiber and fabric construction have been resolved, yet others remain enigmatic, including the precise relationship of some of the fabrics to the wooden furniture. Separating the accidental synergy of various degradation processes from intentional workmanship remains a challenge. However, it is clear that the fabrics, like the furniture, show a high level of technological achievement, skill, inventiveness, and sophistication.

[59] Dalley, "Ancient Assyrian Textiles and the Origins of Carpet Design," 121–123.

[60] See Montegut, "Moth or Mollusc? A Technical Examination of Byssus Fibers."

[61] Author's measurement, National Museum of Natural History, Smithsonian Institution.

[62] See Handschin, "Wild Silk Moths."

[63] See W. Forbes, "Silkworm of Aristotle."

[64] See Seves, et al., "Microbial Degradation of Silk."

APPENDIX 9

CONCORDANCE

Furniture, fragments, and associated objects from Tumulus MM	Illustrations	Gordion inventory number	Tumulus MM number (Gordion I)
Inlaid table	Figures 1, 4–28, 30I Color Plates III, VIII–IX Plates 1–35, 124A–B, 129–132, 145A–B, 150D, 151A	5212 W 80	MM 388
Table 1	Figures 29A, 30A, 31 Color Plate IIIA Plates 36A, 37–41, 125B, 126A–B	5203 W 79	MM 380
Table 2	Figures 29B, 30B, 32–34 Color Plate V Plates 36B, 42–45, 128, 143A–B	12516 W 124	MM 382
Table 3	Figures 29C, 30C, 35 Color Plate V Plates 36B, 46–49	12517 W 125	MM 384
Table 4	Figures 29D, 30D, 36 Color Plate IIIA Plates 36, 50–53, 128, 141D, 142C–D	12518 W 126	MM 381
Table 5	Figures 29E, 30E, 37–40 Color Plate IIIA Plates 36A, 54–59, 127B, 146C, 151C–D	5202 W 78	MM 383
Table 6	Figures 29F, 30F, 41 Plates 36B, 60–62, 126C, 141A–B, 144, 146A, 152B	12519 W 127	MM 385
Table 7	Figures 29G, 30G, 42 Plates 36B, 63–65, 141C, 143C–D, 146B, 152A	12520 W 128	MM 386
Table 9	Figures 29H, 30H, 43 Color Plate IIA Plates 66–68, 100, 108A, 142A–B, 146E–F	12521 W 129	MM 387
Serving stand A	Figures 2, 44–51, 60, 62–63, 66, 67A, 68–69, 71–73 Color Plates IIIA, IVA, X, XII–XIII Plates 69–79, 90–91, 93, 94D, 95A, 96A–B, 97A–B, 98A–B, 99A–D, 133–134, 135A, 136A, 137, 138B, 145C–D, 150A–B, 157–158 CD-Figures 66–69	5229 W 81	MM 378
Serving stand B	Figures 52–59, 61, 64–66, 67B, 68, 70–71, 74–75 Color Plates IIIA, IVB, XI, XIV–XV Plates 69, 80–89, 92, 94, 95B, 96C–D, 97C–D, 98C–D, 99E–F, 124C, 133A, 134B, 135–136, 137A–B, 138, 146D, 150A–C, 151B CD-Figures 70–73	5230 W 82	MM 379
Furniture from the northeast corner	Figures 76–78 Color Plate IIB Plates 100–106, 127A, 155–156		

Furniture, fragments, and associated objects from Tumulus MM	Illustrations	Gordion inventory number	Tumulus MM number (Gordion I)
Carved stretcher, northeast corner	Figures 77–78 Plates 100–101, 104–105A, 127A	12522 W 130	
Stool leg ("short leg"), northeast corner	Figure 76 Plates 100–101, 105B	12538 W 131	
Coffin	Figures 3, 79–90 Color Plates IB, IIA, XVIA Plates 107–115, 147, 148A–C, 149, 153–154	12210 W 123	MM 389
Coffin, associated iron fragments	Plates 113, 114A–B	12209 ILS 766	

BIBLIOGRAPHY

Translations of ancient texts cited appear here under the names of the ancient authors.

Ahlberg, Gudrun
　　1971　　*Prothesis and Ekphora in Greek Geometric Art*. Göteborg: Paul Åströms Förlag.

Akurgal, Ekrem
　　1949　　*Spaethethitische Bildkunst*. Ankara: Ankara University.
　　1955　　*Phrygische Kunst*. Ankara: Ankara University.
　　1961　　*Die Kunst Anatoliens von Homer bis Alexander*. Berlin: Walter de Gruyter.
　　1962　　*The Art of the Hittites*. New York: Harry N. Abrams.
　　1968　　*The Art of Greece: Its Origins in the Mediterranean and Near East*. New York: Crown.

Albenda, Pauline
　　1978　　"Assyrian Carpets in Stone." *Journal of the Ancient Near Eastern Society of Columbia University* 10:1–34.

Aldred, Cyril
　　1971　　*Jewels of the Pharaohs: Egyptian Jewellery of the Dynastic Period*. London: Thames and Hudson.

Allen, Max
　　1981　　*The Birth Symbol in Traditional Women's Art from Eurasia and the Western Pacific*. Toronto: Museum for Textiles.

Alp, Sedat
　　1968　　*Zylinder- und Stempelsiegel aus Karahöyük bei Konya*. Ankara: Türk Tarih Kurumu.

Arias, P.E., and Max Hirmer
　　1962　　*A History of Greek Vase Painting*. London: Thames and Hudson.

Aruz, Joan, Kim Benzel, and Jean Evans, eds.
　　2008　　*Beyond Babylon: Art, Trade, and Diplomacy in the Second Millennium B.C.* New York and New Haven: Metropolitan Museum of Art and Yale University Press.

Ataç, Mehmet-Ali
　　2006　　"Visual Formula and Meaning in Neo-Assyrian Relief Sculpture." *The Art Bulletin* 88, no. 1:69–101.

Athenaeus
　　1928–1951　　*Deipnosophistae*, trans. C.B. Gulick. Loeb ed. Cambridge, MA: Harvard University Press.

Aytuğ, Burhan
　　1986　　"Kral Midas'la Gömülen Mobilyalar (The Furniture Buried with King Midas)." In *Arkeometri Ünitesi Bilimsel Toplantı Bildirileri* 6, 3–11. Ankara: Tübitak.
　　1988　　"Le mobilier funéraire du roi Midas I." In *Wood and Archaeology, Acts of the European Symposium, Louvain-la-Neuve, October 1987, PACT 22*, edited by T. Hackens, A.V. Munaut, and C. Till, 357–368. Strasbourg: Council of Europe.

Azarpay, Guitty
　　1968　　*Urartian Art and Artifacts: A Chronological Study*. Berkeley, CA: University of California Press.

Bachmann, W.
　　1927　　*Felsreliefs in Assyrien: Bawian, Maltai und Gundük*. Leipzig: J.C. Hinrichs'sche Buchhandlung.

Bahrani, Zainab
　　2001　　*Women of Babylon: Gender and Representation in Mesopotamia*. London: Routledge.

Baker, Hollis S.
　　1966　　*Furniture in the Ancient World, Origins and Evolution: 3100–475 B.C.* London: The Connoisseur.

Baker, Tim
   1992   "Glue." In *The Traditional Bowyer's Bible* 1, edited by Jim Hamm, 195–206. New York: Bois d'Arc Press.

Ballard, Mary
   2008   *MCI Report #5277: The Gordion Project.* Museum Conservation Institute Archives, Smithsonian Institution.

Balter, Michael
   2005   *The Goddess and the Bull.* New York: Free Press.

Barber, Elizabeth Wayland
   1991   *Prehistoric Textiles: The Development of Cloth in the Neolithic and Bronze Ages, with Special Reference to the Aegean.* Princeton: Princeton University Press.
   1994   *Women's Work: The First 20,000 Years.* New York: Norton.
   1999   *The Mummies of Ürümchi.* New York: Norton.
   1999   "The Curious Tale of the Ultra-Long Sleeve." In *Folk Dress in Europe and Anatolia: Beliefs about Protection and Fertility*, edited by Linda Welters, 111–134. Oxford: Berg.

Barber, Elizabeth Wayland, and Paul Barber
   2004   *When They Severed Earth from Sky: How the Human Mind Shapes Myth.* Princeton, NJ: Princeton University Press.

Barclay, R.
   1981   "Wood Consolidation on an Eighteenth Century English Fire Engine." *Studies in Conservation* 26:133–139.

Barnett, Richard D.
   1950   "The Excavations of the British Museum at Toprak Kale Near Van." *Iraq* 12:1–43.
   1954   "The Excavations of the British Museum at Toprak Kale, Near Van–Addenda." *Iraq* 16:3–22.
   1975   *A Catalogue of the Nimrud Ivories, with Other Examples of Ancient Near Eastern Ivories in the British Museum.* London: British Museum.
   1976   *Sculptures from the North Palace of Ashurbanipal at Nineveh (668–627 B.C.).* Oxford: Oxford University Press.

Bass, George
   1987   "Oldest Known Shipwreck Reveals Splendors of the Bronze Age." *National Geographic* 172, no. 6:693–733.

Baumann, Hellmut
   1993   *The Greek Plant World in Myth, Art and Literature.* Portland, OR: Timber Press.

Beck, Roger
   2006   *The Religion of the Mithras Cult in the Roman Empire: Mysteries of the Unconquered Sun.* Oxford: Oxford University Press.

Beckman, Gary
   1995   "Royal Ideology and State Administration in Hittite Anatolia." In *Civilizations of the Ancient Near East* 1, edited by Jack M. Sasson, 529–543. New York: Scribner's.

Bellinger, Louisa
   1962   "Textiles from Gordion." *The Bulletin of the Needle and Bobbin Club* 46, nos. 1–2:5–33.

Bergmann, Bettina, and Wendy Watson
   1999   *The Moon and the Stars: Afterlife of a Roman Empress.* South Hadley, MA: Mt. Holyoke College Art Museum.

Berndt, Dietrich, and Horst Ehringhaus
   1994   "Langsam stirbt Kybele: Fortschreitende Zerstörung phrygischer Felsdenkmäler." *Antike Welt* 2:166–171.

Berndt-Ersöz, Susanne
   1998   "Phrygian Rock-Cut Cult Façades: A Study of the Function of the So-called Shaft Monuments." *Anatolian Studies* 48:87–112.
   2004   "In Search of a Phrygian Male Superior God." In *Offizielle Religion, lokale Kulte und individuelle Religiosität*, edited by Manfred Hutter and Sylvia Hutter-Braunsar, 47–56. Münster: Ugarit-Verlag.
   2006   *Phrygian Rock-Cut Shrines: Structure, Function, and Cult Practice.* Leiden: Brill.

Bianchi, Robert
    1985   "Reflections of the Sky's Eyes." *Source* 4, nos. 2/3:10–18.

Bittel, Kurt
    1963   "Phrygisches Kultbild aus Boğazköy." *Antike Plastik* 2:7–21.
    1970   *Hattusha: The Capital of the Hittites*. New York: Oxford University Press.
    1976   *Die Hethiter: die Kunst Anatoliens vom Ende des 3. bis zum Anfang des 1. Jahrtausends vor Christus*. Munich:
                    C.H. Beck.
    1981   "Kubaba: Ikonographie." *Reallexicon der Assyriologie* 6:261–264.

Black, Jeremy, and Anthony Green
    1992   *Gods, Demons and Symbols of Ancient Mesopotamia: An Illustrated Dictionary*. London: British Museum
                    Press.

Blackburn, Graham
    1977   *Illustrated Furniture Making*. London: Robert Hale.

Blanchette, Robert A.
    1998   "A Guide to Wood Deterioration Caused by Microorganisms and Insects." In *The Structural
                    Conservation of Panel Paintings*, edited by K. Dardes and A. Rothe, 55–68. Los Angeles, CA: J. Paul
                    Getty Museum.
    2000   "A Review of Microbial Deterioration Found in Archaeological Wood from Different Environ-
                    ments." *International Biodeterioration and Biodegradation* 46:189–204.
    2003   "Deterioration in Historic and Archaeological Woods from Terrestrial Sites." In *Art, Biology, and
                    Conservation: Biodeterioration of Works of Art*, edited by Robert Koestler, Victoria Koestler, A. Elena
                    Charola, and Fernando Nieto-Fernandez, 328–347. New York: Metropolitan Museum of Art.

Blanchette, Robert A., Kory Cease, André Abad, Robert Koestler, Elizabeth Simpson, and G. Kenneth Sams
    1991   "An Evaluation of Different Forms of Deterioration Found in Archaeological Wood." *International
                    Biodeterioration* 28:3–22.

Blanchette, Robert A., and Elizabeth Simpson
    1992   "Soft Rot and Wood Pseudomorphs in an Ancient Coffin (700 B.C.) from Tumulus MM at
                    Gordion, Turkey." *Journal of the International Association of Wood Anatomists* 13, no. 2:201–213.

Boardman, John
    1955   "Painted Funerary Plaques and Some Remarks on Prothesis." *Annual of the British School at Athens*
                    50:51–66.
    1998   *Early Greek Vase Painting, 11th–6th Centuries B.C.: A Handbook*. London: Thames and Hudson.

Boehmer, Rainer
    1973   "Phrygische Prunkgewänder des 8. Jahrhunderts v. Chr. Herkunft und Export." *Archäologischer
                    Anzeiger* 2:149–172.

Bonfante, Larissa
    2005   "The Verucchio Throne and the Corsini Chair: Two Status Symbols of Ancient Italy." In *Terra
                    Marique: Studies in Art History and Marine Archaeology in Honor of Anna Marguerite McCann*, edited by
                    John Pollini, 3–11. Oxford: Oxbow.

Bradsher, Keith
    2005   "More Than a Billion Chinese but So Few Coffins." *New York Times*, November 10.

Breu, Marlene
    1999   "Traditional Turkish Women's Dress: A Source of Common Understandings for Expected
                    Behaviours." In *Folk Dress in Europe and Anatolia: Beliefs about Protection and Fertility*, edited by Linda
                    Welters, 33–51. Oxford: Berg.

Brixhe, Claude
    1981   "Les graffites du grand tumulus." In R.S. Young, *Three Great Early Tumuli, The Gordion Excavations
                    Final Reports* I, 273–277. Philadelphia, PA: University of Pennsylvania Museum of Archaeology
                    and Anthropology.
    2002   "Corpus des inscriptions paléo-phrygiennes. Supplément I." *Kadmos* 41:1–102.

Brixhe, Claude, and Michel Lejeune
    1984   *Corpus des inscriptions paléo-phrygiennes*. Paris: Éditions Recherche sur les Civilisations.

Bryce, Trevor
    2004   *Life and Society in the Hittite World*. Oxford: Oxford University Press.

Buck, Susan, and John Childs
    1990   "Sample Analysis: Gordion Furniture from Tumulus MM." Gordion Furniture Project Archives.

Budin, Stephanie
    2003   *The Origin of Aphrodite.* Bethesda, MD: CDL Press.

Buluç, Sevim
    1979   *Ankara Frig Nekropolünden Üç Tümülüs Buluntuları* [Doçentlik Tezi]. Ankara: Ankara University (DTCF).
    1986   "Ankara Kabartmaları." In *IX. Türk Tarih Kongresi-Bildiriler,* 423–433. Ankara: Türk Tarih Kurumu.
    1988   "The Architectural Use of the Animal and Kybele Reliefs Found in Ankara and Its Vicinity." *Source* 7, nos. 3–4:16–23.

Burke, Brendan
    2005   "Textile Production at Gordion and the Phrygian Economy." In *The Archaeology of Midas and the Phrygians. Recent Work at Gordion,* edited by Lisa Kealhofer, 69–81. Philadelphia, PA: University of Pennsylvania Museum of Archaeology and Anthropology.

Burkert, Walter
    1983   *Homo Necans: The Anthropology of Ancient Greek Sacrificial Ritual and Myth,* trans. Peter Bing. Berkeley, CA: University of California Press.

Burnham, Dorothy
    1980   *Warp and Weft, A Dictionary of Textile Terms.* New York: Scribner's, 1980.

Calmeyer, Peter
    1996   "Achaimenidische Möbel." In *The Furniture of Western Asia: Ancient and Traditional,* edited by Georgina Herrmann, 223–231. Mainz: Philipp von Zabern.

Carpenter, Edmund. See Schuster, Carl, and Edmund Carpenter.

Cartwright, Caroline
    2005   "The Bronze Age Wooden Tomb Furniture from Jericho: The Microscopical Reconstruction of a Distinctive Carpentry Tradition." *Palestine Exploration Quarterly* 137, no. 2:99–138.

Caubet, Annie, and François Poplin
    1987   "Les objets de matière dure animale. Étude du matériau." In *Ras Shamra-Ougarit 3. Le centre de la ville, 38ᵉ–40ᵉ campagnes (1978–1984),* edited by M. Yon, 273–306. Paris: Éditions Recherche sur les Civilisations.

Caubet, Annie, and Marguerite Yon
    1996   "Le mobilier d'Ougarit (d'après les travaux récents)." In *The Furniture of Western Asia: Ancient and Traditional,* edited by Georgina Herrmann, 61–72. Mainz: Philipp von Zabern.

Chen, Hsiou-lien, Kathryn A. Jakes, and Dennis W. Foreman
    1998   "Preservation of Archaeological Textiles through Fibre Mineralization." *Journal of Archaeological Science* 25, no. 10:1015–1021.

Clagett, Marshall
    1995   *Calendars, Clocks, and Astronomy. Ancient Egyptian Science* 2. Philadelphia, PA: American Philosophical Society.

Cohen, Andrew
    2005   *Death Rituals, Ideology, and the Development of Early Mesopotamian Kingship: Toward a New Understanding of Iraq's Royal Cemetery of Ur.* Leiden: Brill.

Cohen, Mark
    1993   *The Cultic Calendars of the Ancient Near East.* Bethesda, MD: CDL.

Coldstream, J.N.
    1968   *Greek Geometric Pottery: A Survey of Ten Local Styles and Their Chronology.* London: Methuen.
    1977   *Deities in Aegean Art before and after the Dark Age.* London: Bedford College.
    2003   *Geometric Greece: 900–700 B.C.* London: Routledge.

Collingwood, Peter
    1982   *The Techniques of Tablet Weaving.* New York: Watson-Guptill.

Collins, Billie Jean
    2001   "Ritual Meals in the Hittite Cult." In *Ancient Magic and Ritual Power,* edited by Marvin Meyer and Paul Mirecki, 77–92. Leiden: Brill.

2002   "Animals in the Religions of Ancient Anatolia." In *A History of the Animal World in the Ancient Near East*, edited by Billie Jean Collins, 309–334. Leiden: Brill.

2004   "The Politics of Hittite Religious Iconography." In *Offizielle Religion, lokale Kulte und individuelle Religiosität*, edited by Manfred Hutter and Sylvia Hutter-Braunsar, 83–115. Münster: Ugarit-Verlag.

Collon, Dominique
2001   *Cylinder Seals V: Neo-Assyrian and Neo-Babylonian Periods*. London: British Museum.

Cornelius, Izak
2004   *The Many Faces of the Goddess: The Iconography of the Syro-Palestinian Goddesses Anat, Astarte, Qedeshet, and Asherah c. 1500–1000 B.C.* Orbis Biblicus et Orientalis 204. Fribourg: Academic Press Fribourg.

Crowfoot, Grace M.
1954   "Textiles, Basketry, and Mats." In *A History of Technology* 1: *From Early Times to Fall of Ancient Empires*, edited by Charles Singer, E.J. Holmyard, and A.R. Hall, 413–447. Oxford: Clarendon Press.

Curtis, John
1996   "Assyrian Furniture: The Archaeological Evidence." In *The Furniture of Western Asia: Ancient and Traditional*, edited by Georgina Herrmann, 167–180. Mainz: Philipp von Zabern.

Dalley, Stephanie
1991   "Ancient Assyrian Textiles and the Origins of Carpet Design." *Iran* 29:117–135.

Davis, P.H.
1965–2000   *Flora of Turkey and the East Aegean Islands*. Edinburgh: University of Edinburgh Press.

De Grummond, Nancy
1985   "The Etruscan Mirror." *Source* 4, nos. 2/3:26–35.

2000   "Mirrors and *Manteia*: Themes of Prophecy on Etruscan and Praenestine Mirrors." In *Aspetti e problemi della produzione degli specchi etruschi figurati*, edited by M.D. Gentili, 27–67. Rome: Aracne.

Dentzer, Jean-Marie
1982   *Le motif du banquet couché dans le Proche-Orient et le monde grec du VIIe au IVe siècle avant J.-C.* Rome: École française de Rome.

Depuydt, Leo
1997   *Civil Calendar and Lunar Calendar in Ancient Egypt*. Leuven: Peeters.

Detienne, Marcel
1989   "Culinary Practices and the Spirit of Sacrifice." In *The Cuisine of Sacrifice among the Greeks*, edited by Marcel Detienne and Jean-Pierre Vernant, 1–20. Chicago, IL: University of Chicago Press.

DeVries, Keith
1980   "Greeks and Phrygians in the Early Iron Age." In *From Athens to Gordion: The Papers of a Memorial Symposium for Rodney S. Young*, edited by Keith DeVries, 33–49. Philadelphia, PA: University of Pennsylvania Museum of Archaeology and Anthropology.

2002   "The Throne of Midas?" *American Journal of Archaeology* 106, no. 2:275.

DeVries, Keith, Peter Kuniholm, G. Kenneth Sams, and Mary Voigt
2003   "New Dates for Iron Age Gordion." *Antiquity* 77, no. 296 (http://antiquity.ac.uk/ProjGall/devries/devries.html).

Diodorus. See Pollitt, *The Art of Ancient Greece: Sources and Documents*.

Doob, Penelope Reed
1990   *The Idea of the Labyrinth from Classical Antiquity through the Middle Ages*. Ithaca, NY: Cornell University Press.

Dörtlük, Kayhan
1988   "Elmalı Bayındır Tümülüsleri Kutarma Kazısı." *X. Kazı Sonuçları Toplantısı* 1:171–174.

Drews, Robert
1993   "Myths of Midas and the Phrygian Migration from Europe." *Klio* 75:9–26.

Dunbabin, Katherine
1999   *Mosaics of the Greek and Roman World*. Cambridge: Cambridge University Press.

Dunn, Emily
   1989   "Banquet Table 1." Conservation report, Gordion Furniture Project Archives.

Dusinberre, Elspeth
   2002   "An Excavated Ivory from Kerkenes Dağ, Turkey: Transcultural Fluidities, Significations of
                   Collective Identity, and the Problem of Median Art." *Ars Orientalis* 32:17–54.

Easton, Donald
   2002   *Schliemann's Excavations at Troia, 1870–1873.* Studia Troica 2. Mainz: Philipp von Zabern.

Eaton-Krauss, Marianne
   2008   *The Thrones, Chairs, Stools, and Footstools from the Tomb of Tutankhamun.* Oxford: Griffith Institute.

Eliade, Mircea
   1964   *Shamanism: Archaic Techniques of Ecstasy.* Princeton, NJ: Princeton University Press.

Ellis, Richard
   1981   "Appendix V: Textiles: The Textile Remains." In Rodney S. Young, *Three Great Early Tumuli, The
                   Gordion Excavations Final Reports I,* 294–310. Philadelphia, PA: University of Pennsylvania Museum
                   of Archaeology and Anthropology.

Emery, Irene
   1966   *Primary Structure of Fabrics.* Washington, DC: Textile Museum.

Erbek, Mine
   2002   *Çatalhöyük'ten Günümüze Anadolu Motifleri (Anatolian Motifs: From Çatalhöyük to the Present).* Ankara:
                   Ministry of Culture of the Republic of Turkey.

Erden, Attila
   1998   *Anadolu Giysi Kültürü (Anatolian Garment Culture).* Ankara: Ministry of Culture of the Republic of
                   Turkey.

Evans, James
   1998   *The History and Practice of Ancient Astronomy.* New York: Oxford University Press.

Evershed, R.P., S.J. Vaughan, S.N. Dudd, et al.
   1997   "Fuel for Thought? Beeswax in Lamps and Conical Cups from Late Minoan Crete." *Antiquity*
                   71:979–985.

Eyre, Christopher
   1995   "The Agricultural Cycle, Farming, and Water Management in the Ancient Near East." In
                   Civilizations of the Ancient Near East 1, edited by Jack M. Sasson, 175–189. New York: Scribner's.

Feigl, Fritz
   1966   *Spot Tests in Organic Analysis,* in collaboration with V. Anger, trans. R.E. Oesper. Amsterdam:
                   Elsevier.

Filley, Timothy R., Robert A. Blanchette, Elizabeth Simpson, and Marilyn L. Fogel
   2001   "Nitrogen Cycling by Wood Decomposing Soft-Rot Fungi in the 'King Midas Tomb,' Gordion,
                   Turkey." *Proceedings of the National Academy of Sciences of the United States of America* 98, no. 23:13,346–
                   350.

Finkel, Irving
   2007   "On the Rules for the Royal Game of Ur." In *Ancient Board Games in Perspective,* edited by Irving
                   Finkel, 16–32. London: British Museum.

Forbes, Robert J.
   1964   *Studies in Ancient Technology 4.* Leiden: Brill.

Forbes, William T.M.
   1930   "The Silkworm of Aristotle." *Classical Philology* 25:22–26.

Ford, James, and Clarence Webb
   1956   "Poverty Point, A Late Archaic Site in Louisiana." *Anthropological Papers of the American Museum of
                   Natural History* 46, part 1:1–136.

Frankfort, Henri
   1948   *Kingship and the Gods.* Reprint, Chicago, IL: University of Chicago Press, 1971.

Frid, Tage
   1979   *Tage Frid Teaches Woodworking, Book I. Joinery.* Newtown, CT: Taunton.

Gardiner, Alan
    1973   *Egyptian Grammar*. London: Oxford University Press.

Gentili, Gino Vinicio
    1987   "Verucchio." In *La Formazione della città in Emilia Romagna: Verucchio*, edited by Giovanna
                Montanari, 207–263. Bologna: Nuova Alfa Editoriale.
    2003   *Verucchio Villanoviana: Il sepolcreto in località Le Pegge e la necropoli al piede della Rocca Malatestiana*.
                Rome: Giorgio Bretschneider.

Gervers, Michael, and Veronica Gervers
    1974   "Felt-making Craftsmen of the Anatolian and Iranian Plateaux." *Textile Museum Journal* 4,
                no. 1:15–29.

Ghirshman, Roman
    1939   *Fouilles de Sialk près de Kashan, 1933, 1934, 1937* 2. Paris: Librairie orientaliste Paul Geuthner.

Gillard, Robert D., and Susan M. Hardman
    1996   "Investigation of Fiber Mineralization Using Fourier Transform Infrared Microscopy." In
                Archaeological Chemistry: Organic, Inorganic, and Biochemical Analysis, ACS Symposium Series 625,
                edited by Mary Virginia Orna, 173–186. Washington, DC: American Chemical Society.

Gimbutas, Marija
    1982   *The Goddesses and Gods of Old Europe: 6500–3500 B.C.* Berkeley, CA: University of California Press.
    1989   *The Language of the Goddess*. New York: HarperCollins.
    1991   *The Civilization of the Goddess: The World of Old Europe*. New York: HarperCollins.
    1999   *The Living Goddesses*, edited and supplemented by Miriam Dexter. Berkeley, CA: University of
                California Press.

Glendinning, Matt
    2005   "A Decorated Roof at Gordion: What Tiles Are Revealing about the Phrygian Past." In *The
                Archaeology of Midas and the Phrygians: Recent Work at Gordion*, edited by Lisa Kealhofer, 82–
                100. Philadelphia, PA: University of Pennsylvania Museum of Archaeology and Anthropol-
                ogy.

Glob, Peter V.
    1971   *Denmark: An Archaeological History from the Stone Age to the Vikings*. Ithaca, NY: Cornell University
                Press.
    1974   *The Mound People: Danish Bronze-Age Man Preserved*. Ithaca, NY: Cornell University Press.

Goff, Beatrice
    1963   *Symbols of Prehistoric Mesopotamia*. New Haven, CT: Yale University Press.

Goff, Clare
    1969   "Excavations at Baba Jan, 1967: Second Preliminary Report." *Iran* 7:115–130.
    1970   "Excavations at Baba Jan, 1968: Third Preliminary Report." *Iran* 8:141–156.

Goldberg, Lisa
    1988   "Conservation Report." Gordion Furniture Project Archives.

Goodenough, Edwin R.
    1954   *Jewish Symbols in the Greco-Roman Period 4: The Problem of Method; Symbols from Jewish Cult*. New York:
                Pantheon.

Goodison, Lucy, and Christine Morris
    1998   "Beyond the 'Great Mother': The Sacred World of the Minoans." In *Ancient Goddesses: The
                Myths and the Evidence*, edited by Lucy Goodison and Christine Morris, 113–132. Madison, WI:
                University of Wisconsin Press.

Gorny, Ronald
    1996   "Viticulture and Ancient Anatolia." In *The Origins and Ancient History of Wine*, edited by Patrick
                McGovern, Stuart Fleming, and Solomon Katz, 133–174. Amsterdam: Gordon and Breach.

Grjaznov, Michail
    1984   *Der Grosskurgan von Aržan in Tuva, Südsibirien*. Munich: Beck.

Gubel, Eric
    1987   *Phoenician Furniture: A Typology Based on Iron Age Representations with Reference to the Iconographical
                Context*. Studia Phoenicia 7. Leuven: Peeters.

Gunter, Ann
  1990   "Artists and Ancient Near Eastern Art." In *Investigating Artistic Environments in the Ancient Near East*, edited by Ann Gunter, 9–17. Washington, DC: Arthur M. Sackler Gallery, Smithsonian Institution.
  1991   *The Bronze Age. The Gordion Excavations Final Reports III*. Philadelphia, PA: University of Pennsylvania Museum of Archaeology and Anthropology.
  1996   "Furniture in Elam." In *The Furniture of Western Asia: Ancient and Traditional*, edited by Georgina Herrmann, 211–218. Mainz: Philipp von Zabern.

Gunter, Ann, and Margaret Cool Root
  1998   "Replicating, Inscribing, Giving: Ernst Herzfeld and Artaxerxes' Silver Phiale in the Freer Gallery of Art." *Ars Orientalis* 28:3–38.

Gwinnett, A. John, and Leonard Gorelick
  1987   "The Change from Stone Drills to Copper Drills in Mesopotamia: An Experimental Perspective." *Expedition* 29, no. 3:15–24.

Haas, Volkert
  1995   "Death and the Afterlife in Hittite Thought." In *Civilizations of the Ancient Near East* 3, edited by Jack M. Sasson, 2021–2030. New York: Scribner's.

Hadzisteliou-Price, Theodora
  1971   "Double and Multiple Representations in Greek Art and Religious Thought." *Journal of Hellenic Studies* 91:48–69.

Handschin, Eduard
  1946   "Wild Silk Moths." *Ciba Review* 53:1915–1922.

Hanfmann, George M.A., and Jane Waldbaum
  1969   "Kybebe and Artemis: Two Anatolian Goddesses at Sardis." *Archaeology* 22, no. 4:264–269.

Hannah, Robert
  2005   *Greek and Roman Calendars: Constructions of Time in the Classical World*. London: Duckworth.

Hargrave, Michelle
  1999   "The Remounting of Serving Stand B, 1999." Gordion Furniture Project Archives.

Harper, Prudence, Joan Aruz, and Françoise Tallon
  1992   *The Royal City of Susa: Ancient Near Eastern Treasures in the Louvre*. New York: Metropolitan Museum of Art.

Haspels, C.H. Emilie
  1971   *The Highlands of Phrygia: Sites and Monuments*. Princeton, NJ: Princeton University Press.

Hawkins, J.D.
  1981   "Kubaba at Karkamiš and Elsewhere." *Anatolian Studies* 31:147–176.
  1981   "Kubaba: Philologisch." *Reallexicon der Assyriologie* 6:257–261.
  1994   "Mita." *Reallexicon der Assyriologie* 8:271–273.

Hayward, Charles H.
  1979   *Woodwork Joints*. New York: Sterling.

Helbaek, Hans
  1964   "First Impressions of the Çatal Hüyük Plant Husbandry." *Anatolian Studies* 14:121–123.
  1970   "The Plant Husbandry of Hacılar: A Study of Cultivation and Domestication." In James Mellaart, *Excavations at Hacılar*, 189–244. Edinburgh: University of Edinburgh Press.

Heller, Steven
  2000   *The Swastika: Symbol beyond Redemption?* New York: Allworth.

Hemelrijk, Jaap, and Dietrich Berndt
  1999   "The Phrygian Highlands, a Postscript: Wilful Destruction of the Rock-Monuments." *Bulletin Antieke Beschaving* 74:1–20.

Hepper, F.N.
  1996   "Timber Trees of Western Asia." In *The Furniture of Western Asia: Ancient and Traditional*, edited by Georgina Herrmann, 1–12. Mainz: Philipp von Zabern.

Herodotus
  1976   *Histories*, trans. Aubrey de Sélincourt. Harmondsworth: Penguin.

Herrmann, Georgina
1986   *Ivories from Room SW 37 Fort Shalmaneser. Ivories from Nimrud (1949–1963) Fascicule IV*, 1–2. London: British School of Archaeology in Iraq.
1992   *The Small Collections from Fort Shalmaneser. Ivories from Nimrud (1949–1963), Fascicule V.* London: British School of Archaeology in Iraq.
1996   "Ivory Furniture Pieces from Nimrud: North Syrian Evidence for a Regional Tradition of Furniture Manufacture." In *The Furniture of Western Asia: Ancient and Traditional*, edited by Georgina Herrmann, 153–165. Mainz: Philipp von Zabern.

Herrmann, Georgina, ed.
1996   *The Furniture of Western Asia: Ancient and Traditional.* Mainz: Philipp von Zabern.

Hesiod
1982   *Works and Days* and *Theogony*, trans. H.G. Evelyn-White. In *Hesiod, the Homeric Hymns, and Homerica.* Loeb ed. Cambridge, MA: Harvard University Press.
2006   *Works and Days* and *Theogony*, trans. Glenn W. Most. In *Hesiod: Theogony, Works and Days, and Testimonia.* Loeb ed. Cambridge, MA: Harvard University Press.

Hoadley, R. Bruce
2000   *Understanding Wood: A Craftsman's Guide to Wood Technology.* Newtown, CT: Taunton.

Hodder, Ian
2003   "The Lady and the Seed: Some Thoughts on the Role of Agriculture in the 'Neolithic Revolution.'" In *Archaeology beyond Dialogue*, edited by Ian Hodder, 155–161. Salt Lake City, UT: University of Utah Press.
2006   *The Leopard's Tale: Revealing the Mysteries of Çatalhöyük.* London: Thames and Hudson.

Hofenk de Graaff, Judith
1974   "A Simple Method for the Identification of Indigo." *Studies in Conservation* 19:54–55.

Hoffman, Marta
1964   *The Warp-Weighted Loom.* Studia Novegica 14. Oslo: Norsk Folkemuseum.

Homer
1951   *Iliad*, trans. Richmond Lattimore. Chicago, IL: University of Chicago Press.
1965   *Odyssey*, trans. Richmond Lattimore. New York: Harper and Row.
1982   *Homeric Hymns*, trans. H.G. Evelyn-White. In *Hesiod, the Homeric Hymns, and Homerica*, 286–463. Loeb ed. Cambridge, MA: Harvard University Press.

Hunger, Hermann, and David Pingree
1989   *MUL.APIN: An Astronomical Compendium in Cuneiform. Archiv für Orientforschung*, Supplement 24. Horn, Austria: Ferdinand Berger und Söhne.
1999   *Astral Sciences in Mesopotamia.* Leiden: Brill.

Işık, Cengiz
1986   "Tische und Tischdarstellungen in der urartäischen Kunst." *Belleten* 50:413–445.

Işık, Fahri
1991   "Zur Entstehung der tönernen Verkleidungsplatten in Anatolien." *Anatolian Studies* 41:63–86.

Jagels, Richard
1981   "Crook Timber." *Wooden Boat* 40:120–122.

Jakes, Kathryn A., and J. Hatten Howard III
1986   "Formation of Textile Fabric Pseudomorphs." *Proceedings of the 24th International Archaeometry Symposium*, edited by Jacqueline Olin and M. James Blackman, 165–177. Washington, DC: Smithsonian Institution Press.

James, Peter
2002   "The Dendrochronology Debate." *Minerva* 13, no. 4:18.

Jesus, Prentiss de
1980   *The Development of Prehistoric Mining and Metallurgy in Anatolia.* Oxford: BAR.

Johnston, Sarah Iles
2004   "Mysteries." In *Religions of the Ancient World: A Guide*, edited by Sarah I. Johnston, 98–111. Cambridge, MA: Harvard University Press.

Kalter, Johannes
    1984   *The Arts and Crafts of Turkestan.* London: Thames and Hudson.

Karageorghis, Vassos
    1969   *Salamis in Cyprus: Homeric, Hellenistic, and Roman.* London: Thames and Hudson.
    1973–1974 *Excavations in the Necropolis of Salamis III.* Nicosia: Department of Antiquities, Republic of Cyprus.

Katz, Dina
    2003   *The Image of the Netherworld in the Sumerian Sources.* Bethesda, MD: CDL Press.

Keenan, Douglas
    2004   "Radiocarbon Dates from Iron Age Gordion Are Confounded." *Ancient West and East* 3, no. 1:100–103.
    2006   "Anatolian Tree-Ring Studies Are Untrustworthy." www.informath.org/ATSU04a.pdf.

Kelly, Mary
    1989   *Goddess Embroideries of Eastern Europe.* McLean, NY: Studiobooks.
    1999   "Living Textile Traditions of the Carpathians." In *Folk Dress in Europe and Anatolia: Beliefs about Protection and Fertility*, edited by Linda Welters, 155–178. Oxford: Berg.

Kenyon, Kathleen M.
    1960   *Excavations at Jericho I. The Tombs Excavated in 1952–4.* London: British School of Archaeology in Jerusalem.
    1965   *Excavations at Jericho II. The Tombs Excavated in 1955–8.* London: British School of Archaeology in Jerusalem.
    1970   *Archaeology in the Holy Land.* London: Benn.

Kern, Hermann
    2000   *Through the Labyrinth: Designs and Meanings over 5,000 Years*, rev. English ed., edited by Robert Ferré and Jeff Saward. Munich: Prestel.

Killen, Geoffrey
    1980   *Ancient Egyptian Furniture 1: 4000–1300 B.C.* Warminster: Aris and Phillips.
    1994   *Ancient Egyptian Furniture 2: Boxes, Chests and Footstools.* Warminster: Aris and Phillips.
    1994   *Egyptian Woodworking and Furniture.* Buckinghamshire: Shire.
    1996   "Ancient Egyptian Carpentry, Its Tools and Techniques." In *The Furniture of Western Asia: Ancient and Traditional*, edited by Georgina Herrmann, 13–20. Mainz: Philipp von Zabern.

King, L.W., ed.
    1912   *Babylonian Boundary-Stones and Memorial-Tablets in the British Museum.* London: British Museum.

Kohler, Ellen L.
    1995   *The Lesser Phrygian Tumuli, Part I: The Inhumations. The Gordion Excavations (1950–1973), Final Reports II.* Philadelphia, PA: University of Pennsylvania Museum of Archaeology and Anthropology.

König, Friedrich
    1955   *Handbuch der chaldischen Inschriften.* Archiv für Orientforschung, Supplement 8, part 1. Graz: Ernst Weidner.

Kopcke, Günter
    1967   "Neue Holzfunde aus dem Heraion von Samos." *Mitteilungen des deutschen archäologischen Instituts, Athenische Abteilung* 82:100–148.

Körte, Gustav, and Alfred Körte
    1904   *Gordion: Ergebnisse der Ausgrabung im Jahre 1900. Jahrbuch des kaiserlich deutschen archäologischen Instituts* 5. Berlin: Georg Reimer.

Kramer, Samuel
    1960   "Death and Nether World According to the Sumerian Literary Texts." *Iraq* 22:59–68.

Krzyszkowska, Olga
    1996   "Furniture in the Aegean Bronze Age." In *The Furniture of Western Asia: Ancient and Traditional*, edited by Georgina Herrmann, 85–103. Mainz: Philipp von Zabern.

Kuhn, Hans H.
    1998   "Adsorption at the Liquid/Solid Interface: Metal Oxide Coated Textiles." In *Book of Papers: 1998 International Conference and Exhibition*, 281–289. Research Triangle Park, NC: American Association of Textile Chemists and Colorists.

Kuniholm, Peter
  1977   "Dendrochronology at Gordion and on the Anatolian Plateau." Ph.D. diss., University of Pennsylvania.
  1993   "A Date-List for Bronze Age and Iron Age Monuments Based on Combined Dendrochronological and Radiocarbon Evidence." In *Aspects of Art and Iconography: Anatolia and Its Neighbors, Studies in Honor of Nimet Özgüç*, edited by Machteld Mellink, Edith Porada, and Tahsin Özgüç, 371–373. Ankara: Türk Tarih Kurumu.

Kuniholm, Peter, Bernd Kromer, Sturt Manning, Maryanne Newton, Christine Latini, and Mary Jaye Bruce
  1996   "Anatolian Tree Rings and the Absolute Chronology of the Eastern Mediterranean, 2220–718 B.C." *Nature* 381:780–783.

Kupper, J.-R.
  1992   "Le bois à Mari." In *Trees and Timber in Mesopotamia. Bulletin on Sumerian Agriculture* 6, edited by J.N. Postgate and M.A. Powell, 163–170. Cambridge: Sumerian Agriculture Group.

Kurtz, Donna, and John Boardman
  1971   *Greek Burial Customs*. Ithaca, NY: Cornell University Press.

Kyrieleis, Helmut
  1969   *Throne und Klinen, Studien zur Formgeschichte altorientalischer und griechischer Sitz- und Liegemöbel vorhellenistischer Zeit. Jahrbuch des deutschen archäologischen Instituts* 24. Berlin: Walter de Gruyter.
  1980   "Archaische Holzfunde aus Samos." *Mitteilungen des deutschen archäologischen Instituts*, Athenische Abteilung 95:87–147.

Lange, Kurt, and Max Hirmer
  1968   *Egypt: Architecture, Sculpture, Painting in Three Thousand Years*. London: Phaidon.

Larsen, Mogens Trolle
  1996   *The Conquest of Assyria: Excavations in an Antique Land, 1840–1860*. London: Routledge.

Layard, Austen H.
  1849   *The Monuments of Nineveh*. London: John Murray.

Legrain, Leon
  1936   *Ur Excavations III. Archaic Seal-Impressions*. Oxford: Oxford University Press.

Liebhart, Richard, and Jessica Johnson
  2005   "Support and Conserve: Conservation and Environmental Monitoring of the Tomb Chamber of Tumulus MM." In *The Archaeology of Midas and the Phrygians*, edited by Lisa Kealhofer, 191–203. Philadelphia, PA: University of Pennsylvania Museum of Archaeology and Anthropology.

Lloyd, Seton
  1989   *Ancient Turkey: A Traveller's History of Anatolia*. Berkeley, CA: University of California Press.

Loud, Gordon
  1939   *The Megiddo Ivories*. Chicago, IL: University of Chicago Press.

Lu, Peter, and Paul Steinhardt
  2007   "Decagonal and Quasi-Crystalline Tilings in Medieval Islamic Architecture." *Science* 315:1106–1110.

Luckenbill, Daniel D.
  1926–1927 *Ancient Records of Assyria and Babylonia*. Chicago, IL: University of Chicago Press.

Lucretius
  1992   *De Rerum Natura*, trans. W.H.D. Rouse, rev. Martin F. Smith. Loeb ed. Cambridge, MA: Harvard University Press.

Luschey, Heinz
  1939   *Die Phiale*. Bleicherode am Harz: Carl Nieft.

Mallowan, M.E.L.
  1965   *Early Mesopotamia and Iran*. New York: McGraw-Hill.
  1975   *Nimrud and Its Remains*. London: Collins.

Mallowan, M.E.L., and L.G. Davis
  1970   *Ivories in Assyrian Style. Ivories from Nimrud (1949–1963), Fascicule II*. London: British School of Archaeology in Iraq.

Mallowan, M.E.L., and Georgina Herrmann
    1974   *Furniture from SW.7 Fort Shalmaneser. Ivories from Nimrud (1949–1963), Fascicule III.* London: British
                School of Archaeology in Iraq.

Mandrus, Janis
    1999   "The Remounting of Serving Stand A, 1999." Gordion Furniture Project Archives.

Manning, Sturt, Bernd Kromer, Peter Kuniholm, and Maryanne Newton
    2001   "Anatolian Tree Rings and a New Chronology for the East Mediterranean Bronze-Iron Ages."
                Science 294:2532–2535.
    2003   "Confirmation of Near-Absolute Dating of East Mediterranean Bronze-Iron Dendrochronol-
                ogy." *Antiquity* 77, no. 295 (http://antiquity.ac.uk/projgall/manning/manning.html).

Marinatos, Nannó
    2000   *The Goddess and the Warrior: The Naked Goddess and Mistress of Animals in Early Greek Religion.* London:
                Routledge.

Matthews, W.H.
    1970   *Mazes and Labyrinths: Their History and Development.* Reprint of *Mazes and Labyrinths: A General Account
                of Their History and Developments* (London, 1922). New York: Dover.

Matthiae, Paulo
    1977   *Ebla: An Empire Rediscovered.* London: Hodder and Stoughton.
    1977/1989   *Ebla: Un impero ritrovato.* Turin: Giulio Einaudi.

Maxwell-Hyslop, K.R.
    1971   *Western Asiatic Jewellery, c. 3000–612 B.C.* London: Methuen.

Mayer, Walter
    1983   "Sargons Feldzug gegen Urartu—714 v. Chr. Text und Übersetzung." *Mitteilungen der deutschen
                Orient-Gesellschaft zu Berlin* 115:65–132.

McGovern, Patrick E.
    1997   "Wine of Egypt's Golden Age: An Archaeochemical Perspective." *Journal of Egyptian Archaeology*
                83:69–108.
    1999   "Retsina, Mixed Fermented Beverages, and the Cuisine of Pre-Classical Greece." In *Minoans
                and Mycenaeans: Flavours of Their Time,* edited by Yannis Tzedakis and Holley Martlew, 206–208.
                Athens: Greek Ministry of Culture/National Archaeological Museum.
    2000   "The Funerary Banquet of 'King Midas.'" *Expedition* 42, no.1:21–29.
    2003   *Ancient Wine: The Search for the Origins of Viniculture.* Princeton, NJ: Princeton University Press.

McGovern, Patrick E., Donald L. Glusker, Lawrence J. Exner, and Gretchen R. Hall.
    2008   The Chemical Identification of Resinated Wine and a Mixed Fermented Beverage in Bronze
                Age Pottery Vessels of Greece." In *Archaeology Meets Science: Biomolecular Investigations in Bronze
                Age Greece,* edited by Yannis Tzedakis, Holley Martlew, and Martin Jones, 169–218. Oxford:
                Oxbow.

McGovern, Patrick E., Donald L. Glusker, Robert A. Moreau, Alberto Nuñez, Curt W. Beck, Elizabeth
    Simpson, Eric D. Butrym, Lawrence J. Exner, and Edith C. Stout
    1999   "A Funerary Feast Fit for King Midas." *Nature* 402:863–864.

McGovern, Patrick E., Ulrich Hartung, Virginia R. Badler, Donald L. Glusker, and Lawrence J. Exner
    1997   "The Beginnings of Winemaking and Viniculture in the Ancient Near East and Egypt."
                Expedition 39, no. 1:3–21.

McGovern, Patrick E., and Rudolph H. Michel
    1993   "The First Wine and Beer: Chemical Detection of Ancient Fermented Beverages." *Analytical
                Chemistry* 65:408A–413A.

McGovern, Patrick E., Mary M. Voigt, Donald L. Glusker, and Lawrence J. Exner
    1996   "Neolithic Resinated Wine." *Nature* 381:480–481.

McGrail, Seán
    2004   *Boats of the World from the Stone Age to Medieval Times.* Oxford: Oxford University Press.

McGrail, Seán, and Geoffrey Denford
    1982   "Boatbuilding Techniques, Technological Change and Attribute Analysis." In *Woodworking
                Techniques before A.D. 1500,* edited by Seán McGrail, 25–72. Oxford: BAR.

McMahon, Gregory
    1995   "Theology, Priests, and Worship in Hittite Anatolia." In *Civilizations of the Ancient Near East* 3, edited by Jack M. Sasson, 1981–1995. New York: Scribner's.

Meador, Betty De Shong
    2000   *Inanna, Lady of Largest Heart: Poems of the Sumerian High Priestess Enheduanna.* Austin, TX: University of Texas Press.

Meiggs, Russell
    1982   *Trees and Timber in the Ancient Mediterranean World.* Oxford: Clarendon Press.

Mellaart, James
    1962   "Excavations at Çatal Hüyük. First Preliminary Report, 1961." *Anatolian Studies* 12:41–65.
    1963   "Excavations at Çatal Hüyük, 1962. Second Preliminary Report." *Anatolian Studies* 13:43–103.
    1964   "Excavations at Çatal Hüyük, 1963. Third Preliminary Report." *Anatolian Studies* 14:39–119.
    1965   *Earliest Civilizations of the Near East.* London: Thames and Hudson.
    1967   *Çatal Hüyük: A Neolithic Town in Anatolia.* New York: McGraw-Hill.
    1970   *Excavations at Hacılar.* Edinburgh: University of Edinburgh Press.

Mellaart, James, Udo Hirsch, and Belkis Balpınar
    1989   *The Goddess from Anatolia.* Milan: Eskenazi.

Mellink, Machteld J.
    1956   *A Hittite Cemetery at Gordion.* Philadelphia, PA: University of Pennsylvania Museum of Archaeology and Anthropology.
    1965   "Mita, Mushki and Phrygians." *Anadolu Araştırmaları* 2:317–325.
    1971   "Excavations at Karataş-Semayük and Elmalı, Lycia, 1970." *American Journal of Archaeology* 75:245–255.
    1977   "Temples and High Places in Phrygia." In *Temples and High Places in Biblical Times*, 96–104. Jerusalem: Hebrew Union College–Jewish Institute of Religion.
    1983   "Comments on a Cult Relief of Kybele from Gordion." In *Beiträge zur Altertumskunde Kleinasiens: Festschrift für Kurt Bittel*, edited by R. Boehmer and H. Hauptmann, 349–360. Mainz: Philipp von Zabern.
    1993   "Midas-Stadt." *Reallexicon der Assyriologie* 8:153–156.

Merhav, Rivka, ed.
    1991   *Urartu: A Metalworking Center in the First Millennium B.C.E.* Jerusalem: Israel Museum.

Meskell, Lynn
    1995   "Goddesses, Gimbutas and 'New Age' Archaeology." *Antiquity* 69:74–86.
    1998   "Twin Peaks: The Archaeologies of Çatalhöyük." In *Ancient Goddesses: The Myths and the Evidence*, edited by Lucy Goodison and Christine Morris, 46–62. Madison, WI: University of Wisconsin Press.

Mesnil du Buisson, R. du
    1948   *Baghouz: L'Ancienne Corsôtê.* Leiden: Brill.

Metin, Mustafa, and Mehmet Akalın
    2001   "Frigya'da bulunan İkiz İdol." In *Anadolu Medeniyetleri Müzesi 2000 Yıllığı*, 183–188. Ankara: Museum of Anatolian Civilizations.

Metropolitan Museum of Art: Egypt and the Near East. New York: Metropolitan Museum of Art, 1987.

Metropolitan Museum of Art: Greece and Rome. New York: Metropolitan Museum of Art, 1987.

Metzler, Dieter
    1990   "Historical Perspectives on Artistic Environments." In *Investigating Artistic Environments in the Ancient Near East*, edited by Ann Gunter, 143–147. Washington DC: Arthur M. Sackler Gallery, Smithsonian Institution.

Michel, Rudolph H., Patrick E. McGovern, and Virginia R. Badler
    1992   "The Chemical Confirmation of Beer from Proto-Historic Lowland Greater Mesopotamia." *Nature* 360:24.

Miller, Naomi F.
    1993   "Plant Use at Gordion: Archaeobotanical Results from the 1988–1989 Seasons." *American Journal of Archaeology* 97:304.
    1995   "Archaeobotany: Macroremains." *American Journal of Archaeology* 99:91–93.

1999   "Interpreting Ancient Environment and Patterns of Land Use: Seeds, Charcoal and Archae-
              ological Context." *TÜBA-AR* (Turkish Academy of Sciences Journal of Archaeology) 2:15–
              29.

Mladenovic, Vesna
   1999   "Threads of Life: Red Fringes in Macedonian Dress." In *Folk Dress in Europe and Anatolia: Beliefs
              about Protection and Fertility*, edited by Linda Welters, 97–110. Oxford: Berg.

Montegut, Denyse
   1999   "Moth or Mollusc? A Technical Examination of Byssus Fibers." In *The Materials, Technology,
              and Art of Conservation: Studies in Honor of Lawrence J. Majewski on the Occasion of His 80th Birthday,
              February 10, 1999*, edited by Rebecca A. Rushfield and Mary W. Ballard, 186–203. New York:
              Conservation Center, Institute of Fine Arts, New York University.

Moorey, P.R.S.
   1980   "Metal Wine-Sets in the Ancient Near East." *Iranica Antiqua* 15:181–197.
   1994   *Ancient Mesopotamian Materials and Industries: The Archaeololgical Evidence*. Oxford: Clarendon Press.

Moran, William, ed. and trans.
   1992   *The Amarna Letters*. Baltimore, MD: Johns Hopkins University Press.

Muhly, Polymnia
   1996   "Furniture from the Shaft Graves: The Occurrence of Wood in Aegean Burials of the Bronze
              Age." *The Annual of the British School at Athens* 91:197–211.

Müller, Hans, and Eberhard Thiem
   1999   *Gold of the Pharaohs*. Ithaca, NY: Cornell University Press.

Munn, Mark
   2006   *The Mother of the Gods, Athens, and the Tyranny of Asia*. Berkeley, CA: University of California Press.

Murray, H.J.R.
   1951   *A History of Board-Games Other Than Chess*. Oxford: Clarendon Press.

Muscarella, Oscar White
   1967   "Fibulae Represented on Sculpture." *Journal of Near Eastern Studies* 26, no. 2:82–86.
   1982   "King Midas' Tumulus at Gordion." *Quarterly Review of Archaeology* (December):7–10.
   1988   *Bronze and Iron Ancient Near Eastern Artifacts in The Metropolitan Museum of Art*. New York:
              Metropolitan Museum of Art.
   1989   "King Midas of Phrygia and the Greeks." In *Anatolia and the Ancient Near East: Studies in Honor
              of Tahsin Özgüç*, edited by Kutlu Emre, Machteld Mellink, Barthel Hrouda, and Nimet Özgüç,
              333–344. Ankara: Türk Tarih Kurumu.
   1995   "The Iron Age Background to the Formation of the Phrygian State." *Bulletin of the American Schools
              of Oriental Research* 299/300:91–101.
   2003   "The Date of the Destruction of the Early Phrygian Period at Gordion." *Ancient West and East* 2,
              no. 2:225–252.

Muscarella, Oscar White, ed.
   1981   *Ladders to Heaven: Art Treasures from Lands of the Bible*. Toronto: Lands of the Bible Archaeology
              Foundation.

Naumann, Friederike
   1983   *Die Ikonographie der Kybele in der phrygischen und der griechischen Kunst*. Tübingen: Ernst Wasmuth.

Negbi, Ora
   1970   *The Hoards of Goldwork from Tell el-Ajjul*. Studies in Mediterranean Archaeology 25. Göteborg:
              Lund.

Nelson, Bryan, Miguel Goñi, John Hedges, and Robert Blanchette
   1995   "Soft-Rot Fungal Degradation of Lingin in 2700 Year Old Archaeological Woods." *Holzforschung*
              49, no. 1:1–10.

Neugebauer, Otto
   1942   "The Origin of the Egyptian Calendar." *Journal of Near Eastern Studies* 1, no. 4:396–403.

Newman, Richard, and Margaret Serpico
   2000   "Adhesives and Binders." In *Ancient Egyptian Materials and Technology*, edited by Paul Nicholson and
              Ian Shaw, 475–494. Cambridge: Cambridge University Press.

Oates, Joan, and David Oates
    2001   *Nimrud: An Assyrian Imperial City Revealed*. London: British School of Archaeology in Iraq.

Öğün, Baki
    1978   "Die urartäischen Bestattungsbräuche." In *Studien zur Religion und Kultur Kleinasiens: Festschrift für Friedrich Karl Dörner*, edited by Sencer Şahin, Elmar Schwertheim, and Jörg Wagner, 639–678. Leiden: Brill.
    1982   "Die urartäischen Paläste und die Bestattungsbräuche der Urartäer." In *Palast und Hütte: Beiträge zum Bauen und Wohnen im Altertum von Archäologen, Vor- und Frühgeschichtlern*, edited by Dietrich Papenfuss and Volker Michael Strocka, 217–236. Mainz: Philipp von Zabern.

Ohly, Dieter
    1953   "Holz." *Mitteilungen des deutschen archäologischen Instituts*, Athenische Abteilung 68:77–126.

Oppenheim, A. Leo
    1949   "The Golden Garments of the Gods." *Journal of Near Eastern Studies* 8, no. 3:172–193.

Orchard, J.J.
    1967   *Equestrian Bridle-Harness Ornaments. Ivories from Nimrud (1949–1963) Fascicule I*, 2. London: British School of Archaeology in Iraq.

Orthmann, Winfried
    1975   *Der alte Orient. Propyläen Kunstgeschichte* 14. Berlin: Propyläen Verlag.

Otten, Heinrich
    1958   *Hethitische Totenrituale*. Berlin: Akademie-Verlag.

Ovid
    1977–1984   *Metamorphoses*, trans. Frank J. Miller, rev. G.P. Goold. Loeb ed. Cambridge, MA: Harvard University Press.
    1996   *Fasti*, trans. James G. Frazer, rev. G.P. Goold. Loeb ed. Cambridge, MA: Harvard University Press.

Özgen, Engin, and İlknur Özgen, eds.
    1988   *Antalya Museum*. Ankara: Ministry of Culture and Tourism of the Republic of Turkey.

Özgen, İlknur, and Jean Öztürk
    1996   *Heritage Recovered: The Lydian Treasure*. Ankara: Ministry of Culture of the Republic of Turkey.

Özgüç, Nimet
    1965   *Kültepe Mühür Baskılarında Anadolu Grubu (The Anatolian Group of Cylinder Seal Impressions from Kültepe)*. Ankara: Türk Tarih Kurumu.
    1968   *Kaniş Karumu Ib Katı Mühürleri ve Mühür Baskıları (Seals and Seal Impressions of Level Ib from Karum Kanish)*. Ankara: Türk Tarih Kurumu.
    1980   "Seal Impressions from the Palaces at Acemhöyük." In *Ancient Art in Seals*, edited by Edith Porada, 61–86. Princeton, NJ: Princeton University Press.

Özgüç, Tahsin
    1950   *Kültepe Kazısı Raporu, 1948*. Ankara: Türk Tarih Kurumu.
    1969   *Altıntepe II: Mezarlar, Depo Binası ve Fildişi Eserler (Tombs, Storehouse and Ivories)*. Ankara: Türk Tarih Kurumu.
    1982   *Maşat Höyük II: Boğazköy'ün Kuzeydoğusunda bir Hitit Merkezi (A Hittite Center Northeast of Boğazköy)*. Ankara: Türk Tarih Kurumu.
    2003   *Kültepe: Kaniš/Neša*. Tokyo: Middle Eastern Cultural Center in Japan.

Özgüç, Tahsin, and Mahmut Akok
    1947   "Die Ausgrabungen an zwei Tumuli auf dem Mausoleumshügel bei Ankara." *Belleten* 11:57–85.
    1958   *Horoztepe: Eski Tunç Devri Mezarlığı ve İskân Yeri (Horoztepe: An Early Bronze Age Settlement and Cemetery)*. Ankara: Türk Tarih Kurumu.

Pain, Stephanie
    1999   "Grog of the Greeks." *New Scientist* 164, no. 2214:54–57.

Parr, Peter
    1996   "Middle Bronze Age Furniture from Jericho and Baghouz." In *The Furniture of Western Asia: Ancient and Traditional*, edited by Georgina Herrmann, 41–48. Mainz: Philipp von Zabern.

Payton, Robert
    1982   "Second Conservation Report." Gordion Furniture Project Archives.

1983   "Third Conservation Report." Gordion Furniture Project Archives.
1984   "The Conservation of an Eighth Century B.C. Table from Gordion." In *Contributions to the Paris Congress on Adhesives and Consolidants*, edited by N.S. Brommelle, Elizabeth Pye, Perry Smith, and Garry Thomson, 133–137. London: International Institute for Conservation of Historic and Artistic Works.
1984   "Conservation of Screens A and B." Gordion Furniture Project Archives.
1991   "The Ulu Burun Writing-Board Set." *Anatolian Studies* 41:99–106.

Peacock, E.E.
1996   "Biodegradation and Characterization of Water-Degraded Archaeological Textiles Created for Conservation Research." *International Biodeterioration and Biodegradation* 38, no. 1:49–59.

Petronius
1969   *Satyricon*, trans. Michael Heseltine, rev. E.H. Warmington. Loeb ed. Cambridge, MA: Harvard University Press.

Piggott, Stuart
1962   "Heads and Hoofs." *Antiquity* 36, no. 142:110–118.

Pinches, Theo. G.
1885   "The Antiquities Found by Mr. H. Rassam at Abu-Habbah (Sippara)." *Transactions of the Society of Biblical Archaeology* 8:164–171.

Pindar
1937   *Odes*, trans. John Sandys. Loeb ed. Cambridge, MA: Harvard University Press.

Pitard, Wayne
1978   "The Ugaritic Funerary Text RS 34.126." *BASOR* 232:65–75.

Pittman, Holly
1984   *The Art of the Bronze Age: Southeastern Iran, Western Central Asia, and the Indus Valley*. New York: Metropolitan Museum of Art.

Pliny
1942–1986   *Natural History*, trans. H. Rackham, W.H.S. Jones, and D.E. Eichholz. Loeb ed. Cambridge, MA: Harvard University Press.

Pollitt, J.J.
1990   *The Art of Ancient Greece: Sources and Documents*. Cambridge: Cambridge University Press.

Polosmak, Natalya
1994   "A Mummy Unearthed from the Pastures of Heaven." *National Geographic* 186, no. 4:80–103.

Popham, M.R., P.G. Calligas, and L.H. Sackett
1993   *Lefkandi II: The Protogeometric Building at Toumba. Part 2: The Excavation, Architecture and Finds*. Athens: British School of Archaeology at Athens.

Popham, M.R., E. Touloupa, and L.H. Sackett
1982   "The Hero of Lefkandi." *Antiquity* 56:169–174.

Powell, Marvin A.
1992   "Timber Production in Presargonic Lagaš." In *Trees and Timber in Mesopotamia. Bulletin on Sumerian Agriculture* 6, edited by J.N. Postgate and M.A. Powell, 99–122. Cambridge: Sumerian Agriculture Group.
1996   "Wine and the Vine in Ancient Mesopotamia: The Cuneiform Evidence." In *The Origins and Ancient History of Wine*, edited by Patrick McGovern, Stuart Fleming, and Solomon Katz, 97–122. Amsterdam: Gordon and Breach.

Prag, John, and Richard Neave
1997   *Making Faces: Using Forensic and Archaeological Evidence*. College Station, TX: Texas A&M University Press.

Prayon, Friedhelm
1987   *Phrygische Plastik*. Tübingen: Ernst Wasmuth.

Pritchard, James
1969   *Ancient Near Eastern Texts Relating to the Old Testament [ANET]*. Princeton, NJ: Princeton University Press.

1969   *The Ancient Near East in Pictures Relating to the Old Testament* [*ANEP*]. Princeton, NJ: Princeton University Press.

Pulak, Cemal
1998   "The Uluburun Shipwreck: An Overview." *International Journal of Nautical Archaeology* 27, no. 3: 188–224.
2002   "The Uluburun Hull Remains." In *On Ship Construction in Antiquity*, TROPIS 7, no. 2, edited by Harry Tzalas, 615–636. Athens: Hellenic Institute for the Preservation of Nautical Tradition.

Randsborg, Klavs, and Kjeld Christensen
2006   *Bronze Age Oak-Coffin Graves: Archaeology and Dendro-Dating.* Copenhagen: Blackwell Munksgaard.

Record, Samuel, and George Garratt
1925   "Boxwoods." *Yale University School of Forestry Bulletin* 14:7–81.

Reiner, Erica, ed.
2006   "T": *The Assyrian Dictionary of the Oriental Institute of the University of Chicago* 18. Chicago, IL: Oriental Institute.

Reisner, George
1955   *A History of the Giza Necropolis II: The Tomb of Hetep-heres the Mother of Cheops.* Cambridge, MA: Harvard University Press.

Renfrew, Jane
1995   "Vegetables in the Ancient Near Eastern Diet." In *Civilizations of the Ancient Near East* 1, edited by Jack M. Sasson, 191–202. New York: Scribner's.

Richter, G.M.A.
1966   *The Furniture of the Greeks, Etruscans, and Romans.* London: Phaidon.

Ricketts, Michael
1960   "Furniture from the Middle Bronze Age Tombs." In Kathleen M. Kenyon, *Excavations at Jericho I*, 527–534. London: British School of Archaeology in Jerusalem.

Ridgway, David
1997   "Nestor's Cup and the Etruscans." *Oxford Journal of Archaeology* 16, no. 3:325–344.

Rig Veda
1981   *The Rig Veda: An Anthology*, trans. Wendy Doniger. London: Penguin.

Robinson, David M.
1934   "The Villa of Good Fortune at Olynthos." *American Journal of Archaeology* 38:501–510.

Rochberg, Francesca
1995   "Astronomy and Calendars in Ancient Mesopotamia." In *Civilizations of the Ancient Near East* 3, edited by Jack M. Sasson, 1925–1940. New York: Scribner's.
2004   *The Heavenly Writing: Divination, Horoscopy, and Astronomy in Mesopotamian Culture.* Cambridge: Cambridge University Press.

Roehrig, Catharine
2002   *Life along the Nile: Three Egyptians of Ancient Thebes. The Metropolitan Museum of Art Bulletin* (Summer). New York: Metropolitan Museum of Art.

Rogowski, Gary
2002   *The Complete Illustrated Guide to Joinery.* Newtown, CT: Taunton.

Roller, Lynn
1983   "The Legend of Midas." *Classical Antiquity* 2, no. 2:299–317.
1984   "Midas and the Gordian Knot." *Classical Antiquity* 3, no. 2:256–271.
1987   *Nonverbal Graffiti, Dipinti, and Stamps. Gordion Special Studies I.* Philadelphia, PA: University of Pennsylvania Museum of Archaeology and Anthropology.
1989   "The Art of Writing at Gordion." *Expedition* 31, no. 1:54–61.
1999   "Early Phrygian Drawings from Gordion and the Elements of Phrygian Artistic Style." *Anatolian Studies* 49:143–152.
1999   *In Search of God the Mother: The Cult of Anatolian Cybele.* Berkeley, CA: University of California Press.

Rosenthal, Elisabeth
2005   "Pilgrims Pay Last Respects Before Papal Funeral Today." *New York Times*, April 8.

Rubinson, Karen
 2002   "Through the Looking Glass: Reflections on Mirrors, Gender, and Use among Nomads." In *In Pursuit of Gender: Worldwide Archaeological Approaches*, edited by Sarah Nelson and Myriam Rosen-Ayalon. Walnut Creek, CA: AltaMira Press.

Rudenko, Sergei I.
 1960   *The Culture of the Population of the Central Altai in Scythian Times*. Moscow: USSR Academy of Sciences.
 1970   *Frozen Tombs of Siberia: The Pazyryk Burials of Iron-Age Horsemen*. Berkeley, CA: University of California Press.

Rybakov, B.A.
 1965   "Cosmogony and Mythology of the Agriculturalists of the Eneolithic," part 1. *Soviet Anthropology and Archaeology* 4, no. 2:16–36.
 1965–1966   "Cosmogony and Mythology of the Agriculturalists of the Eneolithic," part 2. *Soviet Anthropology and Archaeology* 4, no. 3:33–52.

Sale, D.
 1993   "An Evaluation of Eleven Adhesives for Repairing Poly (Methyl Methacrylate) Objects and Sculpture." In *Symposium '91, Saving the Twentieth Century: The Conservation of Modern Materials*, 325–340. Ottawa: Canadian Conservation Institute.

Saleh, Mohamed, and Hourig Sourouzian
 1987   *The Egyptian Museum Cairo*. Mainz: Philipp von Zabern.

Salonen, Armas
 1963   *Die Möbel des alten Mesopotamien nach sumerisch-akkadischen Quellen*. Helsinki: Suomalainen Tiedeakatemia.

Salvini, Mirjo
 1994   "The Historical Background of the Urartian Monument of Meher Kapısı." In *Anatolian Iron Ages 3. The Proceedings of the Third Anatolian Iron Ages Colloquium Held at Van, 6–12 August 1990*, edited by A. Çilingiroğlu and D.H. French, 205–210. Ankara: British Institute of Archaeology at Ankara.

Sams, G.K.
 1977   "Beer in the City of Midas." *Archaeology* 30, no. 2:108–115.
 1989   "Sculpted Orthostates at Gordion." In *Anatolia and the Ancient Near East: Studies in Honor of Tahsin Özgüç*, edited by Kutlu Emre, Machteld Mellink, Barthel Hrouda, and Nimet Özgüç, 447–454. Ankara: Türk Tarih Kurumu.
 1993   "Gordion and the Near East in the Early Phrygian Period." In *Aspects of Art and Iconography: Anatolia and Its Neighbors, Studies in Honor of Nimet Özgüç*, edited by Machteld Mellink, Edith Porada, and Tahsin Özgüç, 549–555. Ankara: Türk Tarih Kurumu.
 1994   "Aspects of Early Phrygian Architecture at Gordion." In *Anatolian Iron Ages 3. The Proceedings of the Third Anatolian Iron Ages Colloquium Held at Van, 6–12 August 1990*, edited by A. Çilingiroğlu and D.H. French, 211–220. Ankara: British Institute of Archaeology at Ankara.
 1994   *The Early Phrygian Pottery. The Gordion Excavations, 1950–1973, Final Reports IV*. Philadelphia, PA: University of Pennsylvania Museum of Archaeology and Anthropology.

Sasson, Jack M., ed.
 1995   *Civilizations of the Ancient Near East*. New York: Scribner's.

Schaeffer, Claude
 1954   "Les fouilles de Ras Shamra-Ugarit, quinzième, seizième et dix-septième campagnes (1951, 1952 et 1953)." *Syria* 31:14–67.

Schiering, Wolfgang
 2003   "Löwenbändiger und Midas-Thron in Delphi." In Ἐπιτύμβιον Gerhard Neumann, 57–68. Athens: Benaki Museum.

Schletzer, Dieter, and Reinhold Schletzer
 1983   *Old Silver Jewellery of the Turkoman: An Essay on Symbols in the Culture of Inner Asian Nomads*. Berlin: Dietrich Reimer.

Schliemann, Heinrich
 1881   *Ilios: The City and Country of the Trojans*. Reprint, New York: Arno Press, 1976.

Schuster, Carl, and Edmund Carpenter
  1986–1988   *Materials for the Study of Social Symbolism in Ancient & Tribal Art: A Record of Tradition & Continuity.*
               New York: Rock Foundation.
  1996   *Patterns That Connect: Social Symbolism in Ancient & Tribal Art.* New York: Harry N. Abrams.

Scurr, Donald
  1989   "The Mask of Midas." *Aramco World* 40, no. 5:36–41.

Seidl, Ursula
  1996   "Urartian Furniture." In *The Furniture of Western Asia: Ancient and Traditional,* edited by Georgina
               Herrmann, 181–186. Mainz: Philipp von Zabern.

Seiler-Baldinger, Annemarie
  1994   *Textiles: A Classification of Techniques.* Washington, DC: Smithsonian Institution Press.

Seves, Annamaria, Maria Romanò, Tullia Maifreni, Silvio Sora, and Orio Ciferri
  1998   "The Microbial Degradation of Silk: A Laboratory Investigation." *International Biodeterioration and
               Biodegradation* 42, no. 4:203–211.

Sevin, Veli
  1991   "The Early Iron Age in the Elazığ Region and the Problem of the Mushkians." *Anatolian Studies*
               41:87–97.

Sherratt, Susan
  2004   "Feasting in Homeric Epic." In *The Mycenaean Feast,* edited by James Wright, 181–213. Princeton,
               NJ: American School of Classical Studies.

Shiloh, Yigal
  1984   *Excavations at the City of David* 1. *Qedem* 19. Jerusalem: Hebrew University.
  1985   "The Material Culture of Judah and Jerusalem in Iron Age II: Origins and Influences."
               In *The Land of Israel: Cross-Roads of Civilizations,* edited by E. Lipinski, 113–146. Leuven:
               Peeters.

Simon, Erika
  1972   "Hera und die Nymphen: Ein böotischer Polos in Stockholm." *Études de céramique et de peinture
               antiques offertes à Pierre Devambez* 1. *Revue Archéologique* 2:205–220.

Simpson, Elizabeth
  1981   *Gordion Field Book* 175.
  1983   "Reconstructing an Ancient Table: The 'Pagoda' Table from Tumulus MM at Gordion."
               Expedition 25, no. 4:11–26.
  1983   "Report on the Conservation and Restoration of the Wooden Furniture from Gordion, Turkey,
               1983." Gordion Furniture Project Archives.
  1984   "Report on the Conservation and Restoration of the Wooden Furniture from Gordion, Turkey,
               1984." Gordion Furniture Project Archives.
  1985   "The Wooden Furniture from Tumulus MM at Gordion, Turkey." Ph.D. diss., University of
               Pennsylvania.
  1988   "The Phrygian Artistic Intellect." *Source* 7, nos. 3/4:24–42.
  1990   "Midas' Bed and a Royal Phrygian Funeral." *Journal of Field Archaeology* 17:69–87.
  1993   "A Carved Stretcher from the Big Tumulus at Gordion." In *Aspects of Art and Iconography: Anatolia
               and Its Neighbors, Studies in Honor of Nimet Özgüç,* edited by Machteld Mellink, Edith Porada, and
               Tahsin Özgüç, 569–572. Ankara: Türk Tarih Kurumu.
  1995   "Furniture in Ancient Western Asia." In *Civilizations of the Ancient Near East* 3, edited by
               Jack M. Sasson, 1647–1671. New York: Scribner's.
  1996   "Phrygian Furniture from Gordion." In *The Furniture of Western Asia: Ancient and Traditional,* edited
               by Georgina Herrmann, 187–209. Mainz: Philipp von Zabern.
  1998   "Symbols on the Gordion Screens." *Proceedings of the XXXIVième Rencontre Assyriologique Interna-
               tionale, Istanbul, 1987,* 629–639. Ankara: Türk Tarih Kurumu.
  1999   "Early Evidence for the Use of the Lathe in Antiquity." In *Meletemata: Studies in Aegean Archaeology
               Presented to Malcolm H. Wiener,* edited by Philip P. Betancourt, Vassos Karageorghis, Robert
               Laffineur, and Wolf-Dietrich Niemeier, 781–786. Liège: Université de Liège.
  2001   "Celebrating Midas: Contents of a Great Phrygian King's Tomb Reveal a Lavish Funerary
               Banquet." *Archaeology* 54, no. 4:26–33.
  2002   "The Andokides Painter and Greek Carpentry." In *Essays in Honor of Dietrich von Bothmer,* edited
               by A. Clark and J. Gaunt, 303–316. Amsterdam: Allard Pierson Museum.

2003   "The Conservation of the Wooden Objects from Gordion, Turkey: Methods for the Treatment of
            Dry Archaeological Wood." In *Art, Biology and Conservation: Biodeterioration and Works of Art*, edited
            by R.J. Koestler, Victoria Koestler, A. Elena Charola, and Fernando Nieto-Fernandez, 359–369.
            New York: Metropolitan Museum of Art.

2008   "Banquet Tables at Gordion." In *Aykut Çınaroğlu'na Armağan (Studies in Honour of Aykut Çınaroğlu)*,
            edited by Elif Genç and Duygu Çelik, 135-155. Ankara: Ekici Form Ofset.

Forthcoming *The Gordion Wooden Objects II. The Furniture and Wooden Artifacts from Tumulus P, Tumulus W, and the
            City Mound.* Leiden and Boston: Brill.

Simpson, Elizabeth, and Robert Payton
1986   "Royal Wooden Furniture from Gordion." *Archaeology* 39, no. 6:40–47.

Simpson, Elizabeth, and Krysia E. Spirydowicz
1999   *Gordion Wooden Furniture (Gordion Ahşap Eserler): The Study, Conservation, and Reconstruction of the
            Furniture and Wooden Objects from Gordion, 1981–1998.* Ankara: Museum of Anatolian Civiliza-
            tions.

Simpson, Elizabeth, Krysia Spirydowicz, and Valerie Dorge
1992   *Gordion Wooden Furniture (Gordion Ahşap Eserler): The Study, Conservation, and Reconstruction of the Wooden
            Furniture from Gordion, 1981–1990.* Ankara: Museum of Anatolian Civilizations.

Siu, Ralph G.H.
1951   *Microbial Decomposition of Cellulose.* New York: Reinhold.

Slackman, Michael
2006   "Out of Desert Poverty, a Cauldron of Rage in the Sinai." *New York Times*, May 7.

Sloane, Eric
1964   *A Museum of Early American Tools.* New York: Ballantine.

Smith, Sidney
1938   *Assyrian Sculptures in the British Museum, from Shalmaneser III to Sennacherib.* London: British
            Museum.

Spirydowicz, Krysia E.
1990   "Table 1, Tumulus MM." Treatment Record, Gordion Furniture Project Archives.
1990   "Table 2, Tumulus MM." Treatment Record, Gordion Furniture Project Archives.
1990   "Table 3, Tumulus MM." Treatment Record, Gordion Furniture Project Archives.
1990   "Table 4, Tumulus MM." Treatment Record, Gordion Furniture Project Archives.
1990   "Table 5, Tumulus MM." Treatment Record, Gordion Furniture Project Archives.
1990   "Table 6, Tumulus MM." Treatment Record, Gordion Furniture Project Archives.
1990   "Table 7, Tumulus MM." Treatment Record, Gordion Furniture Project Archives.
1990   "Table 9, Tumulus MM." Treatment Record, Gordion Furniture Project Archives.
1992   "Furniture from the NE Corner, Tumulus MM." Treatment Record, Gordion Furniture Project
            Archives.
1993   "Table 1, Tumulus MM." Treatment Record, Gordion Furniture Project Archives.
1994   "Table 1, Tumulus MM." Treatment Record, Gordion Furniture Project Archives.
1996   "The Conservation of Ancient Phrygian Furniture from Gordion, Turkey." In *Archaeological
            Conservation and Its Consequences*, edited by Ashok Roy and Perry Smith, 166–171. London:
            International Institute for Conservation of Historic and Artistic Works.
1998   "Table 2, Tumulus MM." Treatment Record, Gordion Furniture Project Archives.
1998   "Table 4, Tumulus MM." Treatment Record, Gordion Furniture Project Archives.
1998   "Table 5, Tumulus MM." Treatment Record, Gordion Furniture Project Archives.
1999   "Table 1, Tumulus MM." Treatment Record, Gordion Furniture Project Archives.
1999   "Serving Stand A, Tumulus MM." Treatment Record, Gordion Furniture Project Archives.
1999   "Serving Stand B, Tumulus MM." Treatment Record, Gordion Furniture Project Archives.
2001   "Furniture from the NE Corner, Tumulus MM." Treatment Record, Gordion Furniture Project
            Archives.

Spirydowicz, Krysia E., and Elisabeth Joy
1999   "Table 3, Tumulus MM." Treatment Record, Gordion Furniture Project Archives.
1999   "Table 6, Tumulus MM." Treatment Record, Gordion Furniture Project Archives.
1999   "Table 7, Tumulus MM." Treatment Record, Gordion Furniture Project Archives.
1999   "Table 9, Tumulus MM." Treatment Record, Gordion Furniture Project Archives.

Spirydowicz, Krysia E., Elizabeth Simpson, Robert Blanchette, Arno Schniewind, Mauray Toutloff, and Alison
Murray
2001   "Alvar and Butvar: The Use of Polyvinyl Acetal Resins for the Treatment of the Wooden
            Artifacts from Gordion, Turkey." *Journal of the American Institute for Conservation* 40, no. 1:43–57.

Stanley, Alessandra
2005   "When Mourning Becomes Television: Even Anchors Stay Behind the Cameras at Vatican."
            New York Times, April 9.

Steffy, J. Richard
1994   *Wooden Ship Building and the Interpretation of Shipwrecks*. College Station, TX: Texas A&M University
            Press.

Steinkeller, Piotr
1980   "Mattresses and Felt in Early Mesopotamia." *Oriens Antiquus* 19, no. 2:79–100.
2002   "Stars and Stripes in Ancient Mesopotamia: A Note on Two Decorative Elements of Babylonian
            Doors." *Iranica Antiqua* 37:359–371.
2002   "Archaic City Seals and the Question of Early Babylonian Unity." In *Riches Hidden in Secret Places:
            Ancient Near Eastern Studies in Memory of Thorkild Jacobsen*, edited by Tzvi Abusch, 249–257. Winona
            Lake, IN: Eisenbrauns.

Stierlin, Henri
1993   *Das Gold der Pharaonen*. Paris: Terrail.

Strabo
1917–1935   *Geography*, trans. H.L. Jones. Loeb ed. Cambridge, MA: Harvard University Press.

Strommenger, Eva, and Max Hirmer
1962   *Five Thousand Years of the Art of Mesopotamia*. New York: Harry N. Abrams.

Stronach, David
1993   "Patterns of Prestige in the Pazyryk Carpet: Notes on the Representational Role of Textiles in
            the First Millennium B.C." In *Oriental Carpet and Textile Studies* 4, edited by Murray Eiland, Robert
            Pinner, and Walter Denny, 19–34. Berkeley, CA: San Francisco Bay Area Rug Society and OCTS
            Ltd.
1996   "The Imagery of the Wine Bowl: Wine in Assyria in the Early First Millennium B.C." In *The
            Origins and Ancient History of Wine*, edited by Patrick McGovern, Stuart Fleming, and Solomon
            Katz, 175–195. Amsterdam: Gordon and Breach.

Strong, Donald
1966   *Greek and Roman Gold and Silver Plate*. London: Methuen.
1976   *Roman Art*. Harmondsworth: Penguin.

Summers, Geoffrey, and Françoise Summers
2006   "The Kerkenes Project in 2006." *Anatolian Archaeology, British Institute at Ankara Research Reports*
            12:32–33.

Summers, Kirk
1996   "Lucretius' Roman Cybele." In *Cybele, Attis and Related Cults: Essays in Memory of M.J. Vermaseren*,
            edited by Eugene Lane, 337–365. Leiden: Brill.

Symington, Dorit
1996   "Hittite and Neo-Hittite Furniture." In *The Furniture of Western Asia: Ancient and Traditional*, edited
            by Georgina Herrmann, 111–138. Mainz: Philipp von Zabern.

Symmes, Harrison
1984   "Native Stands of Boxwood in Modern Turkey." *The Boxwood Bulletin* (April):76–79.

Szarzyńska, Krystyna
1993   "Offerings for the Goddess Inana in Archaic Uruk." *Revue d'Assyriologie* 87:7–27.

Talalay, Lauren
1987   "Rethinking the Function of Clay Figurine Legs from Neolithic Greece: An Argument by
            Analogy." *American Journal of Archaeology* 91:161–169.
1993   *Deities, Dolls, and Devices: Neolithic Figurines from Franchthi Cave, Greece*. Bloomington, IN: Indiana
            University Press.

Temizer, Raci
    1959   "Ankara'da bulunan Kybele Kabartması" ("Un bas-relief de Cybèle découvert à Ankara").
                    Anadolu 4:179–187.

Tezcan, Burhan
    1968   "1968 Göllüdağ Kazısı" (1968 Göllüdağ Excavations). *Türk Arkeoloji Dergisi* 17, no. 2:211–235.

Theophrastus
    1916–1926   *Enquiry into Plants*, trans. Arthur Hort. Loeb ed. Cambridge, MA: Harvard University Press.

Thureau-Dangin, F., A. Barrois, G. Dossin, and Maurice Dunand
    1931   *Arslan-Tash*. Paris: Librairie orientaliste Paul Geuthner.

Todd, Andrew, and Emily Dunn
    1989   "Table 5." Treatment Record, Gordion Furniture Project Archives.
    1989   "Table 6." Treatment Record, Gordion Furniture Project Archives.
    1989   "Table 7." Treatment Record, Gordion Furniture Project Archives.
    1989   "Table 9." Treatment Record, Gordion Furniture Project Archives.
    1989   "Northeast Corner Fragments." Examination Report, Gordion Furniture Project Archives.

Toynbee, J.M.C.
    1982   *Death and Burial in the Roman World*. London: Thames and Hudson.

Treasures of Tutankhamun. New York: Ballantine, 1976.

Tuck, Anthony
    2006   "Singing the Rug: Patterned Textiles and the Origins of Indo-European Metrical Poetry."
                    American Journal of Archaeology 110:539–550.

Türck, Ulrich
    2004   "Die phrygischen Muster und ihr Weiterleben." *Boreas* 27:193–231.

Ucko, Peter
    1962   "The Interpretation of Prehistoric Anthropomorphic Figurines." *Journal of the Royal Anthropological
                    Institute of Great Britain and Ireland* 92:38–54.
    1968   *Anthropomorphic Figurines of Predynastic Egypt and Neolithic Crete with Comparative Material from the
                    Prehistoric Near East and Mainland Greece*. London: Andrew Szmidla.

Ulansey, David
    1989   *The Origins of the Mithraic Mysteries: Cosmology and Salvation in the Ancient World*. New York: Oxford
                    University Press.

Ulrich, Roger
    2007   *Roman Woodworking*. New Haven, CT: Yale University Press.

Van Buren, E. Douglas
    1939   "The Rosette in Mesopotamian Art." *Zeitschrift für Assyriologie* 45, nos. 2/3:99–107.
    1945   *Symbols of the Gods in Mesopotamian Art. Analecta Orientalia* 23. Rome: Pontificium Institutum
                    Biblicum.

Van De Mieroop, Marc
    1992   "Wood in the Old Babylonian Texts from Southern Babylonia." In *Trees and Timber in
                    Mesopotamia. Bulletin on Sumerian Agriculture* 6, edited by J.N. Postgate and M.A. Powell, 155–161.
                    Cambridge: Sumerian Agriculture Group.

Van der Toorn, Karel
    1998   "Goddesses in Early Israelite Religion." In *Ancient Goddesses: The Myths and the Evidence*, edited by
                    Lucy Goodison and Christine Morris, 83–97. Madison, WI: University of Wisconsin Press.

Vassileva, Maya
    2005   "The Belt of the Goddess: Phrygian Tombs versus Greek Sanctuaries." In *Studia Archaeologica
                    Universitatis Serdicensis*, Supplementum 4:91–101.

Ventris, Michael, and John Chadwick
    1973   *Documents in Mycenaean Greek*. 2nd ed. Cambridge: Cambridge University Press.

Vermaseren, Maarten J.
    1977   *Cybele and Attis: The Myth and the Cult*. London: Thames and Hudson.

Vernant, Jean-Pierre
    1989   "At Man's Table: Hesiod's Foundation Myth of Sacrifice." In *The Cuisine of Sacrifice among the Greeks*, edited by Marcel Detienne and Jean-Pierre Vernant, 21–86. Chicago, IL: University of Chicago Press.

Virgil
    1999–2000 *Aeneid* and *Georgics*, trans. H. Rushton Fairclough, rev. G.P. Goold. Loeb ed. Cambridge, MA: Harvard University Press.

Vitruvius
    1931–1934 *De Architectura*, trans. Frank Granger. Loeb ed. Cambridge, MA: Harvard University Press.

Voigt, Mary M.
    1983   *Hajji Firuz Tepe, Iran: The Neolithic Settlement*. Philadelphia, PA: University of Pennsylvania Museum of Archaeology and Anthropology.

Von Bothmer, Dietrich
    1984   *A Greek and Roman Treasury. The Metropolitan Museum of Art Bulletin* (Summer). New York: Metropolitan Museum of Art.

Von der Osten, H.H.
    1929   *Explorations in Central Anatolia: Season of 1926*. Chicago, IL: University of Chicago Press.

Von Eles, Patrizia
    1995   *Museo Civico Archeologico, Verucchio: Guide to the Museum*. Rimini: Province of Rimini Museum System.
    2002   *Guerriero e sacerdote: Autorità e comunità nell'età del ferro a Verucchio. La Tomba del Trono*. Quaderni di Archeologia dell'Emilia Romagna 6. Florence: All'Insegna del Giglio.

Von Luschan, Felix
    1943   *Die Kleinfunde von Sendschirli*. Mitteilungen aus den orientalischen Sammlungen, Ausgrabungen in Sendschirli 5. Berlin: Walter de Gruyter.

Ward, Cheryl
    2000   *Sacred and Secular: Ancient Egyptian Ships and Boats*. Philadelphia, PA: University of Pennsylvania Museum of Archaeology and Anthropology.

Warnock, Peter, and Michael Pendelton
    1991   "The Wood of the Ulu Burun Diptych." *Anatolian Studies* 41:107–110.

Weeks, Jane
    1982   "Roman Carpentry Joints: Adoption and Adaptation." In *Woodworking Techniques before A.D. 1500*, edited by Seán McGrail, 157–168. Oxford: BAR.

Welters, Linda, ed.
    1999   *Folk Dress in Europe and Anatolia: Beliefs about Protection and Fertility*. Oxford: Berg.

Werr, Lamia al Gailani
    1996   "Domestic Furniture in Iraq, Ancient and Traditional." In *The Furniture of Western Asia: Ancient and Traditional*, edited by Georgina Herrmann, 29–32. Mainz: Philipp von Zabern.

Wessel, Carl J.
    1954   "Textiles and Cordage." In *Deterioration of Materials: Causes and Preventive Techniques*, edited by Glenn A. Greathouse and Carl J. Wessel, 408–506. New York: Reinhold.

Westenholz, Joan
    1998   "Goddesses of the Ancient Near East: 3000–1000 B.C." In *Ancient Goddesses: The Myths and the Evidence*, edited by Lucy Goodison and Christine Morris, 63–82. Madison, WI: University of Wisconsin Press.

Weyl, Hermann
    1952   *Symmetry*. Princeton, NJ: Princeton University Press.

Whitley, James
    2002   "Too Many Ancestors." *Antiquity* 76:119–126.

Wilford, John
    2002   "Statuette is Traced to Midas; Alas, Not Golden, Just Ivory." *New York Times*, January 3.

Wilkinson, Charles K., and Marsha Hill
  1983   *Egyptian Wall Paintings.* New York: Metropolitan Museum of Art.

Williams, Patricia
  1999   "Protection from Harm: The Shawl and Cap in Czech and Slovak Wedding, Birthing and
                Funerary Rites." In *Folk Dress in Europe and Anatolia: Beliefs about Protection and Fertility*, edited by
                Linda Welters, 135–154. Oxford: Berg.

Wilson, Thomas
  1896   *The Swastika: The Earliest Known Symbol, and Its Migrations; with Observations on the Migration of Certain
                Industries in Prehistoric Times.* Washington, DC: United States National Museum.

Winter, Irene J.
  1976   "Carved Ivory Furniture Panels from Nimrud: A Coherent Subgroup of the North Syrian Style."
                Metropolitan Museum Journal 11:25–54.
  1976   "Phoenician and North Syrian Ivory Carving in Historical Context: Questions of Style and
                Distribution." *Iraq* 38:1–22.
  1981   "Is There a South Syrian Style of Ivory Carving in the First Millennium B.C.?" *Iraq* 43:101–
                130.
  1999   "Reading Ritual in the Archaeological Record: Deposition Pattern and Function of Two Artifact
                Types from the Royal Cemetery of Ur." In *Fluchtpunkt Uruk: archäologische Einheit aus methodischer
                Vielfalt. Schriften für Hans Jörg Nissen*, edited by Hartmut Kühne, Reinhard Bernbeck, and Karin
                Bartl, 229–256. Rahden: Verlag Marie Leidorf GmbH.
  2003   "Ornament and the 'Rhetoric of Abundance' in Assyria." *Eretz-Israel* 27:252–264.
  2007   "Representing Abundance: A Visual Dimension of the Agrarian State." In *Settlement and Society:
                Essays Dedicated to Robert McCormick Adams*, edited by Elizabeth Stone, 117–138. Los Angeles and
                Chicago: Cotsen Institute of Archaeology, UCLA, and The Oriental Institute, University of
                Chicago.

Woods, Christopher
  2004   "The Sun-God Tablet of Nabû-apla-iddina Revisited." *Journal of Cuneiform Studies* 56:23–103.

Woolley, C.L.
  1921   *Carchemish, Report on the Excavations at Jerablus on Behalf of the British Museum II. The Town Defences.*
                London: British Museum.

Woolley, C.L., and R.D. Barnett
  1952   *Carchemish, Report on the Excavations at Jerablus on Behalf of the British Museum III. The Excavations in the
                Inner Town.* London: British Museum.

Xenophon
  2001   *Anabasis*, trans. Carleton Brownson, rev. John Dillery. Loeb ed. Cambridge, MA: Harvard
                University Press.

Young, Rodney S.
  1951   "Gordion—1950." *University Museum Bulletin* 16, no. 1:3–20.
  1956   "The Campaign of 1955 at Gordion: Preliminary Report." *American Journal of Archaeology* 60:249–
                266.
  1957   *Gordion Field Book* 63.
  1957   *Gordion Field Book* 70.
  1957   Draft for "The Gordion Campaign of 1957: Preliminary Report." Gordion Archives, University
                of Pennsylvania Museum of Archaeology and Anthropology.
  1958   "The Gordion Campaign of 1957: Preliminary Report." *American Journal of Archaeology* 62:139–154.
  1960   "The Gordion Campaign of 1959: Preliminary Report." *American Journal of Archaeology* 64:227–
                243.
  1962   "The 1961 Campaign at Gordion." *American Journal of Archaeology* 66:153–168.
  1963   "Gordion on the Royal Road." *Proceedings of the American Philosophical Society* 107:348–364.
  1965   "Early Mosaics at Gordion." *Expedition* 7, no. 3:4–13.
  1969   "Doodling at Gordion." *Archaeology* 22, no. 4:270–275.
  1974   "Phrygian Furniture from Gordion." *Expedition* 16, no. 3:2–13.
  1975   *Gordion: A Guide to the Excavations and Museum.* Ankara: Ankara Turizmi, Eskieserleri ve Müzeleri
                Sevenler Derneği.
  1981   *Three Great Early Tumuli. The Gordion Excavations Final Reports I.* Philadelphia, PA: University of
                Pennsylvania Museum of Archaeology and Anthropology.

INDEX

For illustrations of furniture, fragments, and associated objects from Tumulus MM, see also Appendix 9/Concordance, pp. 225–226.

abrasives, 160, 201. *See also* scraping/smoothing/rubbing.

abstract/abstraction, 38, 41, 44, 48–49, 75, 84, 106 n. 277, 192–193

abundance, 45, 55, 88 n. 137, 90, 91 n. 166, 101 n. 239, 102, 105 n. 271, 106–107

Acemhöyük, Turkey, 85 n. 111, 116 n. 46

acetone, 137, 141, 146, 149–150, 152–153, 155, 163

acetonitrile, 177

Achilles, 109, 128 n. 17

acids, 127 n. 3, 127 n. 5, 171, 178–179, 182–186, 221. *See also* alkali/alkalinity; fatty acids; pH.

acrylic sheet, 142, 159–162. *See also* Plexiglas.

Acryloid (B-44/B-72), 141, 152, 155, 158, 161, 163

acrylonitrile, 205 n. 12, 217 n. 43

adhesives/cement, 31 n. 3, 142, 144, 146, 148, 150, 152–155, 158, 161–163, 202 n. 43, 217. *See also* glue.

    Acryloid B-72, 152, 155, 161, 163

    Butvar B-98, 139–142, 146, 148, 150, 152–155, 158

    contact cement, 161

    dichloromethane/methylene chloride, 159–161

    hot-melt, 157

    nitrocellulose/HMG, 142, 144, 158

    "Weld-on"/acrylic solvent cement, 160–161. *See also* dichloromethane/methylene chloride.

Adılcevaz, Turkey, 63

Aditi, 108 n. 281

adze, 197–199

Aegean. *See* Greece/Greek, Bronze Age.

aesthetic, Phrygian, 15–16, 18, 33–34, 36–38, 48–56, 72 n. 42, 74–75, 77–83, 85–86, 93–97, 99–110, 117, 135

Africa, 84 n. 104, 182

agriculture/crops/farming, 53–54, 99, 101–107. *See also* abundance; astronomy/astronomical canon; earth; Hesiod, *Works and Days;* Virgil, *Georgics.*

    agricultural cycle/year, 103–106, 107 n. 277; CD-Figure 94

    and the Tumulus MM serving stands, 99–110

    autumn/winter rains, 105

    festivals, 103, 105–106, 106–107 n. 277, 109. *See also akītu* (new year's) festival.

    growing season, 106

    harvest, 103–105, 107

    planting, 101 n. 240, 104–106, 107 n. 277

    plowing, 104–106, 107 n. 280

    solar year, 103–105

    summer preparations, 105

    threshing/winnowing, 105

    voice of the crane, 105

    winter activities, 105

    and Matar/Magna Mater, 98 n. 218, 99, 102–110

    and the state economy, 103–106, 130 n. 36

    at Çatalhöyük, 53–54

    at Gordion, 106

    at Hacılar, 53

    crop yield/agricultural production, 53–54, 91, 105–106

        fruits and vegetables, 105. *See also* food and drink.

        grain, as main subsistence food, 105. *See also* grain.

    cultivation, 53, 54 n. 157, 101, 106, 109 n. 292

    "Debate between Summer and Winter," 105 n. 271

    equinoxes/solstices and agriculture, 103–107. *See also* astronomy/astronomical canon.

    farmer's world, 101, 105

    fertility, 52–55, 56, 88 n. 136, 90, 98 n. 218, 99, 101 n. 240, 102, 106, 106–107 n. 277, 107 n. 278, 109, 130 n. 36

    saved seeds, 90, 91 n. 166, 107 n. 277

    "sown field," 53

Ahiram of Byblos, 43 n. 73, 44 n. 79

Akhenaten, 43

akītu (new year's) festival, 105 n. 271

akroterion, 92–94, 96, 100, 101 n. 236

Alacahöyük, Turkey, 52, 84–85; CD-Figure 80

Alalakh, Turkey, 89 n. 147

alcohol (in conservation treatment), 13, 15, 18, 65, 137–139, 142–143, 145
  ethanol, 139–142, 146–155, 161, 172
  isopropyl alcohol, 143–144

Alden, Harry, xxxviii, 165, 205 n. 12

Alexandria/Alexandrian, 40, 104 n. 258, 104 n. 263

Alışarhöyük/Alışar IV pottery, 117 n. 53

alkali/alkalinity, 171, 207. See also acids; pH.

Alkinoös, 106 n. 276

Alp Reklam, Ankara, xxxviii, 159–160, 162

Alpüren, Cemal and Celal. See Alp Reklam.

Altai Mountains, Siberia, 46, 124

Altıntepe, Turkey, 46, 63, 76 n. 66

aluminum, 172
  present in textiles, 205, 207–209, 212, 214, 218, 221

Alvar (polyvinyl acetal resin), 13–14, 31 n. 3, 111, 137–139, 138 n. 9, 145, 148, 155–156, 158 n. 92

Alyattes, 76, 131 n. 42

Amarna/Amarna letters, 43, 198

amber, 117 n. 52

Amenhotep III, 43

Amiternum, relief, 109; CD-Figure 100

amphora, 10 n. 41, 49 n. 122, 50, 108, 128–129, 183–184

analyses, 41 n. 55, 94, 95 n. 194, 197
  Gordion, 106 (plant use), 133–134 (dating)
  Tumulus MM artifacts, 165–187, 203–223.
    See also entries for individual analytical techniques.
    consolidants, 138–139, 141, 158 n. 92
    dendrochronology, 119 n. 3 (coffin corner block)
    designs, serving stands, 77–83, 97, 193; Color Plates X–XI; CD Figures 66–73
    drink/beverage residues, 9 n. 26, 31, 74, 123, 177–183, 186–187
    early analyses, 9 n. 26, 14, 16 n. 25, 19, 31 n. 2, 57 n. 4, 178 n. 3, 203–204
    food remains, 9 n. 26, 31, 74, 123, 127, 177–178, 183–187
    furniture finish residues, 202 n. 39
    glue residues, 31 n. 3, 200 n. 32
    textiles associated with the furniture, 114, 122–123, 130, 203–223; Plates 153–158; CD-Figures 1–65
    wood pathology, 156, 171–176, 203 n. 6, 221 n. 51; Plates 139–149
    wood species, 7 nn. 6–7, 14, 16 n. 25, 19, 31 n. 2, 57 n. 4, 122 n. 22, 139, 145, 165–170; Plates 139–149
    wood strength tests, 158 n. 92

Anat, 88, 89 n. 145

ancestors, 41, 43, 55, 84, 106, 107 n. 277, 108 n. 281, 109 n. 291, 135 n. 78

animal legs, 46, 76

animal paw/hoof (feet), 9, 38 n. 30, 44–45, 66, 75
  hooves/hoof feet, 42, 63 n. 55, 76, 112 n. 7. See also heads and hoofs.
  lion-paw feet, 38, 43 n. 73, 44–45, 76–77
  "scroll" feet, 9, 19–20, 66, 68, 71, 73–75, 95, 96 n. 203

animals. See motifs (designs); sacrifice/sacrificial ritual; individual entries.
  carved stretcher, Tumulus MM, 112, 114 n. 17, 117, 155; Figures 77–78; Plates 101, 104, 105A
  pairs of, 88–89, 94 n. 193
  Tumulus P, 117, 162

anise/fennel, 127 n. 3, 186

Ankara, Turkey, 8 n. 17, 24 n. 101, 35 n. 15, 76 n. 63, 92–93, 96 n. 202, 100, 101 n. 236, 117 n. 56, 123–124, 131 n. 39, 143, 156–159, 162. See also Bahçelievler; Etlik; Great Tumulus, Ankara; Museum of Anatolian Civilizations.

apotropaic (design). See protective device/ protection/apotropaic design.

Apsû, 87 n. 134, 102 n. 246. See also Enki/Ea.

archaeological context, 53, 63, 75, 89 n. 147, 92, 115, 135 n. 78, 178, 213, 217. See also plunder/robbery/thieves; unexcavated artifacts.

architectural terra-cottas/tiles, 95 n. 194, 97 n. 207, 117 n. 54

architecture
  architectural labyrinths, 51 nn. 135–136
  Greek, 94 n. 193
  Phrygian, 8 n. 12, 92–99, 101 n. 239, 110, 117 n. 56, 134 n. 75, 198 n. 12

Argos/Argive, 50, 131 n. 40

Ariadne, 51

Arinna. See Sun Goddess of Arinna.

armor, 89 n. 150, 129

Arnhem Land, Australia, 55 n. 168; Plate 116C

Arslan Kaya, Turkey, 93–96, 97 n. 209, 98, 134 n. 75; Plates 120, 121A; CD-Figure 74

Arslan Taş, Turkey, 96 n. 204, 134 n. 75; CD-Figure 77

Arslan-Tash, Syria, 46 n. 97

artist/artisan/designer, xxxv, xxxviii–xxxix, 2, 18, 28, 31, 34, 40 n. 44, 54, 73, 76–79, 82–83, 95, 116, 128, 192–194, 200–202. See also craftsmen.

Aržan, Siberia, 124

Asherah, 88 nn. 142–143

Ashurbanipal, 44, 50 n. 127, 91, 103 n. 257, 117 n. 51, 128 n. 10

Assur, 45 n. 88

Assurnasirpal II, 45, 77 n. 75, 91, 199 n. 16

Assyria/Assyrian, 44–46, 50, 55, 76–77, 86–87, 89, 91, 92 n. 182, 95, 99, 101 n. 239, 102 n. 246, 103, 109 n. 296, 116, 117 n. 51, 128 nn. 10–11, 129 n. 20, 131 n. 42, 132–133, 134 n. 75, 178, 199, 222, 223 n. 59; CD-Figure 98. *See also* individual entries.

Assyrian Colony Period, 85 n. 111, 92 n. 178

Astarte, 88–89

astrological, 106 n. 271, 195 n. 24

astronomy/astronomical canon, 103–106. *See also* calendar; celestial/celestial phenomena; cosmos/cosmic; moon/lunar; star/astral; sun/solar.
    Alexandrian astronomical canon, 104 n. 263
    and calendars, 103–106
    "equinox year," 105
    equinoxes and solstices, 103–107; CD-Figure 94
        autumnal (fall) equinox, 105, 106 n. 272
        vernal (spring) equinox, 103, 105, 105–106 n. 271, 106 n. 272, 107
        winter solstice, 105
    morning (cosmical) setting, 105 n. 265
    morning (heliacal) rising, 103–104 n. 257, 104 n. 258, 105 n. 265
    MUL.APIN ("Plough Star"), 103–104 n. 257, 105 n. 264
    Pleiades, 105, 109
    Ptolemy, 104 n. 259, 104 n. 263
    Sirius/Sothis, 104 n. 258, 105

asymmetry, 33–34, 36–38, 50, 77–78, 80, 94

ATA, 90 n. 160

Atalia, queen of Sargon II, 91

Athenaeus, 39 n. 38, 40, 76, 127 n. 6

Athens/Athenian, 50–51

attachments/fittings, 9, 32 n. 4, 34–35, 39, 41, 44–46, 76, 93, 116, 129, 134, 199. *See also* furniture.

aviation fuel/AVGAZ, 137. *See also* solvent, gasoline.

AVIS, 90 n. 160

awl, 20, 33, 197–198

axe, 197

Aytuğ, Burhan, xxxv, xxxviii, 31 n. 2, 38 n. 31, 61 n. 31, 165–170, 173, 198 n. 11, 200 n. 26

Baba Jan, Iran, 50 n. 128

Babylon/Babylonian, 46 n. 96, 87, 89, 96 n. 203, 104 n. 263, 116 n. 42, 197, 199 n. 15; Plate 116A
    astronomy/astrology, 105 n. 264
    calendar, 103, 104 n. 258

Baghouz, Syria, 42–43, 62 n. 43, 64, 116, 202 n. 41

Bahçelievler (Ankara), Turkey, 92 n. 177; Plate 118B

Bakşeyiş Monument, 98 n. 210

Balawat gates, 76

Balkans, 54, 85, 108 n. 286

Ballard, Mary, xxxvi, xxxviii, 203–223

balsa wood, 142

Baniti, 91

banquet/feast. *See also* food and drink; funerals/funerary ritual; sacrifice/sacrificial ritual.
    archaeological evidence for, 42, 47–48, 63–64, 124, 187
        from Gordion, 31, 40–41, 62, 73–75, 123, 127, 130–132, 177–187
        from Salamis, Cyprus, 129
    courses, 40
    depictions of, 42, 44–46, 76–77, 128 nn. 10–11, 178
    Greek, 130 n. 36, 131 n. 38
    Homeric, 128–129
    in the netherworld, 131 n. 39
    textual evidence for, 39–40, 76, 128–130

banquet furniture, 39–48, 62–64, 73–77, 123, 127, 137–138, 143–146, 148

Banquet Stele, Nimrud, 91 n. 170

Bard Graduate Center, xxxvii

barley, 45 n. 84, 53, 103, 106, 107 n. 280, 127–128, 134, 178, 182–184, 186. *See also* grain; seeds/grains/peas/cereals.

Barrekub, 195 n. 24

Bashadar, Siberia, 124

bast (plant fiber). *See* textiles.

Batdorf, Lynn, 199 n. 23, 201 n. 35

batting. *See* textiles.

Bavian, monument of Sennacherib, 134 n. 75

Bayındır, Turkey, 46 n. 97, 108 n. 282, 124, 131–132

Beck, Curt, xxxviii, 127 n. 2, 177, 179, 183–184

"bed," Tumulus MM, 2, 8, 13, 21–27, 31, 120–123, 155–156; Figure 3. *See also* coffins, Tumulus MM.

beds/couches
    Egyptian, 115 n. 37, 197 n. 6
    Greek, 47, 127 n. 1
    Lydian, 46 n. 96, 131 n. 42
    Mari, 199
    Nimrud, 116
    of Ptolemy Philadelphus, 40
    relief from Amiternum, 109; CD-Figure 100
    relief from Nineveh, 44, 117 n. 51
    Salamis, Cyprus, 129
    Tumulus K-III, 41

beds/couches (*Continued*)
 Tumulus P, 113–114, 123
 Ugarit, 88 n. 144, 89 n. 147
 Urartian, 45
beer/ale, 106, 127, 128 n. 7, 128 n. 11, 178,
 182–183, 186. *See also* barley; "mixed bever-
 age"/mixed fermented beverage; wine.
beerstone. *See* calcium, oxalate.
"bell idol." *See* dolls/"bell idols."
Bellinger, Louisa, 106 n. 276, 203–204, 206–211,
 213, 216, 221–222
Belorussia (Belarus), 53 n. 153
belts, 41, 109 n. 289, 215
 Assyrian, 91 n. 171
 Bayındır, 124, 132
 dedicated in sanctuaries, 131 n. 40
 Ivriz, 86
 of Matar, 92, 131 n. 39
 Tumulus K-III, 132 n. 46
 Tumulus K-IV, 132 n. 46
 Tumulus MM, 8 n. 15, 10, 65 n. 2, 130
 Tumulus P, 49, 132 n. 46
 Tumulus W, 49, 132 n. 46
bending/training (of wood), 14, 17, 19, 38, 58, 66,
 200; Plate 152C. *See also* wood.
benzine. *See* gasoline.
Berecynthus (district), Turkey, 199
Berndt-Ersöz, Susanne, 92 n. 177, 93 nn. 185–
 186, 94 n. 193
beverage. *See* food and drink; "mixed beverage"/mixed fermented beverage.
Bible, 46 n. 97, 199
bier, 109, 123, 127. *See also* beds/couches; coffins.
bilateral symmetry. *See* symmetry.
bird, 52 n. 143, 54 n. 162, 84, 90, 92, 98–100,
 106 n. 277, 108–109, 129–130. *See also* AVIS;
 hawk/bird of prey.
birefringence, 209, 219, 222
birth symbol, 54 n. 163
bitter vetch, 106, 186
Black Sea, 199
Blanchette, Robert, xxxv, xxxviii–xxxix, 31 n. 2,
 38 n. 31, 137, 145 n. 38, 156, 165–176, 200 n. 27
boats. *See* ships/shipwreck.
Boeotia/Boeotian, 54 n. 162, 108, 109 n. 289;
 Plate 117C; CD-Figures 82–85
Boğazköy, Turkey, 88 n. 141, 92, 98, 100 n. 233,
 108 nn. 288–289, 129; Plate 119A
bone/bones, 31 n. 3, 41–42, 48 n. 112, 127–129,
 185, 192 n. 7, 193, 197, 222 . *See also* ivory;
 skeleton, Tumulus MM.
Bor stele, 86; CD-Figure 97
Botel Tobago/Taiwan, 55
bow drill. *See* drill/bow drill.

bowls/cups, 10, 43–44, 48, 52 n. 143, 76, 84,
 90, 92, 101, 102 n. 242, 124, 127 n. 6, 128 n.
 7, 128 nn. 9–10, 131–132. *See also* omphalos
 bowl/phiale mesomphalos/phialai.
 attribute of Matar, 92
 Megaron 3, Gordion, 75
 Phrygian dedications, 131 n. 40
 Tumulus K-III, 75, 130 n. 33, 132
 Tumulus MM, 8–10, 15, 57, 74, 90 n. 160, 127–
 128, 130, 131 n. 38, 134 n. 70, 151, 178–179,
 194
 Tumulus P, 74, 132
 Tumulus W, 75, 132
 with graffiti, 193–194
 with saved seeds, 90, 91 n. 166, 107 n. 277
boxes/chests, 43, 48, 68, 114 n. 23, 120, 157–158
boxwood/*Buxus sempervirens* L., 16, 19, 31–33,
 38–39, 43–45, 57–61, 65–66, 68 n. 25, 70–71,
 73 n. 47, 75, 111–112, 119, 121–122, 139–140,
 143–146, 148, 150, 152, 154, 166–169, 172–173,
 175, 195 n. 24, 197–199, 200 n. 26, 201, 202 n.
 39; Plates 139C–F, 143, 146E–F, 152C. *See also*
 taskarinnu.
brass (for display mounts), 142, 144, 161, 163
bread, 39–40, 91 n. 166, 106, 131. *See also* grain.
 bread wheat, 53, 106
 dough, 106
 kneading trough, 62 n. 41, 106
British Institute of Archaeology, Ankara, xxxv,
 xxxvii, 159
British Museum, 44–45, 46 n. 97, 49, 76 n. 64, 87
 n. 132, 115 n. 35, 117 n. 51, 128 n. 10
Brixhe, Claude, 96 n. 205, 194
bromine, 208, 212
bronze, 10–11, 18, 31, 52, 65, 73–75, 85, 89, 94 n.
 193, 117 n. 55, 128, 130–132, 134
 belts, 8 n. 15, 10, 49, 65 n. 2, 130, 131 n. 40,
 132
 cauldrons, 9–10, 50 n. 131, 65, 74–76, 124, 127–
 130, 131 n. 40, 132, 134 n. 70, 142, 178–179,
 182–184, 218 n. 46
 corrosion product, 73–75, 151
 fibulae, 9–10, 21, 111, 113–114, 124, 130, 131 n.
 40, 132, 215, 223
 fittings/attachments, 9, 45–46, 93, 129, 134 n.
 70
 furniture, 41, 76
 studs/tacks, 8 n. 15, 41, 49, 75
 tools, 197
 vessels, 8–10, 15, 18, 31–32, 40, 57, 73–75, 90 n.
 160, 123–124, 127–128, 130–132, 134 n. 70,
 139, 142, 145, 151, 177–182, 186–187, 194,
 218
brush/brushed, 139, 141, 144, 149–154, 160, 205

bryton, 127. *See also* "mixed beverage"/mixed fermented beverage.
Buck, Susan, xxxviii, 202 n. 39
Buildings A and G, Gordion. *See* Gordion (site), city mound.
bull, 42, 84, 90, 96 n. 162, 106 n. 271, 108, 112, 116–117. *See also* heads and hoofs.
    attachments, 9, 129
    blood, 133
    glue, 202 n. 43
    hooves (as furniture feet), 42
    legs, 84 n. 98
bull-men, 96 n. 203
Buluç, Sevim, xxxix, 134 n. 74
burial customs. *See* funerals/funerary ritual; tombs/burials; individual entries.
burr clover, 206; CD-Figures 10, 13
Butrym, Eric, xxxviii, 127 n. 2, 177, 179, 184
Butvar B-98 (polyvinyl butyral), 158
    as consolidant, 139–158
    for adhesive, 146, 148, 150, 152–155, 158
    for fill/paste, 150, 152–155, 158
Büyük Kapı Kaya, 93, 97–98; Figure 93; Plate 121B
byssus, 222–223

cabinetmaker. *See* woodworker/woodworking.
Calagione, Sam, xxxviii, 127 n. 5, 128 n. 11
calcium
    oxalate ("beerstone"), 127 n. 5, 178–179, 181, 183–184
    present in textiles, 205, 207–209, 212, 214, 218–219, 221
    tartrate, 179, 181–184. *See also* tartaric acid/tartrate.
calendar, 64 n. 65, 103–106, 132. *See also* agriculture/crops/farming; astronomy/astronomical canon; seasons.
    agricultural/agricultural cycle, 103–106
    Alexandrian, 104 n. 258, 104 n. 263
    and the Tumulus MM serving stands, 105–106
    as a manifestation of the cosmic order, 103
    Assyrian, 103
    Babylonian, 103, 104 n. 258, 104 n. 263
    Egyptian, 103 n. 253, 104
    embroidery, 107 n. 277; CD-Figure 94
    "equinox year," 105
    equinoxes and solstices, 103–107
    Greek, 104
    Gregorian reform, 104
    intercalation, 103–104
    Julian, 104
    leap year, 104 n. 259, 104 n. 261
    lunar, 103–104
    luni-solar, 103–104
    new year's festival, 105 n. 271
    solar, 103–105
    star, 103–104
Callixeinus, 40 n. 42
Canaanite, 43
carbon-14/radiocarbon (dating), 133–134
carbonized (wood/textiles), 41, 62 n. 41, 85, 115
carbonyl, 179, 182–184
carboxylate, 179, 182, 184
Carchemish, Turkey, 89–91, 92 n. 182, 95 n. 196, 98, 133 n. 63; Plate 118D; CD-Figure 99
carnelian, 46 n. 97, 53 n. 151
Carpenter, Edmund, xl, 55. *See also* Schuster, Carl, and Edmund Carpenter.
carpet/carpets
    Anatolian (carpets/kilims), 52 n. 145, 54
    Assyrian (threshold slabs), 87, 91
    at the funeral of Pope John Paul II, 131 n. 37
    patterns/symbols/meaning, 52 n. 145, 54
    Pazyryk, 87
carver/carving/woodcarving, 37, 70, 112 n. 5, 198, 202. *See also* woodworker/woodworking.
cashmere, 206
Çatalhöyük, Turkey, 50 n. 126, 52 n. 149, 53–54, 84, 101 n. 239; CD-Figures 86–87. *See also* agriculture/crops/farming; figurines/statuettes.
cauldron attachments, 9, 129, 134 n. 70
cauldrons, 9–10, 50 n. 131, 65, 74–76, 124, 127–130, 131 n. 40, 131 n. 42, 132, 134 n. 70, 142, 178–179, 182–184, 218 n. 46; Color Plates IVB, VB, VIA-B; Plates 1, 36B, 70
cedar/*Cedrus libani* Loud., 7 n. 7, 35 n. 19, 119–120, 123–125, 165–166, 169–170, 172–174, 176, 197, 198 n. 12, 199; Plates 140A–B, 147A–B, 148C
celestial/celestial phenomena, 86 n. 125, 88 n. 138, 99, 101 n. 240, 102–106, 109. *See also* astronomy/astronomical canon; cosmos/cosmic; moon/lunar; star/astral; sun/solar.
    and the Tumulus MM serving stands, 102, 105–106
    importance for agriculture, 99, 101 n. 240, 104
    observation and recording of, 103, 105 n. 271
cellulose, 146, 173, 176, 203–204, 215–216
cereals. *See* grain; seeds/grains/peas/cereals.
chairs/thrones, 53, 77, 87–88. *See also* "throne-backs," Tumulus MM.
    Acemhöyük, 116 n. 46
    Assyrian, 45, 76; CD-Figure 98

chairs/thrones (*Continued*)
    depictions of, 43 n. 73, 45, 53, 76–77, 85, 87–
        88, 90, 92 n. 178, 100, 115–116
    Ebla, 41
    Egyptian, 116
    Greek, 48
    Hittite, 92 n. 178, 130
    ivory fittings, 44 n. 76
    Megaron 3, Gordion, 75
    Nimrud, 45, 76
        Room SW.7, Fort Shalmaneser, 44 n. 76,
            116–117
    of Kubaba, 90; CD-Figure 99
    of Nabû-apla-iddina, 87; Plate 116A
    of Narundi, 88; Plate 116B
    orthostat, city mound, Gordion, 85, 115; Plate
        119C
    rock thrones, Phrygia, 100
    Salamis, Cyprus, 116 n. 49, 129
    Terrace Building, Gordion, 115 n. 31
    throne of Midas, Delphi, 10, 16, 47, 131
    tomb of Tutankhamun, 35
    Tumulus K-III, 41, 75, 115
    Tumulus MM (northeast corner), 2, 31, 112–
        117, 129–130, 198, 200 n. 29; Figure 78;
        Plate 105A
        carved stretcher, 2, 111–113, 114 n. 17, 155,
            166, 169; Figures 77–78; Plates 101, 104,
            105A
        conservation of, 13, 111, 155
        early interpretation of ("stool #2"), 21–22,
            111; Plate 103
        excavation, 8, 113; Color Plate IIB; Plates
            100, 103
        textiles associated with, 8, 21–22, 113–114,
            123, 211–216, 222–223; Plates 155–156;
            CD-Figures 25–55
        wood species analysis, 166, 169
    Tumulus P, 46 n. 96
    Urartian, 45 n. 83, 46 n. 93
    Verucchio, 48
chalcolithic, 52, 54, 84, 101. *See also* individual
    entries.
Chaos/Chasm, 107, 108 n. 281
chariot, 19, 129
cheese, 128, 186
cherry/*Prunus* sp., 57, 60, 145 n. 38, 165–167, 175,
    197, 198 n. 13
Childs, John, xxxvii–xxxviii, 202 n. 39
Chile, 84 n. 104
chisel, 70, 197–198, 200; Plate 150B–C
chlorides, 171
chlorine, present in textiles, 221
chloroform, 177, 186

cholesterol, 185
chromatograph, 177. *See also* GC-MS; HPLC;
    LC-MS.
cinnabar, 64
Circe, 128
city mound, Gordion. *See* Gordion (site).
clamp/clamping, 22, 27, 68, 69 n. 25, 120, 143,
    159, 202
clan/tribe/"genealogical clans," 55–56, 84, 90 n.
    165. *See also* "genealogical patterns."
claws/toes, 35 n. 19, 75, 86, 95–96. *See also*
    animal paw/hoof (feet).
clay, 206
    at Gordion, 7–8, 106, 173, 176
    figurines, 53; Plate 117A
    stamps, 54; CD-Figure 86
Clear-View boxes, 157–158
climate control, 157
clothing. *See* costume/dress/clothing.
coffins. *See also* "bed," Tumulus MM; bier.
    Ankara, 123–124
    Bayındır, 124
    boat-shaped, 125
    Denmark, 124
    Egyptian, 202
    joinery, 2, 68, 202
    Luidao, China, 124–125
    Qäwrighul, 124
    Siberia, 124
    Tumulus B, 123, 133 n. 62
    Tumulus C, Gordion, 123
    Tumulus MM, 2, 31, 57, 61, 114 n. 23,
        119–125, 127, 130. *See also* drawings;
        photography/photographs.
        conservation of, 13, 137, 155–156
        construction/assembly (ancient), 119–120,
            123, 127, 130 n. 35
        corner blocks, 8, 22–27, 119–123, 156, 165–
            166, 169, 173, 176, 197; Plate 115
            "cuttings," 23, 25–26, 119 n. 5, 121 n. 17,
                169; Plate 115A
        early interpretation of (as a bed), 2, 8, 13,
            22–27, 31, 120–123, 155–156; Figure 3
        excavation, 8, 22–27, 145; Color Plates IB,
            IIA; Plates 107–110
        form, 120–123
        function, 120, 123, 127, 130
        funeral ceremony prior to burial, 31, 74,
            120, 123, 127–128, 130, 177–178, 186–187;
            Frontispiece
        iron bars/bosses/reinforcements, 8 n. 19,
            22–23, 25–27, 119–120, 121 n. 16, 122–
            123, 156, 169, 173, 176, 221; Plates 111–
            113, 114A

placement in the tomb chamber, 8, 10, 23–
24, 27, 120–123, 127, 130
rails, 2, 8, 22, 24–27, 119–123, 156, 166, 169,
197; Figure 3D; Plates 110, 114C–D
replica, Museum of Anatolian Civilizations,
Ankara, 130 n. 35; Color Plate XVIA
textiles, 8, 21–25, 27, 119–123, 155–157, 169,
174, 204–212, 220–223; Plates 153–154;
CD-Figures 1–24
wood degradation/deterioration, 156, 165,
171, 173–174, 176; Plates 147, 148A–C
wood pseudomorphs, 156, 173, 176, 221 n.
51; Plate 149
woods, 119–122, 165–166, 169, 197
contrast in color, 8, 24, 121–122, 156, 197
n. 10
Tumulus S-1, 123
collars/collar-and-tenon joinery, 14, 17, 25, 32,
38–40, 42–44, 47–48, 57–64, 145–154, 167–168,
200, 202; Figures 27, 39. See also joinery.
color. See textiles; wood.
color diagrams (designs on serving stands), 3, 77–
83, 97; Color Plates X–XI; CD-Figures 66–
73
Comacchio, Italy, 201 n. 35
compass, 20, 61, 66, 70–71, 73, 189–192, 193 n.
14, 197, 200; Plate 152A–B
conidia, 205
conservation, xxxv, xxxvii–xxxviii, 11, 13–15, 27,
31 n. 3, 58, 65, 66 n. 13, 73, 112, 137–159, 161–
163, 171, 202, 204–205; Plates 124–128. See also
individual entries.
early treatments, 11, 13–15, 18, 58, 65, 67 n.
18, 111, 137–139, 143, 145–146, 148, 150–152,
154–156
in situ, 13–14, 137–139, 141, 145, 148, 151, 153,
155–156
consolidant/consolidation, xxxv, 31 n. 3, 112,
138–157, 159, 161–163. See also Acryloid; Alvar;
Butvar B-98; conservation; Rutapox; solvents;
wax.
penetration of/absorption by wood, 138–141,
144, 146–147
pipette/syringe application, 140–141, 146, 151–
154
removal of, 138–141, 143, 146–154
tank/tray, 140, 143, 147, 149, 153–154; Plates
125A, 126C
testing, 138–139, 141, 158 n. 92
under vacuum pressure, 140, 143, 147, 149,
152–155, 157–158
constellation, 103, 105, 109
Copernicus, 104 n. 259
copper, 89, 200 n. 31

adjacent to/present in textiles, 203, 207–209,
212–214, 217–219, 221
cord/cording, 114, 124, 211, 213, 222. See also
upholstery/cushions.
"cat gut," 213
rush, 114 n. 18, 213
corrosion, 171
bronze, 151
iron, 10, 119 n. 7, 123, 154, 156, 173, 176, 205,
221 n. 51
Corsica, 199
cosmical setting, 105 n. 265
cosmos/cosmic, 99, 101–103, 106, 109–110, 130.
See also celestial/celestial phenomena.
costume/dress/clothing, 8, 53–55, 86–87, 90–
91, 95, 99, 106–107 n. 277, 131 n. 42. See also
crown/headdress; textiles.
Assyrian, 50 n. 127, 86–87, 89, 91, 99, 109 n.
296; CD-Figure 98
ethnographic/traditional, 53 n. 151, 54–55,
106–107 n. 277; Plate 116C; CD-Figures
88–96
"golden," 86 n. 125, 87 n. 127, 91 n. 175, 109 n.
296
Greek, 54 n. 162, 108, 108–109 n. 289; Plate
117C; CD-Figures 82–85
of the king buried in Tumulus MM, 8
of Warpalawas, 86–87, 99 n. 220; Plate 119D;
CD-Figure 97
panel decoration on, 86–87, 89–90, 91 n. 171,
99, 109 n. 296
Phrygian, 86–87, 92–93, 99, 101 n. 237; Plates
116D, 118A–C, 119A–B, 120–121
couches. See beds/couches.
Cox, Dorothy, xxxix, 10, 13 n. 2, 15–24, 26–28,
32, 36–37, 41 n. 54, 57, 72, 111, 113, 120
craft/craftsmanship, 1, 16, 124, 202, 219
craftsmen, 2, 16, 18 n. 42, 31, 34, 38 n. 30, 40 n.
44, 47, 50 n. 126, 51, 54, 68 n. 25, 69, 72 n. 42,
73, 76–79, 82–83, 94, 97, 116, 133 n. 62, 158,
160, 192–194, 197, 200–202, 203 n. 8, 221 n.
52. See also woodworker/woodworking.
crazing (Plexiglas/acrylic sheet), 39 n. 36, 142,
161–162; Plate 124B
creator deity, 55–56, 106, 108–109, 135 n. 78. See
also goddess/female deity; mother/mother
goddess.
crescent, 67, 87–88, 93, 103 n. 254, 109. See also
lunette/half-circle.
Croesus, 46 n. 96, 131 n. 42
Cronus. See Kronos.
crook timber, 200 n. 27
crops/yield. See agriculture/crops/farming.
cross. See motifs (designs).

crown/headdress, 54, 88–93, 95–96, 99–103, 107 n. 280, 108–109 n. 289. *See also* fillet.

cryo-cut freezing microtome, 172

Cucuteni (Tripolye), Moldavia, 52–53, 101, 108 n. 281; Plate 117A

Çulha, Abdurrahim, xxxviii

cuneiform, 195 n. 24

Cunningham, Roland, xxxviii, 205 n. 12

curls/curled tendrils, 89–90, 92, 95–96, 101

Daedalus, 51

dance, 51, 108 n. 286

dark/light interplay. *See* inlay; wood, color contrast.

datalogger, 157, 162–163

dating, 10–11, 62 n. 43, 89 n. 155, 119 n. 3, 132–134, 194 n. 20. *See also* carbon-14/radiocarbon (dating); dendrochronology; individual entries.

deer/stag, 84, 112, 117, 124 n. 48

Değirmen Monument, 98 n. 210

deity/divinity, 52, 55–56, 87 n. 134, 88 n. 141, 90–91, 95 n. 196, 98 n. 218, 101, 102 n. 246, 103 n. 252, 106–108, 116 n. 43, 130 n. 36, 131 nn. 38–39, 132 n. 56, 135 nn. 77–78, 199. *See also* creator deity; god/male deity; goddess/female deity; individual entries.

Delikli Taş, 98 n. 210

Delphi, Greece, 10, 16, 46 n. 96, 47, 76, 116 n. 43, 131

Demeter, 107, 109 n. 290

"demon," 9, 92

dendrochronology, 119 n. 3, 132–133, 194 n. 20

designs. *See* motifs (designs); pattern, underlying.

destruction level. *See* Gordion (site), city mound.

diacylglycerides, 184, 186

diamond/lozenge. *See* motifs (designs).

dichloromethane/methylene chloride. *See* adhesives/cement.

"Dilbat necklace," 89 n. 147

dinos, 10 n. 41, 183–184

Diodorus Siculus, 51 n. 137, 132

Dipylon amphora, 50

dirt/grime/debris. *See* wood, cleaning/dirt removal.

display cases
    angle deck, 160–161; Plate 131B–C
    custom-designed (1997), 142, 162–163; Plate 138B
    early, 65, 67 n. 18, 142–143, 159 n. 1, 160–163; Plates 129B, 132B
    humidity, 142, 157, 160, 162–163
    temperature, 162
    ventilation of, 142, 160

display mounts, xxxviii, 35 n. 15, 39, 142, 144,

159–163; Plates 129–138

divination, 90 n. 165, 97–98, 135 n. 78

Djeser-ka-re-seneb, 76 n. 64

Dogfish Head Brewery, 127 n. 5, 128 n. 11

dolls/"bell idols," 54 n. 162, 107 n. 277, 109 n. 289; CD-Figures 82–83

"doodles"/"doodle stones" (Megaron 2, Gordion), 99–100; Figures 94–99

Dorge, Valerie, xxxv n. 2, xxxvii, 38 n. 31, 137 n. 4

dowel/pin/peg. *See* joinery.

dowry textiles, 54

drawings, xxxv, xxxviii–xl, 1, 3, 28, 45 n. 85, 49 n. 123, 53 n. 150, 77 n. 75, 82, 91 n. 175, 108 n. 284, 159, 210 nn. 26–27. *See also* compass; "doodles"/"doodle stones"; graffiti.
    field/early drawings, xxxv, 11, 13, 28, 31, 49 n. 113, 62 nn. 38–39, 75 n. 55, 113 n. 11, 114 n. 24, 138
        "bed" (coffin), Tumulus MM, 13 n. 2, 22, 24 n. 105, 24 n. 107, 26–27; Figure 3
        furniture from the northeast corner, Tumulus MM, 111, 113
        inlaid table, Tumulus MM, 13, 15–18, 32, 36, 41 n. 54; Figure 1
        plain tables, Tumulus MM, 13–14, 57, 59
        "screens" (serving stands), Tumulus MM, 13 n. 2, 19–21, 66 n. 6, 66 n. 10, 67–68, 72; Figure 2
        tomb plan, Tumulus MM. *See* Tumulus MM, tomb plan.
    incised
        on faces of serving stands, 70–71, 73, 200–201; Figure 70
        on tenons of serving stands, 70–71, 73, 189–195, 200; Figures 63, 65; Plates 93–94
    reconstruction drawings, 1, 14–22, 26, 41 n. 50, 47 n. 106, 62 nn. 38–39, 62 n. 46, 63 n. 53, 63 n. 55, 75 n. 55, 85, 113 n. 11, 199
        coffin, Tumulus MM, 119 n. 2, 119 n. 7, 120 n. 15, 121–123, 130 n. 35; Figures 79–90
        furniture from the northeast corner, Tumulus MM, 112; Figures 76–78
        inlaid table, Tumulus MM, 15–18, 32 n. 5, 36, 39, 41 n. 54; Figures 4–28
        plain tables, Tumulus MM, 14, 58 nn. 15–16, 59–60, 61 nn. 29–30, 146; Figures 29–43
        serving stands, Tumulus MM, 19–21, 65, 66 n. 6, 67–68, 69 n. 31, 72, 144; Figures 44–75
    "sown field," 53 n. 153

dregs/lees, 182

dress. *See* costume/dress/clothing.

DRIFTS (Diffuse-Reflectance Infrared Fourier-Transform Spectrometry), 177–185

drill/bow drill, 20, 33, 35 n. 19, 68, 70, 159–161, 163, 197–198, 200–202

drilling program (Tumulus MM), 7–8, 65, 137, 174–175

drink. *See* food and drink; "mixed beverage"/mixed fermented beverage.

Dunn, Emily, xxxvii, 146–147, 152

Dussubieux, Laure, xxxviii, 203–223

dust, 31 n. 3, 142–143, 146, 148–153, 156, 161–162, 210

dye/dyeing, 202 n. 39, 204, 208, 212, 217–219
    "crocking," 218
    indigo, 130, 212, 217–220, 223
    mordant, 217
    Tyrian purple, 114, 123, 208, 212
    vat/vatting, 217–218

Eanna precinct (Uruk), 88

earth, 7, 8 n. 21, 87, 102 n. 246, 107 n. 280, 109, 124, 128–129, 134–135, 137

Earth (deity), 105, 107–109. *See also* Gaia/Ge; Tellus.

Ebla (Tell Mardikh), Syria, 41–42

ebony, 43

Egypt/Egyptian, 35, 40, 43–44, 53 n. 152, 64, 76, 103 n. 253, 104, 112, 115–116, 183 n. 6. *See also* individual entries.
    calendar, 103 n. 258, 104
    deities, 88, 90 n. 165
    games, 135 n. 78
    glue, 31 n. 3
    labyrinth, 51
    primeval hill, 135 n. 77
    symbols/attributes, 90, 94 n. 193, 96 n. 203, 102
    tombs, 35 n. 19, 43, 64, 76 n. 64, 116 n. 44, 197
    tools/woodworking techniques, 197–198, 200 n. 26, 202

El, 88

Eleusinian mysteries, 186

Ellis, Richard, 8 nn. 18–19, 204, 206–209, 211, 213, 216, 218 n. 46, 220–221

Elmalı, Turkey, 124

embroidery, 53 n. 151, 86 n. 122, 106–107 n. 277

Enheduanna, 88 n. 135

Enki/Ea, 102 n. 246

Ephesus (statuettes), 108 n. 282

equinoxes, 103–107; CD-Figure 94. *See also* agriculture/crops/farming; astronomy/astronomical canon; calendar.
    and the Tumulus MM servings stands, 105–106, 106 n. 272

autumnal (fall), 105, 106 n. 272
    "equinox year," 105
    in 750 B.C., 106 n. 272
    means of determining, 105 n. 264, 105 n. 271
    symbols in the cult of Mithras, 105–106 n. 271
    vernal (spring), 103, 105, 105–106 n. 271, 106 n. 272, 107

Erebos, 108 n. 281

esters, 179, 183

estimated measurement, 1

eternity/*aeternitas*, 96 n. 203, 109. *See also* shen sign.

ethafoam, 142, 148, 155–158, 161

ethanol, 139–142, 146–155, 161, 172

Ethulose 400, 152

Etlik (Ankara), Turkey, 92

Etruscan, 51 n. 136, 90 n. 165

evil eye, 54, 162–163; Plate 132B. *See also* protective device/protection/apotropaic design.

excavation, Tumulus MM. *See* Tumulus MM.

excavation/field photographs. *See* photography/photographs.

Exner, Lawrence, xxxviii, 127 n. 2, 177

Expedition (magazine), 13–15, 18–19, 21, 25–26, 67

Faharet Çeşme, 100–102; Plate 119B. *See also* "idols."

faience, 91 n. 175

farming/farmers. *See* agriculture/crops/farming.

fatty acids, 184

Faustina, 109

feast. *See* banquet/feast.

feathers, 223

Feigl spot tests, 178, 183–184

felt, 8, 114, 122–123, 160–161, 203, 207–208, 210–213, 221–222

fenugreek, 186

fertility/reproduction, 52–56, 88 n. 136, 90, 98 n. 218, 99, 101 n. 240, 102, 105–107, 108 n. 286, 109, 130 n. 36, 135 n. 77. *See also* agriculture/crops/farming; goddess/female deity.
    symbols, 52–56, 88 n. 136, 90, 99, 101 n. 240, 102, 106, 106–107 n. 277

festivals, 40 n. 43, 103, 105–106, 107 n. 277, 109, 132. *See also* akītu (new year's) festival; ritual.

fiber. *See* textiles.

fibula/fibulae, 9–10, 21, 86, 101 n. 236, 111, 113–114, 124, 130, 131 n. 40, 131 n. 44, 132, 215, 223; Color Plate IIA; Plates 108, 119D

figurines/statuettes, 40 n. 41. *See also* dolls/"bell idols"; "idols."
    animals, 50 n. 131, 92 n. 179, 117

figurines/statuettes (*Continued*)
  associated with grain, 53–54
  female, 52–54
  from Bayındır, 108 n. 282, 124
  from Çatalhöyük, 53–54
  from Cucuteni, 52–53, 101 n. 240; Plate
    117A
  from Delphi, 10 n. 53
  from Ephesus, 108 n. 282
  from Gordion, 50 n. 131, 92 n. 179, 117
  from Hacılar, 53–54
  from Samos ("Hera"), 109 n. 289
  neolithic/chalcolithic, 52–54, 101 n. 240
fill/filler
  balsa wood, 142
  beeswax and sawdust, 146–148
  glass microsphere/Butvar paste, 150, 152–155,
    158
  inlay, 69
  lead (Tumulus B coffin), 123, 133 n. 62
  plaster-like, 114
  white glue and sawdust, 146
fillet, 91
filling ornament. *See* motifs (designs).
finials, 45. *See also* terminals.
finish/finishing, 199–200, 201 n. 38, 202. *See
    also* abrasives; scraper; scraping/smoothing/
    rubbing.
fish, 31 n. 3, 45, 48, 84, 92 n. 179, 108, 117, 129,
    201 n. 38
flavonoid, 217
flax, 45 n. 84, 106, 114, 134 n. 69, 203–204, 215–
    216, 221–223
Fleming, Stuart, xxxix, 127 n. 2
"flipping" (of designs). *See* symmetry.
floral motif/ornament. *See* motifs (designs).
"flowing vase," 102. *See also* spring/water.
flute, 92, 107, 199 n. 21
food and drink, 9 n. 26, 10, 31, 40, 42, 45, 47,
    74, 76, 88 n. 137, 105, 123, 127–132, 177–187,
    223. *See also* banquet/feast; grain; "mixed
    beverage"/mixed fermented beverage;
    seeds/grains/peas/cereals.
  beer/ale, 106, 127, 128 n. 7, 128 n. 11, 178,
    182–183, 186
  bread, 39–40, 91 n. 166, 106, 131
  cheese, 128, 186
  fish, 45, 48, 129
  fruit, 105, 109, 130 n. 36, 182
  grapes, 48, 86, 105, 127, 128 n. 7, 128 n. 11,
    178, 182, 184
  honey/mead, 127–128, 178, 182–187
  legumes, 184, 186
  lentils, 106, 127, 134 n. 69, 185–187

meat, 39, 42–43, 47–48, 127–128, 130, 183–187.
    See also goat; lamb/sheep.
  roasted on spits, 127–129, 185
  nuts, 48
  on tables, 39–40, 42–43, 45–48, 63–64
  poultry, 129
  spices, 121, 127, 186–187
  stew, 127, 183, 185–187
  vegetables, 105, 127, 186–187
  wine, 105, 127–129, 131 n. 37, 178, 182–
    187
footstools/footrests, 45 n. 83, 47 n. 106, 48, 88,
    116 n. 41
frass (insect), 173, 175
free tenon/floating tenon. *See* tenon.
frieze, 42, 92, 112
frozen tombs. *See* Pazyryk, Siberia; Ukok,
    Siberia.
FTIR (Fourier Transform Infrared Spec-
    troscopy), 205, 215–216, 218–221
funerals/funerary ritual (and evidence for). *See
    also* coffins.
  funerary procession, 109
  Greek, 47, 50, 127 n. 1, 128–129
  Hittite, 129–131
  Homeric, 128–129
  Lydian, 124, 131–132
  Pazyryk, 124
  Pope John Paul II, 131 n. 37
  Salamis, Cyprus, 129
  Thracian, 129
  Tumulus MM, 31, 39, 43, 74, 120, 121 n. 17,
    123–125, 127–135, 174, 186; Frontispiece
funerary banquet/meal. *See also* banquet/feast;
    food and drink.
  Baghouz, 43
  Bayındır, 124
  Gordion, 132
  Hittite, 129–130
  Homeric, 128–129
  "leftovers," 123, 130, 177
  "mixed beverage"/mixed fermented bever-
    age, 127–128, 177–187
  Pazyryk, 64
  stew, 127, 183–187
  Thracian, 129 n. 18
  Tumulus MM, 31, 40, 73–75, 123, 127, 130–
    132, 177–187
  Verucchio, 48
funerary games, 129 n. 18
fungus/mold/fungal decay, 7 n. 7, 18, 61, 65, 120
    n. 11, 137, 143–145, 153, 156, 165, 171–176, 205,
    220
  brown rot, 171, 174

soft rot, 7 n. 7, 61, 120 n. 11, 137, 156, 165, 171–176

white rot, 171

fur, 47–48

furniture. *See also* "bed," Tumulus MM; beds/couches; chairs/thrones; coffins; northeast corner, Tumulus MM; serving stands; stools; tables; individual sites.

Acemhöyük, 116 n. 46

Altıntepe, 39 n. 37, 46, 63, 76 n. 66

Anatolian, 39 n. 37, 40 n. 43, 41–43, 45–46, 53, 63, 76–77, 90, 115, 116 n. 41, 116 n. 46, 117, 130, 131 n. 42, 199

Assyrian, 44–46, 76–77, 116–117

attachments/fittings, 34–35, 39, 41–47, 76, 88 n. 144, 116, 129, 134, 199 n. 25

Babylonian, 46 n. 96, 87, 116 n. 42, 197

Baghouz, 42–43, 64, 116, 202 n. 41

bronze, 35 n. 19, 41, 45–46, 49, 75–76

city mound, Gordion, 1, 41, 75, 85, 115

depictions of, 40 n. 41, 41–47, 76–77, 85, 90, 109, 115–116, 131

Ebla, 41–42

Egyptian, 35 n. 19, 40, 43, 64, 76, 112, 115–116, 197

gold, 35 n. 19, 40, 45, 46 nn. 96–97, 130, 131 n. 42, 199

Greek, 39–40, 43, 47–48, 50 n. 129, 64 n. 63, 66 n. 8, 116 n. 43, 127 n. 1

Hittite/Neo-Hittite, 40 n. 43, 43, 46, 77, 90, 130

Homeric, 39, 47 n. 104, 48

Horoztepe, 41

in Linear B texts, 43

Iranian, 45, 88

ivory, 35 n. 19, 43–46, 76, 88 n. 144, 89 n. 147, 115–117, 129, 201

Jericho, 42–43, 47, 62–63, 115–116, 197 n. 1, 199–200 n. 25, 200 n. 28, 202 n. 41

Jerusalem, 44, 199, 202 n. 39

Karatepe, 46, 77

Kerkenes Dağ, 117

Kültepe, 42

Lydian, 46 n. 96, 76, 131 n. 42

Mari, 199

Mycenae, 43 n. 75

Pazyryk, 40 n. 43, 46–47, 63–64

Phoenician, 44, 46, 76 n. 65

portable/collapsible, 39–40, 42, 47, 62–64, 96–97, 101 n. 238, 115, 132

Roman, 40, 109

Salamis, Cyprus, 116 n. 49, 129

Samos, 47 n. 106, 50 n. 129, 64 n. 63, 66 n. 8

silver, 35 n. 19, 43, 45–46, 48, 76, 117, 131 n. 42, 199

Syrian, 41–44, 46, 88 n. 144, 89 n. 147, 115–117, 199

Thera, 43 n. 75

Thracian, 39–40

throne of Midas, Delphi, 10, 16, 47, 131

tomb of Hetepheres, 35 n. 19, 116 n. 44

tomb of Tutankhamun, 35 n. 19, 43, 64, 115 n. 35

traditional, 64

Tumulus K-III, 41, 75, 115, 130 n. 33, 132

Tumulus K-IV, 75 n. 63

Tumulus P, 13, 16 n. 25, 19, 20 n. 65, 40–41, 46 n. 96, 48–49, 62, 68 n. 25, 73–75, 95, 97, 113–115, 123, 132, 162

Tumulus W, 13, 75, 132

Ugarit, 43, 88 n. 144, 89 n. 147

Urartian, 39 n. 37, 45–46, 63, 76–77, 115, 131 n. 42, 199

Verucchio, 48, 64, 202 n. 44

Zincirli, 46 n. 98, 116 n. 41

gable, 7, 92–94, 100, 101 n. 236

Gabov, Alexander, xxxvii–xxxviii

Gaia/Ge, 105, 107–108. *See also* Earth (deity).

games/puzzles, 34, 88 n. 137, 94, 135. *See also* funerary games.

gaming boards, 88 n. 137, 135 n. 78

gasoline/"benzine" (as wood treatment), 15, 18, 31 n. 3, 65, 137–139, 143

gazelle, 89 n. 145, 89 n. 148, 90

GC-MS (Gas Chromatography-Mass Spectrometry), 178–179, 183–184, 186. *See also* TD-GC-MS.

genealogical clans. *See* clan/tribe/"genealogical clans."

"genealogical patterns," 52, 55–56, 87, 99, 106, 117 n. 54; Plate 116C; CD-Figures 86–93, 95–96

Geometric (Greek) pottery/vases/repertoire, 47–48, 50, 91 n. 175, 127 n. 1

geometric ornament. *See* motifs (designs).

gesso, 43

gilding. *See* plating/sheathing/gilt.

Gimbutas, Marija, xxxix, 53 nn. 152–153

glass, 74 n. 50

attachments, 46 n. 97

for conservation, 140, 143–144, 152, 154

for display, 142, 160–162

microspheres/microballoons, 150, 155, 158. *See also* Butvar B-98, for fill/paste.

glass paste/frit, 43 n. 72, 46 n. 97, 117 n. 52. *See also* faience.

Glaucus of Chios, 76 n. 71
glue, 14–15, 19–20, 34, 68–69, 73, 146, 159–161,
    163, 200–202. *See also* adhesives/cement.
    analysis, 31 n. 3, 200 n. 32
    animal, 31 n. 3, 202 n. 43
    bull's, 202 n. 43
    casein, 31 n. 3
    Egyptian, 31 n. 3
    white, 146, 160–161
    with clamping, 68–69, 202
Glusker, Donald, xxxviii, 127 n. 2, 177
glyoxalic acid, 178
gnomon, 103–104 n. 257
goat, 42, 47, 84, 89, 92, 96, 112, 117, 127–128, 130
    n. 36, 183–184, 186–187
goat hair/wool, 204, 206, 208, 221
god/male deity, 45, 86–87, 90, 93 n. 183, 101, 102
    n. 246, 107, 107–108 n. 281, 130 n. 36, 135 n.
    78. *See also* deity/divinity; individual entries.
    moon-god/Sin, 87
    of vegetation, 86, 105 n. 270
    sun-god, 87, 129
goddess/female deity, 53, 87–110, 129, 131–132,
    134–135, 199. *See also* deity/divinity; individual
    entries.
    creator deity, 55–56, 106–109, 135 n. 78
    double/multiple images (or aspects), 100–102
    enthroned, 53, 88, 90, 92 n. 178
    fertility, 90, 99, 101 n. 240, 102, 106–107, 109
    "house of the goddess," 92, 98, 135
    images on textiles, 106–107 n. 277
    mother goddess/Matar, 87, 91–102, 105–110,
        117 n. 56, 131–132, 134–135, 199; Plates
        118A–C, 119A–B, 120–121
    "Mother of the Gods," 88, 107, 108 n. 281,
        109, 199
    nude, 88–89, 90 n. 158; Plate 117B
    prehistoric figurines, 52–54
    sun-goddess, 88 n. 141, 129
    with lions, 88–90, 92 n. 178, 93, 94 n. 191, 95–
        96, 98–99, 100 n. 226, 107–108, 117 n. 56,
        134 n. 75; Plates 117C, 120–121; CD-Figures
        85, 99
    with rosette(s), 87–92, 95–96, 99–100, 102 n.
        251, 108–109 n. 289, 132, 135 n. 78; Plates
        116B, 117B, 118C–D; CD-Figure 84
goethite, 123, 205–206, 218–219, 221
gold/precious metal, 11, 35, 39–40, 45–46, 48,
    89, 91, 109 n. 296, 128 n. 7, 130–131, 134, 172,
    199. *See also* furniture; plating/sheathing/gilt;
    textiles.
Goldberg, Lisa, xxxvii, 148, 150–154
Göllüdağ, Turkey, 95; Plate 122A
Gordias, 10, 133

Gordion archives/catalogue cards. *See* University
    of Pennsylvania.
Gordion field books/notes, 8, 13–15, 17–19, 21, 22
    n. 91, 24 n. 103, 25–27, 68, 111 n. 1, 114, 119 n.
    2, 122 n. 23, 137–138, 143, 145
Gordion Furniture Project, xxxv–xl, 138, 146,
    156, 158–159, 161
    archives, 31 n. 3, 145 n. 43, 199 n. 23, 200 n.
        27, 201 n. 35
Gordion (site). *See also* Tumulus MM, Gordion;
    other individual entries.
    city mound, 49, 85, 106, 115, 117, 186, 197,
        222
        architectural terra-cottas, 97 n. 207
        Building A, 46 n. 97
        Building G, 95, 99 n. 225
        destruction level, 1, 11 n. 55, 44, 75, 85, 89,
            95 n. 199, 99, 102, 106, 115, 117 nn. 53–
            54, 133–134, 193, 204
            dating of, 11 n. 55, 132–134
        Megaron 2, 95 n. 199
            graffiti ("doodle stones"), 99–100;
                Figures 94–99
            pebble mosaic, 49, 52 n. 146, 99; Figure
                92
        Megaron 3, 41, 75, 115
        Terrace Building, 62 n. 41, 89, 91, 96, 106,
            115 n. 31, 127 n. 3, 134 n. 69
    Hittite-period burials ("Hittite cemetery"), 89,
        129
Goretex, 148, 156–158, 162
graffiti, 189–195. *See also* "doodles"/"doodle
    stones"; inscriptions.
    letters/alphabetic marks, 73, 191, 193–194
    on bowls from Tumulus MM, 90 n. 160, 194
    on the Midas Monument (Yazılıkaya), 96, 132
        n. 58; CD-Figure 76
    on the Tumulus MM chamber, 194 n. 22
    on the Tumulus MM furniture, 70–71, 73,
        189–195, 200; Figures 62–65; Plates 93–94
    on the walls of Megaron 2, 99–100; Figures
        94–99
grain, 53–54, 86, 90, 105–107, 109, 130 n. 36,
    183. *See also* agriculture/crops/farming; food
    and drink; seeds/grains/peas/cereals; wood,
    grain.
    and clay figurines, 53–54
    barley, 45 n. 84, 53, 103, 106, 107 n. 280, 127–
        128, 134 n. 69, 178, 182–184, 186
    bread wheat, 53, 106
    cultivation, 53, 54 n. 157, 105–106, 109 n. 292
    einkorn, 53, 106
    emmer, 53, 128 n. 7
    grinding of, 106

saved seeds, 90, 91 n. 166, 107 n. 277
wild, 53–54
Great Tumulus (METU), Ankara, 76 n. 63, 131 n. 39
Greece/Greek, 9, 40, 47–48, 50–52, 86, 89, 90 n. 164, 91 n. 175, 94 n. 193, 96 n. 202, 101 nn. 239–240, 104–105, 107–109, 116 n. 43, 127–129, 131, 133, 135, 186–187, 195 n. 24, 199. *See also* architecture; calendar; furniture; Geometric (Greek) pottery/vases; individual entries.
astronomy, 104 n. 260, 104 n. 263, 105 n. 264
Bronze Age, 43, 51, 108 n. 283, 183, 187
deities, 46 n. 96, 98, 101 n. 239, 105, 107–109, 131 n. 42, 135. *See also* Kybele/Cybele; Meter; "Mother of the Gods"; individual entries.
pottery/vases, 47–48, 50, 54 n. 162, 108, 108–109 n. 289, 127 n. 1
sacrifice, 108, 128, 130 n. 36, 131 n. 38
grid (design), 54–55, 73–74, 80 n. 88, 83, 85–87, 97, 99, 103, 132, 201. *See also* motifs (designs), lattice.
griffin, 85 n. 111, 94 n. 191, 117, 128 n. 9, 129
guardian figures, 50 n. 127, 55, 87–88, 94, 95 n. 201
guidelines. *See* inlay.
guilloche. *See* motifs (designs).
Güneş, Hanife, 107 n. 277; CD-Figure 93
Gyges, 10, 131 n. 42

Hacılar, Turkey, 53–54, 84, 101–102. *See also* agriculture/crops/farming; figurines/statuettes; pottery/vases.
Haldi, 45, 93 n. 183, 131 n. 42
hare/rabbit, 48, 108
Hargrave, Michelle, xxxviii, 163 n. 8
Harlin, Greg, xxxix, 128; Frontispiece
Haspels, Emilie, 93 n. 185, 93 n. 189, 94 n. 193, 96 n. 206, 97 n. 209
Hassuna, Iraq, 52 n. 143
Hathor wig, 88, 90, 92, 96 n. 203, 100, 101 n. 236
hawk/bird of prey, 92, 98, 100, 108, 117. *See also* bird.
headdress. *See* crown/headdress.
heads and hoofs, 108 n. 287. *See also* sacrifice/sacrificial ritual.
Hegesander, 76
Held, Benjamin, xxxv, xxxviii, 31 n. 2, 165–170, 176
heliacal rising, 103–104 n. 257, 104 n. 258, 105 n. 265
hemp, 106 n. 276, 204
Hepat, 88 n. 141
Hephaestus, 109

Hera/Heraion, 47 n. 106, 51 n. 136, 64 n. 63, 107 n. 278, 109 n. 289, 131 n. 40
Herodotus, 10, 16, 46 n. 96, 47, 51 n. 136, 76, 104 n. 263, 129, 131, 133
Hesiod, 104–105, 107, 108 n. 281, 200 n. 26
Theogony, 107, 108 n. 281
Works and Days, 104–105, 107, 200 n. 26
Hetepheres, 35 n. 19, 116 n. 44
hieroglyphs
Egyptian, 43, 96 n. 203, 102
Luvian, 90 n. 160
Hittite, 40 n. 43, 43, 88–89, 91 n. 166, 100 n. 234, 103 n. 252, 127 n. 3, 128 n. 7, 129–131, 132 n. 56. *See also* agriculture/crops/farming; funerals/funerary ritual; furniture.
"Hittite cemetery," Gordion. *See* Gordion (site).
HMG (adhesive), 142, 144, 158
Hoadley, Bruce, xxxviii, 2 n. 8, 165
Hodder, Ian, 53 n. 156, 54 n. 157
Homer/Homeric, 39, 47 n. 104, 48, 51, 107, 128 n. 7, 128 n. 13, 129, 134, 186, 195 n. 24, 199 n. 19
Iliad, 48 n. 109, 51 n. 140, 109, 128–129, 186, 189 n. 19
Odyssey, 39 n. 38, 48 n. 109, 106 n. 276, 128, 186, 202 n. 242
Homeric hymns
to Demeter, 107 n. 280
to Earth Mother of All, 107
to the Mother of the Gods, 107
honey/mead, 127–128, 178, 182–187
hoof/hooves. *See* animal paw/hoof (feet); heads and hoofs.
hook (design). *See* motifs (designs).
hook (for display mounts), 142, 144, 159–163
Hopwood, Walter, xxxviii, 203–223
horns, 52 n. 143, 84, 86, 88, 90, 92, 95–96, 198. *See also* crescent; lunette/half-circle.
Horoztepe, Turkey, 41
horse, 47, 77, 88 n. 143, 112, 117 nn. 55–56, 128–130
trappings/frontlets, 89, 91, 96
horsehair (stuffing), 221 n. 53
"house of the goddess." *See* goddess/female deity; Matar.
HPLC (High-Performance Liquid Chromatography), 177–179, 183–184, 221
humidity, 141–142, 144, 157, 160, 162–163, 173. *See also* datalogger; moisture/moisture content.
hunt/hunters, 91 n. 171, 98, 100
Hurrian, 88–89
Hyades, 109
hydrocarbon, 179, 183, 185

hydrogen peroxide, 178
hydroxyl/water of hydration, 179
hyphae, 176, 205. *See also* fungus/mold/fungal
    decay.

iconography, 52 n. 146, 88 n. 143, 89–91, 92 n.
    178, 98 n. 214, 99–100, 102 n. 246, 105, 106 n.
    271, 108, 110, 132
ICP-MS (Inductively Coupled Plasma Mass
    Spectrometry), 212
"idols," 37, 52, 55 n. 168, 100–101. *See also*
    dolls/"bell idols"; figurines/statuettes; motifs
    (designs).
    "double idol," 100–101
    Faharet Çeşme, 100–102; Plate 119B
    Gordion, 100 n. 233
    Kerkenes Dağ, 101 n. 239
    Midas City, 100
    Troy, 52 n. 144, 102 n. 248; CD-Figure 81
Inanna, 87–88. *See also* Ishtar.
incense, 121 n. 17, 131 n. 44
indigo, 130, 212, 217–220, 223. *See also* Tyrian
    purple (6,6'-dibromoindigo).
infrared, 177, 203 n. 5, 205, 215–216, 218 n. 45,
    221
inlaid table, Tumulus MM. *See* tables, Tumulus
    MM.
inlay, 1, 9, 15–20, 27, 31–43, 45, 46 n. 97, 48–50,
    65–67, 69–75, 77, 78 n. 83, 79, 81–84, 87–88,
    95–97, 100–101, 104, 106, 112, 117 n. 52, 121
    n. 17, 132, 139–144, 166–168, 189, 192–193,
    198–202. *See also* motifs (designs); pattern,
    underlying.
    dark/light interplay, 19, 33, 49–50, 72, 79, 85
    errors, 82–83, 201
    guidelines/incised grid, 70, 73, 201; Figure 70
    missing, 16–17, 35–36, 39, 45, 46 n. 97, 134,
        201
    pattern drawn with a knife, 70–71, 73, 200–201
    practice designs, 70, 73, 192–193, 200
    (precious) metal, 35, 39, 45, 46 n. 97, 134, 199,
        201
    process/technique, 20, 31 n. 3, 33, 69–71, 73,
        81–82, 200–202
    template, 78 n. 77, 201
    wedge/shim, 202; Plate 95
inscriptions. *See also* graffiti.
    Kubaba, 90 nn. 160–161, 91 n. 166
    Meher Kapısı (Urartu), 93 n. 183, 98
    Mita/Mushki, 133
    Nabû-apla-iddina (Sippar), 87
    Paleo-Phrygian, 194
        Arslan Kaya, 94; Plate 120
        Matar, 91, 94, 96, 98, 132

Midas, 96, 132; Plate 123; CD-Figures 75–
    76
    Midas City, 100 n. 235
    Midas Monument/Yazılıkaya, 96, 132;
        Plate 123; CD-Figures 75–76
    Tumulus MM
        on bowls, 90 n. 160, 194
        on roof beam of tomb chamber, 194 n.
            22
        on serving stands, 73, 191, 193–194;
            Figure 66A; Plate 94A
    Qedeshet/Anat/Astarte/Asherah, 88
    "Villa of Good Fortune," Olynthos, 52
insects, 76, 173, 175, 222. *See also* frass (insect).
    larvae, 173, 175
    moth (silk), 222–223
    wood-boring beetle, 173, 175
Iran/Persia, 45, 50, 52 n. 143, 84, 86 n. 124, 88,
    103, 104 n. 258, 104 n. 263, 128 n. 9, 135 n. 78
Iraq Museum, Baghdad (looting of), 46 n. 97
iron. *See also* coffins, Tumulus MM; goethite;
    Tumulus MM, Gordion, tomb chamber.
    bars/bands/bosses (coffins), 22–23, 25–27,
        119–120, 121 n. 16, 122–124, 156, 169, 173,
        176, 221; Plates 111–113, 114A
    coating. *See* goethite.
    fire dogs, 129
    for displays, 159 n. 1, 160, 162
    nails, 8 n. 19, 10, 18, 22, 27, 65, 74, 120, 123,
        130, 156, 173, 176, 205
    present in textiles, 205–209, 212–214, 217–219,
        221
    pseudomorphs, 156, 173, 176, 221; Plate 149
    rust/corrosion, 10, 23, 25–27, 119 n. 7, 120 n.
        13, 123, 154, 156, 173, 176, 205, 221 n. 51
    spits, 129
    stands, 9, 74–76, 128 n. 11, 129, 131 n. 42, 159
        n. 1, 160, 162
    tools, 197
Ishpuini, 76 n. 68
Ishtar, 86 n. 125, 87–89, 91. *See also* Inanna.
Istanbul University, Faculty of Forestry, 31 n. 2,
    166
ivory, 43, 91, 96 n. 202, 116 n. 41, 195 n. 24
    Acemhöyük, 116 n. 46
    Aegean, 43
    and the inlaid table, Tumulus MM, 46 n. 97,
        201
    Bayındır, 46 n. 97, 124
    Delphi, 10 n. 53
    Egyptian, 35 n. 19
    furniture inlay/attachments, 35 n. 19, 43–
        46, 76, 88 n. 144, 89 n. 147, 115–117, 129,
        201

Gordion, 46 n. 97, 89, 91, 96, 115; Plate 117B
horse trappings, 89, 91, 96; Plate 117B
Kerkenes Dağ, 117
Megiddo, 43
Nimrud, 44, 46 n. 97, 76, 89, 116–117
Salamis, Cyprus, 116 n. 49, 129
Syrian, 44, 89, 91, 96, 116
Ugarit, 43, 88 n. 144, 89 n. 147
Urartian, 45–46
Ivriz, Turkey, 86, 105 n. 270; Plate 119D

Japanese tissue, 152
Jericho, furniture
joinery/woodworking techniques, 42–43, 47, 62–63, 116, 197 n. 1, 198, 199–200 n. 25, 200 n. 28, 202 n. 41
stools, 115–116
tables, 42–43, 62–63, 199–200 n. 25
woods, 197 n. 1
Jerusalem, 44, 199, 202 n. 39
jewelry/gems, 53 n. 151, 54 n. 162, 55 n. 169, 89, 91, 96 n. 202, 131 n. 43
gems/stones on furniture, 43 n. 72, 45, 46 n. 97
joinery, 2, 9, 14–15, 17–20, 32–37, 39, 41–44, 46–48, 57, 60–64, 66–69, 71–73, 76, 79, 81–82, 112–114, 121, 143, 159, 189, 192, 200–202
acrylic sheet/Plexiglas, 159–162
and inlay, 18–20, 67, 69–71, 72 n. 39, 81–82, 189, 201–202; Plates 96–98
clamped, 68, 69 n. 25, 202
coffin, 2, 68, 121–122, 202; Figure 3D
collar-and-tenon, 14, 17, 32, 38–40, 42–44, 47–48, 57–64, 145–154, 167–168, 200, 202; Figures 27, 39
dowel, 2, 9, 15–16, 18–21, 24, 31–33, 35 n. 18, 37–39, 42, 69, 140, 159–160, 162, 166, 200; Figure 4
square dowel, 38, 200
edge/butt, 32 n. 4, 39, 41–42, 62 n. 45, 68, 73, 202
free/double tenon, 2, 42, 62 n. 45, 67–69, 73, 189, 192, 202; Figures 49, 57
glued, 14–15, 19, 31 n. 3, 68, 68–69 n. 25, 73, 201–202
halved joint, 2, 37
locking joint, 2, 33, 36, 66; Figures 60–61
mortise-and-tenon, 2, 15, 31 n. 3, 32–38, 48, 59–60, 62–63, 64 n. 63, 67–69, 72–73, 111–112, 115–116, 142, 189–192, 197 n. 7, 200, 202; Figure 26
open mortise/corner bridle joint, 2, 33–34; Figure 24; Plate 23
pin/peg, 2, 14–16, 18–20, 24, 31, 33–34, 35 nn. 17–19, 36, 41–42, 47, 57, 58 n. 16, 59–71, 73, 122, 162, 163 n. 7, 166–168, 189–191, 200–202
repair, 36; Plate 151C. See also repairs, ancient.
sheathed (corner), 34, 46 n. 97, 199; Figure 25
shim/wedge, 42 n. 62, 47, 57, 61, 63, 200 n. 28, 202; Plate 95
ship, 68, 202
T bridle joint, 2
terminology, 2
through-mortise/through-tenon, 111, 115–116
joint sealant (Goretex), 162

jugs/juglets, 10, 74, 92, 102 n. 242, 130–132, 134 n. 70
juniper/Juniperus sp., 7, 16 n. 25, 31, 33, 39, 65–66, 70–71, 111, 139, 143–144, 166–169, 172, 174, 197–200; Plate 140C–D

Karaburun, Turkey, 128 n. 9
Karatepe, Turkey, 46, 77
Karhuhas, 90
Kaş shipwreck. See Uluburun shipwreck.
Kashinawa Indians, Peru, 55 n. 168
Kelly, Mary B., xxxviii, xl, 107 n. 277
Kerkenes Dağ, Turkey, 101 n. 239, 117
Kheruef, 76 n. 64
Khorsabad, Iraq, 45, 87, 91, 128 n. 11, 131 n. 42, 178
kilim. See carpet/carpets.
Kimmerian, 10, 133–134
king post, 94, 97, 134 n. 75
Klucel HF, 146, 148, 151–153, 158
knife, 41, 70–71, 197, 200–201
Knossos, Crete, 51, 89 n. 145
Kohler, Ellen L., xxxv n. 1, xxxix, 145
Koles, Joseph, xxxviii, 203–223
Konya, Turkey, 86
Körte, Gustav and Alfred, 41, 128 n. 11
Kress, Samuel H. (foundation), xxxvii
Kronos, 108 n. 281
Kubaba, 90–92, 98; Plate 118D; CD-Figure 99
Küçük Kapı Kaya, 93
Kültepe, Turkey, 42, 85 n. 111, 87 n. 126, 101–102
Kumca Boğaz Kapı Kaya, 93
Kutkam, Mehmetçik, xxxviii
Kybele/Cybele, 98, 101 n. 239, 109, 131 n. 39, 199. See also Matar.
Kybelon, 98
kykeon, 128 n. 7, 186. See also "mixed beverage"/mixed fermented beverage.
Kytoros, 199

labyrinth. *See* maze/labyrinth.
ladles
   Ankara tumuli, 76 n. 63
   Bayındır, Tumulus D, 124, 131–132
   Gordion
      Megaron 3, 75
      Tumulus K-III, 75, 132
      Tumulus K-IV, 75–76 n. 63, 132
      Tumulus MM, 9, 65, 74, 127–128, 130, 178;
         Color Plates IVB, VIC
      Tumulus P, 74, 132
      Tumulus S-1, 76 n. 63
      Tumulus W, 75, 132
   Karaburun, 128 n. 9
   "Lydian Treasure," 131
lamb/sheep, 42–43, 91 n. 166, 98 n. 212, 117,
   127–128, 130, 183–187, 203, 221
lapis lazuli, 43 n. 72, 46 n. 97, 49 n. 124
Lars Porsena, 51 n. 136
lathe/turned, 14–15, 17, 38 n. 30, 44, 63 n. 60,
   197, 200
lattice. *See* motifs (designs).
LC-MS (Liquid Chromatography-Mass
   Spectrometry), 178–179, 183–184
leather, 8, 10, 47, 49, 115, 124, 207
Lebanon, 199 n. 18. *See also* cedar/*Cedrus libani*
   Loud.
Lecoff, Albert, 38 n. 30
Lefkandi (Euboea), Greece, 91 n. 175
legumes, 184, 186
Lejeune, Michel, 96 n. 205, 194
lentils, 106, 127, 134 n. 69, 185–187
Levant, 44, 46
libation, 44, 90, 98, 128–130. *See also* sacri-
   fice/sacrificial ritual.
lignin, 215
lily, 43 n. 68
limestone, 49 n. 124, 173
Linear B (tablets), 43, 108 n. 283
linen, 8, 21, 123, 129, 155, 216. *See also* flax.
lintel, 92–94, 97
lions/feline imagery, 35, 38, 41–46, 53, 76–77,
   88–90, 92–93, 94 n. 191, 95–96, 98, 107–
   108, 115–116, 117 n. 56, 128 nn. 10–11, 129,
   134 n. 75. *See also* animal paw/hoof (feet);
   tigers.
   from Gordion, 9, 65, 74, 95–96, 99–100, 112,
      117, 127 n. 5, 178–179, 218 n. 46
literacy, 192
log casing. *See* Tumulus MM, Gordion.
log coffins, 31, 120–125, 133 n. 62, 156. *See also*
   coffins.
loom, 203, 205, 210. *See also* weaving.
   weights, 106, 222

looting/looted. *See* plunder/robbery/thieves;
   unexcavated artifacts.
lotus, 45, 50 n. 127
Louvre Museum, 45 n. 88, 52 n. 143, 54 n. 162,
   76
Love, Nancy, xxxvii
lozenge. *See* motifs (designs).
lozenge-and-dot pattern. *See* motifs (designs).
Lucretius, 109, 202 n. 43
lunette/half-circle, 9, 20, 37, 48–49, 66–67, 70–
   72, 74, 78 n. 83, 84, 87, 95, 99–103, 190. *See*
   also crescent.
   lunette "crown," 100–103
   rosette/lunette complex (on serving stands), 9,
      48–49, 66–67, 70–72, 74, 78 n. 83, 84, 87,
      95, 97, 99–103; Plates 77, 87
Lydia/Lydian, 46 n. 96, 76, 104 n. 263, 131
"Lydian Treasure," 131

Macedonia/Macedonian, 64, 104 n. 258, 199
magic/magical, 52, 90, 99
Magna Mater, 109, 135, 199
magnesium, present in textiles, 207–209, 212, 214,
   218, 221
Mahmatlar, Turkey, 84
"main" designs. *See* serving stands, Tumulus
   MM.
Mal Taş, 98 n. 210
Malatya, Turkey, 90 n. 162, 91, 95 n. 201
Malkata, Egypt, 183
mallet, 197 n. 7, 198
Mandrus, Janis, xxxviii–xl, 163 n. 8
manganese, present in textiles, 209
maple/*Acer* sp., 14, 45, 57, 60, 145 n. 38, 165–167,
   175, 197, 198 n. 13
Maraş, Turkey, 91 n. 167
Mari, Syria, 199
marriage ritual/dowry, 53 n. 153, 54
MASCA (Museum Applied Science Center for
   Archaeology, University of Pennsylvania), 9 n.
   26, 31 n. 3, 127 n. 2, 177–178, 186–187
Matar, 87, 91–102, 106–110, 117 n. 56, 131–132,
   134–135, 199. *See also* Kybele/Cybele; Magna
   Mater; Meter; mother/mother goddess;
   "Mother of the Gods."
   and lions, 93, 94 n. 191, 95–96, 98–100, 107–
      108, 117 n. 56, 132, 134 n. 75
   and Midas, 96, 132, 134, 199
   and rosettes, 87, 91–92, 95–96, 99–100, 102
   as creator deity, 106–109
   as fertility deity, 99, 101–109
   deconstruction of, 98–99
   "house of the goddess," 92, 98, 135
   iconography, 91–110

images of, 91–93, 95–97, 100–101, 108, 134; Plates 118A–C, 119A–B, 120–121

inscriptions, 91, 94, 96, 98, 132

Matar Kubileya/"Mother of the Mountain," 98

shrines of, 92–100, 101 n. 238, 108, 132, 135

symbols of
   on the inlaid table, Tumulus MM, 48, 99, 106, 132, 135
   on the serving stand, Tumulus P, 95
   on the serving stands, Tumulus MM, 87, 92, 95–97, 99–102, 106, 110, 132, 135
   on the walls of Megaron 2, Gordion, 99–100

"mattress"/"bed" covering, 21 n. 82, 22–23, 208, 211, 221

maze/labyrinth
   connection to dance, 51
   Cretan, 51
     on coins from Knossos, 51
   Egyptian, 51 n. 136
   Etruscan labyrinth/tomb of Lars Porsena, 51 n. 136
   "Lemnian" labyrinth/Samian Heraion, 51 n. 136
   maze-like patterns on ancient artifacts, 51
     from Çatalhöyük, 54; CD-Figure 86
     from Gordion, 49
   multicursal, 34, 37, 51
   mysteries/path to the afterworld, 135
   on the inlaid table, Tumulus MM, 34, 37–38, 50–51, 97 n. 207, 99–100, 135; Figures 9, 17
   on the walls of Megaron 2, Gordion, 99–100; Figure 98
   "starting point," 34, 37, 50
   swastika as maze, 37, 50–51; Figure 17B
   symbolism, 34, 50–52, 99–100, 135 n. 78
   terminology, 51
   unicursal, 34, 37, 51

McGovern, Patrick, xxxv, xxxviii, 9 n. 26, 127 n. 2, 177–187

MCI. See Smithsonian Institution, Museum Conservation Institute.

MDF (Medium Density Fiberboard), 162

meander, 18 n. 42, 38, 50, 94 n. 193

meander square, 33, 48, 66–67, 69–72, 77–85, 99–100, 102–105, 106 n. 272, 201; Figures 69, 71–72, 74
   origin of the term, 66 n. 14

measurements/dimensions (and accuracy of), 1, 13, 16 n. 27, 24 n. 107, 25 n. 110, 39 n. 34, 58, 112–113, 119 n. 2, 122, 139–141, 144, 223 n. 61

meat. See food and drink.

medallion, 9, 13 n. 2, 19–20, 48, 66, 70–71, 72 n.

36, 73–75, 77, 78 n. 83, 79 n. 86, 81–83, 89, 95–96. See also rosette.

Megalesia, 109

Megaron 2. See Gordion (site), city mound.

Megaron 3. See Gordion (site), city mound.

Megiddo, 43, 135 n. 78

Meher Kapısı (Urartu), 93 n. 183, 98

Meketre, 197

Melgunov kurgan, 46 n. 91

Mellink, Machteld J., v, xxxv, xxxix, 1, 19, 92 n. 177, 100 n. 226, 101 n. 237

mensa, 40

Mesopotamia, 44, 76 n. 65, 84, 87, 88 n. 137, 88 n. 142, 89 n. 147, 89 n. 156, 90–91, 92 n. 180, 101 n. 239, 102–103, 105, 129 n. 27, 135 n. 77

Meter, 98, 101 n. 239, 107, 109, 135

methanol, 177, 186

Metropolitan Museum of Art, xxxvii, 46 n. 97, 76 n. 73, 89 n. 147, 115 n. 35, 116 n. 46, 131 nn. 43–44

METU. See Middle East Technical University (METU), Ankara.

Micronesia, 84 n. 104

microtome, 172

Midas, 7, 10–11, 16, 47, 56, 96, 129 n. 20, 131–134, 186, 199, 221
   throne of Midas, Delphi, 10, 16, 47, 131

Midas City, Turkey, 96, 100, 101 n. 236, 132

"Midas Feast," 127 n. 5

Midas Monument. See inscriptions; monuments, stone/rock; Yazılıkaya/Midas Monument.

"Midas Mound," 10. See also Tumulus MM, Gordion.

"Midas Touch," 127 n. 5. See also Dogfish Head Brewery.

Middle East Technical University (METU), Ankara, 76, 124

milk, 186

Miller, Naomi, xxxviii, 186–187

Minet el-Beida, Syria, 89 n. 145

Minos, 51. See also Knossos, Crete.

minotaur, 51

mirror, 90, 91 n. 167

mirror image/reflection. See symmetry, bilateral.

"Mistress of Wild Beasts," 89

Mita of Mushki, 133. See also Midas.

Mithras, 105–106 n. 271

"mixed beverage"/mixed fermented beverage, 127–128, 177–187. See also beer/ale; bryton; honey/mead; kykeon; "Midas Touch"; wine.

Mob (design firm, Ankara), 162–163

mohair, 204, 208, 220–221

moisture/moisture content, 8–9, 65, 124, 137–139, 155, 157, 173–176, 207 mold. *See* fungus/mold/fungal decay.

mold/casting, 53, 142, 160

Moldavia, 101

molding, 45, 63, 71, 95, 111, 115

mollusc, 223

Mongolia, 84 n. 104

monuments, stone/rock, 91. *See also* Phrygian highlands; relief, stone; individual entries.
   Bavian, 134 n. 75
   Ivriz, 86, 105 n. 270; Plate 119D. *See also* Bor stele.
   Phrygian, 92–98, 100, 110, 132, 134 n. 75, 135 n. 78
      Arslan Kaya, 93–96, 97 n. 209, 98, 134 n. 75; Plates 120, 121A; CD-Figure 74
      Arslan Taş, 96 n. 204, 134 n. 75; CD-Figure 77
      Büyük Kapı Kaya, 93, 97–98; Figure 93; Plate 121B
      Küçük Kapı Kaya, 93
      Kumca Boğaz Kapı Kaya, 93
      Midas Monument/Yazılıkaya, 93 n. 186, 96–98, 132, 134 n. 75; Plate 123; CD-Figures 75–76
   Urartian
      Meher Kapısı, 93 n. 183, 98
      Taş Kapısı, 93 n. 183

moon/lunar, 87, 90 n. 165, 101 n. 240, 103–104, 109, 134, 195 n. 24

moon-god. *See* Sin.

Moreau, Robert, xxxviii, 127 n. 2, 177, 179, 183–184, 186

mortise and tenon. *See* joinery.

mosaics. *See also* tables, Tumulus P, Mosaic Table.
   cone (Uruk), 88
   Megaron 2, Gordion, 49, 99; Figure 92
   pebble, 49, 52, 99
   "Villa of Good Fortune," Olynthos, 52

mother/mother goddess, 55, 87, 91, 98, 105–109, 135. *See also* Kybele/Cybele; Magna Mater; Matar; Meter; "Mother of the Gods."

"Mother of the Gods," 88, 107, 108 n. 281, 109, 199

motifs (designs). *See also* pattern, underlying.
   animals, 41, 43, 52, 84, 108, 112, 117, 124, 155. *See also* animal legs; animal paw/hoof (feet).
   checkerboard, 49–50, 74–75, 93, 95 n. 196
   chevrons, 66, 75
   circles, 20, 49, 66, 70, 72, 84 n. 104, 96, 189–190, 192–193, 200
   crescent, 67, 87–88, 93, 109
   cross, 37–38, 48 n. 111, 49, 52, 55, 72, 78, 84–86, 93, 96 n. 202, 97, 99–100, 108, 193; Figure 71

cross-hatching, 50

diamonds. *See* motifs, lozenge/diamond.

droplets, 66, 71

figure-eight, 49, 79, 85

filling ornament, 71 n. 35, 101, 108

floral/leaf/plant, 34–35, 43–46, 50 n. 127, 55, 63, 76, 94 n. 193, 108, 109 n. 289

geometric, 1, 9, 15–16, 32–33, 39, 47–50, 54 n. 162, 55, 66, 85–87, 91 n. 175, 93, 95, 100, 101 n. 238, 117, 139, 142, 144, 192–193. *See also* individual motifs.

guilloche, 33, 85 n. 111

hook, 33–34 , 37–38, 49–50, 54–55, 66–67, 72 n. 38, 77, 78 n. 83, 79, 80 n. 88, 83–86, 92, 99–100, 115

human figures, 42, 45, 52 n. 143, 55, 84–85, 89, 100

"idol," 37, 52, 55 n. 168, 100–101

lattice, 33, 49, 50 n. 128, 52, 55, 67, 71, 74–75, 83, 99, 115. *See also* grid.

lines, 73, 100–102, 108, 190–193

lozenge/diamond, 19, 33, 37–38, 48–50, 52–55, 63, 66–67, 70–72, 74–75, 83–87, 92–94, 96–97, 99–100, 124, 131 n. 37, 190–193. *See also* motifs, net.
   as/on the abdomen, 52–54, 55 n. 168
   lozenge-and-dot, 52–54, 55 n. 168, 84, 86–87, 88 n. 136, 91 n. 175, 99, 107 n. 277, 108 n. 289
   lozenge cross, 38, 52, 55, 97, 99–100
   quadripartite/quartered lozenge, 52–54, 55 n. 168, 85. *See also* quadripartite designs.

lunette/half-circle, 9, 20, 37, 48–49, 66–67, 70–72, 74, 78 n. 83, 84, 87, 95, 97, 99–103, 190

meander, 18 n. 42, 38, 50, 94 n. 193

meander square, 33, 48, 66–67, 69–72, 77–85, 99–100, 102–105, 106 n. 272, 201

net, 37, 52, 54, 55 n. 168, 86–87, 100, 108 n. 289

palm tree/frond, 44 n. 77, 96 n. 203

quatrefoil, 87, 97, 108

rosette, 9, 19–20, 33, 37, 42–43, 48–49, 51 n. 139, 66–67, 70–75, 84, 86–92, 95–97, 99–100, 102, 107 n. 277, 109 n. 289, 109 n. 296, 115–116, 132, 135 n. 78, 142, 189–192, 200. *See also* rosette.

spiral, 37, 43, 50, 85 n. 111, 95

square, 9, 15, 17–20, 32–38, 46 n. 97, 48–50, 52, 53 n. 153, 54 n. 158, 55, 66–67, 69–72, 74–75, 77–87, 93–94, 97, 99–105, 106 n. 272, 132, 166, 201

star, 54 n. 162, 87–89, 91 n. 175, 102, 109

star rosette, 66, 71, 87–89, 91 n. 170, 95. *See also* rosette.

swastika, 19, 33, 37, 48–52, 54 n. 162, 71 n. 35, 78–79, 83–86, 91 n. 175, 94, 99, 100 n. 231, 101 n. 237, 102, 107 n. 278, 108, 109 n. 289; Figure 71. *See also* swastika.

triangle, 19, 35–38, 48–50, 63, 66–67, 71–74, 83, 88 n. 136, 99–100

U-shaped, 37–38, 49

volute, 86

wheel, 49, 50 n. 128, 52, 84 n. 98

whorls, 84 n. 104, 85 n. 111

winged disc, 35 n. 19, 89, 96

zigzag, 48 n. 111, 49, 75, 85, 88 n. 136, 100–102

mount

display, 35 n. 15, 39, 142, 144, 159–163; Plates 129–138

storage, 148, 150–155, 157; Plates 127–128

mountain/primeval hill, 46, 89 n. 145, 93 n. 187, 98, 107–108, 124, 135, 199

mounts/attachments. *See* attachments/fittings; furniture.

MUL.APIN ("Plough Star"), 103–104 n. 257, 105 n. 264. *See also* astronomy/astronomical canon.

Musasir (Urartu), 45, 131 n. 42, 199

Muscarella, Oscar White, xxxix, 11 n. 55, 134 n. 69

Museum of Anatolian Civilizations, Ankara, xxxv, xxxvii–xxxix, 8 n. 17, 90 n. 157, 90 n. 161, 91 n. 168, 92 nn. 176–177, 92 nn. 180–181, 102 n. 242, 138, 143

galleries, 39, 63 n. 53, 65, 67 n. 18, 130 n. 35, 142, 159–163

laboratory, xxxv, 59, 138, 146, 159–163

storeroom, 16 n. 28, 65, 67 n. 18, 156–157

Mushki, 133

musical instruments, 92, 107, 199 n. 21

musicians, 92, 108 n. 289, 109, 116; Plate 119A

Mut, 90 n. 165

Mycenae/Mycenaean, 43 n. 75, 183, 187

Mylar, 149, 157

myrrh. *See* incense.

mystery cults/mysteries, 106 n. 271, 109, 135, 186

Nabû-apla-iddina, stone tablet (Sippar), 87, 91 n. 170; Plate 116A

nails, 41, 123, 205

Tumulus MM chamber, 8 n. 19, 10, 18, 65, 74, 130

Tumulus MM coffin, 22, 25 n. 113, 27, 120, 156, 173, 176; Plate 113A

naiskoi, 101 n. 239, 108. *See also* niche monuments.

Narundi, 88; Plate 116B

National Endowment for the Humanities, xxxvii

National Geographic Society, xxxvii, 128 n. 12, 162

National Science Foundation, xxxvii, 177

Navaho, 84 n. 104

negative pattern, 67. *See also* play with/manipulation of designs, dimension, symmetry.

neolithic, 53–54, 84, 101, 177 n. 1. *See also* individual entries.

Nestor's cup, 128 n. 7, 186 n. 9

net. *See* motifs (designs).

New Caledonia, 55 n. 168; CD-Figure 95

New York Times, 10 n. 53, 64 n. 65, 125 n. 54, 131 n. 37

niche monuments, 92–100, 108, 134 n. 75, 135 n. 78. *See also naiskoi*.

nickel, present in textiles, 207, 214, 218

Nimrud, Iraq, 44–45, 46 n. 97, 76–77, 86 n. 125, 87, 89, 91, 96 n. 203, 116–117, 195 n. 24

Banquet Stele, 91 n. 170

Burnt Palace, 44

Fort Shalmaneser, 44, 116

ivories, 44, 46 n. 97, 76, 89, 96 n. 203, 116–117, 195 n. 24

Northwest Palace, 44, 77, 91 n. 170

tomb II, 91

1984 Foundation, xxxvii, 157

Nineveh, Iraq, 44, 50 n. 127, 91 n. 171, 117 n. 51, 128 n. 10

nitrogen, 156, 174, 203 n. 6, 222 n. 55

nomads/nomadic, 47, 90 n. 165

North Syria/Syrian, 44, 46, 89, 90 n. 159, 91, 94 n. 193, 96 n. 203, 102 n. 251, 132

northeast corner, Tumulus MM, 2, 8, 13, 21–22, 111–117, 129–130, 137, 155, 166, 169, 198, 211–216, 222–223

carved stretcher, 2, 111–113, 114 n. 17, 117, 155, 166, 169; Figures 77–78; Plates 101, 104, 105A

red pigment, 112, 114 n. 17, 155

chair ("stool #2"), 112–117, 129–130, 198, 200 n. 29; Figures 77–78; Plates 103–104, 105A

stools/stool legs, 2, 8, 21, 111–116, 130, 155, 166, 169, 200 n. 29; Color Plate IIB; Figure 76; Plates 100–103, 105B

textiles, 8, 21–22, 111–114, 116, 123, 155, 211–216, 222–223; Plates 155–156; CD-Figures 25–55

impression of cording from seat, 114, 211–213, 222; Plates 106B, 155A–B

uncatalogued artifacts, 21, 114, 130; Plate 106A

woods, 111–112, 166, 169, 198

Novus 1 and 2 (plastic polish), 161
nude/nudes, 88–89
Nuñez, Alberto, xxxviii, 127 n. 2, 177, 179, 183–184, 186
nuts. *See* food and drink.
Nux/Night, 108 n. 281

oak, 124
Odysseus, 202 n. 42
offerings, 1, 10, 48, 76, 88 n. 138, 90–91, 103 n. 252, 109 n. 289, 114, 121 n. 17, 124, 127 n. 3, 128–131, 174. *See also* sacrifice/sacrificial ritual.
off-gassing/fumes/vapors, 140, 142, 157, 161
Okeanos, 180 n. 281
olive oil, 127 n. 3, 185, 187
Olson, Daniel, xxxvi–xxxix
Olympos (Macedonian), 199
Olynthos, Greece, 52
omphalos bowl/phiale mesomphalos/phialai, 9, 75, 128, 130–132, 151, 178–179; Color Plates III, IVA, V; Plates 1, 36, 54, 69–70
oracle. *See* divination.
Orion, 109
Orta Doğu Teknik Üniversitesi. *See* Middle East Technical University (METU), Ankara.
orthostat, 134 n. 75. *See also* relief, stone; sculpture.
    Ankara (and vicinity), 96 n. 202, 117 n. 56
    Carchemish, 89–90; Plate 118D; CD-Figure 99
    Gordion, 85, 115, 117 n. 56; Plate 119C
    Karatepe, 46
Ouranos, 107
ovens, 106
Ovid, 109 nn. 291–292, 199
Özen, Latif, xxxviii–xxxix

"Pagoda Table"/"pagoda" struts, 15, 17, 31. *See also* tables, Tumulus MM, inlaid table.
paint/pigment, 150, 160. *See also* textiles; wall painting.
    acrylic paint, 142, 144, 161, 163
    body paint, 54–55
    on furniture, 13, 43, 44 n. 78, 202 n. 39
    on the carved stretcher, northeast corner, Tumulus MM, 112, 114 n. 17, 155
Paleo-Phrygian. *See* inscriptions.
palm tree/frond. *See* motifs (designs).
paraffin. *See* wax.
Paraloid. *See* Acryloid (B-44/B-72).
parasol, 19, 162
Parthenon, 116 n. 43
Pasiphae, 51

patching. *See* repairs.
pattern, underlying
    Arslan Kaya, 94–95; CD-Figure 74
    negating/obscuring of, 82–83, 94, 95 n. 194, 135, 201
    Tumulus MM furniture, 33–34, 77–83, 201; Color Plates X–XI; CD-Figures 66–73
Payton, Robert, xxxv, xxxvii–xxxviii, 31 n. 3, 138–144, 149, 159
Pazyryk, Siberia, 40 n. 43, 46–47, 63, 86 n. 124, 87, 124, 203 n. 1
peas. *See* seeds/grains/peas/cereals.
pectin, 215
pediment, 92, 94, 96–97
Pergamon, Turkey, 109 n. 291
Persephone, 107 n. 280
Persia/Persian. *See* Iran/Persia.
Pessinous, Turkey, 109 n. 291
petroleum ether, 146, 148
Petronius, 40
pH, 137, 173. *See also* acids; alkali/alkalinity.
phenol, 127 n. 4, 185
phenylhydrazine, 178
phiale. *See* omphalos bowl/phiale mesomphalos/phialai.
Phoenicia/Phoenician, 44, 76 n. 65
phosphorus, present in textiles, 205, 207–209, 212, 214, 218–219, 221
photography/photographs, xxxv, xxxviii, xxxix–xl, 53 nn. 150–151, 55 n. 165
    city mound, Gordion, 49 n. 123, 100 n. 228
    Phrygian monuments, 93 n. 184, 93 n. 189
    Tumulus MM furniture, 1, 3, 21
        coffin, 23, 25, 27, 120–122
        furniture from the northeast corner, 21, 111–113, 114 n. 18, 213
        in situ, 14–15, 17, 21, 23, 27, 32, 36–37, 41 n. 54, 65, 111–113, 121
        inlaid table, 15–18, 32, 35 n. 15, 36, 41 n. 54, 140, 160
        1957, 13 n. 2, 14, 20, 58 n. 19, 73, 111–113
        plain tables, 14, 57, 58 n. 17, 58 n. 19, 59, 145–146, 152 n. 61
        serving stands, 13 n. 2, 19 n. 54, 20, 65, 66 n. 6, 72 n. 40, 73, 143–144, 163, 191 n. 4, 202
Phrygia, xxxv, 7, 10, 31, 46 n. 97, 85, 98, 102, 106, 107 n. 278, 109, 123, 132–133, 135, 187, 198 n. 12. *See also* individual sites.
Phrygian highlands, 93–100, 101 n. 236, 134 n. 75, 135. *See also* monuments, stone/rock.
Phrygian language/writing, 90 n. 160, 98, 130, 194–195. *See also* inscriptions.
Pindar, 40

pine/*Pinus* sp./*Pinus sylvestris* L., 7, 119, 121, 165–166, 169–170, 172–174, 176, 197, 198 n. 12, 199; Plates 147C–F, 148A–B

plane (*runcina*), 197 n. 5

planet, 88 n. 138, 104 n. 257, 109, 195 n. 24. *See also* astronomy/astronomical canon.

plants, 34, 43, 45 n. 84, 53 nn. 155–156, 76, 94 n. 193, 101 n. 240, 104–106, 109 n. 289, 123, 183, 185, 204, 215. *See also* individual entries.

plaque/panel, 44, 46, 49–50, 53 n. 151, 54 n. 162, 75–76, 84–85, 88 n. 144, 89, 93, 94 n. 193, 96 n. 203, 97, 98 n. 210, 100–102, 108, 109 n. 289, 116–117, 129 n. 23, 135 n. 78, 197, 202. *See also* furniture, attachments/fittings.
 carved stretcher, Tumulus MM, 112, 114 n. 17, 117, 155
 inlaid table, Tumulus MM, 16–17, 18 n. 42, 32–33, 35–37, 46 n. 97, 49 n. 116, 50–51, 97 n. 207, 199, 201
 panel decoration on textiles. *See* costume/dress/clothing.
 serving stands, Tumulus MM, 9, 18–19, 72, 79 n. 86, 81 n. 90, 87, 97, 143, 189–191, 201

plaster, 114, 160

platelets, 178, 183

plates/saucers, 21, 48, 74 n. 50, 114, 129, 132, 162, 197

plating/sheathing/gilt, 41, 45–48, 63, 129. *See also* furniture.
 gold, 35 n. 19, 43 n. 72, 45, 117 n. 52
 inlaid table, Tumulus MM, 34–35, 39, 45, 46 n. 97, 134, 199, 201
 silver, 45–46, 48

play with/manipulation of designs, dimension, symmetry, 31, 33–34, 36–38, 40 n. 44, 48, 50, 67, 77–86, 94, 193. *See also* pattern, underlying.

Pleiades, 105, 109

Plexiglas, 39 n. 36, 68, 142, 144, 148, 157–158, 159 nn. 1–2, 160–163. *See also* acrylic sheet.

Pliny, 51 n. 136, 86 n. 122, 121 n. 17, 186, 197 n. 5, 199, 201 n. 38, 202 n. 43

plunder/robbery/thieves, 44, 46 n. 97, 63 n. 58, 116 n. 46, 124 n. 49, 129, 131 nn. 42–43. *See also* unexcavated artifacts.
 inlaid table, Tumulus MM, 35, 39, 46 n. 97, 134
 Phrygian rock monuments, 93, 98 n. 210

polarized light microscopy, 215

polish (Plexiglas), 160–161

polos, 89–93, 95, 108 n. 289; CD-Figure 84. *See also* crown/headdress.

polyester, 158, 161, 205 n. 12, 217 n. 43

polyethylene, 140–141, 144, 146
 sheet/sheeting, 141, 143–144, 147, 149–153, 155, 157

polyvinyl acetal resin. *See* Alvar.

polyvinyl acetate (AYAF), 141

polyvinyl butyral. *See* Butvar B-98.

pomegranate, 90, 92

Pope John Paul II (funeral), 131 n. 37

poppy-head, 90

Porada, Edith, 15 n. 15

potassium
 bromide, 177
 gluconate, 183–184
 present in textiles, 207–209, 212–214, 218, 221
 tartrate/bitartrate, 182

pottery/vases. *See also* "flowing vase"; Geometric (Greek) pottery/vases/repertoire; Uruk, Uruk vase.
 Alişarhöyük, 117 n. 53
 chalcolithic, 52, 84, 101
 Cucuteni (Tripolye), 101
 Gordion, 49, 102, 106 n. 276, 108 n. 288, 117, 132, 186, 193–194
 Greek, 47–48, 50, 101 n. 240, 108, 108–109 n. 289, 127 n. 1, 187
 Hacılar, 54, 84, 101–102
 Hassuna, 52 n. 143
 Kültepe, 101, 102 n. 242
 neolithic, 52, 54, 84, 101–102
 Phrygian, 49, 86, 102, 108 n. 288, 117, 124 n. 39, 132, 193–194
 Salamis, Cyprus, 129
 Susa, 50 n. 126, 52 n. 143
 Tumulus MM, 9–10, 27, 74, 127, 129, 177, 183–185, 194; Color Plate VIA

poultice, 146–148, 151–153

Poverty Point, Louisiana, 134 n. 73

precious metal. *See* gold/precious metal; silver.

preserved measurement, 1

procession, 90, 91 n. 166, 92, 103 n. 252, 116
 funerary, 109

prophecy. *See* divination.

protective device/protection/apotropaic design, 52, 54–55, 83, 87, 88 n. 136, 90 n. 165, 91, 98 n. 218, 99, 101 n. 240, 102, 106, 130 n. 36, 132 n. 56

protome, 85 n. 111, 129

pseudomorphs
 textile, 203, 221
 wood, 156, 173, 176, 221 n. 51

Ptolemy (astronomer), 104 n. 259, 104 n. 263

Ptolemy II Philadelphus, 40

Ptolemy III, 104 n. 259

Puzur-Inshushinak, 88 n. 140

Pylos (tablets), 43, 108 n. 283

Pyrenees, 199

Qäwrighul. *See* coffins.

Qedeshet, 88, 89 n. 145

quadripartite designs, 52–54, 55 n. 168, 84–
    85, 93, 97. *See also* meander square; motifs
    (designs), lozenge/diamond; swastika.

querns, 106

Quetol, 172

Quinn, Chad, xxxviii, 127 n. 2, 177, 179, 183

rabbit/hare, 48, 108

radial patterns, 84, 85 n. 111, 96, 101–102. *See
    also* motifs (designs); swastika; symmetry,
    rotational.

radiocarbon (dating). *See* carbon-14/radiocarbon
    (dating).

raft of Odysseus, 202 n. 42

rain, 53, 101, 102 n. 245, 105. *See also* spring/
    water.

ram, 9, 42, 45, 62, 65, 74, 117, 127 n. 5, 178–179,
    218 n. 46. *See also* sheep.

ramie, 114 n. 19, 215, 223

ramp (Tumulus MM), 7–8, 130

rebirth/regeneration, 90, 135
    games/gaming boards, 135 n. 78
    mirror as symbol of, 90

Reilly, George, xxxviii, 31 n. 3

Rekhmire, 197–198

relief pithos/pottery, 108 n. 289, 117

relief, stone. *See also* "idols"; monuments,
    stone/rock; *naiskoi*; niche monuments; stele;
    individual entries.
    Amiternum, 109; CD-Figure 100
    Assyrian, 44–45, 86
        Khorsabad, 45, 87, 91, 128 n. 11, 131 n. 42,
            178
        Nimrud, 45, 77, 86 n. 125, 87, 91 n. 170
        Nineveh, 44, 50 n. 127, 91 n. 171, 116–117 n.
            51, 128 n. 10
        threshold, 87, 91
    Bor, 86; CD-Figure 97
    Egyptian, 76 n. 64, 197
    Greek
        Parthenon, Athens, 116 n. 43
        Siphnian Treasury, Delphi, 116 n. 43
    Hittite/Neo-Hittite/Aramaean
        Boğazköy, 88 n. 141
        Carchemish, 89–91, 92 n. 182; Plate 118D;
            CD-Figure 97
        Karatepe, 46, 77
        Malatya, 90 n. 162
        Maraş, 91 n. 167
        Zincirli, 46 n. 98, 91 n. 168, 195 n. 24
    Ivriz, 86, 105 n. 270; Plate 119D
    Phrygian, 134 n. 75

Ankara, 92–93, 96 n. 202, 117 n. 56; Plate
            118B
        Boğazköy, 92, 98, 108 n. 289; Plate 119A
        Faharet Çeşme, 100–102; Plate 119B
        Gordion, 85, 92, 115, 117 n. 56; Plates 118A,
            119C
        Sincan, 101 n. 236
    Sardis, 101 n. 239
    Susa, 45
    tablet of Nabû-apla-iddina, 87, 91 n. 170; Plate
        116A
    tomb of Ti, Saqqara, 197

relief, wood/ivory. *See also* ivory.
    Kerkenes Dağ, 117
    Tumulus MM, northeast corner (carved
        stretcher), 2, 111–113, 114 n. 17, 117, 155,
        166, 169; Figures 77–78; Plates 101, 104,
        105A

religion, 102, 108 n. 281. *See also* deity/divinity;
    worship; individual entries.
    Phrygian, 84, 132, 135

religious year/holidays, 103–105, 132. *See also*
    calendar.

repairs
    ancient, 32 n. 4, 36, 39–40, 60, 134, 191, 200,
        205; Plate 151C. *See also* tables, Tumulus
        MM, inlaid table, construction/assembly
        (ancient).
        inlay wedge, 202; Plate 95
        patching, 33, 39, 114, 200 n. 30; Plates 28–
            29, 97A–B
    modern, 31 n. 3, 100, 152–154, 163

resin canals, 172, 176

resins, 141, 145–146, 151, 157–158, 202, 220. *See
    also* Acryloid (B-44/B-72); Alvar; Butvar B-98;
    Rutapox.

Reynolds, Nancy, xxxviii

Rhea, 107, 108 n. 281

Rig Veda, 108 n. 281

ritual, 53 n. 153, 90 n. 165, 92 n. 180, 97–98, 103,
    105, 108 n. 286, 109 n. 290, 127 n. 3, 129–
    131. *See also* festivals; funerals/funerary ritual;
    religion; sacrifice/sacrificial ritual; worship.
    objects, 102 n. 242, 132 n. 51
    Phrygian, 98, 128, 130–132, 135

ritual towels/cloths, 54, 106–107 n. 277

Rohm and Haas (Plexiglas), 142, 158, 159 n. 2,
    161

Roller, Lynn E., xxxvi, xxxviii, xl, 90 n. 165, 93
    n. 185, 94 n. 193, 98 n. 214, 98 n. 218, 99 n.
    223, 100 n. 228, 100 n. 230, 100 n. 233, 107 n.
    278, 107 n. 280, 189–195

rosette. *See also* medallion; motifs (designs).
    and abundance, 88 n. 137

and birds, 54 n. 162, 99–100, 108–109 n. 289
and Hathor wig, 88, 90, 92
and lions/lion legs, 42, 88–89, 95–96, 99–100
and lunette, 9, 37, 48–49, 66–67, 70–72, 74, 78
    n. 83, 84, 87, 95, 97, 99–103
and star/star rosette, 54 n. 162, 66, 71, 87–89,
    91 n. 170, 95
and swastika/maze, 51 n. 139, 54 n. 162, 99–
    100, 107 n. 277, 108–109 n. 289
and the agricultural year, 107 n. 277
and winged sun-disc, 96
as ivory furniture decoration
    from Gordion, 115
    ivories from Ugarit, 43
    Nimrud ivories, 96 n. 203, 116
    North Syrian ivory furniture attachments,
        96 n. 203, 116
as protective device, 91
as royal insignia
    at Gordion, 99, 132
    in Assyria, 91, 132
as symbol/attribute of Matar, 87, 91–92, 95–
    96, 100, 102 n. 251, 132
as symbol/attribute of Near Eastern and
    Greek goddesses
    "Astarte" plaques, 89
    goddesses depicted on early Greek artifacts,
        108–109 n. 289
    Inanna/Ishtar, 87–89, 91
        tablet of Nabû-apla-iddina, 87
    Kubaba, 89–90
    Narundi, 88
    other western Asiatic goddesses, 87 n. 131,
        88–89
compass-drawn, 20, 66, 70–71, 73, 191–192,
    200
on animal haunches, 42, 95, 96 n. 202
on furniture from Gordion
    from the city mound, 115
    inlaid table, Tumulus MM, 33, 37, 48, 99
    "screen," Tumulus W, 75
    serving stand, Tumulus P, 49, 74, 95
    serving stands, Tumulus MM, 9, 19, 48, 74,
        84, 87, 92, 95–97, 99–100, 102, 142, 192,
        200
        serving stand A, 20, 66–67, 72, 189–190,
            192, 200
        serving stand B, 20, 70–73, 191–192, 200
    stool, Tumulus P, 49
on gaming boards, 88 n. 137, 135 n. 78
on Gordion artifacts
    belts, 49
    graffiti/"doodle stones," 99
    ivory horse trappings, 89, 96

    medallions, "Hittite cemetery," 89
    mosaic floor, Megaron 2, 49 n. 123
    omphalos bowls, 9
  on Greek artifacts, 51 n. 139, 54 n. 162, 91 n.
    175, 108–109 n. 289
  on horse trappings, 89, 91 n. 171, 96
  on jewelry/belts, 49, 89, 91
  on textiles/headdresses
    Assyrian, 87, 89, 91
    Bor stele, 86
    fillet, 91
    polos/headdress, 89–92, 95, 99, 108–109 n.
        289
  "rose window," 9, 20, 66, 70
  solar/celestial significance, 88–89, 96, 99, 102,
    109 n. 296
rot. *See* fungus/mold/fungal decay.
rot/decay resistance (of woods), 174–175
rotational symmetry. *See* symmetry.
royal insignia/device, 84, 87, 91, 99, 132
rubble fill (Tumulus MM), 7, 134, 173
rush (seating), 114 n. 18, 213
Rutapox, 141–142

sacrifice/sacrificial ritual, 46 n. 96, 90, 91 n. 166,
    97–98, 108, 128–132. *See also* libation; offerings;
    ritual.
    and feasting, 128–132
    and the state, 130–131
    heads and hoofs, 108 n. 287
Sahara, 84 n. 104
Sakçagözü, Turkey, 95 n. 201, 96 n. 203
Salamis, Cyprus, 116 n. 49, 129
Salmanköy, Turkey, 91; Plate 118C
Samarra culture (Hassuna), 52 n. 143
Samos, Greece, 47 n. 106, 50 n. 129, 64 n. 63, 66
    n. 8, 89, 109 n. 289, 131 n. 40
Sangarios (river), 92 n. 177
Saran, Erkal, xxxix, 162
sarcophagus
    Gordion, 41, 75 n. 63, 102, 123
    of Ahiram, 43 n. 73, 44 n. 79
Sardis, Turkey, 98, 101 n. 239, 104 n. 263
Sargon of Akkad, 88 n. 135
Sargon II, 45, 86–87, 91, 129 n. 20, 131 n. 42, 133,
    178, 199
saw (tool/technique), 197–198; Plate 150A
    flatsawn/flat cut, 2, 199 n. 24
sawdust, 146–147
scalpel, 144, 146–147, 152
scarab, 96 n. 203; CD-Figure 79
Schenck, William, xxxviii–xl
Schniewind, Arno, xxxviii, 38 n. 31
Schuster, Carl, and Edmund Carpenter, xl, 55

scientific analyses. *See* analyses, Tumulus MM artifacts; individual entries.

scraper, 197, 201 n. 38

scraping/smoothing/rubbing (furniture), 70–71, 197, 200–201. *See also* abrasives; scraper.

"screen." *See also* Amiternum, relief; serving stands.

    Megaron 3, 75

    Tumulus MM, 2, 9, 13, 18–21, 31–32, 65, 73, 75

        function, 18–20, 73–74

        "screen A," 9, 13 n. 2, 19–21, 32–33, 65, 67–68, 72

        "screen B," 13 n. 2, 18, 20–21, 32, 65, 70, 72 n. 40

    Tumulus P, 16 n. 25, 18–19, 20 n. 65, 73, 75

    Tumulus W, 18, 75

"scroll feet." *See* animal paw/hoof (feet).

sculpture. *See also* animals, Tumulus P; figurines/statuettes; "idols"; monuments, stone/rock; orthostat; relief, stone; relief, wood/ivory; stele; individual entries.

    Anatolian, 46, 77, 86, 88 n. 141, 89–91, 92 n. 182, 95, 105 n. 270, 195 n. 24; Plates 118–122; CD-Figures 81, 97, 99

    double/multiple representations, 100–101; Plate 119B

    East Greek, 108

    fibulae represented on, 86, 101 n. 236; Plate 119D

    from Gordion, 85, 92, 95, 99, 100 n. 233, 115, 117; Plates 118A, 119C, 122B–C

    Kubaba, 89–91; Plate 118D; CD-Figure 99

    Kybebe, 101 n. 239

    Kybele, 101 n. 239

    Magna Mater, 109 n. 291

    Matar, 91–93, 95–98, 100–102, 108, 117 n. 56, 134, 135 n. 78; Plates 118A–C, 119A–B, 120–121

    Narundi, 88; Plate 116B

    Phrygian, 85, 91–102, 108, 115, 117, 134, 135 n. 78; Plates 118A–C, 119A–C, 120–121, 122B–C

sealant, 142–143, 161–162

seals/seal impressions, 42, 52 n. 143, 54, 76 n. 65, 84, 85 n. 111, 88, 89 n. 145, 89 nn. 153–154, 108 n. 283, 200 n. 31

seasons, 84 , 99, 101, 103 n. 257, 105–106, 107 n. 280. *See also* calendar; Hesiod, *Works and Days*.

seating furniture/cushions/hassocks, 14, 19, 113–115, 129 n. 23, 212, 220. *See also* chairs/thrones; stools.

seeds/grains/peas/cereals, 45 n. 84, 48, 53–54, 86, 90, 91 n. 166, 103, 105–107, 109, 127–128,

130 n. 36, 133–134, 178, 182–184, 186. *See also* agriculture/crops/farming; food and drink; grain.

    and Demeter, 107 n. 280

    at Çatalhöyük, 53–54

    at Gordion, 106, 133–134

    at Hacılar, 53

    at Verucchio, 48

    dating of seeds, Gordion, 11 n. 55, 133–134

    dots as symbols of ("sown field"), 53–54. *See also* motifs (designs), lozenge/diamond.

    impressed as ornament, 53

    inserted into clay figurine, Çatalhöyük, 53–54

    pomegranate/poppy seeds, 90 n. 164

    saved seeds, 90, 91 n. 166, 107 n. 277

    Tumulus MM

        mixed fermented beverage, 127–128, 178, 182–184, 186

        serving stand B, 105–106

    wild vs. cultivated/domesticated, 53–54

selvage, 204, 220

SEM (Scanning Electron Microscopy), 165, 172–173, 176, 208, 213

SEM-EDS (Scanning Electron Microscopy with Energy Dispersive Spectroscopy), 205, 207–209, 212, 214, 218, 221

Sennacherib, 87 n. 128, 134 n. 75, 199 n. 16

sequential coincidence/repetition, 33–34, 45 n. 84, 50, 77, 83 n. 96, 101 n. 239. *See also* symmetry.

serving stands. *See also* drawings; photography/photographs; "screen"; vessel/cauldron stands.

    Assyrian, 76–77

    bronze vessels as evidence for, 75–76 n. 63, 130 n. 33, 132

    depictions of, 76–77, 109

    Megaron 3, 75

    Tumulus K-III, 75, 130 n. 33

    Tumulus MM, 9, 13, 18–21, 31–32, 40, 48, 56–57, 60, 65–110, 116–117, 123, 127–128, 130, 132, 135, 171, 175, 178, 189–195, 198–202

    and Phrygian monuments, 92–98, 135 n. 78

    as portable shrines, 96, 99, 101 n. 238, 132

    back leg (missing), 9, 19–20, 65–68, 70–74, 142–143, 162–163; Color Plates XIII, XV; Figures 2, 51, 59; Plates 79, 89

    back piece, 18, 20, 65–67, 68 n. 19, 70–72, 74, 162–163; Figures 48, 51, 56, 59; Plates 75A, 85A

    conservation of, 13, 18, 65, 137–138, 142–145, 149–150, 157; Plates 124C, 125A

    construction/assembly (ancient), 9, 18–20, 65–73, 97, 142–143, 189, 192, 199–202

designs, 9, 19–20, 48–49, 52, 56, 66–67, 71–74, 77–87, 94, 97, 99–103, 105–106, 109–110, 135, 142, 144, 192–193. *See also* motifs (designs); symmetry.
  and agriculture/agricultural year, 102–109. *See also* agriculture/crops/farming.
  and calendars, 103–106. *See also* calendar.
  and celestial phenomena, 86 n. 125, 87–88, 89 n. 147, 90 n. 165, 96 n. 203, 99, 100–107, 107–108 n. 281, 109–110. *See also* celestial/celestial phenomena.
  and "doodles," 99–100
  and equinoxes/equinox years, 103–105, 105–106 n. 271, 106 n. 272, 107
  and Faharet Çeşme, 100–102
  and "genealogical patterns," 84, 87, 99, 106
  and royal prerogative/insignia, 86–87, 91, 99, 132
  and textile patterns, 85–87, 91, 99, 106–107 n. 277, 109 n. 296, 132
  and the goddess Matar, 87, 91–102, 106–110, 132, 135
  apotropaic/protective, 83–84, 87, 88 n. 136, 91, 98 n. 218, 99, 102, 106
  color diagrams, 3, 77–83, 97; Color Plates X–XI; CD-Figures 66–73
  derivatives, 79 n. 83, 80–83; Figures 72, 74
  error, 82–83, 201
  "flipping" of, 78–83, 85–86, 94, 100 n. 229, 103, 201
  "main" designs/groups, 78–83, 85–86, 106; Figures 72, 74
  rosette/lunette, 9, 20, 48, 66–67, 70–72, 74, 78 n. 83, 84, 87, 95, 97, 99–103
  rosette/medallion, 9, 13 n. 2, 19–20, 48, 66–67, 70–75, 77, 78 n. 83, 79 n. 86, 81–84, 87, 92, 95–97, 99–100, 102, 142, 189–192, 200. *See also* rosette.
  scribe lines/guidelines, 70, 73, 201; Figure 70
  square/meander square, 48, 66–67, 69–72, 74, 77–85, 99–100, 102–105, 106 n. 272, 132, 201
  subsidiary designs, 78–83, 103
  swastikas, 19, 48, 52, 71 n. 35, 78–79, 83, 86, 99, 102; Figure 71. *See also* swastika.
  symbolism, 83–110, 135 n. 78
  underlying pattern, 77, 82–83, 103, 201
    intentional obscuring of, 82–83, 94–95, 135, 201

early interpretation of, 13, 18–21, 65; Figure 2. *See also* "screen"; "throne-backs."
excavation, 9, 18, 65, 74, 127, 130; Color Plates IIIA, IV; Plates 69–71, 80–81
front "legs," 19, 65–73, 75, 79–84, 87, 95–97, 103, 142–144, 162–163
function, 18–20, 65, 73–74, 97–98, 128, 130–132, 178–187
graffiti on tenons, 70–71, 73, 189–195, 200; Figures 62–65; Plates 93–94
inlay technique, 18–20, 66–67, 69–71, 72 n. 39, 73, 81–82, 83 n. 93, 97, 189, 192–193, 200–202; Figures 68–70
joinery, 2, 18–20, 62 n. 45, 65–73, 143, 189, 192, 200–202
lion legs/paw feet, 95–96, 99; Plates 90–92
reconstruction of, 65, 68, 144, 162–163; Color Plates XII–XV; Figures 47–51, 55–59; Plates 78–79, 88–89, 133–138
scroll feet, 9, 19–20, 66, 68, 71, 73, 74 n. 53, 75, 95, 96 n. 203
side pieces, 9, 18, 20, 65–67, 70–72, 74, 77, 162, 202; Figures 45–46, 53–54; Plates 76, 86
struts, 9, 19, 21, 65–68, 70–72, 73 n. 44, 74, 142, 162–163; Figures 47–48, 51, 55–56, 59; Plates 75, 85
surface finish (ancient), 199, 202
textiles found behind serving stand A, 130, 216–220, 223; Plates 157–158; CD-Figures 56–65
top piece, 9, 19–21, 65–67, 70–74, 128, 130, 142–144, 162–163; Figures 44, 52; Plates 74, 84
vessels used with/analysis of contents, 31, 73–74, 123, 127–128, 130, 132, 177–187; Frontispiece
wedge/shim, 202; Plate 95
woods, 19, 65–66, 70–71, 73, 75, 144, 166, 168–169, 198–199; Plates 145C–D, 146D
  contrast in color, 9, 18–19, 66, 79, 143–144, 198–199
Tumulus P, 16 n. 25, 18–19, 20 n. 65, 41 n. 49, 49, 73–75, 95, 97, 132; Figure 91
Tumulus W, 18, 75, 132
Urartian, 76
Seuffert, Andy, 13 n. 2, 72 n. 36
shaman/shamanism, 90 n. 165
Shamash, 87. *See also* sun-god.
Shaushga, 88
shearling, 207
sheathing. *See* plating/sheathing/gilt.
sheep, 43, 91 n. 166, 98 n. 212, 117, 127–128, 130, 184, 187, 203, 221. *See also* ram.

shellac, 161

shen sign (Egyptian hieroglyph), 96 n. 203

shield, 55
    of Achilles, 109

shim/shimming, 42 n. 62, 47, 57, 61, 63, 200 n.
    28, 202; Plate 95

ships/shipwreck
    boat-shaped (coffins), 125
    Comacchio, 201 n. 35
    Egyptian, 202
    joinery, 2 n. 3, 68, 120 n. 15, 202
    Uluburun (Kaş), 89, 195 n. 24, 202

shrine, 46 n. 96, 50 n. 126, 53 n. 156, 54 n. 160,
    87, 92 n. 180, 197 n. 8
    of Matar/Kybele, 93, 95–100, 101 nn. 238–
        239, 132, 135

Sialk, Iran, 50 n. 128

Siberia, 40 n. 43, 46–47, 63, 84 n. 104, 90 n. 165,
    124. See also Pazyryk, Siberia.

silicon, present in textiles, 205, 207–209, 212–214,
    218, 221

silicone sealant/gasket, 142–143, 157, 161

silk, 203, 207, 222–223
    Coan silk, 223
    "sea silk." See byssus.

silk moth, 222–223
    Bombyx mori, 222–223
    Pachypasa otus Drury, 223
    Saturnia pyri, 223

silkscreen (fabric), 146–147, 149–150, 153–155,
    158; Plate 126C

silver, 35 n. 19, 43, 45–46, 48, 53 n.151, 76,
    117 n. 52, 124, 131–132, 161, 199. See also
    gold/precious metal; plating/sheathing/gilt.

Simpson, Carlos, xxxviii, 34 n. 9

Sin, 87

Sinai (desert), 64

Sincan, Ankara, Turkey, 101 n. 236

sinew, 222

"singing the rug," 54 n. 163

Sippar. See Nabû-apla-iddina, stone tablet.

Sirius, 104 n. 258, 105

situla/bucket, 9, 65, 74, 127–128, 130, 178–179,
    218 n. 46; Color Plate VII

skeleton, Tumulus MM, 8, 10, 22 n. 84, 23–24,
    155; Color Plate IB; Plates 107–108, 109A

sleeves, 108

Smith, Ron, 137–138

Smithsonian Institution, xxxvii, xxxix, 203–204,
    205 n. 12, 206 n. 15, 217 n. 43, 221 n. 54, 223
    n. 61

snakes, 84, 88, 135 n. 78

sodium, present in textiles, 205, 209

sodium hydroxide, 178

soft-rot fungus. See fungus/mold/fungal decay.

solder, 161

Solomon Islands, 84 n. 104

solstice, 103–104 n. 257, 104–105, 105 n. 264, 106
    n. 272, 107 n. 277

solvents, 139–144, 148, 151, 158, 177
    acetone, 137, 141, 146, 149–150, 152–153, 155,
        163
    alcohol/isopropyl alcohol, 13, 15, 18, 65, 137–
        139, 142–145
    crazing from, 39 n. 36, 142, 161–162
    ethanol, 139–142, 146–155, 161, 172
    evaporation of, 139–140, 144, 147–148, 151
    gasoline/"benzine," 15, 18, 31 n. 3, 65, 137–
        139, 143
    methanol, 177, 186
    off-gassing of, 142, 157, 161. See also solvents,
        crazing from.
    petroleum ether, 146, 148
    solvent cleaning of textiles, 205 n. 12, 217
    solvent-gel poultice, 146–148, 151–153
    toluene, 138–144, 146–155
    vapor, 140, 142, 161
    "Weld-on"/acrylic solvent cement. See
        adhesives/cement.

Sothis, 104 n. 258. See also Sirius.

soumak, 209–210

"sown field," 53

spectrometer, 177

sphinx, 43 n. 73, 89, 117 n. 56
    confronted, 94

spices. See food and drink.

spinning/spun (yarn/textiles), 45, 102, 106, 204,
    208, 213, 217–219, 222–223

spiral. See motifs (designs).

Spirydowicz, Krysia, xxxv, xxxvii–xxxviii, 137–
    158

spits, 127–129

spoons. See also ladles.
    Tumulus MM, 21, 114
    Tumulus P, 132, 162

spring/water, 90, 98 n. 211, 99–102, 109, 130, 134

square. See motifs (designs).

stag. See deer.

stamps/stamped ornament, 49 n. 121, 54, 84, 85
    n. 111, 117. See also seals/seal impressions.

standard, 19, 49, 52 n. 144, 85

star/astral, 87–89, 91 n. 175, 102–105, 107,
    109, 195 n. 24. See also celestial/celestial
    phenomena; constellation; cosmos/cosmic;
    Inanna; Ishtar; motifs (designs); Pleiades;
    Venus.
    morning/evening star, 88

star rosette. See motifs (designs); rosette.

steam bending. *See* wood.

steel (for conservation, display, and storage), 140, 143, 149, 157–158, 162

stele. *See also* relief, stone.
    Banquet Stele, Nimrud, 91 n. 170
    Bor, 86; CD-Figure 97
    Sincan, 101 n. 236
    Zincirli, 91 n. 168, 195 n. 24

stools, 19, 199. *See also* footstools/footrests; seating furniture/cushions/hassocks.
    Assyrian, 45, 76, 116 n. 42
    Baghouz, 116,
    city mound, Gordion, 115
    depictions of, 42, 45, 76, 115–116, 197
    Egyptian, 43, 64, 112, 115–116
    Greek, 47 n. 106, 116 n. 43
    Jericho, 115–116
    Salamis, Cyprus, 129
    Tumulus K-III, Gordion, 115
    Tumulus MM (northeast corner), 8, 21, 31, 111–116, 123, 130, 155, 200 n. 29. *See also* northeast corner, Tumulus MM.
        conservation of, 111, 155
        early interpretation of, 21, 111
        excavation, 8; Color Plate IIB; Plates 100–103
        fill/patching material, 114; Plate 106C
        form, 21, 111–112
        joinery, 21, 111–113
        legs, 2, 8, 21, 111–115, 155, 200 n. 29
            long legs ("stool #2")/chair, 21, 111–117, 129–130, 198, 200 n. 29; Plate 103
            medium legs ("stool #3"), 21, 111–114; Plate 102
            short legs ("stool #1"), 21, 111–113, 115; Figure 76; Plates 101, 105B
        small objects associated with, 21, 114, 130
        stretchers, 2, 21, 111–113, 114 n. 17, 115, 117, 155, 166, 169
        textiles associated with, 8, 21–22, 111–114, 116, 123, 155, 211–216, 222–223; Plates 155–156; CD-Figures 25–55
            impression of cording from seat, 114, 211–213, 222; Plates 106B, 155A–B
        unplaced leg fragments, 114; Plate 106A
        woods, 111–112, 166, 169
    Tumulus P, 40 n. 44, 49, 74 n. 50, 114, 162
    Urartian, 45 n. 83, 46, 115
    Zincirli, 116 n. 41

storage, 16 n. 28, 65, 112, 114, 138, 143–144, 146–147, 149–150, 152–154, 156
    cabinets, 157–158; Plate 128
    mounts, 148, 150–157; Plates 127–128

Stout, Edith, xxxviii, 127 n. 2, 177, 179, 183–184

Strabo, 10 n. 54, 98, 133

straw (for seating), 114 n. 18

straws, 127 n. 6

stretchers, 35 n. 19, 43–46, 49, 76–77, 115–117. *See also* stools, Tumulus MM (northeast corner).

strut/strutwork, 41–46, 48, 62, 76, 115. *See also* serving stands, Tumulus MM; tables, Tumulus MM, inlaid table.
    boxwood, 44
    floral, 43–45, 55
    ivory, 43–44

studs. *See* tacks/studs, bronze.

Styrofoam, 157–158

sulfur, present in textiles, 205, 207–209, 212–214, 218, 221

sulfuric acid, 178

Sumer/Sumerian. *See also* Ur; Uruk.
    deities, 87–88. *See also* individual entries.
    funerary customs, 131 n. 39, 132 n. 51, 135 n. 77

sun/solar, 87, 89, 90 n. 165, 96, 101, 103–105, 109, 134, 195 n. 24
    solar year, 103–105

sun-disc, 87–89, 96 n. 203, 102, 106 n. 277

sun-god, 87, 129. *See also* Shamash.

Sun Goddess of Arinna, 88 n. 141

sun-goddess of the earth, 129

Susa, Iran, 45, 50 n. 126, 52 n. 143, 86 n. 124, 88

swastika
    as apotropaic device, 52, 83, 91 n. 175, 99, 102
    as good luck symbol, 51 n. 142, 52, 102
    as maze symbol
        Crete, 51
        inlaid table, Tumulus MM, 37, 50; Figure 17B
    as multivalent symbol, 102
    as Nazi emblem, 51 n. 142
    associated with a goddess/"idol," 52 n. 144, 54 n. 162, 102 n. 248, 108, 108–109 n. 289; Plate 117C; CD-Figures 81–84. *See also* Faharet Çeşme.
    based on the cross, 78; Figure 71
    early forms of the design, 51–52, 84
    from Olynthos, 52
    in Anatolian art, 52
        Alacahöyük standard, 52, 84–85; CD-Figure 80
        Bor stele, 86; CD-Figure 97
        carpets/kilims, 52 n. 145
        Faharet Çeşme relief, 100 n. 231, 101 n. 237; Plate 119B
        Ivriz relief, 86; Plate 119D
        Troy artifacts, 52, 102 n. 248; CD-Figure 81
    in China, 51 n. 142

swastika (*Continued*)

    in India, 51 n. 142

    Native American, 51 n. 142, 84 n. 104

    on a Hallstatt textile, 54 n. 162

    on artifacts from Gordion

        pebble mosaic, 52 n. 146; Figure 92

        textiles, 85 n. 114

    on Greek artifacts, 91 n. 175

        "bell idols," Boeotia, 54 n. 162; CD-Figures 82–83

        ceramic polos, Boeotia, 108–109 n. 289; CD-Figure 84

        coins of Knossos, 51

        pottery/vases, 50, 108; Plate 117C

    on the façade of Arslan Kaya, 94; CD-Figure 74

    on the Tumulus MM furniture

        inlaid table, 33, 37, 48, 50; Figures 5–8, 14–16, 17B

        serving stands, 19, 48, 52, 71 n. 35, 78–79, 86, 99, 102; Figures 50, 58, 69, 71–72, 74; Plate 99

            variant in stand A's lunette, 102; Figure 50; Plate 77

    on Tumulus P artifacts, 49; Figure 91

    symmetry of, 78

        as radial design, 78, 84, 102

    with broken central bar, 78–79, 86; Figure 71

    with rosette

        calendar embroidery (Russia), 107 n. 277; CD-Figure 94

        Cretan coins, 51 n. 139

symbol/symbolism, 34, 43 n. 68, 50–56, 75, 83–110, 125, 131–132, 135, 193. *See also* individual entries.

    multivalent, 102

    "paradox" of, 102 n. 247

symmetry, vii, 16, 24, 31, 33–34, 36–38, 50, 77–86, 112, 122

    bilateral, 33, 36, 49 n. 118, 50, 77–78, 80, 83 n. 96

    "flipping" of designs, 78–83, 85–86, 94, 100 n. 229, 103, 109 n. 289, 201

    lattice (complete symmetry), 83

    play with, 31, 33–34, 36–38, 48, 50, 77–86, 94, 193

    rotational, 49 n. 118, 52, 78–80, 83 n. 96, 84–86, 94, 100 n. 231, 102; Figure 71

        90-degree, 49 n. 118, 52, 78, 83 n. 96, 84, 85 n. 111, 94, 100 n. 231

        180-degree, 78–79, 84–86; Figure 71

    translational, 83 n. 96. *See also* sequential coincidence/repetition.

Syria/Syrian, 41–44, 46, 64, 91, 94 n. 193, 96, 102 n. 251, 115–117, 132, 199. *See also* furniture; ivory.

    deities, 88–89, 90 n. 159

tables

    Aegean, 43

    Altıntepe, 46, 63

    Anatolian, 41–42, 45–46, 63, 77, 130. *See also* individual entries.

    Assyrian, 44–45, 76

    Babylonian, 46 n. 96, 197

    Baghouz, 42–43, 64, 202 n. 41

    banquet, 39–48, 62–64, 76–77, 123, 127, 132, 137–138, 143–146, 148

    corner pieces, 34–35, 39, 45–46, 134, 199

    depictions of, 40 n. 41, 41–42, 43 n. 73, 44–47

    Early Bronze Age, 41–42

    Ebla, 41–42

    Egyptian, 40, 43, 64

    evidence from Jerusalem, 44, 199

    first millennium B.C., 44–48, 63–64. *See also* individual entries.

    four-legged, 40 n. 41, 40 n. 46, 41, 43 n. 65, 44, 46–47, 62 n. 38, 63–64

    gold and silver, 35, 39–40, 43, 45–46, 134, 199

    Greek, 39–40, 43, 47–48, 64 n. 63

    Hittite, 40 n. 43, 43 n. 74, 130

    Homeric, 39, 47 n. 104

    Horoztepe, 41

    in ancient texts, 39–40, 43, 45, 46 n. 96, 130

    Iranian, 45

    ivory tables/fittings, 43–46, 129

    Jericho, 42–43, 47, 62–63, 199–200 n. 25, 200 n. 28, 202 n. 41

    Late Bronze Age, 43–44, 130

    later examples/ethnographic parallels, 64

    Megaron 3, Gordion, 41

    Middle Bronze Age, 42–43, 62–63. *See also* individual entries.

    multiple/sets, 39–40, 42, 62. *See also* tables, Tumulus MM, plain tables.

    Pazyryk/Ukok (Siberia), 40 n. 43, 46–47, 63

    portable/collapsible, 39–40, 42, 47, 62–64

    Roman, 40, 109

    Salamis, Cyprus, 129

    Samos, 47 n. 106, 64 n. 63

    Thracian, 39–40

    three-legged/tripod, 8, 14–15, 16 n. 25, 31, 39–44, 47–48, 57, 62–64, 139, 145. *See also* tables, Tumulus MM; tables, Tumulus P.

    tray top, 9, 14–15, 39–45, 47, 57, 59–60, 62–64, 68–69 n. 25, 139, 145, 199. *See also* tray/"kneading trough."

    Tumulus K-III, 41

Tumulus MM
inlaid table, 9, 15–18, 31–56. *See also*
drawings; photography/photographs.
and inlaid stool, Tumulus P, 40 n. 44, 49
conservation of, 13, 15, 18, 31 n. 3, 137–
145; Plate 124A
construction/assembly (ancient), 15–18,
31–39
internal bracing system, 2, 9, 15–16,
31–33, 37, 39, 159–162; Figure 4;
Plate 2
patching/repairs, 32 n. 4, 33, 36, 39–
40, 134, 200; Plates 4A–D, 5C–F,
16E–F, 20A–D, 24B, 25B, 26–29
corner pieces (missing), 32 n. 4, 34–35,
39, 45, 46 n. 97, 134, 199; Figure 25;
Plate 23
designs, 33–35, 37–39, 48. *See also* inlay;
motifs (designs).
fertility symbols, 52–56, 106
"genealogical patterns," 52, 55–56,
99, 106
hooks and swastikas, 33–34, 37–38,
48–50, 92, 99. *See also* swastika.
swastika as maze, 37, 50; Figure
17B
interplay, 33, 36–38, 48–50, 72
lozenge/square cross, 38, 52, 97, 99
lunette, 37, 48, 99
mazes, 34, 37–38, 49–51, 97 n. 207,
99, 135; Figures 9, 17. *See also*
maze/labyrinth.
obscuring/negating of, 95 n. 194, 135
rosettes, 33, 37, 48, 99. *See also* rosette.
symbols of Matar, 99, 106, 132, 135
early interpretation of ("Pagoda Table"),
15–18; Figure 1
excavation, 9; Color Plate III; Plate 1
frame, 15–17, 31–39, 48–50, 97 n. 207,
99, 134, 139–141, 160–161, 166, 198–
199; Figures 4–8; Plates 3, 6, 11, 13,
15, 17, 19, 22
glue/residues, 15, 31 n. 3, 34, 200 n. 32,
202 n. 43; Plate 23
handles, 16–17, 32, 34–39, 46 n. 97, 48,
50, 67 n. 15, 134, 141–142, 160, 192,
199, 201; Figures 13–16; Plates 4A–D,
5C–F, 20A–D, 21C–F
missing inlay, 16–17, 35–36, 39, 45, 46
n. 97, 134, 199, 201; Plates 4B, 5D,
20B, 21D, 151A
repairs, 36, 39; Plates 4A–D, 5C–F,
20A–D
inlay technique, 31 n. 3, 33, 35, 200–201

joinery, 2, 15–17, 32–39, 200
collar-and-tenon, 17, 23, 32, 38–40,
200; Figure 27
leg struts, 2, 15, 17–18, 31, 37–38, 49, 55
n. 168, 66 n. 11, 67 n. 15, 159, 161;
Figures 10–12; Plates 7–10, 14, 18
legs, 15–17, 19, 31–33, 37–39, 42, 48–
49, 139–140, 142, 197 n. 3, 198–200;
Figures 4, 18–20, 27–28; Plates 24–31
reconstruction/display, 39, 141–142, 159–
162; Color Plates VIII–IX; Figure 21;
Plates 33–35, 129–132
reputation, 15–16, 18
surface finish (ancient), 199–200, 202
table top, 15–17, 31–32, 34–36, 38–39,
139, 141–142, 161, 200; Plate 32
top struts, 15–17, 31–32, 34–37, 45, 49,
160–161; Figures 5–8; Plates 3A, 11A,
15A, 19A
type-1, 16–17, 34–37, 44 n. 77, 48, 99;
Plates 4E–F, 5A–B, 12A–B, 12E–F,
16A–B, 16E–F, 20E–F, 21A–B
strut C3, 16, 35, 39–40, 99 n. 222,
167; Plate 16E–F
type-2, 16–17, 35, 36 n. 22, 37, 44 n.
77; Plates 4G–H, 12C–D, 12G–H,
16C–D, 16G–H, 20G–H
use, 39–40, 127, 130–132
woods, 16, 19 n. 57, 31, 39, 139, 166–167,
198; Plate 145A–B
contrast in color, 9, 16, 33, 39, 49–50,
139–140, 198–199
plain tables, 8–9, 13–14, 31, 57–64;
Color Plates II, IIIA, V; Figures 29–
43; Plates 36–68. *See also* drawings;
photography/photographs.
as a set, 14, 21
cataloguing errors, 2, 13–14, 57–60
conservation of, 13–14, 58 n. 17, 144–155;
Plates 38, 125B, 126, 127B, 128
early interpretation of, 13–14
excavation/removal from the tomb, 8–9,
13–14, 57, 145; Color Plates II, IIIA,
V; Plates 36–37, 42, 46, 50, 54–56, 60,
63, 66, 108
form, 14, 57–62, 145
joinery, 14, 57–62
collar-and-tenon, 14, 23, 57–62, 145,
200, 202; Figure 39
legs, 13–14, 19, 42, 57–62, 145–155, 198–
200. *See also* bending/training (of
wood).
repairs (ancient), 60, 200; Plate 151C
shimming, 57, 61, 63

tables (*Continued*)
>storage, 146–158; Plates 127B, 128
>textile fragments ("bag") associated
>>with, 9, 111, 113
>tops, 13–14, 57–62, 145–155, 198–200
>use, 39–40, 62, 127, 130–132
>woods, 13–14, 57–62, 145, 165–168, 197–
>>198; Plates 141–144, 146A–C, 146E–F
>contrast in color, 13, 60
>>Tumulus P, 132
>>>Mosaic Table, 16 n. 25, 40–41
>>>plain tables, 16 n. 25, 40, 62, 74 n. 50
>>>Tripod Tray Table, 41, 68–69 n. 25
>>Ugarit, 43
>>Urartian, 45–46, 63
>>Verucchio, 48, 64
tacks/studs, bronze, 8 n. 15, 49, 86
>Megaron 3, Gordion, 75
>"screen," Tumulus W, 75
>stool, Tumulus P, 49
>Tumulus K-III, 41, 75
>Tumulus K-IV, 75 n. 63
tamarind, 182
Tarhunzas, 90
tartaric acid/tartrate, 127 n. 5, 178–179, 181–185.
>*See also* calcium, tartrate.
Taş Kapısı (Urartu), 93 n. 183
taskarinnu, 199
tattoos, 55 n. 168; CD-Figure 96
tauroctony/bull slaying, 106 n. 271. *See also*
>Mithras.
TD-GC-MS (Thermal Desorption-Gas
>Chromatography-Mass Spectrometry), 179,
>184, 186. *See also* GC-MS.
Tell el-Ajjul (goldwork), 89 n. 147
Tellus, 109. *See also* Earth (deity).
temperature fluctuations, 157, 162–163. *See also*
>datalogger.
template, 78 n. 77, 159, 201
tenon, 1–2, 14–17, 19–20, 25–26, 31–38, 39 n. 34,
>40, 42–44, 47–48, 57–73, 111–112, 115, 148–
>150, 162, 167–169, 189–194, 200, 202. *See also*
>joinery.
>free/double tenon, 2, 42, 62 n. 45, 67–69, 73,
>>189, 192, 202
>graffiti, 70–71, 73, 189–195, 200
>mortise and tenon, 2, 15, 31 n. 3, 32–38, 48,
>>59–60, 62–63, 64 n. 63, 67–69, 72–73, 111–
>>112, 115–116, 142, 189–192, 197 n. 7, 200,
>>202
>tenon and pin/peg, 14–15, 18–20, 42, 47, 57,
>>58 n. 16, 60–64, 67–69, 73, 162, 166–168,
>>189–191, 200–202; Figure 39
>as clamping mechanism, 68, 202

terminals, 37, 46. *See also* finials.
Terrace Building. *See* Gordion (site), city mound.
tetrad, 84. *See also* quadripartite designs.
>cardinal points, 84, 104 n. 257, 190
>four quarters of the universe, 84
>(four) seasons, 84, 99, 101, 103 n. 257, 106, 107
>>n. 280
>(four) winds, 51 n. 142, 84
>genealogical system, 84. *See also* "genealogical
>>patterns."
textiles. *See also* byssus; carpet/carpets; cos-
>tume/dress/clothing; linen; loom; ramie; silk;
>weave types; weaving; wool.
>and the Amiternum stand, 109 n. 296
>and the Tumulus MM serving stands, 85–87,
>>99, 109 n. 296, 132
>and woodworking, 107 n. 277
>as offerings, 114, 116, 131
>as carriers of artistic tradition, 53 n. 151, 54,
>>85, 91, 106–107 n. 277
>Assyrian, 86–87, 91, 99, 109 n. 296, 132
>bacterial immunity/antibacterial protection
>>of, 203, 223
>bacteriostatic coating on, 205–206
>"bag"/container, 9, 21, 111, 113–114, 209, 211,
>>213, 215, 223
>batting, 114, 123, 212, 221
>"blanketing," 21, 114, 211, 213, 215, 222
>"calendar embroidery," 107 n. 277; CD-Figure
>>94
>Çatalhöyük, 54
>city mound, Gordion, 85, 106, 204
>coated/coating, 123, 204–206, 213, 215–217,
>>219, 221, 223
>color/colorant, 203–208, 210–213, 215–222.
>>*See also* dye/dyeing; goethite; indigo.
>cording/cordage, 114, 211, 213, 222
>decay/deterioration/degradation, 8, 23, 111,
>>114, 119, 122, 156, 174, 203–208, 210 n. 27,
>>212, 215, 219–223
>depictions of, 54, 85–87, 91–92, 95, 108, 108–
>>109 n. 289, 115
>dowry textiles, 54
>ethnographic/traditional, 53 n. 151, 54–55,
>>106–107 n. 277; CD-Figures 88–94
>felt, 8, 114, 122–123, 160–161, 203, 207–208,
>>210–213, 221–222
>fiber/fibers, 203–209, 211–223
>>bast, 114, 123, 204, 215, 220, 223. *See also*
>>>flax; ramie.
>>cellulosic, 203–205, 215–216
>>hair/mohair, 204, 206–208, 211, 220–221
>>lofted, 123, 212, 221
>>monofilament, 204, 222. *See also* silk.

for conservation, 140, 147. *See also* Gore-tex; silkscreen (fabric).

for museum display, 160–161

from Pazyryk, 47, 86 n. 124, 87, 203 n. 1

from Verucchio, 48

gauze, 209–210

gold (yellow)/"golden," 8, 22, 109 n. 296, 122–123, 204, 206, 215–221. *See also* goethite.

Greek, 86

Hallstatt period, 54 n. 162

Hittite, 129

"mattress," 22–23, 208, 221

mineralization, 207, 220–222

napped, 203, 205–206

net/knotted netting, 222–223

of the gods, 86, 89, 91, 132

of Warpalawas, 86–87, 99 n. 220

pattern/patterns, 54, 85–87, 99, 102 n. 244, 106–107 n. 277, 108, 210–211, 215, 222–223. *See also* "genealogical patterns"; motifs (designs).

Phrygian, 85–87, 99

pillow/cushion, 14, 85, 113, 129 n. 23, 212, 220, 221 n. 53, 223

ply/plied, 204, 211, 215–220, 223

production at Gordion, 106, 222

protective function of, 52 n. 145, 54–55, 87, 91, 99

pseudomorphs, 203, 221

ritual cloths, 54, 106–107 n. 277

royal, 86–87, 91, 99, 132

selvage, 204, 220

soumak. *See* weave types.

spinning, 45, 102, 106, 204, 208, 213, 217–219, 222–223

distaff, 106 n. 276

spindle whorls, 52 n. 144, 106 n. 274

starting border, 211, 220

storage, 114 n. 23, 120, 157, 218, 223

tarry (tar-like), 215, 217–219

Tumulus MM, 203–223

coffin, 8, 22–25, 27, 119–123, 155, 157, 169, 204–212, 220–223; Color Plates IB, IIA; Plates 107–110, 153–154; CD-Figures 1–24

east wall, 216–220, 223, 130; Plates 157–158; CD-Figures 56–65

northeast corner, 8, 21–22, 111–114, 123, 130, 155, 211–216, 222–223; Color Plate IIB; Plates 100, 155–156; CD-Figures 25–55

preliminary study and publication, 8 n. 18, 106 n. 276, 203–204. *See also* Bellinger, Louisa; Ellis, Richard.

used to wrap bronzes, 9, 130

Tumulus P, 85

twined, 114, 123, 208–213, 215, 222–223

"union" cloth (mixed fabric), 219–220, 223

unprovenanced (from Gordion), 114 n. 23, 120

yarns/thread, 51, 130, 204–206, 208–223

bicomponent/striped, 130, 204, 218–221, 223

floss, 211, 213

painted, 218

S-plied, 204, 215–217, 219–220

twist of, 204, 222

Z single, 204, 215–220

Z-spun, 208, 219

Thebes (Boeotia), Greece, 108 n. 289

Thebes, Egypt, 76 n. 64, 197–198

Theophrastus, 199

Theseus, 51

Thracian, 39, 127, 129

"three-burner stove," 19–20, 67. *See also* serving stands, Tumulus MM, top piece.

threshold slabs, stone, 50 n. 127, 87, 91

"throne-backs," Tumulus MM, 18–19. *See also* serving stands, Tumulus MM, early interpretation of.

thrones. *See* chairs/thrones.

Ti, tomb of, 197

tigers, 47. *See also* lions.

Tiglath-pileser III, 86–87; CD-Figure 98

tinfoil, 47 n. 101, 149

titanium, present in textiles, 209, 214

Toba (Argentina), 55 n. 168; CD-Figure 96

toluene, 138–144, 146–155

Tomb of the Lord of the Goats, Ebla, 42

tombs/burials, 35 n. 19, 40 n. 43, 41–43, 46–48, 51, 54 n. 162, 62–64, 75–76, 85, 86 n. 124, 89, 90 n. 165, 91, 92 n. 177, 108 n. 282, 114–116, 121 n. 17, 123–125, 127 n. 1, 128–129, 131–132, 135, 197, 203. *See also* funerals/funerary ritual; Tumulus MM, Gordion; other individual entries.

burial mounds, 1, 7, 10, 124, 128, 129 n. 18, 134 n. 73, 137. *See also* mountain/primeval hill.

grave markers, 91 n. 167, 107 n. 277

on the tomb of Midas, 134

Phrygian monuments identified as tombs, 96 n. 204, 134 n. 75

reuse of monuments/shrines as tombs, 134 n. 75

tools. *See also* individual entries.

bronze, 197

early American/traditional, 197

Egyptian, 197–198

from Gordion, 197

tools (*Continued*)
  iron, 197
  Jericho, 42 n. 62
  Old Babylonian, 197
  Phrygian, xxxviii, 2, 158, 192, 197–202
    adze, 197–199
    chisel, 70, 197–198, 200; Plate 150B–C
    compass, 20, 61, 66, 70–71, 73, 189–192, 193
      n. 14, 197, 200; Plate 152A–B
    drill, 20 n. 65, 33, 35 n. 19, 68, 70, 197–198,
      200–202; Plates 150D, 151
    knife, 70–71, 197, 200–201
    lathe. *See* lathe/turned.
    saw, 2, 197–198, 199 n. 24; Plate 150A
    scraper, 197, 201 n. 38
  Roman, 197 n. 5
Topal, Ekber, xxxix, 159
toys, 95 n. 198, 96 n. 202, 117
transmission electron microscopy, 172, 175
tray/"kneading trough," 62 n. 41, 106
tray (table). *See* tables, tray top.
tree, 2, 16, 34, 38, 43, 44 n. 77, 54 n. 162, 55
  n. 168, 94 n. 193, 96 n. 203, 99, 106–107 n.
  277, 109, 112, 117, 120, 125, 134, 165, 172, 175,
  182, 199, 201. *See also* motifs (designs); wood;
  individual entries.
tribe/tribal. *See* clan/tribe/"genealogical
  clans."
triglycerides, 184–185
Trimalchio, 40
tripod stands, 75, 76 n. 66, 129
  for display mounts, 159 n. 1, 160–162; Plate
    130D
Tripolye. *See* Cucuteni.
Troy, Turkey
  lead "idol," Troy III, 52 n. 144, 102 n. 248;
    CD-Figure 81
  spindle whorls decorated with swastikas, 53 n.
    144
Tuekta, Siberia, 124
Tumulus 1 (Atatürk Mausoleum), Ankara, 123–
  124
Tumulus I (METU I), Ankara, 76 n. 63
Tumulus II (METU II), Ankara, 124
Tumulus B, Gordion, 123, 133 n. 62
Tumulus C, Bayındır, 132 n. 45
Tumulus C, Gordion, 123
Tumulus D, Bayındır, 46 n. 97, 108 n. 282, 124,
  131–132
Tumulus, Great (METU). *See* Great Tumulus,
  Ankara.
Tumulus K-III, Gordion, 41, 49, 50 n. 131, 75,
  102, 117, 123, 130 n. 33, 132
Tumulus K-IV, Gordion, 75–76 n. 63, 132

Tumulus MM, Gordion. *See also* coffins, Tumulus
  MM; northeast corner, Tumulus MM; serving
  stands, Tumulus MM; tables, Tumulus MM.
  burial goods, 8–10. *See also* individual entries.
  catalogue of finds, 2
  construction of the mound, 134
    Poverty Point (calculation of workload), 134
      n. 73
  dating, 10–11, 119 n. 3, 132–134, 194 n. 20
  drilling program, 7–8, 65, 137, 174–175
  excavation, 7–11; Color Plates I–V, VIA; Plates
    1, 36, 54, 69–70, 80, 100, 107–110
  inscriptions
    on artifacts, 73, 90 n. 160, 191, 193–194
    on roof beam, 194 n. 22
  interment, 8, 122–123, 127–128, 130
  log casing, 7–8, 10, 132–133, 174
  "Midas Mound," 10
  moisture/water (in chamber), 8–9, 65, 137,
    155, 173–176
  reconstruction of funeral ceremony and
    banquet, 120, 123, 127–128, 177–187;
    Frontispiece
  robbery (evidence for), 35–36, 39, 46 n. 97,
    134
  tomb/tomb chamber, 7–8, 130 n. 35, 165, 171
    conservation, 8 n. 12
    construction, 7–8
    floor boards, 7 n. 7, 165–166, 170, 174
    iron nails, 8 n. 19, 10, 18, 65, 74, 130
    woods, 7, 165–166, 170, 174
  tomb occupant, 8, 10–11, 23, 24 n. 101, 132–
    133
  tomb plan(s), viii, xxxix, 8, 10, 13, 21–23, 26–
    27, 57, 75 n. 56, 111, 113, 120, 130
  uncatalogued/unlabeled finds, 2, 8 n. 15, 8 n.
    22, 13–14, 57–62, 68 n. 22, 111, 114, 119–120
Tumulus P, Gordion, 13, 16 n. 25, 19, 20 n. 65,
  40–41, 46 n. 96, 48–49, 62, 68 n. 25, 73–
  75, 85, 95, 96 n. 202, 97, 113–114, 115 n.
  28, 117, 123, 132, 138, 162. *See also* serving
  stands, Tumulus P; stools, Tumulus P; tables,
  Tumulus P.
Tumulus S-1, Gordion, 76 n. 63, 123
Tumulus W ("Tumulus Pauline"), Gordion, 13,
  49, 75, 132, 138, 197. *See also* serving stands,
  Tumulus W.
Turkmen/Turkmenistan, 53, 64; CD-Figures 88–
  89
turning/wood turning. *See* lathe/turned.
Tutankhamun, 35 n. 19, 43, 64, 96 n. 203, 115 n.
  35; CD-Figure 79
Tuva, Siberia, 124
twinning/dualism, 101 n. 239

Tyrian purple (6,6'-dibromoindigo), 114, 123, 208, 212

Ugarit, Syria, 43, 88, 89 n. 147, 129 n. 27
Ukok, Siberia, 47 n. 103, 63 n. 58
Uluburun shipwreck, 89, 195 n. 24, 202 n. 42
underworld/netherworld, 64, 131 n. 39, 135
unexcavated artifacts, 46 n. 91, 46 n. 97, 76 n. 66, 76 n. 68, 89 n. 147, 94 n. 193, 116 n. 46, 131 n. 43. *See also* plunder/robbery/thieves.
University of Minnesota, Department of Plant Pathology, xxxvii, 31 n. 2, 165–166, 171, 176
University of Pennsylvania, xxxv, xxxviii–xxxix
    Gordion archives/catalogue cards, 1 n. 1, 15 n. 15, 16, 32 n. 5, 37 nn. 23–24, 66 n. 14, 70 n. 34, 111 n. 1, 113 n. 9. *See also* Gordion field books/notes; bibliographic entries.
    Gordion Furniture Project archives, 31 n. 3, 145 n. 43, 199 n. 23, 200 n. 27, 201 n. 35. *See also* Gordion Furniture Project.
    MASCA (Museum Applied Science Center for Archaeology), 9 n. 26, 31 n. 3, 127 n. 2, 177–178, 186–187
    Museum of Archaeology and Anthropology, xxxv, xxxvii–xxxviii, 7, 127 n. 5, 138, 178
upholstery/cushions, 14, 85, 113–114, 123, 212, 220, 221 n. 53, 222–223
    corded seats, 114, 211, 213, 222
Ur, Iraq
    lyre, Royal Cemetery, 41, 49
    Royal Game of Ur, 88 n. 137
    seal impressions, 52 n. 143, 84, 85 n. 111
    Standard of Ur, 49
Urartu/Urartian, 45–46, 63, 76–77, 86, 93 n. 183, 98, 115, 131 n. 42, 133 n. 63, 199. *See also* individual sites.
Uruk, Iraq
    Eanna precinct, 88
    texts, 88 n. 138, 102
    Uruk vase, 45 n. 84
UV (ultraviolet), 178
Uygur, Nazif, xxxviii, 159

vacuum, 140, 155, 158
    glass desiccator, 140, 152, 154
    low-suction vacuum cleaner, 149–154
    tank, 140, 149, 153; Plate 125A
    vacuum pump, 140, 143, 147, 149, 158; Plate 125A
Van (Tushpa), Turkey, 93 n. 183, 98
Velcro, 157
Venus, 88 n. 138. *See also* Inanna; Ishtar; star/astral, morning/evening star.
Verucchio, Italy, 48, 64, 202 n. 44

vessel/cauldron stands, 74–77. *See also* serving stands; tripod stands.
    Assyrian, 76–77
    depictions of, 76–77, 131 n. 42
    Egyptian, 76
    Lydian, 76, 131 n. 42
    Salamis, Cyprus, 129
    Tumulus K-III, 75
    Tumulus MM, 9, 74, 128 n. 11; Color Plate VB; Plate 36B. *See also* serving stands, Tumulus MM.
    Urartian, 76, 131 n. 42
Virgil
    Aeneid, 199 n. 21
    Georgics, 105 n. 271, 200 n. 26
Vitruvius, 198 n. 12
Volara, 144, 157–158, 163

wall painting, 50 n. 126, 52, 76, 102 n. 245, 128 n. 9, 197
walnut/*Juglans* sp./*Juglans regia* L., 31, 32 n. 4, 39, 46 n. 93, 57–62, 65–66, 70–71, 73, 139, 143–146, 148, 150–154, 165–169, 172–173, 175, 197–199; Plates 139A–B, 141C–D, 142, 145, 146B–D
Warpalawas, 86, 99 n. 220, 105 n. 270; Plate 119D; CD-Figure 97
water. *See* rain; spring/water.
water clock, 105 n. 264, 105 n. 271
water damage. *See* Tumulus MM, moisture/water (in chamber).
waterlogged (wood), 48 n. 110
wavy lines. *See* motifs (designs).
wax
    as a base for inscriptions, 194–195
    as a consolidant, 13, 15, 18, 31 n. 3, 58 n. 17, 65, 137–139, 143, 145–147, 163
    beeswax
        as a consolidant, 137–138, 146–147
        as an indicator for honey, 127 n. 3, 127 n. 5, 181, 183–185
    paraffin, 137–138, 146
    removal, 138–140, 143, 146–152, 154
weave types
    gauze, 209–210
    plain/tabby, 204, 206, 209, 215–217, 219–220, 223
    soumak, 209–210
    twill, 206
    twining, 114, 123, 208–213, 215, 222–223
weaving
    errors, 204–206, 211
    loom/loom weights, 106 n. 274, 203, 205, 210, 222

weaving (*Continued*)
    patterns. *See* textiles.
    "singing the rug," 54 n. 163
    spindle/spindle whorl, 52 n. 144, 91 n. 167,
      106 n. 274
    tablet/card, 209–210, 215
    warp, 204, 209–211, 214–215, 217, 219–220,
      222
    weave count, 204–205, 211, 213, 215–217,
      223
    weaver's knot, 205
    weft, 204, 209–211, 215, 217, 219–220, 222
wedge. *See* shim/shimming.
wedge (inlay), 202; Plate 95
wheat. *See* grain.
wheel. *See* motifs (designs).
wheel construction, 202 n. 42
wicker, 76
Wilson, Thomas, 51 n. 142
wind/winds, 51 n. 142, 84, 104 n. 257, 124, 128 n.
  16
wine, 48, 105, 127–129, 131 n. 37, 132 n. 52,
  178, 182–187. *See also* beer/ale; "mixed
  beverage"/mixed fermented beverage.
winged disc, 35, 89, 96, 102 n. 251
Winnebago (tribe), 51 n. 142, 84 n. 104
Winter, Irene, xxxix
Winterthur Art Conservation Program, xxxvii, 31
  n. 3, 202 n. 39
wood. *See also* individual entries.
    anatomy/cell structure, 137, 165, 171–176
    archaeological, xxxv, 138, 157–158, 171, 176
    carbonized, 41, 62 n. 41, 115
    checking, 153, 156, 176
    cleaning/dirt removal, 66 n. 13, 112, 113 n. 16,
      138–140, 143–144, 146–155, 163
    color, applied/on, 44 n. 78, 64, 112, 114 n. 17,
      155, 202 n. 39
    color change, 1, 18, 39, 138–141, 143–144, 148,
      198–199
    color contrast, 1, 8, 18–19, 24, 33, 39, 49–50,
      60, 66, 79, 121–122, 139–140, 143–144, 156,
      198–199
    consolidation, 31 n. 3, 112 n. 6, 138–159, 161–
      162. *See also* conservation.
    cupping, 147
    delamination, 58 n. 11, 147–148, 150, 152–154
    deterioration/degradation, 165, 171–176;
      Plates 139–149. *See also* fungus/mold/
      fungal decay.
        biological/microbial decay, 171, 173, 175
          soft rot, 7 n. 7, 61, 120 n. 11, 137, 156,
            165, 171–176
        non-biological decay, 171, 176

distortion/warping, 1, 18, 37, 58, 60 n. 26, 137,
  141–143, 148–151, 155, 159
drying/seasoning, 18, 65, 133, 175, 199
expansion/swelling, 58 n. 11, 139, 144
failure, 59 n. 22, 200 n. 27
fibers, 139, 172, 174
grain, 2, 20, 38–39, 57–62, 66, 68–71, 121, 141,
  147–150, 152–154, 198–200
identification/wood species analysis, xxxv,
  xxxviii, 7 n. 6, 14, 16 n. 25, 19, 31 n. 2, 119
  n. 1, 122 n. 22, 165–169, 173, 176, 197–198.
  See also individual entries.
micromorphology, 165, 172, 174–176
mold growth on, 18, 65, 143–145, 174
pruning, 200 n. 26
pseudomorphs, 156, 173, 176, 221 n. 51; Plate
  149
sample/sampling, 7 nn. 6–7, 14 n. 12, 16 n.
  25, 19 n. 57, 57 n. 4, 119 n. 3, 122 n. 22, 137,
  139, 156, 165–169, 171–175
shrinkage, 23, 58 n. 11, 60–61, 72, 137, 139,
  143, 147, 155
softening (during treatment), 148, 151
sources, 197–199
steam bending, 14, 17, 19, 38 n. 31, 58 n. 10,
  200
strength/hardness tests, xxxviii, 158 n. 92
trained/curved branches, 58, 66, 200; Plate
  152C
turning. *See* lathe/turned.
unprovenanced (from Gordion), 68 n. 22, 114,
  119 n. 7, 120, 139
wooden objects
  animal figures, Tumulus P, 117, 162
  parasol, Tumulus P, 162
  plates/saucers, 21, 74 n. 50, 114, 132, 162,
    197
  spoons, 21, 114, 132, 162
woodworker/woodworking, 2, 16, 31, 38 n. 30, 42
  n. 62, 47–48, 63, 68–69 n. 25, 72 n. 42, 82–83,
  94–95, 107 n. 277, 133 n. 62, 158, 160, 192–
  194, 197–202. *See also* artist/artisan/designer;
  carver/carving/woodcarving; craftsmen.
  depictions, 116 n. 42, 197
  techniques/traditions, 197–202. *See also*
    joinery; individual entries.
    at Jericho, 42, 47, 62–63, 115–116, 197 n. 1,
      199–200 n. 25, 200 n. 28, 202 n. 41
    at Pazyryk, 46–47, 63, 124
    Egyptian, 31 n. 3, 43, 64, 115–116, 197–198
    Phrygian, 197–202. *See also* individual
      entries.
    Roman, 197 n. 5, 199 n. 24, 201 n. 38, 202
      nn. 42–43

terms, 2

tools, xxxviii, 2, 20, 33, 35 n. 19, 42 n. 62, 61,
66, 68, 70–71, 73, 158, 189–192, 193 n. 14,
197–202. *See also* tools; individual entries.

traditional, 64, 107 n. 277, 124–125, 197

wool, 21, 155, 203, 207–208, 211, 220, 223

for display, 160–161

goat, 204, 206, 221. *See also* cashmere; goat
hair/wool; mohair.

sheep, 203, 221

worship, 88–89, 98, 103 n. 252, 107, 109 nn. 289–
290, 134–135, 199 n. 21. *See also* religion; ritual;
individual entries.

writing boards, 195 n. 24

writing/texts. *See* graffiti; hieroglyphs; inscriptions; individual entries.

Xanthus of Lydia, 104 n. 263

Xenophon, 39–40, 127 n. 6

xylene, 205 n. 12, 217 n. 43

Yaba, 91

Yami, 55

Yazılıkaya (Boğazköy), 88 n. 141

Yazılıkaya/Midas Monument (Midas City), 93
n. 186, 96–98, 132, 134 n. 75; Plate 123; CD-
Figures 75–76

yeast, 182–183

yew/*Taxus baccata* L., 7 n. 7, 16, 19, 31, 43, 70,
73, 119, 120 n. 11, 121, 122 n. 22, 144, 165–166,
168–169, 172–173, 176, 197–198; Plates 140E–F,
148D

misidentification of, 7 n. 7, 16 n. 25, 19, 31, 120
n. 11, 121 n. 17, 173, 176

Young, Rodney S., xxxv, 1–2, 7–11, 13–28, 31–39,
57, 65–69, 73, 75 n. 60, 78 n. 82, 95, 99–100,
111–114, 115 n. 27, 119 n. 2, 120–123, 133, 137–
139, 143, 145, 155–156, 208

zigzag. *See* motifs (designs).

zinc, 178

present in textiles, 209

Zincirli, Turkey, 46 n. 98, 91 n. 168, 95 n. 201, 96
n. 203, 116 n. 41, 195 n. 24